Armageddon Films FAQ

Series Editor: Robert Rodriguez

Armageddon Films FAQ

All That's Left to Know About Zombies, Contagions, Aliens, and the End of the World as We Know It

Dale Sherman

APPLAUSE
THEATRE & CINEMA BOOKS
An Imprint of Hal Leonard Corporation

Published in 2013 by Applause Theatre & Cinema Books
An Imprint of Hal Leonard Corporation
7777 West Bluemound Road
Milwaukee, WI 53213

Trade Book Division Editorial Offices
33 Plymouth St., Montclair, NJ 07042

All images are taken from the author's personal collection except where otherwise specified.

The FAQ series was conceived by Robert Rodriguez and developed with Stuart Shea.

Printed in the United States of America

Book design by Snow Creative Services

Library of Congress Cataloging-in-Publication Data

Sherman, Dale, 1964–
    Armageddon films FAQ : all that's left to know about zombies, contagions, aliens, and the end of the world as we know it / Dale Sherman. — First paperback edition.
        pages cm. — (FAQ series)
    Includes bibliographical references and index.
    ISBN 978-1-61713-119-6
1. Horror films—United States—History and criticism. I. Title.
    PN1995.9.H6S475 2013
    791.43'6164—dc23
                                                                    2013027444

www.applausebooks.com

To Tony, who patiently sat on the patio one warm summer night
as a six-year-old boy tried to explain the plot of *This Is Not a Test*

And to Maddie, who will hopefully grow up
to find all these movies pretty silly

Contents

Acknowledgments

Thanks go to all that helped shape my thinking on movies over the years: magazines like *Starlog, Fangoria, Video WatchDog* and *It's Only a Movie*. The great video stores of my yesterdays and todays: Video Central and Aardvark Video back in Columbus, Ohio, and the still-going-strong Wild & Woolly Video in Louisville, Kentucky (and thanks to Todd Brashear for his dedication to Wild & Woolly). The video companies that have released a lot of oddball films over the years, too many to be named in fairness to all. Shout-outs to theaters that had or still do attempt to keep the movies in the theaters, such as the New Beverly in Los Angeles and the Drexel Marathons of old in Columbus, Ohio, as well as all the others in between.

Thanks to Brian Schnau and Mike DeGeorge for their takes on portions of the book over time, as well as everyone at Applause and Hal Leonard for their help in seeing that this project got going, especially that of Jessica Burr, Gary Morris, Marybeth Keating and Robert Rodriguez and their hard work on the book. Thanks to my agent Robert Lecker, who kept after me as well.

Thanks to Tony Kazmerrick, Hunter Goatley, Misha at Wrong Side of the Arts, and James Thompson for their help with visuals for the book. Thanks to Tim Lybarger for verifying the *Day After* rumor about *Mister Rogers' Neighborhood* for me. Thanks to everyone who had suggestions for movies while I was working on the book. I hope I covered a few that interest you.

Thanks to Jill for putting up with the long hours I spent getting this project done, although she seemed to love watching as many of the movies as I did. Thanks to other family and friends for putting up with it as well. Special thanks to Maddie for her patience. Now, let's go outside and play.

Introduction

Spoiler Alert!

I'm not kidding! Spoiler alert! Well, in a moment, actually. Best to warn you now, though.

Back in 1997, my wife and I drove a distance to see the Charlton Heston version of *Planet of the Apes* at a small-town movie theater. Sure, as movie fans we had seen it before—to the point where we knew it backward and forward—but this was a rare chance to see it on the "big screen" with a large audience instead of on television.

We went in figuring we weren't alone in having seen it numerous times. After all, it had been made reference to in so many other films and television programs that it was a cliché to riff off of Heston's epic line-reading of such gems as "Take your stinkin' paws off me, you *damn, dirty ape!*" and "Goddamn you all to *HELLLLLLLLLLLL!*" (Surprisingly, the two most remembered quotes from the movie are about the only times profanity appears, but that's perhaps a story for another book.) The film had four sequels, a television live-action series, a Saturday morning cartoon series, comic books, and even *The Simpsons* had based a very popular episode on a musical version of the movie that—and here's the kicker—gives away the ending of the film.

And that's just it. Out of everything in that movie, it is the ending that people remember the most once they've seen it (and here's that *SPOILER* for you): Taylor, played by Heston, is riding a horse along a beach with his girl Nova by his side like those old "Love Songs" K-Tel Record ads you used to see on television. Before the soundtrack can break into "If" by Bread, Taylor comes to a halt after finding the half-buried remains of the Statue of Liberty and realizes he had been on Earth the entire time. So well known was, and is, the image of Heston kneeling in the surf at the . . . well . . . head of the statue that one of the DVD releases of the movie prominently featured the destroyed monument on the cover. There was outrage by some fans over this because "it gives away the end of the movie." However, it clearly wasn't done to anger people. Nor were the references and parodies over the years meant to upset anyone; the moment had become so iconic in film that it is nearly impossible *not* to make commentary (either dramatically or in humor) on its most powerful image. Therefore, it is hard to conceive of people watching the movie not anticipating this moment.

Yet a fascinating response occurred in that theater in 1997 when the audience saw what had made Taylor fall to his knees in shock. A collective gasp escaped the audience of people from all walks of life and ages, as the camera

THE APES ARE COMING!

ALL FIVE FILMS IN ONE UNIQUE BOXSET,
INCLUDING NEVER-BEFORE-SEEN
INTERVIEWS AND FOOTAGE.

pLANET ... APES
BENEATH ... pLANET ... APES
ESCAPE ... pLANET ... APES
CONQUEST ... pLANET ... APES
BATTLE ... pLANET ... APES

BUY IT ON VIDEO 25ᵀᴴ JANUARY 1999

DIGITALLY THX MASTERED
FOR SUPERIOR SOUND AND PICTURE QUALITY

Planet of the Apes ad displaying the video cover that raised a ruckus among fans. For those who don't want it spoiled, just ignore the object on the left and assume Taylor found a shiny new penny in the surf.

panned the silhouette of Liberty's crown and then cut to Heston in front of the partially buried statue. "Oh, my God," people could be heard whispering to each other in the theater. "That's the Statue of Liberty! He was on Earth! This is Earth!" There was a buzz in the audience as ticket buyers compared notes with their friends and reflected on how they had never known it was Earth until that final moment.

My wife and I sat in the theater in stunned silence, but due to the revelation of the audience rather than what was on the screen. Was it possible that this many people had never heard of the ending to the movie before? Had never seen it? How was that possible? If we had jokingly referred to the ending earlier to each other, would we have spoiled the evening for those around us who may have overheard?

Which in a roundabout way brings you and me to a major point as we begin this trek into the various cinematic ends of the world: there's no way any examination of these films can be done with absolute merit without discussing *how* things go kablooey. Perhaps that's not really a point that needs to be made—after all, if you're reading this book, you probably already have some good ideas of how several of these movies end, move on from, or even start with "the end." Yet the moment one thinks that anything can be discussed without worry is exactly when someone is going to get upset that I have "ruined the ending of that movie" for them.

So let us cut to the chase right here. If you really do not want to know what happens in the films included in this book (and, to be honest, not that many really *end* with the end of the world . . . but more on that topic further on), then you may want to put this book aside for a while until you've caught up on a few. If, however, you know the genre and want to take a look back at such films or find new ones here that may be of interest to you even if the endings are "spoiled," then I think you'll enjoy what's ahead.

Certainly more than the people in the movies experiencing the end of the world. Of course, some were quite happy to see it go, which is another topic for later in the book.

But anyway . . .

Of course, the biggest spoiler to these movies is right there out in front—it's the demise or the threat of the end of the world in some fashion within all of them. (My personal favorite is the movie trailer for *End of the World* from 1977. The trailer ends with the earth blowing up. Yup—that's the end of the world there, I guess.) The big difference is how they occur or even if they occur at all. As we'll see, most appear to have more to do with the death of society or civilization than with the death of the planet or the human race. Others—typically named "postapocalyptic" and usually the cheapest ones, because it is easier to film in abandoned lots with bows and arrows than with expensive sets and special effects—deal with a world structure decades, even centuries after the "end." Still others deal just with the spark of the coming disaster that will wipe most of us out; just as a good number deal with the ramifications effective immediately after such a crisis occurs. Of course, as many times as the films covered end with someone wiping his brow saying (to paraphrase the late Roger Ebert on the subject), "We narrowly avoided disaster once again, let's kiss!," so too do we have a handful that end with people standing in silence as everything turns to darkness.

This is what makes the genre so interesting—for a topic that appears narrow and self-evident (the world is doomed—then boom—the end), there are endless variations to just how such incidents occur and how they will be emotionally as well as physically resolved. It reflects our particular poisons (to use a turn of phrase) that we love in our darkest hours. Will it come from the stars by aliens attacking? Some natural disaster that we gosh-darn didn't expect? Nuclear war? A contagion? Zombies? Monsters? Satan? God, or the gods, having a well-deserved laugh? Will we take it well? Will we sit and bitch? Will we lose our minds or find our salvation? We're driven to watch these films because the dangers we see within them reflect something within ourselves, no matter what variation of the end suits us best. Those of us that can't get enough of brain-eating undead, and those that gobble popcorn by the nuclear blast's flashes of light may have little interest in some of the other scenarios, but ultimately we all find the end fascinating.

Of course, in a number of the films listed, the filmmakers have some type of statement they want to make to the audience. Sure, typically, the more realistic the menace (especially those dealing with nuclear war), the more serious the message, but even in the most absurd of these films there is a message trying to sneak out. Do they deal with some preordained fate, and can it be avoided? Are we looking for closed-room dramas where the last few people alive must deal with emotional issues (not as uncommon as you might think)? Perhaps the ultimate disaster movies where we want to see which movie star will survive the end of the world? Do we like to speculate on what we'd do if we survived? Better yet, what if we could get some really cool cars and guns and check out all the hot babes that are miraculously surviving the apocalypse? (Heston, son, I'm looking at you.)

Thus, while it is easy to dismiss the apocalyptic film genre as being "all the same," it rarely is the case. Which is why a book dealing with the ramifications of these films and some—perhaps "final" makes it sound like a pun, so let's say defining—comments on what we see in them are in order. We know the movies, but what are the last things we need to learn from them? Perhaps most important of all, what do they really say about us as a culture? Why are we so driven to pay to see such films?

End of the World (1977), a movie that has no qualms about giving the audience exactly what they paid for, although not in the form of a giant alien head bursting through the planet's crust.   *Courtesy of Vintage Cinema Ads*

No doubt about it, there have been plenty of terrible movies made about the end of the world. There've also been some classics in the genre, and not all are so easily dismissed from your mind or can be laughed off after viewing. Thus, do not expect everything in this book to be a laughfest, although on such a topic it is worthwhile to try to be lighthearted at times. After all, one never knows when a movie that looks like pure cheese from the beginning will come up with at least one moment where it will smack one in the face with a pure cinematic image that makes the eighty-plus minutes of silliness around it worth all the trouble. Just as likely, one can be surprised at how a movie striving to make striking emotional moments about such a catastrophe can fall on its face in foolishness as well.

Yet perhaps the last thing to discuss before we dive into the various topics surrounding these films is what actually constitutes an "apocalyptic movie"? Unless we put some guidelines in place, we could end up with multiple volumes detailing every movie that has ever used the threat of a nuclear war in the plot, or a possible villain that wants to control the world. To help avoid that, here are four criteria to consider before jumping headfirst into the rest of this book.

Bond, No Bond

The setup: After ninety minutes of good guy/bad guy cat-and-mouse games, our hero finds out that he has twelve minutes to deactivate the computer never discussed before or else the missiles will go off and World War III will begin! Resolution: he does it. In other words, a possible doomsday is in the movie, but only as a climactic arc in the last half-hour and not as the focus of the picture. This is one reason why you will not find the Matthew Broderick movie *WarGames* (1983) within these pages. Yes, it does involve a theme about nuclear war being unwinnable, but it's namely set up as an action-comedy that only deals with the possibility of the end of the world in the last few minutes of the film. Otherwise, there are five gazillion espionage movies that are similar, and then you'd be reading a book mostly about Bond movies, of which the FAQ series has been there and done that.

Think Larger

Speaking of cat-and-mouse games, *The Bedford Incident* (1965) deals with such a situation between an American ship and a Soviet submarine for much of the duration of the film. In the final moments, a soldier accidentally fires a missile to destroy the submarine, and one comes from the submarine in retaliation. Result is the death of everyone in the movie and a strong moral/political statement that one simple human error can lead to the death of all.

Yet, as far as we the audience know, those are the only deaths that occur as a result of that error. Would it mean a larger war throughout the world? We never know; the movie ends as the bombs go off. In all likelihood, cooler heads would at least want to investigate the situation and, in all probability, sweep it under the rug before the press and public found out (after all, it's a message that supports nuclear disarmament at a time the big boys in power wouldn't have dreamed of such a thing). So we have a film that deals with death by nuclear destruction and asks questions about how much power we can responsibly hold, but it doesn't quite fall into the same category of such films as *Dr. Strangelove* or *The Day After* where even accidental nuclear attacks lead to bigger responses.

To put it another way, a movie that is considered the genesis of the zombie mythology most of us know these days, *Night of the Living Dead*, could be seen as an "isolated incident" story, due to an ending that suggests the zombie plague is over after one night. However, this is disproven with the sequel, *Dawn of the Dead*, and subsequent films. The Italian follow-up, *Zombie*, appears as a one-off incident as well . . . that is, until its final moments where we witness a swarm of zombies on their way to New York. However, there have been a large number of zombie films over the past nearly fifty years that deal with little incidents—mainly on small islands—where people come, scream, get killed by a zombie or leave. Or if there is a final "twist" that suggests it may continue, there's no sense that it means some type of pandemic zombie explosion. (More like, "Oooh, little Sally has turned into a zombie! End of film?" Which in reality, would have continued after that moment with "BAM! End of Sally. No more zombies.") Thus, they fall outside of the Armageddon factor we will see in this book.

In relations to isolated incidents . . .

Even *Big* Disaster Movies Are Not Necessarily Apocalyptic Movies

From a critical standpoint, it would be easy to take many disaster movies from over the years and put them down as "end of the world" scenarios. *Earthquake* (1974) ends with nearly everyone in the cast—heck, everyone in L.A.—dead. But that's it. It affects a city in California, not the world. *Volcano* (1997) featured a volcanic eruption in L.A. (Boy, Hollywood sure does like offing itself in the movies, doesn't it? Well, give the public what they want . . .) The city is destroyed, but not the world.

The thing that throws some viewers off, however, is that for the two hours we're watching that movie, it becomes our world. Thus, even though we may look at it later and objectively say, "Yeah, those aren't really apocalyptic," there is a kneejerk reaction for a moment of "Hey, where's *Earthquake*? Where's *The Poseidon Adventure*?" Perhaps a better way to put it is in biblical terms (and believe me, critics have over the years tied in the Bible with the above disaster movies): such disaster films are not Noah's Ark—God is sick of men's evil and he's gonna drown everyone in the world except some lucky survivors and a mess of livestock—but rather Sodom and Gomorrah—God is sick of men's evil but he's only gonna wipe out these cities and let that be a lesson to the rest of you. The reasoning is the same in both for people's demises, but the results are a

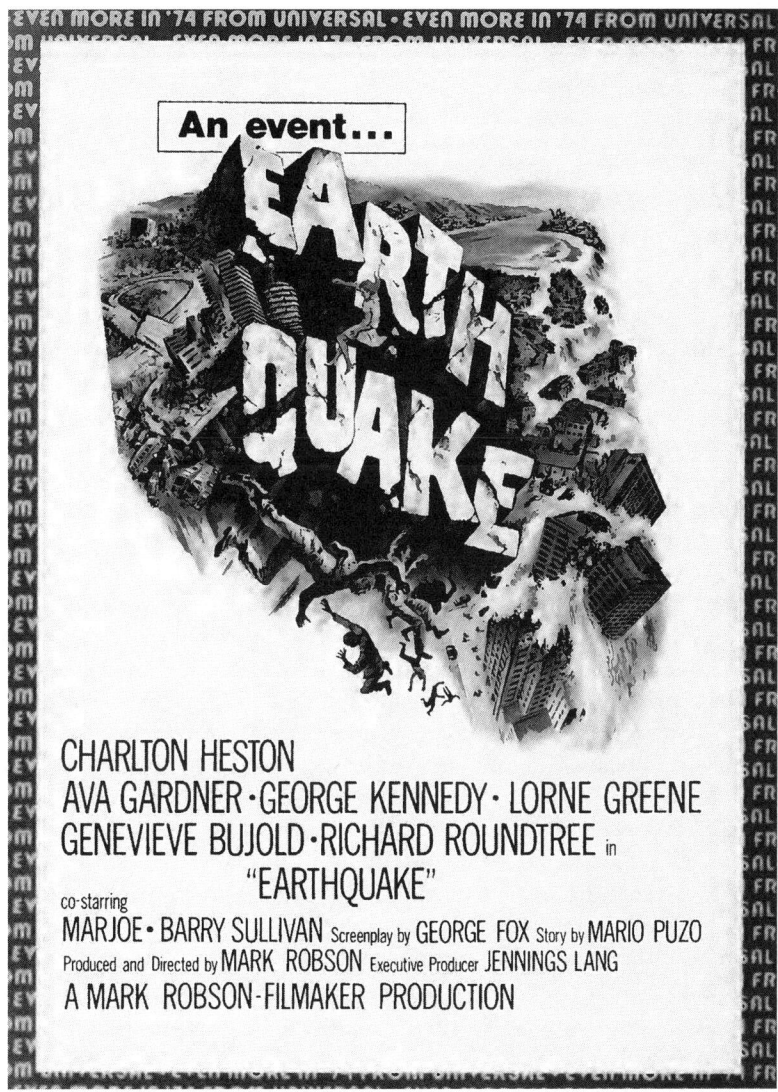

Although thought of as one, *Earthquake* (1974) is not an apocalyptic movie, and not covered in this book. Ah . . . but neat poster, right?

Courtesy of Vintage Cinema Ads

difference between that of the whole world and a city or two. (As an aside, some researchers believe Sodom and Gomorrah were consumed by earthquakes, which in a roundabout way to get us back to the Heston flick . . . not that Heston had anything to do with the real events, of course. At least as far as we know.) So, final verdict: end-of-the-world movies can be disaster movies (and there certainly will be a few within the following pages), but not all disaster movies are end-of-the-world movies.

Of course, this is not to say that movies that feature the above are not worthy of seeing and discussion. Merely, for the topic of this book, the focus is on movies where apocalyptic events propel the stories, rather than ones that do not quite fit the definition. As to what categories each movie falls into, read on.

Hey, Why Isn't *Def-Con 4* in That Chapter Instead of This One?

First off, if you're paying that close attention to the categories for something like *Def-Con 4*, then you're probably being a bit anal. Like me, the author, who worried enough about it to make it a point here. So come over and we'll chat like a couple of schoolgirls having a slumber party. As for those of you who are now saying, "What the hell is *Def-Con 4*?" Well, well, well. Lookie, we have some outsiders come into town today. . . .

Admittedly, there may be times where the categories listed in the following chapters may pull at certain flicks in two or even three ways. *Def-Con 4* does show us characters who missed the Apocalyptic event, and thus fits into chapter 3, but it also features our hero falling into a futuristic world with scavengers living amid what they can find of the modern world and a big gimmicky car like the car-theme chapter later on (okay, it's a rather shabby dress-up on a bulldozer, but it's obvious that the idea of something like *Mad Max* was there). In such cases, I have attempted to put movies into chapters where I felt they were best suited, but don't be surprised if you may personally feel that a movie "here" may fit better "there," no matter how strong of an argument I make for my positioning. If so, hopefully, I can persuade you along the way.

No doubt, there's going to be a few movies that everyone feels should be in here that didn't make it. Namely because there's just not enough room to name every movie that has some means of killing off humanity. Hopefully, this book will at least scratch the surface of what is out there to be seen.

End spoiler alert, as the journey into the land of our doom awaits. The first step comes in the form of the novels that have helped shape our views of how the end will come . . . and yet for some reason have never quite made it to the screen.

A great poster for the rather iffy *Def-Con 4* (1985)—a movie that manages to cross over various apocalyptic film genres.   *Courtesy of Wrong Side of the Art*

Armageddon Films
FAQ

Ten Famous Apocalyptic Novels Never Turned into Major Films

The Pitch Meetings

ollywood has never feared going to other sources to come up with plots for movies. Give them a real-life incident, a fable they heard as a kid, a comic book, or even a short story, and they're bound to think it over just long enough to say, "How can we make some money off of this?" No need to rack one's brain coming up with a fresh idea when one is simply out there ready to be bought and used, after all. Novels are especially easy targets of Hollywood producers because if a book was/is a bestseller, then obviously the story is one that has reverberated with the public and therefore would be a prime target for acquisition to become a film. This is why some of the most famous movies covered within these pages are those that had been adapted from literary sources.

What may seem odd from a twenty-first century standpoint is how essentially "recent" the concept of the apocalyptic novel really is. Of course, some would throw the Bible in there as one of the first because they think they're being scandalous by calling the Bible "a novel," but certainly other religions have their own concepts of "end-times." However, neither the Bible nor other holy books are an all-encompassing work about Armageddon; they are mainly a means to describe man's birth and interaction with God since the beginning of time. Besides, no matter what your views of it may be, the Bible was created to educate rather than to entertain in some fashion, as is the same with most religions' end-time theories and prophecies. Besides, we have really only two major apocalyptic tales in the Bible: Noah's Ark and Revelation, and both have surfaced in movies over the century time and time again, and therefore they wouldn't place a status in the focus of this chapter anyway.

Which brings us back to when tales about the end of the world began being published for mass consumption. Most historians tend to look to two early nineteenth-century works as the beginning of . . . well, the end, really. The first being *Le dernier homme* (aka *The Last Man*) by Jean-Baptiste Cousin de Grainville in 1805, with the second coming twenty-one years later with Mary Shelley's *The Last Man*. At least, in retrospect, they are considered the first, even though no one focused much time on them when they were published. Further, Shelley's novel was considered a critical failure and forgotten, only to be finally republished in the twentieth century. Yet what brought on this sudden attraction to such a concept in popular literature at the beginning of the nineteenth century that would grow into a mass market in the twentieth century?

Perhaps because in some ways, the public began to realize that the world was becoming a smaller place. There may have been areas of countries we hadn't "discovered" yet, but there wasn't much to add either. Upon establishing the "New World" and getting a clear understanding of the landmasses of the world, the earth suddenly became rather finite, and with it so did our feeling of safety. Before, there was always the chance of saying, "I can get out of here and go somewhere no one will find me. I can stop the world and come back to it when I choose." That wasn't the case anymore. Discoveries making the news then made clear that people were everywhere—maybe different in mysterious ways, but still people, and still doing most of the same dumb things as everyone else was everywhere else. You catch a cold here, you'll catch it there. Maybe even give them something you have that will kill them (like smallpox to the American Indians) or vice versa. Now there was no escape, no brave new worlds. No place to hide.

And with that came the realization for some that a spark "here" could travel to an explosion at the other end of the world, wiping us all out. Or worse, a spark "there" would travel back to us. Amazingly, as we revealed to ourselves the marvelous wonders of existence throughout our planet, our minds turned to how to destroy it—hopefully, as an appreciator of art who loves a painting and then worries if it is safe from someone destroying it; unfortunately, and more commonly, as a cynic who figured someone was bound to mess things up. At first, such dreams of the end were few, but as we became closer to each other due to communication and available travel, so too did our concerns about our neighbors' actions drop into our minds. The smaller our world becomes, the more paranoid our thoughts turn to the future, and thus the greater the fascination with our worldly demise.

Thus, the genre grew, and from the first steps by Grainville and Shelley a variety of books about society collapsing—if not all-out Armageddon—hit the publishing houses and began to sell well with the public. Into the twentieth century, and especially after World War II and the knowledge that a nuclear war could potentially wipe most of us off the planet (with "us" victorious or not), the number of novels about "the end" grew even faster. Into the twenty-first century we see even more appearing, finally breaking away from the nuclear fears of the Cold War, only to drop ourselves knee-deep into that of unstoppable natural disasters or contagions of one type or another (and, for the sake of argument, most zombie movies fall into that category as well).

As stated at the beginning of this chapter, the success of certain novels automatically led to an interest from Hollywood. Many of the best novels in the apocalyptic genre have made their way to the small and big screen over the years, and will be discussed in this book. Three in particular—*The War of the Worlds*, *Invasion of the Body Snatchers* and *I Am Legend*—practically corner the market for major themes in such movies made over the years and merit their own chapters in this book. Yet, ironically, there are several well-remembered novels over the years considered classics outside of, as well as within, the genre that have never made it to the big screen. In some cases, there have been widespread discussions about doing such, to the point where the trade papers have occasionally dropped hints about such-and-such studio or so-and-so beginning production," but—with the exception of one lone *Playhouse 90* production for one of the books to follow here and less than a handful of radio plays—none has occurred.

Why is this? What has driven people to these books time and again that have made some of them prototypes of the genre? And, if so, why has Hollywood not been able to cash in on such properties?

Below are ten such important apocalyptic novels that have failed to make it to the big screen—and to show how Hollywood thinks, appraised in as typical a studio fashion as possible. First up will be a look at the script reader's summary. A script reader is someone paid by the studio to read a script or book and then write a report about it, giving a summary of the plot, potential pluses and minuses of the novel and even some historical notes if they feel they are relevant. Such reports are a quick way for an executive to see if going any further—like actually *reading* the material—is worth their time.

Second is that of—for lack of a better analogy—the author's agent. Of course, most of the writers discussed here are long gone, but let us just assume that someone who holds rights to the property is trying to get a movie deal. She will want to push all the good things she can about the book in order to see that the studio picks it up. So, it's not uncommon for her to brush aside some issues that may not put the most positive light on the material. It's a hard sell and a tough job, but someone's got to be the cheerleader.

In typical opposition to the agent is the studio bean counter. Although certain creative types tend to see him as the evil dark lord who stops anything good from happening, his main job is to examine a property and be forthright in saying what he thinks can and can't work. Even an idea that may look great on paper may not be doable on film and it's the bean counter's job to make sure the studio doesn't burn money on a project that isn't feasible.

Finally, there's the studio executive who takes all of the previous opinions, facts and figures into consideration before concluding if the studio will go forward with the project or not. It all begins with a time warp, as a smartphone from a poolside in L.A. falls through a wormhole and into the lap of Mary Shelley's agent in 1826.

The Last Man by Mary Shelley (1826)

Script Reader's Analysis: *The Last Man* was written by Mary Shelley (1797–1851), who is best known today as the author of *Frankenstein: or, The Modern Prometheus* (1818). She was married to the poet Percy Shelley from 1816 until his death in 1822, having become inseparable since 1814 and only wed after the death of Shelley's first wife in 1816. The couple traveled extensively through Europe during their years together, sometimes with their friend and fellow poet Lord Byron, with Mary giving birth to four children in that time, of which three died while still very young. After Percy Shelley's death, Mary Shelley settled in England with her son and continued to write, while vacationing in Europe on occasions. She died in 1851 at the age of 53.

Note that Shelley's novel usually is compared with a work by Jean-Baptiste François Xavier Cousin de Grainville commonly translated under the same title and posthumously published in 1806. Grainville's epic poem deals with the last fertile man on Earth searching for the last fertile woman on Earth in a world rapidly reaching an end. They meet, but then Adam, the first man, persuades the protagonist to let the world end, as per God's plans, by not procreating and extending human existence on Earth. The protagonist agrees and the world ends. It is an interesting work; fascinating for having been written when it was in that it combines elements of biblical prophecies with fantasy, set in a future vision of the world; but it is a work known mainly by those interested in apocalyptic and/or early traces of science fiction in literature.

Shelley's work was written a couple of decades later and is sometimes referenced as having some elements similar to Grainville's work; although a plot dealing with the end of mankind is obviously going to have some similarities no matter what. Shelley's work is better known due to her recognition as an author, and it being a novel that modern audiences can still absorb, unlike Grainville's work, which tends to be viewed as having more scholarly than entertainment value.

The Last Man was published in 1826 as a novel in "three volumes." Reviews savaged the novel to the point that Shelley moved on quickly to other novels to try to please her publisher, while the book was not officially reissued in English until 1965, during a period where the public rediscovered Mary Shelley's various novels. Reviews were kinder in 1965, but today Shelley's work is once again mostly forgotten, with the exception of the ever-popular *Frankenstein* novel.

It is widely accepted that the book is somewhat autobiographical in terms of the characters: Adrian, Earl of Windsor representing Shelley's deceased husband Percy Shelley; Lord Raymond being a variation of Lord Byron; Perdita, Lionel's sister, as a portrait of Mary's stepsister and lover to Byron, Claire Clairmont; and finally the protagonist—the male "wild child," Lionel Verney—being that of Mary herself. Even a child in the novel, Clara, is named after one of Shelley's deceased children. The multiple travels of the group of characters over time also reflects somewhat the constant travels of the Shelleys during their years together, while the theme of all those around the protagonist dying no doubt was also influenced by Mary Shelley's life, with Adrian's drowning obviously a parallel with Percy's own death at sea.

The Plot: It is the late twenty-first century in England. Lionel Verney is the son of a man who was once the favorite of the king. A letter, to be sent upon Lionel's father's death, asking for the King's protection of Lionel and Perdita, never reaches the king, and the son and daughter grow up uncivilized and loathing the royal family. Later, after the fall of the monarchy, Lionel becomes friends with the potential heir to the throne, Adrian, Earl of Windsor.

Between ongoing wars and star-crossed love affairs facing our protagonists and others, eventually there is talk that a plague is moving toward Europe. The plague is of little consequence for a good chunk of the novel, with pressing personal problems and conflicts being the focus instead. It is only as the plague begins to engulf the entire world halfway through the text that characters take notice of it, especially after refugees from America attempt to invade England in hope for safety. Although the protagonists try their best to resolve the crises due to the invasion, and mostly succeed, the plague soon takes a good majority of those left, and a handful of survivors attempt to seek shelter elsewhere.

Near the end of the novel, there are only four survivors left: Lionel, Adrian, Lionel's son Evelyn and Perdita's daughter Clara. Evelyn dies while the group is in Switzerland, and both Adrian and Clara drown while attempting to sail to Greece. Lionel continues with his journeys in hopes of finding some other survivors, but is unsuccessful and admits that he must be the last man on Earth. Even so, as the novel ends, he writes down his memories about his life and the end of mankind in hopes that someone somewhere will have survived and find his story to read someday.

Agent's Pitch: First off, it's Mary Shelley—one of the few classical writers, like Mark Twain, William Shakespeare and Ernest Hemingway, that everyone knows of, even if they have never read any of their work. She wrote *Frankenstein* and everyone knows that one. *Frankenstein* is a classic of horror, and *The Last Man* is considered a classic of science fiction. As already mentioned, it's defined as one of the first novels to deal with an apocalyptic theme, certainly one of the first to deal with a pandemic that kills off most of the human race. It is obvious that Shelley had vision—nowadays, such novels are commonplace, but here was someone talking about the end of the world nearly two hundred years ago.

Let's not forget we have the whole visual look of the book, what with the spectacular visions of war in futuristic places across the globe. If not set in a future we can see today, it could easily be reworked in a "steam punk" fashion to make it the future as would have been seen by Shelley in 1826, which is a style that goes down well with audiences. It also has a variety of romances in the style of Jane Austen, with good deeds leading to good things like Charles Dickens; even the whole business with the letter to the king that is never sent is straight out of something like *Jane Eyre* or *Sense and Sensibility*. We've got action for the men in the audience and romantic drama for the women. It's epic in scope; sci-fi in looks; full of adventure and romance; plus, the built-in curiosity of those that will see Shelley's name in the title as *Mary Shelley's The Last Man* and want to check it out. How can it not succeed?

Bean Counter's Response: Have you ever read the novel? It's nearly five hundred pages long, and it's not until chapter 2 that you find out it takes place in the future. The book is nearly a third over before the first mention of the plague occurs. One has to give credit to Shelley for presenting how people ignore telltale signs of encroaching danger, thanks to the emphasis being placed on elements outside of the plague until it is essentially too late for the characters to do anything about it. However, anyone coming into the novel expecting the story to be about people trying to survive the plague and not on political and domestic drama that fall outside of that scope probably struggle with the various romances and military escapades that fill most of the pages until late in the novel.

It would help as well if there were firmer guidance as to how the plague occurs and what it is, especially after Lionel contracts the plague but somehow survives without any real acknowledgment that it means others possibly survived as well. But for a novel by someone who would not have had the research available to her that most people have today with the clicking on a keyboard via the Internet, one again has to give Shelley credit for doing the best she can with describing what such a plague would be like. However, a bigger issue at hand is that Shelley obviously had to set the story in the future in order to get to the ending she desired (that of the end of the world), but has nothing to show us of that future world beyond balloons as transportation. Everything else is of horses and ships, letter-writing and long chats in the parlor on a lazy day. It could still be 1826 in many ways, and any attempt to present this story to audiences today would involve some major rethinking as to how such an epidemic would be presented in what we commonly see today as the present or the near future.

One thing the agent has said that is true is that the story reads like Jane Austen; hence, a major problem with making it a film—as mentioned, most of the story is that of romantic entanglements, rivalries and intrigue. Audiences coming into the film to see an apocalyptic movie will be bored by the courtships and such, and will probably have little patience for the various trips to war and battles that propel the characters storywise but would be hard-pressed to show adequately in the context of a movie. Those coming in to see something like Austen would be devastated by the sudden shift to contagion horror and ultimately the death of everyone but Lionel, who is doomed to die alone and in defeat as the movie fades to black. Also, while the novel is epic in scope, it seems to be a lot of running around that only brings the characters back to square one. There is also the possibility of a hard sell to audiences in the survivors of the world finding England is the only place safe, and if so, that Americans would be the only ones to try to muscle in on the territory. While not the intention of Shelley, it plays out in the book as nearly xenophobic in nature and probably would be best eliminated or pushed into the background (say, as Americans arriving as welcomed refugees rather than pirates or gangsters ready to take over).

A potential script based on the novel would be best set in the near future and have some of the romantic and battle scenes cut out. Okay, most of the romantic and battle subplots. An attempt at steam punk may have some success; perhaps the story dealing with an alternate Earth where the timeline is different and progress had shot off in another direction due to the constant wars. Speaking of which, the idea of a war being fought that keeps everyone preoccupied until the plague is upon everyone has some potential, especially if perhaps the plague was the result of a combination of modern science combined with the logistics of germ warfare developed during World War I (thus, the plague would have hit the trenches first before slowly working its way back to the masses not being affected by the wars fought in foreign lands).

Let's face it, the ending is a downer—mankind has no salvation, and the last man wanders around for a while until he (will likely) die. Although lyrical in the form of the novel, a film depicting Verney looking for people that never turn up for a good chunk of screen-time would have trouble even working in art movies today. The case of Verney surviving naturally leads to a revised ending that finds him locating others, but to do so—or many of the other suggestions here—means nearly reinventing the story from scratch. If we want to make *Mary Shelley's The Last Man*, it seems pointless to strip away so much of what makes it *Mary Shelley's The Last Man* in order to make a bankable movie.

Studio's Decision: Pass, with reservations. Agree with bean counter that the work involved in bringing it to the screen would either give us an expensive art movie that will have a limited audience or a science fiction movie that will confuse audiences. The steam punk idea has some promise, but we could make our own movie with that type of thing and without bothering to make it Mary Shelley's version.

Intrigued by script reader's historical background on the novel and how Shelley based so many of the characters of that in her life. Perhaps we're looking at this from the wrong end of things. A type of *French Lieutenant's Woman* adaptation may be more in order—one that juxtaposes Shelley's real-life drama with that of her image of those same events that work their way into *The Last Man*, using the same actors for both the novel's characters and their real-life counterparts. This could be a way to avoid the whole "downer ending" of the novel, as we could cut back to Shelley's life after the story's narrative and find some type of message to wrap things up that will satisfy audiences and leave them a little more "up." If we had some developments in this direction, we may reconsider the project as a biopic, but the idea of a science fiction film seems dead in the water.

After London by Richard Jefferies (1885)

Script Reader's Analysis: Richard Jefferies (1848–1887) dealt namely with subjects of man's interaction with nature in his writings. Not so much in the style of someone like Jack London, who wrote adventure yarns structured around elements of nature, but more as to man's reaction to nature and vice versa in much quieter tones. As Jefferies focused most of his writing on nonfiction essays about nature and inner thoughts, this isn't much of a surprise. After all, much has been made in biographies about Jefferies' frustration in a short life less ventured into the world than he had anticipated. This comes through in his work, as well as his novels, including *After London.*

The Plot: The novel is broken down into two parts. The first, "The Relapse into Barbarism," demonstrates Jefferies' love of the outdoors and his strength as an essayist. At nearly one-fifth of the total pages of the novel, the first part covers background information as to how nature would reclaim the world at some future point where mankind is no longer there to dominate. Most reviewers have pointed out that Jefferies never defines exactly what wipes out humanity, but ultimately such concerns are beside the point in terms of where Jefferies is going with the novel anyway: The story is one that does not need anything known about what caused such a catastrophe, only that it had occurred, especially as the second part of the novel takes places hundreds of years after the "fall."

The second part of the book, "Wild England," really is quite separate from the first, as it is a more traditional coming-of-age adventure story rather than the dry, "factual" aspects of the first part. With mankind devolving into a feudal society, small towns and villages sprinkle throughout what remains

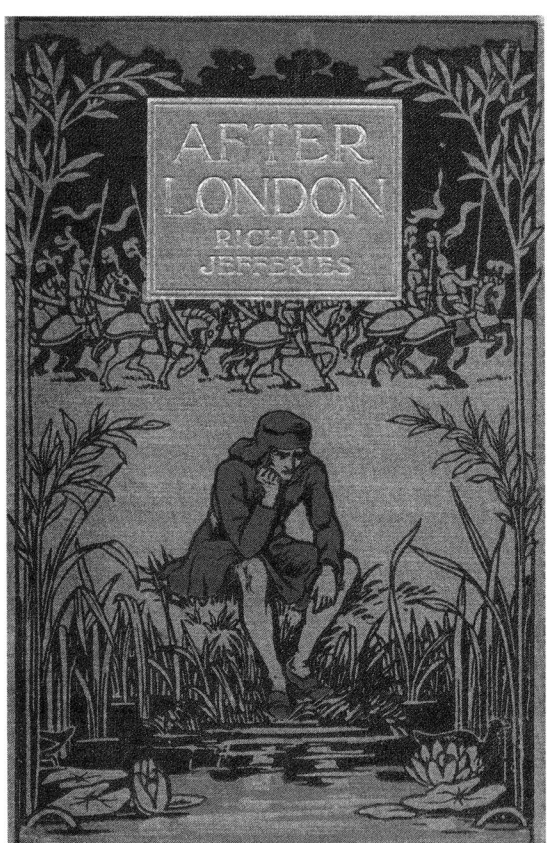

The cover to the 1905 edition of Richard Jefferies' *After London,* one of the first novels to use a postapocalyptic Earth as a setting for fantasy adventure.

of England after the "relapse," along with gypsies, pirates and "bush men" that pose a hazard for those within such communities. Felix, the third son of a baron, is a bit of an outcast due to his thirst for knowledge. He sets out to make a name for himself in order to win the hand of a girl, Aurora, the daughter of another baron. After a series of adventures in a world where bits and pieces of the past (Jefferies' present) peeks through, Felix ends up becoming a king and returning for Aurora.

Coincidentally, the book has been seen by critics as much an autobiographical study of Jefferies as Shelley with *The Last Man*. The only difference is that Shelley's position is one of "Here is my life, dressed up for your amusement," while Jefferies' is "Here's how I wish my life had been." One is a venture into fantasy to tell a true-life story, the other is wish fulfillment. Jefferies was a farm boy who had been to private school, educated but drawn to nature, quick-thinking but lacking when it came to work beyond what he chose to do. He was an outsider who eventually married a woman living on a nearby farm after succeeding in the release of his first novel, *The Scarlet Shawl*, in 1874. All of which are mirrored in the character of Felix from *After London*.

Most importantly, as a young man Jefferies had envisioned a life for himself that would involve travel around the world, only for fate (an attempt to travel to Russia and then America were both dashed due to circumstances Jefferies had not foreseen) and his health—what would eventually be determined to be tuberculosis—to thwart such attempts. Although he found some success through his writing—regularly featured in newspapers for his local historical essays, later published in volumes, as well as his novels—people considered him a quirky sort, aided by his lack of concern about his appearance and the results of his various illnesses that left him appearing weak and malnourished. Of course, most writers "write what they know," hence Jefferies using elements of his life in his novels beyond that seen in *After London* alone. For example, his book *Bevis*—a second book of two about a boy—also features a protagonist that builds his own boat in order to sail across the waters to a new, strange place. Yet it is easy to see how much of *After London* is how Jefferies would have wished his life to have been—sailing free, being brave, being shined upon by fortune, and grandly winning the hand of the woman of your dreams. Not to mention seeing the fall of London, which has been reported in some biographies as being a city for which Jefferies had little fondness.

However, all this would have little relevance to an audience watching such a film made of the novel. One intriguing element of the book is that there is no dialogue between characters. Nor is the book written in the first person, as typical for such a narrative. Instead, it is all descriptive, even that of characters' conversations, which would give a scriptwriter the opportunity to go her own way with dialogue while keeping the flavor of Jefferies' writing in place. On a further upside, most of the story takes place in the wildness and the shells of what once was today's world, now hundreds of years gone to pieces, so concerns about special effects may be limited, depending how scenes are shot. Also, the novel takes the perspective of a young man having adventures in a fantasy world, so it may appeal to more of a younger audience if pursued.

Agent's Pitch: I won't lie, Richard Jefferies is not a name that attracts attention to itself these days, so we don't have the ability to play off of the name as we did with Mary Shelley. The title, *After London*, probably needs revamping as well, as it doesn't really sell the audience on what the movie is about. However, we do have a fine piece of writing that imaginatively builds up a postapocalyptic world some hundreds of years after the fall of mankind. In the past few years, we have had several documentaries and films made that attempt to show the world after mankind has bowed out, but *After London* was there nearly a century before many such visual studies, and this may be something we can play off of in a movie.

Besides, we have nasty villains, a boy hero, and a girl waiting at home he wants to impress. This could easily be set up as a multifilm epic, with the boy's adventures going to seek his fortunes and his finally becoming king, or work as a single feature as well. Hit the youth market, throw a good-looking young actor (like a Justin Bieber type) in the role and you have a built-in audience of teenage girls that will be dying to buy tickets. The title and the historical data about the author may not suggest it, but it is a fantasy novel for young adults and easily adaptable for film.

Bean Counter's Response: The script reader's view that the feudal setting is one that could prove cost-effective is a good one. It's all dependent on the director's vision and on whether he decides to CGI the hell out of it to make it all look like ruined landscapes everywhere or if he's happy with maybe one or two money shots of a destroyed London popping up on the screen. A fantasy film full of action with bows and arrows against bad guys with a young popular actor on his way up or even one of the newer pop stars probably would do respectably at the box office if advertised correctly. Cash in on some of the popularity of such titles as *The Hunger Games* and *Twilight* that way.

Doubt we could make it into a franchise, however, as there just isn't enough story to make into a series. It's strictly a one-film concept here. Maybe a two-part miniseries for one of the cable channels if we can't get it going as a theatrical film. This one may have legs.

Studio's Decision: Let's get it into development and see where it heads. As the bean counter mentions, we may be able to sell it to the networks or cable if we can't push it as a feature film. See how cost-effective we can do the shooting and put in a young cast willing to work for less money, plus one or two stars in featured roles for box office (get Sean Bean as one of the lords; he plays rough and tough monarchy in everything anyway), and we may have a winner here. All dependent on what interest we can get at this point. It may be one of the lighter-weight books we're looking at here, but a breezy action film doesn't have to be *2001*. Maybe we can keep the ending open enough that we can build it into a franchise if box-office returns support it.

The Scarlet Plague by Jack London (1912)

Script Reader's Analysis: Jack London (1876–1916), although from a different background than Richard Jefferies, had a similar career in writing for newspapers and magazines, as well as writing books, with an emphasis on nature. The main difference is that, while Jefferies tended to lovingly look at the environment in the raw, London sensationalized man's need for and conflict with nature. He certainly is the better remembered of the two, with a much-publicized life as he built up his career, along with a steady stream of popular works, including such novels as *Call of the Wild, The Sea Wolf,* and *White Fang* (all titles that were essentials of American Literature for children . . . at least until more recent times).

The Scarlet Plague is a novel—sometimes referred to as a short story or novella, since it's a very slim book—that was written near the end of London's life, as he experienced growing health problems and considered his writing career more of a financial necessity than one of love for the art or need of expression. Uniquely, London's work began to expand toward writing material that some would suggest as being science fiction in nature, with strong social-political implications, such as his novel *The Iron Heel* (about the rise of an oligarchy in early twentieth-century America) and his short story "The Unparalleled Invasion." *The Scarlet Plague* is along similar lines.

The Plot: The story is told in flashback to a group of young boys around a fire. James Smith is a professor working at a college in 2013 (a hundred years into the future for London at the time of publication, although presented in the book as "modern times") when a quick-acting contagion known as the "Scarlet Plague" sweeps through the world. Smith attempts to barricade himself with fellow college professors, students and their families in a building at the university, but eventually all are forced out as the disease takes hold. The band of people dwindles over time, as some depart to go their own way, others die from the disease, and still others are killed by the brutality of man against man (for example, one is shot and killed by a passing drunk for no reason). Eventually, Smith is alone and travels on his own for a time before meeting up with others.

The remainder of the book follows Smith as he gains a family and builds a small society of survivors around him, while also dealing with those wishing to cause conflict for the group. The book ends as it begins, with Smith finishing the story to the boys, who half-believe Smith's story as the truth, but soon dismiss it all as simply a story told by a crazy old man.

It is interesting that this early piece of apocalyptic fiction is rarely mentioned today in comparison with others such as Shelley's *The Last Man* and Jefferies' *After London,* as the story flows much better for modern readers than those of the previous authors. Certainly in light of the fact of how similar it is in plot and

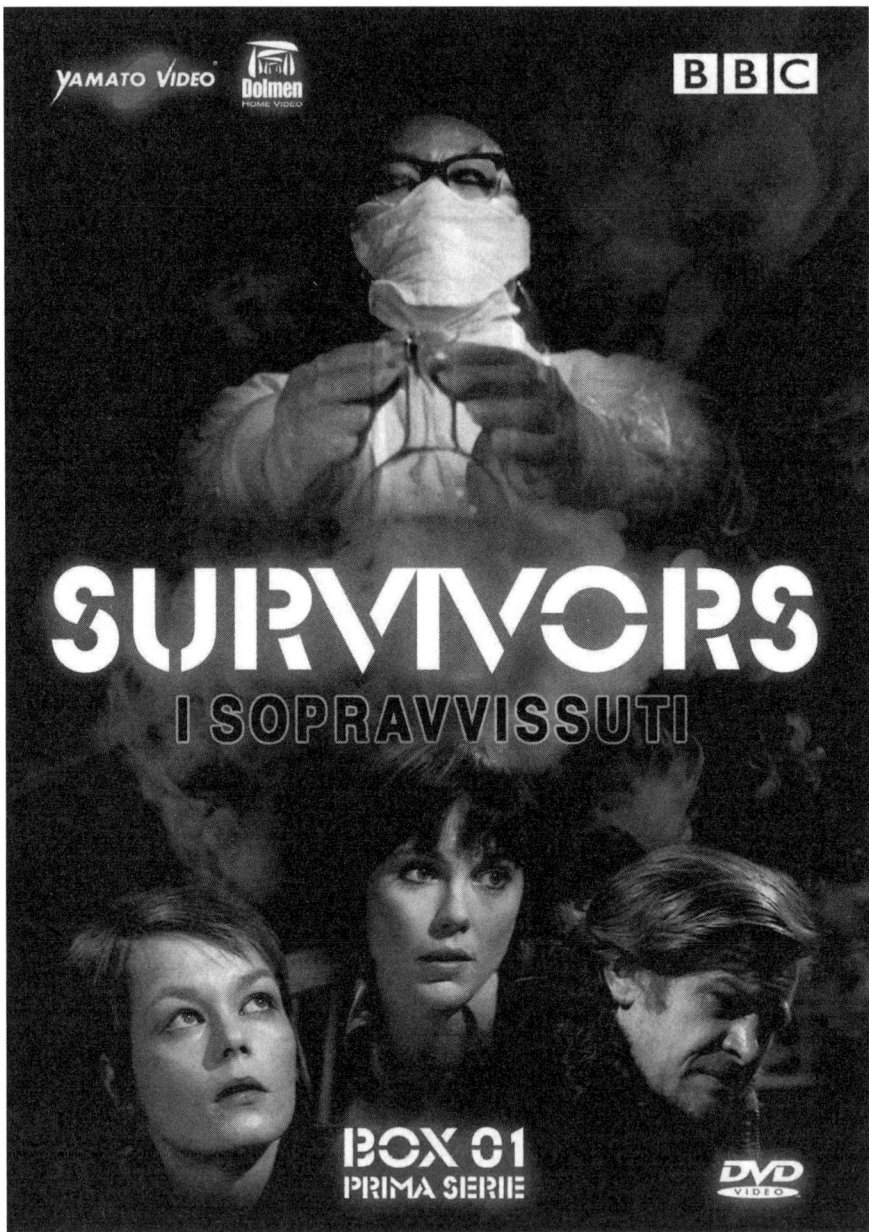

Contagions wiping out all but those immune are the basis for both *Earth Abides* (1949) and *The Scarlet Plague* (1912)—two classic apocalyptic novels never filmed, although many movies and television programs, such as *Survivors* (1975–1977), have told similar stories.

scope to George R. Stewart's *Earth Abides*. Some have complained about London's tendency to write in a sporadic manner, but such a style has become more of the norm and certainly acceptable today, which makes the relatively short work easy to read in gulps instead of as one sit-through.

Agent's Pitch: Okay, we're back to a recognized author's name, which is always a plus when selling a movie to audiences. Maybe most people who recognize London's name don't know he wrote an "end of the world" novel, but that could be generated into swell advertising to those "in the know"—"The Forgotten Science Fiction Epic!"—or some such. Better yet, it starts in a recognizable world, which means audiences will be able to immediately link to the surroundings before it veers off into the whole "contagion" thing. Even better, it is a series of adventures over time and places and could be a chance for an actor to give one of those "Oscar-worthy" studies of a man who ages from mid-twenties to late eighties within one film. Get Tom Hanks on it, and you'll have a blockbuster.

Bean Counter's Response: That may be pushing it a bit. I will grant that the episodic nature of the novel does make for distinct possibilities of a miniseries or even a continuing series for one of the networks based on the book. As stated, the book takes place in modern times, so special effects will be easy to keep to a minimum, and since nature hasn't completely overtaken the world in the early moments of the book, it would be a fairly cheap show to produce. I'm not too keen on London's eventual look of the characters, which finds them in furs and bits of cloth, as if they are cavemen, but we can certainly work around that factor. A continuing series would also avoid the somewhat depressing ending of the book by not even venturing there (unless perhaps in a concluding episode that wraps up everything, and even there we can tweak it enough to not make it seem as if mankind was over and done with).

One element that may pose problems is that of London's tone toward the class system—a socialist at heart, London tended to write in a rather ironic fashion about how the upper class could be reduced to that of the "barbarian," as demonstrated in *The Scarlet Plague* by depicting a once-rich woman who was now the slave of her former chauffeur. The ending may also be seen as a bit of a downer, as it shows society has fallen to a savage level after roughly a generation, although there are certainly other works that have similar premises (such as George R. Stewart's *Earth Abides*, not to mention numerous *Mad Max* rip-offs and films such as *Threads*). Even so, there's still lingering feelings of hope at the end of *The Scarlet Plague*, and the frequent moments of action make this quite promising. Certainly more so than the previous two novels discussed.

A series about people surviving a contagion has certainly been done before. There was a series called *Survivors* on British television in the 1970s (and redone just a few years ago) that touched on the same theme, so it's possible. Stephen King's *The Stand* is set up as the survivors of a plague dealing with issues after the "end," which was made into a lucrative miniseries for one of the networks.

There is also the Showtime cable series *Jeremiah* (2002–2004), which used a similar concept. While a theatrical version may be too ambitious, a series format just may work, and of the three projects looked at so far, this one merits the best chance of success. That nothing more has been done with this novel beyond a one-off radio adaptation on the CBS program *Escape* back in 1954 is surprising.

Studio's Decision: Agree that this property has a good chance of being turned into some type of series, be it a miniseries or something ongoing. Suggest we check into formats done in the past to see what should be avoided, tone down some of the political stuff London tied into it, and develop a stronger female lead for the project (maybe even make Smith a woman?) to attract a female audience and I think we may have something. Everything about *The Scarlet Plague* rings as a winner, and it is surprising nothing has been done with it already.

Last and First Men by Olaf Stapledon (1930)

Script Reader's Analysis: Olaf Stapledon (1886–1950) wrote books and essays on the nature of philosophy, while also dabbling in fiction. Most of his novels and stories deal with aspects of philosophy as well, as he found he could present his thoughts to a broader audience rather than with nonfiction essays on the topic. His first work of fiction, *Last and First Men*, is one of his two best known (the other being *Star Maker*, published in 1937) and deals with a speculative history of mankind starting just a short period of time after the publication of the book in 1930 and expanding billions of years into the future. Stapledon's attention to detail while being able to navigate storylines set over such a long stretch of time made him a renowned figure in science fiction and typically considered an inspiration to many famous writers in the genres of science fiction and fantasy, such as Arthur C. Clarke, C. S. Lewis, and Stanislaw Lem. Coincidentally, Stapledon leaned politically in the same direction as Jack London before him in that they both believed in certain aspects of socialism winning out in time over capitalistic ideals, although Stapledon was much more explicit in his dislike for capitalism. This is certainly the trend in the early chapters of *Last and First Men*.

The Plot: In a narrative told from the viewpoint of a modern man who is receiving messages from someone in the far-flung future, a history of mankind begins with a look at "things to come" in the 1930s and how man evolves. Eventually, man falls, only to rise again, fall again, rise again, fall, divert, rise and fall, battle aliens, conquer aliens, fall, rise, etc., etc., until—billions of years in the future—mankind realizes that it has exhausted its reach and will soon be extinguished. In those thousands of thousands of years, there are men who are artificial, can fly, of a group mind, giants and dwarves in various periods of evolution. Ultimately, the future messenger's actions are not an attempt to point out the futility of mankind (it is even admitted at one point that attempts at communication are not working as well as hoped), but rather to point to the "music" of mankind and a celebration of life continuing no matter what the consequences or changes that occur throughout history.

Finally, there is a certain irony in a book that obviously takes a humanist's attitude toward life being written in a style that is much like that of the New Testament; with a "future man" telling a writer in the past what is to come, rather than God doing the honors.

Agent's Pitch: It's . . . um . . . hmm. Well, as stated already, the book does cover a vast amount of material that one can take and make into a variety of projects. It certainly has the clout of many respected writers in the science fiction genre and is pointed to as the basis of many works that came after it. We probably wouldn't even be talking about *2001* or half of the movies and books that have come out in the past eighty years if it weren't for *Last and First Men.*

Okay, the writing isn't very fiery, but there is a poetic passion there that those who read it will see as being something that we can grasp onto for a movie. The script reader's mention of the "New Testament" rendering of the text is perhaps the way to go? Make the movie about the man in the present who receives the information and wonders, "Is it God? Is it an alien?" Then it turns out to be from the future! Imagine having to live with the idea of knowing exactly when the end was going to come and how everyone would eventually be just fine and dandy with it! This may work, or perhaps develop it as the framework to an anthology series that goes back and forth with stories developed out of what Stapledon presents in his book.

Bean Counter's Response: No argument that this is an iconic science fiction book and that the number of ideas therein are fascinating to consider. However, it is also a book that would be nearly impossible to translate to the screen.

While the novel is long on plot—covering the rise, fall, and rise again of mankind obviously would create a need for epic storytelling, after all—there is little in the way of audience identification: mankind as a whole rather than the acts of individuals propels the plot, and the story is told in a clinical, textbook style. Even Clarke's *Childhood's End*, which also covers the evolution of mankind, manages to avoid keeping such a distance between reader and characters [but more on that particular book later]. Although the textbook style is an interesting angle, and understandable for a man of letters like Stapledon, it leads to a rather dry read for those expecting something a bit more adventurous. On the other hand, it is exactly this method of storytelling that readily supports *why* the book would be a springboard for so many writers that come after Stapledon—he throws out so many ideas that one could easily take one or two, reshape it in its own way and make multiple films or novels. Yet, as a whole, *Last and First Men* refuses—adamantly so—to present anything that would transfer readily to a theatrical film or a television series (unless one wanted to create some type of Carl Sagan–like *Cosmos* series out of it for PBS). Even the wars discussed are presented as more to do with their ramifications rather than being written as action set pieces.

What do we cover? Just the first fall of mankind? Do we blaze through the subsequent evolutions in minutes in order to fit everything in? A miniseries may cover more ground, but most of the book is "this happened, then this, then this," without much structure in the way of narration that typically exists for fiction; there is no three-act structure here—it's a series of timely events until the end.

There are also immediate problems with the opening of the book: Stapledon has no way of avoiding getting immediate history of the 1930s onward incorrect for those of us reading from more than eighty years on. Moreover, Stapledon has little compassion for the American way of life and plants his future history with America being an instigator that destroys the world in the early chapters, which may not sit well with viewers (to be fair, China does not necessarily come off well in these chapters either). More than one source, including an introduction in one edition of the novel, suggests that readers either read those chapters with a "grain of salt" or skip over them and get to the meat of the novel afterward, and this would be a good suggestion for any film production made out of the book.

The agent has hit upon some possibilities—dealing with the issues a writer of the present would have in receiving by telepathy or another form (it's never quite stated how in the book) these stories of the future. Maybe something can be made of this concept into a movie, with visions of the future of mankind flashing through the film as the present-day writer comes to grip with what is happening to him and how it is ultimately all a story about the beauty of mankind rather than him losing his mind. It would take a lot of effort to mold the novel into such a concept, if we did go that way.

Studio's Decision: I think everyone needs to take a step back from this project and reassess. We're getting too far away from the book by concentrating on an element that isn't even presented in the text—that of the author's trials and tribulations upon getting messages from the future. The script reader mentioned it as being ironic, not the end-all for turning the book into a movie, for gosh sakes! Honestly, I grant you that it's an intriguing concept, but it's not Stapledon's book. There's a reason this book has been placed on a pedestal, and there's a reason that it's never been made into a movie—good books don't always make for entertaining movies. Any attempt to do this will be a gamble that no major studio would want to risk, and any independent studio would have trouble finding the funds to complete. Let's move on.

(Oh, but keep that "writer getting messages from the future" idea around for a possible script—that sounds interesting and we won't have to pay Stapledon's estate anything. Eh . . . No one is keeping notes here, right?)

Earth Abides by George R. Stewart (1949)

Script Reader's Analysis: George R. Stewart (1895–1980) is an example of another well-educated writer who used his own background as his starting point when putting together his most famous novel, *Earth Abides*. Stewart was an English professor at the University of California, Berkeley, and author of several nonfiction books about the evolution of American names, interstate roads within the U.S., a book about the Donner Party (*Ordeal by Hunger*), and a novel (*Storm*) that was the foundation of the National Weather Service beginning to give first names to tropical storms.

All this study came together in *Earth Abides*, with Stewart telling a story that incorporates his love of road travel, ecology, survival of man in inhospitable environments, and even the evolution of names into one story. Many will note that there are several similarities to Jack London's earlier *The Scarlet Plague* (including *Earth Abides* also being produced as a radio drama for the CBS series *Escape*; it was the only two-parter done for the series and came more than three years before *The Scarlet Plague* adaptation). Both deal with a man who survives a plague and wanders the cities in search of others. Both also find the protagonist trying to continue with civilization in some form as he had known it only for it to crumble into a more barbaric one as he reaches old age, as well as having a descendant in the final pages who may one day carry on the fight to bring civilization back. There are certainly other books that deal with lone survivors after a worldwide disaster searching for others and trying to find hope in the years following—Shelley's *The Last Man*, as well as the lesser-known *The Purple Cloud* (1901) by M. P. Shiel are a couple of examples from the years before London and Stewart. Significantly, *Earth Abides* is typically remembered most of the "contagion-survivor" novels because it is one of the first to take place in "modern times" and in recognizable circumstances for readers of the twentieth century and even into the twenty-first.

The Plot: Isherwood Williams, commonly referred to as "Ish," is bitten by a rattlesnake while in a mountainous area located on the West Coast of America. Thinking himself near death, Ish holes up in his cabin for a time, but eventually recovers. Taking a mining hammer he found right before being bitten, Ish returns from the mountains only to discover that a plague has wiped out or scared off everyone in town.

Eventually he travels back to his home to discover the same, and, picking up a stray dog that keeps following him, he begins a drive through America to see who is still around. In his travels, he finds both people who he believes will survive (a makeshift family already starting to farm what they can) and those who certainly won't (a couple living it up in the city with no preparation for the future). He also comes across the crazed and the lonely, before finally returning to the West Coast.

There he meets Emma, and the two decide to stay together to build a family and to establish a community of other survivors in hopes of bringing back civilization. Ish attempts to teach everyone elements of sciences and other subjects of the world before, but has little success except with his son, Joey. When Joey dies, Ish gives up trying to rebuild the past and instead focuses everyone on basic survival through hunting and farming. Eventually Ish is the last of those still alive from before the plague, seen as nearly a legend by the younger generations and his hammer a symbol of power. Before his death, he speaks with his great-grandson Jack, who shows some of the same promises as a leader that Ish's son Joey had. Ish passes his hammer on to Jack and contemplates all that he has been through, and what the future will hold for those left. As he looks at nature around him, and how it has devoured what mankind once saw as progress, he remembers a passage from the Bible stating that men may go and come, "but the earth abides."

One similarity between Stewart and previous writer Jefferies is their fascination (perhaps even obsession) with how nature will reclaim the land after mankind has been depopulated. In Jefferies' case, he devotes the first part of his novel to such descriptions, but Stewart intermingles his text between that of a second-person narrative and descriptions that appear to be Ish's observations. Early on, it appears to be Ish's fever dreams and read in such a fashion, but later such commentaries on nature pop up nearly at random and can be disconcerting. However, these moments would be visually rendered in a movie and thus are of little concern for a film project.

Two elements that are intriguing from the novel—one of which may not even be worth pointing out. The main physical relationship in the novel is that between a Caucasian man (Ish) and an African American woman (Emma). Little is made of this interracial relationship in the text, even after Stewart raises such issues earlier in the book with Ish's meeting with the impromptu family that is farming. One can speculate how Middle America may question that setting up such a romance in the movie was a "Hollywood stunt," even though it's right there in the novel.

The other notable observation this script reader has made is that Ish luckily avoids the effects of the contagion on society and comes back in time to see the final results. One would first assume that the rattlesnake bite at the time of infection somehow helped him survive, but as others obviously outlasted the plague as well, his layup in the cabin at the beginning of the novel merely sets up him, along with readers, to slowly discover what happened after he "left." Perhaps Stewart believed describing those details "as they happened" brought little to the story besides a lot of depressing and unnecessary backstory (unlike London's *The Scarlet Plague*, where the protagonist describes everything that happens during those days of panic and sickness as part of his process to understand his new world). There are certainly movies that skip over the end of the world [several famous ones are mentioned in chapter 3, in fact], and we can do the same here with an adaptation, but some viewers do see avoiding such details as a bit of a cheat.

Agent's Pitch: Fantabulous! As the script reader mentioned, we have a known writer with a book that—at least until recently—was well remembered by the public. We got an interracial relationship here, which always entices known actors into playing something still considered slightly "risky" even today, and those roles are both strong alpha characters that are involved with most of the action of the novel (Ish more than Emma, but Emma still gets a good deal to do as the "mother" to the community created). There's also a number of supporting parts that have much to do, with a series of storylines that can be used or dropped depending on where we go with a script. It's even got a smart dog in it! People love dogs in end-of-the-world movies!

Not mentioned by the script reader is the detail that Stephen King stated that *Earth Abides* was in his mind when writing *The Stand*, and we know how famous that book is! Maybe we can even get a quote from King to help promote the thing! It's a class-act story, with a beginning, middle and end. Sure, there's a sense of loss here and there (loss of family, loss of the world we once knew), but the book ends on a positive note, and the movie can end the same way. We even have a symbol that can be used for promotional purposes on posters and such—Ish's hammer, which is a symbol of his life and his hope for the future. This is a winner all the way!

Bean Counter's Response: As much as I would like to disagree with the agent just for using the word "fantabulous," I think *Earth Abides* is a possible winner. Avoiding the whole "everyone is dying" part of the story may not work for all audience members, but there is so much going on in the novel that it is of little consequence if missed. Although the script reader doesn't mention it, the agent is correct that there are plenty of supporting characters after the first third of the novel that have dramatic moments that would work well on film—the whole social-political crisis of Charlie, who may be bad news for the community, for example. The main characters of Ish and Emma would certainly be of interest to big-name stars if correctly pitched, as well.

I do have a slight disagreement about King's endorsement of *Earth Abides*. His comment about Stewart's novel appears in King's nonfiction book *Danse Macabre* and is mainly about his process in figuring out the plot of *The Stand*. While King does point out that *Earth Abides'* plot helped plant the seed of his epic novel, he also made clear that he didn't think the second part of the novel worked quite as well as the first. Further, he puts much emphasis on trying to write a book that was an American *Lord of the Rings*, which is about as far as you could possibly get from *Earth Abides*. It is also interesting to note that, while King respects and endorses *Earth Abides*, he references many elements besides the book that led to him creating *The Stand*, and it is not quite a case where we can stand there and say, "If you like *The Stand*, here's where it all started!" While it's a nice tidbit, emphasis has been placed a bit too strongly on this aspect over the years when it comes to *Earth Abides*.

The above are just minor nitpicks, however. Overall, much like *The Scarlet Plague* before it, there does seem to be some room to make a good movie or even a series out of the material. Moreover, there is a history of other attempts to do just that with the novel, so we know the book is workable. Fortunately, such projects are far enough in the past that any new attempt would appear fresh to modern audiences.

Studio's Decision: Agree about the similarities, but that merely means that if we cannot get one rolling, we can go with the other. The elements of the novel that may be hard to do, such as the ecological notes Ish makes, can be easily rendered for the big screen in a visual sense, so no problems there. The ending may come across as a bit of a downer to some, but we can easily tack on a scene with the great-grandson emerging with the hammer in triumph after seeing Ish and showing that a new, better world is in the offing. Some swelling operatic music there as the masses rise up and cheer. Voilà—instant classic ending.

Okay, maybe that's looking a bit too *Lion King*-ish there, but something of that tone would work to get around any chances of people leaving the theater depressed. It may be the end of the world, but we want people leaving happy.

Childhood's End by Arthur C. Clarke (1953)

Script Reader's Analysis: For many years Arthur C. Clarke was considered one of the "Big Three" in science fiction, along with Robert Heinlein (*Starship Troopers*) and Isaac Asimov (pretty much everything else . . . okay, that's a rare joke from this reader, but Asimov was prolific as a science author and science fiction writer, including *I, Robot*, which was adapted as a hit movie for Will Smith). Clarke (1917–2008) may not have been quite as busy as Asimov, but he certainly contributed in abundance to the printed page, with written pieces on scientific advances as well as his short stories, novellas and novels over the years. Best known is his collaboration with Stanley Kubrick on the movie and novel *2001: A Space Odyssey*, which was originally pitched between the two as an adaptation of his short story "The Sentinel," although there are certainly aspects of *Childhood's End* in the finished work as well. Besides *2001*, *Childhood's End* and "The Sentinel," Clarke created some of the better-known short stories and novels in the genre, from *Rendezvous with Rama* to "The Nine Billion Names of God" (an apocalyptic short story) to *The Sands of Mars*.

Childhood's End has been seen as evidence that Clarke was still engaged with the paranormal (a belief he discarded later in life, although he did use telekinesis as a plot device in the novel), but the book mainly shows his early faith in science. Although sci-fi writers tend to portray the negative consequences of science on mankind, Clarke typically saw it as beneficial. This can be seen in *Childhood's End*, for while it could be viewed as a gloom-and-doom tale of the end of civilization, Clarke himself saw it as focusing on the positive advancement of the human race to another level of existence.

The Plot: It is the time of the Cold War's Space Race between the U.S. and the Soviet Union when aliens arrive, offering advancement and peace for all of humanity. After some hesitation, the people of Earth begin to cooperate with the aliens, and peace does come quickly to the world, but at the cost of creative interest in the arts and sciences. Many years later, children are born who exhibit telekinetic abilities that separate them from their parents mentally and, soon after, physically as they relocate to a continent of their own.

Before this occurs, however, the aliens—now known as the Overlords and who are satanic in appearance—find that a human named Jan Rodricks had stowed away on one of their supply ships. He

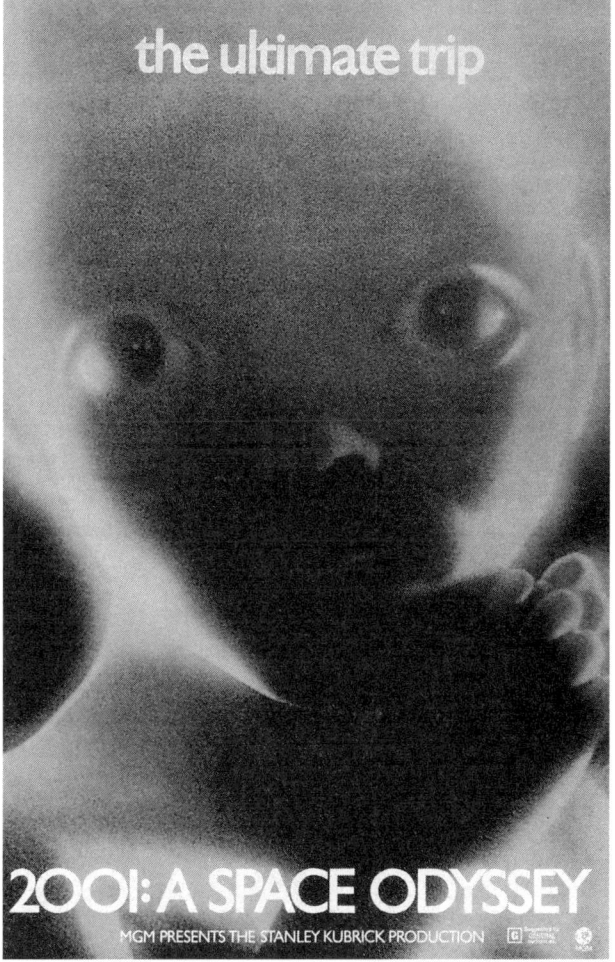

2001: A Space Odyssey (1968)—a classic film that found inspiration in Arthur C. Clarke's never-filmed novel *Childhood's End*.

arrives on the Overlords' home world and discovers that the aliens are merely servants of a greater power called the Overmind—made up of various alien races that have moved beyond the physical level and joined together as one entity. The Overlords' task is to find worlds where the inhabitants are close to achieving a new stage of evolution, much as has occurred with the children on Earth, and prepare them to join with the Overmind.

By the time Jan returns to Earth many decades after his departure, the children are mainly the only ones left, as most of those that came before them have died or are in the process of dying. The Overlords and Jan observe the final stages of preparation for the children to become part of the Overmind, with Jan staying to report to the Overlords firsthand what occurs as the aliens back off to a safe distance in space. With the startlingly rapture-like departure of the children, Jan feels a wave of fulfillment for the human race as they move up on the evolutionary scale even as he dies and the Earth crumbles around him and disappears. With the disappearance of Earth, the Overlords move on to their next assignment.

As noted above, Clarke's suggestion of aliens coming one day to help propel mankind into a greater era can readily be found in *2001* with the usage of the monolith (elements of such alien involvement stopping dead a Cold War can also be seen as a major plot point in the sequel film and novel, *2010*; not to mention being used as well in James Cameron's *The Abyss*). However, Kubrick hid that revelation behind a lot of special effects and metaphorical images, intentionally obscuring the meaning in the process. The television series *Babylon 5* also used many elements about the Overlords as part of the alien species in the series called the Vorlons; down to the revelation that they are helping mankind move to a higher evolutionary plane, as well as their physical appearance being biblical in nature (albeit as angels instead of demons). Still, the plot of the film hasn't really been pushed much in film over the years, and once the late topical element of the Cold War is excised, the story could stand as-is for a movie. The element of children gaining telekinetic powers soon after the arrival of aliens may be seen as a bit reminiscent of *The Midwich Cuckoos* (1957 and adapted into film as *Village of the Damned* in 1960 and 1995), but that book saw such children as pretty much alien invaders, while Clarke's *earlier* work saw it as an evolutionary step up for mankind. The main thing would be to avoid comparisons, even if our argument would readily be, "Clarke was there first." In reality, he was there second in many ways, as it is easy to see elements of Stapledon's *Last and First Men* in the novel—a work that Clarke freely admitted was very influential on him in his early career.

Agent's Pitch: Once again, another known author's name is involved with the project we are reviewing, which is always a plus. People know *2001*, and the sequel film is a bit of a cult-favorite among sci-fi fans, so there is a safety net right there in terms of building a picture around one of Clarke's novels. There is also a lead character, Jan, who is intertwined into the story, so we don't have the loss of audience identification that comes with some of the other novels—like *Last and First Men* and *A Canticle for Leibowitz* where actions take place over centuries and there is no consistent character to root for. Okay, admittedly he disappears for the good chunk of the story on Earth as he sails off to the Overlords' planet, but at least he comes back and has explained to him what has occurred. Even better, we could build the story around Jan's adventure solely and we avoid some of the depressing material about parents losing their kids to the "next evolutionary step" and killing themselves in despair (which appears in the novel). Make him the one that discovers what they look like, and conflate the time-period things occur so that it can be within Jan's lifetime and you've still got *Childhood's End*, with a meaty part for a major actor like Will Smith.

Bean Counter's Response: I was going to suggest that, much like Stapledon's book earlier discussed, this may be more to bite off than we can chew. However, the agent does have a good point that we may be able to move a few things around, make this more about the one character, and still have it drive home the same message as the book. However, let me point out that earlier attempts have been made to get a script into shape for *Childhood's End*, with Universal looking into making it into a film in the early 2000s, but nothing came of it. This may be enough of a history to show that, while the intentions may be good, the project just won't gel. Might be best to avoid.

Studio's Decision: Have to agree with the bean counter here. There are certainly enough projects out there to spend time on getting to completion rather than one that seems to have been batted around for decades with no resolution. A movie about how we're all insects and the kiddies are going to destroy Earth just because they want to leave home probably would be a difficult sell to the American public. Maybe if the agent can solicit someone to throw together a script that can impress, or actually can get Will Smith to express interest, we'll take another look at it.

Alas, Babylon by Pat Frank (1959)

Script Reader's Analysis: Pat Frank was a pseudonym used by writer Harry Hart Frank (1908–1964), whose first novel was actually another tale about the end of the world called *Mr. Adam*. *Mr. Adam* (1946) was a satirical novel about the only fertile man left on the planet after radiation sterilizes every other man. Pat would author other novels over time, but it would be *Alas, Babylon* that would make him a household name. The book is considered one of the first novels to deal with the aftermath of a nuclear war in America and the dangers of radioactivity at a time when most people still thought of radiation as something you could avoid by ducking behind a tree or holding your breath for a while.

The Plot: Fort Repose is a (fictional) small town in Central Florida that managed to avoid destruction in a short-lived nuclear war between the Soviet Union and the United States. With communication outside of the town pretty much gone, the townsfolk slowly have to come to grips with the reality of living in a new world where they have to make do on their own. Randy Bragg has his brother's wife and children staying with him when the attack occurs, leaving Randy struggling to keep the family together while also helping others through various problems that arise from their ignorance as well as keeping one's sanity after the "end of the world."

Frank's book remains immensely popular after over fifty years due to a modern setting for a book dealing with a subject that weighed on people's minds since the bombing of Hiroshima. Before the end of World War II, novels tended to head in the direction of those already discussed—with a contagion (even if in the form of a gas, it still functions in the same manner) wiping out people in a way that is instantaneous. Thus, once a period of outbreak had occurred, everyone else still around has little to worry about beyond finding shelter, food and company. *Alas, Babylon* moved in an alternate direction most readers probably knew would be the case if bombs started to drop: that surviving the blasts would be only the beginning of a long process, and one where someone else's mistake may cost your life. Although the book doesn't go quite as dark as later books in how mankind will turn on itself pretty quickly [such as *Lucifer's Hammer*, which is discussed later in this chapter, or *The Road* (2009)], it is still a solemn look at how the world would change forever, even for the lucky ones.

Of course, fifty-plus years have passed since the book was published, and some of the dialogue dealing with life-and-death issues such as radiation comes off as rather stilted—with Frank's background as a government observer and newspaperman that is forgivable in some ways. Today, most of the information (some of which may be seen as misinformation in this more informed day and age) about radiation poisoning and the effects of nuclear bombing may be common knowledge to readers, but at the time, it would have read as startling. On the upside (or perhaps downside, depending on your views), common knowledge about such topics has slipped with today's audience, so it may be just a surprising today for some readers.

Alas, Babylon did make its way to the small screen back in 1960 as the premiere episode of *Playhouse 90*'s fourth season. It starred Don Murray as Randy, with Kim Hunter, Dana Andrews and Burt Reynolds and was considered a misfire by critics and Pat Frank. The consensus was that the broadcast gutted most of the dramatic action for a "love story," although a play version based on the teleplay does not support this criticism. Frank, on the other hand, while feeling that the broadcast had action, thought it had no narrative point to make and was missing a segment or two to get his story points across. There has been speculation for years that CBS may hold a copy of the program, yet it has never reappeared for public viewing since its airing back in 1960. Thus, there is no concern that a new adaptation of the book would conflict with anything that the public could or would be interested in seeing.

Agent's Pitch: If we're talking iconic doomsday novels, you don't get any more iconic than *Alas, Babylon*! It has a small-town feel, with lots of parts for character actors and a strong lead, a character who has to grow to become the real leader of the town over time. The sister-in-law and another character are heavy female parts, so actresses would love to work in it as well. Sure, some of the dialogue is a bit textbook-ish, and we may need to find a better reason as to why this one town avoids most of the problems that would come after such an attack, but it's action-packed and has an "up" resolution. There's a reason *Alas, Babylon* is remembered, and a film adaptation would prove the same.

Bean Counter's Response: It would be remembered all right—as something viewers have already seen, perhaps multiple times. There was a television series a few years back called *Jericho*, about a town that survives a nuclear war and the struggle of the community to deal with the aftermath. It lasted for a season, was canceled for low ratings, renewed for seven more episodes and then canceled for good. At this point, an adaptation of *Alas, Babylon* would look like we're merely ripping off a CBS series that only had limited appeal. That's just one of many examples from over the past thirty-plus years. Nothing against the book itself—definitely a page-turner, if a bit antiseptic in its dialogue at times—but the timing is all wrong for it. Best to avoid, even though it is a classic of the genre.

Studio's Decision: Gotta agree. It's a bit too much of "been there, done that," even if the novel can be seen as the genesis of where many movies and television shows to follow came from (a recent example appears in the NBC series *Revolution*, which used the idea of the brothers sending a coded message to each other at the time of the end-of-the-world event just as in *Alas, Babylon*). Maybe someday someone can come back to it, but other postapocalyptic movies where average people try to survive—such as *Testament*, *The Day After* and *Threads*—have pushed the boundaries of the topic far beyond what appears in *Alas, Babylon*. To make it any grimmer would be a drastic change to the story; not to change it at all would have audiences bored. It may be a great book, but making it a movie would be a no-win situation for the time being.

A Canticle for Leibowitz by Walter M. Miller Jr. (1960)

Script Reader's Analysis: Walter M. Miller Jr. (1923–1996) was a prolific science fiction writer of the 1950s. His last book was the one he is best known for, *A Canticle for Leibowitz*. He was known to be very private about his life and became more so as the years went by. He would never write another book after *Leibowitz*, but was working on a follow-up to the book when he committed suicide in 1996. That manuscript was eventually completed by another writer and released as *Saint Leibowitz and the Wild Horse Woman*. The book is actually not a sequel as much as an additional story that takes place between those told in *A Canticle for Leibowitz*.

The Plot: The novel is broken into three parts: "Fiat Homo," "Fiat Lux" and "Fiat Voluntas Tua." Each part—which were originally written as separate novellas and then forged into one novel by Miller—deals with a period of mankind centuries after the destruction of America in a nuclear war. The main thread that runs through the parts is that of an order of monks who secretly preserve books and files that detail scientific achievements after civilization destroyed most of them in reaction to the war.

"Fiat Homo" focuses on a lowly monk who locates a six-hundred-year-old buried bomb shelter that has works written by the soon-to-be-sainted Isaac Leibowitz, one of the architects of the world-destroying bombs and the creator of the monastic order that is attempting to preserve the work. Much political

The series *Babylon 5* (1994–1998) paid homage to both *A Canticle for Leibowitz* (1960) and *Last and First Men* (1930).

scandal is suggested by the recovery of the "memorabilia," as some in the order think the find could jeopardize Leibowitz being proclaimed a saint. Eventually the monk is able to pass on some of the material to the pope but dies on his trip back.

"Fiat Lux" takes place six hundred years after the first part and deals with more political intrigue as mankind begins to emerge from its ignorance of the past twelve hundred years and is embracing some elements of science again.

"Fiat Voluntas Tua" is centered on an era six hundred years after the second (twelve hundred years after the first), where mankind began using science once again. However, along with space travel and other major advances, there have come even more political issues, with another war set to occur that will pretty much wipe out Earth and all the knowledge the monks have spent centuries collecting.

The book has plenty of moments of humor, almost Douglas Adams–like, especially in its first part where Miller makes much of how wordage common today would be taken to mean a number of other things in the future. This humorous side slips a bit later in the novel but remains enough throughout in order to give the reader a sense of bemusement as the world rises and falls in a future era. It also has a sense of hope emerging from the ashes, as those who seek to protect mankind's legacy leave for "greener pastures" with (pretty much) the end of human existence on Earth itself.

Years have passed with potential adaptations of the novel being mentioned here and there in the trade papers, but none has ever been done. In all probability, this is due to the same problems that plague *Last and First Men*: besides one possible character—one that may be that of the "Wandering Jew" of legend and appears briefly in all three parts—characters live and die within the frameworks of their particular section of the book. As stated above, the book really is three novellas that exist within the same futuristic framework, and with only the goal of preserving science through this religious order as a standard throughout. A very entertaining book, but probably a hard sell as a movie. It should be mentioned that an episode of the 1990s series *Babylon 5* played tribute to *Canticle* in the episode "Deconstruction of Falling Stars," which dealt briefly with a monk preserving the science of an earlier era in a postwar future of Earth, as well as radio adaptations that have been done by the BBC and NPR in the past. So it has been tried.

Agent's Pitch: Once again, the script reader has brought up an important point—this is a project that has been around in Hollywood for a while and is not simply a case of someone having a pet project, but rather such an enticing novel that many have wanted to put it up on the big screen. Yes, there is the problem of no running character, but as also mentioned there is the one character that could be the Wandering Jew. Or perhaps even Leibowitz himself? There have been many interpretations of the legend through the centuries, so why not Leibowitz as the embodiment of such a character, left to wander the earth for his careless, selfish sin against God by allowing the nuclear war that killed off so many? The novel opens with a stranger in a beard who sets things in motion, and it ends over a thousand years later with a monk in a beard leaving Earth. Okay, making a connection due to a beard is a stretch, but it is one way to go with a film.

Work within those boundaries and a doable film or even a miniseries of some type to tell each part could work. If not, perhaps at least the "Fiat Homo" as a film on its own?

Bean Counter's Response: I don't think just "Fiat Homo" alone would cut the mustard as a film; certainly not with an ending that has our reluctant hero shot in the head with an arrow and no real resolution to the story. You'd be better off going with the third part, "Fiat Voluntas Tua," and using brief flashbacks to the other sections of the novel. That could work, but we'd probably get a backlash from fans for discarding so much in such a manner.

Miller's writing is excellent and does have some funny situations, but these mainly work on the printed page and would be hard to pass off as dialogue in a movie (or would come off as repetitive), since a good chunk of it is inner dialogue. The first two-thirds of the novel does at least seem cost-effective in allowing us to shoot in barren areas without worries about showing advanced technologies; of course, that's all saved for the final third, which is where the money would probably have to go.

There are also potential problems with religion. Not only is there the Wandering Jew, which can be provocative when used for entertainment purposes, but also the religious order created to "keep the faith" in a sense, as it obviously has elements of Catholicism and could be construed a parody. It's a delicate, dicey area to consider and may explain why there has always been some holding back in creating a film out of the book beyond reshaping the story to fit one hundred minutes of screen-time.

Studio's Decision: Yes, it looks like there have been some attempts to get this one off the ground, but it appears to be a very difficult book to convert in movie terms. Perhaps it is best to stay that way, especially with some concerns about the religious aspects of the novel, even though it is mainly dealing with mankind's ignorance. The studio is tempted but not convinced with what we have in front of us so far. Saying that, if someone managed to unlock the plot in a way to make it work as a film, they probably could have a blockbuster on their hands.

Lucifer's Hammer by Larry Niven and Jerry Pournelle (1977)

Script Reader's Analysis: First off, we finally have come to authors of a novel that are still alive. Larry Niven (b. 1938) and Jerry Pournelle (b. 1933) are famous science fiction writers who have worked on several books separately and a dozen books together, of which *Lucifer's Hammer* is one of their earliest collaborations.

Meteor—the 1979 film that some contend used the novel *Lucifer's Hammer* (1977) as its basis. As a movie, it made for a great pinball machine.

The novel deals with the prediction, preparation for and aftermath of a comet breaking up in Earth's atmosphere and leading to the destruction of most of the planet.

The Plot: Tim Hamner, the protagonist, is a rich amateur astronomer who spots the comet that will be nicknamed "The Hammer." Due to faulty calculations, scientists realize too late that the comet will hit Earth. When it hits the atmosphere, it breaks up into several smaller asteroids slamming into multiple places around the world, creating a series of natural disasters that wipes out millions. A panicky political situation leads to nuclear bombing between Russia and China and even more devastation for the planet. Besides Hamner and his wife, multiple other characters struggle to survive—some working together to rebuild a community, while others join a deadly armed, cannibalistic religious cult that attempts to wipe out all others in their path.

The book is somewhat unique out of the group of novels being discussed, as there are nearly as many pages written about the "before" and "during" aspects of such a disaster as with the struggle to survive (typically most such novels only briefly look at the "before" aspects of such a situation, concentrating more on the aftereffects of such an event). While some of this would no doubt need to be trimmed for a movie, it does allow for the writers to flesh out characters in a way that is not seen in some other novels of this type. Of course, smashing things into Earth is nothing new—going back to such titles as *When Worlds Collide* up to the present with more recent films like *Seeking a Friend for the End of the World* and *Melancholia* (2012 and 2011)—but one rather intriguing aspect is that the book attempts to end on a positive note. Instead of the rather downbeat "our children and their children will be barbarians" aspect of most other apocalyptic novels and films, *Lucifer's Hammer* has an upbeat ending suggesting that mankind would be able to not only progress from the disaster but advance further.

One side note about the novel—many people who read the book as kids or teenagers came away with a vivid lesson in learning to do things to help one survive. This is reflected in the novel after the comet hits, when people attempting to join the community must prove their worth in order to be accepted. In a world where technology was secondary to simple survival, knowing how to build a fence becomes more important than building a computer, and kids came away from the book with the focus of learning a certain number of skills "just in case" they ever became necessary to use in real life.

The book does bog down a bit in the final third, as the group tries to fight off the religious cult (oddly, a similar factor comes into play in Stephen King's *The Stand*, although in his book the villains have more supernatural intentions than those in *Lucifer's Hammer*), as it seems a bit rushed and too definitive in its resolution after such a buildup. Some modern readers have also found the dialogue and actions of certain "bad guys" a bit off-putting, thanks to being a product of the times (the 1970s), but that could be easily changed in a script.

The major problem here is that, as stated, there've been enough movies like this that there may not be much call for another. It has been pointed out that the film *Meteor* (1979) appeared to use the book as a leaping-off point toward very different conclusions. If so, it is not unusual in Hollywood—Arthur C. Clarke wrote a book about such a possible collision in *The Hammer of God*, which eventually was changed so much in script form that the movie based on it, *Deep Impact*, looked nothing like the novel it sprang from.

Agent's Pitch: Sure, there've been a few movies like this, but in most of those cases, the earth gets off pretty well (or in *When Worlds Collide*, the survivors go to a better place anyway). This one digs in to show the rugged adventures of those that live through it and then find a way to deal with the new world they find themselves. Plus, you have the major action sequence of an ongoing battle with the religious fanatics late in the story that will give everything before it an exciting conclusion. Again, another story with multiple casting opportunities for a number of different characters and the added strength of a protagonist that makes it to the end of the novel in triumph.

Besides *Melancholia*, which ended on a depressing note, there hasn't been a major studio movie about planet smashing in a while and certainly not one as jam-packed with action and food for thought as this one. Tie it in with the Boy Scouts on that whole "knowing multiple skills to be of vital use" thing ("Be prepared" is their motto, after all) or other activity groups like it, and it connect with the kids.

Bean Counter's Response: It's an intriguing idea to deal with the long process involved with a coming catastrophe and the resulting consequences of it. The fanatics fighting the protagonist's group near the end is a bit of a problem, as it nearly seems like something out of a different book after all that has come before it. Yes, it may make realistic sense, and marauding groups of vicious killers certainly have popped up in other works, such as several zombie movies (and *The Walking Dead* series) as well as the novel and film of *The Road*. Still, the fanatical aspects of such a group may be hard to work into the movie without fear of offending a real-life organization. Perhaps some changes to their alliances to avoid this?

Even so, we would run into the potential problems of previous works already out there that have covered this territory to some degree. Looks like another case of a book that helped set up several similar-themed movies, but actually producing a movie now about it would look like we were ripping off everyone else.

Studio's Decision: A bit hesitant about this one. This could work, but it would need a strong first two-thirds to make the final third—the battle with the fanatics—gel properly in a two-hour movie; otherwise it'll look like we ran out of story and shoved in the battle just to eat up time. The final message of technology not being the enemy of mankind is a promising concept—perhaps this can be worked more into being the central theme of the movie instead of a clever upbeat idea at the end? Also, it may be a case that we're looking too hard at the cause of the situation rather than all the plotting that happens around it. It may be *Lucifer's Hammer*, but the story is about the people involved and not so much the comet itself. With that in mind, trimming most of the "before" section of the book to get to the accident itself and then spend the final hour of film-time with the results may be a way to go. There's been potential to get this one going before; let's give it a roll and see what we can come up with for it.

Y: The Last Man by Brian K. Vaughan and Pia Guerra (2002–2008)

Script Reader's Analysis: The last book discussed here is the most recent. It is also the only comic-book series discussed out of the novels here. The concept—about the last man on a planet full of women—isn't anything new to books (Pat Frank's *Mr. Adam* has already been mentioned) or movies, but the comic-book series was a vastly successful one that ran for sixty issues and covers a variety of topics within those pages.

The writer/creator of the series, Brian K. Vaughan, had been writing for Marvel and DC Comics before coming up with *Y: The Last Man* for DC's mature-audience line, Vertigo. Vaughan eventually would break into television, working as a script editor, writer and producer for the series *Lost*, as well as working on scripts for various projects, including those based on his own work. Pia Guerra was the artist who penciled the series (for those who aren't familiar with comic-book terms, which means she created the artwork, with others doing the inking to finalize the images).

The Plot: A plague of unknown origins (suggestions are made as to what causes it—from manmade to natural) kills all males of every mammal species in the world, with the exception of a young man named Yorick Brown and his pet capuchin money, Ampersand. The sixty-issue series follows Yorick as he travels to locate his fiancée, Beth, in a world devastated by the loss. He is pursued by those who wish him dead either for political or other reasons. Eventually he does meet up with Beth, but they both realize they have no relationship. Evading those that wish him dead, Yorick grows old in a stabilized world that regroups through the cloning of both men (Yorick) and women.

Y: The Last Man had a variety of plots and subplots intertwined into the mix as Yorick continued on his journey. A number of characters appear throughout the series, but there is really a minimal cast that contributes to the main thrust of the tale, so it would not be that difficult to come up with a core number of actors to fill roles or write the script to mainly focus on them (unlike some of the earlier novels discussed, which have such a large group of characters working together that it may be hard to keep the film focused without going all over the place to cover them all). Some comic-book fans may howl at this suggestion, but with the somewhat episodic nature of the story, a lot of material from the sixty issues could be jettisoned in order to create a ninety-minute movie without losing the plot. Otherwise, it would have to be something bigger, or perhaps even be turned into a television series in order to incorporate all the twists and turns that happen in the series.

Of course, it should be noted that New Line Cinema has been struggling to get a film adaptation off the ground since 2007, including with Vaughan himself writing a script. At one time there was even talk of turning it into a trilogy of films to tell the entire story, with actor Shia LaBeouf playing Yorick. September 2012 saw a script come through from writers Matthew Federman and Stephen Scaia that the studio felt was promising, and they are again looking to make the film.

Agent's Pitch: If New Line doesn't work things out, then this is a hot project that we should snatch up! It's got action, a strong role for a geek-like actor who can then play the tough guy at the end, it's science fiction, end-of-the-world stuff and it's populated by mostly women. Lots and lots of women. Tell me that doesn't sell on the big screen. The only guy left in the world who all the girls are trying to catch? That's money in the bank. Especially if it gets sexy (and there certainly is some sex in the comic). Is Cinemax still around? Maybe we can make it a weekly "after-hours" show there or something.

Bean Counter's Response: Well, I think the agent is being wrongheaded here. And in need of a cold shower. The story definitely is action-packed, and there is some heat involved through sex, but the emphasis is on characters and their interaction due to the apocalyptic crisis on their hands. Those sixty issues would suggest something more along the lines of AMC's *Walking Dead* series if done at all, however, as such character development works better in such a serial style than as a one-off film. Saying that, a trilogy seems a bit much for the material, as it is essentially a chase mixed in with the "whodunit" aspect as to why Yorick is alive when most other men are dead. To extend it that far could make those not familiar with the series think we were simply stretching things out to make a buck.

Agree that the subject matter may appeal to young men and boys, but there's more here than that. Big question is, is this just one movie or something more? May be best, if done at all, to stick with the one-film concept, but everyone wants a franchise these days, so I doubt that is what the studio really wants to hear.

Studio's Decision: Agree that a one-off movie, with perhaps room for a sequel, would be the way to go here. Oddly enough, that would mean that anything to come in a sequel would fall outside of what was already written in the comic, unless we pulled some of the storylines out to save for such a sequel. It would also mean losing the epilogue of the series, where we see Yorick at the end of his days. Still, probably the best way to go, if at all. Of course, New Line has it and may finally get it going, so perhaps our even discussing it is moot at this point.

Still, it means that out of these ten novels, at least one of them may finally see a proper theatrical release. Some were better ideas than others, some had better execution in the writing than others, but all are iconic in how other novels and especially the movies would be created based on their concepts in the years to come. Will they all eventually make it to the big screen? Probably not; at least some of them look to be hard to conform to a script that would put popcorn eaters into seats. If not those, however, there are plenty of other novels that have come out over the years we can take a look at. Certainly a cash opportunity here, as it seems people are never going to get tired of movies about the end of the world, be it from contagions or aliens or whatever. The audiences of today love this stuff. Wonder if they always did?

2

When Film Was Young, the Earth Was Doomed

Early Examples of Armageddon

hings to Come, scripted by H. G. Wells from his own novel *The Shape of Things to Come*, was released in 1936. It features a world war that would go on for decades, creating a postapocalyptic world where mankind slowly reassembles itself to greater glory. It perhaps is not quite on the level of the rises and falls seen in Olaf Stapledon's *Last and First Men* (mentioned in the previous chapter), but it does see Man working to reverse the Hell it has unleashed on Earth and for this reason is commonly referred to as the first true postapocalyptic movie of cinema.

Yet that's not quite true. Between the beginning of the movies and 1936, there were a handful of movies that used apocalyptic devices in their films to entice audiences. Of course, spectacle is the spice of filmmaking, and showing things blowing up real good certainly catches the eyes more than simple dramatic responses between characters, so a good horse chase in a western, a daring cliff-jump in an action film or the acrobatics of stars like Keaton and Fairbanks spoke volumes to the masses. Thus, a good disaster sells, and when the sinking of the *Titanic* saw money being made with films such as *Saved from the Titanic* (*1912*, starring survivor Dorothy Gibson), the German *In Nacht und Eis* (1912), as well as August Blom receiving international attention with his film *Atlantis* in 1913 (featuring an ocean liner sinking at sea after being hit), filmmakers saw that audiences were fascinated by seeing such epic visuals on the big screen. The public's shocked reaction to Winsor McCay's animated documentary *The Sinking of the Lusitania* (1918), which was educational in its intent, fortified such spectaculars. With that in mind, disaster films began to be cranked out, and what better way to have a big special-effects moment than something as astonishing as the world stopping? Or using the end of the world to tell a dramatic story?

What follow are five films released before 1936 featuring the end of the world in one context or another: comet, natural disaster, scientific intervention or contagion. Three are dramas, two are comedies. Oddly enough, two of the dramas are somewhat similar in story setup and execution, while one of the

Although *Things to Come* (1936) is commonly considered the first apocalyptic movie, there were a handful of films before that also show the end of the world.

comedies was remade twice before 1936 (and one of those times as a musical). In reflecting on so many decades past, it is interesting to see how much had changed as well as remained the same between these early attempts to show the end and those that come out today.

No doubt, some may wonder why *Metropolis* isn't on this list, but more about that film in chapter 6.

The End of the World (aka *Verdens Undergang*) (1916)

Atlantis, as mentioned before, had given Danish director August Blom worldwide attention—or, rather, some infamous attention, as some thought showing such a sinking so soon after the *Titanic* disaster was in poor taste, even if the event was taken directly from the book being adapted. Such notoriety was not necessarily why Blom moved on to an epic end-of-the-world film soon after, however. He had already made a name for himself with a variety of early films, some of which had fantasy elements in them (such as adaptations of *Dr. Jekyll and Mr. Hyde* and *Robinson Crusoe*, as well as a modern variation on Jack the Ripper), so another fantastical film was certainly not that unusual a step for him at the time.

The film stars Olaf Fønss as Frank Stoll, a ruthless businessman who steals away one of a coal mine owner's daughters, Dina (Ebba Thomsen), early in the film. Meanwhile, Dina's sister, Edith (Johanne Fritz-Petersen), finds shy courtship with a sailor named Reymers (Alf Blutecher). An astronomer named Wisemann (listed as Wissmann in some sources and played by K. Zimmerman) discovers that a comet may hit the earth. Word leaks about the comet, forcing the stock market to plunge, which allows Stoll to buy cheap, expecting the comet to avoid Earth. However, Wisemann confirms with other scientists that the comet will indeed collide with Earth on a certain date and only informs his friend Stoll, as the scientists agree not to panic the public with the truth. Stoll convinces the newspapers to report that the comet will miss the earth, leading to a rally in the marketplace and his being able to sell off stocks at a premium.

Stoll returns to the coal mining village of his wife to do some business just as the comet is to hit. The miners, fueled by Dina's angry ex-fiancé, try to attack the Stolls as they arrive, while Dina's father curses her before flamboyantly dying from heart failure. The Stolls go on to their mansion to have a party to celebrate the "failed" coming of the comet with many rich friends. As the meteors begin to shower Earth with flaming death, the coal miners agree to attack the mansion in retaliation (and mainly to allow Dina's ex-fiancé to take vengeance). The miners interrupt a dance by Dina and some other women and, in a gun-battle with the rich men inside, shoot Dina. Stoll drags the dying Dina through a secret passage in the house and into the mines, hoping to avoid the miners and the meteors. On the surface, meteors crash into buildings, fires erupt, flooding washes through the cities, and . . . well, cows seems to be roaming aimlessly, which isn't much of a threat unless you have a fear of cows, but anyway, nature's chaos brings death to most. In the mines, poison gases pour out, sending Stoll and the ex-fiancé to join Dina in death.

The next morning, a preacher saves Edith from the roof of her home and takes her to a cave. When she awakens, she finds a church and begins ringing the tower's bell in order to see who is still left. Her sailor boyfriend emerges from the sea after having to abandon ship during the night and hears the bell. They run to meet each other in a field and then fall to their knees in a prayer of thanks to God for allowing them to find each other as the film comes to a close.

As one can expect from a movie made in 1916, the pantomime acting of the cast may seem a bit heavy for modern consumption, but beyond Fønss and the actor playing the father this is fairly rare overall (to be fair, European films tended to be a bit more sedate about such scenery-chewing compared to American films of the time). The meteors shown—mostly model work, depicting smoking nuggets from the sky raining on the village as well as showers of sparks falling over the cast outdoors—do convey the sense of hellfire from above, especially for a film at such an early phase of special-effects work.

The most intriguing aspect of the story is the focus on characters. Typically such films would concentrate on the "good" daughter and her sailor beau, yet that is not the case here. The audience's focus is on Frank and Dina Stoll, and for nearly half the picture (with the exception of Frank beating down Dina's ex-fiancé) they could be seen as the protagonists. It is only when Stoll convinces the newspaper editor to plant false information about the upcoming comet collision that Stoll really comes into play as the villain of the piece. Dina isn't even given that clear a definition, as her only fault is evidently believing her husband's false claim that the comet will not hit the earth. True, Dina participates in an exotic dance at the party (the closest the film comes to the decadence of the orgy scene from the similarly plotted *End of the World* [1931]), but it hardly seems fair that she ends up shot in the mayhem and then poisoned in the mines soon after.

After this serious effort, there would be a brief delay before the next film depicting a desperate world in turmoil. Surprisingly, when it does come, it is in the form of a comedy.

The Last Man on Earth (1924)

The November 1923 issues of *Munsey's* (a popular magazine of nonfiction and fiction of the time) featured a novelette by John D. Swain, who did a number of stories for the pulps of the early twentieth century. The novelette deals with a virus, Masculitis, which has wiped out every male in the world upon reaching puberty. Ten years after the fact see a vaccine created that can be given to the few remaining boys left alive, but there is no certainty they have not already been weakened to the point of no return. Then suddenly, a man who had become a hermit after his fiancée left him ten years before emerges, making him the last man on Earth, with the world full of women eager to make sure he helps repopulate the planet.

Swain's story starts with some serious overtones, but slowly evolves into an examination of what a culture completely full of women would resemble. Then comedy imposes on the narrative, as a female gangster, Greenwich Gertie, locates the last man, Elmer Robinson, and positions herself to capture and ransom him off to the government. After testing and prodding by scientists and such, the government displays Robinson for a possible auction to the highest bidder. When he happens to see his former fiancée in the crowd, the two reunite and are allowed to marry, leading to the birth of twin boys and the promise of humanity once again prospering.

The novelette was popular enough that Fox Studio picked up the rights to the story and released it as a full-length comedy in 1924. John G. Blystone, who was certainly no slouch when it came to filmmaking and comedy, directed the film, which follows the novelette closely. Blystone worked on over one hundred films in his career, including Buster Keaton's *Our Hospitality* (1923), features for Will Rogers, and two Laurel and Hardy features, *Block-Heads* and *Swiss Miss* (both 1938).

Although the novelette goes for a mixture of pathos, social evaluation and humor, the movie is played just for laughs, with Earle Foxe—typically cast as a villain in various comedies of the time—as the hillbilly/hermit Elmer Smith. The film, a popular hit in 1924, prints of which have survived (from an era where many movies have not made it to the present day due to neglect and abuse), is rarely shown today, and reviews of the film seem somewhat mixed as to what changes were made to the plot from Swain's original novelette. Still, the main thrust of the plot is the same, what with our hero surviving in the Ozark Mountains when discovered several years after a plague has killed off all mature men on the planet. Kidnapped by Greenwich Gertie (Grace Cunard) for sale to the government, Smith suffers through a number of tests before being presented to the president (or "presidentess," as stated in the film). Two senators ("senator-esses" . . . the humor doesn't rise much higher than that, folks) then stage a mix of bathing-suit modeling and a prizefight in order to prove who should have Smith for their own. Eventually, Smith is reunited with his love, Hattie (Derelys Perdue), who he was taken from when kidnapped by Gertie in the mountains.

The film did well enough at the box office that the storyline was brushed off and given another go in front of the camera nine years later. In this case, Fox decided to not only add some musical elements to the story, but also film the movie twice with the same star, Raul Roulien. This is not as odd as it may sound today, for at the time dubbing of films into various other languages was still in its infancy, and most studios found it simpler to shoot a movie that they deemed would be popular more than once—first in English and then one or more times typically with the same major stars phonetically speaking another language while other roles were recast with native-speaking actors. *Dracula* (1931) is one popular example out of many from the period—filmed during the day at the studio with Bela Lugosi and cast in English, while a Spanish-language version with an entirely different cast and director was shot during the evening on the same sets. In the case of the 1933 remake of *Last Man on Earth*, Raul Roulien was a logical choice as the star—he could perform in English and Spanish, was being promoted by Fox as a popular "Latin Lover" type at the time, and, most importantly, he could play comedy and sing—starring in several Spanish-language musicals for Fox in the 1930s and appearing in such films as the Astaire-Rogers musical *Flying Down to Rio*).

The English version was released as *It's Great to Be Alive*, a much cheerier title than that used for the Spanish-language version, *El último varon sobre la Tierra* (*The Last Man on Earth*, as with the 1924 production). Roulien plays Carlos Martin in the English version, while his name was changed to that of Ralph Martin in the Spanish one, but otherwise, with the exception of different costars, the films are essentially the same, although with some slight variations from the 1924 movie. In these cases, our hero no longer simply disappears into the mountains but heads out for a crossing of the Pacific Ocean after being jilted by his girl Dorothy/Dolores (played by Gloria Stuart in the English version and Rosita Moreno in the other; Stuart is best known for her work in such films as *The Old Dark House*, *The Invisible Man* and the 1997 James Cameron film *Titanic* as the older Rose). He crashes on an uncharted island, where he is found six years after the virus has wiped out men from the planet. The film follows the standard plot, although much of it—from what can be surmised from reviews of the time—appears to be more about showcasing comedy set pieces and vaudeville acts than examining the ramifications of the "last man on earth" plot. While Fox heavily promoted Roulien's involvement in the film, most reviews appear to favor Edna May Oliver as the head scientist in the English version and any scene that takes attention away from Roulien, who played the role as a Latin Maurice Chevalier. After that, Roulien went back to playing secondary roles in English films. The director of the English remake, Alfred L. Werker, would go on to direct the first movie in the Sherlock Holmes film series starring Basil Rathbone (*The Adventures of Sherlock Holmes*) and the dismal Laurel & Hardy feature *A-Haunting We Will Go* (1942), among other films. The director of the Spanish language film, James Tinling, would go on to work on both the Charlie Chan and Mr. Moto film series, and worked steadily in movies until the 1950s, when he moved to television.

Intriguingly, while it is clear that *The Last Man on Earth* was a forerunner of such novels as *Mr. Adam* in the 1940s as well as the *Y: The Last Man* comic-book series discussed in the previous chapter, there have been no other adaptations of the novelette since 1933. One would think at least someone would have taken such a concept as a single man left in a world full of women and run with it in these very un-PC days (one can almost visualize the Rob Schneider movie poster). Alas, while there have been hints of such elements in films based on reproduction not being possible for one reason or another, *The Last Man on Earth* sits waiting to be reborn (pun intended) in the new century.

At 3:25 (aka *The Crazy Ray*, aka *Paris qui Dort*, aka *Paris Asleep*) (1925)

This may be seen by readers as a bit of a cheat once the plot is known; after all, it does not deal with a real apocalyptic event (although the consequences of it could readily lead to one), but rather an experiment that leaves the world devoid of human contact with the exception of a handful of people. On the other hand, since most films dealing with the aftermath of the end of the world typically deal with a situation exactly as the above, perhaps it is not that far from the mark.

The movie is the first directed by René Clair, who would go on to write and direct many films in a forty-year career, both in Europe and for a time in the United States. Some of his best-remembered work came from a short span in the 1940s when he worked in America, such as the 1945 adaptation of Agatha Christie's *And Then There Were None* (aka *Ten Little Indians*) and a handful of films dealing with a mixture of fantasy and comedy, such as *I Married a Witch* (a Veronica Lake vehicle that was an obvious source for the later U.S. television series *Bewitched*) and *It Happened Tomorrow* (with Dick Powell as a reporter who gets the next day's newspaper). In fact, many of his films are spiced with fantasy elements, and *The Crazy Ray* is no different.

The movie begins with a night watchman (Henri Rollan) at the Eiffel Tower waking up one morning to discover that everyone in Paris (and presumably elsewhere in the world, based on information given later in the movie) has been frozen in time at exactly 3:25 a.m. After traveling around the city for a bit, he runs into a group of five people who had just landed in a plane. The group goes around together, gathering riches and having a good time in Paris on their own, but they soon grow bored and begin to fight a bit over the one woman in their group. Later, they receive a message from the daughter of a scientist who activated a ray that has frozen everyone but them (it turns out that the plane was outside of the ray's influences when it was in the air). The watchman convinces the scientist to put things right, and after a sequence involving variation of speed with those reviving, things are back to normal. As the group of travelers goes about their own ways—some finding that they miss the "sleeping Paris" they had, while others use what they saw to their advantage—the watchman meets up again with the scientist's daughter at the Eiffel Tower, and the watchman finds an expensive ring, left over from their escapades in the city, giving it to the woman as their relationship begins to blossom.

The film is definitely a comedy and mainly built on the premise of seeing people "frozen" in everyday situations while those not affected react around them. An interesting aspect for viewers of "sole survivor" films of the future (such as the *I Am Legend* adaptations discussed later and certain postnuclear movies) are scenes set in the "empty" streets of Paris and our main character adjusting to a life where he is essentially on his own. Such a novelty wears off soon after when the plane passengers arrive, turning the comedy more on the group annoying each other than reacting to their consequences, but for a time at least, it is easy to get into a feel of this being a true apocalyptic film. It should be stated that shots in and around the Eiffel Tower—especially those of the actors climbing up and down the structure and sitting on the edge of higher platforms—are rather dazzling to watch as well.

End of the World (aka *La fin du monde*) (1931)

Abel Gance is considered one of the finest filmmakers ever. Certainly as one of the most innovative of the silent age, with his work on such early films as *J'accuse* (1919) and *Napoleon* (1927) cementing his place in film history. His films for the time were epic in scope, with *Napoleon* in particular considered a must-see for anyone interested in cinematic history.

And, in all irony, it took *End of the World* to bring about his downfall.

True, that's perhaps a bit overly dramatic, but in some ways it is fitting in describing what happened with Gance's 1931 movie. Gance spent two years filming France's first all-talking motion picture, before it was eventually taken away from him in the editing process by his financiers. Wishing to recoup costs, they had the film edited without Gance's involvement from approximately three hours into a 105-minute feature, which curtailed much of Gance's sweeping look as to the follies of mankind and the hopes of redemptions found with the promise of a comet hitting Earth. Further damage to Gance's vision was inflicted on the project when more than fifty additional minutes were cut for its American

End of the World (1931) by famed director Abel Gance. Considered a disaster by the studio, critics and audiences at the time, the film has been difficult to locate in anything approaching its original intended length.

release and it was exploitatively retitled *Paris After Dark*. Such editing no doubt made the plot rather choppy, and both versions were considered commercial and critical duds by those who saw them in the 1930s. In later years, after appreciation of Gance's work became known worldwide, there have been some reevaluations of *End of the World*, but most of those who have more recently seen it agree that the project seems to have been a misfire even if Gance's original three-hour-long version had remained in place. This is because the story just doesn't captivate in a way to make even the end of the world something that would revolutionize the world the way Gance saw it.

The plot is surprisingly rather similar to that of the earlier *The End of the World*, only with a longer character-driven and religious-intoxicated subplot twisted through the picture. The movie starts with a passion play being presented for an audience. Actress Genevieve (Colette Darfeuil) is attracted to Jean, the actor playing Jesus in the play (played by director/writer Gance), but he refuses her, convinced that his path leads to the salvation of the world. Jean eventually is falsely accused of a rape and ends up being sent to an asylum from a head wound he suffered in a mob attack, but his words to Genevieve live on through a number of recordings he made that begin a peace movement at a time of possible world war. Jean's brother, an astronomer (Victor Francen), sees a comet on a collision course with Earth but is convinced by Jean to hold off on telling the world and to look to Genevieve as a possible mate in the new world of peace to come.

Meanwhile, financier Schomburg (Samson Fainsilber) is infatuated with Genevieve and, after molesting her, announces he plans to marry her. When Jean's brother announces the coming of the comet in order to head off a war, stocks plunge, but Schomburg keeps buying in hopes that it will pass and a world war will increase his investments in weapons. Schomburg manages to denounce the news of the comet and accuses Jean's brother of trying to destroy the economy. As the brother avoids capture, Genevieve decides to reconcile with Schomburg. An announcement by radio of the war is stopped by the brother and others at the Eiffel Tower, and Schomburg and Genevieve are killed when those with the movement cut the cable to their elevator as they attempt to leave the monument, sending them crashing to the ground.

With the only major character remaining being Jean's brother, he announces that the world needs to come together as one. As many pray around the world in their various religions for salvation, a good number of others let loose with drunken orgies as natural disasters begin to wipe out civilization due to the approaching comet. However, in the final moments, even those happy in chaos finally stop and begin to pray as well.

The comet does pass without hitting Earth, but with its passing comes a new unity to the world, and a one-world government is accepted by all to help rebuild in a new age of enlightenment, as the movie comes to an end.

As stated before, there are many similarities here between the similarly titled 1916 film and this one: a comet approaches; scientists hold off on announcing the coming of doom; a financier who buys when the market is down manages to control world events, parties it up as doom approaches, and dies when it appears he has triumphed; even the religious praise to God in a new world shattered by the comet are all there to link the two films. Yet Gance manages to take the same material and, even in truncated form, seems to lose sight of his objective by focusing too much on his vision.

Obviously, Gance saw the film much as a continuation of his earlier projects where human need for sanity and peace avoids future wars, just as in *J'accuse*. In the case of *End of the World*, Gance would go down an avenue that would be pounced upon by other creative sources over the years, from the pages of *Watchmen* and such television series as *The Outer Limits* ("The Architects of Fear") to movies from good to duds (*Meteor*)—that a greater crisis will lead to world governments uniting against a common enemy. Perhaps if the film had stayed on that premise and given viewers such a worldview, the ending where everyone is brought together might have yielded a better result. Instead, we have the majority of the movie taken up with what boils down to a domestic drama (which isn't *that* uncommon for such films, as will be seen in a later chapter). Jean may have a vision of world peace, but we're mainly focused on our villain doing dastardly (and very localized) things in order to make himself rich while driving Jean's brother underground—essentially the plot of numerous melodramas, which just happens to have the comet's approach as a different hook to hang all the brouhaha upon. Thus, when we get to the moment when everyone falls to their knees in prayer, it comes off even more forced and hokey than the sailor and the daughter in the 1916 film falling to their knees in the exact same manner.

Perhaps part of the problem is the passing of time. We have a worldview today where we realize that major tragedy tends to bring people together only briefly. We feel for our brothers at moments of crisis, but only for so long. Then we get back to watching football and playing our video games, glad that it wasn't us that got caught in madness. A world government comes about in the film because of a passing comet. Our real world cannot even unite when thousands die after planes ram into buildings. That said, maybe it would be better if we were a bit more like Gance's vision than our own. Alas, we don't even have the convenience of a shorter running time to get there someday.

As it turns out, Gance would continue to work in the film industry for years to come, but mostly as a work-for-hire and seldom in a position where he could bring more of his epic storytelling to the screen. He survived the end of the world, but just as his dream in *End of the World* doesn't match what most probably would happen in reality, his vision of a film that would sweep public perception and create such a world was not to be as well.

Deluge (1933)

The final film here is one that has been seen by probably the most people of any of those listed in this chapter. At least parts of it anyway. And those parts being mainly the rather spectacular special effects that pop up early in the proceedings.

The film, which was considered lost for many years until a copy dubbed in Italian turned up in 1987, kicks into gear with suspense as scientists agree that some type of predicament (it's never quite clear what, but an eclipse of the sun seems to be the lynchpin to the disaster) will cause a series of natural disasters around the world. Soon after, cities are ripped apart by earthquakes that have buildings falling like cards, and the people in them disappearing from the screen as they hurtle down below.

Elsewhere, a rich family (one can only assume they're rich by the way they are dressed and their house on the moors) worries about the earthquakes destroying the house around them. The husband, Martin (Sidney Blackmer, who is probably best remembered today as the leader of the satanic apartment dwellers in *Rosemary's Baby*), takes the wife, Helen (Lois Wilson), and children out to the rocks by the sea. It doesn't seem like the safest place to be, either, but it turns out that the wife is injured while still in the house. Soon, the tidal waves hit, sending New York underwater and finding the husband waking up in the middle of nowhere, with wife and children lost.

Elsewhere, a championship swimmer by the name of Claire (Peggy Shannon) has washed up on land near a cabin holding two desperate men, Norwood (Ralf Harolde) and Jephson (Fred Kohler). At first, things appear to be normalizing between the threesome, but when Norwood attacks Claire, Jephson kills him and Claire heads to the waters to swim away. Jephson follows by boat to catch what he considers his woman now.

Claire once again is found passed out on the shores, only this time by Martin, who has spent his time holed up in a small cottage and stockpiling supplies he has found in a cave that looks suspiciously like Los Angeles' Bronson Canyon (the cave is even presented as being a tunnel much like one that is actually in Bronson Canyon). After a time together, Martin demands to know if Claire will stay with him or move on. Realizing that her chances on her own are bleak and that Martin has been kind to her, she agrees to stay and they begin to set up house in the cottage. Jephson, however, turns up—now as part of a roving gang of criminals—and steals Claire away. Martin saves her, but Jephson knows where they are and knows there are supplies in the cave nearby.

Even farther away, Helen and the children are found by a man named Tom (Matt Moore) and taken to a devastated town where the townsfolk are trying to reestablish civilization. Tom believes Martin is dead and wants Helen as his wife (in fact, new laws in the town make it clear that she will need to marry), but Helen

Considered a lost film for years (an Italian-dubbed copy was found in 1987), *Deluge* (1933) has not only advanced special effects but also a rather adult storyline for the era.

is holding out hope that Martin is still alive. The people in the town find out that the gang is nearby and decide to rally the men to deal with them finally after the gang has attacked several members of the community. They track the gang down just as they attack Martin and Claire in the cave and save the pair. Both are willing to join the community, and Martin quickly becomes a leader thanks to his ideas about distributing the supplies he has. However, problems arise when Martin finds that Helen and the children are still alive. Tom takes it well and moves on, and even Helen is willing to suggest that the three of them work something out, but Claire refuses to give up Martin. In the finale, she takes off for the waters once again and disrobes, swimming away into the distance while Martin calls out to her onshore.

The movie is based on a novel by S. Fowler Wright, which has the action taking place in England instead of New York, but otherwise, much of the plot is similar. Wright was a late bloomer as a successful author, finding success in his fifties after self-publishing *Deluge* and getting a movie deal. He wrote a number of science fiction stories and crime novels in his remaining years, including a quasi-sequel to *Deluge* named *Dawn*, a book about another determined, athletic woman who fights for her role in the new world, much like Claire in *Deluge*. As it stands, one could easily modify *Dawn* to be the story of Claire arriving on another shore and her further adventures in a sequel picture, but it was not to be. A third book in a planned trilogy by Wright was never completed. As for the director, Felix E. Feist, he is probably best remembered for the 1953 remake of *Donovan's Brain* and his later work directing television in the 1950s through 1960s (including a handful of episodes from *Voyage to the Bottom of the Sea*).

The film is remembered so well today because of the special effects that show Manhattan being wiped out, first by earthquakes and then by tidal waves (if a viewer had seen *The Day After Tomorrow* [2004] or *2012* [2009], it isn't hard to wonder if the writers had *Deluge* in mind when showing Manhattan being wiped out in flooding). Although with today's audiences' more mature eye to special effects, the crumbling cityscape may appear as merely a shaking of a table to break up model buildings, but they were convincing enough to be used in various other productions afterward, most commonly in serials of the time, such as *King of the Rocket Men* (and further reused in the parody *J-Men Forever* years later). Beyond that, the tidal waves swallowing the city are even better effects and quite remarkable.

Yet there are other elements that seem somewhat advanced for the times. In a movie era when bad things may happen, but never to the point of man turning against man, *Deluge* bothers to go a tad darker. Our main heroine is stuck with two crazy men who are willing to kill each other to have her. Later, a gang of men are roving around looking to take what they can, killing other men and (as the characters state) doing even worse to the women they come across. As the 1930s progressed and the Hollywood censorship codes came into play, such talk would be virtually wiped clean from movies, only slowly returning to the genre in the late 1950s and especially in the 1970s and onward. Yet in between, while there may have been concerns after apocalyptic events, everyone kept their hands about the waist and played "fair." Although *Deluge* doesn't suggest complete anarchy, it doesn't back away from suggesting that the world wouldn't be happily reset to noncrisis mode immediately after a major disaster has wiped out civilization. Those who survive may have lived through the worst, but there would still be plenty of hardship in front of them in the years to come.

Unlike the characters we find in the movies covered in the next chapter.

Okay I'll stop.

3

Congrats! You've Slept Through Armageddon

Movies Where the Protagonist Missed the End of the World

Okay, so you want to write a story about a modern man stuck in a world he doesn't understand. Fine—understandable, really. Classic concept in literature, as it's one most readers can identify from experiences in their lives where things seemed recognizable but completely alien to them at the same time. You can go about this in a realistic manner by placing your hero in a foreign country, like James Clavell's *Shogun*, in order to address cultural issues. Maybe put the character in some backwater location and show how savage mankind can be. Better yet, why not place your protagonist into some other reality, where you don't have to worry about getting some of the facts about a location correct (or upsetting the natives once the movie comes out)? This brings to mind material like *The Wizard of Oz* and *Alice in Wonderland*, but isn't *Deliverance* in a sense like taking modern-day characters and placing them in an alien landscape? So where is your location for such a film? An alien world? Maybe, but then you have to explain a culture that truly is "alien," and that either takes a lot of creative work or you end up having to excuse why Planet X looks so much like downtown Los Angeles.

The future. That's the answer. Place your story in the future. Yet how do you explain all the changes from the modern day—the style of dress, the architecture, and the way people talk? You can't get away with people of the future talking to each other like, "My, what a lovely public execution hall built here fifty-six years ago after the flooding of the plains due to the nuclear strikes, eh, Borad? This is why we also wear rubber accessories and eat only plankton today, of course!" Okay, maybe on *Doctor Who*, but otherwise, not very often. Plus, you want to get back to that grand idea of a "stranger in a strange land" that you had when you first sat down to create.

Resolution? A modern-day man somehow plucked out of time, only to rejoin the world after the destruction has occurred. You get to have a character that the audience can identify with that uses modern inflections and concepts to juxtapose against that of your "future world." It also allows for conversations easier to swallow, like, "Oh, you've noticed the lovely public execution hall! That was built fifty-six years ago when the flooding occurred due to the nuclear strikes, Mr. Smith! Of course, you missed all that while you were frozen for two hundred years! Here—have some plankton; it's all we eat today." There! That works great. Exposition that doesn't look quite like exposition.

Thus, it has worked in movies for years, from the days of obscure films such as *Just Imagine* (1930) to more recent times in Sylvester Stallone's *Demolition Man* (1993). It also has been beneficial as a plot-device in postapocalyptic movies; sometimes as a surprise during or near the end of such films, oftentimes as a matter of convenience for the production in ways of financial and storytelling devices. For example, as briefly suggested in chapter 1, it's a lot cheaper to show a ruined landscape *after* the catastrophe that destroyed civilization than to show millions of people dying as they panic and run *from* the catastrophe. Not to mention how long it would take for many to die in a postnuclear Earth from radiation or from a contagion. You either have to play that all out on the screen in some fashion (like in *The Day After* or *Testament*) or stick your character(s) in a hole somewhere to avoid it (such as *Def-Con 4* putting its heroes in a spaceship for the duration, where they are witnesses to the nuclear destruction but only through audio and visual transmissions). Further, you have to deal with how such visuals will affect the story. Not only is it cost-prohibitive, but it's hard to build up much enthusiasm for a comedy after showing the suffering of the masses, for instance.

It also is effective in plots where you want one or more character to somehow survive such an outcome without any of the repercussions of enduring it. It's easier to write a character who can do action, and one suffering from the full effects of nuclear fallout isn't going to be realistic in running away from the new masters and their fire-spewing dump trucks. The best solution? Our heroes missing out on all the "bad stuff" due to the luck of the draw. Jack London's *The Scarlet Plague*, discussed earlier, is an example of this—our hero is sick in a cabin far away from the contagion that kills nearly everyone, so there's no need to show the slow demise of humanity. *The Last Man on Earth* (and its two remakes) mentioned in chapter 2 has our protagonist in a remote location to avoid the plague that wipes out the male population. As seen below, a few films do this (and two are admitted homages to a third)—sometimes merely days or even hours after the worldwide crisis that sets up the story of humans in a postapocalyptic world. If so, typically as the mystery that must be resolved by the characters as to what happened while they were "out."

Whatever the reason, what follow are a series of films that deal with apoca-lyptic events for which our heroes never actually have to endure the cause of their "new world" surroundings.

Buck Rogers (various; 1933–1981)

Buck Rogers first saw the light of day in the pages of the first science fiction pulp magazine, *Amazing Stories*, in 1928. The story, written by Philip Francis Nowlan and called "Armageddon 2419 A.D.," was popular enough that a sequel story, "The Air Lords of Han," appeared half a year later in 1929. The two stories were then combined and released as the novel *Armageddon 2419 A.D.* years later, but it would be the original stories and the subsequent comic-strip version that started in early 1929 that generated interest in bringing the character to the big screen. Along the way, however, some changes occurred as to what brought, no pun intended, Buck to the future.

That version of the character fell into a deep sleep after breathing in a mysterious gas during a cave-in at a mine. He awakens nearly five hundred years later in 2419 and finds a scorched America, conquered by the advanced weaponry of the enemy from Asia (specifically China), now known as the Hans. Buck goes on to join a "gang" that is fighting the enemy to win back America.

The comic strip had the same background story (although the Hans became the Mongol Reds), and the radio show and two short films to come—a World's Fair short in 1933 and one from 1935 done to promote Buck Rogers merchandise—didn't argue the point, but things changed with the 1939 movie serial starring Buster Crabbe. In the serial, Buck and his companion Buddy Wade crash while flying near the North Pole. Fearing a length of time passing before rescue, they release an experimental gas called Nirvano that supposedly will keep them in short suspended animation. They are then found five hundred years later and join with others to fight the villainous dictator Killer Kane, who has conquered the world.

Yet in all of these cases, the new world Buck enters is one created through political strife over many years—hence, it's dystopian but not apocalyptic (a theme examined more thoroughly in a later chapter). It was only with the 1979 television series *Buck Rogers in the 25th Century* that world destruction really came into play. The series was put into development by Glen A. Larson (who had just come off of working on *Battlestar Galactica*, which also had an apocalyptic theme—survivors of a world destroyed by villains searching for a new home) and Leslie Stevens (creator of the science fiction anthology series *The Outer Limits*). The idea was, of course, to play off the success of *Star Wars* with a series based on what many saw, along with the *Flash Gordon* serials of the 1930s, as the genesis of George Lucas' movie. When the pilot was completed, the studio decided to reedit the film slightly and release it as a feature in theaters—an idea that worked well enough to help generate additional interest from the NBC network to bring the series to television in the fall of 1979.

Gone, of course, was the politically incorrect and obviously dated threat of the "Yellow Menace" that had haunted the original stories and the comic book, and in its place came Draco, Princess Ardala and the Draconian ship that wants to conquer Earth in 2491. Rogers' method of getting to the future also changed, with Buck (Gil Gerard) found drifting in a space shuttle from 1987, stuck in suspended animation due to a malfunctioning life-support system in the shuttle (no doubt, a lucky break for Rogers there). Upon returning to a very clean and white Earth, he discovers that most of the world was destroyed in a nuclear war soon after he left in the shuttle. Hence, there is no evil to conquer to restore an old regime as in the earlier versions of the characters; Buck simply works as a policeman to protect Earth from evildoers. This makes the series a rather mixed bag: on the one hand, it at least kept the series away from being about a "red menace" and Buck arriving on a war-torn Earth. On the other hand, it means that there is no central goal for the character in the series beyond what could be dreamed up in the next episode and the occasional anarchic word usage and comparisons of "1987 versus 2491," such as an embarrassing disco dance early on in the series.

With a lot of the momentum surgically omitted from the character and the plot, it is understandable in some ways why the series only lasted for less than a season and a half, dying completely in 1981. Of course, there are many who consider Buck Rogers and Buster Crabbe's other famous role in the series for *Flash Gordon* to be a major influence on George Lucas and his *Star Wars* franchise, but one famous producer who must also be noted here as looking at *Buck* is *Star Trek* creator Gene Roddenberry. Not only will *Star Trek* use accidental long-term suspended animation for the character of Khan in the original series (who, of course, would become a major well-remembered villain in the second *Star Trek* movie, *Wrath of Khan*, and in the second movie of the revamped *Star Trek*, *Into Darkness*), but Roddenberry would also feature the same accidental route for characters in an early episode of *Star Trek: The Next Generation* ("The Neutral Zone"). He would also make it a major plot point for the protagonist in three television pilots produced in the 1970s, as *Genesis II*, *Planet Earth* and *Strange New World* all feature a main hero from the twentieth century waking up in a new postapocalyptic society of the future. Finally, Dylan Hunt, the name used for essentially the same character in *Genesis II* and *Strange New World*, would reemerge as the name of Kevin Sarbo's character in the 2000 television series devised by Roddenberry called *Andromeda*, which managed to run for five seasons in syndication. Hunt, as could be expected, began the series as someone who too was revived after accidentally skipping through time. Roddenberry just seemed intent on finding a way to bring the Buck Rogers myth to one of his programs, although the one best remembered, Khan, turned out to be the villain of the piece.

One final bit of trivia about *Buck Rogers* tying into the postapocalyptic worlds being reviewed: after the start of the 1979 television series, it was decided to reprint *Armageddon 2419 A.D.* With its release, the publisher, Ace, began looking into the idea of continuing the series on its own terms. To do this, they worked with writers Jerry Pournelle and Larry Niven to come up with storylines for such a series, and outlines were produced by the pair that were used for one novel by John Eric Holmes, *Mordred*; two by Richard S. McEnroe, *Warrior's Blood* and *Warrior's World*; and *Rogers' Rangers* by John Silbersack. If you have read this book from chapter 1 on, you may recognize the names of Pournelle and Niven as the authors of *Lucifer's Hammer*, a novel dealing with a comet hitting Earth (and discussed in chapter 1). This is of interest to *Buck Rogers* fans, for the pair managed to tie in the end-of-the-world event of their novel directly into their outlines, making the *Buck Rogers* sequel novels actual sequels to *Lucifer's Hammer* as well.

Buck Rogers may not have gotten there first in the "freeze-dried heroes" sweepstakes. Harry Houdini's *Man from Beyond*, from 1922, is a movie that has a man frozen in ice from an earlier age and thawed in modern times, and one could even equal the classic "Rip Van Winkle" as being a story about a man displaced by time—but it is the one best remembered in placing a man from today into the future through suspended animation of one type or another. After this, when such an element is used—as with *Captain America*, or in Mike Judge's *Idiocracy* (see chapter 6) and the animated series *Futurama*—one is immediately reminded of *Buck Rogers* and the first man of the present arriving in a chaotic world of tomorrow.

Speaking of which, at one time a Hollywood producer worked for a while on bringing H. G. Wells' 1910 novel *The Sleeper Awakes* to the screen. This story is about a man who unintentionally sleeps for two hundred years after drinking a potion and awakens to find himself in a dystopian future. The producer was George Pal, and he would produce three movies based on other H. G. Wells novels; two of which will be discussed in subsequent chapters, and the other being the next movie on this list.

The Time Machine (1960)

George Pal (1908–1980) was an animator who made his mark in America with a series of short subjects for Paramount Studio, the Puppetoons. In 1950, he moved over to producing live-action films, nearly all of which contain elements of fantasy and science fiction. After producing two big hits in the 1950s based on H. G. Wells novels (*When Worlds Collide* and *War of the Worlds*), it was only natural for Pal to look to other works of Wells to bring to the cinema. He finally settled on *The Time Machine*, which was released in 1960 with Rod Taylor as H. G. Wells (called George throughout the picture), Alan Young as his friend David and Yvette Mimieux as Weena. Although the movie makes some departures from Wells' original novel, it stays faithful in many ways as well: our narrator (who is not named in the book) showing his guests a tiny version of the time machine in order to prove his point; Weena, the future Eloi who is saved from drowning and helps him in the year 802,701 A.D.; the Morlocks, who cannibalize the Eloi and steal the time machine. Even the narrator taking the handle that controls the time machine is there.

But there are vast differences as well: Weena is the love interest in the movie and assumed to be who the narrator goes back to at the end, but she is presumably killed in a forest fire in the book; the narrator goes 30 million years into the future, instead of just to the era of the Morlocks, to find the human race gone and little left of Earth; and travel is mainly to 802,701 A.D., 30 million years in the future and then back again. And it is this area where the biggest changes occur. In the novel, Wells sets up the Morlock/Eloi era as a mystery that the narrator ends up with several theories as to how they came to pass, all of which are environmental and/or political in nature. However, he never can be conclusive about what caused the human race to evolve to this level.

Yet the 1960 movie goes in a different direction by giving George several stops along the way to 802,701 A.D. This not only allows some clever visual effects that would gain the movie an Oscar (stop-motion effects were perfectly in line with Pal's earlier work with the Puppetoons), but also advances the plot in both George's understanding of the future world and why the perfect-looking Eloi behave like cattle to the slaughter for the monstrous Morlocks. George at first stops for a brief visit with David's son during World War I, is rattled by bombing in 1940, and then reemerges in 1966 (six years after the release of the film) to find that a nuclear attack is occurring. He soon jumps into the time machine to save himself from the carnage and emerges in 802,701 A.D. A trip to the "talking rings"—metallic bracelets that speak when spun on a table—tells him that the war had continued for centuries, eventually leading to one group of survivors staying underground while the other went to the surface, thus producing the Morlock and Eloi in an evolutionary process. (It is interesting to note that such an evolutionary process after a global nuclear war was used by writer Terry Nation to explain the evolution of the monstrous Daleks and the Thals—who look like the Eloi even down to the light hair and ignorance of conflict—when writing the first Dalek story for *Doctor Who* just three years after *The Time Machine* was released.) It is also established that the Eloi are conditioned to go to the Morlocks after hearing the sirens, just as the public earlier fled to the fallout shelters in the 1966 sequence.

Because of these changes, the tone of the story becomes quite different between the novel and the movie, even though much remains the same. In the book, the narrator's ultimate goal is to get back into the time machine and find evidence to deliver to his friends so he can prove his journeys (beyond that of the flowers he brings back, much like in the movie). In the film, his motives are more heroic—a chance to go the future and teach mankind to once again be progressive and create (going so far as to take three books with him for the journey . . . although the question has always been which three books would someone take to help reboot the world?). The narrator goes from a journey into vanity into one of nobility, thanks mainly to having witnessed the demise of civilization through his various hops in time, even if it meant he really didn't have to endure the devastations of those destinations.

There have been several adaptations of *The Time Machine* over the years, mainly as audio plays for radio and other sources, as well as an early BBC television version in 1949, with most attempts following the original novel and avoiding the narrator being aware of any apocalyptic event as in the 1960 version. Two other film adaptations since Pal's film—a 1978 made-for-syndication-television version and a theatrical film in 2002—do dip into such territory, however.

The 1978 movie (starring John Beck, probably best remembered by readers of this book as the costar in the 1975 version of *Rollerball* as well as the rebel leader in Woody Allen's *Sleeper*) uses relatively little of the novel and 1960 film beyond that of a time machine and the Morlock/Eloi plot. It instead begins in modern times and makes the plot center on how the protagonist's involvement with military weapons leads to the destruction that creates the postapocalyptic future he eventually finds himself. As for the 2002 version, it attempts to stick somewhat closer to the source novel, but does at least pull in an additional side trip just long enough in 2037 to see the destruction of the moon, which causes the apocalyptic event that changes the world in the future. Even so, it is the Pal version that remains best known today.

But it appears we have done a little time traveling of our own, as there's an earlier movie with *The Time Machine* star Rod Taylor that features him missing out on the end of the world.

World Without End (1956)

Rod Taylor is one of the stars of this little gem, which is pretty much in the grand tradition of such films as *Rocketship X-M*, *Queen of Outer Space* and . . . well . . . *Abbott and Costello Go to Mars*, to be honest: robust men arriving on another planet, running into monsters, keeping the women-types safe and shooting with revolvers at anything that may get in the way of a pure, he-man future for all. This is pretty much what we get in *World Without End* as well, with Taylor and his gang of astronauts in trouble when their rocket orbiting Mars goes out of control. Upon crashing on the planet, they discover over time that not only are they in the future (2508, to be exact), but the barbaric people they've met are all earthlings, as they have actually crashed on Earth instead of Mars. (Hmm . . . a story where astronauts land on a barbaric planet that they eventually discover is actually Earth after most of humanity is wiped out in a nuclear war . . . that sounds like another movie from a few years later, but I can't quite put my finger on the title. It's bound to turn up at some point in this chapter, though.)

Eventually the crew finds a group of humans underground and works with them to resolve their differences with the mutants (pronounced Mutates) on the surface, mainly through bloodshed, and they all begin to repopulate the earth together (the astronauts with the future humans, I mean, not just the astronauts alone). To give credit where it is due, it is one of the few examples of people mistakenly going to the future and deciding to stay there, unlike our next movie.

Beyond the Time Barrier (1960)

The same year *The Time Machine* was released saw this little quickie from producer and star Robert Clarke (*The Hideous Sun Demon*) and director Edgar G. Ulmer (*The Black Cat*, *Detour*, *The Man from Planet X*), which sees a man who ventures into space only to end up landing in the future not by choice but by mistake, as in *World Without End*. As will be seen, accidents seem to be the most popular way for such evasions of destruction to occur in these films from this point onward.

In this case, Major Bill Allison is test-piloting a jet for space flight when a maneuver propels the craft sixty-four years into the future. He lands, finding only the remains of the airbase and a futuristic city off in the distance. Captured by the city dwellers, he is smitten by the psychic daughter (Darlene Tompkins)

Beyond the Time Barrier (1960) is one of the earlier examples of a hero who manages to miss the destruction caused by an apocalyptic event.   *Courtesy of Wrong Side of the Art*

of the leader (Vladimir Sokoloff) and thrown in with three prisoners who had arrived in the same manner he had from the past. Eventually, he discovers a way to get back to his own time, but one of the prisoners decides to let loose the mutants being held in another part of the city, leading to much chaos and the death of all the major characters besides Allison before he returns to his own time.

The most interesting aspect of this feature is that of people left on Earth due to radiation slowly mutating them, as it is not due to the standard motif of nuclear fallout. Instead, the mutations occur after cosmic radiation has seeped into the atmosphere due to the destruction of the ozone layer. True, it turns out that nuclear testing leads to this ozone layer depletion, but an alternative source for the end of the world was a nice change of pace for the time. Further, the possible eradication of the ozone layer became big news in the 1970s and onward, and comic-book fans certainly remember that cosmic radiation played a role in the eventual creation of the Fantastic Four in Marvel Comics. Nevertheless, those things were still in the future in 1960 when *Beyond the Time Barrier* arrived in theaters, making what is a rather dull actioner somewhat prophetic with the method used to bring about the end of the world.

Unlike some other characters listed in this chapter, Allison does face physical ramifications with his skip over troubled times by the end of the film. Although he avoided the radiation mutation in the future, his return trip finds him aging the sixty-four years' difference, making him an elderly man whom the authorities at first do not believe to be Allison. On the hopeful side, the military seems to be listening to him as the movie concludes, and we do have Allison's noble motives in trying to warn the past about nuclear testing, yet Allison's swift demise makes the ending rather downbeat. Such will be the norm for many of the subsequent movies listed.

The Day of the Triffids (1962, 1981, and 2009)

There have been three major adaptations of John Wyndham's 1951 science fiction novel *The Day of the Triffids,* and all three deal with the same plot, which finds peril coming from two directions that forces a global change in society and a "survival of the fittest" atmosphere . . . with the "fittest" perhaps not being mankind. The first issue at hand is a rather large carnivorous plant called a triffid that seems to have intelligence, can walk, and uses a poisonous stinger to trap animals (including humans). While this may seem to be a good reason to just get rid of the nasty things—suggested in the novel as being the results of an experiment—the plant's oil can be made into fuel. This makes it valuable and—as per natural human insanity—at the start of the novel and films a plant that has been harvested in abundance for many years.

In the book and first two adaptations, a freakish meteor shower is watched by many (the 2009 miniseries makes this a solar eruption instead, but the results are the same). Bill Masen (Howard Keel in the 1962 movie, John Duttine in the 1981

BBC miniseries and Dougray Scott in the 2009 BBC version) is in the hospital with his eyes wrapped up due to an accident related to the triffids and is unable to witness the event in the sky. This turns out to be a lucky break for him, as the event blinds all who watch it. With most of the public unable to see, the triffids cannot be managed in their pens and they soon break loose to prey on the blind. Masen, who studied the triffids in the past, and a few other survivors have to deal with the breakdown in society, mad schemes to reverse the problems, and other, crazed survivors who want to set themselves up as ruler in the new world.

As with *Beyond the Time Barrier*, our hero manages to avoid disaster merely by being in the wrong place at the right time. Better yet, *Day of the Triffids* also sets up for a brief time the traditional mystery that such films as these have in common—in essence, because the protagonist is confined at the time of the "incident," he has to piece together exactly what occurred that allowed him to avoid the same outcome as everyone else.

These moments of Masen waking up in an abandoned hospital, not comprehending what has occurred, are striking. So much so that two other well-known apocalyptic works would borrow that concept in homage: *28 Days Later*, which opens with Jim (Cillian Murphy) waking up from a coma in a deserted hospital after the raging dementia virus has wiped out much of London; and *The Walking Dead* television series, which has Rick (Andrew Lincoln) waking up from a coma in a deserted hospital after the zombie contagion has wiped out most of the country. While some fans of *28 Days Later* have commented on how *The Walking Dead* copies its opening, it should be noted that the comic-book series *The Walking Dead* used the same situation and was started in 2003, before its creator knew that *28 Days Later* would make the same homage. Besides, the creators of both have clearly stated that having their protagonists wake up in the hospital after the fact was a direct homage to *Day of the Triffids*, so neither was a rip-off of the other.

Planet of the Apes (1968)

The *Planet of the Apes* series of five films (1968–1973), not to mention its various sequels, certainly have a place in any book about apocalyptic futures. It's also a very downbeat run of films, seeing the rise of a new order with the apes that is in every way just as prejudiced and mad as the humans before them—plus, the world gets blown up at least twice. Even the fifth and final movie, *Battle for the Planet of the Apes*, which spends much of the film trying to suggest an alternate "happy" ending for the world in the future, can't quite escape from the predetermined insanity of hate and war in its final scene.

While terrible things do happen, and there are certainly ramifications for the characters once they "arrive" after these events, the first film opens with the biggest "you've slept through it" moment in cinema history, namely because it's supposed to be a mystery until the final moments of the movie. That mystery I already spoiled for you at the beginning of this book, but the reason behind it has not been discussed. At the beginning of *Planet of the Apes*, we have Charlton Heston as Taylor, an astronaut on a spaceship traveling away from Earth in 1972. Upon wondering what the future will be like and foreshadowing the daylights out of the whole "will the world be a better place?" thing, Taylor goes

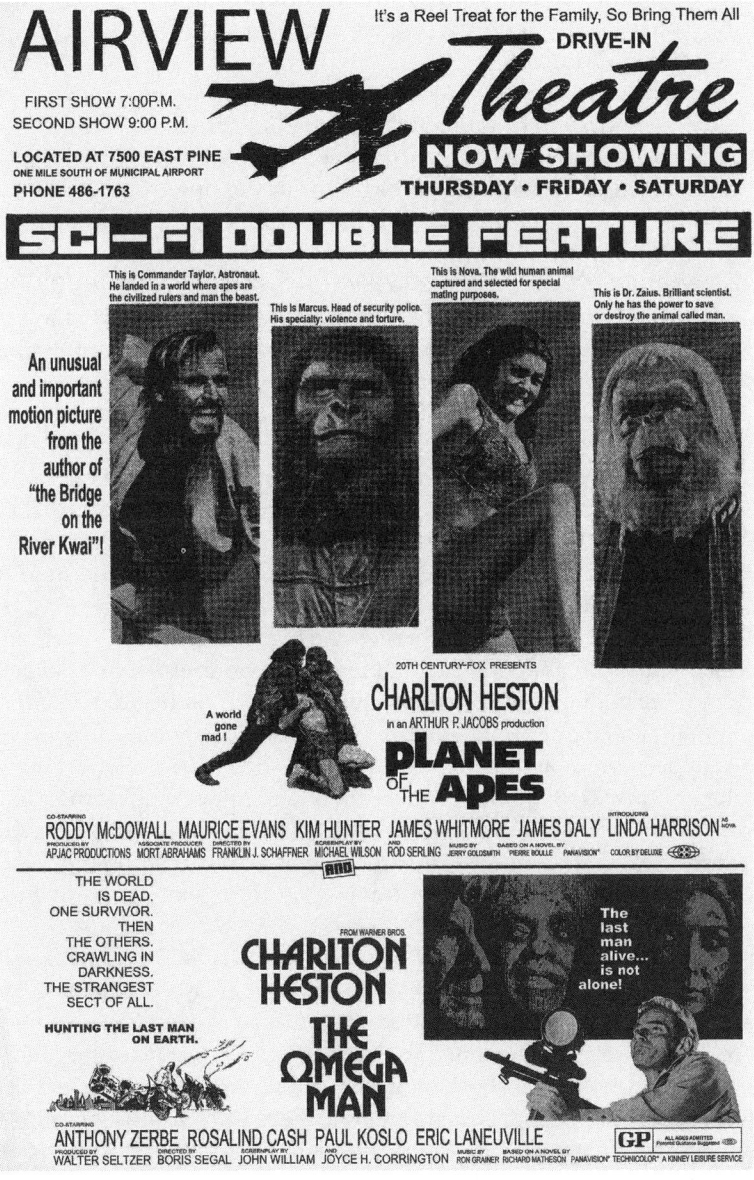

Two Chuck Heston apocalyptic tales for the price of one! *Planet of the Apes* (1968) is probably the best-known film featuring a character who comes into the story after the worst has happened to the planet.

Courtesy of Steve Clark and Hunter Goatley

into hibernation with the other three astronauts. He awakens in 3978 with the ship having crash-landed in a lake and rapidly taking on water. Taylor and two of the others (the lone female astronaut died previously in the journey due to a malfunction with her hibernation chamber) escape the sinking ship and head to land. There they ponder where they are and what they will find on the planet that they assume to be in the correct trajectory for their ship, somewhere in the constellation of Orion.

They eventually meet up with mute and rather mindless human scavengers just as they are attacked by humanlike apes on horseback. One of the astronauts dies at the scene, another is eventually seen to have been lobotomized, and Taylor is shot in the throat and thrown in with the other humans in Ape City. (This brings to mind—are there other cities full of apes? Is this it? If not, how did they get away with calling their city Ape City? Do the other ape communities wince a bit at that? "Oh, why can't we have a nice name like Ape City instead of being Monkeytown?" And, really, isn't this a bit pretentious? We don't see a lot of Human Village or Mankind Junction locations on the map, after all. Maybe a few Peckerwoods. But this is a huge digression. Sorry.)

After various adventures in the city, with Taylor trying to communicate with the apes and attempting to plead his case to those in charge, he finally breaks out and travels into the "forbidden zone." What he finds is the Statue of Liberty and the realization that somehow the spaceship had returned the crew to Earth in 3978. Taylor makes the (as we later discover) correct assumption that mankind destroyed itself, resulting in the mute, simple-minded humans still left on the planet.

The reveal of the Statue of Liberty is the big shocker of the movie—the one discussed in the introduction that left the audience stunned in disbelief. Up to this point, the audience could center their reactions on the idea that the movie is essentially a metaphor of man's inhumanity to those not like themselves (only with juxtaposition of apes being man and man being animals). Yet throughout the plot are sprinkled moments where there's an underlying mystery to resolve: how did this world come into being? Taylor's jump into the future allows for the surprise ending and could only be done if—up to that point—we have no awareness that this is Earth in the future instead of some unnamed planet in the constellation of Orion.

As it stands, the original novel by Pierre Boulle, *La planète des singes* (1963) isn't even set on Earth—the protagonist lands on an ape-dominated, Earthlike planet, although in a final twist the protagonist returns to Earth to find it now run by apes as well (an element Tim Burton would return to in his 2001 adaptation). For this reason, and others in the novel, there is no mystery as to why apes are the dominant species; it is merely there for purposes of satire dressed in elements of science-fantasy. Thus, although the novel deals with the elements of the protagonist being hurled into the future and finding a strange new world waiting for him, there is no sense of some type of world-ending menace having hit Earth (or the Earth equivalent). It is only with the Heston movie that the point is driven home that Taylor missed the death of his world and has returned to see the results.

A postapocalyptic Earth that we are not to recognize as such wasn't new to cinema by 1968. Roger Corman's *Teenage Cave Man* with Robert Vaughn (looking anything but a teenager or a caveman, even in his loincloth) had covered the same "shock ending" ten years before Heston and crew. The film also draws itself from the age-old science fiction plot of the battle-scarred lone male and female survivors of a nuclear war finding each other and becoming Adam and Eve (commonly referred to as a "Shaggy God" story, as per writer Brian W. Aldiss). Elements of this can be seen in episodes of *The Twilight Zone* as well, such as the episodes "Two" (featuring Charles Bronson and Elizabeth Montgomery as two enemies who must come together after the end of the world), "Probe 7, Over and Out" (which ends with nuclear war survivors becoming Adam and Eve), and even Richard Matheson's "Third from the Sun" (featuring a group of people leaving a doomed planet to find Earth), just to name one program. Perhaps it is no wonder that *Twilight Zone* creator Rod Serling would cowrite the script to *Planet of the Apes*—its final twist makes the movie one long *Twilight Zone* episode.

The Doomsday Machine (1972)

If ever there was a movie that suggests the pain of living through the apocalypse, it's *The Doomsday Machine*. To clarify, you don't actually get to witness Armageddon in the film; it's just that having to sit through it will feel like watching the death of billions. This is a movie that is almost mesmerizing in its ineptitude; one that you'll end up sitting through waiting for at least one plot thread to pull together and go somewhere, only to find in the end it just isn't going to happen. I take that back, mainly because there is *no ending* to this movie. It just stops like a fever dream, making you wonder if maybe you just hallucinated it. If this movie doesn't have you shouting "WHAT?" at the screen when it ends, then you've either fallen asleep or have crumbled before the might of *The Doomsday Machine*.

Nevertheless, the movie (also known as *Doomsday Plus Seven, Armageddon 1975* and *Escape from Planet Earth*) falls into our category of people who miss out on the end of the world. In this case, the reason is intentional, although the characters don't realize it at first. One could almost suggest that the cast and crew didn't realize it either, but as much as there is loopy about *The Doomsday Machine*, it is pretty clear that the end of the world was part of the picture from the start. It was only in its final stages of production that things seem a bit iffy.

The events of the movie (I can't imagine anyone saying there is actually a plot here) finds a group of astronauts about to be sent out on a mission to Venus. Three of the seven men are then replaced by women right before the rocket takes off. While the men huff and puff in anger—and later in lust at the women—it is only once they are in space that they realize the switch occurred because of a "doomsday machine" the Chinese have activated on Earth. Sure enough, a short time later, the earth is destroyed through stock footage from other films. This is somewhat witnessed by the astronauts, although it appears most of it is them reacting to a reddish glowing ball in space.

As the men try to pair up (with the women, of course), everyone soon realizes that they will be unable to land on Venus due to lack of fuel unless they get the crew down to three. Of course, this seems to be very bad form for Earth's one last great hope of survival there, NASA. Then again, hoping against not hope but science that somehow a trip to Venus would find a sustainable atmosphere for humans was a bit of a reach in the first place. But it was all last-minute planning, of course.

Anyway, the fuel problem is resolved when an attack on one of the women leads to two members being accidentally sent out an airlock (the most unsettling and funniest thing in the movie), and two other members go out into space to fix the ship and discover a lost Soviet ship that can accommodate the two. However, just as they are get set to head on to Jupiter, the first ship disappears and we get a voice-over—evidently from Venus—telling the two on the Soviet ship that the first ship was "gone" and that they would not be allowed to land on Venus. They suggest something about "life beyond the universe," which probably isn't much help for people with little fuel. The Venusians then

A fantastic foreign poster for *The Doomsday Machine* (1972), a movie that has nothing in it to match the poster.

Courtesy of Wrong Side of the Art

appear to blow up the final ship, and we see a long shot of space before the words "The End" appear on-screen.

So there you have it—the world is blown up by the Chinese for no reason other than it sounded like a good idea at the time, and the last remaining hopes of the human race are wiped out pretty much off camera by a planet with a "No Vacancies" sign out front. We also have a movie where the shape of the rocket taking the crew to Venus changes several times, and where the Soviet rocket scenes are shot with actors hiding in costumes so that they don't have to reveal they are not the same actors as seen earlier in the film. Not to mention an abrupt ending where characters disappear from the screen without visual confirmation. This would have been okay for someone just starting off in films, but there are so many professional names and faces in the movie, it makes *The Doomsday Machine* even stranger: director Herbert J. Leder (*Fiend Without a Face, The Frozen Dead, It!*); pulp writer Stuart J. Byrne (who also wrote scripts for the 1950s series *Men into Space*); and stars like Grant Williams (*The Incredible Shrinking Man*), Denny Miller (*Wagon Train*), Mala Powers (*The Colossus of New York*) and Bobby Van (a song-and-dance man at MGM before moving on to television game shows). There's even Mike Farrell (B.J. of the television series *M*A*S*H*) as a reporter in one scene and Casey Kasem looking just fabulous as the voice of mission control.

So what happened? It appears the production began in 1967, with much of the footage shot that took place before the flight and in the first rocket completed. Then the production shut down, and people went on with their lives until 1972 when the footage was bought and additional footage was shot (that of the Soviet ship) in order to get the film up to a length that could be released to theaters. This means that all the special effects were probably thrown together from other sources in 1972 and the movie was finally put together without the cast having ever seen any of it.

For this reason, *The Doomsday Machine* fits in this category of "Missed Armageddon" as a double whammy—as neither the characters nor the cast ever got to really witness the end of the world.

Idaho Transfer (1973)

This rarity from 1973 was directed by Peter Fonda and costars Keith Carradine in a small role. Sadly, those are probably the best selling points of the movie, as it's a rather trivial, yet convoluted, mess of a film that seems to be really, really wanting to say something and be entertaining, but just kind of sits there for about eighty minutes until everyone decides to wrap it up with a quickie nonsensical ending.

The concept in the movie is that a scientific group is working on a government project that will allow matter to be transmitted between two separate points. While it appears the project is a success, the scientists discover that they've also managed to transfer people fifty-six years into the future into what appears to be a depopulated Earth. Because of reasons not given very clearly, people over the age of twenty quickly lose the function of their kidneys after traveling through time, so only younger people can do it, and thus a group of teenagers is sent into the future to try to figure out what happened and perhaps repopulate the earth. There's a catch, however, as it appears that the transfer leaves the people sterile, and the government soon cuts off funding, leaving the kids in the future (so the whole project seems a bit hopeless and unnecessary). Eventually some of them discover that there appears to have been some type of plague that wiped out most of civilization and that there are a few cavemen-like survivors around.

As luck would have it, one of the girls from the past goes crazy and kills a few of the others (including Keith Carradine's character). One of the other girls, Karen (Kelley Bohanon), manages to escape back into the past and reset the matter-transference machine to another time. She arrives sometime past the point of fifty-six years into the future, where she is picked up by a husband, wife and child in a futuristic car, whereupon the audience discovers that they plan to do something to her body, making her whole survival up to that point rather meaningless.

And thus, another case of someone avoiding the horrors of the apocalypse (the plague in this case), only to yield to other terrible things waiting on the other side. It appears many of these movies seem to think that if one doesn't suffer, then one must pay for that sin in another way. Perhaps it is all down to scriptwriters wishing to make some type of ironic statement, but it does make one wonder if God just doesn't like time travelers. At least the next movie avoids the perils of time travel, although it is another case of being in the "wrong place at the right time."

Where Have All the People Gone? (1974)

A rare television outing in these categories (besides series television, which is another chapter) finds Peter Graves in an *NBC Movie of the Week* from 1974 as a father of two teenaged children (one being a young Kathleen Quinlan before the days of *Warning Sign*, a film discussed in a later chapter). The family, including the mother, and some others are on a camping trip when the mother heads home, while the father takes the kids out to study the insides of a cave. While Graves and the daughter and son are in the cave, a weird solar event (possibly a flare) occurs that causes a brief earthquake, the loss of most electricity, and dogs turning rabid and somehow striking nearly every human with a virus that eventually turns them into powder within a day or two. Possibly by being underground at the time of the flares the three survive, although it is later suggested that they may be one of the few that have immunity to the virus, or perhaps a combination of both. As they trek home to see if the mother is still alive, a young woman and a boy join them as they try to avoid the mad dogs and the paranoid few remaining humans roaming the countryside.

The setup for *Where Have All the People Gone?* isn't that unusual—the premise of being in the wrong place at the right time has already been discussed briefly with *The Day of the Triffids*, but *Where Have All the People Gone?* physically places the protagonists in a location where they are out of harm's way. Such a placement isn't that out of the ordinary for apocalyptic drama either—going back to the days of "Time Enough at Last" for *The Twilight Zone* (Burgess Meredith as the book reader who accidentally is saved from nuclear devastation thanks to having gone to a bank vault to read when the missiles strike). Several postnuclear films of the 1960s also begin with this premise, such as the family driving away from L.A. as the bombs drop in *Panic in the Year Zero!*, the trio of characters of Roger Corman's *The Last Woman on Earth* scuba diving as most of the oxygen leaves the planet, and even *The World, the Flesh and the Devil* finds Harry Belafonte's character underground like the family in *Where Have All the People Gone?* as the bombs drop. The only big difference is that these other films tell us and our heroes pretty much right off the bat what has occurred. In the case of *Where Have All the People Gone?*, that mystery is part of the foundation of the plot, which is one reason why this movie is mentioned here and not all of these others (but don't worry, they'll get their space here soon enough).

In many ways, the concerns about what happened are a contrivance. We never quite make out what caused the situation to occur or why such a virus would be triggered by the solar flares beyond a letter left by the mother that is read in the last ten minutes of the movie and comes off as more of a bone thrown to the audience for making it that far rather than any type of logical series of events. Still, it allows the moviemakers working on a television budget to make a film that wipes out most of the human race without actually having to show it—the family is up in the mountains when everyone is destroyed—or even pay for extras to lie around as dead bodies, as the virus turns everyone into white powder after death, which makes cleanup a breeze, no doubt. Even with these shortcuts and a resolution that never quite explains things, however, the film actually holds up fairly well and even managed to get around the whole "what if there's another solar flare" question that some viewers may have by suggesting that those still alive are immune to its effects. Certainly not a classic film in any sense, but it does just squeak by on its premise in the end. The movie was directed by John Llewellyn Moxey, who directed a lot of television in the 1970s and onward, including the already mentioned *Genesis II* for Gene Roddenberry. Sometimes Hollywood just seems like a close-knit circle.

The Quiet Earth (1985)

This 1985 film is directed by Geoff Murphy, who would go on to do a lot of sequel work in the 1990s, including *Young Guns II, Under Siege 2: Dark Territory* and *Fortress 2: Re-Entry*, but don't let that fool you—*The Quiet Earth* is not a cheap quickie cash-in. In fact, it is probably one of the stronger artistic entities listed in this book. Saying that, I've probably scared off even more readers from ever giving it a chance. If so, I would suggest a reconsideration, as *The Quiet Earth* is a unique entry in the run of movies where the protagonist has somehow avoided the end of the world.

The movie is based on a 1981 book by Craig Harrison, with some of the plot switched around a bit in order to make it a bit less certain so as to deepen the mystery, especially when it comes to the concluding images. Some, of course, have felt a bit cheated at the ambiguity of that ending, but, in all honesty, it's an improvement over that of the novel.

The film begins with a man, Zac Hobson (Bruno Lawrence), waking up at 6:12 one morning to discover that everyone has disappeared and that a power-grid experiment called Project Flashlight appears to have been the cause of everyone disappearing. Hobson spends some time working through a mental breakdown in his loneliness as being the last person on Earth when he meets a woman named Joanne (Alison Routledge). After the two find one other survivor, Api (Pete Smith), they discover that they all share one thing—all three were in the process of dying when the effects of Project Flashlight occurred, with Hobson's near death being from an attempted suicide after realizing the danger-ous consequences of the experiment. Thus, the trio missed the annihilation of the human race by happenstance.

Realizing there is a chance the situation may recur unless they can stop it, Hobson convinces the others that they need to destroy the building where the experiments took place. Certain of death, Hobson sacrifices himself to detonate explosives at the building only to wake up once again. This time, however, it is definitely not the earth he knew, and he stares in disbelief at his new surround-ings as the film closes.

In this case, the mystery that comes with the protagonist waking up in a strange, new world is one of his own creation, although he doesn't realize that until late in the film. What makes this even more intriguing is that resolving *how* he got there doesn't necessarily tell him *why* or *where*. Could he and the others actually have succeeded in dying and are in purgatory or hell? Did everyone else disappear, or were they the only ones that vanished? More importantly, once Hobson retriggers the incident that put him in a world nearly devoid of people, where exactly did he go next?

The book deals with many similar themes and answers many of them in a way that still leaves some questions as to what is really happening, but also tells us perhaps a bit too much at the same time. Worse yet, when Hobson comes to the end of the novel and tries to commit suicide once again (instead of doing something heroic to save the others), he wakes up to find himself without his memories of the events he went through and reliving the whole situation over again (and possibly over and over again forever). As can be seen, this leads the book to fall into a *Groundhog Day* revisitation of events that, unfortunately, is an age-old cliché in fiction. Thus, in the case of *The Quiet Earth*, while the ending of the film doesn't resolve all the issues, it still leaves the viewer with a better resolution than that of the novel it is based on.

Army of Darkness (1992)

This one may seem a bit of a cheat to some readers, as the moment under discussion is only seen as the "original alternate ending" for the movie. Still, it is one that has become part of the canon of Sam Raimi's series of *Evil Dead* movies fondly remembered by many fans. Even those, like me, who actually prefer the ending used.

The *Evil Dead* trilogy Raimi made with Bruce Campbell starring has a long, twisting history. The premise of the first movie (*Evil Dead*) was revisited for a good chunk of the second (*Evil Dead 2: Dead by Dawn*) and then rewritten into the beginning of the third (*Army of Darkness*) in a way that doesn't quite fit what had already been seen in the first two. To get the essentials across, here's a brief quasi-summary: Ash (Bruce Campbell) goes with friends (or, in the case of the third movie, just his girlfriend, cameoed by Bridget Fonda) to an old cabin in the deep woods. There, a book called the *Necronomicon Ex-Mortis* is found and read from. This book of the dead allows evil spirits to inhabit those in the cabin and eventually Ash himself, who has to chainsaw off his own now-possessed right hand to prevent the evil from taking him over. By the end of the second film, he has seen so much that he has gone from sane to insane to back again. He manages to destroy the book, but in the process ends up opening a time portal that sends him back into the fourteenth century. There, he helps King Arthur fight off the "deadites" and is given a potion that allows him to go back to his own time by putting him to sleep for centuries.

At this point, near the end of the third movie, the scene cuts to Ash working at a department store and telling his story to a bored coworker. Suddenly there's a commotion as a deadite appears and Ash dispatches the demon without any hesitation in quite a heroic manner as the movie ends with Ash in triumph.

But this wasn't the original ending. What had been planned, and was filmed, was one where Ash had been given the potion to drink, but then—as only Ash can do—he messes up the dosage and winds up sleeping way past his own time. Instead, he wakes up in postapocalyptic London, looking at a torn-up city landscape and a demolished Big Ben as he begins hysterically singing "London Bridge" to himself. To the minds of those working on the movie, this was a perfect ending for Ash, as he had been shown time and again (more specifically in the second and third film rather than the first) to be a bit of a screwup, so him mistakenly taking too much of the potion seemed fitting.

The studio, however, didn't care for it once they got a chance to see it on the big screen. To them, it sent theatergoers out on a downer after all the silly and fun stuff seen before it. It seemed a bit unfair after everything Ash went through to end up being, seemingly, the last man on Earth, muttering to himself in a half-crazed way. In hindsight, it also would have suggested that it was a setup for another sequel (Ash in the future fighting deadites), when everyone agreed that the third film was a good way to end the cycle of films (no matter how often fans have clamored for an *Evil Dead IV* over the years). Thus, showing us an Ash as just a guy in a department store who still can kick demons' butts all over the place works better as an ending than one where he sleeps through the apocalypse. As for those who made it, even Raimi stated in Bill Warren's book

The poster for the third *Evil Dead* film, commonly known as *Army of Darkness* (1992), but in this Japanese poster as *Captain Supermarket*. Ash manages to sleep through Armageddon, but only in one version of the film.

Courtesy of Wrong Side of the Art

The Evil Dead Companion (St. Martin's Griffin) that he liked how the movie has two endings, one with Ash crazed in the future and the other as a "cheesy hero." Of the films discussed here, *Army of Darkness* is almost unique—the end of the world isn't the premise of the movie, as with many of those listed in this chapter about "missed Armageddon." In fact, it's a final punch line at the end of the film. Yet it's not alone in doing that, as the last film listed here will show.

Resident Evil (2002)

It's a video game. That should have ended the whole series right from the start, as it usually means a quickie movie made for kids and little more. Cap that status off with one where a premier director of horror films—more specifically the father of the modern zombie picture—George Romero was canned from the project after his script was deemed "too close" to the video game by the studio and most fans would have assumed that any film made would be a quickie rip-off not worthy of their time.

But a strange thing happened—the movie eventually released in 2002 (also known as *Resident Evil: Ground Zero*) turned out to be a somewhat stylish monster movie. Obviously styled after James Cameron's *Aliens* film, with a military team sent to investigate a location that has large homicidal creatures lurking in the dark, and a dash of the more recent zombie movies of the time that featured fast-moving cannibalistic dead infecting others, it still finds its own groove in the mix to stand by itself as a decent little thriller. At least, if nothing else, it is a passable time waster in a large pile of zombie movies that have been made before and since its release.

The premise of the film was originally conceived, and in many ways still functions, as a prequel to the first *Resident Evil* video game, released back in 1996 for the PlayStation and a tremendous hit. The shooter game allows players to kill various monsters and zombies while attempting to figure out a series of puzzles in a mansion that sits over a facility where the trouble has originated. Its success has led to a number of sequel games as well as books, and animated films beside the movie series listed here.

When the movie was broached in 1999, Sony sought out George Romero to put together a script, which made a certain amount of sense. Who else to write such a zombie movie than the person that pretty much invented the genre with films like *Night of the Living Dead* and *Dawn of the Dead?* Yet what they got didn't sit well with the studio heads: they essentially wanted a cash-in that took the general premise of the game and name and went off in its own direction. Romero, on the other hand, based his script on the plotline of the game and even included various characters and situations from it. Oddly, the studio felt that such a direction for the movie would be a bad idea—to their way of thinking, a movie not enough like the game would upset gamers while alienating viewers who didn't know the game at all. Instead, Paul W. S. Anderson arrived after succeeding with his movie version of the game *Mortal Kombat* in 1995, as well as making such films as *Event Horizon* and *Solider*. While those films didn't do well at the box office, Anderson had proven himself able to write and direct action-fantasy material, and the studio felt his script for *Resident Evil* fit what they were looking for in what they hoped would be a franchise. Which is exactly what it became—the first film made nearly three times what it cost to produce and has led to four sequels and more yet to come.

The premise of the first film finds Milla Jovovich (who is remembered first by many for her role in *The Fifth Element*) as Alice, an amnesic woman who later recalls she works for the Umbrella Corporation in a facility underneath a mansion. The corporation is a pharmaceutical company that is so big it is essentially a government entity with its own military force and had been working on genetically engineered creatures and viruses. An outbreak of something called the T-Virus has led to the shutdown of the facility by the supercomputer, called the Red Queen, running the facility to stop contamination. A commando squad arrives and, in trying to find out what happened to shut down the place, may end up spreading the plague created by the T-Virus that turns people into zombies and some into mutated monsters, as well as releasing mutated dogs and other creatures that kill. At the end of the film, Alice manages to get out of the facility with another survivor after giving herself the antivirus to the T-Virus. Unfortunately for Alice and the other lone survivor, members of the Umbrella Corporation arrive to take them both away. Later, Alice wakes up alone in a deserted lab (as in *Day of the Triffids*, *28 Days Later* and *Walking Dead*) and manages to make it outside. It is there that she discovers a disaster area where Raccoon City once stood. It is made clear that all Alice and the others did to stop the contamination was futile, as the Umbrella Corporation had gone back in and accidentally released the virus and the mutated creatures. Knowing that her trials are not over, Alice grabs a shotgun from a police car and gets ready to go to war.

The movie certainly isn't a masterpiece, but it does achieve what it sets out to do—give us action set pieces with zombies and horror creatures while tossing in a little bit of a mystery (as to who Alice is and what occurred that caused this situation). In a way it also gives us the "slept through the apocalypse" twice in one movie—the first time when Alice wakes up after the contagion starts in the locked-down facility and again at the end of the film in a twist that shows her story is far from over. Plus, it allows us to see a character who has a take-charge attitude and is in prime physical condition to do battle in the new world she discovers, just like many of the movies earlier described. Just as in the final two examples here, both of which came out in 2013.

Oblivion (2013)

This film, directed by Joseph Kosinski and starring Tom Cruise, deals with a man who believes he is the last man on Earth after an alien invasion had destroyed most of the planet decades before he was born. His job is to help with the harvesting of material from the planet to help fuel another world where he believes

Tom Cruise's second attempt to see the end of the world, this time in *Oblivion* (2013) as one of the few humans still alive after an alien invasion.

the rest of humanity has moved. Instead, he eventually discovers (in a twist not unlike that in Duncan Jones' 2009 movie, *Moon*) that he is just one of many clones of a man who is being used to harvest the planet for the use of the aliens that conquered Earth years before. The premise is similar to another "lone soul on a devastated Earth" movie, *WALL-E*, the Pixar animated film dealing with an ages-old robot left on an unpopulated, polluted Earth who finds plant life returning to the surface of the planet. In fact, the two films share other elements: each features a protagonist who is left to do a duty on an Earth no longer inhabitable (due to pollution in *WALL-E*, alien invasion in *Oblivion*); both protagonists are from an earlier age, which neither is aware of; and both movies bring humanity back to Earth after the devastation of the planet. In some ways, both films follow the premise of *Buck Rogers*—in a sense "awakening" in the future to fix things so that mankind can once again inhabit the planet. Meanwhile . . .

After Earth (2013)

Just a month after the release of *Oblivion* came *After Earth*, a movie directed by M. Night Shyamalan and starring Will Smith and his real-life son Jaden Smith. The movie deals with a father and son who crash on an abandoned Earth after some type of event that made the planet uninhabitable for humanity. The father is injured in the crash, and it is up to the son to keep them safe, both from aliens who wish to kill them and from the inhospitable planet, while setting up their rescue. Surprisingly, the film got somewhat angry reviews, but the film is exactly what it sets out to be—a young-adult adventure story about a boy growing up. Of course, the advertising for the film didn't exactly present it that way, but that is essentially what the film gives us, and why it is in this chapter—the boy had missed what occurred on Earth, and to him it is a new landscape rather than a remembered one. With that in mind, the film ends as it should, with no sense of the son wishing to "fight" to put things right like most of the protagonists in the other films listed here. Rather, he just wants to get out of there. Even so, *After Earth* does fulfill the requirement of the previous "slept through the apocalypse" films listed here.

In many of the movies here, the aim is to give these characters that missed the "big event" a chance to resolve a mystery and right some wrongs. Of course, in some cases, such as *Planet of the Apes* and *Where Have All the People Gone?*, the protagonist finds that there is nothing he can do but move on and survive. In the next chapter, it turns out that there really isn't even that much hope left for the heroes, even though they pretty much know from the start that the world is doomed.

4

Five Years Left to Cry In

Movies Where the End Is a Foregone Conclusion

Nearly all of the movies discussed in this book deal with two types of plots when it comes to the end of the world. The first features a crisis slowly and meticulously rising, followed by people trying to save themselves (such as in *Deep Impact* or *When Worlds Collide*); a few minutes of special effects at the climax; and, finally, a brief wrap-up of either the crisis being avoided or the survivors looking at the aftermath in stunned disbelief (before—usually—kissing passionately). The second is a brief look at the world before the crisis (if at all), followed by a majority of the movie played in disaster-movie mode, with the catastrophe occurring (such as in most zombie movies, *Independence Day*, *Invasion of the Body Snatchers*, and others), and then back to the quick resolution (and kissing). The main emphasis in all of these movies is one thing, however—survival. Billions of people may die along the way, but the protagonists are determined to make it out alive—at least some of them—and we watch as we would in any disaster movie to see who of those famous faces at the bottom of the movie poster makes it to the end.

Such movies are not the focus of this chapter. Instead, it centers on movies where the end happens and—even if there are some survivors somewhere—there are no winners. That may seem as if it's a rather dull topic to cover. After all, what is the point of following characters if it is just going to end with them dying? Yet this very question is where expectations usually are different from the results. These films are not so much about gosh-wow special effects—many end in brief flashes of light rather than huge *Star Wars* special effects, after all—but character studies based on the knowledge that the end is probably just around the corner.

Such a threat to life for the characters in these movies—from a handful to in some cases to everyone still alive on the planet—is what their stories hang on: can they find a way out if given enough time? If not, how would any of us act knowing that everything we've ever known will cease to exist by a certain date—not just ourselves but everything that has come before us? That you, me, our kids, the little doggy in the window—everyone will cease to be and nothing more will ever come? How do we ground ourselves, fight on, or give up, with such knowledge in front of us? In digging into such bleakness, the movies look past the typical theme of survival and rather into something we never can quite escape—the final blackness of death and the end of our memories. The end of our worlds.

There are three scenarios used for such films: the premonition ("Why won't someone believe me?"), the race against time ("How can we survive if you do believe me?"), and the inevitable ("Okay, everyone believes me, but what's the point in trying?"). Of course, these same themes appear in many of the movies covered in this book—heck, in most action films, period—but in those cases, they are simple plot-points or arcs that move the story along to the next story point. For example, John Woo's *Broken Arrow* features a ten-minute climactic escape for a man and a woman from a nuclear device about to go off and then moves on with the story; *Miracle Mile*, in comparison, finds a man and a woman spending nearly the entire length of the movie desperately attempting to get out of town before a nuclear warhead kills everyone. Both showcase the same concept of a couple racing to get away from a nuclear device that *will* be detonated, but the first film uses it merely as a thrilling set piece on a larger canvas; the other makes it the entire point of the movie.

What may be most surprising about the collection of films listed here is how they succeed in being different types of movies even though they share the same conclusion. Some are mysteries, some are action films, some act as domestic dramas, and a rare few even comedies. Many share these elements, but the emphasis usually leads to a road less traveled by the majority of apocalyptic movies, which is that of penetrating doom for the human race, with no winners to be found—making nearly all of them unique, memorable and sweetly melancholy.

The Premonition

Movies about premonitions are not anything new. Going back to the silents, we've had many films where characters for one reason or another have the ability to predict something that is to come. And be it happenstance, a mental ability or some type of prophecy, typically the films will demonstrate such predictions as being correct. End-of-the-world movies are no stranger to them either—it's not that unusual to have one character have a type of dream sequence showing the end occurring, or another announcing his fears to the public (and seen as insane, as in examples found in *Independence Day* and *2012*). In typical fashion, while such warnings are laughed off by the majority, the protagonist and his friends usually have faith in prophecy. Not quite so much in the cases that follow.

The first solid example of such premonitions revealing the results of an all-out Armageddon—beyond those that reference biblical prophecies—appears in David Cronenberg's adaptation of Stephen King's book *The Dead Zone* (1983). In that movie (as in the book), Johnny Smith (Christopher Walken) obtained "second sight" after a car accident that allows him to see images from a person's past or future when he touches them. He later discovers that he can also alter future events that he "sees" and sets out to stop a political candidate running for senator (played by Martin Sheen) that will eventually cause a nuclear war after he becomes president. Although the film is not actually a true representation of this category's theme—after all, Johnny manages to derail the vision from coming true, saving everyone in the process—it is easy to see *The Dead Zone* being the trigger for several of the films that follow.

Although *The Dead Zone* does not end with an apocalyptic event actually occurring, it does at least hint at the idea that the person having such visions may be in the right and not just "lucky" at predicting what is to come. It could be suggested that several end-times movies fall into this category as well—after all, they feature characters "in the know" who are trying to save others from what is to come—but these are built on the Book of Revelation and fall under their own banner (and into their own chapter in this book). The only real exception in the case of end-times movies would be the 1991 movie *The Rapture*, starring Mimi Rogers, and that is because it takes a different tack from those done for "Christian audiences"—mainly in that it keeps the audience guessing as to whether the protagonist is right or wrong in her belief of "things to come."

Written by Michael Tolkin (whose novel *The Player* was filmed by Robert Altman in 1992 and who would go on to cowrite the scripts for *Deep Impact* and the 2004 remake of *Dawn of the Dead*), *The Rapture* deals with a strongly amoral woman who eventually joins a cult that believes the Rapture (the ascending of those who believe in God to Heaven, leaving nonbelievers behind to face the rise of the beast) will soon arrive. Over time she marries and has a daughter, but begins to question her faith after her husband is murdered. Nevertheless, she is convinced that the Rapture will happen, taking her daughter with her to the desert to wait. When nothing occurs for quite some time, and as her daughter's health weakens, the woman struggles as to what to do. Killing her daughter in an attempt to send her on to heaven, the woman is arrested for the murder. As she sits in jail, the Rapture actually does occur. While others who had not believed give their lives over to God and are taken to heaven, and despite the pleas of her daughter from above, the woman refuses to accept God after feeling forsaken by Him and thus will linger in purgatory forever.

What is fascinating about the movie is that the audience is never quite sure how far we can trust Mimi Rogers' character. She is portrayed as an excessive personality who goes from one extreme to the polar opposite once she joins the sect, giving herself wholeheartedly to the sect's beliefs without any true concerns. It also becomes increasingly clear that she is not mentally balanced, and thus the audience's sympathy is never quite certain. In other movies of this type from Hollywood, the audience would stand confident that the protagonist and her cult are wrong; if done by those within the Christian cinema movement, there would be no doubt that she was absolutely right. Yet the element that makes *The Rapture* stand away from other such films is that it refuses to play either of those

MIMI ROGERS   DAVID DUCHOVNY

THE
RAPTURE

A FILM BY MICHAEL TOLKIN

"IT GOES PLACES MOVIES
SELDOM DARE TO GO"

MARSHALL FINE-GANNET NEWS

The Rapture (1991) is a rare film detailing a Christian prophecy in a decidedly agnostic manner.

games—we are never sure until we actually see the Rapture occur on-screen that she was correct, and her refusal to accept God now stands as a mental and physical experience instead of just one that deals with faith. She can move on to be with her daughter in paradise at any time if she lets God back into her heart, and the audience is pulling for her to do so because by that point they can see this is exactly what she should do. Instead, she refuses, due to the betrayal she feels. In some irony, a film that actually shows the audience the Rapture as a true event ends up being not about *that.* Her premonitions were correct— the end of the world did occur—yet in the end it is not about the Rapture or even religious faith, but solely her excessive emotional stubbornness that has always controlled her life, even to the point of ascension into heaven. And it is this type of examination of how characters tick at moments of such a crisis that makes it much more unique than if it had played it safe by going in either of the conventional directions ordained (no pun intended) by Hollywood and Christian cinema.

An oddly similar revelation comes to the protagonist of the 2011 film *Take Shelter,* starring Michael Shannon and written and directed by Jeff Nichols. Shannon plays Curtis LaForche, a man who has apocalyptic visions. He begins to work on a storm shelter, convinced that a storm with yellow rain will arrive and obsessing to the point of looking to have lost his sanity as he also loses his job. Eventually, just as Rogers' character in *The Rapture* does, he is convinced to turn away from his prophetic dreams, going away with his wife and daughter to a beach on vacation. Once there, it turns out that his dreams were a real warning, as yellow rain begins to fall, and what appears to be the end of the world (or at least his world) rapidly approaches the shores of the beach.

But is that what the film really is saying in the end? Some viewers took issue with an ending that leads to the same as in *The Rapture*, the protagonists may seems to have possible mental issues but ultimately are right in their assumptions about the ending of the world (in their own ways, Rogers' character via the Rapture and Shannon's character via a storm). Most of the film deals with the possibility that Curtis is suffering from the beginning stages of schizophrenia (a condition his mother had at a similar age), with the dreams being merely a part of this diagnosis. In the end, it appears he realizes that he needs to deal with this problem, with the first step being to get away from his shelter, only to discover that he was right all along. To some viewers, this felt like a cheat; after all the buildup to show the serious ramifications of mental illness, it turns out that "the crazy guy was right all along!" Others felt that the moviemakers were in a sense laughing at the character—making him suffer until he abandons his dreams, only for his dreams to be proven correct the second he gives them up and can no longer save himself or his family. Thus, it is merely a cosmic joke at the expense of Curtis.

However, a few viewers have interpreted the ending to be his dreams instead of reality: that this storm approaching him is simply a manifestation in his mind of the rapidly approaching stages of schizophrenia. Yet, unlike in earlier dreams he had, his wife and daughter are now there to witness the "storm" that will take him into madness, as he finally faces the challenges of his oncoming schizophrenia with his family at his side instead of on his own. In a sense, he really has given them shelter in preparation for his descent, thanks to all that has occurred before. Whether that means he will succumb to it or be able to rise above it is never stated, but it does mean that what appears on the surface to be an apocalyptic film actually isn't one at all.

And if that is the case, and there are so many recognizable similarities to *The Rapture*, can we say the same for *The Rapture*? Is Rogers' character actually experiencing the Rapture, where she can be safe with the knowledge that her daughter is in heaven for sure, even as she rejects God's love and stays in purgatory? Or is it possible she is trapped in purgatory because it resides only in her own mind and not in reality? If so, it means she had waited so long for the Rapture to occur, and even killed her own daughter in hopes of speeding up the process, that she decided to create the moment in her mind in order to be able to live with it. Which would explain why she cannot leave purgatory, as there is no way she can even if she did accept God back into her heart, as the Rapture is real only in her mind. If this is actually the situation, then it turns both of these films into character studies pertaining to mental illness rather than apocalyptic visions (and more like such endings found in a movie like *Brazil*, which will be discussed in a later chapter).

Whether one views these two films as dream or reality—and, to be fair, what is to keep us from the possibility that Walken's character in *The Dead Zone* isn't just ending his life with wish fulfillment of what he hopes would be rather than what will be—at least the last film in this category has no analogies that can be made about it. Oddly enough, it ends up possibly fitting another category in our discussion later on, rather than that of premonitions.

The movie is *Knowing* (2009), starring Nicolas Cage as a professor whose young son begins seeing the "whisper people" that want him and a girl named Abby to go away with them. Near the beginning of the film, the son is shown picking out items from a fifty-year-old time capsule, including papers that give a series of numbers the professor is able to decipher as dates when fatal disasters have occurred. The father's investigation of the papers suggests that the world will be ending soon, and the whisper people want the children for some reason. Coincidentally (and in a convenience of storytelling), the father also finds out that massive solar flares will quickly reach the earth, killing everyone. Soon after, the whisper people arrive in their spaceship. It is revealed that the papers were a prophecy by the aliens about what was to come, and now they wish to take the two young children away to safety as the world ends. The father lets them go as he stays behind to die with the rest of humanity, knowing that his son and the girl might possibly be able to recreate the human race somewhere else in the galaxy.

So what does this tell us about premonitions and prophecies? Well, in the case of *Knowing*, it appears that aliens have much more advanced knowledge about our solar system, our sun and future tragic human events, and they will try to warn us about such dangers. Unfortunately, they do so in such a cryptic manner that it is told only to one little girl and then hidden away in a time capsule for fifty years. As it turns out, it is by chance that a boy just happens to open it and find the numbers. What's more, that the boy will have a father who will be able to decipher the numbers in order to put the boy and the granddaughter of the girl who wrote it all fifty years ago (not to mention being the right age for the boy to grow up with) in the right place and at the right time to be saved. With that much advanced knowledge you would think they could have come up with some way to save a few more people, or even a few more kids than just the two and a couple of rabbits (and lucky for them that the earthlings managed to do most of the work for them in even giving them the two). Or maybe even stop the solar flares. But no, we're supposed to be thankful for them doing as close to the least they could possibly do to help at all. Sure, we're supposed to leave the theater thinking how noble the aliens are for saving the two children, but it really looks like the aliens just had a shopping list to pick up a few items on the way home. "Oh, Kqytim! Be sure to pick up a couple of human children on the way back from the Sol System, will you? Oh, and a couple of rabbits." "Good thinking, Srbyrm! The bunnies will make good stew for the children to eat on the way home!"

In other words, boy, those aliens are jerks. But that's a topic for another chapter. As for now, attention should be on the next category in movies that ultimately show us the possible ends of the world, but with some at least given a chance to skedaddle.

The Race Against Time

As discussed earlier in this chapter, the "race against time" category of apocalyptic films deals with movies that have one central theme—the characters within the film know the end of the world is approaching. The difference with this category is, unlike the first where people cannot be certain that the world will end today, tomorrow or even years from now, everyone in the room pretty much knows that death is coming and it's coming before the night is out. Which, as before, reverberates in most action and disaster movies—after all, James Bond always seems to stop the satellite from detonating the bomb that will blow up the world with seven seconds to spare—yet, in those movies, such situations are momentary and done typically as the film's climax. In the case of the movies below, there is no deviation from that task; from the start or near start of such movies it is solely about surviving the upcoming apocalyptic event. There may be some mixed results by the time the end credits appear, but in all the movies listed next there are a lot of casualties along the way and no true redemption for any of the characters who try to challenge fate.

To kick things off, a look at a movie that, at first glance, appears not to be correct for this category at all, *Rocket Attack, U.S.A.* (1961). Up front, I should remind readers that this film should not to be confused with *Invasion U.S.A.* (1952), which is about an all-out, ground-forces military attack against America by gentlemen who are never quite stated to be, but probably are, "dirty commie Russian scum." Nor should it be confused with *Invasion U.S.A.*, the Chuck Norris movie from 1985, with Chuck resisting an all-out, ground-forces military attack against Americans by "dirty commie Cuban scum." (So much has changed in thirty years—now it only takes one American to wipe out the Communists when it took an entire country to lose to them in 1952.) Instead, this movie from 1961 involves . . . well, what do you know . . . "dirty commie scum."

As typical for this book, we have avoided the various American takeover movies such as *Red Dawn* (1984), because they don't involve an apocalyptic-altering affect. True, that movie involved the takeover of . . . well, it seems, mainly a high school and some irritating kids in the middle of nowhere, but the movie is about occupation—perhaps bordering on dystopian in nature—but certainly not apocalyptic (and that's playing it favorably, it's rather more like a male teen fantasy of playing bang-bang with guns rather than what would commonly be seen of an occupation). Yet *Rocket Attack, U.S.A.* is the exception that proves the rule. For as much as it tries to play it cool and come off as quasi–James Bond in tone (specifically Ian Fleming's books and other Cold War novels being produced at the time), it involves a movie-length "race against time" to avoid a nuclear war by stopping a missile from being launched behind the iron curtain. This involves our hero, John Manston (John McKay), making his way to Moscow with the help of a female agent, Tannah (Monica Davis), in hopes of finding out what the Soviets may have learned about U.S. military secrets thanks to Sputnik (the first satellite, put into space by the U.S.S.R. soon before the film's release).

Rocket Attack, U.S.A. (1961) is one in a series of movies where people ineptly try to stop World War III and . . . fail.   *Courtesy of Wrong Side of the Art*

As it turns out, they've learned enough to create a nuclear missile and have aimed it at New York to start World War III. Why? Mostly because they're "dirty commie scum." In the last few minutes of the film, Manston manages to get within yards of the rocket; just seconds before liftoff, and . . . he gets himself killed. This allows the Soviets to fire the missile at their leisure and wipe out a lot of friendly, happy, innocent people in New York who are really engrossed in the topic of neckties, it appears. And so, after roughly sixty minutes of anticipation in seeing our spy behind the iron curtain winning one for the good ol' U.S. of A., we are instead invited to witness the destruction of New York in the first of a wave of assaults on the country. Which seems very anticlimactic in many ways—it's like Bond being shot by Blofeld before he can flip that switch to cancel the satellite that will end the world—yet it seems to be a common thread in many of the nuclear annihilation films that were to come.

This Is Not a Test (1962) may have arrived a year, not four years, later, but it certainly is in the same line as *Rocket Attack, U.S.A.* As with the earlier picture, it stars actors that look vaguely familiar, but not so much, and is written and produced by people who had solid, workmanlike careers in television and films but no obvious ambitions with this movie except to make a quick buck. The film tells a story about vastly confused people waiting for a missile to hit what appears to be the Los Angeles area at the start of World War III (once again, Hollywood loves to destroy Hollywood when it comes to the end of the world). In some ways the movie even works as a sequel to *Rocket Attack, U.S.A.*—for while the earlier film shows the incompetence of our spies in the Soviet Union to stop the war, the latter shows the same for the civilians waiting for the end to come. As Gary Westfahl mentions in a brief overview of director Fredric Gadette (who worked mainly in television for *You Asked for It* and *ABC's Wide World of Sports*), this is a film that "perfectly reflects the genuine ineptness that ordinary people would display in the face of nuclear weapons" (www.sfsite.com/gary/gade01.htm), for it shows them hemming and hawing, unsure of what to do, until they are obliterated by the missile approaching from the Soviets.

The plot starts off with some predictability, as Deputy Dan Colter (played by Seamon Glass, who would go on to play hill-people bit roles in movies like *Deliverance* and *Damnation Alley*) is shown out on a mountain road near Los Angeles. He has been ordered to stop any vehicles from entering the city due to a possible missile attack. That's logical; after all, there's no point in sending people into what could be a nuclear holocaust at any moment, plus it makes sense to keep roads clear. Great—make sure people have an exit away from the city as the news spreads.

Then it gets weird. As he begins to halt people from going into the city, he also refuses to let them leave, taking away their car keys. Evidently, his orders are to make sure no one goes to the city *and* also keep them at his present location—on an isolated mountain road, far too close to the city to save anyone from potential screaming death coming from the sky. This also means that any military vehicles, much less civilian cars, frantically heading out of the city are pretty much going to be stuck at this roadblock once they see all the cars and trucks littering the place. As it stands, it doesn't make much sense and immediately calls into question the deputy's leadership—either he's completely misunderstanding his instructions (which I even suspected was the case when I saw the movie as a boy), or he's gone loopy with power. Either way it looks, he soon has a number of people pulled over and afraid to try to make a break for it thanks to the deputy aiming a shotgun at them and even handcuffing one man to the fender of a car when he tries to escape.

The assumption to make while watching is that perhaps the people who made the film didn't realize what an actual bomb would do to the area. After all, it's still early enough in the 1960s that the general public assumed a quick "duck and cover" will save you from anything the bomb would bring; yet dialogue makes clear that everyone knows they are sitting ducks just waiting to die if they stay there. Their only real chance is to get in their cars and gun it toward anywhere other than where they are, but everyone is simply too scared to fight the increasingly irrational deputy. Instead, they clear out a truck in hopes it will give them protection for two weeks until the radiation settles, then people either kill themselves, take a run for the hills or dive into the truck and go slightly screwy while waiting for the end. The deputy certainly comes off that way, especially after he strangles one couple's dog to save air in the truck; as if a poodle will squander more air than six people stuck in the back of a truck for two weeks.

With the missiles starting to fall, a group from the city arrives with their vehicle out of gas. Having faced the chaos of the city, they have little fear of the deputy and knock him out, grabbing one of the women while taking off as fast as possible in the deputy's car. Those remaining then hurry back inside the truck and seal it tight (how they do this from the inside of the truck is questionable at best, but they do). Soon, the deputy wakes up and pounds on the door, realizing that his best-laid plans to save himself have left him on the outside. The movie ends as the bomb detonates in the nearby city, turning the scene to white in a flash. While it is clear the deputy has died, there is no resolution for the characters inside the truck, nor message to be found—death came from the sky, and as one character calmly watches the deputy frantically (just as others would no doubt do in a real-life situation) tries to save himself, he realizes that it matters little as they are all to be obliterated anyway.

Perhaps unintentionally, due to the limitations of a mostly unknown cast and the strictly-by-the-paces shooting of these two films, there's actually a depressing starkness to them that says much more in reflection about our own concerns in the Cold War than the hysterical superhero antics of characters like Bond. Because we like to see ourselves on the side of the righteous and the good, we tend to want our movie heroes to be able to succeed for the same reasons. "It's the U.S.A." (or Britain, or what-have-you), "so we're going to figure out a way to beat the commies and stop them from killing us," is what we were supposed to and did shout out to the world during the Cold War. Our movie heroes from John Wayne to James Bond to Chuck Norris and beyond have always been there in the movies to prove that righteousness. Yet always lingering was and is the doubt that is strongly projected by films such as *Rocket Attack, U.S.A.* and *This Is Not a Test*. They pretend to showcase our macho posturing, but conclude with the final message we all have thought of in the pit of the night, which was, "Oh, God, we're going to screw this up, aren't we?" We at first assume the deputy and the spy know what they're doing, but ultimately their plans are crackpot at best and do nothing to save anyone in the end. All that's left is hoping someone somewhere was a bit more on the ball and survives.

Which leads right into a subcategory here—movies where those in charge are witness to oncoming devastation and attempt to stop an escalation of attacks in the brief window of time available to them. Three films fall into this subcategory, with the two most famous, *Fail-Safe* and *Dr. Strangelove, or How I Learned to Stop Worrying and Love the Bomb* (both from 1964), even sharing the same plot, but more about that in a moment.

Dr. Strangelove is based on the 1958 novel *Red Alert* by Peter George, while *Fail-Safe* was adapted from the 1962 novel of the same name by Eugene Burdick (coauthor of *The Ugly American*) and Harvey Wheeler. *Red Alert* deals with renegade U.S. Air Force Brigadier General Quinten, who decides to initiate an attack on the Soviet Union himself by sending out a squadron of B-52 bombers under the directions of a war plan that gives him the authority to do so if the leaders of the U.S. government are wiped out in a first strike. The men on the bombers don't realize that this is all a ruse and go out on their mission assuming that World War III has begun.

The U.S. president and his cabinet attempt to work with the Soviets to stop the mission from being completed, although there are suggestions from the military that, with the mission ongoing, they might as well see it through and finish off the Soviets for good. This doesn't sit well with the president, who reveals that the Soviets have planted a "doomsday device" in the Ural Mountains—a number of hydrogen bombs that would release enough cobalt into the atmosphere that any attempt to bomb them will lead to the annihilation of everyone on the planet.

An attack on the bombers knocks out two of them, but the others remain, and a final one, the *Alabama Angel*, has its radio damaged. The recall code that will void the mission is finally found and transmitted, allowing the bombers to return to the U.S. with the exception of the *Alabama Angel*, which did not receive the code due to the damage received to their radio in the previous contest with the Soviets. With the bomber racing to its target, the Soviet premier suggests that they be allowed to bomb a U.S. city in retaliation, and the president reluctantly agrees.

As it turns out, the bomber's payload is a dud, and there is no explosion. The Soviets, however, are insistent on bombing an American city anyway, which draws a threat from the president that all of the U.S. military would be brought against them if it occurs. The Soviets back down, and the end of the novel finds the president deciding that more needs to be done to beef up the U.S. arsenal of weapons in order to keep the Soviets in their place and ensure peace. Which is fascinating for viewers of *Dr. Strangelove* and other movies in this book, as it is the exact opposite conclusion found in most of them and certainly in the Stanley Kubrick movie.

Nevertheless, the general plot of the novel intrigued Kubrick, who was coming off the success of *Spartacus* (1960) and *Lolita* (1962)—and would later do *2001: A Space Odyssey* (1968) with Arthur C. Clarke—and was looking for a project dealing with the arms race. Kubrick's point, however, was to show the insanity of such a thing, certainly in light of the chance that someone some-where was bound to make a mistake and end up getting a lot of people killed by accident. Directed to George's book, Kubrick liked what he saw, but initial scripting found him and others (including George himself) getting more out of making up parodies of the crisis than keeping the situation serious. After some struggle with what to do with the plot, it was decided that making it a dark comedy was the way to go, and thus we ended up with one of the first black comedies pertaining to the new atomic age. And although Veljko Bulajic's *Rat* from 1960 beats it to the punch by four years (more about this movie in a later chapter), it is considered the apocalyptic comedy that every film after it has to stand up against.

Throwing in the additional spice of satirical author Terry Southern (who had written both *Candy* and *The Magic Christian* by this point), the script digs deep into random silliness amid the serious threat of nuclear annihilation very early on. Sterling Hayden, who had appeared in Kubrick's earlier *The Killing* (1956), is General Jack D. Ripper, the equivalent of Quinten, who activates the bombers due to concerns about fluoride in American water supplies being a communist plot (an actual conspiracy theory of several in the public at the time) and a reason for his impotence. President Merkin Muffley (played by Peter Sellers in one of three roles) is advised by his cabinet in the war room, specifically General Buck Turgidson (George C. Scott), about Ripper's plan. As the movie bounces from those onboard the *Leper Colony* (the *Alabama Angel* equivalent of the movie) and its commander Major T. J. "King" Kong (Slim Pickens, in a part originally planned for Sellers as well) to the war room and to Ripper's office, where he holds a British officer named Mandrake (Peter Sellers), discussions move from letting the mission be completed to allowing the Soviet premier to shoot the bombers down.

As in the book, the Soviets have created a doomsday device that will wipe out humanity if they are bombed, but the movie makes clear the insanity of having such a device that would be a deterrent if no one knows it exists (the Soviet ambassador then explains that they were going to announce it the following week as a present for the premier's birthday). From there, even with the humor-ous overtones, the movie follows the book rather closely (the shooting down of many of the bombers, the code being found to recall the remainder, and the one damaged bomber that makes it through to drop its payload). There is even a malfunction where the *Leper Colony* should not be able to succeed—just as the

Alabama Angel failed in its mission in the book—but Kubrick and others won't have it, and thus Kong takes matters into his own hands (and legs) and rides the bomb like a wild bronco to the doom of mankind.

And through all this is the late appearance in the film of Dr. Strangelove, a wheelchair-bound German scientist (also played by Sellers) who has a gloved hand with a mind of its own and a plan for all the "important" men there to head to the mineshafts for a few decades "with ten women for every one" of them. It's a plan for survival that, as with everything before it, is played out as a cartoonish male fantasy, with Turgidson's concern not about the general population being slaughtered in the nuclear holocaust but rather if the U.S.' mineshafts are bigger than the Soviet ones. Meanwhile, the Soviet ambassador is taking spy photos of the big board in the war room that will be of no use to anyone in the future, feeling compelled to do so just because. With the images of various atomic explosions filling the screen, Vera Lynn's rendition of "We'll Meet Again" plays, reminding us that the cycle of stupidity (i.e., war) on a grand scale seems to be never-ending, even in the face of total annihilation.

The film plays like a horror movie in many respects, with dread increasing as it closes in on the end of the world at a time when a majority of people were still feeling the anxieties of the Cuban Missile Crisis in 1962 (which many thought would end with World War III starting). Yet, at the same time, the film filters all this tension through outrageous comedy that in some ways ends up negating its own message, even though it probably plays much closer to the reality of such a situation than most of the movies listed in this book. We really do have people in positions of power who are paranoid enough to consider such an attack "good." One could easily see an officer unsure whether to shoot a Coke machine in order to save the world because he doesn't want to have to "answer to the Coca-Cola Company." Even the most famous line in the movie (and one of the most famous in cinema history), "Gentlemen, you can't fight in here! This is the war room!," epitomizes the sheer ironic attempts at normality we would no doubt face in such a situation. Ultimately, *Dr. Strangelove* is too good at its game to really get Kubrick's intended message across: he wants us to examine the manic senselessness of the arms race, but we are too busy laughing at Peter Sellers shouting out "Mein Führer! I can walk!" to worry about it. Plus, allowing Strangelove to advocate the mineshaft plan suggests that a number of humans will survive, even if it's this idiot bunch (although the montage of atomic blasts happens so soon after Strangelove's speech that it could suggest no one had time to initiate his plan). Thus, even though the message is that the Cold War is leading us all to mindless oblivion and we see what could be the end of the world, the film pulls back through comedy to the point that it is somewhat safe. After all, in the film there are only two unique deaths seen on camera, Ripper and Kong—two crazed individuals who probably deserve what they get and both dying in comedic scenes that downplay their demises.

To say all the above is not to disavow the classic status of *Dr. Strangelove*; it is a miracle that such a film balancing the horrors of war with comedy could be done, especially in 1964, and only someone like Kubrick could have pulled that off. Later in this book the discussion will turn to other apocalyptic comedies, but *Dr. Strangelove* is the prototype that other such films can only hope to strive to be. Even so, *Dr. Strangelove* fits more readily in this "race against time" genre as it shows many characters from early in the film working to stop the end from occurring. Moreover, like the two cheap B-movies previously mentioned, the message is the same: no matter how heroic our efforts, mankind is bound to find a way to fail.

The next film, however, while played like a serious version of *Dr. Strangelove*, is different in one major regard from those listed before: it manages to show a resolution that does not find mankind destroyed, although it is an outcome that is of little benefit to anyone involved and still sees millions killed. Even so, *Fail-Safe*, starring Henry Fonda as the president of the United States, once again displays how our (and their) macho posturing will lead directly to a massive mistake on a global scale. The movie, directed by Sidney Lumet—whose vast career ranged from early material like *12 Angry Men* to *Dog Day Afternoon*, to the somewhat apocalyptic *Network* and up to his last film, *Before the Devil Knows You're Dead* (2007)—is based on a novel so close in structure to *Red Alert* that a copyright infringement lawsuit was filed against the book after its release in 1962. The case would be settled out of court, but such similarities would be remembered when Lumet began filming the novel while Kubrick was finishing his *Red Alert* adaptation, *Dr. Strangelove*. With the same studio, Columbia, making both films, it was agreed that *Dr. Strangelove* would come out first, and in doing so, it eroded interest in the "serious" version that came out later, leading to *Fail-Safe* not doing as well at the box office as it might have if released before Kubrick's movie. After all, once parodied, it was hard to take a similar story seriously.

The plot of the 1964 film (and subsequently the 2000 television remake by Stephen Frears that starred George Clooney) follows closely that of the novel: an unidentified plane leads to U.S. bombers being sent into action to be ready in case of an attack. As it turns out, it is a minor mistake, and the bombers are recalled. However, a malfunctioning fault indicator in the master computer allows a "Go" command to be sent to a squadron of six bombers who proceed to head toward Moscow with a payload of nuclear warheads. Unfortunately, the Soviets had perfected a radio-jamming system that will not allow the squadron to verify their order, with the assumption being that war has broken out and they must proceed with the attack.

The president, played by Henry Fonda in the earlier film and Richard Dreyfuss in the telefilm, discusses the situation with his advisers. Ignoring the advice of Professor Groeteschele (Walter Matthau and Hank Azaria, respectively), who (much like Turgidson from *Dr. Strangelove*) suggests they should use the mistaken attack to their advantage and bomb the Soviets to avoid any retaliation, the president okays the military to try to shoot down the bombers. When this fails, he involves the Soviets, who are at first distrustful. General Bogan (Frank Overton/Brian Dennehy) at Strategic Air Command begins working with

The main competitor to *Dr. Strangelove* in 1964. *Fail-Safe* has nearly the same story line, told as a serious drama, and did poorly by comparison at the box office.

Courtesy of Vintage Cinema Ads

the Soviets to attempt to stop the radio jamming and/or shoot down the bombers, but paranoia on both sides leads to delays that allow one bomber to make it through. Attempts by the president to talk to the commander of the bomber (as well as family members in the two adaptations) and get him to return are fruitless, and it is clear that the bomber will succeed in its mission to destroy Moscow.

In hopes of stopping what appears to be an all-out war, the president offers to bomb New York City in hopes that such an "eye for an eye" response will keep the Soviets from retaliation. When it is clear that Moscow has been wiped out, the president sends General Black (Dan O'Herlihy/Harvey Keitel) to drop the bomb on New York, knowing full well that the president's wife and Black's wife and young daughter are in the city. The final image is of Black dropping the bomb that will destroy New York City and then committing suicide in the bomber.

No other way to say it, *Fail-Safe* is a bleak story that finds no winners and no saviors. The president does manage to avoid World War III, but the "race" to stop the bombing of both Moscow and (in due process) New York City are failures. Moreover, as with the previous movies mentioned, the audience sees a series of characters who work against the best interest of mankind due to distrust and their own concerns: a Soviet commander shoots down the wrong plane because he assumes Bogan is lying about which planes to ignore (leading to the Soviet commander having a nervous breakdown), Bogan's second-in-command attempts a coup because he cannot contemplate the U.S. working with the Soviets, and the bomber's crew refuses to believe the recall request because it is assumed the Soviets would fake such a command. Man's delusion of being in the right, the assurance of nothing bad being possible, leads to the death of millions. Those in charge may avoid the greater conflict, but delays, arrogance and basic human nature are again demonstrated to lead to greater tragedy. Oddly, the end of the 1964 adaptation has some similarities with that of *Rocket Attack, U.S.A.*, with the camera shifting to showing people going about their daily business in New York City just as it is about to be nuked. Suddenly, the end of *Rocket Attack, U.S.A.* doesn't seem quite as amusing anymore, as survival is impossible for the innocent in both of these films' worlds.

It is nearly two decades before there's another attempt to show a nuclear crisis between the Soviets and the Americans, this time from the National Broadcasting Company (NBC) and their miniseries *World War III* (1982). Well, a title like that certainly does cut to the chase, doesn't it? The movie stars Rock Hudson as the president and David Soul as a colonel who is sent to Alaska to deal with Soviet paratroopers who plan to sabotage the Alaskan pipeline (still very much in the news at the time) in retaliation for the ongoing (and real-life) grain embargo that occurred after the Soviet invasion of Afghanistan. As Soul and his troops try to fight off the Soviets, Hudson tries to negotiate peace with the Soviet premier (Brian Keith, who played another Soviet in a film discussed in chapter 16). It turns out that the premier knew nothing of the attack until it had already started and isn't completely thrilled with the idea. As plans look to be coming together, the premier is killed by a bomb. His underlings take this as a prime opportunity to attack America with nuclear weapons and lie to Hudson about wanting to talk peace further in order to keep the U.S. military off their guard, but the president is too smart for them and has already issued an okay for a full-out nuclear attack of the Soviet Union. The movie ends with the U.S.A. starting the bombing and the Soviets returning in kind. Everyone around the world hears the missiles begin to fall as the movie quickly cuts to black.

While the miniseries appears at first to be heading down the same road as *Red Dawn* and the American television miniseries *Amerika* (both of which focus on a Soviet takeover of America), it quickly veers into the land of *Fail-Safe* and *Dr. Strangelove* territory with the introduction of nuking countries and invasions being kept from people who should have been in the know. As one would expect for a program from American network television of the 1980s, the story is pretty much a white-hat/black-hat, cowboys-and-Indians plot, with the Americans being for truth and justice, while the Soviets (with one exception) are barbarians driven by bloodlust. Ultimately, however, *World War III* is in some ways even worse in its depiction of governments losing their way than the previous films discussed. There, the mistakes made are unintentional, with people trying their best to fix things before they reach the final stages. With *World War III*, the emphasis is on people in control just playing many games over problems, such as the embargo, that could be easily resolved and were in real life. The embargo lasted only two years, with the U.S. creating more problems for itself than it did for the Soviets—U.S. farmers had to deal with large fluctuations in grain prices, while the Soviets simply found other sources for their grain . . . and without having to resort to trying to bomb the Alaskan pipeline to get results.

A final film in this subcategory of movies where those in control make very bad decisions is *By Dawn's Early Light*, a 1990 HBO movie based on the 1983 book *Trinity's Child* by William Prochnau, although so many changes were made to it that the movie stands on its own, using only some of the framework of the novel. Still, at least it plays a tad saner than *World War III*. The story begins when the Soviets believe that a terrorist attack on a city is the doing of NATO and launch a response on the U.S. before realizing their mistake (a reversal of the other two films that start with America initiating the conflict). In a further reversal of *Fail-Safe*, the Soviets state they are willing to take a hit in response from the U.S., but only an equivalent one. Anything more will lead to an all-out war. The president (Martin Landau) agrees to the counterstrike, but soon believes that a further launch has begun by the Soviets and the original request just a ruse. Although this turns out to be directed at the Chinese (as they have decided to strike the Soviets while they have a chance) and not the U.S., the president is not informed of this until after a second strike has been activated and he is soon unable to countermand the order when Marine One, which he is aboard, crashes.

With the president presumed dead, the secretary of the interior (Darren McGavin) takes over and agrees that only the destruction of the Soviets will stop the bombings. When the president is found alive, the secretary refuses to relinquish his command—power mad, paranoid, and positive the request to stand down is a fake. The president and others then work to stop the secretary from giving a final order that will lead to assurance of global destruction, managing to do so just moments before it is to begin.

After the setup of the previous two movies, it is refreshing to see one that deals with a global conflict that goes down a different road than *Dr. Strangelove* and *Fail-Safe*. Moreover, in this post-9/11 age where terrorists being able to pull off grand schemes of destruction are a reality, the setup for the initial attack seems quite possible. Certainly more than in 1990 when the film was broadcast. It also allows the movie to steer away from the Cold War agenda of the "dirty commie scum" that is present in the novel it is based on, which was rapidly becoming an impossible cliché by 1990. In the book, the Soviets see the strike as a way to push the U.S. into doing its bidding; in the movie, it's a mistake and seems more realistic than an elaborate plan that is pretty much set up to start a war. It also allows the movie to appear in this chapter, as everything comes together to lead to a near global nuclear event thanks to the errors of those in power's well-intentioned attempts to do the right thing. After all, the secretary's not believing the president is alive is merely a variation on the bomber's commander not believing the president's pleas to turn back in *Fail-Safe*. While it does not measure up to being a classic like the two movies listed before it (although it does share James Earl Jones from *Dr. Strangelove*), *By Dawn's Early Light* works in the same manner of showing how easily we can come to nuclear war. At least, as with *Fail-Safe* before it, the outcome allows for the survival of the world, although the cost is millions of lives.

Survival is the key point of *Miracle Mile* (1988), starring Anthony Edwards as Harry, a young man who meets up with a woman named Julie (Mare Winningham) one day in L.A. and plans to go out with her later, only to mistakenly pick up a ringing payphone and hear from the other end that World War III will commence in seventy minutes. (With the exception of nearly thirty years between them, one could almost suggest that this is what was happening in Los Angeles while the deputy in *This Is Not a Test* was busy with the travelers after the spy in *Rocket Attack, U.S.A.* failed in his mission. But, admittedly, that may be trying too hard to get them to gel.) A chance encounter with someone connected to the government gives him the opportunity to leave for a military base in Antarctica before the bombs start dropping, but he is intent on finding Julie first and taking her with him. The rest of the film deals with Harry trying to locate Julie and then find a way to get to the waiting plane before time runs out, while avoiding obstacles that appear as panic begins to grip the city. Finally, the two manage to meet up and get to a helicopter that will take them to the waiting plane, but just as they take off, the bombs hit, causing the helicopter to crash in the La Brea Tar Pits. Thus, even with some foresight (much like that of those waiting for the bombs in *This Is Not a Test*), safety is not guaranteed for the protagonists, and the movie ends with them resigning themselves to their fate. The movie fades out as the helicopter fills with water and another bomb soon comes, yet with the two protagonists looking back at their race against time in as positive a light as they can—for at least they tried, and they were able to spend their last moments together before the world comes to an end—a statement that will be seen again in this chapter.

Which leads to the kinship between the movies in this category—there may be much to make of human frailty and fallacy, but there is always a sense of determination to beat the clock and somehow win. A spy is shot, allowing a missile to be launched that destroys New York. A deputy strong-arming civilians leads to him being nuked for his troubles. A guy merely wants to save his new girlfriend from harm and ends up getting them both killed in the process. On a global scale, we see that human errors (intentional or not) may one day find us facing extinction for something trivial. In every case, however, at least some of the characters try their best to defuse the situation and save whom they can. In a few cases, that works: *Miracle Mile* and *This Is Not a Test* both hint at characters who probably were able to get to shelter before the bombs started to drop, while *Fail-Safe* and *By Dawn's Early Light* may feature massive casualties but at least show an ending to such destruction and perhaps a better world coming out of the situations. Yet in all of them, there is a sense of dread in knowing that the end will soon come. The only fortunate thing for the characters is that such moments of fear are fleeting, as their doom will be at hand within minutes.

Such is not quite the case for the final category in this chapter, however.

The Inevitable

Movie posters, especially those for horror films, usually try to convey some feeling of both mystery and terror with their advertising. One of the common clichés of such work is a slogan that reads along the lines of "Those who died in the first few minutes of the monster's attack . . . were the lucky ones."

In some ways, this sums up the difference between the movies found in the previous two categories. In those films, whether it is a race against time or simply a possible end that could happen, there's still a general feeling that things are going to be okay for at least someone, somewhere on the planet. We may see a bomb go off in, say, *Miracle Mile*, but does that mean no one on Earth survived? *The Rapture* suggests the good are ascending to heaven, but others (such as the protagonist) still live on Earth, so it's not quite the end of the world. Even *Knowing* has two kids surviving Earth's destruction so that they can start life anew on another planet (at least let us hope that's what the aliens had in mind there). There is always hope that someone somewhere will get out alive, even if the people in the movie we're watching have no chance of doing so. Further, nearly all of the films listed in this book have one thing in common—whether we fight or flight from the disaster commencing, it usually is presented as something that has come out of the blue and will be dealt with in the very near future. Usually within the next few hours or even minutes.

gregory peck · ava gardner
fred astaire · anthony perkins

stanley kramer's production of
on the beach

introducing donna anderson
screen play by john paxton · from the novel by nevil shute
produced and directed by stanley kramer · released thru [ ] united artists

On the Beach (1959) was not the first to suggest the impossibility of winning a nuclear war, but certainly one of the first to suggest the end of humanity, with no hope for survival.

Then we have the films where there is no escape; there is no way to beat it, we are destined to all die. And we know it. Worse yet, the end is not just a few minutes away or an hour or so, it is destined to happen days, weeks or even months into the future (for example, *On the Beach* is stated to take place nearly two years after the rest of the world has been killed off). Which leads us to wonder what we would do if we knew the world was going to end and there was no way to change that? Would we attempt to find a way to stop it? Would we decide to end it all ourselves so we have some control over our destinies? Would we simply wait it out, going through the motions of our normal lives until the very end?

These questions about mortality are the framework of the last six movies listed in this chapter. In many ways, such films are like "tragic illness" movies on steroids. Instead of Ryan O'Neal pining over the long decline of Ali MacGraw from cancer in *Love Story*, however, we find everyone left on the planet realizing that the days of the earth, their friends, the neighbor's dog, and themselves are rapidly drawing to a close. And we won't even get a chance to see O'Neal come back for *Oliver's Story* years later, because he's just as much a goner as MacGraw. (Saying that, maybe the end of the world isn't such a bad idea.) While some of the movies listed next try to find some mixture of emotions, happy, angry and sad, in those final days, there is really one thing that they all have in common—there is no chance, no hope, and the world will be destroyed pretty much by the time the end credits begin. Of course, such films as *Threads*, *Testament* and *The Day After* also deal with people waiting for the end in a way, but those stand more as morality tales that deal with domestic dramas played out against the fabric of a nuclear holocaust. The following, however, are focused more on simply waiting, with the reasons behind such being more of a MacGuffin (a red-herring plot device) than part of the ongoing storyline. Not that such nuclear disasters as those in *Threads*, etc., don't play into at least the first movie to really deal with the long wait for death due to a global event.

Which is, of course, *On the Beach* (1959), starring Gregory Peck, Ava Gardner and Fred Astaire. Based on the novel by Nevil Shute (who also wrote other well-known novels based in Australia, such as *A Town Like Alice* and *The Far Country*), the movie adaptation pretty much stood on its own for nearly forty years as *the* pinnacle of what could be done in a movie about the last days of mankind on Earth. Directed and produced by Stanley Kramer, who was and still is best remembered for making epic-style "message movies," the film kept anyone else looking to do a similar type of story in the decades that followed tossing up their hands and giving up. It is the movie that all others are compared to when dealing with the end being around the corner and is still quite powerful today, even with a remake in 2000 (directed by Russell Mulcahy and starring Armand Assante, Rachel Ward and Bryan Brown in the Peck, Gardner and Astaire roles of the original).

The plot of the movie and its remake follows very closely that of the original novel. Peck plays Captain Dwight Towers of an American submarine that manages to avoid the fallout after every country in the Northern Hemisphere has wiped itself out. (The book and the later 2000 miniseries attempt to explain the history of the war that occurred, but the 1964 movie ignores it—as realistically most people still alive would do, since knowing who pushed the buttons would have little to do with the results by that point in time.) Towers and his crew are in Melbourne, which is one of the last spots left on the planet that have not been contaminated by radiation. Unfortunately, global air currents are moving the radiation farther and farther into Australia, and those still alive realize there may be little time left.

Towers becomes friendly with an Australian naval officer named Peter Holmes (played by Anthony Perkins), who has a wife (Donna Anderson) and a young daughter. He also spends time with a scientist, Julian Osborn (Fred Astaire), and Moira Davidson (Ava Gardner), a woman who has taken to drinking heavily in light of the approaching end. Early on, she attempts to come on strong with the captain, only to be rebuffed by him due to his devotion to his wife and children. She is then horrified to find out that the captain talks as if his family is still alive in the United States, when it is obvious that no one has survived there.

Or have they? An incomprehensible Morse code message is located in the U.S., making some hopeful that people have survived. Towers and his crew are asked to go up north to check out the signal and also to test a theory that the radiation is dissipating, which could mean a chance for survival. Unfortunately, the crew finds that the radiation is actually increasing, while the Morse code message turns out to be nothing more than a Coke bottle tangled up in a window shade cord and hitting against a telegraph key. The crew heads back to wait out the remaining weeks until the end. Some, including the scientist, get involved with a suicidal auto race, and others wait in line to take suicide pills (eventually the option of Perkins' character and his family). As the ending comes closer, the crew decides that they want to head back to their homeland. Towers, knowing that they do not have the power to make it, decides to go with them anyway, as he sees it as a fitting end for him and his crew. With Moira watching, the sub takes off for the horizon, and the film comes to an end.

The 2000 miniseries takes some mild liberties with the plot—mainly to make it appeal more to viewers of the new century, where some things have changed over how we perceive such a nuclear crisis would occur—but otherwise plays out in much the same manner as the 1964 film and the original novel. While there is some faint hope found in all three, the overall message is one of the foolish nature of mankind even to think that a war fought with nuclear weapons would accomplish anything more than humanity's exit from the realm.

Moreover, it deals with how individuals would react to knowing there is no way back—the end is coming, and one must either put up with the idea of a slow death by radiation poisoning (as some decide to do in the book, although this is mostly eliminated in the two adaptations) or through other means. Astaire's character is happily willing to die in his auto race if that is the way it goes because it means his own exit, and when it doesn't occur (in fact, he wins the race), he asphyxiates himself in his garage to achieve the same results. Rather than see his family suffer, Perkins' character (in a scene that is typically seen as the hardest for most parents to watch) convinces his wife that killing their daughter and then taking pills to end their lives is their best option. Towers heads off with his men on a mission that they all recognize as being impossible, but it at least gives an objective, a meaning, to their end. Moira may end the movie seeing the sub off, but it is clear she soon will join the others on the other side of life as well. As the camera pans through the deserted streets, a sign tells us "There is still time . . . Brother," but that message is not intended for those in the film. Their time had ended. The film is one of hopelessness, sorrow and regret, made clear in the early scene where Moira realizes that the captain is talking about his family in the present tense even though they are dead. Moira breaks down, thinking him driven insane, but Towers freely admits that he knows his fantasy about his family is not real. Still, it is what he has to keep going. His self-worth is all that's left, as it is for all the others there, and it is what he and they will take with them when they go.

If one element stands out beyond the obvious in *On the Beach*, it is the feeling of community in the last days. Nearly all of the movies listed here have no scenes of chaos or even rioting in the final days, unlike other films that ultimately have people surviving (or looking to possibly survive) the apocalyptic event. *When Worlds Collide*, *Miracle Mile* and others may show people crumbling under the weight of their knowledge of what is to come, but we oddly don't see much of in the form of chaos in the films listed here with the exception of *Happy End* (*Les derniers jours du monde*), a 2009 French film written and directed by Arnaud Larrieu and Jean-Marie Larrieu. That film, which is based on a novel of the same name by Dominique Noguez, oddly echoes the structure of Mary Shelley's *The Last Man*—both deal with a protagonist who doesn't seem to ever quite become aware of the end of the world coming until it is much too late (and in this case it's both a virus and nuclear war for a double whammy). Such a theme would suggest a comedy, and the movie poster—which shows the main character, Robinson, happily walking naked with two female characters dressed loosely by his side and all smiles—doesn't try to dissuade us from that view. Instead, the film is a melancholic drama, with Robinson (Mathieu Amalric) obsessed with locating a woman he left his wife and daughter for but who has disappeared.

Through his adventures that find him running into numerous other sexual conquests in the past and present, the world begins to fall around him, with terrorists in the streets, bombs on their way, and people falling apart in the last moments of the world (one woman Robinson beds slices her own throat while sitting next to him at an opera because she has given up on life). In one of the final stages of the film, which makes clear that his ex-wife and daughter have found safe harbor somewhere from the various catastrophes taking place, Robinson arrives at a castle. Inside, much like Abel Gance's *End of the World* (1931), a drunken orgy of the rich occurs while waiting for the end. However, in this case, the servants have poisoned the blue martinis everyone drinks in order to kill them all off so the servants can have the fallout shelter within the castle. In the final moments, he arrives back in Paris to find the woman he had been chasing throughout the film, Laetitia (Omahyra Mota), waiting for him. It is at this point of achieving his objective that Robinson's world ends, with a final fantasy image of the two walking naked through the robust modern world of Paris as one bomb goes off and then a second, ending the film.

Thus we end up with the flip side of the community feeling of *On the Beach* to one of isolation and every man for himself. The plague may be wiping out the world, but terrorists are still insistent on playing political games and the poor outsmart the rich in order to obtain dubious survival. People are killed or kill themselves with no one seeming to mind or care unless it upsets their own day somehow. Reviewers have referred to the movie (and the book it is based on) as nihilist in nature, and while the film seems to suggest this is an external view from Robinson's quest to find Laetitia, and that love is all that matters, it is hard to come away thinking that there is anything internal of worth to Robinson either. The conclusion of his search allows the bombs to finally fall, but it is the end of a dream, much more the end of the world, that leads us back to the same type of thinking that could be propelling the protagonists of *Take Shelter* and *The Rapture*. Has he really found the love of his life, or is it merely a satisfying way for him to die alone to think he has? There is never a sense of searching for love, and so with everyone out for themselves, there is only the possibility of achieving a goal.

Melancholia (2011) is not only a word I have trouble remembering how to spell, but it also follows a similar theme to *Happy End* in that the filmmakers seem to not quite grasp the objective they are trying to reach. As a way to displace our notions of what an apocalyptic movie should be, the first hour focuses on a wedding reception that goes horribly wrong. The cause of this is Justine, the bride, whose disintegrating composure through the night comes from issues with depression. As she ignores her new husband, refuses to take part in the reception, mouths off to her boss (getting herself fired in the process) and tops it all off with sex with a stranger on a golf course at the mansion of her brother-in-law and her sister Claire, one is likely to think she's bad news. Certainly that her husband leaving with his parents the next morning is probably the most productive thing he can do for himself.

Justine from *Melancholia* (2011)—a woman who finds peace at the end of the world, or a manipulator of events that cause it? This poster suggests the latter.

But this is a bit underhanded, for Kirsten Dunst as Justine is fantastic as she plays a woman well on her way to a nervous breakdown (only to recover from it in the second half of the film). Unfortunately, director Lars Von Trier seems more interested in making sure that we understand Justine is depressed and passive-aggressive by overplaying his hand, making the character utterly unlikeable, no matter how hard Dunst tries to give her some warmth. The bigger problem is that there is no true coalition between the first and second halves of the film. The first hour focuses on the wedding reception and plays like a slow Woody Allen drama, with no real references to the upcoming disaster beyond a brief comment by Dunst about something she sees in the sky. The second half of the film finds Justine reintroduced to the narrative, thus making the first hour obsolete; not to mention that the first hour leaves such a sour taste to the character that it is harder to warm up to her in the second, which admittedly may have been Von Trier's intentions.

The second part, named after the sister (just as the first was named after Justine), finds Claire many months after the wedding reception bringing a near catatonic Justine to their home (a mansion far away from everything and the one where the wedding reception was held) for recuperation. Meanwhile, the public knows that a planet is hurtling toward them, but is assured that it will merely pass by Earth. Therefore, there's a certain lack of concern about it, although you would at least think the characters would be a tad more interested in the big ball hanging in the sky than they appear. (Again, as with *Happy End*, personal matters seem of more concern than the world ending.) As the husband (played by Kiefer Sutherland) plays with their son, Leo (Cameron Spurr), Claire tries to get Justine active again. Strangely, it is only as the planet comes closer that Justine appears to spring back to life, just as Claire begins to withdraw from those around her in her worries of what is to come. As expected, on the night of the fly-by, the husband and son are able to prove that the planet is swinging away from Earth, leaving Justine in a bad mood and Claire relieved. Yet the husband discovers the next morning that the planet is actually coming back around and will hit Earth, killing everyone.

A quiz: The father and husband that we had seen throughout the picture being loving, strong and intent on doing anything for his son takes this news by A) keeping it a secret and spending his last day happily with his family; B) tenderly informing them and advising them to be strong in their last moments; or, C) in hysterics, killing himself in the horse stable moments after finding out the news? If you picked C, then you're in luck, because that's what we get, even though it makes no sense in terms of what we have seen earlier in the film. This causes Claire to break down as she hides the body so her son won't see it and realizes that the planet is coming back. Claire seeks some comfort from Justine, who snapped out of her depression now that doom awaits and thus, A) willingly comforts Claire; B) tries to reason with Claire that they need to spend what moments they have together instead of being upset; or, C) angrily tells Claire that she's happy everyone is going to die and that there is nothing anywhere else in the universe besides Earth, so when the planet is destroyed, that's it, and she'll be laughing (okay, not that last part). Again, if you guessed C, you're on your way to writing for Von Trier.

Joking aside, it may seem odd to some viewers that the movie tries to make Justine the heroine of the film after the first two-thirds has her either irritating or a troubled mess. However, Von Trier's statement with *Melancholia*, which he explained in interviews, is that he believes depressed people will ultimately handle bad news—and nothing could be badder than the end of the world—better than those who are optimistic. Yet this message does not come across very well; Justine is a nasty piece of work before her depression and afterward, being bitter, self-centered and uncaring. Again, isolation and self-importance—much like *Happy End* before it—appear to be the name of the game rather than the acceptance of one's fate and looking for one final moment of peace before the end. Although the movie ends with Claire, Justine and Leo sitting together under a teepee that (momentarily) finds Justine giving back to those she loves in an unbelievable Kumbaya kind of way while the planets collide and wipe out humanity, one can't help feeling that Justine got what she wanted all along and is happy in death.

Which brings up one interesting interpretation of this film, and that is Justine being shown time and again in her godlike powers to passive-aggressively get what she wants, even though it greatly hurts all of those around her. Her marriage is off because "that's the way I am," as she tells her soon-to-be-ex-husband; she gets to have her sister cater to her whims because she doesn't want to participate in the world around her; and, ultimately, the rogue planet will reverse illogically on its orbit solely because it allows Justine to fulfill a death sentence at the expense of the human race. Remember, it is Justine who first spots the planet in the sky, as if it is being directing toward her to fulfill her death wish. She proclaims that there is no more life anywhere in the universe because it satisfies her to think so, and with the film's submission to Justine's will, it probably is therefore true within the film's reality.

Oddly, in those final moments where the planet is about to collide (and let's face it, the science in this movie makes no sense, but Von Trier has clearly stated that it was never his intention to bother getting it right; hence another reason to believe the collision is Justine's doing), there is a general feeling that everyone involved with the film suddenly wanted to bring some happiness into the proceedings. Yet after two hours of splashing cold water on the audience's sympathies, the ending that finds the three characters together holding hands feels smarmy and clichéd instead of satisfying. But perhaps that is exactly how Justine would have wanted it anyway, with everyone bowing down to her vision of the world, even in its ending.

This brings us back to our earlier films *Take Shelter* and *The Rapture* (as well as *Happy End*)—if we're to believe that the ending may be Justine's doing, can we accept that it is real? Could her depression have advanced to the point where she merely wants her own world to end, and end in a fashion of her own doing?

The brother-in-law (who obviously has never liked her) suddenly commits suicide, the dominating sister becomes docile and the nephew—the child to her adult—looks up to her as his savior in a death wish that takes out the world; all of these elements play into the fantasy of how Justine wants the world to be rather than how it is. Which means that everything we see in the second half is not real at all, and the "planet" she saw before the wedding reception is merely the catalyst that leads to the entire world's-end scenario she can play out and control in her head.

Yet this is perhaps more of the wish fulfillment of yours truly than that of Von Trier. Whatever the case may be, while the last two recent movies tend to cast a cynical eye upon what people would do in their last days, the final three films represent a more positive finale to mankind. The first is the latest, *Seeking a Friend for the End of the World*, a 2012 comedy that was pushed heavily in the media but received rather lackluster reviews from critics and tepid results from the box office (not quite earning back the film's budget of $10 million). The movie was written and directed by Lorene Scafaria (who had written the screenplay for the 2008 hit movie *Nick and Norah's Infinite Playlist*) and starred Steve Carell as Dodge Petersen and Keira Knightley as Dodge's neighbor Penny.

The story is about another collision with Earth, only this time it is a seventy-mile-wide asteroid that will hit the earth in three weeks if it cannot be stopped before then. The news scares Dodge's wife away, leaving him on his own. As most people struggle to find things to do in their last three weeks on Earth, Dodge is satisfied simply to go to work and keep to his normal schedule. One night he meets his neighbor, Penny, who has broken up with her boyfriend and wants to return to England to see her family.

Upon finding out that his high school sweetheart had tried to contact him months ago, Dodge convinces Penny to join him on a road-trip to see her, promising in return that he will get Penny on a flight to England afterward. After several misadventures, Dodge finds that he has fallen for Penny but sends her on her way to England nevertheless, while he heads home. Penny, instead, returns to join Dodge and admits the same. The movie ends with the two together on a bed, happy to have found each other and able to spend what time they did have together, as the end of the world occurs and the screen fades to white.

The second film, *4:44 Last Day on Earth*, which came a year earlier in 2011, was directed by Abel Ferrara (*King of New York*, *Bad Lieutenant*) and starred Willem Dafoe as Cisco, an actor, and Shanyn Leigh as Skye, a painter. The two live together in New York, and the movie opens less than fifteen hours before the predicted end of the world thanks to radiation destroying the ozone layer; somewhat similar to *Beyond the Time Barrier*, only death for all instead of people becoming mutants (cue Willem Dafoe gag here). Beyond some mild moments of crisis around the apartment they live in—such as a man calmly jumping to his death at the building next door—not much happens. No outlandish crisis, no wacky comedy, no moments of drama (beyond a brief moment where Cisco considers drugging himself up for the end); everything is just lazily heading toward the apocalypse, and this only makes Cisco more anxious as 4:44 gets closer. With the end just minutes away, the two collapse together on top of Skye's finished painting and hold each other. Skye repeats a comforting mantra that the two will be together in what is to come and will help guide others to join them on the next path, as the screen slowly fades to white.

Seeking a Friend for the End of the World (2012) is a rare attempt at an apocalyptic comedy.

Both *Seeking a Friend* and *4:44* go off in their own directions for much of their plot—*Seeking* is a comedy about a road trip with various episodic events occurring over many days, while *4:44* is a drama set for the most part in one apartment and between two characters over the duration of a few hours. Yet, oddly, both end up with the same final image—the two lovers lying together, scared of what is to come but happy to be together in their final moments as the screen turns to the light. While it is interesting to see two vastly different movies conclude the same way, there is another film that came years before them that deals with two people coming together in the final shot of the film in much the same manner and with the screen also fading to a bright light. It is a mixture of comedy and drama and ends up invoking the most positive ending out of any movie featuring humanity being wiped out.

The film is the 1998 Canadian feature *Last Night*, written, directed and starring Don McKellar. It begins with the information that the world has six hours left before the end. What is causing it is never stated, although there is the image of everything looking like high noon as the hour approaches midnight, suggesting something with the sun. McKellar plays Patrick, a recent widower (his wife died of cancer before the announcement came of the imminent apocalyptic event) who wants to spend the last few hours alone, listening to some music and drinking a little wine, and certainly not involved in anyone else's drama. Meanwhile, Sandra (Sandra Oh) is trying to get home to be with her husband, Duncan. Duncan (played by director David Cronenberg, who made *The Dead Zone* referred to at the beginning of this chapter) is busy at his job at the power company, calling each customer to let them know that they will have gas "until the very end." Sandra's brief stop at an abandoned store to pick out supplies for a final supper allows others to strip her car, leaving her to walk. She makes it as far as Patrick's apartment building and by sheer coincidence asks to use Patrick's phone.

Unable to get Duncan on the phone (a rioter had killed him minutes after getting to their apartment), Sandra and Patrick venture out to help get Sandra home. After various run-ins with friends (Callum Keith Rennie plays a friend of Patrick's who is spending his last few hours trying every sexual encounter he had ever fantasized about, while another friend is off to perform a piano concert at a hall before the very end) and strangers, Patrick finds a car for Sandra, but Sandra ends up being stuck in traffic thanks to a huge party in the streets. She returns to Patrick's apartment and finds him on the roof of his apartment building, fulfilling his planned last moment, which is listening to music and drinking some wine. Sandra then asks him to do her a favor as she opens a small case she has carried throughout the film. Inside are two guns, and Sandra tells Patrick that the plan was for her and Duncan to commit suicide in the final moments before the end of the world in order to end things by their own hands instead of some predestined manner.

Patrick is reluctant but finally agrees to help Sandra. As the camera cuts to show what every other character seen in the film is doing as the final countdown

"ONE OF THE YEAR'S BEST MOVIES, PERIOD."
- Brian D. Johnson, MACLEAN'S

it's not
the end
of the world...

there's still
six hours
left.

LAST
NIGHT
(MINUIT)

HAVE A NICE DAY!

A Film By DON McKELLAR

The 1998 Canadian feature *Last Night* is a brilliant realization of people coping with the inevitable end of the world that still hasn't gotten the recognition it deserves.

occurs, Sandra and Patrick sit with guns to each other's heads, ready to pull the triggers. The countdown continues to get closer to the end, but neither can shoot. As a tear runs down Sandra's face and a small smile appears on Patrick's, the two pull the guns away and kiss each other passionately instead while the screen turns to white.

In retrospect, what is fascinating is that *4:44* and *Seeking a Friend* both end with our two main characters coming together and embracing before the screen turns white, but the oldest film, *Last Night*, holds the deepest impact with that same final image. In fact, the entire movie plays better, with many elements coming across in a much more positive light than in the other two. Even the depressing topic of "what will happen to the children" is better addressed in *Last Night* than in *Seeking a Friend*, as an older character remits the idea that the children have it the easiest of all, for they will die in the happiness of their youth, while those who had grown old will be the most remorseful over their accomplishments meaning nothing. The film also plays fair with its various other characters, allowing even incidental ones, such as a coworker of Cronenberg's characters who appears to fancy him, a rather uplifting ending to their lives in the final moments of the film. But most impactful of all is the ending—*4:44* may end with the couple hoping for something positive on the "other side," and *Seeking a Friend* finds the two lovers happy to end it in each other's arms, but *Last Night* is something more. Yes, it may appear that the film is setting up a standard movie "meet-cute" between Patrick and Sandra, but that element really isn't pulled into the movie until the final moments and only because Patrick is just trying to help out a woman who has become his friend over the past few hours. More importantly, unlike some of the earlier films that look upon the end as a negative, or try to make angry statements for or against mankind, *Last Night* challenges us because it refuses to go that route. The world may end, but there is no reason we need to go out afraid.

At the beginning of this chapter, it was mentioned that these movies have one thing in common, that there are no winners. That is not quite correct. True, *Last Night* still ends like the others with everyone dying. But in that brief moment before life on Earth was extinguished, there was a last defiant act of kindness that toppled all the anger, fears and tears.

In the end, it appears, maybe love will conquer all.

5

Oh, Yeah, Babylon

Movies Featuring Apocalyptic Events We Forgot Happened

The previous chapter looked at movies where there was no way to avoid thinking about Armageddon. Somehow, someway, it was going to happen, and even in those cases where the worst was avoided, the next-to-worst did occur. While most of the movies discussed in this book deal with such an event as the focus, there are a sizable number where that is not the case at all. Make no mistake, the films listed below absolutely do involve some type of "day of reckoning" for the human race (be it to its existence or to the structure of society). Nevertheless, a newcomer to the stories told probably was surprised to see such a thing occur in these movies. That, or the end of the world is such a contrivance that we tend to forget it even occurred when placed within the scope of the picture (or pictures, as in the case of the sequel in one popular series listed in this chapter). This may be difficult to understand—how the end of the world would be just another piece in a greater puzzle, but examples below will show this to be true.

As discussed in chapter 3, such a plot development has been used in films such as *Planet of the Apes* and *Teenage Cave Man* in order to give them a final twist by taking the audience's assumption that the movies are located on another planet or earlier time and revealing it to be the earth in the future instead. Movies such as *Captive Women* (1952) and *A Nymphoid Barbarian in Dinosaur Hell* (1990) also go for this kind of twist—although mainly to show off women in loincloths (admittedly much more preferable to Robert Vaughn in same). The emphasis of such films is on prehistoric derring-do and drama such as in *One Million Years B.C.* (1966, with Raquel Welch) and *When Dinosaurs Ruled the Earth* (1970, with Victoria Vetri) but then with the added shock of "It's the future!" Let us not forget the "Shaggy God" plot, also discussed in chapter 3, which involves people left over from the end of the world deciding to become the new (or original in some cases) Adam and Eve, turning up in various books, movies, television programs, radio and—let's face it—every beginning writer's head for many, many years.

One could suggest that the *Mad Max* genre of films—the postapocalyptic car flick, could sit somewhat comfortably within this area as well. After all, more than a couple of them are set up in the same manner, revealing this futuristic world to be a throwback to our own past. Yet, such a twist in the tale is fairly uncommon, normally because once you show a 1969 Charger with monster teeth on the front bumpers, you've pretty much given the game away that this is a postapocalyptic Earth. Either that, or there's a Dodge dealership on Mars.

The movies mentioned above are different from those discussed below because even with these shock endings, they still make that "Damn you all to Hellllll" statement a focal point; the punch line to a movie-length joke, in a sense. That is not the case with the movies listed here. An example of the films in this chapter is the 2002 remake of the Robert Vaughn caveman movie, *Teenage Caveman* (directed by Larry Clark and starring Andrew Keegan). The movie is still set in a postapocalyptic world where mankind has reverted to being cave dwellers, but this is revealed early on instead of at the end as in Roger Corman's original. In doing so, it startles viewers' expectations and then moves on to tell an entirely different story: in the 2002 movie, the protagonist and his woman find themselves with a couple who are from a highly advanced society, thus focusing on the topics of class and race rather than just "you blew it up!" For some, the end of the world is a surprise, but does not really impact the plot at all. In some examples, it is the hidden lynchpin to the plot around it but rarely the true focus of the films. For at least one of the films discussed here, it is just a crazy addition to a whole list of crazy things that happens. No matter what the outcome, however, the one thing these films all have in common is that the end of the world either was not expected or is not the moment one remembers best afterward.

"Peace on Earth" (1939)

To start off, we feature a short film that to some may seem not to belong on the list. After all, it does prominently feature the end of the human race, and this moment is certainly the one that is supposed to stay with the audience after the film is over. But there's another reason why it tends to be forgotten: it's an MGM cartoon. From the company that brought you Tom & Jerry and Droopy the Dog comes a cartoon showing mankind wiping itself out in bloodshed. Something one isn't quite expecting when settling into one's seat for a feature film at the theaters.

Until the 1970s, a trip to the theaters would typically involve a number of shorts, cartoons, newsreels and, up through the 1960s, even a second (shorter) feature. It was considered a night out, and the studios knew that people expected to get their money's worth out of paying for a ticket. Every major studio had some type of ongoing short-subject series (such as *The Little Rascals* or *The Three Stooges*), and either had an in-studio animation department or hired out to an animation company to make cartoons for them. In the case of MGM, they were finally finding their feet after numerous attempts at creating characters that were as popular as Mickey Mouse and Porky Pig at the time and would find major success with Tom and Jerry (the cat and mouse team) in 1940. The cartoons were starting to show a distinctive gloss that made them identifiable as MGM cartoons by 1939, thanks to the work of Hugh Harman and Rudolf Ising (Harman-Ising) and a brief time later William Hanna and Joseph Barbera (who, of course, would go on to become better known as the team Hanna-Barbera in television). In 1939, Harman put together a cartoon in time for the Christmas holiday called "Peace on Earth," just as the Second World War had broken out in Europe. The film begins with a rather startling image of a destroyed Christian church, with the image of Jesus in stained glass shattered, before panning down to show a village of houses that actually belong to squirrels. An old squirrel visits his grandchildren, who ask about men, and the old squirrel tells them about the last war between the humans, ending when the two final men in battle shot each other dead. The animals left in the aftermath slowly emerge and find a book in the destroyed church mentioning such things as "Thou shalt not kill." The book gives them the idea to rebuild, thus creating a community that is humanlike, with houses made out of the steel helmets of the dead and peace for all.

The short is a staggering depiction of the death of the human race at a time when the U.S. was still treading the line of isolationism in terms of World War II, fearing the consequences of a new war after the terrible carnage inflicted on people in the previous war. The trend would change swiftly as more Americans saw how things were going in Europe and the Far East after 1939 and definitely after the bombing of Pearl Harbor on December 7, 1941, but in 1939, it was still a subject openly discussed without being considered unpatriotic. Still, it is quite surprising to see a major studio release a film that suggests war will lead to an apocalyptic event rather than simply the "good" winning over the "bad" and being necessary, at least at some level.

The short would get an Academy Award nomination for Short Subject (losing out to Disney with "The Ugly Duckling"), and there were rumors it was up for a Nobel Peace Prize as well, although no one seems to have records showing such. The cartoon would be revisited in 1955 when Hanna-Barbera would adapt the plot to Cinemascope in a new cartoon called "Good Will to Men." The squirrels have been changed to mice (which, considering Hanna and Barbera's success with such in their Tom and Jerry cartoons, is understandable), and instead of a grandfather talking to grandkids, it is an old deacon telling the story to a group of choirboys. It also depicts mutual assured destruction with atomic weapons (which maybe allows us to assume radiation mutated the animals to want to start wearing clothes and go to church) instead of a lonely final battle between two men, and the book left behind for the animals is shown to be the Bible instead of just "a book," but the remainder of the cartoon is much the same. It too was nominated for an Academy Award, but lost out to "Speedy Gonzales."

Well, it was a different time.

Goke, Body Snatcher from Hell (1968)

This Japanese movie is a very odd bird indeed when it comes to apocalyptic movies, especially with a title like *Goke, Body Snatcher from Hell*. The Japanese title was *Kyuketsuki Gokemidoro*, which suggests a somewhat better translation as *Gokemidoro the Vampire*, but even that doesn't convey the type of horror/quasi–science fiction film it really is. Nor the morality play it seems to insert within the terrors demonstrated.

It starts as an action movie, with a group of people on a plane discovering that one member on the flight has a rifle (and possibly a bomb) and demands the flight be diverted to Okinawa. Yet, just as things go sour on the flight and the hijacker shoots out the radio, the plane loses power after nearly hitting a UFO and crashes in a deserted area. There are a few survivors, including the copilot Sugisaka (Teruo Yoshida) and stewardess Kuzumi (Tomomi Sato)—our heroes—and things now appear to be setting up a traditional "stranded on a desert island" plot, as those still alive bicker over supplies and what they need to do next.

Suddenly, the dead hijacker awakens and bolts from the damaged plane, as we come to realize that they really did almost hit an alien spaceship. One with aliens called Gokemidoro who can take over people's bodies by physically inserting themselves into people's skulls. So now it's an alien invasion flick. Only the dead who rise drink the blood of the living, making it a vampire movie. As a side note, we have the survivors besides Kuzumi and Sugisaka having sinful pasts and exposing themselves as the worst of humanity as the crisis continues to build, making one wonder if perhaps the group has landed in some type of hell or purgatory. Or if perhaps mankind is better off when the aliens begin to bump them off. No matter what, the number of survivors begins to decrease, and it looks like doom for the two innocents left.

Sugisaka and Kuzumi end up being able to outrun the alien pursuing them and look to have good fortune smile on them when the Gokemidoro is killed in a landslide. At this point, most movies would have had the traditional lovers' kiss and a big "The End" appearing (perhaps with a question mark to make it spooky), but that's not *Goke*. Instead, the camera follows the copilot and stewardess running until they reach a highway (which means they were never on a deserted island at all). The highway is littered with cars, showing what is left of the dead inside (a powerful image that has been repeated in many apocalyptic movies—especially zombie flicks—since). As they continue to move through the carnage, they come to realize that they were not the first victims in the alien invasions but actually the last, and the camera pulls back out into space to show a Gokemidoro invasion force beginning to descend, with the earth slowly changing colors to fit a world for its new masters.

And thus we have an end-of-the-world movie in the final minute, which one would not have expected from watching the beginning, even with the weird red sky the plane flies through (which Quentin Tarantino would pay homage

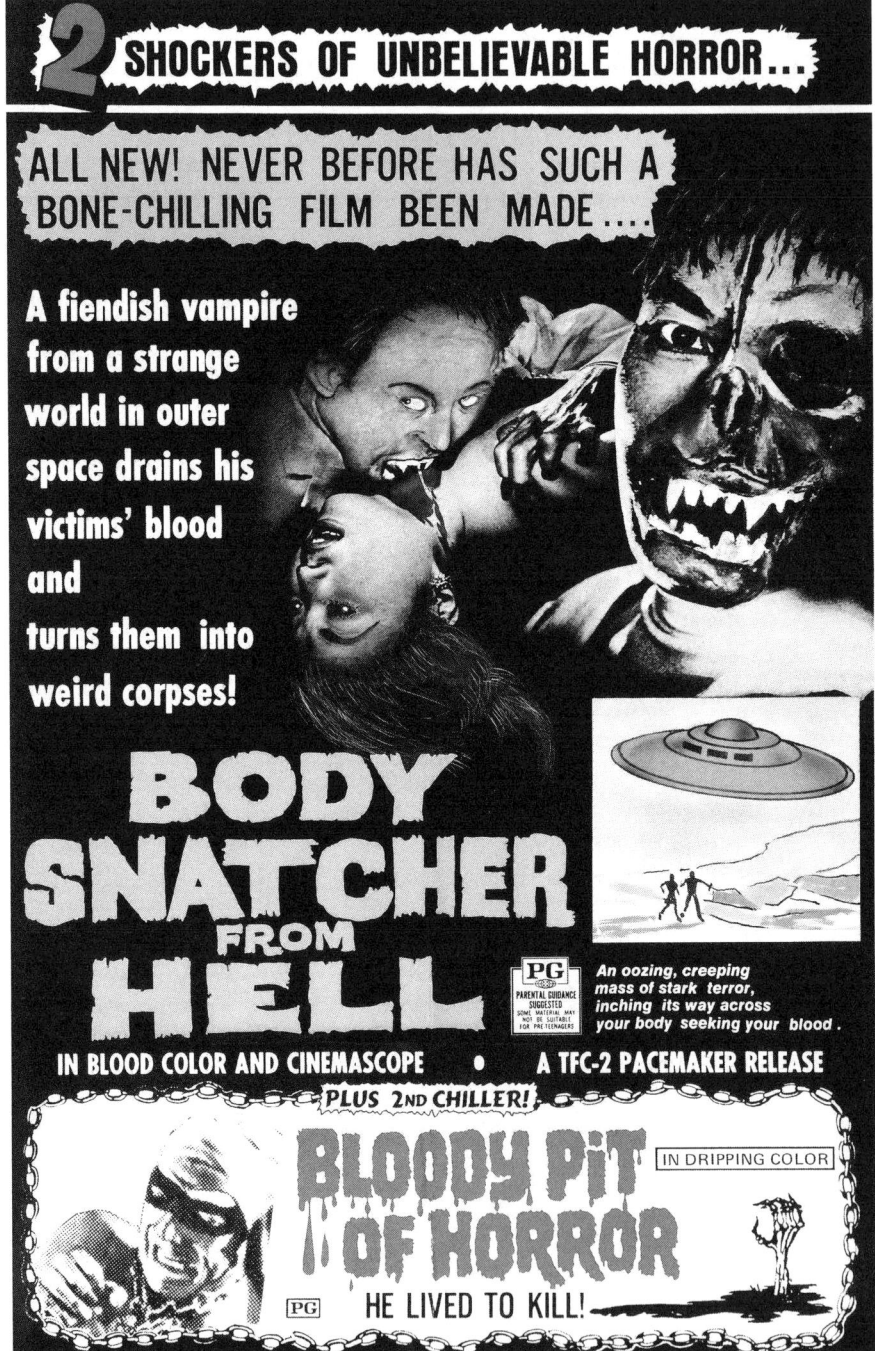

Goke, Body Snatcher from Hell (1968)—a horror/mystery/alien invasion movie that ends up being much more than expected at first glance.   *Courtesy of Wrong Side of the Art*

to in *Kill Bill: Volume 1* in a scene featuring the Bride heading to Japan onboard a plane). The movie poster used in the U.S. tried the best it could by throwing in all the elements of the movie and managed to not really get the point across either ("A fiendish vampire from a strange world in outer space drains his victims' blood and turns them into weird corpses!"). Even the American title doesn't tell us much: Goke is a shortened version of the aliens' name, and he's certainly not from hell, although he does do a bit of body snatching there. The whole vampire thing used in the Japanese title seems confusing as well. What's the use in emphasizing the vampire subplot when it is rarely used? Then again, if the aliens need blood, why are they intent on wiping out the food supply? No doubt that's a question that can be answered by saying, "Because you're worrying too much about it."

With a movie that builds up so many odd layers, it is easy to forget the ending, which comes out of left field (viewers don't realize they're near civilization until the protagonists get there), but in hindsight it is logical. After all, although 99 percent of the alien invasion movies find the "war of the worlds" over after one battle, in all likelihood, there would be more than just one alien or one ship to worry about. You may luck out with a landslide to take out one, but no war is over with just one battle, as proven here.

Beneath the Planet of the Apes (1970)

Well, Taylor couldn't just sit in the surf all day, you know. He had places to go, things to do. Which turned out to be a bad idea, as we'll see.

Planet of the Apes did blockbuster business in 1968, leading to speculations about doing a sequel. That didn't seem too far-fetched, really—Taylor is still on the run at the end of the first movie, and although we get the denouement about the world he is on being a postapocalyptic Earth, there's still more that could be told there. Is Ape City the only civilization around? Could there be other cultures or even other humans that Taylor and his barbarian girlfriend Nova can join? Can you finally get on Space Mountain without waiting in line for five hours at Disneyland? Many directions such a sequel could go.

The only thing stopping that was Heston, who made it clear he had no interest in being involved with a sequel. In 1969, he was more interested in getting other projects going, like working on *Julius Caesar*, a planned production of *Antony and Cleopatra* he wanted to direct, and this thing about the "last man on Earth fighting vampires" that sounded interesting (more on that one in a few chapters). The studio was also unsure of where to take a sequel anyway, with attempts by Rod Serling and the original novel author Pierre Boulle not moving the story in the direction they wanted. Then Paul Dehn—cowriter of this and the three remaining films in the series and who had written scripts for movies involving the threat of rather nasty nuclear devices (*Seven Days to Noon* [1950] and *Goldfinger* [1964])—got involved. With producer Mort Abrahams, the pair came up with a story that received a green light not only from the studio but

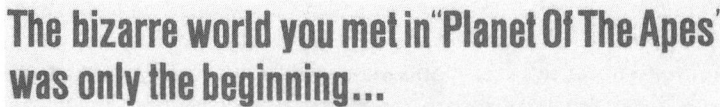

While we all remember how the first one ends, we tend to forget that the second movie in the *Planet of the Apes* series—*Beneath the Planet of the Apes* (1970)—actually shows viewers an apocalyptic event.

Courtesy of Hunter Goatley

with Heston as well (thanks to how they managed to insert his character into the story).

The plot finds Taylor heading off from the broken Statue of Liberty and continuing into the Forbidden Zone. Arriving at a spot where he and Nova (Linda Harrison) envision death here and there (a wall of fire at one point; an earth-splitting quake at another), Taylor investigates, only to vanish. It is the last we see of Heston until the final fifteen minutes of the film. Nova roams the area for a time and meets up with Brent (James Franciscus), another astronaut from Taylor's time, sent to locate Taylor's ship and miraculously arrived at the same destination. Seeing that Nova is wearing Taylor's dog tags, Brent wants to know where Taylor is, but Nova has no place to take him except back to Ape City (for all your ape needs). After reacquainting the audience with characters from the first movie (although David Watson replaced Roddy McDowall as Cornelius for the one picture, due to McDowall being committed to a different project at the time), Brent discovers that he is on a future Earth and is drawn to an underground fortress where mutant humans with telepathy worship a rather large nuclear missile.

Brent is taken to a cell where Taylor sits, and the two are forced to fight by one of the telepaths until they manage to kill him. Knowing that the apes are on their way, the mutants plan to set off the bomb, not quite grasping the fact that it is a doomsday device that will wipe out all remaining life on the planet. Brent and Taylor attempt to stop them, as well as try to talk reason to the gorillas arriving that only seem to be interested in battle. Nova and Brent die in the carnage that follows, while Taylor is bleeding to death. He pleads with Dr. Zaius (Maurice Evans) to stop the killing. Zaius not only ignores his request but also taunts him, telling Taylor, "Man is evil! Capable of nothing but destruction!" In a final rage, Taylor falls on the plunger that activates the bomb. As the screen goes dark, a narrator states, "A green and insignificant planet is now dead."

Well, Heston certainly made sure there was no way he could come back for a further sequel. Not that it stopped the series from continuing (thanks to time travel) for another three movies.

In the framework of the five movies, the best remembered by the general public is *Planet of the Apes*. It is the one that people may have seen out of the group and recognize (for the most part at least, as seen in the introduction to this book) as postapocalyptic. Even though the last three movies in the series (*Escape from the Planet of the Apes*, *Conquest of the Planet of the Apes* and *Battle for the Planet of the Apes*) reference the final destruction of the planet caused by Taylor (with no shout-out to him; such is the price of fame), people have that Statue of Liberty image in their heads and think, "Ah, this is the moment they're speaking of!" Actually, *that* moment—the nuclear event that wipes out much of the human race and allows the apes to take over—occurs between the fourth and final movies in the series. Moreover, it doesn't really look like people are hurting that badly from the incident; living in shacks and roughing it, sure, but nothing like the horrors of postnuclear war we see in so many films. Further, the final film even suggests that a peace between humans and apes will last at least six hundred years, according to the narrative. This makes Taylor's anger at the end of *Planet of the Apes* rather misguided, as it seems the apocalyptic event he is obsessing over was insignificant in reality. Yes, we did blow it up, but it could have been worse.

Meanwhile, it is actually the second movie that features a full-blooded end of the world, which we don't focus on because the image of the Statue of Liberty broken is too powerful. More importantly, the annihilation of Earth was brought about by the guy who was damning everyone left and right at the end of the first movie for "finally doing it" when it actually had been an event that brought apes and humans together in peace.

Good way of proving Zaius' point there, Taylor.

The Lathe of Heaven (1980)

In 1979, the Public Broadcasting System (PBS) went into one of their periodic moments of wanting to produce their own dramatic films for viewers rather than relying on the BBC to give them programming. That time around, they decided to try their hand at adapting work by a number of science fiction authors on the cheap, which is all they could afford. One such attempt that got some press in various newspapers and magazines was based on a book by Ursula K. Le Guin called *The Lathe of Heaven*, directed by David Loxton and Fred Barzyk and starring Bruce Davison (*Willard, X-Men*) as George Orr.

Orr is a young man who discovers that since the age of seventeen his dreams reshape reality. After years of trying to control it through various drugs, he is sent to an oneirologist, William Haber (Kevin Conway), to discuss his dreams. When Haber discovers that what Orr says is real, he begins to manipulate Orr's dreams in order to remedy various "problems" facing society—with mixed results. An attempt to end racial hatred leads to everyone becoming the same dull color, overpopulation is resolved with a plague, world unity through an alien invasion. These incidents are reversed, but Haber learns nothing from the consequences of the quick-fix and is determined to find a way to bypass Orr and develop the same ability himself so he can do it "right." Orr, realizing what Haber has in mind, contacts a lawyer (Margaret Avery) to help him get out of the treatments.

As Haber progresses toward his goal, Orr finally remembers the moment that led to his abilities manifesting in the first place: a nuclear war that destroyed civilization. Nearing death from radiation poisoning and wishing it all to go away, Orr had somehow managed to do exactly that, but once activated, he keeps subconsciously making changes. Now that he understands, he can control it, but Haber has already begun to figure out the process and attempts to make changes himself, which only succeed in the crumbling of the reality created by Orr. Haber is defeated, leaving him catatonic and the earth a jumbled mix of different realities that had been created throughout the film, but it's at least a reality that Orr can live with, and he is willing to let it be.

The Lathe of Heaven, which had heavy involvement by Le Guin, is a story about our dreams and the consequences of playing God, even if with noble intentions. What we want may not be the best for others or even ourselves and certainly not as instant gratification. Le Guin used global nuclear annihilation as the event that triggers Orr's latent powers in order to explain his ability, and uses it as part of the mystery being discovered within the novel. Yet this apocalyptic event is more of a MacGuffin in the proceedings; it may explain the "how" of the plot, but it is inconsequential to the bigger issues of "what" and "why"—Orr may have gained these powers by way of the apocalyptic event, but never mind that—how would people handle such powers if they suddenly had them? Subsequently, we have an "end of the world" movie where it not only is a past event revealed two-thirds of the way through the movie, but also in a sense never happened and isn't quite as important as . . . everything else in the movie. Leading to why people tend to forget the world ending even occurs (which it doesn't, but it has to . . . and we can go around in circles about this for ages).

In 2000, the cable channel A&E remade the movie as *Lathe of Heaven*, starring Lukas Haas, James Caan and Lisa Bonet in the three main roles. It is considered a dud by most fans of the book and the 1980 movie; it is more obsessed with superficial self-centered wish fulfillment by Haber and concentrating on the relationship between the lawyer and Orr, rather than dealing with the big concepts of the book and earlier adaptation. But it does at least keep the nuclear war aspect as a plot device.

The Apple (1980)

Hmm. Yes. *The Apple*. Well, it was bound to show up somewhere in these pages; it might as well be here. Especially with *that* (literally) out-of-the-blue ending.

Directed by Menahem Golan (*Delta Force*, *Enter the Ninja* and producer of *Superman IV: The Quest for Peace*), the film is structured as a rock musical with biblical overtones that is set in the future of 1994 (because making it 1984 would have been so predictable, evidently). It's rather more like an LSD-induced comic-book version of the Garden of Eden story after repeated viewings of the Village People movie *Can't Stop the Music*, to be honest. The plot deals with two young people, Alphie (George Gilmour) and Bibi (Catherine Mary Stewart, *Night of the Comet* and *World Gone Wild*) from Moose Jaw (you'll remember that because it is repeated about a hundred times throughout the film), who participate in the 1994 Worldvision Song Festival. Although their rather torturous love song somehow wins over the hearts and minds of the kids in the audience, they are denied the win thanks to Mr. Boogalow (Vladek Sheybal, *From Russia with Love*, *Red Dawn*, *The Boyfriend*) making sure his song, "BIM," wins. This may all look silly, but to be fair, if this were remade today it would be *American Idol*, with Simon Cowell as Boogalow.

Boogalow is enticed by the pair and tries to sign them up to his talent agency, which also appears to be running America and keeping everyone in line by wearing "BIM" marks on their faces. At the contract signing, Alphie has an apocalyptic vision that briefly shows the earth quaking and Boogalow as Satan, making him reluctant to sign. Bibi, however, has no such misgivings and in one production number is given a giant apple to take a bite of as she becomes the new big star for Boogalow (hence the Adam and Eve motif). Alphie, meanwhile, struggles to get his songwriting career back on track, but Boogalow makes sure that does not occur.

Later, Bibi abandons Boogalow to go back to Alphie, and the two appear some years later with a child and sitting with several people in a type of commune among the trees, singing a song that is about as riveting as a Coca-Cola jingle (you expect them to say how they want to buy the world a Coke). Boogalow then shows up with the police and lawyers to halt the song (good for him), force Bibi back with him and arrest the group. Alphie (wearing one of the worst beards in cinematic history) is sure that things will turn out okay, however, as he expects "Mr. Topps" to arrive at any moment. Sure enough, a golden car appears from out of the clouds, and Danny and Sandy come out to—no, wait, that's *Grease*, but you can see where they got the flying car idea. Anyway, the car appears and Mr. Topps materializes in front of the group to take Alphie, Bibi, their child and all the commune members to a new world where they won't have to worry about Boogalow any longer.

As a result, the viewers end up with the realization that they've just watched a telling of the Book of Revelation done with glitter, silly futuristic costumes and bad disco songs. Here we have the mark of the beast (the "BIM mark") being forced on people to wear or else face fines and arrest, while Alphie discovers that by denouncing Boogalow, he has set himself up to be cast out by society at large. Only those ready for Mr. Topps can follow into a new world, and they ascend to the heavens to do so, leaving those who are with Boogalow behind.

But wait, there's more. We're talking about a musical filled with songs that could only have been done in an era when disco was thought to be (but in actuality wasn't) king; full of repetition and glorifications of the Me Generation, which already made the movie a museum piece by the time it came out in the punk-driven/anti-disco world of 1980. There's also something very odd with the way the musical numbers are staged—typically in tight medium shots with plenty of objects obstructing the dancers in such a way that it looks like they've been forced to dance on different floors of a department store. Not that the dancers are ever given much to do beyond strutting from camera-left to right while staring at the camera, which shows that the film needed a stronger choreographer. Tie into that with costumes and makeup that scream 1974 television instead of 1980 film (and certainly not 1994 reality), and the film begins to look like something aliens would have put together on their assumptions of what Americans were like back in 1980, rather than anything quite human.

With all that said, it is understandable that the most surprising thing about *The Apple* is not that the Rapture happens at the end, but rather that it washed over viewers to the point where it is easy to be blasé about it. "Yeah, the Rapture. Of course. Sure. Fine. Go nuts." With so much else to focus on when discussing the movie, the ending tends to get pushed aside in our memories of *The Apple*.

Executioners (1993)

In 1992, the Hong Kong action-fantasy film *The Heroic Trio*, directed by Johnny To, was released. This movie features well-known actresses from Hong Kong cinema, Michelle Yeoh, Anita Mui and Maggie Cheung, as three women who have superpowers of one sort or another and their battle between themselves and against a supervillain, the Evil Master, who is kidnapping babies to find the next emperor of China. There has been more than one analysis of the film that suggests the three characters represent a reunified China, but for most viewers it is remembered for featuring these impossible superheroes having crazed fights as well as showing the women being the most proactive of the characters rather than the men.

As one could expect with a movie that becomes a big hit (gaining international attention), a sequel was released in 1993 called *Executioners*, which brought the characters back together a few years after the first to fight more foes. The sequel happening isn't surprising, but the setup for the sequel is: sometime between the two movies there was a little thing called a nuclear war that broke out, leaving the population in desperate need of clean water and food, while another villain plans conquest. While it is reasonable to expect more superpower fight scenes, the setup for the second film comes unexpectedly. The first movie takes place in the modern world, but the plot of the second must take place in a postapocalyptic world in order for the "uncontaminated water" plotline to work. Thus, we end up with storytelling for the two films that goes like this: "The Heroic Trio saved the day and defeated the Evil Master in the first movie! Then, blah-blah-blah global nuclear war, yeah-yeah-yeah. Then the next movie begins with the trio searching for uncontaminated water after the end of the world!" A bit of plotting whiplash can be expected from the audience there, and because otherwise the two movies flow so well together, it is easy for one to forget that there's a nuclear event that happens between them. To be fair, however, fans probably are more likely to recall the first movie as being after such an event, rather forgetting it has happened altogether. It certainly makes the first film's fantastic elements more understandable from a viewer's perspective; we've already made the jump to a postapocalyptic world, so people having superpowers would be just one more step in the process.

Star Trek: First Contact (1996)

Like within the *Planet of the Apes* series, this late entry in the cycle of movies based on the various *Star Trek* television series actually involves two apocalyptic events on Earth. Strangely, the one that is part of the series canon since the early days of the original series is the one that viewers tend to miss out on due to a "bigger" threat that appears. Stranger still, the event viewers remember the movie for is the one wiped out of history thanks to that good old *Star Trek* deus ex machina, time travel.

The movie starts with Captain Picard (Patrick Stewart) and crew of the USS *Enterprise* fighting the Borg near Earth. The Borg were villains created for *Star Trek: The Next Generation*; a group of beings from multiple alien cultures that have had their planets wiped out through assimilation and with the survivors turned into cyborgs to continue the race (much like *Doctor Who*'s Cybermen villains). They were brought in as merciless, unstoppable and . . . putting the writers in a corner because they couldn't figure out a way to have the good guys beat them after all the buildup. Thus, over the course of seasons the Borg became rather more of a mild menace; toothless in many ways, as shown in *First Contact* with the Federation wiping them out at the start of the picture.

But not before the Borg ship jettisons a small sphere that opens a vortex into the past. As Picard orders the *Enterprise* into the vortex in chase, the crew can briefly see that the Borg now populates the earth completely, as if they had conquered it sometime in the past.

At the end of the vortex, the *Enterprise* crew finds that they have arrived on April 4, 2063. The date is important because it is the day before a historic one— when Zefram Cochrane (James Cromwell) tested his warp-drive engine for the first time. It is this test that attracts the attention of a passing Vulcan ship, leading to a "first contact" between the two and their eventual alliance that forms the basis of the Federation that will one day prove the better of the Borg. Evidently, the Borg also know of the date and went back in time to stop it from happening and assimilate the planet, thereby stopping the Federation of the future. The *Enterprise* crew figures this out when the Borg attack the location on Earth of Cochrane's ship that is to be used in the test the next day. The *Enterprise* destroys the Borg sphere and works to make sure history goes right, while dealing with the final remaining Borgs, including a Borg Queen, who have managed to board the *Enterprise*. It is this alien invasion apocalyptic event that the crew—namely Picard, with the help of android Data (Brent Spiner), Klingon Worf (Michael Dorn) and Cochrane's assistant Lily (Alfre Woodard)—spends the rest of the movie trying to prevent from happening (and, naturally, succeed in doing, or else Paramount Studios would not have a franchise to continue afterward).

But there's the secondary story on the planet's surface where we find our other apocalyptic event. In the original series and onward, there had been much made of a third world war in Earth's history that wiped out hundreds of millions of people and brought civilization to its knees, which is just ending as Cochrane invents the warp-drive. The invention, as mentioned, led to a "first contact," but that meeting with the Vulcans would also lead humanity to pick up the pieces and strive toward a better tomorrow (to one where, by the time of Captain Kirk and his crew, things such as racial prejudice and common hatred are a thing of the past). Nevertheless, it is an apocalyptic event that sees Cochrane working out of a shack and piecing together what he can to build the warp-drive in surroundings that would not have been out of place in *Battle for the Planet of the Apes*. With half the film detailing how some of the *Enterprise* crew—Riker (Jonathan Frakes), Geordi (LeVar Burton) and Troi (Marina Sirtis)—help Cochrane get his ship and his mental state ready for the historic event, there is certainly enough time to focus on this postapocalyptic Earth that has been mentioned so much in *Star Trek* history but rarely discussed. Unfortunately, most of the material with Cochrane is played for comedy, with Cochrane portrayed as a man who is nothing like the serious, fearless hero he will become in legend. Nor is there an attempt to allow viewers a glimpse into this dark time, and because of this, one would suspect that Cochrane is just an eccentric living in a shack rather than a victim of such a monstrous period of war. Which explains why audiences forget that we're witnessing the aftermath of the near annihilation of the human race, because a nuclear holocaust and death of nearly a billion people just isn't as

Star Trek: First Contact (1996) is a bait and switch; there's a postapocalyptic Earth, but viewers are supposed to be more concerned about the crew of the *Enterprise* fighting Borgs in space.

cool to watch as the zombie-like aliens playing cat and mouse with Picard on the ship above.

But don't those Borgs look neat?

Fight Club (1999)

No doubt, the first question some readers may have is, "What is *Fight Club* doing in a book about apocalyptic movies?" Of course, that question is answered by the same number of people nodding and saying, "But of *course* you have to cover *Fight Club* in the book!" Which is why it has fallen into this chapter rather than another. Some see the movie as satire, a psychological action picture, apocalyptic or all three. But does it really fit in here, and if so, how can it keep itself from appearing as such to more people? In other words, let's ignore the first rule of Fight Club and talk about *Fight Club*.

As to the plot, some feel it is convoluted, but it is actually quite straightforward once you put all the pieces together. The story finds our protagonist (Ed Norton) suffering from insomnia and the boring sameness of his life. He gets some release by attending support groups for things he is not suffering from, where he runs into a fellow faker named Marla (Helena Bonham Carter). He also meets up with a man named Tyler Durden (Brad Pitt), who invites him to join a "fight club." The club is a group of men who have fistfights for no other reason than to feel something in their empty lives, even though it is pure physical pain.

Over time, the fight club becomes a movement, with more and more clubs popping up around the country. Durden then begins to expand the operation beyond men fighting each other and into a modern-day version of the eighteenth-century Hellfire Club, which supported members performing immoral acts against society to prove themselves above the norms accepted by most people. The only differences are that Fight Club involves men of different social classes, rather than strictly the upper class, working together and that their acts are public instead of private, and deadlier. As the numbers of members increase in "Project Mayhem," so does the violence, with a plan in motion to destroy several corporate buildings that control credit card debt and banking records. The protagonist tries to stop Durden and his group, and in the end succeeds in killing Durden (in a way that for once I won't mention so as not to spoil it). Nevertheless, the film ends with Durden's plan succeeding, as Marla and the protagonist watch the buildings blowing up and crumbling to the ground.

And it is with this image that we end up facing the argument of whether to call *Fight Club* an apocalyptic movie or not. Although there is a tremendous amount of fighting, shootings and eventual bombings in the film, *Fight Club* also contains a large amount of humor built on a satire of the myth of American machismo and/or American consumerism. Men feel so empty in a world where they are merely there to work and spend that even something as maniacal as punching each other in the face or blowing up a building feels like an achievement rather than a very stupid idea. Some also see it as a psychological study of how easily manipulated we can be—such as the protagonist and the others who join—when we follow blindly someone with just enough influence to make crazed ideas credible.

Because of this ability, Durden manages to turn his little group of morons that like to beat up each other into a well-oiled machine that can infiltrate the authorities (thus allowing the carnage to follow) and cause mayhem on a grand scale. It is clear that Durden didn't set up the bombing all on his own, but he has already created the environment to have submissive people passively follow

The 1999 movie *Fight Club* attempts to bring us the end of the world, but at a safe distance.

his methods and his madness to achieve those goals for him. Thus, even with Durden's demise, the actions of his "Project Mayhem" group succeed, and the bombing is probably the first of many even bigger plans of destruction to follow. With this, some viewers see the ending of the film as showing us the "lit fuse" of apocalyptic massive death and destruction to come. It is not so much revolution that will follow as sheer bloody anarchy, and all for no reason other than to make some bored men happy in their senseless lives. *Fight Club* tells us that we don't need alien invasions, plagues or bombs to destroy our own world; we can do the job quite well through our own madness. The original 1996 novel by Chuck Palahniuk also makes clear that the bullet train called crazy has already started and can't be stopped (with the protagonist being put into a mental hospital but assured by members of the project that the mission will go on).

Yet the film plays it safe at the end, which was intentional, according to quotes from director David Fincher. It's one thing to "play with fire" as Durden demands of his followers, but ultimately the protagonist has to reject Durden in order for the filmmakers to not be advocating for the destructive powers of Durden's plan. However, in doing so, it also allows Durden's plan to seem exciting and productive with the toppling of the buildings seen from a panoramic view very far away and treated like large, lit dominos falling as Marla and the protagonist watch in wonder. By distancing it, it becomes clean, safe, and leaves the pair as innocents to the actions of those involved.

And played this way for the sake of humor as well. Naturally so, as *Fight Club* ultimately is a comedy, and comedies work best when things don't get too dark. The buildings? Just empty shells that are torn down as an afterthought. Of course, in reality, banking industries work on a twenty-four-hour basis, and thus hundreds of deaths would have occurred with such a bombing, but we as an audience—just like the two watching from the window in the movie—don't have to think about such things as we sit amused by the destruction some distance away. As the movie wraps up, the protagonist is fine, everything is right with the world once again, and there's no need to worry about people like Durden any longer. Because it is filmed this way, however, the ending does not convey an apocalyptic spur unless one really reads more into the story than is represented on the screen.

For those that say the film is not apocalyptic, there is also the argument that one event like this doesn't mean Armageddon on a grand scale. Otherwise, if one jumps on such a bandwagon, then such films as *V for Vendetta* (with the ultimate destruction of Big Ben and Parliament) or even *Star Wars* (the destruction of the Empire's ultimate weapon and some of its highest-ranked members) could be seen as apocalyptic because they suggest a dysfunctional world order being destroyed for a "better one," a process that would always produce some type of anarchy and chaos in the process anyway. There have been some attempts to suggest that *Fight Club* is more of an internal tale of Armageddon, with the protagonist having to deconstruct himself so as to find a new way of thinking and living. But that's a stretch, especially in light of how the book ends with the character realizing all he has done is set things in motion, not rebuild them in a new way. Thus, while there have been many instances where *Fight Club* is brought up as apocalyptic in nature, it doesn't satisfy the definition in a viable way.

Importantly, this film was released before 9/11, and as we found out in 2001, the collapse of a building deemed money based actually didn't lead to some type of Armageddon suggested by those who rank it as an apocalyptic movie. Thus, such conclusions appear to be inaccurate, yet they still exist. Then again, the destruction found at the end of *Fight Club* never seemed quite that fascinating or amusing to watch anymore either.

Dead or Alive (1999)

The only expectation one can get from director Takashi Miike is that you're never going to be sure what kind of movie you're going to see when he is involved. Take *Audition*, which plays for a good chunk of its running time as a quaint domestic comedy about a man searching for a new wife, only to suddenly become sadistically gory when the woman he meets turns out to be a psychotic torturer. *The Happiness of the Katakuris* appears to be a comedy with some zombies thrown into the mix when it suddenly, and with no apologies, bursts into a musical. *Dead or Alive* is the first of a trilogy of crime films that are only connected by way of its stars and director, and even the third one is a science fiction film. The first *Dead or Alive* movie has many flashy visuals, which are in keeping with or go a tad beyond what would normally be acceptable in such a film for the Japanese market, but then it goes one step beyond even that in the final confrontation scene.

The movie deals with two men: Ryuichi (Riki Takeuchi, who looks uncannily like an evil Wayne Newton), a Chinese Triad boss, and Jojima (Show Aikawa), a Japanese detective out to stop Ryuichi. As is typical of such action films, the hero and villain must ultimately meet to deal with their issues one on one. This occurs as Ryuichi and his goons are in a car out in a field. Jojima arrives in his own car, and one of Ryuichi's hoods starts a game of chicken with Jojima, and then another throws a grenade through the window of the car, blowing it sky-high. Still, Jojima survives and, with the two henchmen soon dead, crawls out of the wreckage. Finding one arm useless, Jojima rips it away from his body and tosses it aside, which shows how things are starting to move beyond the realm of sanity. The pair begin shooting at each other at near point-blank range, riddling each other with bullets, but neither will submit first. Jojima then reaches behind his back and pulls out a five-foot bazooka that he somehow had on him all along. Upon seeing this, Ryuichi reaches into his chest and pulls out a glowing orb of energy. Which you do in such situation, obviously.

With Ryuichi throwing the orb at him, Jojima fires the bazooka, hitting the orb. The camera immediately cuts to a shot of the earth from orbit, looking down to show a massive explosion occurring in the location of their fight, the impact of which begins to envelop the earth as the world comes to an end.

While in some circles this is a symbolic visual point to be made about the clash between Japan and China (one man tears out his own heart to use as an attack on the other, leading to an apocalyptic event between the two), for those expecting a more traditional action film, the entire ending comes out of left field. Who is expecting the one character to pull out a bazooka unless the story is being told in the context of a child's game? Then again, who would counter such an act in a game of cops and robbers but another angry child with an orb that will destroy the world? It gives the film a memorable ending, no doubt, but one that may strike viewers as irrational rather than with any subtext that Takashi Miike may have meant to appear there.

The Hitchhiker's Guide to the Galaxy (2005)

There's already been some arguable movies listed in this chapter, so I might as well throw in one more. Of course, as everyone knows, Earth is destroyed in the first few minutes of this famous story by Douglas Adams, which had previously been made into a book, a radio series, another radio series, a play, a television show, a video game, and lastly the movie, along with multiple sequels in various media. As the story begins, Arthur Dent (Martin Freeman) is upset over his house being demolished to put in a bypass, but not as upset as everyone else on Earth when the planet is destroyed in order to put in a galactic bypass by the Vogons. Fortunately for Arthur, his best friend Ford Prefect (Mos Def) is an alien who uses the opportunity to hitchhike a ride on the Vogon spaceship and brings Arthur along. After being discovered and tossed off the ship, they end up on the *Heart of Gold*, a ship being piloted by Zaphod Beeblebrox (Sam Rockwell) and a woman Arthur once met named Trillian McMillan (Zooey Deschanel).

It may look like a goof on the part of yours truly to place this movie in this chapter, for we certainly see the destruction of the earth first thing in the story, and Adams made clear that he wanted to have the destruction in there almost immediately just as a prime joke to set things off with. However, this is material very early in the proceedings, which leads to other, more important matters than this "mostly harmless" planet that is now rubble. After some misadventures, Arthur discovers that the earth was created as a supercomputer to help formulate the question about "life, the universe and everything," for which the answer is "42." With the earth being destroyed, the aliens—who look like mice—have a new Earth built that is an exact replica of the one Arthur had left behind, including the people. Instead of staying on Earth, Arthur decides to join the others in exploring the galaxy.

This is the version of the story that appears in the film. The radio and television versions end slightly differently, with Arthur and Ford stuck on a prehistoric Earth with no way of leaving. Either way, Arthur is around to see Earth yet again as the story comes to a close. Because of this, and all the various comedy touches that Adams threw into the story, one tends to not come out of *Hitchhiker's Guide* thinking, "Oh, no! The earth was destroyed!" as Arthur is fine on Earth in one (albeit in the past) and leaving the earth he knew behind in the movie version. Either way, the earth is there at story end, and therefore there's a tendency to forget that the earth ever got destroyed in the first place, even though it is one of the first things seen in the film.

The Cabin in the Woods (2012)

As I mentioned in the first chapter, there's no way to avoid spoilers if we're going to talk about movies featuring the end of the world. Case in point, *The Cabin in the Woods*, which—much like *Goke* at the beginning of this chapter—knocks audiences' expectations by appearing to be one type of movie and ending up being another. In this case, what at first looks like a slasher film turns out to be a tad more epic in scope by the ending reel.

Produced by Joss Whedon (creator of *Buffy the Vampire Slayer*), who co-wrote with director Drew Goddard (writer on the TV series *Lost* and the film *Cloverfield*), it is obvious from the beginning that the people behind the camera are used to playing with genre expectations in their stories as well as offering some "winking" self-awareness that it's all goofy fantasy. The plot has a group of five college students who fit the standard stereotypes of slasher films, but at first do not quite act the roles: the smart girl is not the innocent virgin of such movies; the jock is book-smart; the sexy friend isn't a bubblehead; the doped-up, unlikable idiot is . . . well, no, he's pretty much a doped-up unlikable idiot in *The Cabin in the Woods*, but you get the idea. They go on a trip to a cabin in the woods, and viewers are set to believe the normal stalker-in-the-woods setup is about to commence, or perhaps some type of supernatural event. That is not quite true, however.

The cabin is actually on top of an installation (like *Resident Evil*) that is commanded by individuals who have a series of mythical monsters and creatures that they can pull up to the cabin to terrorize and kill off the five as part of a sacrifice to the Ancient Ones, a godlike race that sleeps under the surface of the earth. Such a system is established in various parts of the world and based on common preconceptions of horror entertainment (the Japanese one, for example, is a room full of schoolgirls battling ghosts, a common subgenre in Japanese horror films). As events play out, one by one, the other countries make miscalculations that let the intended victims win against the horror released, so it is up to the U.S. counterparts to succeed.

The objective for the U.S. group is to have the victims pick out a storyline to follow by grabbing a particular object in the cellar. Dana, the smart girl (played by Kristen Connolly), grabs a diary that activates the "redneck zombies" story (similar to the event used in *Evil Dead*), and the killers are sent to the cabin to attack. As long as the last surviving victim is the "virgin," then the sacrifice is complete, the Ancient Ones will sleep, and humanity lives for another year. Drugs are dispersed through food, drink and in the air in order to manipulate the five to split off and do other common illogical things as seen in various horror films.

Unfortunately for those in control (and for the human race), the stoner jerk, Marty (Fran Kranz), is able to resist the drugs and is all-knowing about horror movies. Such knowledgeable geekish characters have been around for many years in such films and are typically thrown into the story to try to be "meta" by "winking at the camera" to show the filmmakers know a plotline is a cliché and will therefore subvert expectations because of their omnipotent ability to know

The Cabin in the Woods (2012) gives us slackers who decide to end the world for us because they can't be bothered to do the right thing. Thanks a lot, guys!

their own plotline. Same here with Marty, who looks to triumphantly bite the big one midway through the movie only to turn up alive near the end, thereby putting the mission of the group in the installation in jeopardy. Marty and Dana managed to get below the cabin and into the facility, letting loose all the monsters that then attack those working there. The ambush by the monster is clever, featuring variations of creatures from other movie franchises (*Creature from the Black Lagoon, Hellraiser*, etc.) in a frenzy of killings. With dawn approaching, Dana is told the truth of the situation by the director of the facility (Sigourney Weaver) and given the chance to kill Marty in order to complete the sacrifice and not awake the Ancient Ones. Instead, the director is killed, and Marty and Dana decide to let humanity be destroyed. The two wait and then feel a rumble. On the surface, a giant arm reaches up from the ground, destroying the cabin, before slamming down on the camera to close out the end of the film as the Ancient go about killing off mankind.

Well, awfully nice of the two to make that whole "let's smoke a joint and let the human race torturously die" decision for us. What a good couple of kids!

Escape from L.A. (1996)

We end this chapter by looking back at a sequel that would to many eyes appear to be postapocalyptic from the get-go of the first film. *Escape from L.A.* is the sequel to *Escape from New York*, a 1981 movie directed by John Carpenter (*In the Mouth of Madness, The Thing, Prince of Darkness*) and starring Kurt Russell as Snake Plissken, a former war hero turned criminal who is captured in 1997 and taken to Manhattan, which has been turned into a maximum security prison. Although there are some indications that a war occurred with other countries, it appears to have been very restricted, perhaps European in nature, as little seems to have changed in America beyond Manhattan being turned into a prison. Thus, the setting for *Escape from New York* is not so much postapocalyptic as dystopian. (It should be mentioned that the novelization by Mike McQuay makes no bones about America having been attacked in the war, with the West Coast wiped out, but since this conflicts with the plot of *Escape from L.A.*, it cannot be considered canon.)

The film gained a large amount of popularity through video sales in the years since it was released, so it was decided to make a sequel fifteen years later, *Escape from L.A.* Russell, who cowrote the script with Carpenter and appears to have somehow not aged in fifteen years, has once again been captured and this time is taken to a security prison on the West Coast located on an island of what once was Los Angeles. A massive earthquake had created the island, and a fanatical president had made it a prison for undesirables, which includes everyone who doesn't agree with his religious and political views. The president's daughter, Utopia, steals a remote for a satellite weapon called the Sword of Damocles— which can knock out technology for good to an area or the entire world—and escapes into the L.A. prison, leading to Plissken's recruitment to go in after her and get the remote back.

Plissken manages to bring back the remote and Utopia. The president demands his daughter be sent to the electric chair for her crime, and she is about to be executed when Plissken reveals he still has the remote (he gave the president the wrong one when handing it off). Knowing the code that will activate the worldwide satellite command, and that such a device is impossible for one man to have, Plissken activates the code, shutting down the world's technology and sending mankind to a preindustrial period. As Plissken lights a cigarette, he tells the audience, "Welcome to the human race." Thus, another movie finds that what has come before is nothing compared to things to come.

Like *Beneath the Planet of the Apes, Fight Club, Dead or Alive* and *The Cabin in the Woods, Escape from L.A.* is another movie where the protagonist is the instigator of an apocalyptic event. Furthermore, such characters are quite happy and/or justified in doing exactly that. It is amusing and fitting when Plissken does it, as it saves the life of the girl who had been misled by both her father and the man claiming to love her, while also allowing other innocents to venture into a new world. True, one without technology, but one can go without a hair dryer if it means keeping your head. Taylor, Marty and Dana saw the world as it was and decided that our end was for the best rather than extending it any further for more folly. Tyler, Jojima and Ryuichi may not have really wanted to end the world, but their methods hold no other choice. *Star Trek: First Contact* could be seen in a similar way, as Picard is the reason the Borg first turned up in the series (due to a meddling superbeing named Q in the series who wanted to teach Picard a lesson by giving him a situation he could not resolve without help), so he could be blamed for the apocalyptic event in that film as well. In each of those cases, the protagonist felt trapped, isolated and seeing his or her option (whether right or wrong) as the best for himself and the world.

Several of the films in this chapter also feature other world-ending events occurring before the events of the movie. Because of these happenings, a form of dystopian ideal is either enforced or soon to be: the Ape City, L.A., Orr's city, the Borg future, even the modern worlds of *Fight Club* and *Dead or Alive* suggest crumbling, dictatorial order has fallen into place (or will soon). Dystopian societies are nothing new to the genre of apocalyptic films; most postapocalyptic worlds seem to dictate such societies. However, this can make discussing apocalyptic movies confusing, as sometimes it can be unclear if a dystopian world seen in a film is one that is born out of an apocalyptic event or from other means (usually political). As examined earlier, *Escape from New York* may have been written to be postapocalyptic, but we cannot gather enough information from the film to definitively stand behind that statement. Yes, there was a war, but was the dystopian society born out of the war, or was the war born out of the society? It is this type of "chicken or egg question" as well as others that need examination as we move into the next area of study on Armageddon in films.

6

Apocalyptic or Dystopian?

Futuristic Societies That May or May Not Be Due to the Apocalypse

There are plenty of science fiction movies that take place in dystopian societies; in fact, outside of *Star Trek*, it is hard to find many societies in science fiction movies that are not dystopian in nature. Of course, it is the structure of conflict in many of the films anyway—a classic "man vs. society" setup so that our hero can defeat, or attempt to defeat, the evil power in control. Yet a threatened doomsday or apocalyptic event is not the catalyst to every dystopian culture seen in films.

An iconic example is *1984*, written as a novel by George Orwell and made into features for both television and the movies. It presents a dystopian society where the people are oppressed, yet we cannot be certain how such an environment came to be, namely because history has been rewritten so many times according to government-sanctioned "truth" that no one is sure any longer. Nor do people care, or wish to even suggest they care for fear of being turned into the thought police. It could be from some type of world disaster. War is suggested and figures into the book as ongoing between Oceania (where Winston Smith, the protagonist, lives), Eurasia and Eastasia, but this is suggested to be a cover-up story created by those in power. Winston has some faint memories of a war from his childhood, but he is aware that his memories cannot always be trusted. More significantly, such details are not necessary for the sake of the plot; it doesn't matter how the world of *1984* came about, only that the characters interact within that world. Thus, while *1984* is a seminal work in political and science fiction, leading to adaptations in the theater, radio, television and movies over the years, it fulfills completely the description of a dystopian society, but not one that was born out of an apocalyptic event.

Films similar to the format of *1984* also fall into the same category of perhaps being born of global conflict, but the truth is never established in such a manner that we can say for sure this is the case instead of perhaps some other method. Terry Gilliam's *Brazil* (1985) is a more comical update of *1984*, but the structure of the world is quite similar, with the protagonist, Sam (played by Jonathan Pryce), eventually tortured for sins against the state. George Lucas' 1971 film

THX 1138 shows us a sparkling, white and clean setting in contrast with the dark, rapidly decaying, retro look of *Brazil*. Yet it is a similar totalitarian state where people must conform to strict rules, and finds the protagonist THX (Robert Duvall) having a forbidden love affair with a woman in much the same manner

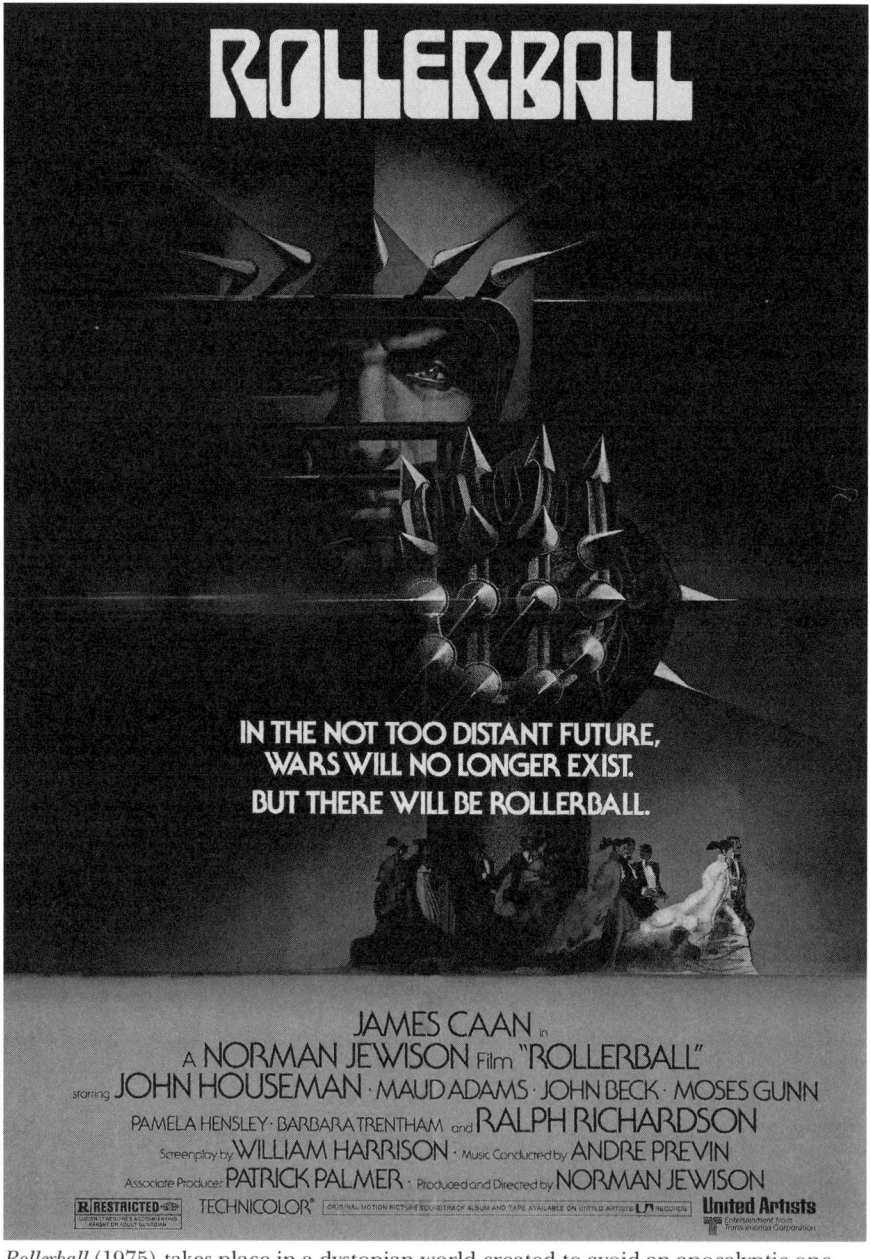

Rollerball (1975) takes place in a dystopian world created to avoid an apocalyptic one.

as in *1984*. It is even as bureaucratic as *Brazil*; for example, the ending chase is resolved when it becomes too cost-prohibitive to continue, which would have fit nicely in the world of the other film. Yet neither *Brazil* nor *THX 1138* gives us a clear reason for the world we're seeing. THX appears to live underground, suggesting some type of protection against a nuclear wasteland, but the work is hazardous, which may be the reason for his location rather than anything that had occurred earlier in the history of this world. Sam's world in *Brazil* appears to be our modern world gone out of control due to paperwork and rules rather than some big event. Hence, while they both have a look that suggests some type of postapocalyptic world, they cannot really be seen as such.

Consequently, there are a number of science fiction films that don't quite meet the standards for apocalyptic film that will be covered in the book. *Blade Runner* (1982) obviously takes place in a dystopian civilization, but there is no way to conclude that it was created by an apocalyptic event. In fact, the film hints more at corporate takeovers and consumerism run wild than some type of catastrophe. This is certainly not a new phenomenon for futuristic movies, with Fritz Lang's *Metropolis* (1927) centering on a society built with the upper class in ivory towers while the workers toil in the slums of the streets to provide for the rich. It is a terrible state for most of the population, but there are certainly no indications that it was created other than through growing social patterns and politics rather than global disaster.

Such corporate lockdown on the world certainly seems to be the case in the *Alien* series, starring Sigourney Weaver, where the Weyland-Yutani corporation runs everything. Elsewhere, Norman Jewison's *Rollerball* (1975) stars James Caan as Jonathan E, a man who plays a roller derby type of game for a team owned by the Energy Corporation who finds that his success and popularity are ruining the meaning of the game, which is to convince the public that individualism is impossible. Jonathan eventually wins over the crowd, and it looks to be the defeat of Energy Corporation's plans, but one wonders if the victor ended up being Weyland-Yutani. (Not surprisingly, the film was remade twenty-seven years later with all its political and cultural plot threads ripped out in order to make it just about the game turning deadly.) In these cases, consumerism and corporate greed have restructured society to become the bedrock on which civilization is based rather than a disastrous event that led us to this outcome (of course, there are those who would be more than willing to say that our present governments are hardly any different).

Speaking of *Rollerball*, perhaps a look at the various movies dealing with televised hand-to-hand (more or less) combat-to-the-death for entertainment purposes can put this into better perspective. Naturally, the first movie people think of today when we discuss this is *Death Race 2000* (okay, the one everyone thinks of today is the popular *Hunger Games* series, but I'll get to that soon enough). This 1974 Paul Bartel movie starring David Carradine as Frankenstein, the two-time winner of "the race" (it's never referred to as "death race"), is set in a world where America is already a tyrannical culture (under the Bipartisan

IN THE YEAR 2000 HIT AND RUN DRIVING IS
NO LONGER A FELONY. IT'S THE NATIONAL SPORT!

DAVID CARRADINE
DEATH RACE 2000

DEATH RACE 2000
A CROSS COUNTRY ROAD WRECK

CO-STARRING SIMONE GRIFFETH SYLVESTER STALLONE · LOUISA MORITZ · DON STEELE
SCREENPLAY BY ROBERT THOM and CHARLES B. GRIFFITH   ORIGINAL STORY BY IB MELCHIOR   PRODUCED BY ROGER CORMAN   DIRECTED BY PAUL BARTEL
METROCOLOR   R   RESTRICTED

While it is easy to believe that *Death Race 2000* (1974) is postapocalyptic, the
film actually shows future America looking like . . . 1974 Southern California.
Courtesy of Wrong Side of the Art

Party, ironically enough) and a yearly game is broadcast showing celebrity drivers
in souped-up cars race across the country. That makes it sound like *Cannonball
Run*, but in this case, additional points are scored by the drivers for the number
of pedestrians they can kill along the way. Everywhere in this America (and
the race is cross-country) shows some minor signs of futuristic trappings, but
otherwise it looks the same as it did in Southern California, 1974, with no signs

or discussion of postapocalyptic hazards (such as "the wastelands," which usually figures so often in such films). There is mention of a global "Crash of '79" that financially ruined most of the world, but the U.S.A. still seems to have stayed at the top of the food chain—the president had moved the capital to another country—although it allowed the society seen here to take charge. (A trilogy of remakes came starting in 2008 that avoid the political and social satire of the original.)

Similar in some ways to *Death Race 2000* is the world of *The Running Man*, the 1987 film starring Arnold Schwarzenegger, with a more visible totalitarian society being set up after an international economic disaster. In this case, the television event is a regular series featuring criminals of the state fighting a number of professional killers in hopes of gaining their freedom (although the winners are killed anyway off camera), with a major one being that of *The Running Man*. Schwarzenegger plays a former military officer who is forced to face the various professional wrestling–styled killers on the show (one is even played by former wrestler Jesse Ventura), where "runners" have to avoid the "stalkers." Surprisingly, unlike *Death Race 2000*, which sees its game abolished due to violence and a new free government replacing the other one, this doesn't appear to be the case in *The Running Man*. Yes, Arnold wins and sends the bad guy (a great role for actor and game show host Richard Dawson) to a rocketing death, but the audience in the studio enjoys the violence, and there is no stopping the totalitarian government's control over the country, thus assuring that all that appears to have happened is the equivalent of the classic *21* game show

The Running Man (1987)—one of many films featuring people trapped in fatal games of entertainment for the masses in a dystopian future.

scandal. Sure, *The Running Man* may have been fixed, but that doesn't mean they all are; so come back next week for a new show featuring criminals of the state risking their lives to win parole!

Either way, both deal with a story placed in an America where a global financial crisis leads to dictatorships. Yet if economic factors could be seen as apocalyptic, then that also means films like Alan J. Pakula's 1981 financial thriller *Rollover* (with Jane Fonda and Kris Kristofferson and dealing with a global financial collapse that causes governmental riots and chaos) are apocalyptic as well. On the other hand, as seen by various financial meltdowns in the past number of years, we know that such risky situations rarely have led to changes in the structure of society or how mankind behaves (perhaps to the lesser of us in not being proactive to making such changes). Therefore, such films ultimately are not truly apocalyptic.

This leaves the other two televised events of the new world order: *Battle Royale* and *The Hunger Games*. As fans of one or the other already know, some controversy was created when aficionados of the book by Koushun Takami and film adaptation of *Battle Royale* (1999 and 2000, respectively) made plain that they felt certain aspects of the plot were lifted for the 2008 novel by Suzanne Collins and 2012 film directed by Gary Ross, *The Hunger Games*. One could see why the comparisons occurred—both deal with television "games" that involve a number of teenagers given a bag and a weapon and sent out into a wilderness area to fight to the death, with only one allowed to live. Yet beyond the initial setup of the games and the eventual outfoxing of the system by the final boy and girl (through help outside of their sphere of influence), they are not very similar at all. Nor is the theme entirely new to either, as other books before them have been written to suggest similar games to produce winners for use by the government in one form or another. Stephen King in his Richard Bachman book from 1979, *The Long Walk*, may often be compared to *The Hunger Games* in its use of young people competing to the death in a race, but William Sleator's 1974 novel *House of Stairs* showcases a group of young people who are slowly conditioned to resort to violence in exchange for food in order to serve the military, which isn't that far away from *Battle Royale*. Yet *The Long Walk* involves all volunteers, which isn't the case with *The Hunger Games*, while *House of Stairs* is an experiment to find new soldiers, and the one in *Battle Royale* is mainly to put fear into the public (although the soldier idea probably isn't far from the surface as well).

But the concept of such games goes back even further—Peter Watkins, who had earlier filmed *The War Game* (covered in the next chapter), had produced a movie in 1969 called *The Gladiators*, which featured world leaders and the world's populace watching games put together to show young people fighting for their lives in combat as a means to pacify the public. In this case, however, the two young people who decide to work together to escape are considered collaborators by both sides of the fight and beaten to death. Doesn't have quite

There has been much debate as to the similarities between *The Hunger Games* (2012) and *Battle Royale* (2000), but there've been plenty of other books and movies before them covering the same theme.

the happily-ever-after ring to it that one can find even in *Battle Royale*, not to mention *The Hunger Games*.

So, while *The Hunger Games* and *Battle Royale* do share some elements, the storyline itself is not so unusual that it could not have been thought of by another writer at another time. In fact, this leads us back to the topic of this chapter—*Battle Royale* gives no indication that this is in some type of postapocalyptic society. In fact, what makes the film so horrifying is that it appears to be today, with the governmental sanction of the game some crazed normality in a new world order (admittedly, the students do not appear to be that familiar with the game to follow, although it is clear in the opening segment that it is televised and celebrated by the public). *The Hunger Games*, conversely, is definitely set in a postapocalyptic world, presumed to be nuclear in origin, although it is never outright stated as being the cause. Of the two, *The Hunger Games* actually does fulfill the definition of what an apocalyptic film should be, while the others involving such killing games do not. Furthermore, while the first film in the *Hunger Games* series doesn't take much into account about the previous nuclear event that led to the society created afterward (thus being more of a MacGuffin than an essential plot element), the two sequel books make that event a catalyst to events that occur later, which furthers the understanding as to why it is there—a seeding of things yet to come—when the story could easily have worked if the setting had been merely a dystopian society.

This leaves a handful of other movies that have a dystopian society that at first glance look to be caused by various "end of the world" circumstances but are actually due to social and political changes. The simplest setup is that of Alex and his droogs (his gang) in Stanley Kubrick's 1971 adaptation of Anthony Burgess' 1962 novel *A Clockwork Orange*. Alex and his gang are crazed young men looking for any kind of violent kick they can find, and it is easy to wish to attribute this to some type of catastrophic incident, like a mutation or such. Alas, this is just the norm for the kids of the future, in a society that is pretty much our own. The world order in *Gattaca* (1997, directed by Andrew Niccol and starring Ethan Hawke and Uma Thurman) is definitely one where societal changes have help to create the story told, since it is one based on eugenics being a major factor in how people are treated and not on anything apocalyptic. *Demolition Man* (1993) with Sylvester Stallone and Wesley Snipes looks like a perfect situation where a little Armageddon would have been involved, but this is not the case; the future world is centered around a utopian vision that borders on the religious fanaticisms of the president seen in *Escape from L.A.* Finally there is the world of *Idiocracy* (2006), directed by Mike Judge, which finds two people from today frozen and revived five hundred years later in a world where mankind has devolved into being mentally stunted due to those with intelligence not having offspring at the same rate as the stupid. A sad tale in a way, but hardly one of Armageddon.

It is certainly easy to see how viewers may instantly see these films as having to have some type of cataclysmic event occur to set up the stories that follow.

However, dystopian does not necessarily mean apocalyptic, even if at first glance it appears to fall within the definition of apocalyptic. The films that truly deal with Armageddon must use such an event as the focal point of everything else in the plot, whether it occurs at the beginning, middle or end of the movie, and appear to possibly affect humanity on a global scale. Once that is set in place, the narrative can go in any direction, from comic to horrific to philosophical and dramatic. In fact, a number of movies use the end of the world to tell cautionary tales of one sort or another. And not always how we should not use the bomb, as will be demonstrated in the next chapter.

7

A Man, a Woman, a Nuclear Bomb

Nuclear Dramas

Many different types of movies discussed so far in the book fit a variety of film genres. *Hitchhiker's Guide to the Galaxy* is obviously a comedy. *Buck Rogers* is science fantasy for kids. *The Quiet Earth* is an "art film," *Goke, Body Snatcher from Hell* a horror film, and *Planet of the Apes* science fiction. Such diversity makes a journey into the world of apocalyptic films (and hopefully the reason you picked up this tome) fascinating, because one can never be sure at the onset if a film will venture down one genre alley or another. Perhaps just as well, as a genre strictly dealing with the end of the world would have to put up with wacky films that do not hold the genre up to prestige. For every *Dr. Strangelove* there are dozens of *Exterminators of the Year 3000* (more about that in a later chapter), and so it is easy for many people to see such films as goofy, mindless fun.

Yet among all the silly films that deal with aliens zapping people and people running from berserkers with bad-pun haircuts in souped-up cars are movies where the filmmakers try to convey some dramatic elements in their stories while using Armageddon as a backdrop. A few, like *Fail-Safe* and *Take Shelter*, appear in previous chapters due to an element in them that stands out beyond such dramatic devices, but in this chapter we're looking at movies that use what in other movies would be perfectly serious dramatic setups, but with this lingering apocalyptic element hanging over everything. Such films make up their own subgenre of apocalyptic films because, for a time, they appear to be setting up a regular dramatic story and then swoop in for the kill by throwing an atomic bomb or such into the center of it all.

Within these films are those that follow similar storylines in order to tell certain types of stories. Some are cautionary, some instructional, some even just "losing the plot" entirely after initial setups, but even for a brief moment there's a sense that someone said, "I'm writing a movie that will shake people up." A few did exactly that.

Drama as Documentary

One thing that can be counted upon by each generation is that they will always look back at the ones before and dismiss them as not being as intelligent as they are. This comes into play when discussing global disasters, with the assumption that everyone after World War II thought the air was clean, food plentiful and there was a great big love affair with the whole darn human race. As for the bomb, it was something we would only use if we needed to protect ourselves from the godless Communists, but if we were attacked, we could close our eyes and wish real big and everything would be just fine.

To be fair, there certainly was enough propaganda after the Second World War that reflects that type of thinking. Documentaries such as *Atomic Café* kick off with this type of nostalgic white-bread, gung-ho lecturing with clips from educational shorts like "Duck and Cover" (where the flash of an atomic bomb going off indicates one should put a newspaper over one's head and wait a few minutes before being all right). Nevertheless, as time crept on, it became clearer that things were not as rosy with the bomb as we wished to believe. True, Americans kept their eyes closed to the horrors of the bombings of Nagasaki and Hiroshima (and still do, unfortunately, in so many ways), and tried to play up the atom as a salvation for the nation, but reality has a way of peeking through our fingers when we try to cover our eyes. The 1950s began to see more reports of how radioactivity wasn't like a momentary flatulent but something we had to deal with, especially once our enemy got the bomb. So we built bomb shelters and staged "Duck and Cover" sessions in schools, but beyond scaring a generation of kids near to death, it wasn't much. Soon enough, we had novels such as *Alas, Babylon* and movies such as *Five*, starting to point out that those left behind may not be quite as fortunate as the government films told us we would be.

By 1959, we began to see films that visually stripped away the "nicety" of the bomb, with films such as *Hiroshima, Mon Amour* showing graphic documentary footage of the survivors from the Hiroshima bombing, while *On the Beach* in 1959 showed that a true and quite possible nuclear war would pretty much spell the end of mankind with a slow radioactive death. The public was becoming aware, but for every step forward, there were those who wanted to take it two steps back in order to prove that the Cold War was for our benefit and the government would protect us all, keep us safe and sound. Besides, if a bomb did drop, there was no cause for concern in most parts of the country, as most of us had absolute and assured planning to save us from the bomb.

Not that those who had already felt the ferocity of the atom bomb were taken in by such promises, if the films released in Japan demonstrate anything. In 1961, the Japanese studio Toho—which was already addressing the issue of nuclear disaster under the guise of *Godzilla, King of the Monsters* (1956)—used the special-effects work of Eiji Tsuburaya (who had done such work on *Godzilla*) to tell a story about how easily a nuclear war could erupt that would trap innocents in the carnage to follow. The film is *The Last War*, which should not be confused with a movie released through the Japanese studio Toei that same year called *The Final War* (although that at least had its title changed to the rather less lyrical *World War III Breaks Out* when it finally arrived in America in 1962). Both films deal with a crisis in Korea leading to an escalation of conflict between America and the Soviets until eventually most of Japan is destroyed in the crossfire.

Oddly, although *The Final War* received a certain number of television airings in the early 1960s and even coverage in the pages of *Life* magazine (due to special effects that show the destruction of the Golden Gate Bridge), it is nearly impossible to see, and only synopses and a few stills can give us a good idea of what occurs in the movie. In *The Final War*, the U.S. accidentally drops a nuclear bomb on Korea (as one can guess from reading this far in the book, the U.S. military seems very accident-prone when it comes to nuclear bombs in movies). The movie follows Tatsuo Umemiya and Yoshiko Mita as a reporter and a nurse who do what they can during the crisis, but eventually most of the world is wiped out with the exception of Argentina. The reporter returns to Tokyo to find his girlfriend, the nurse, had died in the bombing, and he soon dies himself from radiation poisoning. The most curious thing about the film is the aircraft used to destroy the cities, which are hexagon crafts that look more like something alien than what the military on any side of the conflict would have available to them.

The Last War, since it is available for viewing and has a more down-to-earth presentation of such a conflict, is the better remembered of the two. The film begins by following a family located in then-present Tokyo, with their biggest drama being that of the daughter wishing to marry a sailor (and which turns out not to be of any concern by the family, so it is very little drama at that).

Yet there's a bigger picture in mind. Intercut with the goings-on of the family are scenes of an escalating development between the "Federation" (essentially NATO forces) and the "Alliance" (Communist forces) at the 38th Parallel in Korea. This is an ongoing issue even today, with saber-rattling from both North and South Korea making those who live nearby, as in Japan, rather jumpy about what can happen; thus, a film depicting the next steps certainly would be of interest by the public there. As events build up, with characters from both sides of the conflict struggling to ease tension, the family members hear news and rumors while trying to live their lives in rather hopeless hope against the inevitable. The sailor marries the daughter only to end up back at sea with the military. He survives the war that follows, but returns to Tokyo knowing it was destroyed in the attack, and his return means his death by radiation poisoning (hence, a very similar ending to the one in *The Final War*).

It is a rather strange viewing experience for those of us who grew up watching *Godzilla* movies, what with the acting and effects duplicating those monster films. Yes, there is a subtext to the first *Godzilla* film (as well as some other Japanese monster films of the time) that deals with the atom bomb and radiation poisoning, but most of these were seen as kiddie flicks in the U.S. and elsewhere, and all we cared about were the monsters making things blow up. To see a movie within that context—with miniature planes and tanks being destroyed, just like in a *Godzilla* movie—but telling a story that could just as easily be one from *The Day After* or *Threads* (both discussed later on) gives the film an almost deeper feeling of loss than in those other pictures. We can't help but expect someone will save the day and the family will be fine, especially as some scenes try to play up such hope among the military working to stop the crisis, but it is not to be, and the family—these people who have no recourse other than to wait it out and hope—die. It is clear to the Japanese that such a conflict would bring death, and all the silly preparations that such Civil Defense films tried to shove down people's throats were meaningless.

Even with its minor faults, *The Last War* is quite a progressive antiwar film for the time and certainly has the same feel as *On the Beach* and other such films more widely known. In 1974, Toho attempted a remake, *Prophecies of Nostradamus*, better known in the U.S. as *The Last Days of Planet Earth*. Although Toshio Yasumi revised his earlier script from *The Last War*, the remake is not considered very good. The plot deals little with a family, but interspersed are their dealings with ecological dangers thanks to changes in the modern world. We then see a man who supposedly is Nostradamus darting his head back and forth, evidently thinking, "Yes, yes, I thought of that. The giant bats and slugs? The baby with two heads? Killer plants in the subways? Suicidal motorcycle runs featuring the same two guys over and over again? Yes, those too. Mmm-hmm, mm-hmm." Thanks, Nostradamus, for the quatrain about the repetitive motorcycle jumps. Now that's thinking ahead! Seriously, while one has to give them credit for trying to tie global warming into events that will shape the world over the coming decades, one can easily see they were trying too hard and not enough at the same time. Worse, it ends with our protagonist telling a room full of men, "This is what may happen," thus making it all just Mr. Crazy here telling us stories. This is showcased in its attempt to talk about so many pathways to destruction, but then relying on stock footage from many other earlier Toho films, including *The Last War*. Sadly, it is more well-known and available than the original it is based on.

Getting back to the earlier days of the Cold War, Japan was not the only country that quickly dismissed the assurances of the Civil Defense films. Frank Perry's 1963 movie *Ladybug, Ladybug* would tackle the Cuban Missile Crisis of 1962 as a means to deal with our preparations for such an attack, with schoolchildren forced into hysteria and the probable death of one of the girls due to the others refusing to let her into a bomb shelter, because no one in authority (the teachers) appears to know what they are doing. More devastating was the work of Peter Watkins with his 1965 film *The War Game*. Watkins, who had found success with a BBC film he had done in 1964 called *Culloden* (which showed the Battle of Culloden of 1746 as if cameras were there to interview soldiers and others at the time), was requested to make another film, which used the same documentary-style of filming to tell a futuristic story. In this, Watkins attempted to show the everyday happenings leading up to a nuclear attack of Britain in 1965, and in the process expertly demonstrated that the chances of survival were pretty slim, even with the evacuation of women and children days before the attack occurs. While *The Last War* uses a traditional "war is coming" motif, it also goes with a standard "hero looks at the devastation in shock" ending. *The War Game* takes it a step beyond in such a "what if" situation, showing the ramifications of such a conflict, even a brief one.

Using information from government sources and public quotes that contradict the reality of such a situation, Watkins follows the pattern of *Culloden*, only this time setting the interviews and documentary-style footage in the near future rather than the past. As a narrator explains the circumstances—this being a joint provocation in both Korea and Germany by Communist forces—and known facts of such preparation before and ramifications after such an attack, we see members of the public and a scattered number of people in positions of command struggling to survive.

Filmed in black and white and with an amateur cast, the film is devastating in showing how crazed and hopeless such an attack would be, with eventual chaos and the breakdown in society in the days and weeks that followed. The use of black-and-white photography also allows for images of the dead that would simply have not gotten past the censors in later television films if the viewers could see the red blood, making such scenes somewhat more effective than later attempts. More importantly, it demonstrated that government propaganda that attempted to show such a nuclear exchange as being somehow "winnable" was simply unworkable and would leave many unlucky enough to be anywhere in the countryside dead or in the process of dying. As can be expected, *The War Game* clashed with what was acceptable for viewers, and with government pressure, the BBC refused to air the program as scheduled. Attempts were made by the BBC to color the film as an experiment that failed, stating this as their reason for not televising it, but the film would turn up in theaters and end up winning an Academy Award for best documentary feature in 1966, strongly suggesting otherwise. The film continued to be, and remains today, a fixture in college courses on both filmmaking and politics, although it rarely gets as much of a focus as do later films that attempted to do similar things.

The next film to try to bring to viewers the shattering effects of nuclear bombing came in 1983 with ABC's production of *The Day After*. Ironically, it would not only be a television production, but would also face many battles with those controlling the purse strings—in this case, the censors at the network. Director Nicholas Meyer came into the project, having just come off a huge success with the second *Star Trek* movie, *The Wrath of Khan* (1982). He had earlier done a science fantasy called *Time After Time* (1979), featuring H. G. Wells using a time machine he invented to arrive in present-day San Francisco, and earlier had worked in television writing the scripts for movies, including a docudrama depicting Orson Welles' infamous radio adaptation of Wells' *The War of the Worlds*. It would seem that Meyer would be a good person to put on the job, but Meyer was skeptical. He felt the script had too many scenes that were padding so the network could air the film over two nights, but relented after the network requested he continue filming everything. It was then decided that, due to lack of advertising, the film should be shown in one night and could be edited down, which is what Meyer wanted to do anyway. An edited version of the film seemed to go over well with the network, but then came pressure from the censors and others to shorten it even more (as well as making sure that the U.S. did not appear to have an active hand in causing the conflict, a suggestion ignored by the filmmakers). Meyer refused to do anything more and quit the project, but was rehired when ABC realized that Meyer and his editor were the only ones that could put together a version of the film that worked.

Peter Watkins' *The War Game* (1965)—suppressed by the BBC, but the pinnacle of all post-nuclear films to come.

With both films dealing with nuclear bombings near planned bombing sites (Kent, England, in *The War Game*; Lawrence, Kansas, in *The Day After*), there are bound to be some similarities in the story and even the filming (although not the amateur cast of *The War Game*, many of the actors in *The Day After* were little known beyond star Jason Robards). The biggest difference, however, is that *The Day After* reviews the events in a strictly dramatic manner instead of the documentary feel of *The War Game*, thus falling back into the realm of *The Last War*. The story follows several characters in the Lawrence, Kansas, area as an escalation grows between the Soviets and America in Berlin, Germany, a major flashpoint in general at the time, with the Soviets controlling East Germany before reunification in 1990. This is an interesting transformation of hot-points in the conscience of viewers in the U.S. over that of Japanese. To them, there is no greater concern than the house next door that has angry neighbors, and thus the continuing engagement of words between North and South Korea obviously brings to mind images of a nuclear war with Japan caught in the crossfire. By 1965 in England, the Korean War was a little more than a decade away and was remembered, but to those living in the United Kingdom, the bigger concern was East and West Germany. Certainly closer to home than Korea. And *The War Game* would set its sights on America using nuclear tactics in Vietnam—a grow-ing concern in the mid-1960s—causing conflict in Germany, which is more the lynchpin to the bombing than Vietnam (and certainly with no consideration of Korea). By 1983, and thanks to the success of *M*A*S*H*, most in America saw the Korean War as a weekly comedy show, evidently fought by long-haired liberals who were only trying to help out. Occasionally someone would hear a word or two about North Korea, but people were having enough problems trying to keep their minds off of the Vietnam War, more than something thirty years earlier, and there were growing concerns raised by President Reagan and others who felt the more bombs the merrier as a deterrent against the "dirty commies" in the Soviet Union. Thus, Americans' concerns were directed more toward Europe than Asia, as seen in the setup for *The Day After.*

As in *The War Game*, things rapidly unravel and bombs go off, nuking the central United States as well as the Soviet Union. The second half of the film deals with those still alive after the attack and how they cope with the growing realization that they all most probably will die due to radiation sickness. After the death of many of the characters and an overwhelming feeling of hopeless-ness encircles those still alive, Robards' character decides to travel to Kansas City, Missouri—which had been a ground zero in the attacks—to die at home (much like how the crew of the submarine decides to return to America in *On the Beach*). He arrives to find the burnt-out shell of his home and squatters inside and demands they leave, but crumples in emotion when they offer him food as the film concludes.

Unlike the BBC, ABC went ahead with the telecast once it was ready for airing. As expected, there was plenty of controversy with the broadcast, and ABC aired the second half of the film (which takes place after the bombing) without commercial interruption, a rarity for American network television. There was also a panel afterward on ABC (featuring Carl Sagan, Henry Kissinger, William F. Buckley Jr. and Robert McNamara on the pros and cons of the film). Although public response from conservatives leaned toward seeing the film as trying to destroy America, privately many found it effective in showing the pain and suffering such a proliferation of nuclear weapons would cause. As the film premiered worldwide in theaters, there was a growing consensus that things needed to change. Although Meyer would later somewhat downplay the effect the movie had on international relationships, several believe that it helped lead to the Intermediate-Range Nuclear Forces Treaty in 1987. Which gives *The Day After* perhaps an even stronger result than the Academy Award *The War Game* received.

A rather interesting side note to the airing of *The Day After* in November 1983 is that of a week's worth of episodes from the PBS series *Mister Rogers' Neighborhood* the same month. Fred Rogers, the star and writer of the show, would commonly base a strip of five shows (airing Mondays through Fridays at a time children can watch) around a central theme that he addressed directly to the viewers as well as using for the stories told by puppet and human characters in "the Neighborhood of Make-Believe." In this strip of programs that aired in November 1983, the topic was conflict.

The storyline used to convey this topic in "the Neighborhood of Make-Believe" has King Friday learning that another area in the Neighborhood called Southwood has been buying up many parts for a project that Friday fears may be bombs. Friday buys up parts to match those of Southwood, while the children (other puppets) learn about what to do when bombs drop. Before things escalate too far, Friday finds out that Southwood is using the parts to build a bridge. The parts Friday has are used to make a record player instead, and everyone agrees that peace is better than war.

For years, those who had heard about these episodes believed that Rogers had filmed them to be shown to children who may have heard about *The Day After* and to help them understand how mistakes can be made that can possibly lead to terrible results. However, as Tim Lybarger points out on his website about *Mister Rogers' Neighborhood* (www.neighborhoodarchive.com/mrn/episodes/1525/index.html), the airings within the same month were a coincidence, and *The Day After* was not in mind when the storyline for the "Neighborhood of Make-Believe" was created. Further, the episodes of *Mister Rogers' Neighborhood* aired the week of November 7 through 11, 1983, while *The Day After* premiered on ABC on November 20 that same year. (Not to mention that the viewership of *Mister Rogers'* were hardly the type to be up late enough to watch *The Day After*, or care to watch it.) Therefore, while it is intriguing that the two appeared at such a similar time, it does appear to be a case more of an urban legend than truth.

With *The Day After* now setting the standard for dramatic depictions of a nuclear attack, the BBC jumped back into the game looking for a movie that ends up combining the documentary structure of *The War Game* (which they would finally air in 1985, twenty years after its initial broadcast date) with the character-driven drama of *The Day After*. The result was *Threads* (1984), which ends up going further than both the previous productions and yet ends up being weaker than either in the end.

The Day After (1983), an ABC special movie event that led to other, similar postnuclear films, including *Testament* (1983) and *Threads* (1984).

The first half of *Threads* plays out as a domestic drama—Ruth and Jimmy are two young people from opposite sides of the track (and in typically British drama fashion, her family is of a slightly higher class than Jimmy). Learning Ruth is pregnant, the two families meet, find an apartment for the pair and try to go about their lives, while Jimmy begins messing around a bit on the side. Meanwhile, as with Shelley's *The Last Man*, there are plenty of developments happening to suggest the end of the world is approaching, thanks to radio and television broadcasts found in the background of scenes about a war brewing between America and the Soviets. In this case, it is Iran that is the breaking point and, as with the earlier films in this chapter, bombs begin to fall.

It is at this point, about midway through *Threads*, that the narrator—who has been heard off and on earlier in the film—takes over, as he describes what would occur in a nuclear strike, and the aftermath. Directing the action on-screen, both families are eventually wiped out by the bombing, radiation or looters. The only exception is Ruth, who manages to escape the city. She eventually gives birth to a daughter on her own and raises her as they try to grow food in the wastelands during the nuclear winter that follows. Ruth dies and her daughter is left on her own. Years later, all the children grow up to be grunting, barbaric teenagers who scavenge for food. The daughter gets pregnant, gives birth in what is left of a hospital and is about to scream at the results when the movie comes to an end.

To make blunt the horrors of nuclear bombing, the film spends a lot of time on gruesome makeup and horrific incidents as the narrator plaintively explains why "Mom" over there has half her face burnt off. Perhaps the biggest problem with the film is that the first half is rather dull, perhaps intentionally so, with the setup of Ruth and Jimmy and how the two families become related. After a good forty minutes of the people drinking at the pub and eating quietly at the dinner table, one begins to wonder if the wrong movie is in the player; especially once it begins to expand the storyline to include Jimmy drunkenly cheating on Ruth. Of course, the objective of the filmmakers is twofold: give the audience characters to follow so they will become emotionally attached, as in *The Day After*, while also establishing how people respond with varying degrees of safety measures (such as the one family with the basement and food, while the other family is trying to use a door against a wall). Yet the characters are dreary and uninteresting, leaving audience sympathy for the characters rather shallow. Thus, when the attack occurs, all that is left is to watch as the narrator goes through the paces of what would happen next (which makes him somewhat sadistic in a way, as if he really, really doesn't like these characters, so he becomes the instigator of the terrible things that happen to them afterward). The film does get some mileage out of addressing long-term issues that the survivors would face (such as the nuclear winter), but the last fifteen minutes dealing with the daughter on her own over-plays its hand. By the time *Threads* gets to what is supposed to be its final horrific image—of the daughter giving birth to something (we're never told if the baby is a stillborn or something else)—it has drained the audience of emotions. No doubt about it, it is terrible what is happening on-screen, but apathy has taken hold thanks to the assault of terrifying images that come before it.

In attempting to take the narrative of *The War Game* and drape it with a dramatic story like *The Day After*, *Threads* ends up not having the emotional impact of either. To be fair, *The War Game* is so clinical that it does keep the audience at a distance from the occurrences played out on-screen, while *The Day After* reaches occasionally for hysterics that push beyond what would be acceptable in reality (Steve Guttenberg's character's cornfield lecture about radiation is so melodramatic that you nearly expect him to break out in a dance number before it is over).

Between *The Day After* and *Threads* came *Testament* (1983), another film that was produced for television and dealt with the ramifications of a nuclear attack and, like *The War Game*, ended up in theaters instead. Only in this case, it was intentional, as the Public Broadcasting Service (PBS) production for their series *American Playhouse* was deemed strong enough to release as a theatrical feature before eventually being aired on the network. The movie was directed by Lynne Littman and starred Jane Alexander (who turns up in the American adaptation of *The Ring* and *Terminator Salvation*) as a housewife with three children who copes with the aftermath of a nuclear attack on major U.S. cities. It is never explained if the attacks came from terrorists or another country, but as with the previous films it doesn't really matter much to the characters now trying to survive. In the case of *Testament*, however, it at first appears that the city they live in managed to survive the attack due to their location (much like *Alas, Babylon*), but soon radiation sickness begins to take hold of the townspeople. The wife holds on in hopes that her husband (played by William Devane), who had traveled to San Francisco before the attack, has survived, but she eventually realizes it is impossible, and two of her children soon slowly succumb to radiation. Eventually, she and her oldest son take in a handicapped boy, but it is clear that there is probably no turning back and they all will soon die of radiation poisoning, as did the others. She attempts to asphyxiate them all in a closed garage with the car running (like Fred Astaire's character in *On the Beach*), but cannot go through with it. Instead, they celebrate a birthday, and the woman tells the children that they need to remember the good as well as the bad as the film cuts back to home-movie footage of the family in happier times.

The earlier films discussed in this chapter certainly are of a depressing nature—mankind will see terrible things happen, and many will lose their lives, but because of the aims of the filmmakers there is a slight distancing between viewers and the stories told. *The War Game* makes it look as if people will survive; it'll be a mess, but they'll survive. Same with *Threads*, and even *The Day After* could leave some viewers with hope that some of the characters may get through it somehow. Not so with *Testament*. There is no other story than the one in front of us on the screen—it isn't about many characters, it is about one woman trying to make sure her family survives. It isn't about instant death to those we see; we slowly see her children dying in front of us and there is nothing that can be done to stop it. We even recognize the kids—one is Lukas Haas (later in *Mars Attacks!*, *The Lathe of Heaven* and *Solarbabies*), whom most remember as the sweet kid in Harrison Ford's *Witness,* and who also plays a sweet little kid here. There is no parent who can watch Haas' death scene and not want to rip out their own heart at the devastation played out by Alexander as the character watches her child die. All the others have very important things to say about nuclear disarmament and use scare tactics, but *Testament* jabs at the heart and leaves an emotional impact that the other films can't quite match.

The closest story emotionally to *Testament* in this category is the final film here, *When the Wind Blows.* The movie was a 1986 animated adaptation of a graphic novel by illustrator/writer Raymond Briggs directed by Jimmy Murakami (*Battle Beyond the Stars*) and starring John Mill and Peggy Ashcroft as James and Hilda Bloggs. The Bloggs are an older couple who have very little relevant knowledge of what to do in a nuclear attack and slowly begin to weaken from radiation sickness after surviving an attack that has wiped out everyone around them. As the movie goes back and forth between memories of the happy past and the present, the two begin to weaken from radiation poisoning but attempt to stay optimistic about their future, as they crawl into their lean-to made of a door and pray while knowingly waiting for the end to claim them.

As with *Testament, When the Wind Blows* is the simpler, more personal story that grips viewers rather than trying to give us all the facts. Yes, it is interesting to know that there would be a nuclear winter and that the next generation could end up talking in grunts, but our hearts break not for the cypher we see as the barbarian girl in *Threads,* but rather for the child dying in *Testament* and the older couple who are mystified by their slow death. We know these people, just as we can fathom and sympathize with Jason Robards' doctor in *The Day After* and the sailor in *The Last War* both having breakdowns in the end after seeing what devastation has been caused by the stupidity of war. The others have something good to say and think about, but the images of the more personal, character-driven films stay with viewers longer.

Even so, *The War Game* reverberates the strongest of any of the group because it so matter-of-factly tells the tale we all need to know. *Threads* would concentrate on the documentary style of *The War Game*, and the style of "future-tense" documentary filmmaking used in Watkins' film would play a part in series presenting scenarios of doomsday that began popping up around the millennium. *World War III*, a German film made for the ZDF network in 1998, takes a "what if?" scenario—that of the Soviets firing on demonstrators at the Berlin Wall in 1989 instead of allowing the destruction of the wall—and extends it to lead to a nuclear war between America and the Soviets. Using the cold documentary manner of *The War Game*, *World War III* (not to be confused with the 1982 NBC miniseries examined earlier), the film seems to cater to a quite anti-Soviet viewpoint early on and never flinches from it. In a way, this is a bit of a ruse, as although we see numerous real-life political figures going through the paces of this story, the plot hinges on Mikhail Gorbachev being taken out in a coup by a paranoid Soviet general, which filters back to the days of *Dr. Strangelove* and one military man diverting the powers of a nation to his own obsessed dreams of destruction of the "enemy." The only difference is that it happens in the Soviet Union instead of America. With that setup, every advance in the plot that shows NATO and the Americans working to resolve the problem peacefully ends with the Soviet leader igniting another, bigger problem until a false reading on equipment (another flashback to *Dr. Strangelove* and *Fail-Safe*) leads to the Soviets sending all their nuclear warheads toward America and vice versa. It is at that point in the story that the film goes back to the original premise and shows what happened in our own world, with a peaceful resolution found for the Berlin Wall situation. In essence, it was all a dream, or rather a nightmare. It would be easy to knock the film for doing such, yet on the other hand, one does have to give it credit for visualizing what people feared would happen in 1989—feared somewhat more than what we hoped and did, fortunately, get.

World War III takes the documentary form of *The War Game* and attempts to give us a documentary from an alternate Earth. In many ways, it was one of the first of a new type of documentary form that caters to the concept of "what if?" The 1990s would see the start of other various films and series based on the idea of alternate ways for the world to end, but unlike *World War III*, subsequent films would take the clinical approach of its predecessors and mix it with the narrative thread of the drama to give them a more personal touch. *After Armageddon* (2010) is a two-hour documentary from the History Channel, and a good example of this mix, with elements of *The War Game* and *Testament* in a narrative detailing what happens to a man, woman and child who must face life after a virus has wiped out half of the population. Their plight is interrupted every so often by a narrator and a few experts describing what the family would probably face in their current situation (with the father eventually dying of an infection from a wound) and the world forced to use solar energy and revert to a quasi–Iron Age lifestyle. Although it focuses on a plague rather than the nuclear annihilation of most of the material here, it is so reminiscent of the others that it should be mentioned here.

Similar to *After Armageddon* is the BBC documentary *End Day* (2005), which follows one character heading to work as five (four in the American version shown on the National Geographic Channel) different and terrible global events are examined: tsunami, pandemic, asteroid, a super volcano and a scientific experiment involving the characters that destroys Earth. As with *After Armageddon*, experts describe such life-ending situations as the character is seen going through his final day (one way or another). ABC would follow the BBC's lead and do a similar program in 2009 called *Earth 2100*, which sets up a protagonist for viewers to follow during a disaster, this time being environmental in nature—namely that of global warming leading to huge hurricanes and eventually a pandemic. Again, experts are trotted out to explain what and why thing would happen, as the main character goes through her paces. In the end, she survives but with everything about her world having changed in the ninety years she has lived.

Aftermath, a 2010 five-part series showed originally on History Television in Canada, follows a similar pattern to the examples above, with each episode focusing on a different type of disaster and its ramifications. In this instance, however, the sudden crises are extreme to the point of seeming somewhat a grasp for anything that may compel people to watch. Instead of discussing common global disasters such as epidemics and earthquakes, the series dealt with the population doubling overnight, oil disappearing unexpectedly, the sun swallowing the planet and the earth's spin slowing to a halt. Although it probably did drive viewers to watch, it seemed a bit like the Superman comics of the 1950s where the editor would ask his kids what they wanted to see in the next issue and then based stories around their crazy ideas.

But it did give us a plot that has been used many times before and certainly since appearing on *Aftermath*—the "what if everyone suddenly disappeared from the planet?" theme. These environmental episodes deal with everyone on the planet just up and leaving one day, but with everything preserved in perfect order. Of course, such an event wouldn't happen (even the Rapture involves a bunch of poor suckers being left on the planet after all the good people leave), but the filmmakers are not so much concerned about selling the audience on how it happened, but rather what happens to the earth after that point. *Aftermath*'s first episode dealt with this, as did a series started in 2008 on the History Channel called *Life After People* and a thirteen-part series from the BBC in 2002 called *The Future Is Wild.* All of these series used experts once again to discuss differences in the animal kingdom, plant life, etc., while visuals showed our world slowly decaying away. None of them show squirrels building houses out of soldier helmets and dressing in clothes as seen in "Peace on Earth" (see chapter 5), but they do spark reminders of what Jack London in *The Scarlet Plague* and Richard Jefferies in *After London* (see chapter 1 for both) had to say about nature reclaiming man's world.

What is fascinating in the number of documentary films and series showing what would happen after we're gone is that they dig deep into something that perplexes us all about death—what are the ramifications of my being absent? Will it matter? Will any of this make any impact in the thousands or even millions of years to come? Of course, as one would expect, the earth will do just fine and dandy without us (after certain man-made hazards are cleaned up by nature, that is); in fact, it will probably be better off, which could be seen as a somewhat depressing acknowledgment to the legacy of mankind's achievements. Woody Allen in his film *Annie Hall* has his younger self refusing to do schoolwork because "what does it matter" since we're all doomed anyway. Such documentaries press that question home multiple times. There usually is some type of defense to keep one positive about life at the end of each episode, hopeful that it will keep us from diving for the remote (or the arsenic), but it seems a bit lacking. Well, at least watching vines quickly climb over cars and buildings are great visuals.

While there have been various other documentaries detailing what would happen if there was a sudden crisis in the world, there is one other area of the documentary style that has led to a small number of films produced about apocalyptic events: the "live television event" films. Such an idea wasn't anything new; Orson Welles practically invented the genre back in 1938 with his Mercury Theatre production of *War of the Worlds*, which was presented for the most part as if it were a "live news broadcast" about a Martian invasion of Earth, based on H. G. Wells' novel (which is covered in more detail in chapter 13). Although perceived as causing great panic when broadcast—even after interruptions reminding listeners it was just a play—in retrospect, such incidents were blown out of proportion in the newspapers of the day. Still, the broadcast gained a notoriety that has remained with it today, and when anyone attempts a new production that uses a similar theme, there's no way to avoid a mention of the Welles production of 1938.

In 1983, NBC produced *Special Bulletin*, which used video to appear like live-on-the-air television with a cast that wasn't instantly recognizable to viewers beyond Ed Flanders (who had just begun appearing on *St. Elsewhere*) and possibly Rosalind Cash (who had previously appeared in *The Omega Man*, of which more details in the next chapter). The film is not quite apocalyptic, although it involves terrorists who plan to blow up a nuclear device in the harbor of Charleston, South Carolina. Flanders plays the New York anchorman of a cable news network that is covering the crisis with a network reporter and cameraman being held hostage by the terrorists so that they can make their demands on national television. This leads the film into questions about the media that are still being played out today—where is the line crossed between covering the story and becoming the story? Thus, in some ways the story about the terrorists with a nuclear device plays a backseat role to the one about the media. Other films after this would try to copy the formula, but always with varying degrees of success.

Countdown to Looking Glass (1984) was the first to follow-up in the style of *Special Bulletin*, although it cuts away from the "live television" feel for dramatic moments that involve the characters on-screen. The plot of the HBO film deals with trouble in the Middle East that escalates into what appears to be the start of World War III, with the president taking off in Looking Glass (the Strategic Air Command plane that is used to control actions in a nuclear emergency). Structured much like *Special Bulletin*, with a cable news channel that is focusing on the big news story, *Countdown to Looking Glass* breaks up the documentary look with several dramatic "off camera" scenes that attempt to inform viewers about the characters and increase tension where it would be impossible if only told through the news channel's camera. Between this and a cast of actors that are recognizable (such as Scott Glenn, Michael Murphy, along with such well-known figures as Eric Sevareid and Newt Gingrich), the film manages to take the viewers out of the story, making this one of the weaker films in the group here. It also ends before there is a resolution, with the Emergency Broadcast signal taking over for the network and the promise that when it comes time to press the button, no one will do it. Having already stepped outside of the film's framework to give viewers elements beyond what they would have seen on the channel, it seems a bit fainthearted to say at the end, "Oh, we have to stop here, because that's how the channel would end, so we don't have to give you a resolution."

The next film to go this route is the 1994 CBS film *Without Warning*, which is actually an alien invasion film but plays much in the same manner as the films cited earlier. It does at least give us the assurance of the end of the world by the conclusion, even if the plot is not logical. In this, the audience are given a movie of the week to be interrupted (much like how Welles' *War of the Worlds* broadcast interrupts "normal broadcasting") when strange events begin to occur in "real time." In this case, the occurrence is not due to a possible nuclear strike but to the sudden impact of various things that are assumed to be meteors around the globe. The viewers learn more at the same pace as the "news reports" being shown in the program, which suggests that the impact points were intentional and that two of three survivors were found who are now speaking in a language no one understands.

The points of impact the survivors came from begin to transmit a signal to space and various other objects begin to descend to Earth, with three intentionally aimed at the capitals of major countries. When nuclear arms destroy these, the two survivors die. Finally, the translation of their jumbled message is deduced, and it turns out to be the words left on the *Voyager* space probe by the U.N. Secretary General. If this was to be a message of peace, it was understood too late, and the program ends with reports of hundreds more meteors heading our way and set to destroy the world.

Which, as with *Knowing* in a previous chapter, reminds us all of one thing— no, not that we can't judge a book by its cover, but that aliens are jerks. To assume that a new planet you're visiting will welcome you with open arms after you kill numerous people with meteors and then give them a greeting in gibberish is hardly a sign of a civilization brimming with intelligence. Not to mention to keep battering the place with even more meteors when a look at broadcasts coming from the planet would tell you that the people are afraid. Alas, we're not supposed to see it that way; our demise is supposed to be seen as our folly, not that of the boneheads from outer space. We don't even get to see what happens to Loni Anderson in the movie of the week either.

The film did get some reactions from people when it aired, even with numerous warnings during commercial breaks that it was strictly a movie and not real. The airing was on October 30, 1994, fifty-six years to the day Welles had frightened some gullible people with his radio broadcast of *War of the Worlds*. Looks like things never change.

The End as Domestic Drama

There is typically one message to be made with a movie about a nuclear holocaust—it's just a flat-out bad idea. Such a message typically falls into three plot subgroups:

1. Boy, our leaders really know how to screw things up, don't they?
2. Can we survive?
3. If not, how much dignity can we allow ourselves as we wait to die?

Then we have the films that are searching for some other story to tell. In general, such films begin with at least one of these essential questions for the characters to confront; then move on to tell stories of survival, about racial prejudice, class warfare, the sexes, loneliness, other themes—essentially stories played out in many dramas that have nothing to do with some type of apocalyptic event. So why ram those ideas into one dealing with an event that wipes out most of the world?

Because it is a structure that allows no escape, or relatively few options, for the participants involved. In reality, if we don't like something, we can find a way to avoid it; in drama, characters must be forced to deal with the situation in front of them with no detour from it. Take *A Streetcar Named Desire* by Tennessee Williams or Eugene O'Neill's *Long Day's Journey into Night*—considered by many to be two of the best American plays ever written. Both restrict their setting to essentially one room; characters are family (poverty addled in one, drug addicted in another); they have no choice but to face confinement together. The setting is a cage, and there is no freedom for the characters until they resolve their issues in some fashion (*Desire* in violence; *Journey* in acceptance).

Same with the nuclear dramas discussed here—the population shrunk to a cast of a handful, with nowhere to go but out into the radioactive wastelands—the setting automatically establishes itself like that of such plays. This is not to suggest that Roger Corman's *The Last Woman on Earth* (1960) is the equivalent of *Death of a Salesman*, but rather the premise of global annihilation allows for setups that are the equivalent of Jean-Paul Sartre's *No Exit* (one man and two women stuck in a room for all eternity). Corman's film deals with three people—a shady businessman, his trophy wife and his lawyer—who, while scuba diving, survive a global disaster that has asphyxiated everyone on the surface. This suggests that a certain number of lucky people using oxygen from another source are probably still alive, but for the moment there are just the three of them, and they struggle to learn how to survive. As in *No Exit*, although they realize they are stuck together, over time tension begins to mount as the wife and lawyer (played by future *Chinatown* scriptwriter Robert Towne) become closer and attempt to take off together. The businessman and the lawyer have a rampaging fight through the streets until (in a surprise twist) the good-guy lawyer finally falls down dead in a church. The businessman and his wife leave the church, unsure of what is to become of them in their new world.

Now, of course, the film begins with some malarkey that allows for these three to live while everyone else dies (better yet, with everyone in the city conveniently disappearing as well, as there are no dead bodies to clean up anywhere). Nevertheless, let us look more closely at the story being told: businessman goes on a trip with lawyer and trophy wife and soon problems develop. The wife decides to leave with the lawyer, and the two men fight over her. The wife and executive reconcile, but with lingering concerns as to what just happened means to them for their future. Such a tale could have taken place within a swanky apartment on one set, with no need for any of the "end of the world" trimmings. Yet by setting it up the way Corman did, he told his story within a framework of "science fiction." The creator of *Twilight Zone*, Rod Serling, once stated that he used fantasy and science fiction in his show so that he could deal with current themes such as racism and politics that would be censored by the network if explored in any normal fashion. Same here with the domestic dramas of nuclear war. They can tell stories that could be in any film, but dressed as something unnatural they allow the filmmakers to go in directions that other dramas would have to abandon.

Plus, after all this lofty talk, let us just admit one other thing: it's cheaper. No additional cast members to pay for, people stuck in essentially one room for the duration of the film, limited special effects needed except for stock footage of a bomb going off or such and finding a quarry or demolished buildings somewhere. There's still the problem of perhaps giving the audience a money shot of your cast walking through the abandoned streets of a city, but even that is down to shooting footage at a time in the morning when there is daylight but little morning traffic. That is not the sole reasoning behind several of the movies listed in this category, but one can't deny that the filmmakers probably did think about it when they went in the direction they decided.

The first film that kicks off this subgenre is *Five* (1951), which is usually seen as the first drama to deal with the possibilities of a nuclear holocaust and what the survivors would do. It also establishes the essential framework of many more "trapped in a box" nuclear dramas to come. Written and directed by Arch Oboler (who went on to do the same for *The Twonky*—about a television set from the future that controls minds—and *The Bubble*—a 3-D alien invasion movie from 1966), the film starts off with a woman named Roseanne (Susan Douglas Rubes), who has somehow escaped the explosion of a new atomic bomb that has wiped out most of humanity. She finds a house with a man living there, Michael (William Phipps), and soon two more survivors arrive—an old man (Earl Lee) and Charles, an African American (Charles Lampkin). Each has survived due to having the fortune of being somewhere where the radiation could not get them when the explosion hit. (If that sounds like *Last Woman on Earth* or *Where Have All the People Gone?*, get used to it, as it's a very common plot device in many of the movies listed below.) Things are going well for the four until a man is fished from the ocean, Eric (James Anderson), who turns out to be a racist and has the insane notion that they are immune to radiation. The old man dies, but there is new life when the woman gives birth to a son. However, Eric destroys the group's crops in a mad vendetta, kills Charles and convinces Roseanne to come with him to the city. Upon finding her husband's skeleton there, Roseanne wants to go back and soon discovers that Eric is dying from radiation poisoning. She turns back, only for her baby to die on the way. She arrives back at the house with Michael and quietly joins him in starting to replant crops.

They fought for
the Ultimate Prize!

THE
LAST
WOMAN
ON
EARTH

NEW
Eastman 52-50
COLOR
VISTASCOPE

Starring
ANTONY CARBONE / BETSY JONES-MORELAND / EDWARD WAIN

Produced and Directed by ROGER CORMAN
A FILMGROUP PRESENTATION

Roger Corman's *The Last Woman on Earth* (1960) is a prototype of how a domestic drama can be camouflaged with science fiction trappings to make it appeal to kids buying tickets at the theaters.   *Courtesy of Wrong Side of the Art*

As stated above, we have most of the general premise found in such movies as these all in one place—the ratio of men and women being an upset as to who dominates and gets the woman, the racial element, the subject of procreation to restart the human race, the insane member with a gun who wants to ruin it for everyone, and the one safe place for everyone to be until they can't stand being around each other and kill. One or more of these plot elements will appear in nearly all of the movies that follow in this subgenre. One of the best remembered of these is *The World, the Flesh and the Devil* (1959), which works as a better-written and condensed version of *Five*, with some elements of *Last Woman on Earth* sprinkled in as well. Harry Belafonte stars as Ralph, a coal inspector who becomes trapped in a cave-in (again, another lucky break) just as atomic weapons are used. He finds himself in a deserted New York City and comes across a white woman, Sarah (Inger Stevens), who eventually is understandably attracted to him (well, it's Harry Belafonte—who wouldn't be attracted to him?), but he pulls away because he cannot get past the racial prejudices of the time. The two find a third survivor, Ben (Mel Ferrer), who naturally assumes that Sarah is for him. Although they all try to work out their differences for a time, with Ralph trying to push Sarah and Ben together, Ben finally decides to take matters into his own hands and kill Ralph so Sarah will have no alternative but to turn to him. However, unlike *Five* and *Last Woman on Earth*, after chasing each other down, they realize that they cannot pull the trigger to end each other's life. At first, the two wander off, but Sarah brings them together, and in a rare positive ending in such a film, the three walk off hand in hand into the new world.

At least they have each other. In *The Noah* (shot in 1968 but not shown until 1975 and not released on video for decades), Daniel Bourla wrote and directed a movie where there is only one survivor left on the planet (at least, as far as he knows) after a nuclear war. Robert Strauss (who appeared in *Stalag 17* and *The Seven Year Itch* for Billy Wilder) plays a soldier who manages to drift to an island in the Pacific after a nuclear war and tries to keep himself busy. He eventually imagines a man to be his friend, then a woman, then children to teach in a new world. Unfortunately, in his madness, he can't accept the good and brings in the bad, leading to an imagined war that kills those in his thoughts and eventually a return to sanity as he comes to accept he really is the last man on Earth. With radiation finally catching up with him, he dresses up and waits to die with dignity. It's not a complete success as a film—it wanders around in various directions for too long before finally settling down to make a point—but Strauss (in his last role, and a rare dramatic one that didn't find him playing gangster #2) is strong, and the ending makes up for the earlier shortcomings. Still, one can see it is an experiment in filmmaking (it's a one-man art film, really), which allows us a little more leniency toward the bumps along the way.

A similar fate awaits the protagonist in *La città dell'ultima paura* (1975), which—much like *The Noah*—attempts an art-house presentation about the last man on Earth. In this case, it is a young man named Aldo (Emanuel Cannarsa), who is a talented artist but is used by his uncle to make money off of his gifts and has a brief affair with a woman named Eva (Marisa Solinas), who he knows he cannot have. Eventually he goes into a cave to take some photos when there is a nuclear attack on the surface, leaving him as the sole survivor. He stumbles through the bomb-torn city and into the desert, contemplating his life until he falls over dead of radiation poisoning. In both this and *The Noah*, the nuclear war is there to help propel stories about something else. In the case of *The Noah*, the film could have as easily taken place after a shipwreck with Strauss' character trying to hold on to his sanity (most of *Cast Away* with Tom Hanks talking to a volleyball could be taken in the same spirit). *La città dell'ultima paura* is more a metaphor of how the world can crush dreams and the endeavors of the artist, which could have been achieved by other means, but director Carlo Ausino found the extinction of the human race a better way to deal with his goal than other methods.

The same could be said for Andrei Tarkovsky's last film, *The Sacrifice* (1986). Tarkovsky (*Solaris, Stalker*) wrote and directed a story about an older man named Alexander who is celebrating his birthday with a number of friends and family, including his young son. In tribute to Ingmar Bergman (as well as typical for Tarkovsky), a lot of the film is taken up with characters discussing their relationships with each other and inner reflections before, during and after they receive reports about a nuclear war starting that will wipe out everyone. Alexander declares to God that he will give up everything he has—his life, his house, even his son, to stop the madness of the war, and with the help of a witch who works as a maid for him, he does this. Thus, he leaves his life behind in a scene that plays as awkward slapstick, but at least with the world and his young son safe. Although the film is considered a bit of a struggle to get through by even many fans of Tarkovsky (little happens until Alexander commences with his sacrifice), the ending makes the long haul before it rewarding and leaves the viewers with a somewhat happy resolution to the situation. Yet, as with the previous two films mentioned, the story could have been as easily told through other methods—Alexander is mainly concerned about his young son surviving, and any type of danger to the child could have produced the same results. Nevertheless, nuclear destruction made for an easy backdrop to the story being told, as in the two films listed prior to it.

Armageddon plays somewhat lesser roles in other art films, although—unlike *The Sacrifice, The Noah* and *La città dell'ultima paura*—the plots reverberate around or toward such an apocalyptic event. Wim Wenders (*Wings of Desire*) has a nuclear satellite out of control for a good portion of his 1991 film *Until the End of the World*, and it ultimately does create a global disaster by leading to an incident that wipes out most electronics in the world. Yet the film is never really about that incident as much as using it as a plot-point among many others—namely about a camera for blind people that becomes an addictive device that can record people's dreams. In fact, by the end of the film it is evident that the world has gotten back on track with no real concerns due to the disaster, so it's hardly an apocalyptic film. *It's All About Love* (2003), written and directed by Thomas

Vinterberg, showcases a variety of weird things happening around the world that demonstrate impending chaos (people flying, snow in the summer, water freezing when it shouldn't, clones running around, people dropping dead due to loneliness, etc.), but the film is looking more at the concept of how the lack of universal love is destroying the world, rather than offering any type of logical explanation for what is occurring (or resolution for that matter). Chris Marker's *La jetée* (1962) may be remembered more today for being the genesis of Terry Gilliam's *12 Monkeys* (1995, which is covered in a later chapter)—but it tells a story about time travel and fate that only needs the push of a postapocalyptic world to get it going. Could the same story have been told without the apocalyptic setup of the film? Quite possibly, but the device of such a catastrophe occurring makes for easy shorthand to the viewers as to what has happened and why the world they see on the screen appears as it does.

The attempt to get to the "human element" in the above films leads us back to the concept of people trapped in a box. The following four examples find characters stuck in a bomb shelter and—much like the characters stuck in the truck in *This Is Not a Test* (covered in an earlier chapter)—slowly losing their grip on their sanity and their civility. *Refuge of Fear* (aka *Creation of the Damned*) was released in 1974 and features five people locked in a bomb shelter as the bomb begin to drop. This includes a couple, Arthur (Fernando Hilbeck, *Let Sleeping Corpses Lie*) and Carol (Patty Shepard, *The Werewolf Versus the Vampire Woman*), and a family with a grown son, Margie (Teresa Gimpera, *The People Who Own the Dark*), Robert (Craig Hill) and Chris (Pedro Mari Sanchez). They make it to the shelter in time, but as they wait it out to see if the radiation level will go down, they all start to lose it. Arthur pops pills, Carol comes on to Chris, they eat the cat, the son wanders out into the radiation and dies, the husband commits suicide, the father kills the mother, tries to kill the other woman, who kills him instead and then—hey, the radiation is down and they can all leave. Oh. A little too late now, isn't it? Well, at least one of them can leave.

Flash-forward thirty-eight years and we have *The Divide*, directed by Xavier Gens and starring Michael Biehn (*The Terminator*) and Rosanna Arquette. Nine people make it into a bomb shelter of an apartment building before the door is sealed by the superintendent. Their boredom and reckless behavior is compounded by a group of soldiers who break down the door—allowing radiation to seep in—and steal a young daughter for experiments of some kind elsewhere in the building. Eventually, as in *Refuge of Fear*, one woman manages to make it outside, although in her case it appears that her chances of survival are remote from the looks of the destroyed cityscape.

Neither of these movies paints a very happy picture of those having to wait in the shelters constructed to allow people to live after the nuclear war. This would seem to set up the standard question seen in nuclear films—are the dead the lucky ones? However, in both of the above cases, it plays out more like traditional disaster movies, where the audience tries to figure out which member of the cast is going to make it to the end. *Refuge of Fear* at least attempts to give the ending some thought, with the film flashing back to a happier time for the five before the nuclear blast to show how people can rapidly change under stress, but *The Divide* seems most interested in carnage, even throwing in the troops and the experiment on children just to spice up the proceedings a bit more.

Two final "in a box" movies look at experiments in what people would do in such a situation. Oddly enough, both are from 1974 (as was *Refuge of Fear*) and feature a large cast of characters being shoved into a bomb shelter with information fed to them to make them believe a nuclear war is ongoing in order to see how they react. The first is *Le troisième cri* from Israeli director Igaal Niddam, which deals with ten people of varying professions being trapped when supposedly a nuclear war breaks out. To be honest, it's not a bad group of people to have with you—a military man, a doctor, a librarian, a radio technician, a dietician, two firefighters, a businessman and even two maids to help clean up. Over time, they wonder what is happening and suspect that something is fishy about the whole thing—the problem is who can they elect to go outside and make sure?

Chosen Survivors, directed by Sutton Roley and starring Jackie Cooper (*Superman: The Movie*) and Richard Jaeckel (*Day of the Animals*), features a group of ten people picked by the government to be drugged and sent into an underground shelter when war is imminent. As it turns out, it is just an experiment to see how people would do in such a situation, but there is a big problem in that the shelter was built into a cave system that is full of vampire bats. In particular, bats who can not only get in but attack in packs that can kill a person. Or several. The group tries to leave, but the button that will allow them to refuses to work. Eventually, after a couple of attempts to either stop the bat attacks or get to the surface fail, the military comes in and takes out everyone left alive and the movie ends.

Perhaps *Chosen Survivors* is a fitting end to the "trapped in a box" apocalyptic movie anyway. *The Divide* attempted to do it again in 2012, but the cycle had pretty much worn itself out by 1974, what with having to drag in aspects that appear to be playing off of the "killer rats" phenomenon that kicked in with the release of *Willard* in 1971 (and more about those types of movies in another chapter). Perhaps only so much dramatic tension can be created about people in a room. Even the producers of movies for Christians found limited interest in the topic, although such a concept would certainly seem to be in line with their endeavor; after all, as the old saying goes, "There are no atheists in fox-holes." Still the only big "Christian cinema" movie to play with the concept is *Six Hundred and Sixty-Six* (1972), featuring Joe Turkel (*The Shining*, *Blade Runner*) as a colonel stuck in an underground bunker with other military men with limited air and limited patience. By the end of the film, everyone has either murdered each other or committed suicide with the exception of the colonel, who finally discovers that the Day of Reckoning is at hand. That may seem like a bit much for a nuclear "trapped in a box" movie, but at least it's a better payoff than the "just an experiment" one of *Chosen Survivors*. Curiously enough, it does follow the trend of the previous films in that nearly everyone ends up going insane by the final reel. Even if it is supposed to be about the end-times.

Panic in the Year Zero! (1962) is a slightly different beast, but still heads down the same brutal road as the earlier films. The movie starts with a typical "nuclear family" of the era—Ray Milland, Jean Hagen, Frankie Avalon and Mary Mitchell—heading out with their trailer on a camping trip. After getting many miles away from Los Angeles, they see an atomic explosion in the direction of their home city. At first, they attempt to head back against the flow of traffic to find the wife's mother, but eventually decide their best efforts should be to turn back toward an area the father thinks will be safe for a time while the panic subsides and the authorities regroup.

Turning to all methods to buy, trade and steal supplies, the family manages to make it to their isolated spot, but instead of heading toward a nearby home or staying in their trailer, the father moves them to a cave. This turns out to be a good idea, as a gang of hooligans the family had run into earlier (which Frankie managed to scare off with a rifle blast) have taken over the house and killed the family there with the exception of a teenage daughter who they keep for their own amusements. The hooligans are finally killed, but Frankie gets hurt in one of the gunfights, and the family takes off again to find a doctor. Running into others at night, they fear the worst, but it turns out to be the military, who direct them to a place of safety, noting that they were one of the few that seemed to have gotten out of it alive and without radiation poisoning.

Panic in the Year Zero! has some of the standard observations about humanity as seen in the earlier films, but it is remarkable in portraying society at large easily starting to grab at each other's throats soon after the blast appears. Moreover, it rationalizes Milland's actions in attacking others to get things to help them survive (although he does pooh-pooh Frankie's enthusiasm after shooting at the punks they meet along the road). The one thing that may be troublesome about the movie is that Milland's character is 100 percent correct across the board on every action he takes. Nevertheless, in an era when the apocalypse was done with taste and dignity, *Panic in the Year Zero!* is a rare exception. It has Frankie Avalon shooting at people to survive, folks. Shooting at people! Not to mention the subtext of the girl found in the house (whose reasons for being there are explicitly explained in the movie trailer, although not in the film itself). It's strong stuff from an American studio in 1959 and shows that the "end" may be just the beginning of terrible things to come.

The End as . . . Oh, Look—a Monster! Argh!

So we've had a handful of movies that took the idea of a nuclear apocalypse, began to set up their stories as if they were to become domestic dramas and then finally gave up on that idea and threw in a monster. Of course, none of the writers or producers involved were sitting there saying, "I really hate to use the monster, but—" Their objective from the beginning was, "Okay, give me ten

Panic in the Year Zero! (1962)—all that needs to be said is, "It's Frankie Avalon with a rifle, people!"   *Courtesy of Wrong Side of the Art*

pages to establish the characters and then we'll give them the money shot of a monster and start bumping off everyone until the hero kills it." It's *Frankenstein* or *The Thing* with different window dressing on it. The point is the monster; the way it got there for the good guys to fight is beside the point. Nuclear radiation just made it easy to create a man-made monster, just as it made animals and insects grow super-big in a number of films over the years.

Nothing wrong with that—well, the science is screwy, but if we're talking about people being able to survive a nuclear attack because they just happen to be in a cabin in the woods, science is going to take a backseat anyway. Besides, you're trying to drag kids into the theaters, not critics wanting to contemplate the universe (plenty of other movies for that, as has already been seen). The downside is that you end up with a number of movies that can be considered postapocalyptic due to a nuclear disaster that use it mainly as a means to get to a new dystopian future world where our hero or heroes have to fight to make right. In some cases, the movies find something in the past to pull out into the present—as in the *Mad Max* car films discussed in a later chapter—but to many it's just a monsterfest.

Nevertheless, previous plot points established for other movies in this chapter stand firm here as well: the good guys and gals wanting to start a new world, the bad guy with a gun, radiation all around, cutting off escape. Plus, the added bonus of a monster, and there you have it: monster movies of the Atomic Age.

One of the first examples of the nuclear monster is featured in Roger Corman's 1956 movie *The Day the World Ended.* The setup is all right there: an older man and his attractive daughter (Paul Birch and Lori Nelson) living in a cabin in a valley that makes it a natural bomb shelter. Stumbling into the cabin are three other survivors—Rick (Richard Denning, *Target Earth*), the dashing young geologist, who is an expert on radiation; Tony (Mike "Touch" Connors, *Mannix*), a gangster set to kill the men and keep the women; and Roby (Adele Jergens), his girlfriend. As everyone worries about the next storm—which could bring radioactive rain with it, contaminating the area—and about Tony itching to use his gun, there's also a monster loose that will attack anything. It grabs Louise but eventually lets her go, and the creature turns out to be Louise's boyfriend (from before the apocalypse, when he still looked like Roger Corman). The rains come, killing the creature; the father pulls out a surprise gun he always had on him to shoot Tony when needed; and Rick and Louise venture out into the clean rain and their new world for "The Beginning." At least Corman didn't name them Adam and Eve.

The Day the World Ended would be remade in 1967 by Larry Buchanan under the title *In the Year 2889.* It takes place in 1977 (yep, 2889 has nothing to do with anything in the movie really) and is pretty much a photocopy in color of the original. Amazingly, Buchanan manages to make it look even cheaper than Corman did, setting the entire story in a house and its garden that make it look more like home-movie footage than a film. Even the monster is better in the original.

Speaking about "on the cheap," *Robot Monster* (1953), written and directed by Phil Tucker, is certainly remembered by most bad-movie enthusiasts for trying to give us the end of the world and a monster for a buck-ninety-five. The set is Los Angeles' Griffith Park, in particular Bronson Canyon, which also turned up in *The Day the World Ended* and . . . just about any other television show or movie that needed a cave over the years (the other opening of the cave is the Batcave from the old *Batman* television series, for example). The monster is actually an alien in this case, but it's really just a guy in an ape costume with a helmet on his head. He is one of the Ro-Mans (Ro-Men?) who has wiped out everyone on Earth but eight people who are immune to the death ray. Which means he can wipe out millions but has a problem getting little Johnny, who outwits him for much of the movie. To be fair, Ro-Man does eventually catch up with Johnny, but his delay is too late and his boss, the Great Guidance, steps in to finish off everyone with stock footage from other movies. Then it turns out to be all a dream that Johnny is having. Or is it? Yes, it is. Or is it? Maybe so. Or is it? Well, it's over, whatever it is.

All kidding aside, although *Robot Monster* could be seen as an alien invasion movie, it does still fall into the dramatic premise of films we're discussing here, with the exception of no evil guy or a guy who tries to take charge. Ro-Man is a combination of those two characters ("to be like the hu-mans . . .") and the monster in order to get the same plot-points across.

Two other films that use this premise are *Creepozoids* (1987) and *Parasite* (1982). Both have a nuclear event a few years in the past, but instead of concentrating on the typical *Mad Max*–like future, these two movies deal with characters fighting man-made monsters that are born out of the apocalypse. *Creepozoids* in some ways anticipates *Resident Evil*, with laboratory-created monsters lurking in the dark and taking out members of a group of army deserters in a postapocalyptic world. *Parasite* (an early role for Demi Moore and featuring rock singer Cherie Currie in a smaller role) is much more in the spirit of the killer-animal movies that will be discussed in a future chapter, with small creatures created in a lab after the apocalypse that get loose and start eating people. But the stories are bigger than that, with people trying to survive after the end of the world, only for the monsters to come and attack.

No doubt, the nuclear theme of such movies brings out the obvious—we worry about the monsters within ourselves. That are born of us, or perhaps always there but hidden away until the stress is too great. Who doesn't watch Richard Denning in *The Day the World Ended* and hope they can be the dashing hero while fearing that they'd probably and easily turn out to be the murdering, hysterical scum that is Mike Connors' character in the film? Or that one innocent mistake will create an even bigger problem for us after there is no one else to turn to?

The final film to be listed in this chapter is *The People Who Own the Dark*, directed by Leon Klimovsky (*The Werewolf Versus the Vampire Woman*) and starring genre star Paul Naschy, as well as Teresa Gimpera. This 1976 movie sets out in the early stages as almost an alternate universe to the party scene of *The End of the World* (discussed in chapter 2): we have the party of the rich and decadent as the world falls around them outside their castle (somewhat in the spirit of Roger Corman's *Masque of the Red Death*, which also features such a party in a castle that ends tragically for all involved). Because of their location, they survive, but they soon run across people in a small village nearby that are blind from the blast and have gone insane. In a variation of the blind dominating the seeing in *Day of the Triffids*, the blind here are intent on killing all those who still can see. The rich survivors are outnumbered and begin to panic, killing each other off as they try to escape. The two main protagonists do manage to make their way out and are picked up by a bus of soldiers at the end of the movie, but the contamination suits of the men should have been a giveaway, as the two are then killed and dumped into a mass grave. In the end, the enemy was always us and always there.

The 1960s had movie producers seeing that audience appetite was ready for films dealing with the Cold War's threatening preoccupation with someone dropping a bomb on Hooterville, U.S.A. We wanted to know what would happen, and that continued into the 1980s, especially after we had a president who reinforced the concept of stopping the "dirty commies" (although he didn't use that term). Then the Berlin Wall fell and the Soviet Union was no more. Suddenly there was no longer this boogeyman called the Russians to scare us, and the threat of a nuclear attack became more remote. In fact, it became a thing of fantasy. In 1984, we weep watching a child die from radiation fallout in *Testament* because it felt so real; ten years later, we're laughing over the antics of Arnold Schwarzenegger and Jamie Lee Curtis kissing in front of a mushroom cloud in *True Lies*.

With the demise of our fear of nuclear annihilation, other factors took over for our joyrides through terror when it came to the movies. Would it be global warming? Some type of religious phenomenon? Nature taking revenge? Aliens or machines taking over? Maybe even a contagion? The dramas and documentaries mentioned in this chapter dealt with a serious subject that somehow lost its punch with modern audiences as they searched for new, perhaps more thrilling ways to off the planet. After all, once you blow up something, there's not much to do after the fireworks but wait to die, as the films have shown us. That may be the numbing truth, but it hardly makes for popcorn sales at the theaters. Other options for Armageddon seemed livelier, and so Hollywood would quickly turn to other possibilities. One such example is a book dealing with a contagion that turns everyone into vampires that was published in the 1950s and led to various attempts to adapt the short novel into a movie in three different decades, and with varying levels of success, as seen in our next chapter.

8

I Am Legend . . . but Mostly to Readers

The Classic Richard Matheson Novel and Its Various Adaptations

"I don't know why Hollywood keeps coming back to the book just to not do it the way I wrote it."—Richard Matheson to John David Scoleri (*I Am Legend Archives*)

arlier I discussed several well-known and well-regarded novels that have never been adapted into movies. This chapter deals with the first of three novels that have fallen to the far opposite of those listed before—books that have become so iconic in apocalyptic fiction that they not only have been adapted to films many times over the years, but also have been used as springboard or had homage paid to them in several later movies and books. The three books under discussion are Richard Matheson's *I Am Legend*, H. G. Wells' *War of the Worlds* and Jack Finney's *Invasion of the Body Snatchers*.

Matheson's book, *I Am Legend*, is unique of the three, as it does not deal with an alien invasion. Nor, as in most fiction like this, is the cause man's own doing or alien forces. Typically, we get bombs going off, contagions accidentally released from the lab or other man-made catastrophes that lead to the end of the world. That's not quite the case with at least the novel the various *I Am Legend* movies have been based on. Although there are hints that mankind helped push a virus to mutate into something that "turns" everyone, Matheson never presses the point; in fact, he instead suggests what occurs was merely something that was bound to happen anyway.

Yet, as those who have seen the two later movies adapted from the novel know, that's really not the case in the films. Instead, mankind is the perpetrator; we are—as typical in apocalyptic fiction—the masters of our own demise. With this, the first drastic change occurs between Matheson's vision and the various adaptations. There would be many changes on top of that, most dependent on the time and social climate when the films were made.

The book has been the basis of three official adaptations—*The Last Man on Earth* (1964), *The Omega Man* (1971) and *I Am Legend* (2007)—as well as the loose foundation for *I Am Omega* (2007). It has also been an obvious blueprint for many other creative works over the years including Stephen King's *'Salem's Lot* (which he has freely admitted was sparked by the modern-day suburban landscape of Matheson's book) and George Romero's *Night of the Living Dead*, both of which will be discussed in detail in subsequent chapters. Specifically, the novel sets up a premise for apocalyptic fiction that would become a genre in itself, both in book and movie forms.

Before the release of *I Am Legend*, such apocalyptic stories gave the protagonist one of two courses of action when facing the end of the world. One was to stand witness to the destruction as a spectator/commentator (such as in *War of the Worlds* and *The Scarlet Plague*); the other course was to struggle to adapt to the crisis out of his control (such as in *When Worlds Collide* and *Earth Abides*). *I Am Legend* is different—it takes the ideal typically found in dystopian fiction of a protagonist fighting against society for a lost cause (such as in *1984* and *Brave New World*) and positions it as the hero's conflict with the apocalyptic world. The purpose of the protagonist was no longer to "watch the parade go by" but rather to stand up and take action to stop what appears to be the inevitable. After this, increasing number of works done in the end-of-the-world genre would use this conflict to the point that it is mostly the norm today (and certainly the designated plotline of most zombie movies done since *Dawn of the Dead*). *I Am Legend* really stands as a prototype of a subgenre within apocalyptic fiction: that of one man against all. Better yet, one *average* man struggling to make sense of his new world without understanding what has hit him. Other works before this would position a protagonist who has nearly superhuman abilities to fight against his fate or his ability to stand off to one side without fear of retribution (e.g., we know our protagonist in *War of the Worlds* can't die, as he is reporting his story after the fact in a first-person tome). *I Am Legend* is about a "Normal Joe" who, out of desperation, has to work out how to survive using common knowledge, luck and determination. Such a premise will be stretched and twisted over the years, but the core sense of loneliness, paranoia, and prevalence will stay the same in many works that came after it.

Even so, perhaps the most intriguing thing about *I Am Legend* is that all three official film adaptations are unique unto themselves thanks to the deviations they take from the original novel. Two even drop the concept of vampires—the lynchpin of the plot—to go with other forms of mutated life, while all three propel our hero into the mode of having foreknowledge of the cause as well as being the salvation of the crisis (two points not presented in the novel). Other variations from the book occur, but perhaps most poignantly, none of the movies deliver on the punch line of the book's title. As Matheson stated many times in interviews, somehow Hollywood keeps going back to this book, and every time they feel the need to change it from what attracted them to it in the first place.

To tell the whole story here, it is best to break down exactly what we as the audience got in the book and its many adaptations, and what was lost in the translations. Of course, the proper place to begin is with the original source itself.

I Am Legend (novel)

Background: The 1954 novel written by Richard Matheson. Published by Gold Medal Books, a paperback division of Fawcett Publications. 150 pages.

The Plot: The book begins in January 1976, months after a plague has turned everyone into what appear to be traditional blood-drinking vampires. As far as he knows, Robert Neville is the only man to have survived the plague, and he spends his time in mind-numbing routine: staking vampires in their hiding places during the day so they can't attack him and huddling inside his "vampire-proof" house at night (with mirrors, crosses and garlic dressed around the perimeter in order to keep the undead away). As the vampires, including his old friend and neighbor Ben Cortman, taunt him from outside, Neville forces back memories of his dead wife and daughter and concentrates on adjusting to his new world. Even so, a visit to his wife's resting place one day leads to a frantic drive back to his house as the sun sets and ends with his car totaled, his house damaged and Neville having a nervous breakdown.

Months later, Neville recovers and rebuilds. Now, instead of simply walking around stalking the vampires as he had been doing, he begins to focus his attention on the many unanswered questions he has about the vampires; mainly, why they behave so much like traditional vampires of lore. To do so, he digs into his memories of the recent past while also researching and experimenting to see what could be the cause and if there's a possible cure. Eventually, he discovers that bacteria carried in frequent dust storms before the outbreak, and possibly mutated through nuclear testing (the only suggestion that such a plague may have been man-made), led to the global plague. Mass hysteria then gave those struck by the plague traditional vampire characteristics, thus creating a combination of natural and psychological reasons for why the plague victims act as they do. In his research, he also discovers that there are two different types of victims: those who are already dead—and act more like traditional vampires—and those who are still alive but being slowly poisoned to death by the bacteria.

More than a year goes by, and Neville has adjusted somewhat to his circumstances, finding that his research and experiments with the vampire victims have given him a purpose in life. Still, disruptions to his routine come when he finds a wounded dog that he manages to befriend for a time before it dies, and later still—and more importantly—when he happens upon a woman walking in the daylight. Convincing the woman, Ruth, to come back to his house, Neville is hesitant to believe the story of her survival, yet he also worries that his years alone have made him overly suspicious. The two eventually begin to accept each other, only for Neville's concerns to get the better of him, and an attempt to take a blood sample leads to Ruth knocking him out and bolting from the house. In a letter left for him, Ruth admits that she has the plague; however, she and others like her have been able to hold it at bay with a drug (a pill) that keeps most of their vampiric tendencies dormant. She admits that she had been sent as a spy to locate Neville so he could be "brought to justice" by those whose family members had been killed by him over the past two years, but she now somewhat sympathizes with him and warns him to flee while he has the chance.

Six months later, a group of men arrives at night to take Neville away. He watches as the men chase down the vampires outside his home and kill them, feeling some remorse as he watches his old nightly nemesis Cortman destroyed. Neville knows that they are there to take him to be executed for killing the others and shoots wildly at the men. Nevertheless, he is subdued and taken away.

Ruth visits Neville in his prison cell, while others wait outside for his pending execution. He admits that he thought of running (and with a six-month head start, he knows he could have succeeded), yet in the end he could not bring himself to leave. After a brief discussion of the world to come—which Neville sees as even more vicious than the world they currently live in—Ruth leaves him with a packet of drugs so he can kill himself before the mob outside his cell can get to him. Slowly getting up to look out at those waiting for his execution, Neville sees some recoil in fear. In his final moments, he realizes that he has become to them exactly as the vampires had been for him. A thing of fear. A thing of legend.

What Is the Same/Unique? As cited in several sources, author Richard Matheson first came upon the idea for *I Am Legend* after seeing the movie *Dracula* as a child and wondering, "What if everyone in town was a vampire instead of just one man?" Working off this premise, Matheson created the novel by surrounding the text with things from his own life; picturing what he would strive to do if such a situation really did occur in the city of Gardena, California, in Los Angeles County, where he was living at the time. By doing so, Matheson created the textbook plotting for zombie movies of the 1970s and beyond: the lone survivors fighting against monsters that were once their friends and neighbors in familiar surroundings. Such a scenario of paranoia is also reminiscent of *Invasion of the Body Snatchers*—both show our hero being unsure of whom he can trust in a horror-house version of his "everyday world"—but such plot developments only come into play in Matheson's novel with the final chapters' introduction of Ruth. Neville's struggle up to that point is more fundamental—he knows everyone is out to get him and has no reason to believe otherwise. It is this element that seems to have drawn movie producers and studios to the work the most over the years, and it's just about the only universal element found in all three official movie adaptations. One man against all . . . for a time; then, a possibility of relief; only to find hope leading directly to death in the end.

The book opens as a mystery. We the readers see Neville puttering around his house and performing rather odd chores, but it is only midway through the first chapter that we see that he is facing a danger outside of his home at night, and only later do we discover that these people outside his house act like traditional vampires. While brief flashbacks to his life before the plague pepper the early chapters, it is not until midway through the novel that we get a better understanding of what happened to him at the time of the plague and learn details of the death of his young daughter and his wife. Further, it is with these segments of the book that we discover along with Neville that, unless destroyed, the supposed dead will come back to life as predatory creatures. This becomes the preferred method of monster-making for zombie movies from *Night of the Living Dead* onward: death leads everyone—not just bad people, but all—into becoming all-evil entities that must be destroyed. In some way, it may seem that Matheson was predicting this way of creating zombies in the movies to come— the dead become our monsters—but it goes right back to traditional vampire lore, in which people can only become vampires once they have "died."

While the basic framework of the novel will stay in place for the various movie adaptations, it is interesting to see major elements of it that never or rarely made their way into the films. The most important difference is right up front—the novel deals with vampires in a very traditional sense: they can't stand garlic, don't like water or mirrors, have to sleep during the day and only come out at night, searching for blood. There is even a sexual tension related to the vampires: many of the women outside of Neville's home try to pose in seductive ways in hopes of driving him out to them, a running theme in the novel that surprisingly never made it into any of the movies even though it has been a common thread in vampire films since the days of Lugosi's *Dracula.* The only vampire element that really comes into play with all the official adaptations is the creatures avoiding sunlight. *The Last Man on Earth* comes closest to using the undead of the novel, and even refers to them as vampires while also giving Vincent Price stakes to use against them. Yet, even with all that, the film treats the undead more like zombies (and typically as the same slow-moving, grunting monsters banging at windows with sticks as George Romero would later use in his *Living Dead* films) who only, conveniently so, can come out at night. Both *The Omega Man* and *I Am Legend* do not even go as far as making those who have the plague "undead." They're just victims changed into other types of creatures who can't stand the daylight. Because of this, Matheson's focus on how vampire traditions and history could actually have a basis in reality, which runs throughout the book, never comes into play in the various movies.

Yet even in the novel Matheson doesn't play by the rules. Traditionally in vampire stories, a group of vampires behave much like a pack of wolves—working toward a common goal to catch food, only to defer to the leader of the pack, waiting for their chance to get to the remains of the fresh game. Such discrimination is due to what the vampires naturally want to survive—fresh blood, which they cannot get from each other—and it is such a logical step in the narrative that they are that way, it is not necessary to explain to the readers. Further, being a Day-One Vampire was the same as someone who had done it for years; once a member of the club, you were a member in good standing, as it were. This is not the case with Matheson's vampires; they willingly prey on each other, with the author emphasizing moments where Neville has to deal with the remains of vampire victims of the mob outside of his home the next day. As we discover later in the novel, this makes sense; some of these so-called vampires are actually still alive, and thus it is only logical for those that have died and become *true* vampires to see others as food rather than fellow monsters waiting for a snack. We eventually see the reverse of this later in the book, when the vampire/humans come to capture Neville and happily take part in slaughtering the vampires staggering around outside his home (leading to a rather ironic moment for Neville when they destroy his longtime vampire nemesis Ben Cortman and Neville feels sadness for his demise). Thanks to the drugs, the new world order may fear Neville, but they hate what they *could* become just as readily. Perhaps even more so.

Thus, Matheson throws out the textbook example of how vampires should react with their own kind and instead shows them as hating, attacking and killing each other just as much as someone like Neville. Strangely, only *The Last Man on Earth* bothers to tackle this theme from the book, and only briefly in the final few minutes of the film (we see Price picking up bodies early on, but there is nothing to assume this is due to the victims attacking each other). Neither *The Omega Man* nor *I Am Legend* bothers to go down this path of examining this caste system within the vampire order created by the plague. In a way, that is understandable for what amounts to action movies about monsters trying to get at our lone hero. To throw the social/political subtext of Matheson's book into the mix at the conclusion of such films would slam the brakes for audiences looking for normal resolutions to the good guy/bad guy conflict of the stories. We want action and resolutions, not insights into the social order of monsters in the new world. As with the zombie movies to come, it is easier and safer to make the monsters a type of natural force that sweeps in and kills, because then the filmmakers can "get on with the chase," keep the monsters mindless and not worry about trying to build them as characters in their own right.

Another interesting aspect of the vampires from Matheson's world is how few of those outside of Neville's home demonstrate the ability to reason, with "fresh" vampires showing at least some potential for intellectual response instead of just moaning and groaning. This is certainly different in a literary sense from vampires of lore, who commonly are able to act "normal" enough to blend in with humans, or even noble, like Dracula and the various vampires of many novelists. Only Ben is shown as one of the *true* vampires that manages to keep some type of awareness around him, mostly though nightly tormenting Neville with taunts and keeping one step ahead of Neville during the day by changing his place of sleep. In fact, one could argue that Ben's actions are not only for self-preservation, but also to keep some part of his human side alive by concentrating on getting the last man alive. In a way, this makes his later death at the hands of the vampire/humans even more sad and a touch ironic, as he is probably closer to them than they would believe.

True, both *The Omega Man* and *I Am Legend* make the "vampires" more intelligent than the zombie-like monsters of the book and first movie. *The Omega Man* goes so far as to make the victims more of an insane religious cult than monsters, while *I Am Legend*'s creatures are the only ones out of the three films to come up with a successful trap for Neville. Yet in the end they can't be portrayed as too intelligent, or else viewers would ask the obvious question—if they know where Neville lives and hang around there every night (as in *The Last Man on Earth* and *The Omega Man*), why don't they just torch the place and be done with it? It's a logic problem that hits all the films and has to be dealt with in various ways, with only *I Am Legend* marginally succeeding (*The Last Man on Earth* has our protagonist stating that it is due to the victims not being able to think straight enough to do so, which is still better than such actions discussed but overruled for phony-baloney reasons in *The Omega Man*).

One element that does make it into all the adaptations is the resolution finding our hero dying at the hands of those he had been fighting (surprisingly, Matheson does not do so in the script he wrote for Hammer based on the book, but more about that in the *Last Man on Earth* section further on). What is different in the book, however, is that Neville does so without having accomplished anything to resolve the problem he set out to explore. The book finds Neville understanding what causes the plague, but then comes to the (perhaps incorrect) conclusion that there's no way to change people back from vampires into humans. When Ruth asks if such a way is possible, Neville dismisses it, stating that his experiments showed him that nothing could fight the plague once it entered a person's system (and we discover that he is possibly wrong, as Ruth comes from a group that has found a way to fight the plague, although not conquer it). All three movies allow Neville the opportunity to "win" in a sense, even as he dies, for his work leads to a way to destroy the plague (*The Last Man on Earth* and *The Omega Man* both do so with transfusions between Neville and another character, which can lead to more transfusions with others and eventually spreading out the antidote little by little; *I Am Legend* does so with the protagonist coming up with an antidote that is handed off to others to use). He gains a victory even in death, which is simply not there in the book. His death is merely that of a passing fable, a man of myth that hurt those who now ruled.

This brings up two topics in the book that are not really dealt with in the films, both of which relate to Neville's experimentations. Each of the films has Neville somehow involved in trying to create an antidote to the plague before the destruction of mankind. *The Last Man on Earth* shows Price working in the lab (with old buddy Ben) to come up with a solution; *The Omega Man* shows Heston as a military bigwig who ends up using an experimental vaccine on himself during the onslaught of the plague; *I Am Legend* combines the two earlier films to give us Smith as a military bigwig who is also a scientist working on a cure. This is not the case in the novel. In fact, it is never quite explained what Neville does for a living, or even if he works with Ben (he is seen getting a ride to work with him at one point, but nothing more). This is one area where the films actually improve on the book, as it certainly makes more sense for someone who actively knows something about the plague to be able to come up with a conclusive deduction as to what is causing it. We could give Neville in the novel a pass in some sense because of how much free time he has available to find a solution, but it makes more sense that a person trained to deal with the plague and continuing to experiment on it would have a more logical chance at success than the Neville of the book. Then again, the one major criticism made of the book since its release is that Matheson may know how to write a tense story, but he's not very good about his science, with explanations that really don't hold together. No wonder Neville can't come up with an antidote. Even in his "Night Creatures" script, Matheson has Neville find the bacteria causing the plague by accidentally knocking over things in his lab—a terrible monster-movie cliché when it comes to resolutions to a crisis—thus showing that Matheson had his heart in the right place but not the background to really come up with a good resolution to the science involved.

More shockingly, although Neville never comes up with a solution in the book, he does seem to be quite interested in continuing his experimentations on unwilling subjects, resulting in their demises. All the films make mention of Neville using victims of the plague in his experiments, with *I Am Legend*'s Smith being the most obvious about it. In the case of Price and Heston, however, they seemingly give up after a time, while Smith has major reservations about what he is doing. The Neville of the book isn't like that, especially after he reaches the point of understanding what causes the plague to work. Notably, he actively looks forward to his experiments on others to see if he can revert them. Late in the book—when it is clear he understands that there is a difference between vampires who are dead and those who are alive but slowly becoming vampires— he confides to Ruth that he is fine with experimenting on the living anyway. To him, it's either death while finding a cure or death by the plague, which will then turn them into vampires, so he feels he is doing them a favor. Of course, as we discover along with Neville, he was actively killing people who had found a way to control the plague (Ruth's husband being one of them), thus leading him to a realization that perhaps he should die for being the monster they see him. Little by little, Neville in the book becomes the monster he thought he was fighting, and he knows it in the end. This is certainly not in the films, as all experimentation is for a "greater good" and Neville never gets any comfort from his failures as Neville in the book does.

Which brings us to the final element of the book that makes no appearance in the films—the title. It is the last line in the book, and it conveys the irony of Neville's position. Readers' sympathy toward Neville's experiments and random killing of others through the book excuses them as for the "greater good." Neville is our hero; we root for him to survive the vampires, hunt them down and find a cure. Yet, over the course of events shown in the book, and especially with the introduction of Ruth, it is clear why those from the outside looking in would see Neville as a monster that attacks their kind during the day, killing them when they're at their most vulnerable. He realizes at that point he has become like the vampire of lore and will be remembered as a boogeyman in the years to come. He truly has become legend.

Yet in the strangest bit of change from the book to the movies, none of the films keeps this ultimate punch line of the novel, and only one keeps the title of the book. Even so, Smith's *I Am Legend* tries to shoehorn in the title in such a ham-fisted manner that it appears to be an afterthought, with a voice-over narrative that makes Neville out to be the Albert Schweitzer of the horror age. Meanwhile, *Last Man on Earth* makes no claim to the title beyond a one-time mention in a piece of dialogue, and although we even get Heston dying in a Christ-on-the-cross position, there is nothing said or made clear that he has become a legend of any sort, and certainly not the one of evil and darkness as portrayed in the book. Ultimately, the very thing that the book is about is thrown out because the results in a movie would be too dark, leaving us with movies that only fleetingly look like the book they were based on.

Nevertheless, the adaptations came. Although there was one attempt that fell through before any finally made it to the screen.

The Last Man on Earth (1964)

Background: An Associated Producers, Inc. presentation. Filmed in 1963 in Rome, Italy. Released March 1964 through American International Pictures. Written by William F. Leicester from an original script by Richard Matheson (credited as Logan Swanson in the film). Italian prints have the script written by Furio M. Monetti and Ubaldo B. Ragona, with no mention of Leicester or Swanson. Directed by Ubaldo Ragona (Italian version) and Sidney Salkow (English version). Starring Vincent Price as Robert Morgan; Giacomo Rossi-Stuart as Ben Cortman; Emma Danieli as Virginia Morgan; Franca Bettoia as Ruth Collins.

The Plot: It is September 1968, three years after the plague has either killed everyone or turned them into zombie-like vampires. Robert Morgan is a scientist who had worked on finding a cure for the plague with others, including his best friend and neighbor, Ben Cortman. Now he goes through the day trying not to think of his past as he wanders the city, staking the plague victims and hiding out in his home at night from Ben and others who wait outside.

After falling asleep visiting the tomb of his wife in a cemetery, Morgan rushes home and manages to get inside the house, pushing back the slow, stalking vampires outside who reach into the partially open door at him. Watching old home movies of his wife and daughter, Morgan becomes emotionally upset, as the film turns to a flashback of his happy life from before the plague.

A series of flashbacks fall much in line with those of the book, only with some additional background to show that Morgan is a scientist who was working on the problem at a lab (the Mercer Institute of Chemical Research) with Cortman. Cortman is the first to suggest—rightly—that the plague is airborne and that it is turning people into vampires, but Morgan dismisses such hysteria until too late. After seeing his young daughter's body being carted away in a truck to be burned, Morgan refuses to do the same to his wife when she dies and buries her instead, only for her revived corpse to arrive at the house, calling to him.

Returning to the present, Morgan wakes the next morning to see a dog outside his house that is still alive. While frantically looking for the dog, he

Although usually dismissed by fans of the novel, Vincent Price's *The Last Man on Earth* (1964) comes the closest to realizing Matheson's *I Am Legend*.

Courtesy of Vintage Cinema Ads

discovers a number of vampires staked to the ground with iron spears, suggesting to him that others may still be alive. Morgan feels hopeful when the dog returns to the house, but after cleaning the dog up, he realizes it has the plague. The scene cuts to another day (it's not clear if it is the next day or a few days later), with Morgan burying the staked dog in a park. As he finishes, he sees a young woman approaching, who he chases down when she begins to run. Noting that the sun would be down soon, Morgan convinces the woman, Ruth, to come back to his house.

At the house, Morgan suspects Ruth has the plague, but Ruth assures him that her gagging due to the garlic he shoves at her is just due to a weak stomach and nerves. It is here that Morgan admits he's not sure why he has survived (he sarcastically suggests it was because he was "chosen"), but mentions a theory that it may have been due to being bitten by a plague-ridden bat in Panama years before, gaining him immunity. Later, Morgan finds Ruth about to inject herself with a vaccine (unlike the pills of the book) that keeps the plague at bay, but in a tussle between the two, they accidentally break the glass syringe. Ruth admits that there are others like her and that it is her mission to see if Morgan knows anything more about the plague than they do. Morgan assumes that Ruth's people want him to join them; however, she informs him that they want him destroyed because he is a monster to them—"a legend," as she states, that goes around by day killing men, women and children who give outward signs of the plague but are not vampires. Morgan is horrified to think that he may have been killing the living instead of the revived dead.

Ruth tells him men from her group are coming that night to get him. She pulls a gun on him to keep him there, only to pass out from lack of the vaccine. To save her, Morgan gives her a blood transfusion, which cures her of the plague. Morgan suggests that the two of them will be able to save the others so they do not need to use the vaccine any longer. While Morgan goes to set up his microscope in order to prove Ruth is no longer infected, Ben manages to break into the house and drag the still weak Ruth away. Morgan goes outside to pull Ben away from Ruth, just as a squad arrives and begins staking all the vampires by the house. Ruth convinces Morgan to run, as the squad refuses to hear her pleas to stop. Avoiding the squad for a time, Morgan is shot while entering a church. Climbing up to the altar, Morgan is then speared as he calls those present "freaks" and says that he is a man. With his head cradled by Ruth, Morgan repeatedly mumbles in horror, "They were afraid of me," and then dies.

With the immunity now in her blood, Ruth walks away from Morgan's body and comforts a crying baby held by a mother from Ruth's group, telling the child that there is nothing to cry about, as they are now all safe. Ruth walks out of the church as the others stare at the legend now dead.

What Is the Same/Unique? After the release of *I Am Legend* in paperback, Richard Matheson was approached by Anthony Hinds of Hammer Film Production in England to adapt the book into a script. In many ways at the time, Hammer's interest in the book makes a certain amount of logical sense. The company was just coming off great success with their first color horror film, *The Curse of Frankenstein*, in early 1957 and felt that future adult-oriented fantastical horror films were a goldmine for the company. Meanwhile, Matheson was not only a name in both horror and science fiction, but had also just seen his script adaptation of another of his novels, *The Shrinking Man* (filmed as *The Incredible Shrinking Man*), released to much success in the spring of 1957. Further, Hammer had been making a certain number of low-budget action-thrillers sold as second features on the American market for some time, mainly through the assistance of producer Robert Lippert, who insisted films use a known American actor in the lead to beef up potential sales in the U.S. marketplace. Rumors of Val Guest (*The Day the Earth Caught Fire*, discussed later in this book) directing seemed logical as well, as Guest did many film projects for Hammer during this period (*The Quatermass Xperiment*, aka *The Creeping Unknown*; *Quatermass 2*, aka *Enemy from Space*; and *The Abominable Snowman*—all of which featured American leads frontlining a British cast and connected to Lippert). Everything seemed to be in place for the project to happen.

Yet it didn't, and the main reason may have been thanks to Hammer's newfound fame. The company had already had run-ins with the British Board of Film Censors (the BBFC) with their earlier films, but had pretty much blown the doors off the hinges when *The Curse of Frankenstein* completed filming with most of the BBFC's suggestions on the script ignored. Now the agency began looking at Hammer's ascent (or descent, depending on which side of the fence you were on) into horror films with intense interest. Compounding the issue was Matheson's script (entitled "Night Creatures"), which, with Matheson still fresh to scriptwriting and knowing that British filmmaking usually allowed a tad more freedom than the American studios, featured cursing and dramatic, violent action. The BBFC returned the script with a number of suggestions in order to make a movie that would be passable by the board but that Hammer felt gutted the film of its intensity. A similar review by the Motion Picture Association of America (MPAA) garnered pretty much the same results. With the requested changes considered too extensive, Hammer decided to pass on making the film.

Matheson stated in several interviews over the years that he at first found it difficult to fathom why the censoring issues would be the sole reason for cancellation of the project. This actually is somewhat understandable once one reads the MPAA two-page report on the script (reprinted in *Visions Deferred*, a book reproducing "Night Creatures" along with two other unfilmed screenplays by Matheson), as the changes requested seem head-scratchingly simple to fix. Nine of the eighteen suggestions made by the MPAA to get the script passable had to do with coarse language (a few damns, hells and bastards sprinkled through the script); the remainder were warnings on how some scenes should be shot in order to avoid overt gruesomeness, as well as what appears to be Ruth and Morgan cohabiting for some time. Yet reading the script itself makes it more evident why the violence probably pulled the studio and certainly the censors away from it. As with the book, Matheson focuses the middle section of the script on Neville (the name of the protagonist in the "Night Creatures" script) and his "experiments" with various vampires to find out what makes them tick. On the printed page, with Matheson's writing to support Neville's point of view, it reads as logical, even clinical (the more to support the later horror of what he was doing to those still alive). However, in the visual medium of film such scenes make Neville look like a sadistic lunatic (especially with the sight of whimpering candidates for his research unable to get away from him). Further, staking would be shown on camera, blood would have been prevalent on-screen and the subplot of Neville's dog ends with Cortman not only breaking its neck but also grinningly holding up the dead dog by the neck like a trophy for Neville to see. And all this in a recognizable suburban landscape gone mad in shocking blood-soaked color. In comparison, Hammer's next project, *Horror of Dracula*, would have violence, blood and stakings as well but presented off camera and within the context of a fantasy-land-like previous era (much like *Curse of Frankenstein* and a majority of their horror films to come in the '60s and '70s). With a choice to fight to make "Night Creatures" or to go with a proven horror character like Dracula, Hammer may have felt some relief in being able to use the censors' comments as a means to drop out.

As hinted at above, the script for "Night Creatures" follows the plot of the novel closely, although it adds a bit more for Ben Cortman to do, as well as the genesis of Kathy's birthday party seen in Morgan's flashback in *The Last Man on Earth*. In fact, Cortman has a much expanded role in the script—first as Neville's friend who begins to get more hysterical as the plague spreads and later as Neville's nemesis outside his house (and, as with the killing of Neville's dog, much more calculating and vicious than in the book . . . or in any of the later adaptations), rounding out his character much more than in any of the films made. Yet, while fans would have been happy to see a movie that looks like the novel, one opposing problem with the script is that it sticks *too close* to the book, especially in the area of Neville's long research into the probable cause of the plague. Not just because of the violence of the scenes, but also because they are repetitive and only reinforce a point already accepted by the audience. Viewers coming into the film would know from the opening scenes that everyone is now a vampire because of a plague and that Neville is defenseless to stop it. Thus, there's no suspense in watching Neville reiterating that fact over and over again for half the picture. Nor are the scenes with Neville and Ruth discussing such matters gripping in any way.

What is the most interesting in Matheson's "Night Creatures" script is the somewhat happy ending. Instead of the book's climactic arrival of troops from Ruth's people who fight with Neville until they capture him for execution, the script has the troops asking Neville to help them study his immunities and see if they can be passed on to others in their group. Considering all three of the movie adaptations kill off the Neville character in the end, it is surprising to see that Matheson himself wrote his original script to have the character survive.

On reflection, Matheson admitted in interviews that this came about due to his wanting to please those he was working with on the script and readily making the change when asked, more than him thinking it was a great twist to the story.

Even with the positive ending, everyone passed on the script as is, although Hammer associate Robert Lippert saw potential. Buying the property from Hammer, Lippert went to Matheson with the idea of working up a new script to be filmed with Fritz Lang directing and possibly with Jack Palance—an actor Matheson enthusiastically saw as the best for the role—as Neville. Furthermore, Lippert was working through Twentieth Century-Fox with his company Associated Producers Incorporated at the time, so the promise of a major release (even as a B picture coupled with an A picture from Twentieth Century-Fox, as was the norm for API) was there on a platter. A second script was prepared by Matheson of which little is known, beyond the author mentioning that he had gone back to the ending in the novel for the new script. Passed on to Lippert, Matheson was later disappointed to find out that the company had decided to shoot the picture in Italy with Vincent Price in the lead and Sidney Salkow directing. Salkow had just come off *Twice-Told Tales* with Price, and the critical review had been tepid at best, which no doubt did little to enthuse Matheson. Speaking of which, as an American-Italian coproduction, a second director is listed in the credits, Ubaldo Ragona, who is also listed as coscreenwriter with Furio M. Monetti, dropping William F. Leicester and Logan Swanson from the credits. Yet a comparison of the two versions of the film (released in Italy as *L'ultimo uomo della terra*) shows no differences in staging, camera movements or plot, which suggests that Ragona was there mainly to help the Italian cast and most probably rewrote the script's dialogue to suit their purposes as well. In all probability, the majority of the directing is by Salkow, who does a perfectly fine job getting the cast to work with the material, helped in part by the stark camera work of Franco Delli Colli showing the empty city.

The cast, if one forgives the dubbing given to them in the American version, certainly isn't as bad as some reviews have made them out to be over the years, with only the girl, Christi Courtland, playing the daughter going over-the-top (but no doubt it wasn't an easy task for a little girl to suddenly play blind for about thirty seconds of screen-time). Franca Bettoia is quite good as Ruth, which is vital to the overall tone of the last segment, while Giacomo Rossi-Stuart does what he can with the role of Ben Cortman (Rossi-Stuart is one of the better-known actors in the film, having starred in such genre material as *Caltiki—The Immortal Monster, Kill, Baby, Kill* and *The Night Evelyn Came Out of the Grave*). Even Emma Danieli, in the rather nothing role of Virginia Morgan, is allowed the chance to get into monster makeup and play the undead when the wife comes back from the grave.

Most important, of course, is Vincent Price in the title role. Examination of his acting job in the film has been hampered a tad by comments Matheson made over the years that he didn't feel Price was right for the movie. However, it has already been stated that Matheson had an image of Neville for such a film and—since the character is admittedly patterned after Matheson himself—that vision was of a true, fighting-man lead. For example, the discussion of Jack Palance in the role was one that enticed Matheson because he saw Palance being this heroic image of himself. With that in mind, while Price could play determined, driven men in his films, the term "macho" is not one commonly association with the actor. Even so, there's nothing in the novel or the various scripts that makes Neville out to be that type of action-man; furthermore, the story works better if Neville is as common as they come—an average Joe who stumbles upon his path as the "last man on Earth" due to sheer fate. That type of role Price could pull off, and he does remarkably well with a script that is mainly monologue and internal dialogue for two-thirds of the film. One needs to look no further than the scene of Price's character having a breakdown while watching home movies of his forgotten past life to see an actor really digging into a character and giving him depths where he has no choice but to visualize it. The only times Price falters at all, in my opinion, come once he finally gets to interact with other actors near the end of the film. His defiance toward Ruth and certainly his howls at the troop as he stands at the altar with a spear in his chest come off as stagey and take away from an otherwise fine performance. Nevertheless, Price comes closest to what Neville was in the book—a guy way out of his league who becomes a legend to others due to the world around him rather than his own actions.

Matheson's disagreement with Price's casting may have more to do with the surroundings of the making of the film anyway. Not only was the location changed to Rome instead of something more like the suburban location of his novel and his script; not only was the lead changed from a rugged he-man actor like Palance to Price; not only was the selection of a director a disappointment—there was also what happened to his script. After refining the "Night Creatures" script back into a closer adaptation of his novel, Matheson discovered another writer, William F. Leicester, had been brought in to refine it for Lippert. Leicester was known at the time and later in his career for his writing on television westerns, and his changes to the script led to Matheson wanting his name off the screen credits (for financial reasons he instead used his professional pseudonym, Logan Swanson).

It is Leicester's revised script that would become *The Last Man on Earth*, and with it came changes from the book in more than just a different title. The most obvious is that of Neville's name being changed to Robert Morgan in order to make the character sound more Middle America. One interesting development is Morgan's job before the plague, never described in any detail in the novel and briefly mentioned as that of a plant worker in the "Night Creatures" script. In the revised *Last Man on Earth*, however, Morgan is a scientist working on a cure for the plague. To some fans, this seemed to be missing the point of Neville not really understanding what is happening around him and slowly building his knowledge. Yet with the middle section of the script gutted, making him a scientist studying the plague before it wiped out everyone else resolves his later ability to do something about it when he has a chance and explains the scientific equipment in his house when verifying Ruth's (admittedly quick) recovery from the plague. Saying that, it doesn't explain why Morgan hadn't thought about such a resolution before on any of the previous vampires he had run into or perhaps trying to look for a cure through his own immunity—something even Neville at least discusses in some detail in the novel. Even so, intriguingly, the two subsequent adaptations follow the lead of *The Last Man on Earth* by making their Neville character a scientist and/or authority figure who has professional foreknowledge of the plague before trying to find some remedy for it. On the flip side of that, although he is a scientist, *The Last Man on Earth* loses the middle section of the novel dealing with Neville's many experiments—a loss in the script that reverberates in *The Omega Man*, although Smith's film of *I Am Legend* works the premise back into its script.

One element that many have touched upon, including Vincent Price in subsequent interviews about the project over the years, is the location filming in Rome. As Price told a crowd of fans at the *Fangoria Weekend of Horror* convention in 1990, "The problem was that it was supposed to be set in Los Angeles, and if there's a city in the world that doesn't look like Los Angeles, it's Rome!" For this comment and for fans of the novel who came to view the setting as a sleeping suburb in the Los Angeles area, the Rome setting in *The Last Man on Earth* seems not only contrary but inept. Price's words are true—the Rome of 1963 certainly did not look like Los Angeles in that year. However, there is a glaring problem with this criticism—nothing in the script ever states that this *is* Los Angeles. Additionally, the setting is roughly five years in the future, and thus for the landscape to look somewhat alien to viewers is quite closer to what they would have expected than seeing, say, Andy Hardy's street from the Hollywood backlot. In a strange new world that Neville/Morgan inhabits, to see a locale that "looks" similar to how we expect it to be but not quite "right" makes for a richer look to the action in the film.

With the loss of the middle of the book, the film instead focuses on the more dramatic set pieces of the novel: Neville's panic-run back to his house after visiting his wife's tomb, the flashback to the death of his daughter and wife, the dog, Ruth's arrival and the subsequent appearance of the squad to deal with him. While the violence has been toned down (no shouts of "bastards" and Morgan firing a gun indiscriminately into the crowd of vampires, for example), the main thrust of the plot is the same as in the book. Over the years, Matheson admitted that this Price vehicle—for all its warts and issues—is the adaptation that came closest to being like his book, as the ones that followed veered further and further away from the original, in particular the second film, *The Omega Man*.

The Omega Man (1971)

Background: A Warner Bros. production. Filmed in 1970–1971 in Los Angeles, California. Released August 1971. Written by John William Corrington and Joyce

H. Corrington (with dialogue rewrites from an uncredited William Peter Blatty). Directed by Boris Sagal. Starring Charlton Heston as Robert Neville; Anthony Zerbe as Brother Matthias; Rosalind Cash as Lisa; Paul Koslo as Dutch; Eric Laneuville as Richie; Lincoln Kilpatrick as Zachary.

The Plot: It is 1977, two years after a plague has killed most of society and left just a few infected stragglers alive. Colonel Robert Neville appears cruising in a fancy car through the deserted streets of L.A., only to momentarily stop to shoot at a caped figure in one of the skyscrapers with a machine-gun. After wrecking one car, he drives a new one out through the plate-glass window of a car dealership and then stops to watch scenes from *Woodstock* in an empty theater, mumbling along with the words. He leaves to find that the sun is going down and rushes to his car, only to halt in his tracks when he hears a ringing phone. He panics, undecided which payphone nearby to go to, before convincing himself that the phone is not ringing.

Caught in a fiery ambush when he reaches the apartment building he is living in, he kills several of the men in black robes waiting there. He soon closes up the building and flicks on powerful lights to the outside (forcing more robed figures away). As he makes his way up to an apartment at the top of the building, he flashes briefly back to what cause his present situation. A war between the Soviets and China led to germ warfare and finally a man-made plague that begins to wipe out most of civilization. Working for the military as a scientist, Neville jumps onto a waiting helicopter with a test vaccine, only for the pilot and him to be stuck by the quick-acting plague while in-flight. The helicopter crashes and, dying of the plague, Neville injects himself with the test vaccine, curing himself but eliminating the chances of recreating the vaccine in the process.

Although it is never mentioned in the film, it is evident that not all those infected die instantly; some are instead turned into lesion-riddled albinos who cannot stand sunlight or bright lights, and it is these that attack Neville at the building. Those infected in this manner have banded together under the name of the Family, led by a former newscaster, Jonathan Matthias, now known simply as Brother Matthias. Matthias sees Neville as their nemesis, mainly because Neville is a product of the world that brought the

The Omega Man (1971) was one of several attempts to bring Richard Matheson's classic novel *I Am Legend* (1954) to the big screen, only to jettison various parts of the plot along the way.

end to humanity (although it is never quite clear if they know he was directly involved with the military or trying to find a cure). The Family is intent on ridding the world of everything connected to civilization, burning books and art as well as destroying any advanced technology they can find. It is for this reason that Matthias has convinced the others not to attack Neville's apartment building with anything stronger than fire and spears (as well as a catapult they've found), as he believes all are crutches that will lead them back to the ways of the world they want to leave behind.

After a night of dealing with the mob outside his building, Neville spends the next day clearing out areas of the city of the infected, while wondering where Matthias and his followers stay during the day. A search of a hotel turns up one of Matthias' Family members dead, and Neville notes that it is not the first time he's found one that way. A turn in a department store leads to the discovery of an uninfected woman, Lisa. He pursues but loses her and assumes that he may have just imagined her.

Stopping off in a restaurant for a drink, he ventures into the wine cellar, where the Family attacks him and takes him to a mock trial in front of Brother Matthias. Sentenced to death by the Family, Neville is taken to a stadium for burning in a pile of debris from the past. In a daring rescue, Lisa and an apparently uninfected man called Dutch help Neville escape and take him to a group of young people who haven't turned yet. Dutch, a former medical student who has read about Neville's work in germ warfare in various journals, states that they are not sure why the children seem resistant to the plague, but some of them are showing signs of light-sensitivity, and Lisa's brother Richie is definitely turning, which is why the group helped Neville escape, hoping that Neville can help Richie.

Neville believes his blood may be a serum that could reverse the process, yet he needs to go back to his home with Richie in order to do the experiments. Neville mentions that he tried once to recreate the vaccine and give it to one of Matthias' people, but nothing worked; later, Lisa mentions that she and Richie were once part of the Family but left them when it became clear that the Family only wanted members who had turned. With Richie in recovery, and after a brief firefight with Matthias' second-in-command Zachary, Lisa and Neville get intimate.

Seeing that a serum is now possible and having one batch ready, Neville suggests that they collect Dutch and the kids and head away from the city and the Family (who Neville notes are slowly dying off from the plague anyway). Neville, however, wants to create one more batch before they leave, and with Richie still recovering, Lisa goes out "shopping" for their departure.

Neville tells the rapidly recovering Richie that anyone can turn at any time, so best to have more serum on hand. Richie believes the serum can also cure the Family and wants to take it to them, but Neville believes they are "half-dead" already and thinks the risk is too great to even try to approach them with the cure. Richie, knowing where the Family is located due to his previous association with them, ventures out of the apartment to see them when Neville drives out to let Dutch know about the serum's success and the plan to leave the area. Matthias, however, ignores Richie's pleas, assuming that Richie's visit is a trap for the Family. Instead, the Family set Richie up as bait for Neville, who arrives too late to save him.

Neville goes back to his apartment to find that Lisa has turned, bringing the Family with her to destroy the place and kill him. Neville escapes with the serum and Lisa, but Lisa is drawn back to the apartment by Matthias' voice. Matthias spears Neville in the chest just as the sun begins to rise, and the Family disperses, pleased with the idea that they have finally killed Neville. Lisa stays by Neville's side as the sun rises.

Neville manages to stay alive long enough to give Dutch the serum when he arrives with the kids. Slumping down in a fountain, arms outstretched, Neville dies, as Dutch gathers up the turned Lisa and they head off to start mankind over somewhere else, leaving the Family to slowly die.

What Is the Same/Unique? March 1957: Charlton Heston is working on the film *Touch of Evil* with Orson Welles when Welles mentions that he has just read a science fiction novel about the end of the world. At the end of the month, Welles hands a copy of the book to Heston to read, and the two discuss the possibilities of making a film out of it. However, the two eventually head off in other directions with other projects. Thus, the adaptation of *Earth Abides* never occurs.

So why the mention of *Earth Abides* here in a chapter about *I Am Legend*? Because rumors persisted for years that the novel handed off to Heston by Welles was Matheson's. It turns out that much of this confusion came about from an article by Marilyn Beck in 1971 (reproduced in part on the Orson Welles website www.wellesnet.com [www.wellesnet.com/?p=196#more-196]) that mistakenly ties in the *Earth Abides* history between Heston and Welles with the *Omega Man* film, which was then in postproduction. A glance at the article readily shows something was up: Beck mentions delays due to the only book they could find with the novel's title as a "1,400-page anthropological text" (which would certainly make the title *Earth Abides* more logical than *I Am Legend*, at least unless the author of the tome wanted to impress everyone with having written a 1,400-page anthropological text). Of course, both books deal with one man's perspective on fighting to stay alive after a plague wipes out most of the human race, yet the two are vastly different in scope and presentation. *Earth Abides* is a study of the changes mankind would face in the decades after a pandemic, while *I Am Legend* is an action-adventure novel set in a world of vampires.

Not that *The Omega Man* ever got around to mentioning vampires. But more about that in a moment; first, a look at how the movie came about. Charlton Heston's book *The Actor's Life: Journals 1956–1976* gives a chronological background on the trials of getting the movie running and completed, with a first mention of the project coming in November 1969 as he discusses it with producer Walter Mirisch, with a possibility of Sam Peckinpah as the director.

The project then moves to Warner Bros. with Peckinpah still as a possibility. In January 1970, Heston begins work on an outline for the movie to show how he sees the film's story just as those involved find out about the earlier Vincent Price film. A showing of *The Last Man on Earth* makes everyone feel better about their chances, however, and Heston would go on to say that he found that film to be "soporific," "sloppily written" and "ill-acted."

February 1970 saw John William Corrington and his wife, Joyce, brought in to work on the script after Heston had read some stories from the husband that he felt could make him a good possibility for the script. Meanwhile, Heston was also looking at getting a script called *Killer Kane* kick-started somewhere, as well as one based on a book called *Make Room, Make Room* (which Heston finally got made a short time later as *Soylent Green*, and which will be discussed a bit later in this book). By August, the studio was nearly set to go with the production, but wanted the dialogue punched up a bit; meanwhile, the production team began looking for a director, as Peckinpah was not a possibility. Christopher Miles, director of such quirky British films as *The Maids* and *Priest of Love*, was considered before television director Boris Sagal was brought on board. Meanwhile, Heston went to bat to get Anthony Zerbe hired for the second lead of Matthias after the studio hedges, while Rosalind Cash got the role of Lisa over Diahann Carroll.

Mid-November 1970 saw the production of the film begin with problems starting very early on between the director and cinematographer Russell Metty (who had filmed *Touch of Evil* with Heston and Welles, among a large volume of movies from the 1920s onward). Still, shooting was completed by the middle of January 1971, and the film was released in August of that year. In the end, Heston would reflect on the movie (at least in his diaries) as being not as good as he had hoped, later commenting that his subsequent film *Skyjacked*, in which he had little involvement beyond acting in it, made more in a month than *The Omega Man* did in a year's time. His opinion would reverse a bit as the film found an audience on video and DVD, overlooking the fact that many enjoy it for its over-the-top, campy nature rather than the chills and thrills he had expected for it. The presentation of the film can only be described as early 1970s, with a flat television look (not necessarily the fault of Sagal, as it was a style to be found in many studio films of the 1970s) and odd lapses of undercranked film that speeds up the action (take note of the jerky movement of Heston as he first grabs the machine gun very early in the picture, as well as the attack on his apartment at the end). The actors do a good job with what they have to work with—some claim Zerbe is overripe, but with the dialogue he is given, there is not much he can do to avoid it—but Heston has moments where he doesn't quite seem to be acting in the same movie as everyone else, with his earlier scenes on his own working better than those once he has to interact. Regrettably, his love scene with Cash seems stilted and forced, merely to throw in such a scene rather than advancing the movie (besides throwing off the obvious character balances, in that Lisa probably would find Dutch of more interest to bed down with than

Neville). Perhaps the biggest offense for viewers is the unsatisfactory ending: Matthias kills Neville and the Family rejoices in what they've done, with no retribution to come to them. Sure, we're told that they'll all die soon enough from the plague, but after such obvious "twirling mustache" clichés given to Matthias and the Family, one wishes there was some on-screen response to the death of Neville instead of everyone merely moving on with their lives. There is also the infamous "Christ at Crucifixion" pose for Neville at the end that drives the point home of Neville as savior to the world past the breaking point. In the end, it is clear that the reason for the film's existence is not to tell the story of Robert Neville of *I Am Legend,* but rather as a macho fantasy of how Charlton Heston will still get to go to bed with a beautiful woman even after the apocalypse and save the human race in the process.

This certainly makes reluctant sense. Heston was a prime mover in bringing the book back to the screen, mainly based on wanting to make an action picture that involved being the "last man on Earth." As it turns out, that may have been about the only thing that really drew him to the project in the first place. As reported by Mark Phillips in *Flimfax* #91 (October 2002), coscriptwriter Joyce Corrington remembered seeing a copy of the Vincent Price film but could not recall ever seeing the original novel on which they were basing *The Omega Man.* Instead, Joyce and her husband, John William Corrington, used Heston's outline and his suggestions along with their own thoughts about how they felt they could make the story plausible in the modern days of 1970. Because of the wide latitude given to them (and no doubt the production team as a whole), the film only vaguely resembles the novel and mainly in five ways:

1. A plague wipes out nearly everyone.
2. Robert Neville is the name of our hero, and he is immune to the plague.
3. He stays in his fortified home at night, because bad people with the plague want to kill him.
4. He hunts them down during the day because they want to kill him.
5. He is hopeful things will change once he meets a woman who is out in daylight, but she turns out to be infected and leads him to his death.

Everything else is pretty much another story.

Sensing changing times, one of the first things the production team felt needed to be revamped was the plague turning everyone into vampires. In the age of man on the moon, technology getting smaller and the general public becoming more aware of science being able to explain much more—not to mention with horror films at a low ebb in theaters—it seemed to not be fitting for a science fiction film of the sort Heston wanted to make to suddenly dip into the supernatural. The public in 1970 were no longer afraid of vampires; what they were afraid of were hippies and cults—especially after the recent arrest of Charles Manson and his "family" in the Helter Skelter murders of 1969. Thus, a cult of infested, half-crazed albinos that blindly follow their long-haired leader (he even bears a mark on his forehead in much the same way Manson had an

"X" carved into his skin at the time of his trial) replaces the ramshackle group of vampires from the book and first film. There are, of course, Dutch and Lisa to represent the youth of the day, but Dutch clearly states he was a college student looking to get involved in biochemical research for the war effort and would readily kill someone who has "turned," while Lisa is eventually corrupted by the Family. Dutch is saved because he is part of the establishment; Lisa isn't and therefore momentarily becomes the enemy, just as parents feared their own loved ones would turn on them in the new decade dawning.

With the elimination of the vampires also came the dismissal of one of the book's most important revelations—Neville's experiments on victims he assumed were dead vampires instead of actually being a mix of the dead and living. Thus, we only see Neville referring to one tried experiment with a member of the Family, and even that is presented as him trying to save the victim, not simply experimenting as with rats for a greater cause down the road somewhere. In doing so, Neville's guilt is eliminated from the plot.

Losing the motivation of those trying to kill Neville, since the plague victims were not vampires searching for "lunch" (or the vampire-humans of Ruth's group who feared Neville), meant the reason for those with the plague gunning for Neville had to be drastically altered. Instead, the Family is a fanatical group that suffers from dementia due to the plague and is spellbound by their leader, Brother Matthias, a former newscaster (back at a time where the "most trusted voice in America" was that of Walter Cronkite, the newsreader on the *CBS Nightly News*). Matthias' goal is the eradication of the modern past that had led them to the destructive near end of mankind (although they still believe in mass-produced robes and really groovy sunglasses). Such a plan also includes the death of Neville, which evidently has led to a nightly ritual of the Family doing little more than shaking their fists at Neville, while Neville picks them off with his "advanced weaponry."

It is suggested by some reviewers that Matthias knows Neville was a part of the problem in the first place—Neville obviously was working with the military, which was connected in some ways with the germ warfare that led to the plague killing most of them. Yet that is never evident in the film itself. Matthias makes mention of Neville being a doctor and a soldier, but he never states (nor seems to care) that Neville was involved with the very plague that killed everyone (in fact, he's dismissive that Neville could possibly come up with a cure later in the film, even though Neville is obviously immune). All Matthias sees is a thing from their past, as well as a man who is clever enough to keep them at bay *and* kill them off one by one over time. So Neville's conflict with the plague victims is strictly a game of cat and mouse, with none of the subtle undercurrent of the novel and the first film that we can sometimes become the thing we fear the most.

Also lost in translation is any emotional evidence of Neville's past. We learn he was involved in studying the plague, which allows him all the scientific and medical study needed for the second half of the film, and that he is still living in the apartment he had before the plague, but that's it. Unlike the other two adaptations, gone are any mentions of a family or a wife (or even any romantic relationships before the plague). This Neville is one that is emotionally unattached to anything but his apartment for reasons that only amount to stubbornness in light of the Family wanting to drive him out and kill him. Sadly, this also extends to his relationship with the Cortman surrogate of the film, Matthias. Although we have scenes with the two, they appear to know each other only from a distance. There is no personal history there, and certainly they are not the odd "soul mates" of the novel: Neville knows Matthias from television; Matthias knows Neville as the immune guy down the block. Nothing more. Because of this, there is no richness to their joint scenes that would have come out of having established them at least knowing each other and discussing the plague in much the same way as in the novel and Price film (a scene or two of Matthias interviewing the "military expert" for the nightly news could have set up such a conflict easily enough). Such scenes do at least provide a brief echo of the novel it was based on, however. After the mock trial, Neville complains to Matthias that the Family has been trying to kill him for two years, while Matthias casually mentions that Neville has killed off a number of the Family just within the past day and certainly many before that. "You're the Angel of Death, doctor, not us," Matthias points out, giving us a fleeting glimpse into the "Neville as monster" seen in the other films and the novel. Instead, we get at least one scene of a child seeing Neville as God (and another filmed but jettisoned of a child offering a gift in prayer to their "god"). Neville of *The Omega Man* isn't the mistaken man of the past—he has no past—he's an infallible all-mighty being.

The elimination of Neville's past, beyond a brief flashback that shows him injecting himself with the test vaccine, also affects the structure of the story— some of which doesn't make much narrative sense. Neville's delay back to his home is no longer due to spending too long at the tomb of his wife but because he's sitting in a darkened theater watching *Woodstock*. (Which brings up the point that a *dark* theater is hardly the place to hang out when being attacked by people who thrive in the dark, but the movie is naturally bright, so maybe that's Neville's excuse. Still, you would think he would keep better track of the time if he knows the movie well enough to recite passages of it.) Neville isn't immune for reasons he doesn't understand—as in the book—but because he injected himself with a vaccine; yet he is never shown trying to alert others that the test vaccine worked. (Things must have really been bad in those last few days of the plague if he couldn't do so.) The Family is intelligent enough to know exactly where Neville lives and have tools to easily get him out or even lock him out of the house, and Zachary even addresses the illogic of their actions to Matthias at one point. Yet Matthias' response that using more modern methods would just set them back on a path to the "bad old days" is merely an excuse by the scriptwriters to avoid an obvious plot hole. So using, say, fire to burn the place down would be too "advanced"? One nearly expects Matthias to say, "Use weapons? No, that would be too easy." Even the Price movie has a better excuse—that the vampires are too far gone to do the obvious as a means to get to him—while the Smith film makes it clear that Neville is in hiding and the creatures after him have no clue as to where he is located until a couple of vital mistakes lead them to him.

Two of the oddest jumps in the story happen early on and detour *The Omega Man* into a different direction from the other films and the book. The first is the elimination of Neville's isolation and despair at his fate. The first five minutes of the film wrap this up, with Neville denying the ringing of the payphones. After that, we get clear knowledge that the Family isn't merely zombies or vampires but a working number of half-crazed people who don't like Neville, which means he is just a lone cowboy against a vast tribe of Indians in the Future West. By the half-hour mark, we are introduced to Lisa, and, soon after, Dutch and the kids (who look like lost Brady kids or as if they walked out of the "Miri" episode of the original *Star Trek* series). Neville may have been on his own, but there is little evidence he was ever alone. The other—and more abrupt—jump is Neville being captured a third of the way through the picture when the character does not face such a fight for his life until the final pages of the novel and the last ten minutes of the other two films. Essentially, this amounts to the audience getting the ending of *I Am Legend* early on: Neville being put to death for his crimes against those he has fought, with the final hour being the macho fantasy of Heston saving kiddies, shooting bad guys and cracking wise with Matthias.

Such wisecracking leads to an interesting side note about the movie. For the most part the production team was happy with the script that the Corringtons had put together. As reported in Matthew R. Bradley's book *Richard Matheson on Screen: A History of the Filmed Works* (McFarland), Joyce Corrington had a PhD in chemistry and "was teaching at a black university at the time and this was the '70s, and Black Power was very big." Thus, Corrington could write about the germ-warfare aspects of the plague and toss in some two-dollar words to make things sound like Neville and Dutch knew what they were talking about, plus work in the biracial love story that would have still seemed very edgy for a general audience in 1971. However, this was only the second produced script by the husband-wife team, and it had been pushed back by the studio as lacking in good dialogue (Heston in his diaries agreed this was a problem with the script as well). Hoping that a punch-up in dialogue might do the trick, the production team brought in William Peter Blatty to work over the script. Blatty was an established scriptwriter who up to that point had worked on comedies (*Shot in the Dark, Promise Her Anything*, among others) and had written a script based on his 1966 novel *Twinkle, Twinkle, Killer Kane* that Heston has seen and tried to get a studio behind (it would eventually be made in 1980 under the title of *The Ninth Configuration* without Heston's participation). Blatty, still a time away from the success that would come with the release of his 1971 novel *The Exorcist*, was happy to have a paying writing job. The results—Blatty trying to throw some humor into the story—did not particularly make some of the people on the production team happy (nor the Corringtons once Blatty requested his name be added to the credits for what they saw as merely "adding a few lines of dialogue"). Still, the changes were used, and it's strikingly evident where they appear in the script as Neville suddenly becomes a loose, fancy-free smart-ass at times when one would think he would be the most sedate. Certainly, the mock trial and subsequent scene with Matthias and Neville show Blatty's contributions, with Matthias playing straight man to Neville's quips ("Are you fellows really with the Internal Revenue Service?")—an aspect that seems out of line with the rest of the film.

Yet in light of the action heroes of the 1980s and onward, especially the films of Schwarzenegger, Stallone and Willis, it seems like an early prototype of what was to come. Of course, there were action heroes before Heston's turn as Neville who used quips—Bond was certainly a big contender—but most made silly puns related to the action at hand and usually after the danger. Here we have Heston about to be put to death and telling the villain that he is "full of crap" and soon after letting loose with the IRS gag. The evidence points to Blatty being responsible for this unique characteristic of Neville, and such cynical, sarcastic humor will reverberate in the films to come later from other actors who looked up to Heston. It is certain that one reason Schwarzenegger was tied to the later *I Am Legend* remake for years was due to his wanting to play the role Heston had. Which leads us to the final film adaptation to date.

But before that, two last notes about *The Omega Man*. Even if the film itself isn't that good, it does have the best tagline of the three films: "The last man alive . . . is not alone!" (*I Am Legend* would adapt the tagline for its movie poster.) On the other hand, in the first twenty seconds of the movie, which shows Neville driving down the deserted streets of L.A. to demonstrate that he is all alone in the world, a white car can be seen driving around in the distance. Must have been Dutch heading to the department store to look for a shirt to wear.

I Am Omega (2007)

Background: The Asylum presentation. Filmed 2007 in Los Angeles, California. Released November 2007 through the Asylum. Written by Geoff Meed. Directed by Griff Furst. Starring Mark Dacascos as Renchard; Jennifer Lee Wiggins as Brianna; Geoff Meed as Vincent; Ryan Lloyd as Mikey.

The Plot: Renchard is stranded in Los Angeles after a plague has turned everyone into crazed cannibals with festering sores. Renchard has kept himself safe, but flashbacks to a happier life before the plague and his constant use of prescription medication to keep on his toes are starting to get the better of him. In a mad moment, he decides to end it all by placing a series of time bombs around the city in hopes of killing off those with the plague.

He is finally contacted by another survivor, Brianna, who is trying to locate a safe haven called Antioch. Renchard brushes her off and she disappears, just as two men arrive—Mikey and Vincent—who are looking for the woman, as she appears to be immune to the plague. Renchard is forced to help them find her, losing Mikey in the process and with Vincent showing himself to be insane. Vincent leaves Renchard for dead as he takes off with Brianna in order to rape and then kill her, as he is satisfied with the world as it is. Renchard chases Vincent down, saves Brianna, and drives her out of the city just as the time bombs go off, killing all those with the plague.

I Am Omega (2007) was a "mockbuster" attempt to play off Will Smith's *I Am Legend* remake, but does have a couple of good moments in it, even if it plays more like a zombie movie.

What Is the Same/Unique? The same? Well, there's the "I" and the "Am," and you've got "Omega" there from the Heston film. Unique? Just about everything else.

The movie needs perspective of where it came from, and I should cover it here, as this will come up again when we get to *War of the Worlds* and *Invasion of the Body Snatchers*. The Asylum is a film studio that is mainly interested in making one type of picture that can be referred to as a homage, a rip-off, a drafting opportunity or even—as those in charge of the Asylum state themselves—a mockbuster. What they produce is something that has been around since the early days of cinema: if a movie is a blockbuster, studios might be able to get ticket buyers back in the door (or, in this case, buying DVDs) if a similar movie with a similar name is released. For example, after *The Exorcist* came out, there were several movies released that tried to look like *The Exorcist* even if they weren't anything like it (e.g., Mario Bava's afterlife movie *Lisa and the Devil* was released in America as *The House of Exorcism*, with additional scenes featuring Robert Alda as a priest doing an exorcism of Elke Sommer). *Jaws* saw rip-offs like *Great White* hit the screen soon after its success, *Star Wars* with the rather entertaining *Battle Beyond the Stars* and the coulda-been-better *Starcrash*. The idea is to give people something similar for their money, and if by chance some get confused about the titles sounding similar, hopefully they'll enjoy the movies anyway.

The Asylum started in the late 1990s putting out a couple of films but really hit its mark when they released their first mockbuster (a term usually attributed to *New York Post* writer Lou Lumenick), a version of *War of the Worlds* in 2005 that was to coast on the success of Steven Spielberg's version of the same story. There was no turning back after that, with the Asylum producing movie after movie that kinda sorta looked like another movie but not quite, such as *Snakes on a Train, Transmorphers, The Day the Earth Stopped* and—of course—*I Am Omega*.

One positive thing that can be said is that, after the premise has been set up for each of these films, they tend to go their own ways, with stories and plots that periodically make them worth the trouble of tracking down. If not that, at least being so off-the-wall from expectations that they're worth a look just for laughs (like shoving a lesbian scene into their *Transformers* mockbuster). In the case of *I Am Omega*, the movie reflects very little of earlier attempts to make Matheson's novel, and certainly nothing of his book is there either. We have one man fighting against creatures after a plague, but it turns out there's a lot of other people still around, he himself is not the cure (Brianna is), and the creatures are just a variation on zombies instead of anything like those from the book or film adaptations. The main character isn't even named the same as the one in the novel, and he manages to survive (which Smith's version nearly did as well, but more on that in a moment). If the name of the film had not been similar to two others, there wouldn't really be any similarities at all, and it would just be seen as another in the vast number of zombies movies made over the years.

On the other hand, it's not a failure as a postapocalyptic movie; certainly not in comparison to other movies with a similar theme. Mark Dacascos is solid as the lead, playing a role that teeters between trying to stay focused in reality and letting his drug intake and personal issues get the better of him. That in itself makes for an interesting character side of the lead in such a film, and the concept of our hero deciding to blow up everything and then having to race against a clock he created for himself works pretty well. The material with Brianna and the two men looking for her derails the film a bit, but overall it's a decent little movie for one that was simply intended to be nothing more than a mockbuster to coincide with the release of Will Smith's version of the story.

Speaking of which . . .

I Am Legend (2007)

Background: A Warner Bros. production. Filmed in 2006–2007 in Los Angeles, California, and New York City. Released December 14, 2007. Written by Mark Protosevich and Akiva Goldsman, based on the script for *The Omega Man* by John William Corrington and Joyce Corrington and *I Am Legend* by Richard Matheson. Directed by Francis Lawrence. Starring Will Smith as Robert Neville; Salli Richardson as Zoe; Willow Smith as Marley; Alice Braga as Anna; Charlie Tahan as Ethan.

The Plot: The movie begins with a television clip from 2009 (two years in the future from when the movie was released) of a Dr. Alice Krippin on a news program discussing an amazing new vaccine to eliminate cancer. The process involves reengineering the common measles virus so that it kills cancer instead. The clip ends on a high note with all 10,009 test subjects being cancer free and the future looking bright for the human race.

The film jumps to "present day," September 2012, three years later. The scene is Manhattan, with the city overrun by vegetation and flooding. A lone car races through the deserted streets, much like in *The Omega Man*, only this Dr. Robert Neville is hunting game from his car with his dog, Sam, by his side. Stopping to go after a deer on foot, Neville stops in his tracks when a lioness kills the deer instead. In frustration, he points the rifle at the lioness and is ready to fire when a lion and their cubs step forward to gather around the deer. Neville walks away.

The early evening is spent with Neville in a relaxed mood as he goes back to his townhouse and fixes dinner for himself and Sam, then washes the dog. However, an alarm on his watch soon reminds him of his situation; after clearing his mind of memories of the past, he boards up the house and hides in the bathtub with Sam. Through a series of flashbacks that kick in at this point and are inserted through the rest of the movie, the audience learns that Neville was working with the military to find a cure for the plague. With the plague having gone airborne and New York quarantined, Neville initiates getting his wife Zoe and young daughter Marley (played by Smith's real-life daughter, Willow) out of the city before it is too late. Although his wife pleads with him to go with them, he insists on staying, as he is determined to "save everyone," and loads them onto a helicopter to leave the city. Marley hands her father their puppy Samantha to keep him company and shows him a trick she can do with her hands to make a butterfly as Neville steps back from the craft. Unfortunately, as the helicopter takes off to send his wife and daughter to safety, a malfunctioning helicopter nearby slams into it, killing all onboard.

In the present, Neville is shown going through his daily ritual of a workout and then a trip to his basement lab to see how a number of rats are responding to the various serums he has created to counteract the plague. One rat appears to be responding well, and Neville is hopeful as he heads out to complete his testing by finding a human subject. A stop at a video store shows that Neville has tried to deal with his lack of human contact by setting up mannequins around the store so he can talk to them as if in normal conversation. He plays at being attracted to one mannequin in particular but then holds off on the fantasy and heads back out. Neville then sweeps through a building, marking it off his map, to find supplies; and at noon each day, he arrives at a dock on the South Street Seaport (the same area where he last saw his wife and daughter alive) to wait for any other survivors to turn up after announcing such intentions on all AM frequencies.

A search for more game leads to Sam entering a darkened building and Neville following, ready to shoot. The search finds him running into a huddled group of survivors of the plague that are animalistic, power creatures who attack. Neville manages to escape them by jumping out a window with one of the mutants, with the plague victim burning to death in the rays of the sun. Setting a trap, Neville captures one of the female mutants, only to discover a male roaring at him at the entrance of the building, briefly exposing himself to sunlight. Neville assumes it is merely a sign that the victims are regressing to a point where survival instincts no longer are functional, however. He takes the female mutant back to his lab, but the test vaccine nearly kills her, and, after reviving her, he reports his disappointment in a video diary. While relating that dogs still appear to be immune to the airborne strains, he mentions that although he is immune to both "the airborne and contact strains" of the virus, he still cannot figure out a way to pass on the immunity to the victims.

Another day finds Neville and Sam going about their normal routine up to the point where he sees one of the mannequins from the video store out in the streets. The sight disturbs him, and he has a short breakdown before trying to figure out how the mannequin got there. Investigating the area, Neville falls into a trap very similar to the one he had set up for the female mutant. He manages to escape, only to see one of the dogs that has the plague attacking Sam and biting her. Neville tries to save Sam with one of the vaccines, but it doesn't work, and he ends up having to kill her.

With his last link to his previous life gone, Neville is an emotional wreck and sets out at night to the dock in order to take out as many of the mutants as he can before they kill him. They nearly succeed in doing so when someone arrives with bright lights to send off the mutants and take Neville back to his house. This turns out to be Anna and Ethan, a woman and a young boy. Both are the only survivors of a group of five who were on their way to a supposed safety zone in Vermont when they heard Neville's radio broadcast. Neville at first has difficulty adjusting to the sudden appearance of two other uninfected individuals, even though it means there are others besides himself who have immunities to the plague.

In the basement, Anna sees Neville working on the female mutant again and then sees the number of photos on the wall that represent all his earlier failed tests on human subjects. Anna suggests he leave with them tomorrow to go to Vermont, but Neville refuses to leave his home and give up his determination to "still fix this thing." As they continue to argue while setting up the house for the night, they become aware that the mutants have been able to track them to the house and are attacking.

Booby traps take out many of the mutants attacking, but a few get through, including the one that had nearly come out into the sunlight the previous day and who appears to be a leader of the group. Neville manages to get Anna and Ethan down to the basement lab, with the mutants in pursuit. Ironically, as the mutants ceaselessly pound on the glass barrier between them and the trio, Neville discovers that the vaccine he gave the female mutant is actually working. With a cure so near, he tries to halt the mutants, but it is obvious they will not stop until they get through. Sending Anna and Ethan out through a coal hatch along with a sample of the cured female mutant's blood, Neville then decides that his work is done now that a cure has been found. He pulls out a grenade from a desk drawer and, running toward the lead mutant on the other side of the glass, sets off the grenade, killing himself and the mutants.

Anna and Ethan are shown the next day driving to Vermont. They arrive at the safety zone and are happy to discover that it exists and is running properly. They give the blood to a leader there as Anna states in a voice-over that Neville had given his life to find a cure and that those who survived were his legacy. "He is legend," she says.

What Is the Same/Unique? In the '60s we still feared the dark and vampires. In the '70s, we feared the youth of the day and cults. In the 2000s, we feared science. Rumors had traveled for years by those with reasons of their own that discredit vaccinations for children and adults based on the assumption that "the cure is worse than the disease." The swine flu vaccine crisis of 1976 pretty much kicked things off, and even though it turned out to be media hype and nothing to do with the vaccine itself, the public was already starting to turn to distrust. Even with the support of a majority of scientists that readily could prove such falsehoods, it wasn't for many years that urban legends about vaccines causing

ADD and other issues were put to rest (and even then, many people still do not trust the science to get vaccinations, putting theirs and other children at risk over a fallacy). All of that, in a nutshell, is at the jumping-off point of the 2007 version of *I Am Legend*. What better way to show the fallacy of science than to have a doctor proudly inform us at the beginning that we are saved only for it to be the unleashing of a worldwide, man-made epidemic? Then compound that position by having the one doctor left only finding the cure after someone tells him that he has to have faith and everything is part of God's plan, as if his years of work had little to do with it?

But in the end, it's still a better and closer translation of the *I Am Legend* novel than what came before it . . . and what had been planned in the years leading up to its release. After the Heston film came and went, there was not much talk about another adaptation for years. Matheson remarked (in an interview with Paul Sammon in *Midnight Graffiti* #7 [Fall 1992] mentioned in Bradley's book *Richard Matheson on Screen: A History of the Filmed Works*) that producer Dan Curtis had tried to get the rights from Warner to make his own version of the novel years after the Heston film, but Warner saw there may still be life left in the vehicle and refused to negotiate a deal. Curtis, who had helped create the vampire/horror soap opera *Dark Shadows, Kolchak: The Night Stalker* and the well-remembered telefilm based on three of Matheson's short stories, *Trilogy of Terror*, would have been an excellent choice for such a movie, but it simply was not to be.

Instead, the first true evidence that another adaptation was possible sank the hearts of many who were hopeful for a more faithful version when in 1997 the announcement came that Arnold Schwarzenegger was to star in a new version, with Ridley Scott directing. Not that having Scott on board was unsettling, but at a time when Schwarzenegger was winding down his movie career and his films were becoming more and more like live-action cartoons with wisecracking ultra-man character shooting bad guys left and right, fans pretty much assumed the results would be *The Omega Man* times a hundred. As it turns out, Warner was a bit unsure as well. Both Scott and Schwarzenegger were known for films costing millions more than most projects, and the combination of the two would mean a good chance that a final budget could be out of sight. Which is exactly what happened. A projected cost of over $100 million stalled the project, and even when cuts were made to bring it down a few million, Warner finally decided to shutter the project for the time being. The next few years saw various directors and actors being tied to it (Michael Bay, Rob Bowman, Guillermo del Toro, Nicolas Cage, Kurt Russell, and even Will Smith once before coming back to it a few years later), before it was finally settled with Francis Lawrence signing on as the director and with Will Smith as the star.

The script—as one would expect when starting as a Schwarzenegger project—went through various changes over the years as a variety of writers worked on it. From artful to full-fledged, gun-blazing action, and finally back to a more thoughtful approach, the script started under the guidance of Mark Protosevich and additional material from producer Akiva Goldsman. From information that came out after the movie, it is clear that the few scattered moments that are similar to *The Omega Man* came from Goldsman's input, although this was mainly

A third official attempt to make Matheson's book came in 2007 with Will Smith starring. At least this time the original title appeared, even though the film fails to use the title in the manner presented in the novel.

in the first few minutes of the film as we see Neville driving his car through the deserted city as well as Neville being a military scientist working on finding a cure. For the most part, the film falls back more on the Price version, showing a man desperately trying to cling to hope in a world where he is very much alone.

One interesting aspect of the film that none of the others, nor the novel, has is the delay in showing that the few survivors left besides Neville are monsters of a sort—in this case, animalistic hairless mutants that are super-strong, cannot venture out into daylight and will kill anything for food. In the other films, we sees glimpses of the crazed "dead" who are after Neville very early on, and thus we know the risk he falls into with beings that want to see him dead. That doesn't happen in the same way in Smith's *I Am Legend*. Instead, the audience is shown that there must be concerns he has that keep him trigger-ready as he goes through the streets, but we first see him ready to use the gun for hunting, and then we see that wild animals are loose. Thus, it makes sense he would have the gun ready to protect himself, and audience members unfamiliar with the story have no idea what is to come with the mutants until they show up for the first time at the thirty-minute mark, a good third of the way through the film. Indeed, the mutants are not even given a name until near the end of the picture when Anna refers to them once as "dark-seekers" and never again. (Closed-captioning refers to the mutants as "hemocytes," but this term does not appear on-screen.) Yes, there are screams heard earlier on, but for all the audience knows it could just be the cries of the final victims waiting to die.

Once again, plague victims in the film are not quite the vampires of *The Last Man on Earth* and the novel, although certainly more so than in *The Omega Man*. These creatures at least can be physically harmed by sunlight, attack humans, are super-strong and work in packs like the vampires of old. Otherwise, they are more like zombies of recent films (many have pointed out their ability to move fast, making them more like the crazed people in *28 Days Later* and the zombies in the *Dawn of the Dead* remake), although not necessarily cannibalistic as much as simply looking for food to eat. Reports are that earlier versions of the script had the mutants as being more intelligent, somewhere between the vampires in *The Last Man on Earth* and the Family members in *The Omega Man*, but this idea was jettisoned early on. Instead, the mutants seen are wild and seemingly out of control, although this appears to be more to keep the audience on the side of Neville and have them willingly go along with his conclusion that the mutants have lost their last elements of humanity. As we see later in the movie, they know how to set traps like those of Neville's and can stage an attack on the house in a way to infiltrate by following a leader, so the audience is supposed to be as misled as Neville until the revelation that the creatures really have stayed human, just have moved into another direction.

Which would have nicely dovetailed with the originally planned ending of the film—an ending that was shot and then replaced with something that is actually a bit more downbeat. As originally scripted and shot, the ending still has the mutants arriving in the basement lab, but instead of shrieking and trying to smash through the glass as in the version released in theaters, the leader smears a butterfly image on the glass. Neville then realizes the female subject he has been experimenting on has a butterfly tattoo and that all the leader wants is the girl back, nothing more. In this ending, Neville realizes that he has completely misjudged the creatures as being mindless, and therefore his capturing and experimentations border on him being the monster, not them (leading us back to the original punch line of the novel). Neville then gives the female back to the leader, and he—after eyeing the many dead experiment subjects on the wall for a moment—goes on his way, leaving Neville to set off with Anna and Ethan on a trek to see if the safety zone really does exist. This ending still gets to the essence of the novel—that Neville could be seen as the monster from a different perspective—while also allowing him to live and perhaps even find some type of happiness after finally finding a cure and being able to leave his past behind.

That ending was not what made it into theaters. Evidently, the feeling was that the original ending too neatly set up a sequel (Neville and the others on their trek to a safety zone), while allowing the "bad guys" to not have to suffer any consequences for their actions (although, in terms of what actually happens in the film, their actions do make sense). Thus, we end up with the testosterone-filled ending with Neville and the leader screaming at each other while blowing themselves up. Mindless action trumps the thoughtful, peaceful one, as can unfortunately be expected in action films.

One does have to give the film credit for opening up the way Neville deals with his loneliness, in particular not having human companionship—in a modern age, especially in showing how much has changed in the fifty years since Matheson first wrote the book. Most of this has to do with Will Smith's outstanding performance in the role. Vincent Price had one brilliant moment in *Last Man on Earth* that conveys that type of struggle on the end of a mental breakdown, but Smith manages to sustain it through most of his film with only reaction shots and with little dialogue. Still, there were visual changes made to convey how a man would try to get by as best he could that simply would not have been available for consideration in the earlier movies. For example, the videos of old news programs are pretty much an updating of Neville watching the old home movies in *The Last Man on Earth*, while the mannequins around the video store play the same part as the Caesar bust in *The Omega Man* (while also giving the writers a good way to link Neville's declining mental health and a setup for the trap set for him). However, the one area that some fans have questioned is that of allowing Neville to have the dog, Sam, as a companion much earlier and for a longer duration than in the novel and Price film.

As discussed, the dog in the book and in *Last Man on Earth* is more of a fleeting glimpse of hope for Neville near the end of the story, followed almost immediately by his sighting Ruth for the first time. Some may wonder about the proximity of the two events (the dog and then Ruth, one right after the other), but the idea by that point is to show how Neville is ready to sacrifice what little safety he has for any sense of companionship after so many years alone. He risks the vampires in order to track down the dog, and—more importantly—he risks inviting into his home someone who he heavily suspects is infected (and is one of the few elements from the book that makes its way into *The Omega Man*). Yet the Neville of Smith's *I Am Legend* only briefly deals with being ultimately alone in a world gone mad, and that is at the two-thirds mark in the film with the death of Sam. By doing this, the film loses some of its central theme about loneliness and despair so relevant to the book.

Having the dog there does make some sense from a traditional screenwriting standpoint—Sam allows Neville to communicate out loud plot developments to the audience without the use of voice-overs for internal dialogue or the rather irritating "Am I going crazy for talking out loud" dialogue of *The Omega Man*. It is also obvious that Sam is also a bit of typical Hollywood thinking—a dog briefly appears in the book; audiences love dogs; let's make the dog the costar. Significantly, Sam's death fulfills the need in the script for a moment that triggers the third act, which is important as up to an hour into the movie, there's no reason for any type of emotional trigger to occur for Neville. Neville is safe in his home, whose location is not known by the "villains" (the most sensible of updatings from the book—these victims are not mentally clouded as in the book and *Last Man on Earth*, nor morally obliged as in *The Omega Man*—they simply don't know where he is in order to attack). He's frustrated in his work to find a cure, but is willing to keep working at it, so there is no conflict there. Even the arrival of the "Ruth equivalent" would not bring about the third act in Smith's film, as the mutants show no possibility of the hybrid vampire-humans of the book and first film, so there's no reason for Neville to be suspicious seeing Anna and Ethan or for them to be suspicious of him.

However, Sam, thanks to the flashbacks, appears as the rock to Neville's stability in the film. The audience is shown that Neville becomes emotional when thinking about his wife and child (ironically, not in the same manner as in the first movie and novel—that Neville saw them suffer over the process of the virus and then the horror of having his wife return from the dead; Neville of the Smith film sees them go in a flash due to an accident he has no control over, and thus there is only the pain of loss, without the guilt and frustration of the inability to act as in the novel and first movie). Nevertheless, that pain is diminished by having Sam as a link to the last positive thing in his life before the end of the world. With Sam's death, Neville has an emotional breakdown and is willing to die, thus initiating the third act with Anna's rescue of him and the subsequent attack by the mutants.

The third act is intriguing for the many new elements it brings into the story while also working in themes of the other films. In a complete departure from the novel and the other films, for example, Neville's immunity is not unique—the audience finds out very late in the film that a percentage of people have a natural immunity to the virus, as well as Anna pointing out that the Vermont safety zone occurred due to the cold weather (which means that there could be many more pockets of resistance around the world in colder climates). In setting up the virus to not being omnipotent in its destruction, there is no need to make up a rationale for Neville's immunity; he is just one of several that are immune. (At least this way we avoid him trying to explain it as being due to a bat bite, or the odd "I just happened to use the only vaccine lying around and now I can't make any more" excuse of *The Omega Man*.)

Further, unlike in the other two films, Neville has a reason to stay in the house—it's protected from the mutants (or so he believes), it has a lab for him to look for the cure, and it's a base within the confines of where his mission (both professional and personal) is located. His stubbornness in refusing to leave near the end of the picture has not so much to do with seeing nowhere else to go (and why risk the security of the house for the unknown?), but rather that he lost his life due to his commitment to finding a cure and a need to "fix everyone." To give that up before he found it would mean all he lost was for nothing as well. In a way, this reworking is better than in the novel, as it gives Neville the need and drive to stay put, unlike the other films where one has to seriously question why he would want to stay in an area where everyone left knows where you live and wants to kill you.

As with the other two films, Neville does find a cure and readily right before he dies. Yet unlike the other films, his death comes at his own choosing: setting off a grenade that kills the mutants after them (as well as the "saved" female mutant in the process like some bizarre twist on the ending of *Bride of Frankenstein*) and allowing Anna and Ethan to escape. In some ways this comes off as an unsatisfactory conclusion to what the audience has seen up to that point. After all, we have information pointing out that Neville doesn't understand the mutants, that they are there for reasons that have more to do with the experiments than with simply wanting to wipe out "the human in the house." To have it all end with Neville blowing up the bad guys is . . . well, it's not quite as dismal as Matthias spearing a rather apathetic Chuck Heston in the street, but it seems anticlimactic. In discarding the original ending, the film gives us a definite but unresolved ending for Neville, whereas the original ending allowed a complete character arc for Neville. Ironically, it also led the studio to realize that they never could do a sequel.

There has been talk of doing a prequel to the movie, showing Neville's life as the virus takes over the world, but in some ways that seems to be a rather pointless endeavor; after all, it can only end with Neville in a house, experimenting on mutants and talking to his dog, so there's not much left to say storywise. Looking back over the more than fifty years since the book was written, Matheson himself stated that he didn't see much point in anyone going back to it again after the last one (although he'd have been happy to get any fees associated with it if someone had wanted to try). To him, the story was fine for its time, but the years caught up with and surpassed it now, with no need for anyone to tell the story one more time. Oddly enough, the novel has been the genesis (no pun intended) of other movies and especially of the "small band of humans versus a world of monsters/zombies" stories, so to hear the suggestion that the story has pretty much played itself out doesn't quite ring true, even if it is said by the original author of the piece.

As we'll see with the other two novels that have been perpetually revisited over the years by filmmakers later in this book, it appears that the general theme from *I Am Legend* will never completely go away. No doubt, when the time is right, someone else will see what they can do to bring the novel to the screen. Even if, like the ones before it, it is never quite what Matheson intended.

9

Contagion Movies

Wiping Us Out, One Person at a Time

Next to global nuclear disasters, there's nothing like a pandemic to make for depressing movies. Not to mention generating a feeling of hopelessness. Natural disasters like floods and earthquakes? Well, don't move to that part of the country. Aliens? If they ever do turn up, just don't trust them. Asteroids? Hmm. Well, hopefully they'll be shot out of the sky, or at least known about ahead of time so we'll know not to be around when they land. Yes, as you can see, perhaps it's unrealistic rationalizing about disaster, but it at least lets us sleep at night.

Nuclear threats and contagions are out of our hands. The politicians and the military are the ones handling the bombs, not us, and a slip of the finger could lead to incoming death that we have absolutely no control over. The pandemic is similar—every time there's a notice in the paper about another outbreak of even something as minor as the yearly flu season, we all feel a mild sense of panic. How can I avoid it? Will my kids be safe? Is there some idiot out there happily spreading a disease like Typhoid Mary? Is there a country somewhere planning to wipe us out with a man-made plague? Is my government doing the same? We try to take precautions, but there's always a chance that won't be enough, and the simplest of mistakes can lead to disaster that will be too late to stop once it occurs, whether by accident or design. We're all one handshake away from our deaths, no matter how compulsively clean we try to be.

Horror and action films play up to those fears and give us contagions great and small, all looking to take us out. And even though such films tend to be on the dark side, we flock to the theaters to watch them as we do any disaster film—wondering how the lucky ones will survive and who in the cast isn't going to make it. It helps that these are sanitized Hollywood visions, of course. Rarely are visuals more than "Oh, the movie starlet has a slightly bloody nose! She is deathly ill! But she—or her love interest—will find a cure before all hope is lost! The sidekick can snuff it, but hey . . ." Usually if there is anything ghastlier than a couple of pimple-like rednesses on the face, it's always the bad guy who gets it and usually very rapidly and with a cutaway before things get really bad (which somehow will involve the sounds of something sickening plopping on the floor). There may be some gruesomeness, but only on the level of a monster-movie gross-out and typically only for a character that has done wrong. Perhaps it is just as well. The filmmakers can get the point across without having to put the audience into a spiraling depression, or make them nauseous. Ebola in the real world, for example, not only takes out the frail and innocent, but in horrific ways that simply cannot be described in any pleasant terms, and that's only one of many terrible afflictions floating around in the world.

There's also a tendency to avoid showing children dying, as (same with nuclear dramas) it takes films toward a depressing destination that hardly gets viewers reaching for the popcorn. There are exceptions, of course, to showing both the gruesomeness of disease and children suffering. *Outbreak*—a contagion movie of 1995—has a shocking scene of a small child crying in the middle of a cot holding the dead, rotting bodies of his parents, which does impress upon the mind of all the horror that could happen due to a contagion. Yet, again, it has elements of Hollywood safety—the dead bodies are only seen in the reflection of a dark helmet, thus disguising the horror, while it is an African child, which creates some distance between the image and an American audience. If that seems extreme, think of other children seen in the film—all white and American—held back from getting the disease when possible, and in one particular sequence, a girl survives with no physical side effects after playing for days with the monkey that spread the disease killing everyone else.

Even with such restrictions, there's still the sense of hanging doom over such films, and rarely are they fun to watch. (*Outbreak*, directed by Wolfgang Petersen and starring Dustin Hoffman, is an exception because, as in the descriptions below, it is an action film dressed up with the contagion plot. The scientist in charge holding off the military from bombing a small town by pointing a helicopter at them? Yeah, that's probably a rare occurrence in real pandemic situations. Or in other Hoffman roles for that matter. No wonder he wanted to do the film.) Mainly, films about contagions are there to make us think, much like the nuclear dramas mentioned a couple of chapters back. They attempt to tell something about how we as humans react when our backs are against the wall. Even so, they can go in a variety of directions, which has led to dozens of movies that can follow different paths to tell a very similar story. Below are films that best epitomize such themes, as well as subsequent ones that follow a similar pattern.

Panic in the Streets (1950)—Contagion as Medical Thriller

While there had been films through the early part of the twentieth century that dealt with epidemics, the genre as a whole began to take form with a movie in 1950 by Elia Kazan (*On the Waterfront*) called *Panic in the Streets*. The film involves what at first appears to be a standard film noir crime drama, where Blackie (Jack Palance, *Solar Crisis*, in his screen debut) kills a man during a card game and dumps his body at the docks. A doctor (Richard Widmark, *The Swarm*) gets involved when the dead man's body shows signs of disease, and it turns out the dead man was already dying from the plague. With no identification on the body, the doctor and a police captain (Paul Douglas) work to track down who the man is and who else may have spent time with him. With a limited window before having to tell the public at large and causing a panic, the two men finally track down Blackie and his gang, as they begin to succumb to the plague.

Reading this synopsis, one can see similarities to the aforementioned *Outbreak*, another movie commonly viewed as definitive of the genre. Both deal with a disease popping up in a modern American city that a doctor tries to localize in a limited time span (before citywide panic is exposed in *Panic in the Streets*; before everyone dies and/or the military blows up the town in *Outbreak*). Both even feature the disease essentially being smuggled into the country—an illegal alien criminal in the first and a monkey in the second. *Panic in the Streets* established the medical thriller, leading to other movies such as *Robin Cook's Virus* (1995), *Runaway Virus* (2000), *Quiet Killer* (1992, aka *Black Death*), *Contagion* (2002) and *Contagion* (2011), not to mention occasional use in detective series such as *CSI*, *X-Files* and any other show that needed a deadly, unseen menace for an episode or two. Spider-Man even teamed up with Captain America in an issue of *Amazing Spider-Man* (#187) to track down a villain, Electro, who had kidnapped a boy with the plague. It is no doubt a popular concept for movies, television and even the comics, and elements of such detective-adventure storytelling resonate in most of the other movies listed here.

The Andromeda Strain (1971)—Contagion as Alien Invasion

Okay, it has to be said that Quatermass—as is typical—was there first.

Quatermass was a character created by writer Nigel Kneale in 1953 for the BBC in a six-part television serial that was later made into a film by Hammer Studios as *The Quatermass Xperiment* (1955, aka *The Creeping Unknown*). In the serial, as in the subsequent film, Quatermass is a scientist who is involved with the first occupied trip into space. Upon the rocket's return, only one of the three astronauts is inside. Soon, he begins absorbing things and even people around him, and—since this isn't normal behavior for an astronaut—it becomes clear that he has been infected with an alien spore while in space and is mutating into a creature. Worse, unless destroyed somehow, spores from the creature will be released that will contaminate the world, turning everyone into similar creatures. Quatermass manages to destroy the monster (in the serial by convincing the astronaut(s) to defeat the alien creature within them; in the movie by electrocution). It is an invasion on a microscopic scale that could lead to the possible end of the world, and certainly led to a successful series of Quatermass sequels (one of which is listed later in this chapter). However, although it fits perfectly into this category, the vast majority of contagion movies involving alien infiltration go with a sloppier method for world domination.

The Blob (1958) has an old guy poking at the alien unknown (a small meteor) with a stick, infecting himself and setting loose a monster that absorbs any human it comes in contact (which pretty much makes it a contagion movie in an esoteric stretch of the term). *The War of the Worlds* (1953) has a dumb guy

The early Michael Crichton novel *The Andromeda Strain* was filmed in 1971 and would serve as a prototype for many contagion films.

beating a shovel against the meteor that contains the aliens preparing their onslaught. *Night of the Living Dead* (1968) makes mention of a space probe that brings something back that causes the dead to rise as zombies (but more about zombies in the next chapter). *Creepshow* (1982) features a story, "The Lonesome Death of Jordy Verrill," where a moron (Stephen King . . . not that King is a moron, but his character is) touches the gloop inside a meteor and is eventually covered by an alien fungus that will soon take over the world.

Yes, it is time for "let's poke a stick at space stuff," and the movie that really cornered the market on such a telling is *The Andromeda Strain*.

Based on the book by Michael Crichton (known for a slew of other books and movies, but we'll cut to the chase and just say *Jurassic Park*) and directed by Robert Wise (known for a slew of movies, but we'll cut to the chase and just say *The Sound of Music* . . . oh, all right, *The Day the Earth Stood Still*), *The Andromeda Strain* stars James Olson (playing against type) as a doctor who is sent to investigate the death of nearly everyone, with the exception of the town drunk and a newborn, in a small town in New Mexico. It transpires that a satellite had crashed near the town and the sheriff had decided to pry it open, releasing an alien microbe that contaminates the area and also eats all plastic and rubber, making it hard to contain. The doctor goes with a group of scientists to a secret, underground facility in the desert to study the satellite and the two survivors. Eventually they discover a cure, but two new problems

It's time to start poking alien things with a stick! And Stephen King in *Creepshow* (1982) is going to show us the consequences.

emerge—a faulty communication system forces the government to assume that the scientists are dead and the town should be nuked, while the self-destruct program for the facility is activated due to contamination. The scientists deduce that any nuclear radiation will turn what is rapidly becoming a harmless bug into a variety of superbugs that will expand across the globe, and then have to race against time to avoid either explosion from occurring.

In this case, as in many of the films listed in this chapter, the contagion is contained, but not before those in control nearly make a bigger mess of things before setting them right. In some ways, *The Andromeda Strain* is like the *Fail-Safe* of contagion movies—people with their hearts in the right places, but so duty-bound to follow procedures and using equipment that doesn't work properly that they miss, or nearly miss, the opportunity to do the right thing. Even the incidental element of Dr. Leavitt being epileptic shows how good intentions can go askew (tired and overwhelmed, Leavitt misses a slide that would resolve the crisis because she fixates on a blinking red light). Obviously, the deduction of what is causing the germ to kill people is rather like the detective stories already discussed, with some James Bond–like elements thrown in at the end (Olson avoiding a laser while climbing a ladder to get to the switch that will allow him to shut down the self-destruct system wouldn't be completely out of place in such a film). Yet, besides the idea of something from space leading to our destruction (like a reversal of *War of the Worlds*, only with the Martians bombarding us with the germ instead of the other way around), there's also the focus for a good portion of the movie on the facility itself that makes *The Andromeda Strain* a vital forerunner in contagion films.

The Wildfire Complex, the name of the facility in the film, seems quite derivative of a similar underground building found in the 1954 science fiction movie *Gog*, which probably is no doubt based on actual facilities—a multilevel complex that can only be gotten to by elevator where each level of the building deals with stricter, deadlier projects. Much time is spent in the film showing the scientists making their way down to the lower levels of the building where they can do their studies. It is easy to compare films that take place in other scientific buildings—from the underground structures of *The Cabin in the Woods* and *Resident Evil* to the CDC labs of *Outbreak* and the FBI labs of *The Rock*—and see that *The Andromeda Strain*'s visual journey through the Wildfire Complex made an impression on others.

12 Monkeys (1995) and 28 Days Later (2002)—Contagion as Fear of Science

While on the topic of labs, it is fitting to discuss two types of lab-created contagion movies that are typical for the genre: the accidental release of a virus created in the lab (*28 Days Later*) and the deliberate release of the same (*12 Monkeys*). Or, to put them into context, the first movie's subgenre features the scientist holding a glass vial saying, "Here is the most dangerous virus known to man and—oops . . . no, a mop's not really going to be worth the trouble now." The other features the same scientist saying, "Here is the most dangerous virus known to man . . . and now I'll destroy mankind! Bwahahahahahaha!" The reason they're paired here is because the kickoff to both pandemics is based in laboratory experiments (as well as animal rights groups creating problems) that lead to similar results by way of the two completely different methods.

12 Monkeys, which adapts *La jetée* (discussed a couple of chapters back) as its framework, deals with a criminal (Bruce Willis) in a postapocalyptic future where only a few have survived a virus that started decades before in 1996. Scientists have discovered a way to send people back through time, and the criminal is offered a chance to go back to 1996 to track down the original virus and bring it back to the future so that the scientists can create a vaccine. It is established that a crazed individual bent on destruction of society (Brad Pitt, who would do the same honors in *Fight Club*) plans to release a virus being developed

28 Days Later (2002) shows us the results of the "Oops . . . I didn't mean to release the virus" subgenre of contagion films.

in his father's labs that will destroy most human life. Using the cover of his animal rights group, "The Army of the Twelve Monkeys," Pitt diverts attention by releasing animals from the public zoo, while a scientist from the lab secretly working for him plans to board a plane to release the virus around the world. Willis' character tries to stop the scientist—which relates back to *La jetée* for its conclusion—while a scientist from the future joins the crazed scientist on the plane in order to get the sample they need of the virus. Hence, the mad scientist bent on world destruction (with a brief glimpse of hope that the future will be saved).

In *28 Days Later*, an animal liberation group attempts to free chimpanzees from a lab with no clear understanding that the chimps have been infected with a virus called "rage." Although warned, the dim-witted activists take no notice and instead happily release the chimps. Yet, instead of the warm, loving hugs the activists expect, the chimps attack them, which causes the activists to attack each other and thus leads to the epidemic of the virus that turns people violently insane. Consequently, in *28 Weeks Later*, the virus appears to be eradicated, but it turns out that some people are immune to it and end up spreading it all over again, this time sending it across the waters into Europe by the end of the film. In both films, honest mistakes occur—the animal liberation group doesn't want to end their lives and certainly not the world; they just want to save some chimps from experiments. The government isn't sending people back into London because they think more people can die; they think everything is fine, and they would have gotten away with it too if it weren't for some darn kids. All the kids want to do is bring back their mother who is immune but can spread the disease; the father just wants forgiveness and ends up becoming infected when he kisses his wife. The soldier helping the kids get away doesn't realize one is already a carrier, and onward and onward. Good intentions all, but we know where those lead.

Either by accident or design, the films play with an age-old science fiction cliché of scientists creating a monster that they either cannot control or are bent on using to destroy. A throwback to the atomic age films of the 1950s, it is nothing more than a fear of science and advancement—the journey into the unknown described as the future. Such a theme goes back to the days of H. G. Wells' *The Shape of Things to Come*, which finds a revolution trying to stop the first rocket ship to space for fear of taking mankind's destiny too far. Same with super-bombs created in the drive-in movies of the 1950s, and same with certain contagion movies after our fears from the bomb lessened (as we've seen in the previous chapter with the Will Smith version of *I Am Legend*).

Other films that show accidental releases of viruses from the lab include:

- *Plague* (1978, aka *M3: The Gemini Strain*) Working on a bacterium, a scientist accidentally releases a virus that is quarantined, but with one carrier managing to escape. She begins to spread the virus from person to person until a public panic develops.
- *Warning Sign* (1985) Starring Kathleen Quinlan (from *Where Have All the People Gone?*) as a security officer in a lab where biological weapons are being developed. A vial is broken by accident, releasing a quick-acting virus that turns everyone into homicidal maniacs (hmm . . . wonder if the makers of *28 Days Later* saw this when they were younger) that shuts down the facility, and the husband of the security guard tries to break in to get his wife out.
- *Rise of the Planet of the Apes* (2010) James Franco plays Will, a scientist who creates a drug for Alzheimer's that increases the intelligence of primates. When the lab discovers Will's drug initially does work, they decide to continue developing a stronger version that turns out to accelerate the intellect of the

chimps and apes but kills humans. A worker ends up contracting the virus and spreading it to a neighbor of Will's before dying. The neighbor happens to be an airline pilot who is making multiple stops around the world,

This Spanish-language poster for *Warning Sign* (1985) shows clearly how clumsiness can lead to the apocalypse . . . and the misspelling of the title of the film.

Courtesy of Wrong Side of the Art

thereby creating a fast pandemic that will wipe out most of the human race (leading to the apes taking over the world via contagion rather than by way of a nuclear holocaust as in the original series of films). Gee, thanks, Will!

Films displaying the intentional threat of a pandemic:

- *The Satan Bug* (1965) Richard Basehart plays a maniacal villain who gets hold of a new virus called "the Satan bug" that can wipe out all life on the planet. While at first he plans to use the virus as a threat to close down the biochemical lab that made it in the first place, after getting a vaccine against the virus, he goes mad with power and decides to release it anyway so that he can rule an empty world.
- *I Drink Your Blood* (1970) See Contagion as Gorefest Horror Film later in this chapter.
- *Smallpox 2002* (2002) A mockumentary showing a man intentionally giving himself smallpox in order to infect everyone he comes in contact with. The film then explores how the pandemic would spread from Patient Zero to around the world, and the panic and political unrest that would occur.
- *The Thaw* (2009) Working as a variation of *The Thing*, researchers in the Arctic stumble across a frozen woolly mammoth that, when thawed, reveals ancient bugs that rapidly multiply and eat living creatures. The bugs pass themselves on much like a virus, from one person to another. One member of the team infects himself and aims to return to civilization in order to force people to consider the effects of global warming. Bwahahahaha!
- *Resident Evil* (2002–Present) In the first film it is established that a vial of the T-virus was broken and left to contaminate the staff at a facility called the Hive by Spence (James Purefoy), who needed a diversion as he stole the virus to sell on the black market. In subsequent films, more and more of the public become infected with the virus that turns people into killer mutants, zombies, or hot, superhuman chicks (Milla Jovovich and Michelle Rodriguez).

The Crazies (1973)—Contagion as Madness

The movies have dealt with insanity since the early days of cinema, but typically on a one-on-one basis. There may be scenes of mass hysteria, certainly common for disaster films, but stories involving a group of people who are violently demented were rare. Thus, the 1973 movie *The Crazies*, which features a full town of people becoming homicidal in a contagion that appears to be broadening, set off a genre that has grown in many of the same ways as director George Romero's work in another genre (covered in the next chapter). It was not a success when released, but in the later 1970s, fans of Romero's *Night of the Living Dead* had little else to see of his contributions to horror films in art houses and at college movie nights than bad prints of *The Crazies* (aka *Code Name Trixie*) and possibly *Martin*, so the cult interest rapidly grew. In fact, the 1970s were a period when Romero fixated on themes of mental illness—his 1972 film *Season of the Witch* deals with a woman who lets her imagination control her to the point of killing her husband, while *Martin* (1977) features a young man who thinks he's a vampire. Of the three, however, *The Crazies* is the one that pulled together the blueprint for many other films dealing with a growing madness due to circumstances beyond the control of those involved, while also giving us another film where those in control don't really know what they are doing.

The people who live in a small town named Evans City run into two situations where men have suddenly lost their minds and begin to commit violent acts. Soon, soldiers appear in contamination suits to quarantine the town and shoot anyone trying to escape. A scientist arrives to try to find a cure for what turns out to have been a new bioweapon called Trixie that leaked into the town's water supply, as the military tries to control the increasingly out-of-control populace. The film flips back and forth between the scientist's efforts and those of a firefighter named David who is immune to the virus and tries to escape with a group of people, including his pregnant girlfriend. As the film ends with David recaptured and hopeless and the scientist killed just as he discovers a possible cure, word reaches the military that the same thing is happening in another city.

The film was remade in 2010 by Breck Eisner to favorable reviews, but in comparison with the original, it seems to miss the out-of-control nature of the pandemic and instead focuses more on the standard boundaries of old-fashioned slasher movies (evident in the movie poster showing a bloody pitchfork dragged across a floor, from the big scare scene in the remake). Because the original dealt with both sides of the growing problem and the inefficiency of everyone in trying to work toward a solution, it plays as more drenched in reality, even as a lower-budget movie, than the remake, which plays more as a standard scare-'em horror flick. It also isn't quite as depressingly shocking as the original, with some of the madness played out; the remake may show more blood but nothing quite as unsettling as the scene of kindly old people jabbing knitting needles into helpful people and the insanity-enforced incest and suicide played out later in the film by two characters. The remake does its job and does it well, but the original work by Romero lingers in the mind longer.

As it did with several filmmakers in the years that followed. Forty years later, *The Crazies* has birthed a number of movies that use aspects of the 1973 film in telling similar stories about people slowly losing their minds and the handful that try to escape. Further, it plays with a universal theme of zombie movies—our friends and neighbors suddenly turning against us and the fear that we may do the same to our loved ones. There are so many similarities that it's not uncommon for these to be seen as zombie movies (*28 Days Later* is commonly referred to as one, for example), and such scenarios for contagion films have proliferated much like in the zombie films in the past forty years. All the same, here are some of the more memorable ones from this variation of the contagion genre:

- ***Blue Sunshine* (1976)** Made two years after *The Crazies*, this film takes a somewhat different tack, as it deals with a common drug-related theme, the flashback, and takes it to its violent extremes. A type of LSD called Blue Sunshine has a delayed effect of turning those who took it back in the 1960s into bald, homicidal maniacs. A man at the wrong place and time must figure out why it is happening and if it'll affect the man who helped create the drug and who is now running for senator. What makes *Blue Sunshine* memorable is the concept of people's past misdeeds catching up with them years down the line, but unfortunately some critics tend to fixate on the film being merely a "drugs are bad" warning and miss the bigger picture.

- *Les raisins de la mort* (**1978, aka** *Grapes of Death*) Pesticide in a vineyard has turned those who work in the fields and/or drink the wine from the fields that used the pesticide crazy and covered in bloody sores. A woman traveling through the area ends up trying various ways to escape the madness around her. The film was directed by Jean Rollin, known for a number of erotic vampire films.

- *The Children* (**1980**) Who growing up in 1980 doesn't remember the ad for this movie, which seemed to turn up at all hours of the day and night and shows a school bus slowly driving into a fog that turns out to be nuclear radiation? (Who didn't think about it whenever their own school bus went into a bank of fog on the way to school?) The kids from the bus turn up with black fingernails and start killing adults. Similar movies would deal with maniacal children, such as *Devil Times Five* (1974, aka *Peopletoys*), *Bloody Birthday* (1981), *Who Can Kill a Child?* (1976) and *The Children* (2008).

- *Impulse* (**1984**) Directed by Graham Baker (*Alien Nation* and *Omen III: The Final Conflict*), this movie received quite a bit of airplay on HBO and other cable channels in the 1980s, making it better known for a time than *The Crazies*. An earthquake causes a toxic waste spill that starts to turn everyone in a small town insane. In this case, however, the government succeeds in covering up the problem by killing everyone with a crop duster, with the exception of Meg Tilly's character, who gets away.

- *Nightmare at Noon* (**1988, aka** *Death Street USA*) Dirty commie scum infect the water supply of a small town, turning everyone into green crazy people who want to kill. Well, they would, wouldn't they?

- *In the Mouth of Madness* (**1995**) Considered by John Carpenter to be the third of his "Apocalyptic Trilogy" (*The Thing* and *Prince of Darkness* being the other two), the film is a homage to H. P. Lovecraft, with references to the Old Ones (see *The Cabin in the Woods*) and plenty of characters named after ones in Lovecraft's writing. The story deals with a man who is trying to track down a famous horror author who has disappeared. Turns out that his last manuscript causes people to go insane and kill. In the end, the manuscript is not only published but also turned into a movie called *In the Mouth of Madness*, and humanity is lost.

- *28 Days Later/28 Weeks Later* (**2002/2007**) Discussed earlier under a different theme but mentioned here as well, as the virus released causes violent insanity among those infected.

The Children (1980)—Anyone who saw this as a kid never rode the school bus through a fog the same way again.   *Courtesy of Wrong Side of the Art*

- *Quarantine* (2008) A remake of the Spanish film *Rec*, the American version sticks with a more straightforward story about a viral infection (without the religious overtones of the *Rec* series) that turns everyone in an apartment building into (once again) homicidal maniacs. This time with seemingly superhuman power as well. The CDC quarantines the building, killing anyone who even appears to be looking to leave the building, as those inside—including a television crew filming a report about the firefighters who enter the building before the quarantine—try to escape being turned or killed. A sequel was done featuring a group aboard a plane with the disease, but the *Rec* series does a better job at keeping the premise fresh.
- *Pandorum* (2008) A science fiction film that takes place after the end of all life on Earth (thus a postapocalyptic film before we even get to the plot). The crew of a ship wakes up from a type of suspended animation to find that the ship is full of cannibalistic creatures under the command of another crewmember. Pandorum refers to a type of mental ailment caused by space travel, which several characters suffer during the ship's journey and from which the mutants are directly descended.
- *Doghouse* (2009), *The Taint* (2010) and *The Screwfly Solution* (2006) All three deal with a disease that turns one sex (women in *Doghouse*, men in the other two films) homicidal against the opposite sex. *Doghouse* plays as a comedy, *The Taint* a bit and *The Screwfly Solution* (directed by Joe Dante) not at all. Dante's film was actually for television, as part of the *Masters of Horror* series for the Showtime network.
- **Pretty much anything by David Cronenberg (1975–Present)** This may seem rather flip, but it's true—most of Cronenberg's movies deal with a transference of madness between characters in some form, whether through a virus or through example. Cronenberg himself has referred to his films as dealing with "body horror," and it goes back to even his first full-length film, *Stereo* (1969), which involved telepaths and sexual deviations. His second film, *Crimes of the Future* (1970), even hints at the "last man on Earth" plot with a society made up of men who are trying to adjust to a world without women past puberty. From there, madness is a central theme to many of his films. *Shivers* (1975, aka *They Came from Within*) deals with sexually transmitted parasites that drive people insane with lust to the point of homicide. *Rabid* (1977, starring porn star Marilyn Chambers) has a woman given experimental surgery that causes her to transmit a disease that turns others into blood-craving mindless beings. *Scanners* (1981) features people who have telepathic powers due to a drug their mothers took before their births. *Videodrome* (1983) deals with television programs that are designed to drive people insane and kill them. Even more seemingly traditional dramas by Cronenberg—like *Dead Ringers* (1988), *Naked Lunch* (1991), *Crash* (1996), *A History of Violence* (2005) and *A Dangerous Method* (2011)—deal with people transferring dangerous thoughts and actions to one another. Discussing it as one theme doesn't mean to dismiss a body of work (or, rather, a "body

horror" of work), but merely to point out that it is a premise that Cronenberg has focused on throughout his career, with a wide variety of excellent movies to demonstrate that theme.

David Cronenberg has been proven the master of films dealing with the transference of madness, such as *Rabid* (1977), starring porn star Marilyn Chambers.

Courtesy of Vintage Cinema Ads

Virus (1980)—Contagion as Survival/Adventure

Virus is a Japanese movie directed by Kinji Fukasaku (*Battle Royale*) that tells a global story involving a virus that leaves only a handful of survivors, followed by the ramifications of an unattended world that could cause additional risk to those still alive. In the opening minutes of the film, a Bond-ish agent's attempts to steal back a virus created in U.S. labs that can turn any other virus into a superbug leads to a plane crash. The crash results in the virus spreading through Europe, into America and around the world. Eventually, the only humans left are those on a nuclear sub (shades of *On the Beach*) and a group of individuals stationed in Antarctica (it turns out that the virus will not function in temperatures below freezing).

As the survivors try to figure out their next move and how they can repopulate the earth, a massive earthquake activates a U.S. nuclear missile system that will trigger one in the Soviet Union and lead to a nuclear disaster. (Thus, the U.S. gets to kill the world twice—first with a biological weapon and later with nukes.) A small group of survivors tries to stop the bombing but is unsuccessful, wiping out even more of the survivors. Still, a few make it out alive and attempt to move on.

Virus is an interesting film in a couple of respects. The first is that the film was obviously meant to be picked up for American consumption even though it was made in Japan, what with such actors appearing as Glenn Ford (as the president), Chuck Connors, Sonny Chiba (one reason the film periodically turns up on DVD in America even though it is considered a box-office dud is Chiba's popularity in certain cult-movie circles), Robert Vaughn, and even Edward James Olmos (long before *Blade Runner*, *Miami Vice* and *Battlestar Galactica*). What also makes the film intriguing is that it goes beyond just explaining and showing us a pandemic and what the survivors would do afterward. Much like the zombie films to be discussed next chapter and the *Mad Max*–like movies of chapter 19, *Virus* takes those who have survived and sets them in a world where action-adventure is the point of the plot. The survivors manage to get to a safe haven away from the plague, but they soon realize there are hidden dangers that necessitate their return to the old world, leading to adventures that would not be completely out of place in action films of today.

Such a premise appears in the television miniseries version of Stephen King's *The Stand* (1994), which finds a virus being accidentally exposed to people on a military base that leads to a pandemic, leaving only those who have a rare immunity to the virus alive. Yet that's only part of the story—the survivors then have to deal with outsiders who want to destroy them (with possibilities of a biblical relevance to the proceedings in the mix as well). What occurs to the good guys after the plague and their attempt to deal with those wanting to kill them is just as important as the part about the plague and people struggling to find others after most have died.

In *Adrenalin: Fear the Rush* (1996), a plague that kills everyone in Russia has been found in Boston, and the city has been quarantined. Instead of insight into the human despair of those waiting to die, the movie is an action piece, set in a somewhat futuristic world of eleven years in the future. The main character (Natasha Henstridge, *Species*) works with others to hunt down a creature in the city that is responsible for the virus and will contaminate the city much like the creature from the Quatermass movie mentioned earlier. Thus the film turns into a type of crossbreed between *Resident Evil* and *Predator* as Henstridge's character hunts down the creature. Thus, the film is not really even about the contagion any longer (although if the creature is not caught a contagion will occur) but rather a monster movie.

Doomsday from 2008 is somewhat similar to *Adrenalin: Fear the Rush*, in that people are sent into a quarantined zone (this time Scotland instead of Boston) to find a cure, going through different gangs of people who try to stop them along the way in an adventure that reflects a society gone to seed thanks to the virus. On the other hand, *Carriers* (2009) is much more of a drama with action-adventure elements, featuring Chris Pine (*Star Trek*) as one of two brothers who go with two women on a car trip during the final stages of a pandemic that wiped out much of humanity (*Zombieland* from the same year follows a very similar scenario). The objective is to get to an amusement park resort remembered from their childhood in order to wait out the last days of the dying. The film deals not so much with people getting sick as with the responsibility we have to care and look out for each other. In the end, one brother cannot handle the responsibility, while their numbers fall until only one brother and one of the girls make it to their final destination . . . only to discover that the place really had no meaning without the others there to experience it with them.

Blindness (2008)—Contagion as Social Commentary

Oddly, *Blindness*, the 2008 film directed by Fernando Meirelles (*City of God*) and based on a novel by José Saramago, hints at a similar final message to the one in *Carriers*. The film deals with people suddenly going blind without any explanation. The only exception appears to be the wife of a doctor (Julianne Moore). With the cause of the situation unknown, those who have gone blind are sent to an asylum, with the wife accompanying the doctor. With more and more people arriving, food becomes scarce and the place takes on the feel of *Lord of the Flies*, with a group of men forcing others to do their bidding in order to get food. Eventually the doctor's wife gets a handful of them out of the asylum (the soldiers have also gone blind and have left their posts) to find the whole city in chaos. Eventually, the group settles into a new life—much like the blind do with their seeing help in *Day of the Triffids*—only to find their sight returning for no explainable reason.

To state this is a contagion film is a bit hard—there's never any explanation as to what caused the problem in the first place—yet as seen in previous categories (such as with the Cronenberg films) pandemics may take many forms. In the film, it is obvious that the cause for such an event is punishment for misdeeds or perhaps man's inhumanity to their fellow man leading to retribution on a global scale. Those afflicted at first are shown to have sinned on some level before going blind, and others follow suit because it is just assumed that everyone will get it. Moore's character strives to help others and therefore never goes blind, which suggests that those who work to help others are "saved" from damnation. The responsibility to do things for others is hard but has a reward—in the case of *Carriers*, that of having a purpose to their lives; in *Blindness* it takes on a more physical definition with that of being able to see where others are blind.

Thus, the contagion of the film allows for commentary on society. Many of the films listed here at least pay lip service to such a thing, but there are a few movies that try to say something a bit more. Such as *Il seme dell'uomo* (1969), an Italian movie dealing with a couple contemplating having a baby in a world wiped out by a virus. *Right at Your Door* (2006) deals with a man struggling to do the right thing in a situation where a dirty bomb has set loose a virus in Los Angeles that leaves him unable to allow his infected wife back into the house. None may be giving us the same exact message, but all take the contagion theme and mix it in to take drama and push it to the extreme to tell their tales.

Cabin Fever (2002)—Contagion as Gorefest Horror Film

Then we have the movies that use a contagion in order to set up a whole mess of gross special effects and maybe (just maybe) some social commentary as well. *Cabin Fever* was a huge hit when it was released, making a name for writer-director (and sometimes actor) Eli Roth in the process. Although there is a virus that is the cause for the cast being killed off—with promises of further contamination to come—the film is really out to show as many gross-out scenes as possible, leading to a *Night of the Living Dead*-style ending for the one survivor and a lot of plopping, bloody special effects every few minutes. Essentially, it is the contagion version of a *Friday the 13th* movie—it even takes place in the woods and has a lake where bad things happen—and with no apologies.

As it stands, most movies dealing with viruses and pandemics have little room for anything other than being very serious and moralizing. Which makes sense; after all, we're talking about people dying in horrible, agonizing ways through no fault of their own. There certainly isn't much room for humor, but then we have movies like *Cabin Fever* that play for slapstick (as the *Evil Dead* series—also located at a cabin—did in the 1980s). As one could expect, however, the success of *Cabin Fever* didn't lead to a vast expansion in movies dealing with the wacky side of contagions. Only a few have come to pass over the years, with two of the most memorable appearing years before *Cabin Fever*.

I Drink Your Blood (1970) has a story line involving nasty hippies, nasty construction workers and a rather nasty kid who perpetrates the unintentional death of nearly the entire cast. After a group of hippies that wander into town sexually assault a young woman, the woman's young brother takes rabid blood from a dead dog and injects it into meat pies that the hippies are eating. Meanwhile, the construction worker boyfriend of the young woman has his fellow workers attack the hippies, and thus everyone, the squares and the hippies alike, become rabid, homicidal maniacs. As more and more people wipe each other out in gory ways (so gory that the Motion Picture Association of America first rated the movie X until cuts were made), the young woman, the brother and others struggle to get out of town.

The plot is rather silly, as in *Cabin Fever*, but the reasoning behind the story is simply a setup for a lot of disturbing dismemberments by those infected with rabies. It is all about the effects and really nothing more. Certainly not anything to do with brotherly love, as everyone is rather repulsive in the movie. Much more along the lines of H. G. Lewis' *Two Thousand Maniacs* mixed in with a touch of a biker movie, or *Village of the Giants* with little Ronny Howard gone bat-crap crazy.

Larry Cohen has made a career out of taking one theme and mixing it up to the point that it can be about three other things. At least you can never be sure exactly how things are going to turn out in one of his movies. Among his films are the ecological horror movie *It's Alive* (about a mutant killer baby), the bizarre alien invasion flick *God Told Me To* (featuring a young Andy Kaufman as a crazed policeman in a St. Patrick's Day parade), and the fun monster movie *Q*. All seem to start off with one premise and then investigates a variety of other things in the process, and the same with his 1985 film, *The Stuff*.

The movie stars Michael Moriarty as an investigator who is hired by a cookie company mogul (played by Garrett Morris and suspiciously looking like cookie mogul and icon Famous Amos) to investigate a company selling a product called "the Stuff" that is hurting his sales. It turns out that the "no calorie, sweet-tasting chemical" put into their ice cream is actually a parasite that oozes out of the ground and can turn people into zombies before eventually eating out their bodies into a gloopy mess. In this case, there actually is a bit of social commentary involved, as the public is warned and the Stuff destroyed, only for the company owners deciding to put out a new product that has only 12 percent of the Stuff and given a new name. When that is stopped as well, containers of the Stuff are still sold on the black market to fans of it. Unfortunately, as is too true with American consumerism, things may be bad for us, but we ignore all the warnings anyway.

Grindhouse (2007), a joint production by Robert Rodriguez and Quentin Tarantino, attempts to recreate the days of the 1970s grindhouse movie theaters, where all types of action movies would play twenty-four hours a day, with trailers for "coming attractions" stuck in-between. Tarantino directed one half of the picture, with a "killer on the loose" film called *Death Proof*, while Rodriguez directed the other movie in the "double feature," called *Planet Terror*. *Planet* deals with a former soldier and his stripper ex-girlfriend who, along with a group of others, try to avoid people who have been turned into melting, pulsating, crazed maniacs thanks to the release of a bioweapon in a small town. In some ways, it may appear to be another in the series of "deadly virus of oops" films, but the point is action, with several set pieces dealing with horrible, gruesome attacks and people literally falling apart in front of others (not to mention one major character getting his head blown off on camera more or less as a punch line to a joke). There is even a questionable scene done for laughs of a young boy (played by the director's own son) given a gun and told not to point it at his face . . . only for the boy to point it at his face and blow his own head off. (To be fair, the director has stated that he did the scene to give the film an additional sense of horror with the death of a child, but the action occurs off-screen, has nothing to do with the action occurring around it and is played for comedy rather than tragedy. It should also be noted that the director reshot several segments after this to include the boy so that when his son saw the movie he wouldn't be traumatized that his character was killed off; which in a way means that it could have easily lost this bit of depressing senselessness without any loss to the film. But, I guess, if people really were that worked up about it, they could already recut the movie themselves with the additional bits scene on the DVD and make the movie "kid friendly" in a way.) Then again, there are bound to be filmgoers that would be quite happy to see what happens to Tarantino's character in the film actually happen to Tarantino himself, so there's something for everyone here.

Oh, and that whole social commentary thing I mentioned at the beginning of this section for these films. Hmm. Well, I guess the main lesson to learn from these films is "don't be a jackass to others." Beyond that, it's just splatter and laughter all the way through.

Five Million Years to Earth (1967)—Contagion as Technological Virus

We once again return to Nigel Kneale's character Quatermass (see "Contagion as Alien Invasion" earlier in this chapter) in the third serial (known as *Quatermass and the Pit*) and consequently the third film adaptation of the British scientist's adventures. In this story, Quatermass is helping with the uncovering of some type of ship found as the London Underground is being extended. The ship turns out to be one left millions of years ago by ant-like Martians (whose heads resemble our own preconceived notions of a horned devil). Telekinetic power is leaking from the ship, forcing images of the aliens on certain people and leading to a theory that the Martians millions of years ago had been influential in the development of mankind. Further, that the Martians would eliminate those of their own kind that did not act as the others, and this may be a type of race memory in man as well. Quatermass tries to convince the authorities to

FORCE MORE POWERFUL THAN 1,000 H-BOMBS UNLEASHED TO DEVASTATE EARTH! WORLD IN PANIC! CITIES IN FLAMES!

20th CENTURY-FOX presents

FIVE MILLION YEARS TO EARTH

COLOR BY DELUXE

Starring
JAMES   ANDREW   BARBARA   JULIAN
DONALD · KEIR · SHELLEY · GLOVER   Produced by   Directed by   Screenplay by   A SEVEN ARTS-
ANTHONY NELSON KEYS · ROY BAKER · NIGEL KNEALE · HAMMER PRODUCTION

Five Million Years to Earth (1967) is one of a handful of films using Nigel Kneale's character Quatermass and involves a subgenre dealing with a type of technological virus nearly destroying mankind.   *Courtesy of Wrong Side of the Art*

do something, but they see the ship as a stunt that can be used for promotional purposes and happily bring in cameras and film crews. Unfortunately, their equipment boosts the telekinetic power of the ship, leading to people—including momentarily Quatermass himself—mobbing together to kill the few that are not under its control. As chaos takes hold, and the power starts to disintegrate buildings and other structures, Quatermass and another scientist manage to defuse the power, ending the potential end of humanity.

The film looks like an alien invasion movie, and we even get scary aliens to fear (well, okay, not scary actually—a midnight showing of the film I went to in the 1980s had the audience laughing in hysterics at the rather poor effects used for the ant-like aliens), but the aliens are long gone. Even so, the ship emits a force that grabs hold of people and forces them to do things they would not have otherwise done. The Martians are not around, but their ability to influence us lives on through the ship's power to infect most of us like a plague. Earlier reviews would no doubt mark this down to a type of mass hypnosis, but in many ways *Five Million Years to Earth* is an early example of the idea that images and/ or sounds could work as a virus that mentally or physically changes people. As our technology increases our capabilities, so have our fears increased as to how it could negatively affect us. Machine vs. man will be discussed in more detail in chapter 18, but for this chapter the emphasis is on contagions brought on by technology in one form or another. *Videodrome*, mentioned earlier in this chapter, deals with that concept via signals sent through television, as does Cronenberg's *eXistenZ* (1999) from a video-game side—each incorporating techniques that are to change humans into something "else" while hidden away in entertainment to consume (just as the Stuff in Cohen's movie changes people under the guise of a dessert). Most of the films listed here deal with madness and death, sought after by an individual or group of sometimes unknown origin, but all deal with a compounding element to the method that is unleashed.

- *Ringu* (1998) at first seems to be setting up a traditional horror film based on an age-old urban legend based on a grade-school dare, such as spending the night in a haunted house or standing in front of a mirror saying "Bloody Mary" three times (the *Candyman* series of films is based on such a tale). In the case of *The Ring*, teenagers dare each other to watch a videotape showing a series of odd images that conclude with a stone well in the middle of a field before the tape ends. The story goes that seven days after viewing the tape, those who watch will receive a phone call (hence the first interpretation of "the ring") that will lead to them dying in wide-eyed shock. An investigator watches the tape only to discover that the legend is true. Worse, that her son has accidentally seen the tape and is marked for death as well. She must find out why the tape is cursed before her seven days are up.

  The American version of the film that came in 2002 jettisons many of the more intriguing elements of the original novel by Koji Suzuki. Even so, both come to the same conclusion—the only way to be saved from death is to pass on the video for someone else to watch, hence creating a viral continuation of the curse that will multiply over time. The main difference is the reasoning behind the tape: in the American version, Samara—the girl who was thrown down the well by her father due to her telepathic gifts and the haunted figure who kills—is merely interested in killing others. In the original Japanese version, Samara is Sadako and, as in the books, uses the tape in order to will herself back to life; leading the later books to cloning and finally a scenario that involves a world similar to one from the *Matrix* films.

Perhaps detailing the subsequent books may be putting too much emphasis on the technological side of the story. Even so, the method used by Sadako—of the videotape allowing for an evil to be unleashed one person at a time until everyone in the world is eventually consumed by the image of Sadako—allows even the first film in the series to fall in the category of technological viruses. In one sense *Ringu* does do one thing that many of the others in this category do not—the video seen merely kills, with the ultimate goal being one of creation, although that is not clear in the first film or book.

- *Demons* (1985) This Italian film directed by Lamberto Bava (son of director Mario Bava, who did *Planet of the Vampires*) deals with a group of people attending a free showing of a horror movie in a theater who eventually must contend with people in the theater being turned into monsters after one of them is intentionally marked to be transformed during the course of the movie they're watching. Eventually, the monsters escape the theater and go on a rampage through the city, as more and more people are turned into demons. The film was so successful that a follow-up was released in 1986 by the same director. *Demons 2* makes the technological side of the transformations more evident, with a woman watching a television program about the earlier film that shows one of the demons crawling out of the television set and starting the whole process over again. It is never explained exactly why this is happening in either film, merely that someone somewhere wants this to occur.

- *Halloween III: Season of the Witch* (1982) On the other hand, it is clear how and why the television invasion of a virus occurs in *Halloween III*. The film got off on the wrong foot when released, as it was an attempt by John Carpenter to move the horror series away from the masked killer in the first two *Halloween* movies and turn it into an annual tradition at theaters. Unfortunately, fans of Michael (the killer in the first two movies) hated the idea of losing their favorite, while fans of horror films in general never could quite grasp what the film was supposed to be about from the ads. Another problem was that Carpenter had sought out Nigel Kneale (of Quatermass fame) to write the script, only for the producers to have it rewritten to add gore and shocks that Kneale felt hurt the story. When it became public around the time of the film's release that Kneale's involvement was missing (he requested his name be taken off the credits, although elements of his story remain in the film), certain science fiction fans also tore down the movie.

Which is a shame, as it really isn't that bad. Yes, the violence is overpowering at times, but the story is unique, and the film ends with the end of the world just around the corner. The plot deals with a company that makes masks for kids to wear on Halloween. The masks appear popular, and the ads for them are relentless through the film (suggesting that the ads themselves trigger something in people that makes them buy them). As it turns out, the owner of the company wishes for Halloween to once again appear as something terrifying and reverent to ancient ways. To do this, he has placed slivers of Stonehenge inside a microchip that is installed in each mask. When activated by a commercial the night of Halloween, the masks turn whoever is wearing them into oozing, ghastly creatures and kill all those around the wearer. Which is an intriguing idea.

Not the most thought-out of plans, though. It seems to depend on children wearing the masks at a time of night when most would already be out of the masks and eating candy. Plus, kids must be within audio range of a television set airing the ad, which means those actually out trick-or-treating probably would not be affected either, and those in other time zones where trick-or-treating has not even started are pretty safe as well. In other words, we're talking about a global plan that will ultimately affect probably three kids and two frat guys somewhere. Still, give the guy credit for coming up with something unusual there, using technology to hopefully wipe out a good chunk of humanity and bring back the ancient days of lore.

- *Suicide Club* (**2002**) Made at a time where Japanese horror films were reaching a high in being imported to America for consumption, *Suicide Club* at first seems to be working in the tradition of *Battle Royale* (with its interest in young people doing deadly things), but soon shows signs as being rather about society going mad and about the scarier idea of individuals simply losing their grip on reality. The plot deals with an investigation into why fifty-four seemingly normal, happy schoolgirls would jump as one in front of a moving train as part of a mass suicide. As the investigation continues and more people die, an underground social network on the Internet is revealed as the culprit. Worse, it appears its influence is extending beyond those who view it and into the consciousness of everyone—from a band that crush small animals to music to housewives happily cutting their own fingers off at the kitchen counter for no reason. Unfortunately for the film, there is no ending, as the creators involved planned to continue the story line as a trilogy that only supported one more film, *Noriko's Dinner Table* (2005), without any real revelation as to the meaning of the carnage. The implication is that something about the website is turning everyone insane, but later actions in the first film and second suggest something more. As it stands, all that can be counted on is that the website itself leads to heavier and deadlier concerns, which is enough to put it in this category.

- *The Signal* (**2007**) A low-budget film told from the viewpoints of three different characters during a night when a signal is sent by telephone, radio and television that is driving people to murder one another. It is never explained why the signal is being sent or who is sending it. There is one obvious thing, though: deaf people are going to be looking around wondering, "What the heck is wrong with everyone?"

- ***Pontypool* (2009)** from director Bruce McDonald also deals with a similar theme as *The Signal*, where sound contributes to a virus that turns people insane. The difference is that a certain word in the English language is the trigger to the virus, but the word can be random. Thus, talking in another language helps avoid the virus, as does not talking at all. As the film ends, it is found possible to cure the virus if a word is thought to mean something other than its true definition, but only for so long.

So the contagion by technological virus seems to have hit a bit of a rut. Plans are still ongoing to turn Stephen King's novel *The Cell* into a movie, however. This deals with a pulse signal disrupting every cell phone, causing those who hear it to become homicidal. The novel goes into setting up class distinctions between those who have become "phoners," those who haven't, those who have received a corrupted version of the signal and seem to sway in both directions and those who have had to kill phoners to survive. In the end the problem is stopped, but it points out a consistent issue with several of the technological virus movies as well—there doesn't seem to be much reason for such shenanigans other than just to cause chaos. Perhaps in the tradition of contagions in general, that is the norm, but it seems odd that it so often occurs as well in a format that is obviously man-made.

What is strikingly common in such films is how often people strive to conquer the contagion, do so and move on by the time the credits are rolling. Perhaps this is a sign that we as a people want to believe that we'll rise to the challenge and find a way to make the world a better place once again. On the other hand, it may be our own shortsightedness in the works as well. We have had pandemics in the past that, of course, have not wiped us out. Millions may have died, but we somehow avoided it and found ways to knock such viruses down a peg or two. With that in mind, we have a hard time believing that a bug of any kind will take us all out. Maybe the nuclear missiles will, but not the viruses.

We feel safe from disease. Even if we know that we are heading down a path where our intake of antibiotics has helped develop superbugs. Or that changing climate patterns have introduced what were once remote tropical diseases passed on by insects into what are no longer cooler climates. Not to mention the various biochemical weapons that are out there, the failures of inspections to keep tainted meat and vegetables from the public, and the chances of someday seeing terrorists resort to such low-grade biochemical weapons as dirty bombs. I could go on with a list, but the point is made.

As stated at the beginning of the chapter, contagion movies bring out a most depressing level of discussion in us all, even when the films represented in the genre have everyone happy and healthy by their conclusion. The knowledge of risks that are in front of us in reality makes even the "fun" contagion movies a tough pill to swallow. No pun intended. Honest.

Let's say we move on to something more fun. Something that in a way is still connected to contagions, but take it into the realm of the supernatural as well as science fiction and first-person gaming. Of course, that means one thing: zombies.

10

We Have Become Them

How Zombies Slowly Took Over the World

These days we see zombies as one thing: dead humans reanimated—through various means—that mindlessly search for living human flesh to eat. On top of this definition are various nuances and traditions that have sprung up over the years as to how zombies act, move, run (or not run) and, most particularly, how they can be killed. Naturally, this brings to mind the movie that really kicked off our interpretation of zombies today: *Dawn of the Dead.*

Oh, you were thinking of something earlier than that, I'm sure. In fact, I'm positive most readers know as much as or even more than I do about zombies in this day and age. At one time, such films would have been seen as a subset of another genre, such as the contagion films or monster films in general, but there are literally hundreds of movies that deal with gut-munching zombies now, and they can only be looked upon as a category onto itself. So much so that it would be impossible to be all-encompassing about them within this book, and certainly not in one chapter alone. Instead, this chapter is a primer to zombies in movies: where they came from, the changes they went through, and where we seem to be going with the concept.

The Merriam-Webster Dictionary refers to a zombie as "a mixed drink made of several kinds of rum, liqueur, and fruit juice," and yes, bartender, keep them coming. Above that definition, however, is a better one for what is covered in this chapter: "a will-less and speechless human in the West Indies capable only of automatic movement who is held to have died and have been supernaturally reanimated." This doesn't match our modern conception of zombies, but certainly defines our earlier cinematic portrayals of zombies: namely, a definition based on Haiti folklore and voodoo cultural tradition.

The best-known concept is that zombies are the dead brought back through dark magic to do as one wills. However, note that the above dictionary definition makes no mention of the person being really dead, only "held to have died." Even early interpretations of the concept in books and movies leaned more toward one involving living subjects drugged and hypnotized into believing that they have died and being nothing more than shells to do the bidding of their "masters." This is certainly a major influence on writers such as Wade Davis with his nonfiction book *The Serpent and the Rainbow*, which was made into the 1988 film *The Serpent and the Rainbow*, directed by Wes Craven and starring Bill Pullman (*Independence Day*).

As in *The Serpent and the Rainbow*, and in most zombie movies before the 1970s, a zombie is simply a living, hypnotized servant and nothing more. Perhaps a big hulking one that could break your spine in two like a dusty twig, but still human. They sleep in their "resting place" until needed, and some even eat food—gruel, perhaps, but certainly not human brains and intestines—which surely suggest something much more human than the zombies we know of in fiction today.

While there have been early attempts to show individuals who have been hypnotized into doing the bidding of others, the movie typically considered to have kicked off the zombie craze is *White Zombie* (1932), starring Bela Lugosi (*Dracula*). The film finds Lugosi as a voodoo practitioner who helps a man turn a woman into a zombie so the man can keep her from her fiancé. This works—the woman is pronounced dead and then is resurrected as a zombie—but the man who requested it be done has second thoughts and wants Lugosi to reverse the process. Lugosi, however, is too evil (naturally) and having too much fun to do that.

What is interesting about the movie is that the woman and other zombie slaves of Lugosi's character are controlled only as long as he is consciously doing so. The minute he is distracted, they stumble off blindly and tend to fall off cliffs. When Lugosi does the same at the end of the picture and dies, the woman is snapped back to normal, which shows a psychic bond of the master over the zombies that would be used in many of the films to come, even though this seems to suggest Lugosi would have to be working hard to keep his train of thought. No time for the crossword puzzles, that's for sure.

The film was considered a joke by many critics, but the public loved it, and its success led to other variations of the theme, including a film from the same director, Victor Helperin, in 1936, *Revolt of the Zombies*. By 1940, the genre was already generating enough interest that parodies emerged, such as Bob Hope's big breakthrough in the movies, *The Ghost Breakers*. The next really memorable zombie film came in 1943 with Val Lewton's *I Walked with a Zombie*. The movie was a reworking of *Jane Eyre*, only moved to the Caribbean island of Saint Sebastian and with a dash of Hitchcock's 1940 film *Rebecca* for good measure.

The plot features a first-person narrative by Betsy (Frances Dee), who is a nurse hired to take care of the wife of a plantation owner on the island, Paul (Tom Conway). Betsy sees the wife, Jessica, walking around her first night, but is then informed that Jessica cannot walk and has no willpower of her own. With growing feelings for Paul, Betsy tries to help snap Jessica out of her stupor and begins to investigate reports of voodooism that may be affecting the woman. Meanwhile, she also discovers that Paul's brother had at one point planned to

White Zombie (1932) helped solidify the concept of what zombies were supposed to be . . . for thirty-six years at least.   *Courtesy of Wrong Side of the Art*

leave the island with Jessica and that Paul's mother had placed a curse on her, which turned her into a zombie. By the end of the picture, the brother sends Jessica and himself out to sea, where they finally die, and Paul is free to be with Betsy, who he has fallen in love with.

I Walked with a Zombie is considered a classic horror film, thanks mainly to producer Val Lewton's work on it and a classy script that cribs a lot from *Jane Eyre*. However, after that film, subsequent zombie-related movies reverted to mainly glassy-eyed servants pushing people around, strangling a few and acting in many ways like the mummy in horror films. (And what is the mummy in most horror films but a zombie? Stomping around, doing the bidding of its master who brought it back from the dead or fulfilling a curse.) A shift began to emerge in 1968 with the release of *Night of the Living Dead*.

Night of the Living Dead is a film by George Romero, a director out of Pittsburgh who was producing commercials for television. It was decided to make a film, and the script was based on elements that Romero remembered from reading Matheson's *I Am Legend*—only instead of vampires, Romero decided to use ghouls who ate humans and anything else that was not moving fast enough (such as the crawling insect on a tree in one scene). The black-and-white film deals with Barbra (Judith O'Dea) running to a farmhouse after she and her brother are attacked by what at first appears to be a deranged man in a cemetery. She meets Ben (Duane Jones), who begins to board up the house, while listening to radio and television reports of the recent dead coming back to life as and mindlessly attacking people all along the East Coast. Ben hopes that they can wait out the attacks in the house until help arrives.

Soon after, it is discovered that a husband, wife and daughter had been hiding in the cellar of the house (Karl Hardman, Marilyn Eastman and Kyra Schon, respectively), and a young couple (Keith Wayne and Judith Ridley) joins them a short time after that. The father is a lout who insists the cellar is the safest place and does little to help, but with the daughter becoming sicker after having been attacked before arriving at the house, Ben tries to organize an escape to a nearby truck so that the young girl can be taken to get medical attention. The attempt goes disastrously wrong, with the young couple burnt to death in the truck. Barbra eventually gets swallowed up by an attacking herd of the ghouls—led by her now-dead brother—and the father tries once too often to get Ben killed, leading to Ben shooting him dead in anger. Meanwhile, in the cellar, the daughter has died and comes back to life, killing her mother with a masonry trowel. The ghouls continue to attack, and Ben ends up going to the cellar as a last resort, shooting the family, who are now all ghouls, and waiting for what will happen next. Finally, after dawn, a row of rifle-carrying men arrive, taking out the ghouls with shots to the head. Ben is relieved and leaves the cellar, only to be mistaken for just another ghoul. He is instantly killed and thrown on a fire with the other dead as the film comes to a sullen end.

Released into theaters and drive-ins starting in 1968, *Night of the Living Dead* became a surprise hit. It also faced controversy when it was paired up with the

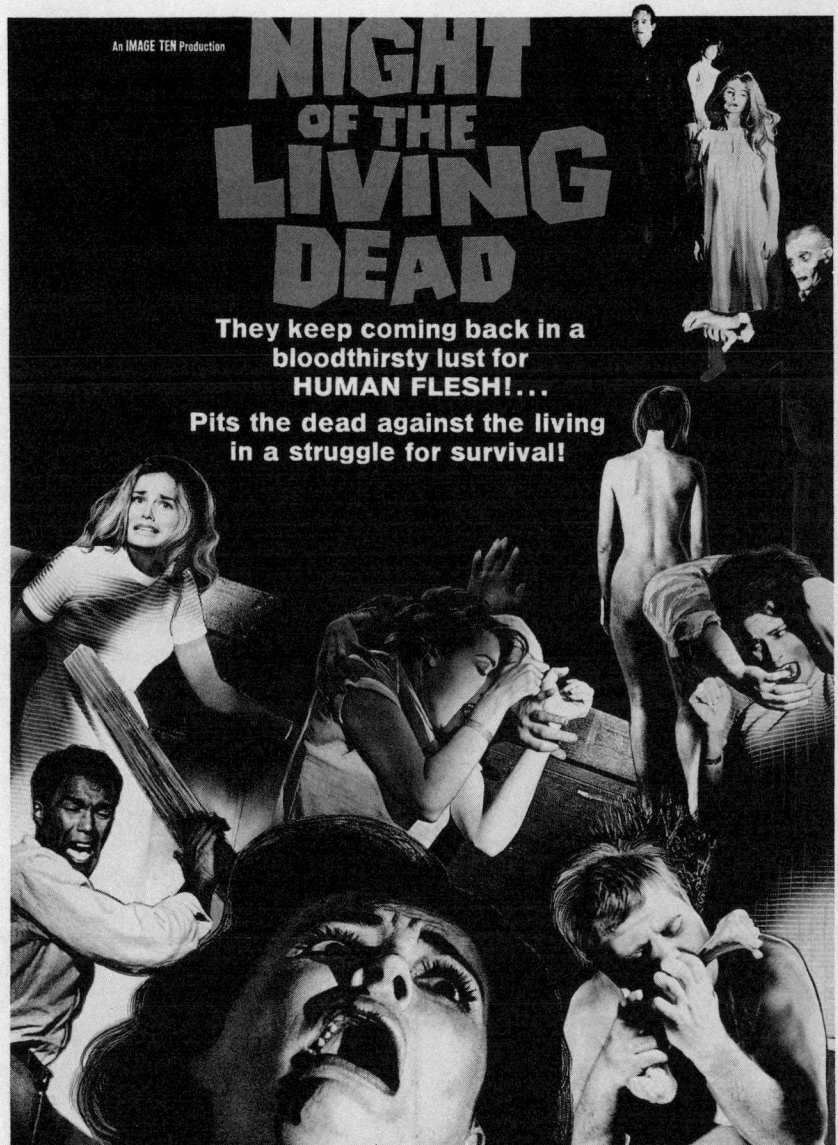

George Romero's *Night of the Living Dead* (1968) gave us zombies who attacked the living for food, a concept that would grow into a successful movie genre in the years to come.

Courtesy of Wrong Side of the Art

very children-oriented *Doctor Who* film adaptation *Dr. Who and the Daleks* for a run as a double feature. The problem was that the films were shown as such during the day for an audience that was full of children, with parents dropping off kids thinking they were going to get typical monster thrills. When critic Roger Ebert attended the double feature in early 1969, he was angered not so much at the movie but that the theater and the distributor would not realize that the film was traumatic to kids and wrote about it in a nationally syndicated column (he mentioned signs of children weeping in their seats as the ending credits began, many too scared to move). The column led to changes being made with the distribution of the film (a Chicago theater soon promoted it as no longer being shown during the day for the double feature, thus lessening the chances of children being sent to see it), but it also attracted even more attention to it, boosting ticket sales to those who had not been familiar with it before Ebert had written his condemnation. *Night of the Living Dead* made millions for the distributor but little for those who actually produced the film.

And this revolutionary concept of the dead that come back not just to kill or maim but to eat the flesh of the living? It didn't seem to really shake things up that much, actually. Zombies kept popping up in movies as mindless dead who do the bidding of others, with little notice of Romero's movie. Granted, the *Blind Dead* series from Amando de Ossorio out of Spain slid in that direction over time, but mainly those films dealt with vengeful ghosts rather than the recent dead eating people. There was a tendency to play zombies as actual dead people instead of simply hypnotized, but they still followed a type of curse, where luckless people would intrude on their domain and the zombies would do terrible things to them in response (such as drowning them in the Peter Cushing movie *Shock Waves*, from 1977). The only significant movie to play off of the whole "dead who eat people" vibe of *Night of the Living Dead* for the next ten years was Benjamin Clark's *Children Shouldn't Play with Dead Things* (1972). Clark (who, as Bob Clark, would go on to do the *Porky's* movies and the holiday classic *A Christmas Story*, making him kind of a Renaissance man in moviemaking) made *Children* very early in his career, and it shows.

The plot deals with a group of actors and their director who go to a small island where there is a cemetery. The director is mainly trying to spook everyone with some rituals that supposedly raise the dead and by digging up a corpse to mistreat for laughs. In vengeance for the corpse, and possibly anyone having to watch the movie, the dead rise and kill the cast of characters, eating them along the way. As stated, zombie movies simply did not follow Romero's path from *Night*, so Clark's film is a significant entry in the genre even though it typically only played in low-rent drive-ins and didn't really find a place in the collection of fans' memories until it was released on video (and certainly after Clark found fame with his other films).

More importantly, *Children Shouldn't Play with Dead Things* brings up an angle that Romero didn't bother with in *Night of the Living Dead*: up to this point, every single one of these movies worked on the stories being isolated incidents. Even

Children Shouldn't Play with Dead Things (1972) was a rarity between *Night of the Living Dead* (1968) and *Dawn of the Dead* (1978) in showcasing cannibalistic zombies, even if they were mainly eating very hammy actors.   *Courtesy of Wrong Side of the Art*

Man from Deep River (1972) not only kicked off a genre dealing with a variety of cannibalistic tribes chowing down on greedy rich, white guys, but also showed how zombies would act from now on, come the time of Romero's *Dawn of the Dead* (1978).

Courtesy of Wrong Side of the Art

Night of the Living Dead focuses on the concept of the hunters actually winning against the ghouls (even if they are stupid enough to not be able to tell any differences between the ghouls and living people). Clark's film, however, shows the dead winning and, better yet, getting on a boat and heading to Miami in the distance for probably more than some fun in the sun. It's an obvious "stinger" to the story line—going back to the old days of monster movies ending with a question mark instead of a card saying "The End"—yet it does drive the narrative in a direction that will become the norm by 1978 when Romero returns to the topic.

But before that, a series of films coming out of Italy should be mentioned that no doubt had some influence on what was to come. In 1972 came a film from director Umberto Lenzi called *Man from Deep River*, which features a man trapped with a cannibal tribe in a rain forest. Such a topic wasn't unusual to movies; several films from the early days of cinema portrayed men of modern society (usually white) having to relate to "the primitives." The Tarzan movies hinted at such on occasion, and there was Cornel Wilde's *The Naked Prey* (1966), which finds Wilde's character naked and on the run from an African tribe that is shown roasting one of his fellow hunters alive in a form-fitting clay. The Richard Harris film *A Man Called Horse* (1970) would also play with a similar theme, leading to a character cruelly treated but ultimately accepted by an American Indian tribe, and it is this film that bears the closest resemblance to Lenzi's. Several grisly events happen throughout *Man from Deep River*, as the man tries to escape only to end up accepted (and willingly so) as a member of the tribe. (For modern audiences, think *Dances with Wolves* but with everyone eating guts.)

As can be expected, the film did excellent business at the grindhouses around the world and led to a subgenre dealing with various cannibalistic tribes and cults in movies over the next several years (such as *Cannibal Holocaust, Trap Them and Kill Them* and the most notorious in American video stores, *Make Them Die Slowly*). All done with vivid special effects—and sometimes with disturbing real-life animal slaughter—that take flesh-eating in a film like *Night of the Living Dead* and compound the gore to a level rarely seen in cinema.

By 1978, audiences were becoming more self-aware, and as films such as *Halloween* and the remake of *Invasion of the Body Snatchers* appeared, showing more vivid special effects, it made sense for Romero to investigate doing something extreme in his comeback zombie movie as well. Seeing the money made off his 1968 movie, which did not trickle down to anyone who actually made the film, Romero decided to revisit the story line after making a series of other pictures (such as *The Crazies* and *Martin*). With the expansion of realistic and gory special effects, Romero decided to do the same and brought in effects artist Tom Savini to create the various effects seen in the film, which created a sensation on their own. Gone were the days of just a ghastly looking dead guy standing there holding what was probably a cow's thigh bone; instead, *Dawn of the Dead* featured effects most audience members had never seen before, such as heads blowing up, bites being taken out of people's necks and legs, and people being ripped apart. So much in fact that it was clear the MPAA would never give the film any rating other than an X, and so the movie was released without any rating whatsoever, which was a true rarity at the time. The posters featured a warning that "no one under 17 will be admitted" to help fight off any problems that occurred back when Ebert saw the first film, but that just led to many teenagers and kids finding theaters near them where the person at the ticket booth didn't care. In other words, it became a bit of a "dare" movie for young people to see if they could handle the gore as well as the horror aspects of the movie. Which made the film even more successful once in theaters. *Dawn of the Dead* would do remarkably well for a film that received no rating from the MPAA, an automatic no-no for some newspapers in running ads for it and with television advertising that usually aired only in the wee hours of the morning. As a moneymaker that came in through the "back door" of respectable theaters, instead of just third-run grindhouses and second-rate drive-ins, *Dawn of the Dead* proved to other filmmakers that there was room to experiment with the gross-outs and produce films that were stronger than what the major studios would ever put out themselves (although some would definitely try after Romero's film succeeded).

The biggest aspect of the movie, however, is that it changes the tide of how zombie stories were told. In *Night of the Living Dead,* as mentioned above, humanity is winning. The ghouls are being knocked off left and right, and everyone is happily tramping around in suits and ties with their rifles having a grand ol' time picking off dead guys. That's not the case as *Dawn of the Dead* kicks off. It is obviously some time later, and it appears the zombies have started to win mainly due to one factor—people have a hard time shooting in the head what were once their friends and family, and thus the population of zombies is allowed to grow because people can't adjust quickly enough to what needs to be done.

The movie begins with Francine (Gaylen Ross) working at a television station where chaos is taking control as a guest speaker tries to convince everyone that the dead are rising and killing, creating more zombies that do the same, and people have to be ready to do what needs to be done. Her boyfriend, Stephen (David Emge), is also the station's helicopter pilot, and he informs her that it's a losing battle and the two will be leaving that night with a couple of friends. His friends are Roger (Scott Reiniger) and Peter (Ken Foree), SWAT members shown dealing with a tenement with a basement full of zombie family members near the beginning of the movie. The foursome take off in hopes of finding a place to hide away until the zombie plague is over, stopping off at an airfield where we see for the first time children as zombies in a movie. They eventually land at a mall, where the generator still works and there are plenty of supplies. Instead of grabbing what they can and moving on, they decide to stay, eventually weeding out the zombies in the mall and moving trucks in front of the doors so more cannot enter. The plan works, but Roger is bitten in the process, and when he dies, he revives momentarily as a zombie before Peter shoots him in the head.

The relationship between a now-pregnant Francine and Stephen deteriorates as the three become bored in their new home. However, a roving motorcycle gang sees the mall and decides to break in, looking to loot the place. At first the three try to defend the mall against the gang and the aggressive zombies who have reentered the building, but soon only Stephen keeps on in a demented attempt to save what is "his." He is eventually bitten and turned into a zombie, mindlessly revealing the location of Francine and Peter in an attempt to go "home." Francine is sent to the roof to leave via helicopter, while Peter plans to stay behind and kill himself, but he decides to live and makes it to the helicopter before Francine can completely take off. The two fly off into a new day, low on fuel and with little supplies, but willing to latch on to staying alive for at least a little longer.

As reported often over the years, *Dawn of the Dead* has more than a simple horror story to tell, focusing on American consumerism and the emptiness and obsession of possession. The zombies flocking to the mall says it all, in a way, with the dead going somewhere they recognize as having been a big part of their lives when they were alive. From there, every so often other zombie films have tried to turn to social commentary in their work, but this wasn't the true breakout element of the film. Although a sequel to the first movie, *Dawn of the Dead* establishes much of the recurring lore of zombie fiction to come. It's even the first in the series to refer to the undead as zombies instead of ghouls. Further, no longer are zombies shuffling, moaning servants who are ordered to do nasty things to others, as had been established in nearly every movie before this about zombies. Now when audiences see zombies they think of dead creatures who crave human flesh. But that's not all. *Dawn of the Dead* also set up other parameters of the genre to come:

- All the dead rise to become zombies (this is a bigger standard than only those being bitten becoming zombies upon death).
- Zombies eat living people.
- They don't moan that much but do shuffle around. (Yes, we'll come back to this one.)
- A bite from a zombie will kill you.
- The dead "die" only if the head is destroyed.
- Society is rapidly crumbling because the zombies are winning.
- Bad guys manage to stay alive just to cause grief for the good guys.

Further, from this point onward, it is no longer an isolated incident on some small island somewhere; it's now a global crisis (or at least appears to be from what information we are given in the films). It's become a pandemic much like what occurs in *I Am Legend*, with only those still human struggling for survival.

Dawn was quickly followed up by the Italians, who turned away from the cannibal series long enough to say, "Hey, we already know how to do those effects; we can make one of these Romero zombie movies ourselves!" Which they did in 1979 with Lucio Fulci's *Zombie* (aka *Zombi II* and released outside of the

George Romero's *Dawn of the Dead* (1978) would define in more explicit terms exactly what to expect from the monsters in zombie movies up to the present day.

Courtesy of Wrong Side of the Art

U.S. as a sequel to *Dawn of the Dead*, which was titled *Zombi* in foreign markets)—a film that not only featured zombies that eat people but even threw in a great white shark that eats zombies as a way to rip off *Jaws* at the same time (and kudos to those who managed to pull off a scene with a guy dressed up as a zombie having to fight a real shark underwater). Even so, it didn't quite escape its heritage, taking place mainly on a small island in the Caribbean. That is, until its final scene, which shows a horde of zombies marching on to Manhattan (further solidifying the concept of the zombies beginning to take over).

After the success of *Zombie*, the screen exploded with . . . well, exploding people and zombies, really. By the mid-1980s, the genre was ripe for parody, which occurred with such films as *Return of the Living Dead* (cowritten with *Night of the Living Dead* cowriter John Russo), *Re-Animator* and *Night of the Comet*, but there were still some new ideas coming along.

Hundreds of zombie movies have come and gone since then, some with minor tweaks to try to freshen up the concept, such as the "running dead" from the 2004 remake of *Dawn of the Dead* (which is also one of a remote few that has the dead *not* coming back as zombies if not bitten). Other films have used the genre as a template for their own visions, such as *28 Days Later*, with its crazed infected individuals. Meanwhile, Romero continues to try out new concepts in subsequent *Living Dead* movies to diminishing results. He attempted a mass-scale ending to the series with *Day of the Dead* in 1985, but found himself rewriting the story to take place in a bunker with a smaller "bad guys vs. good guys with zombies hanging around" story line, which disappointed fans. He would return to the series in 2005 with *Land of the Dead*, followed by *Diary of the Dead* in 2007 (which took the "found video footage" angle of such films as *Cloverfield* and *The Blair Witch Project*) and *Survival of the Dead* in 2009 (a zombie movie bathed in the waters of a Tennessee Williams play). Meanwhile in 1990, Tom Savini tried his hand at directing a remake of the original *Night of the Living Dead* that allows Barbra to be the one who dominates instead of Ben. At the end, she not only survives but has become part of the group of shooters coming back to the house to save Ben, only to find him dead. She shoots the still living (and still sniveling) father character and tells the others that there is "one more for the pile." Looking at some of the poachers teasing and abusing the zombies captured, she realizes that mankind was hardly any different. "We're them and they're us," she says, and even though it appears in a remake, it is a theme that will be driven home in countless other serious zombie films in the twenty-plus years since its release.

Of course, there were dozens, even hundreds more zombie films yet to come. Understandable, really—they're somewhat cheap to make as monster movies and don't exactly involve more than makeup and effects to tell any tale necessary. Yet, just as it felt as if the genre had breathed its last, due to the flood of imitations, new directions were found. Certain comedies sprang up, such as *Shaun of the Dead* (2004), *Fido* (2006) and *Zombieland* (2009)—more on which will be discussed in a later chapter—making fun of the clichés, while the dead rose again with the success of the series *The Walking Dead* on the AMC cable network. The television series is based on a comic book by writer Robert Kirkman and artists Tony Moore and Charlie Adlard, and deals with a small band of people struggling to avoid "walkers" (the term used in the series for zombies) and other humans who have their own agendas against them. The series was developed by Frank Darabont (*The Mist*) and found a large audience, seeing the show into a fourth season by 2013, and takes a position similar to that of *Dawn of the Dead*, with a sheriff and his family working with a group of others to stay out of harm's way. Much of the genre's clichés are in place, including that of the dead rising to be zombies even if they are not bitten (the filmmakers, in a rare misfire, act like this is a startlingly new concept in zombie lore, but as already mentioned, the opposite found in the 2004 remake of *Dawn* is a rarity, not the norm). Nevertheless, the series has done a fine job of creating human-interest stories while at the same time giving viewers the shocks and guts that they want in a zombie program.

2013 finally saw the release of *World War Z*, a film starring Brad Pitt and based on the best-selling novel by Max Brooks. When first suggested as a film, many wondered how it could be done, as the book is an oral history of events by various individuals from around the world who had witnessed the near-destruction of humanity by zombies. While there are many visual moments in the novel, the structure of the book does not readily lend itself to film. Thus, many fans of the book were only mildly surprised when the movie was pushed back from its original release date in late 2012 to June 2013, and that additional filming was done to change the ending of the film (from one featuring Pitt's character fighting off zombies in Russia to that of a somewhat quieter turn of events in Wales). The film faced many problems during production, but because most people involved stayed optimistic, the film was not the scandal or dismal failure that some fans of the book and critics had predicted before its release. As it stands, the movie has done quite well and there are talks once again of doing a sequel.

In the real world, such successes as *The Walking Dead* and *World War Z* have springboard groups online and elsewhere that want to "play dead" in a sense. For most it is just a case of wanting to have some fun with the concept of "What would I do if everyone was a zombie?," thus creating their own fan fiction and playing at makeup to look like a zombie. There are even citywide zombie walks (where everyone marches together dressed as zombies in a parade down a major street of a city) and zombie runs (where runners have to not be tagged by people dressed as zombies hiding along the designated racing area in a park).

There has been a darker side to zombie fandom as well. Most zombie movies take a path that generally is used by films stuck in the Mad Max theme—it's postapocalyptic, but not enough that we can't have cool cars and maybe find neat things to possess. It's a childhood fantasy to find the world empty and be able to be kings and queens of the world, where everything still works and food is still fresh. Sure, there's also zombies around that will try to eat you, but that's just part of the exciting adventure you'll have in your new world. Plus, you get

Based on the novel by Max Brooks, *World War Z* (2013) attempts to tell a global story about zombies quickly advancing against mankind.

to shoot people without the remorse of killing the living. And it is this part of the fantasy where things have gotten a bit uncomfortable. As much as we play with the idea of zombies as entertainment, there are fans who have taken it to the level of survivalists—actively stocking up on weapons and supplies, as if there ever really could be such a thing as a zombie apocalypse.

Even the movies are never definitive as to how it all starts (*Night* makes mention of a space probe, but Romero and others from the film stated it was added mainly to give viewers a reason where none was needed). Most treat it as some type of contagion, much like how it comes about in *I Am Legend*, but in reality any pandemic that comes along to wipe out humanity isn't going to involve being able to drive around in your jeep all day and shoot at former humans as sport. It is just going to involve a lot of dying and probably in agonizingly slow ways.

Still, that doesn't stop some from taking it all a bit too seriously, hoping that someday they'll get a chance to kill what was once their fellow man.

Perhaps Barbra was right. Maybe we have become them.

The Supernatural

When the Undead Just Aren't Enough

Many different trappings of horror movies have been under review for apocalyptic films in the past few chapters. There have been the undead in the zombie movies and vampires (or something like them) in the *I Am Legend* films, but there are still other, more traditional supernatural monsters that have been used to spell the end of the world. Of course, we could include the big monsters of the silver screen, like Godzilla and such; they are, after all, part of our "shock theatre" heritage of movie watching when we were kids and typically thrown in with other horror and science fiction movies; but they're not of the supernatural bent. They're mostly about nuclear accidents and ancient history and will be discussed in a further chapter about nature striking back.

Surprisingly, there are only three areas of the supernatural that have show-cased the end of the world due to the supernatural, and that includes monsters hatched from the mind of H. P. Lovecraft like Cthulhu, the Ancient Ones and Elder Gods in movies already discussed, such as *The Cabin in the Woods* and *In the Mouth of Madness*. *The Dunwich Horror* (1970) deals with a third-act sacrifice by Dean Stockwell's character that nearly brings back the "Old Ones," as do similar attempts to break through barriers between worlds and produce other Lovecraft creatures in such movies as *Cthulhu* (2007) and *The Whisperers in Darkness* (2011). Beyond that, it has been mostly vampires and Satan, with the Devil getting his due, over and over again. First, a look at the bloodsuckers, however.

Traditionally, vampire movies deal with a single vampire fighting humans for one reason or another (usually a woman who reminds the vampire of a more innocent time), but that concept evolved as several movies dealing with groups of vampires moving from place to place like a pack of animals or a force of nature. Typically, however, such groups would work in seclusion. Roman Polanski's comedy *The Fearless Vampire Killers*, from 1967, deals with a large court full of vampires and insinuates that the bumbling "vampire hunters" of the title are about to spread vampirism throughout Europe at the conclusion of the film, but this is a rarity. (The Jim Steinman–penned stage musical based on the movie, *Dance of the Vampires*, even goes so far as to suggest that the vampires have taken over completely in modern-day society.) Most other films about packs of vampires tend to be more low-key and just sneaky. Such vampires appear in films like *Vampire Circus, Thirst, Interview with the Vampire, 'Salem's Lot, Buffy the Vampire*

The Dunwich Horror (1970)—an attempt to bring some of H. P. Lovecraft's concepts to the
big screen.   *Courtesy of Wrong Side of the Art*

Slayer, The Lost Boys, the *Twilight* films and the *Underworld* series, where the vampires really don't want the general public to know who they are and what they're up to (the *Howling* series would do the same for werewolves). They are menaces, but much more interested in their next meal and perhaps some mild level of vengeance, rather than world domination. If there are one or two that do want to rule the world, they are usually the villains of the piece, with other vampires trying to stop them.

Only two films show a postapocalyptic world centering on vampire culture as a global (and thus apocalyptic) experience: *Daybreakers* (2009) and *Stake Land* (2010). There is also the 2011 film *Priest*, which features a dystopian world of vampires and humans fighting each other, but it is more futuristic than apocalyptic (mankind is still going strong, he just has a different enemy to fight). Ironically, both play as if they could be alternate universes from that of Matheson's *I Am Legend* where the vampire plague has occurred—except one is a world continuing without a breakdown in society, and the other is a road picture with several survivors instead of just one. *Daybreakers*, directed by Michael and Peter Spierig (who also teamed on a zombie movie called *Undead*), deals with a worldwide plague that doesn't kill anyone, it merely turns them into vampires. Thus, society continues—the banks are still open and people still get into traffic jams, etc.—with the population feeding on those who did not turn as if they were cattle (a plot rumored at one time as one for Romero's *Living Dead* series). A pharmaceutical company is trying to come up with a way to stretch or substitute blood, as humans face extinction, and without them to harvest, the vampires will first go through a process where they become animalistic, and then berserk, killing anyone around, human or vampire. Meanwhile, more and more vampires are getting fed up with their existence and committing suicide via exposure to sunlight. Thus, the end of the vampires (and of humanity) is rapidly approaching. A scientist working for the company, Edward (Ethan Hawke), unintentionally becomes friendly with a group of humans that includes a man (Willem Dafoe) who was once a vampire but due to an accident had reverted to being human. The group then tries to duplicate the accident, and, upon doing so, deal with a company that realizes a cure may save mankind but will end their monopoly.

Stake Land, directed by Jim Mickle, who directed a vampire/crazed-contagion movie called *Mulberry Street* in 2006, follows two characters trying to travel to a safe haven called "New Eden" after a vampire plague has wiped out most of America. The older, more seasoned man, Mister (played by cowriter Nick Damici), and his young sidekick Martin (Connor Paolo) run into and team up with various survivors as they work their way across the country, while also having to deal with a fanatical band of humans called the Brotherhood and their leader Jebedia Loven (Michael Cerveris).

Both films do a fine job of examining their worlds of vampirism. *Daybreakers* by suggesting a world where the supernatural has intruded and . . . it didn't really make any difference. Everyone acts the same, working for a living and struggling to cope with life as they now know it. It also a mix of the ecological disaster (food supply running out) as well as the plague apocalyptic film, and even though it comes down to mainly a car chase and guys with guns shooting at each other, it at least gives us a look at an alternative to the various zombie plagues that typically turn up in theaters. In comparison to the corporate world satirized in *Daybreakers*, *Stake Land* runs the path of both the zombie landscape mixed in with a bit of *The Stand* and *Lucifer's Hammer* with the paramilitary-fanatic religious group that is out to get them. That may be part of the problem, however: while *Stake Land* is very well made and is certainly worth checking out, just as *Daybreakers* features an intriguing twist on the vampire plague concept, both are reflections of other films and series covering similar territory. It is hard to look at *Daybreakers* and not think of the HBO series *True Blood* (which takes a slightly different tack by having humans and vampires coexisting, side by side, instead of the vampires taking over completely). To be fair, the ends of *True Blood* and *Daybreakers* are not dissimilar from the resolution to Jim Steinman's *Dance of the Vampires* musical, which came before both. Meanwhile, *Stake Land* cannot break away from its heritage as essentially a postapocalyptic zombie movie, even if the angle is shifted to blood drinkers instead of flesh eaters.

This probably explains why we haven't seen much venturing into more films dealing with what humanity would do in apocalyptic situations dealing with the supernatural. Even a good concept is bound to have a studio representative say, "Yes, all fine and good, but why can't this be zombies instead?" And so we go back around once again.

The *Rec* (2007–2013) series of four films out of Spain from Jaume Balagueró and Paco Plaza is a rather unique attempt at mixing in the supernatural with the zombie film. It at first appears to be just another in the series of zombie-like crazy-people movies that came out after the success of *28 Days Later*, but then veers off into heavy religious overtones. *Rec* (as in the record light we see on-screen when using a video camera) deals with a reporter, Angela (Manuela Velasco), filming a television documentary program about firefighters working a late-night shift. The firefighters are called to an apartment complex to help the police with what appears to be a simple case of an old woman stuck in her apartment.

This turns out to be not quite the case. The woman is animalistic and bites one of the police officers, and it turns out that she carried what is assumed to be a fast-working form of rabies that quickly turns people into strong, homicidal maniacs. Yet, just as the film appears to be all set up the way we assume such a horror film would be, we find out that the virus being passed around is actually the result of experiments being done in the penthouse by a high member of the Vatican who was determining if demon possession could be reduced to a biological formula. To do this, he took a possessed girl who is still locked up in the penthouse, while (although it is not made clear) the Vatican scientist appears to have used his results on a neighbor's dog and possibly another child or two. Those left in the building soon find that the entire apartment house has been quarantined, and any attempt to leave results in death by sharpshooters around the building. Meanwhile, more and more of the survivors are dying or being turned, and it is finally left to Angela and her cameraman to try to get out alive.

In *Rec 2* (2009), the religious angle becomes clearer, although the story is stretched a bit thin with the introduction of idiotic teenagers who break into the house while under quarantine, mainly so there will be more characters to kill off as the movie goes along. In the second film, it turns out that a member of the Vatican is part of a squad sent in to find the original possessed girl, as her blood may help others to find a cure. Angela is then found, still alive and with her camera. In the end, however, it turns out that she has also been infected, and as the only one still alive in the house, she manages to be let out, thus releasing the demon contagion upon the world.

Rec 3: Genesis (2012) is a separate story that takes place at the same time as the first and is commonly seen as little more than filler before the final film, *Rec 4: Apocalipsis*, began filming in 2013. However, there are elements that help advance the story line: prayer can halt those infected, freezing them in place for a time in order to get away from them, while the infected cannot enter holy places and feel pain when splashed with holy water. The story deals with a man and woman who are getting married and the infection hitting the wedding party, turning all by the end of the film into what the audience now recognize as demons. As to what will occur in the final battle in *Rec 4*, audiences will have to wait to see when the film is released in 2014.

With the format of the *Rec* film, one can easily tie in the concept of *Demons* and *Demons 2*, as well as other possession films dealing with monsters, but the *Rec* series is the only one that uses religious elements as the basis for the monster's plan for world domination. *Demons* and films like it deal more with some mad scheme to do localized damage, not anything of an apocalyptic nature. Which is why demon possession movies for the most part are not part of the series of film listed here. *The Exorcist* is a classic horror film dealing with demon possession, but beyond the brief narration statement that such events are ways of causing "little deaths" in man's belief in a greater good in the world, it isn't global in its thinking. Nor would it have been a better picture going that route; in fact, it probably would have been the lesser for it as the story about a little girl being possessed becomes too "big" for its own good. Hammer's last picture before closing shop in the 1970s, *To the Devil . . . a Daughter* (1976), featuring Nastassja Kinski, Richard Widmark and Christopher Lee and based on a novel by Dennis Wheatley, also deals with a type of demon possession, but it is hardly the stuff of global concern. Well, at least not at the level we see it in the film.

Now, giving birth or raising a child that is the Antichrist—there's a story we can discuss in further detail here. It falls slightly into the same path as films to be discussed in the next chapter, but the following movies are really not focused so much on following scripture but rather in giving the audience a good horror or adventure movie. After all, when one gets into the Book of Revelation or other text dealing with the end-times, the Antichrist really doesn't have much of a backstory to his tale before we see him achieving world domination. He will come to world power (and it's always a he, so if you want to avoid the Antichrist happening, elect women from now on), then a type of worldwide religious power as well, deceiving the world, make us all wear the "mark of the beast" (oftentimes listed as the numbers "666") and leading us all to the return of Jesus Christ and finally Armageddon. But it's all a bit vague, and there's nothing in scripture about the Antichrist's high school prom or how good he was at basketball as a kid. In other words, filmmakers saw an opportunity to ask themselves, "Hey, what would happen if you knew your baby or your small child was the Antichrist?" and just went hog wild with ideas. He's got to come from somewhere, after all. Besides, who would be able to say, "No, that's not right"? And so a small number of "Bouncing Baby Beelzebub" movies have appeared over time.

The film that really kicked off the whole thing was Roman Polanski's *Rosemary's Baby* (1968), based on a novel by Ira Levin (who also wrote *The Stepford Wives* and the play adaptation of *No Time for Sergeants*). This is really a psychological horror film more than one about monsters or devils, with Rosemary (Mia Farrow) becoming more and more convinced that the neighbors in her apartment are not only Satanists but are working to make sure her pregnancy ends with the birth of the Antichrist. As it turns out, she's right, and although the audience never gets to see the child, Rosemary's cry of "What have you done to his eyes?" makes clear this isn't a normal baby waiting for her in the crib. Still, in a final moment that is both sweet and disturbing, she comes to accept the baby—the Antichrist—as her own.

Of course, then what? Hollywood couldn't leave the story just sitting there, especially after the movie was a big hit in theaters. So a television movie-of-the-week sequel was done featuring Patty Duke (an early contender for the role in the Polanski movie) as Rosemary and her son eight years later in *Look What's Happened to Rosemary's Baby* (1976). Surprisingly, it goes even further by essentially killing off Rosemary and then fast-forwarding into the future where Adrian is now an adult and a bit of a violent loser who doesn't realize his legacy. By the end of the film, he does and runs off scared, but it's too late—Donna Mills has molested him and is pregnant with his son, thereby proposing that Adrian is a lost cause and the Son of the Son of the Devil is going to be the Antichrist. Okay, sure.

Even with that type of ludicrous plot, it still probably is better than Ira Levin's sequel, *Son of Rosemary*, released in 1997 as a novel. It ends with Rosemary waking up before her pregnancy and finding out it was all a dream. Or is it? Yes, turns out it is, actually. So that's all wrapped up in a neat bow, really.

In 1974 came another movie that combined elements of *Rosemary's Baby* with those of *The Exorcist*: *Beyond the Door* (aka *The Devil Within Her*; not to be confused with *The Devil Within Her*, aka *I Don't Want to Be Born*, which features Joan Collins as a stripper whose baby is possessed by an evil dwarf . . . seriously). The film stars Juliet Mills as a woman pregnant with the Antichrist who starts spinning her head around, spitting up soup and doing all kinds of *Exorcist*-like antics. For kids like me that grew up watching Mills as the fun-loving witch-like Nanny on the television series *Nanny and the Professor*, seeing ads where the Nanny is suddenly revolving her head, etc., was particularly memorable, as we ran from the room screaming. In *Beyond the Door*, just as it appears good will win over evil, we find out that that's not really the case and there's a little boy smiling from the silver screen who is supposed to be the Devil's spawn.

A cheap little movie with hardly any real scares, *Beyond the Door* did set up the basic premise of what occurs in the first *Omen* movie (1976). The *Omen* series would last fifteen years and four movies before a remake occurred in 2006, but all deal with the concept of the Antichrist being born and raised. The first film has a fine cast, with stars Gregory Peck as Robert Thorn, the U.S. ambas-

sador to Great Britain, and Lee Remick as his wife, Katherine. When their newborn child dies, Robert agrees to adopt an orphan, soon named Damien, and hides the fact from his wife. Mysterious events begin to occur as Damien reaches the age of five, with first the death of his nanny and then the death of those suspecting something is not quite right about Damien, while Katherine suffers a miscarriage at his hands. Of course, Damien is the Antichrist and even conveniently has the mark on him for easy identification (probably not the best advertising for the Devil's son). This then leads to Katherine's death and Robert obtaining seven daggers that can kill the Antichrist. Where are these daggers discussed in scripture? Never you mind, just take the filmmaker's word for it and keep those daggers in mind, as they'll pop back up in a big way before the series is over.

Robert drags Damien to a church altar and is about to kill him with one of the daggers

An early ad for *The Omen* (1976). It may not have been the first to jump on the "Son of Satan" bandwagon, but it was certainly the most lucrative in franchising the concept.

Courtesy of Vintage Cinema Ads

when the police break in and shoot Robert dead. Damien is then seen at the end of the movie having obtained a new family who were friends of the ambassador—the family of the president of the United States. The second film, *Damien: Omen II* (1978), finds that Damien was adopted by Robert's brother Richard Thorn (William Holden), who is married to Ann (Lee Grant), and that he is now thirteen years old. This film is very much a retread of the first, featuring many elaborate death scenes of those who catch on that Damien is the son of Satan. The only new twists are that Damien is at first panic-stricken when he discovers who he is, and that Ann turns out to be working to help Damien in his destiny. By the end of the film, Ann has stabbed Richard with one of the daggers (I told you those would turn up again), and with everyone pretty much dead, Damien is set to take over Thorn Industries.

Now accepting himself as the Antichrist, Damien grows up to be Sam Neill (of course) and looking to start his role as world dominator in the third film in the series, *Omen III: The Final Conflict* (1981). Damien is now thirty-two, a CEO for Thorn and has just been made the U.S. ambassador to Great Britain when he notes signs that suggest the Second Coming of Jesus is fast approaching. Meanwhile, a group of priests gets hold of the seven daggers and work to get close enough to Damien to kill him before he can do anything to a child born that is Christ. The film ends with everyone pretty much getting a dagger to stab each other until Christ appears and a woman whose son is killed by Damien stabs him in the back with one of the daggers, defeating him at his moment of triumph.

There was one more attempt to resurrect (heh) the series with a movie called *Omen IV: The Awakening*. This was a pilot for a series that dealt with the son of the son of Satan, Alex (if he had only been named Adrian, they could have tied it in with the *Rosemary's Baby* sequel), being born. Evidently, each week would have seen a lot of guest stars being picked off in mysterious ways as they found out the baby was demonic. As one can guess, it bombed and nothing ever came of the idea after the pilot. The book novelizations attempted to carry on the story line in *Omen IV: Armageddon 2000* (1983) and *Omen V: The Abomination* (1985), both by Gordon McGill and also dealing with a "son of the son of" plot, all ultimately ending with the Antichrist losing. Which certainly falls into place with how scripture would have it, although it ends up exposing the true fallacy of producing stories based on the Book of Revelation—we know he can't win. So the only option is to drag out his loss with a bunch of clever death scenes along the way, and thus the story is destined to get stuck in a rut. But more about this in the next chapter. After this, there was an attempt to reboot the series with a remake in 2006 of the first film, directed by John Moore and starring Julia Stiles and Liev Schreiber, with Rosemary herself, Mia Farrow, as little Damien's helper, Mrs. Baylock. The remake was a success, but nothing further has been done to go through the entire cycle again.

Other films have touched upon Satan's spawn or the Antichrist, but most deal with a full-grown man without much reference to his "early days." A few try to take the story of the Antichrist and twist it in different ways, however. The *Hellboy* films by Guillermo del Toro (*Hellboy* in 2004 and *Hellboy II: The Golden Army* in 2008) were based on a comic-book character by Mike Mignola, who appears to be a hellspawn but has rejected his role in Satan's scheme. The 1977 Italian film *Holocaust 2000*, starring Kirk Douglas in the Gregory Peck role, deals with a nuclear industrialist who discovers that his grown son (Simon Ward) is the Antichrist and that their newest nuclear plant is a fulfillment of prophecy—a film that plays more like a mix of entries one and three of *The Omen* series. The 2007 film *The Reaping* (directed by Stephen Hopkins and starring Hilary Swank) appears to deal with a demon child bringing different plagues upon a town, but this turns out not to be quite the case. Before that there was Demi Moore as a pregnant woman in the 1988 movie *The Seventh Sign*, whose story has to do with the birth of her child causing Armageddon through no one's fault but just being essentially the lucky baby in the prophecy lottery, and thus is not a traditional Antichrist tale. *The Crow: Wicked Prayer* (2005), starring Edward Furlong (*Terminator 2*) and Tara Reid (oh, leave her alone), features a ritual that is meant to bring about the Antichrist but instead has Satan take over one of the bad guys, so it doesn't quite fit the mold either. John Carpenter's *Prince of Darkness* (the second in his apocalypse series) involves a variation of the Antichrist that is actually some type of alien force that seeks to bring its "father" out from an antimatter world, keeping a supernatural bent but turning the story of the Antichrist into one that is more geared toward science fiction than the biblical.

Then there's *End of Days*, which takes the tale of the Antichrist and gives us the answer to the burning question, "Yeah, but what if Arnold Schwarzenegger had to fight Satan?" Dealing with no known prophecy ever committed to scripture, the concept of the film has Satan taking over the body of a powerful businessman (Gabriel Byrne) so that he can track down the one woman born on Earth who can give birth to the Antichrist because of a symbol on her arm and who must be impregnated before midnight on New Year's Eve in 1999. Why, yes, it does seem like Satan has to really make things complicated, doesn't he? As many critics pointed out at the time of the film's release, is there a particular time zone Satan has to do this in, or is it just in the one he happens to be in at the time? It makes Damien being born of a jackal rather quaint in comparison.

Vatican knights want to kill the woman, Christine (Robin Tunney), who has no idea any of this is prophesied and ends up under the protection of Jericho Cane (Arnold Schwarzenegger), a former cop with a name out of an old pulp novel. Cane is still depressed over the death of his wife and daughter, but when given a chance by Satan to have them back, he refuses in order to keep Christine safe. With a plot finding characters being hidden Satanists, mercenary Vatican knights ready to kill, and people being resurrected by Satan to help him, Cane still managed to use his wits and a lot of firepower to blow up things and keep Satan on his toes. Eventually, however, Satan possesses Cane, but Cane manages to control his body long enough to throw himself on a sword from a statue of Saint Michael, thus allowing the one-hour time limit Satan established for

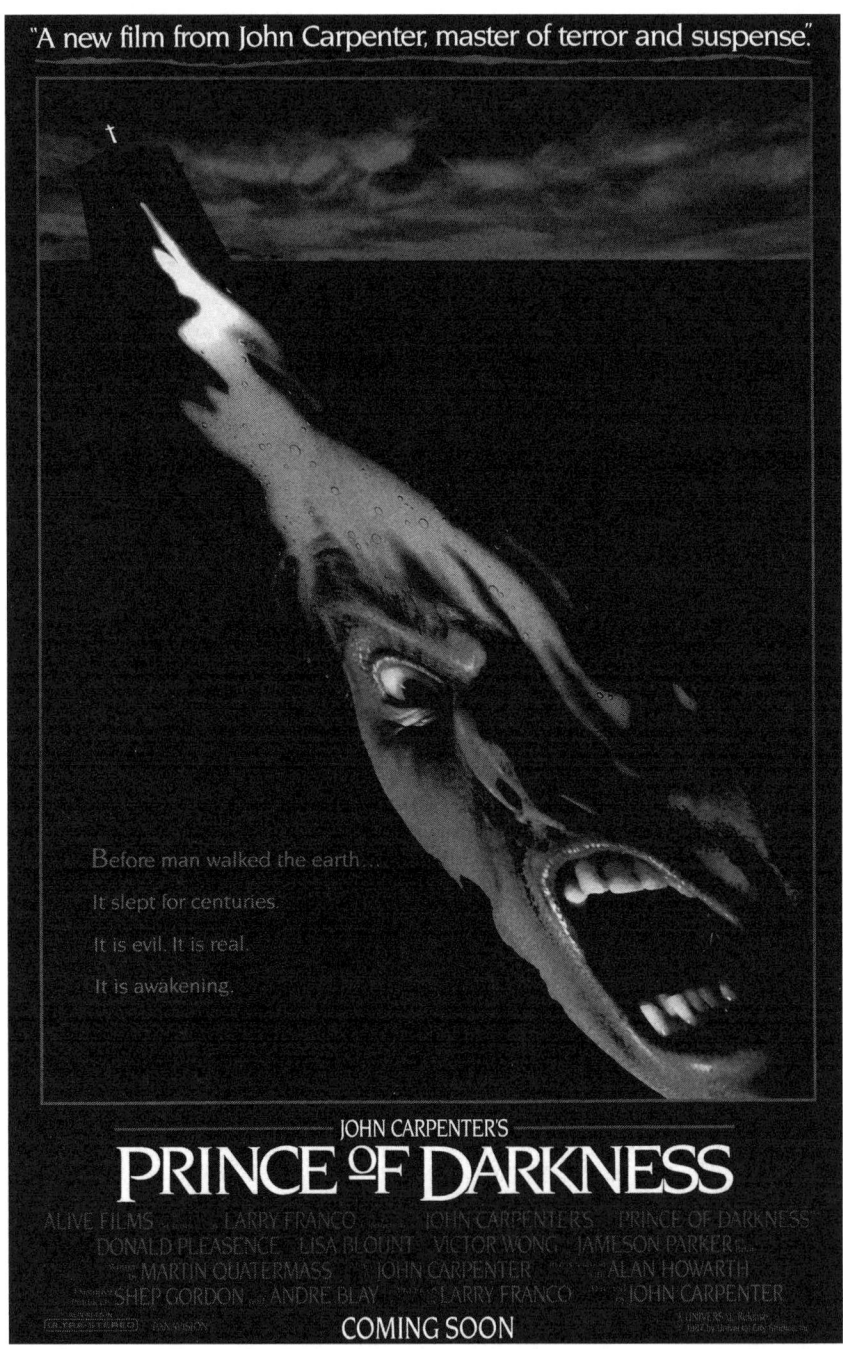

John Carpenter's *Prince of Darkness* (1987) is a rare attempt to reframe the concept of Satan and the end of the world.

251 to end. Satan is sent back to Hell, Cane goes to Heaven to be with his

himself to end. Satan is sent back to Hell, Cane goes to Heaven to be with his family, Christine is safe forever from the bad guy and the Antichrist genre fell in on itself. At least with the major Hollywood studios, which felt the movie underperformed even with a superstar like Schwarzenegger in the cast. Not that it was the end of things from other filmmakers, as we'll see in the next chapter.

There is one other category of religious apocalypses to consider, which really do not quite set up the Antichrist theme. Instead, they deal with an ongoing battle between heaven and hell that uses the people of Earth mainly as cannon fodder. This concept would be a central theme to the Fox network television series *Millennium* for a season before being jettisoned to concentrate on more traditional serial killers and such, but the idea is one that has popped up in a handful of movies over time. As is common with such films, the premise is built on the belief that the angels are not always on the side of God, typically in the status of have fallen or will fall from the grace of God due to some arrogant plan of their own. In some ways, this may appear to be a rather blasphemous concept; after all, angels are supposed to be good, loving, full of kindness, the messengers of God. We grow up with the concept of "guardian angels" that help guide us to the path of righteousness. Then suddenly it's all about them doing bad and trying to kill humans.

Yet the Bible does talk about Lucifer as a fallen angel, and so there is precedence. Thus, it is easy to say, if one angel can fall, why not others? Why not in the present day? If Lucifer can be fallible (and in a sense, human) in his thinking, can other angels be the same? This brings up many theological questions about the nature of man and our relationship with an all-powerful creator that has a secondary group coexisting with us. In some ways, you could say that angels are mankind's first relationship with an alien culture. So what does that mean to Hollywood? Pretty much that we make angels aliens with superpowers that look like us and go around doing a lot of humanlike things, but all for the glory of God or Satan or power. That may seem to go straight back to the topic of blasphemy, but then again, the movie poster for *Legion* (2010) that shows Archangel Michael with his wings spread out and a knife in one hand and an automatic weapon in the other is very striking, even if some may feel it's a bit silly at the same time.

Legion, directed by Scott Stewart (who also directed the dystopian vampire movie *Priest* from 2011) from a script cowritten by him and Peter Schink, starts with Archangel Michael falling from the sky and cutting off his wings. He heads to a diner in the middle of the Mojave Desert to help protect the birth of a child (once again, a child prophesied to do great biblical-rattling things) who will save humanity after God has decided he is fed up with them and wants the angels to wipe them out. Of course, this conflicts with God's promise to Noah from the Bible, but it's God, so evidently he can change the rules if he wants. Plagues appear, such as swarms of flies and people developing boils, but the biggie is a number of humans who become possessed and attempt to take out other humans, including those in the diner.

Michael tries to help in his weakened state, but as the baby is born, the trumpets call and Gabriel comes to deal with the baby himself. This leads to a fight between Michael and Gabriel where Michael is destroyed and Gabriel goes

By 1999 and the release of *End of Days* with Arnold Schwarzenegger, the concept of the Devil looking to start Armageddon was starting to look old-hat.

after the remaining survivors of the diner. When those left are willing to sacrifice themselves in order to save the baby, God decides humanity has redeemed itself enough and calls off the angels, with Michael being redeemed as an archangel. Thus, a battle between the angels, with humanity managing just barely to survive to find a new world waiting for them.

Gabriel is seen again in the 2005 film *Constantine*, based on the popular comic-book series *Hellblazer* (with the characters first created by Alan Moore, who also wrote the quasi-apocalyptic comic-book series *Watchmen*). Constantine (Keanu Reeves) is a man who can see creatures that are derived from angels and demons as they truly are and uses his powers to help keep things in balance between the two, leading to him not being very well liked by either. As the film begins, it is discovered that he once tried to kill himself and that he is dying of lung cancer, leading him to the reluctant conclusion not only that he will die soon but that Satan will come to take his soul to hell. As it turns out, Gabriel has come to Earth because he feels humanity is looked upon too favorably by God and wants to release one of Satan's seven sons, Mammon, on Earth so that humanity will be truly worthy of God's love. Constantine kills himself, stopping the final ritual that would bring Mammon to Earth as Satan appears to drag him to hell. Once Constantine tells Satan Gabriel's plan to usurp his domain with his son, Satan throws Mammon back into hell and God turns Gabriel human for his misdeed, leaving humanity safe and with Constantine given the chance to live again and with his soul intact (at least for the moment).

If this plot sounds somewhat familiar, then perhaps you've seen one of the longer-running series of films dealing with a battle between angels and . . . angels, actually.

The Prophecy (1995), written and directed by Gregory Widen, stars Christopher Walken as the archangel Gabriel. Gabriel seeks the soul of a vicious human in order to use him in his civil war with other angels over who is the favored creation of God—humans or angels. Because of the war, no souls have ever entered heaven, and Satan (Viggo Mortensen) arrives to help mainly because he believes Gabriel is setting himself up to do the job Satan does, and there's no need for two hells around.

At the end of the first film, Gabriel is exposed as the soul escapes his reach, and Satan gladly drags him down to hell with him for seeking to do an evil act, thus appearing to allow the war to end and souls to be released to heaven. However, Gabriel returns in the second film of the series, *The Prophecy II* (1998), directed and cowritten by Greg Spence. In this one, Gabriel returns to Earth to stop the birth of a child born of the angels and man, which will only unite the angels in Heaven and prevent him from restarting the war. Gabriel is again defeated and this time is turned human by Archangel Michael (played by Eric Roberts) at the conclusion of the movie, which is a reversal from *Legion*, which found Michael as a fallen angel and Gabriel doing God's will.

But Gabriel will be back in *The Prophecy 3: The Ascent* (2000). This time around, he has been a human for nearly two decades, watching the boy born of angel and man grow into an adult named Danyael (Dave Buzzotta). Danyael preaches to people that God does not care for humanity, but soon finds that he has a destiny in the battle between the angels. Gabriel tells him that because of who he is, he can stop Pyriel (Scott Cleverdon) from his plan to overthrow God and terminate mankind once and for all. With Gabriel's help, Danyael defeats Pyriel, and for his unselfish actions, God allows Gabriel to once again become an archangel.

And thus ends Gabriel's time in the series, but not the end of *The Prophecy* series itself. The next two movies, *The Prophecy: Uprising* and *The Prophecy: Forsaken* (both 2005), deal with a human named Allison (Kari Wuhrer) who obtains a book that contains new scripture that foretells how the war of the angels will end. *Uprising* is essentially a reprisal of the plot from the first film only with the book being a MacGuffin in the proceedings. *Forsaken*, however, has an interesting twist in that not only does Allison turn out to be another child born of angel and man, but her battle—in which she is the good guy—involves her getting help from Satan and stopping a group from discovering the name of the Antichrist being born. Their plan is to kill the child and stop Armageddon from happening, but for once our "heroes" of a movie actually *want* to protect the Antichrist and see Armageddon through. Thus, the audience cheers (well, within reason) as Allison succeeds, and we're on our way to the Promised Land in a sense.

Ironically, the films covered in the next chapter aren't meant to be cheerleaders for the Antichrist to rise to power as the final *Prophecy* film does. Nevertheless, they certainly do seem to indicate that some filmmakers just can't wait to see the end of the world coming down the path.

12

Onward, Christian Soldiers

The End-Time Flicks

Since the early days of silent movies, filmmakers have produced a variety of biblical stories. There were two reasons for this, the biggest one being that such films were sure moneymakers. Everyone knew at least some stories from the Bible, even if they didn't go to church. So you could slap together a story about Noah, etc., and people would attend because at least it was a story they knew. Secondly, as Cecil B. DeMille discovered rather quickly, you could get away with a lot of vice, sin and women in skimpy outfits as long as it was in the context of a story like *The Ten Commandments* or *Samson and Delilah*. Give the audience what they want and have them leave feeling they got what they needed was the recipe of such filmmaking.

With that in mind, it was not as if the major studios ignored Christians in their films, especially not in the days when many of those studios were managed and owned by those raised in Judaism. More often than not, they bent over backward to produce such films to show their caring for such stories. After all, people are already looking at you a little cockeyed for running a movie studio in the first place; no reason to get Christians—at a time when anti-Semitism was unfortunately quite the norm—upset because not enough films were being made that incorporated Christian ideals in them.

So we did get a lot of films showing rather swashbuckling priests (like Pat O'Brien in *Angels with Dirty Faces* or Spencer Tracy in *Boys Town*) or those who were the caring voice of reason (like Bing Crosby in *The Bells of St. Mary's* and Ward Bond in *The Quiet Man*). Even tough-guy actors like Humphrey Bogart took a crack at it (*The Left Hand of God*). And the studios certainly didn't shy away from allowing religious elements to creep into their stories, as can be seen in movies under discussion in this book, such as the final scene in *The War of the Worlds* (1953), where a group of survivors hold out in a church and pray, only for the Martians to die just before they can obliterate the House of the Lord.

We also got films where the Devil turned up, usually as an instigator to action in the plot and sometimes nothing more than comic relief. Perhaps in those days we felt a little more sure of ourselves and could laugh at the Devil, knowing that as long as we were strong of will, he could never defeat us. Now in our "enlightened times," we ironically seem to view Satan and his minions as something more wicked and uncontrollable (well, besides Adam Sandler's comedy *Little Nicky*, but that was an unbearable evil to audience members in an entirely different way). Also, there wasn't much use for going into religion in science fiction unless taking a biblical story and twisting it a little, or fulfilling the "no atheists in foxholes" formula by having people waiting to be killed by aliens praying for forgiveness or salvation. When it was used in a bigger context, it tended to look a tad silly. *The Next Voice You Hear* is a movie from 1950 that deals with everyone hearing God through the radio and how the moment leads to the overthrow of the Communist regime. Lightning striking Patty McCormack in *The Bad Seed* (1956) looks like none other than God just getting fed up with a character.

More importantly, as we drifted through the twentieth century, we became more aware that not every religious figure was out to do right for mankind in the service of God. Wicked priests, sadistic preachers, dishonest faith healers and just the flat-out "Crazy for God" began to pop up in films mainly because in the real world there certainly were people of this sort, and it made for easy villains to create, especially if such films had a religious tone to them anyway. For example, *Oh God* (1977) may play as a sweet comedy about God making us aware of his existence, but it couldn't resist sticking in a popular religious figure who is only in it for the bucks.

Which has led to a bit of a backlash from Christian viewers. Not that they were greatly upset when Hindus, atheists, Satanists, Islamists or others were painted with a broad brush, but once there were a few films out there dealing with "bad" Christians, the thinking was, "Hollywood doesn't like Christians!" Which led to the development of films being done for Christian audiences by Christian filmmakers (or at least the guys holding the moneybags). The genre is typically seen as slowly emerging through the films of Ron Ormond, who made cheap exploitation films with his wife, June (*The Monster and the Stripper*, for example). In 1968, he began making movies geared to a Christian audience and he became a kind of Cecil B. DeMille of exploitation films, using elements from his past that he could get away with now due to them being dressed up within a Christian narrative (not to say that Ormond wasn't honest in his attempt to preach the gospel; mainly that he knew what would put people into seats). The film that cemented his place the history of Christian cinema was *If Footmen Tire You, What Will Horses Do?* (1971), which dealt with a Communist takeover of America that sees the death and torture of those who are Christian (think of it as a 1960s version of *Red Dawn* cast with people your mom knew at church back then). The film was mainly seen in churches, as were additional films by Ormond and his family before his passing, and more churchgoers took note and decided to do their own films as well.

One can't help but mention the ongoing television series *Insight*, which ran from 1960 until 1983, created by Ellwood E. Kieser, a Roman Catholic priest. There were 250 episodes filmed, mainly of a half-hour variety, in an anthology format like *Twilight Zone*, only dealing with religious issues. One fascinating aspect was how many top-notch television actors, writers and directors were attracted to the series over time, and it was not uncommon to see anyone from Bob Newhart to Martin Sheen to Walter Matthau popping up in episodes directed by Arthur Hiller and Jay Sandrich and Ted Post, and written by people such as Rod Serling and Michael Crichton.

The show lasted a good number of years because, although it could be quite preachy, it was religious programming that entertained, and stations bought the show to air early or late on Sundays to fulfill the requirement of religious programming needed by the FCC. The feel of the show was that of drama for the most part, with little time to get much more across than a situation and then a remedy that involved religious insight into a resolution. Even with good actors, directors and writers, it also came across as quite static at times, which seems to be a lot of the problem with Christian films that came about in the 1970s and onward. *Six Hundred and Sixty-Six* was discussed in chapter 7, but this is a good example of what was occurring in Christian cinema of the 1970s—a rather bare-wall film depicting a handful of characters that do relatively little before the denouement revealing that the Antichrist has come and Armageddon is on its way.

As with *Insight,* many Christian films done by Christian filmmakers to come into the 1980s and onward were simple family dramas that show people in a crisis and coming to God to search for answers. Most certainly they were not of the fire and brimstone variety like *If Footmen Tire You, What Will Horses Do?* or Ormond's follow-up, *The Burning Hell* (1974). Even films that were essentially passion plays rarely got into the gruesomeness that can be drawn out in the story of Jesus' crucifixion (one reason why Mel Gibson's *The Passion of the Christ* in 2004 raised such a ruckus with its focus on what was done to Jesus in shocking detail).

The one area where Christian movies did partake of a more violent nature was on the topic of the end-times. Which, appropriately enough, leads us to a quick summary of what Armageddon is all about; or rather, what some believe it is about from their understanding of the Book of Revelation. The final chapters of the accepted version of the New Testament (some Christians would dispute even that designation) deal with prophecies

If Footmen Tire You, What Will Horses Do? (1971), although not actually an apocalyptic film, helped kick off the concept of the end-times in Christian cinema.

ascribed to John (of which historians question if John is John the Apostle or someone else) and written around 70 AD (or possibly decades later). The chapters deal with a number of things early on, but the focus of everyone today is on John's apocalyptic visions, which are interpreted by Christians in a variety of ways: historical, symbolic or—most importantly for this chapter—futuristic. It is this futuristic interpretation of the Book of Revelation that has led to all the bells and whistles we commonly heard in regard to the end-times: the Rapture, the Day of Reckoning, the Antichrist coming to enslave the world, an actual mark of the beast to be applied, etc.

To those who believe the book to be one of "things to come," the story line goes that the Rapture will take those who believe in Christ up into the air and into heaven, leaving others behind for the Tribulation to follow. It is in this period that the Antichrist will come to power and reign for seven years. In those seven years, the mark of the beast will be placed on the forehead and hand of all who wish to be part of society, and those who refuse will be made Christian martyrs and killed. A series of plagues then will occur involving boils, locust-like creatures that kill, the death of at least a third of those still alive and lots of blood-related incidents. Then, just as the Antichrist is set to deliver a final blow against humanity, Jesus arrives and easily defeats the Antichrist. Those who died without the mark are spirited to heaven, and there's a thousand years of peace on Earth. Then God lets Lucifer off the hook after the thousand years, Satan—not bothering to read the Bible—tries one last attempt to take over, is eliminated for all time after a twelve-minute war and God recreates the earth for the good and righteous forever and ever.

That's the premise most end-times movies are based around, and to do them properly, there can really be no detours from the story line. The only deviation is telling personal stories of those who are caught in the middle of the events that are to come. That is the focus of all the films listed here, with the genre really kicked off in a proper way with the release of *A Thief in the Night* in 1972. The film was produced by Russell S. Doughten Jr., who also cowrote the script and appears in the film, as well as produced the others in the series. It deals with a young woman, Patty Jo Myers (Patty Dunning), who is happily married and thinks of herself as a good Christian, but because she had truly not accepted Jesus into her life, she misses out on the Rapture as her husband and friends disappear from the earth. She then has to face the coming Tribulation on her own and eventually falls from a bridge to her death rather than get the mark of the beast. She wakes to find it was just a dream, but the radio then announces that millions of people have disappeared, and she realizes the Rapture is actually occurring.

While the cast is not very slick, the production values were enough to make the film look more like . . . well, a real film instead of something the Sunday school class had thrown together. Because of this, it was seen by a larger number of people than just those who caught it at special showings and church, and it led to three sequels that tell more of the story. *A Distant Thunder* (1978) continues the story of Patty, who is about to be executed and refuses to accept God as she feels it is his fault that things have turned out as they had. The third film, *Image of the Beast* (1981), finds Patty being saved from the guillotine when an earthquake occurs, but the blade comes down, killing her, when she screams that she'll accept the mark. The story then shifts to four people who have escaped from a detention center and their attempts to fake the mark in order to live within society. Meanwhile, the Antichrist has taken control of the world. Eventually, only a man and a boy survive and are being led to execution, but with the acceptance of Christ on their side as the film ends. In 1983, *The Prodigal Planet* was released, which takes place a few years after the end of the previous movie to show that a nuclear war has wiped out most of the world and that the Antichrist's government is slowly starting to lose out to those believing in the return of Christ. In a truly postapocalyptic movie culture, the man from the previous film has to make his way across a nuclear wasteland and avoid mutants and the Antichrist's military officers to get to a group of believers waiting for the Second Coming. The film

Russell S. Doughten Jr.'s film *A Thief in the Night* in 1972 was the first to set up an end-times franchise for Christian cinema, with multiple others following suit.

ends with some characters surviving, some saved, some not, and everyone still waiting for Jesus to arrive for Armageddon. As of now, there is still talk of at least one more film in the series, *The Battle of Armageddon*, to show what occurs next.

Even as a series still incomplete after over forty years, the initial films had a huge impact on those to follow, including those of the authors of the famous *Left Behind* series, who have pointed to the series as an influence on their work. Although the films rarely rise above their cheap exploitation origins (including a running time that barely passes an hour in length), with the first film ending with a total "it was all a dream . . . or was it?" cliché, the series at least stands by its convictions and tells the story as many Christians believe it will occur. Most films of the genre, including those in other popular series about the end-times, follow the same pattern as the *Thief in the Night* series:

1. People who think they are faithful find they have been left behind.
2. Along with a bunch of bad, wicked people.
3. A military-political group *very* quickly takes over for the Antichrist.
4. While some people seem to move along as if nothing has changed, there are obvious choices to be made as to being either for or against the new world order.
5. The mark of the beast (or BIM if you watched *The Apple*) is given to everyone, and those who refuse are punished.
6. As an underground movement of Christians rise, the Antichrist's world order starts to crumble.
7. Jesus arrives for Armageddon (usually several movies down the line, if at all).

Even as popular as *A Thief in the Night* was, there were not many films that reflected upon the same topic for many years (perhaps due to *Thief* fulfilling the role so well that other filmmakers decided to attempt other stories instead). *Years of the Beast* in 1981 was one of the few, but it was relatively quiet until the *Left Behind* book series began in 1995, finishing in 2007 with sixteen books and various spin-offs series, a trilogy of films, as well as a major studio remake in 2013. The novels were written by Tim LaHaye and Jerry Jenkins, and one has to give them credit for setting their story throughout the entire period described in the Book of Revelation, including the one thousand years of peace and how Lucifer would even have a chance of coming back to fight Jesus again.

The first few books were a huge crossover success in secular sales, obtaining top spots on the *New York Times*' bestsellers list even though it did not record sales of books through Christian bookstores. With that much attention, a movie adaptation was surely in order, but another series of films would hit the marketplace first—this one coming from Cloud Ten Productions, the same company that later produced the *Left Behind* films. The *Apocalypse* series began in 1998, and, while it follows the traditional guideline for the end-times, it does not quite follow one group of characters from film to film like the *Thief* and *Left Behind* series. Instead, the stories told are random events that unfold for characters in each of the four films.

Apocalypse (1998) begins with two reporters who attempt to stop the Antichrist (played by Nick Mancuso) from moving forward with his new world order. *Apocalypse II: Revelations* (1999) stars Jeff Fahey (*Planet Terror, Lost*) as an agent and skeptic whose family vanished in the Rapture. He manages to stop a plot dealing with virtual reality headsets by the Antichrist's world order and converts to God, but is never seen again in the series (most probably because the actor found better gigs). Instead, *Apocalypse III: Tribulation* (2000) picks up a thread of *28 Days Later, Day of the Triffids* and *The Walking Dead* by showing a police officer who wakes up from a coma after the Tribulation has started. The headsets established in the previous movie are reintroduced and allow

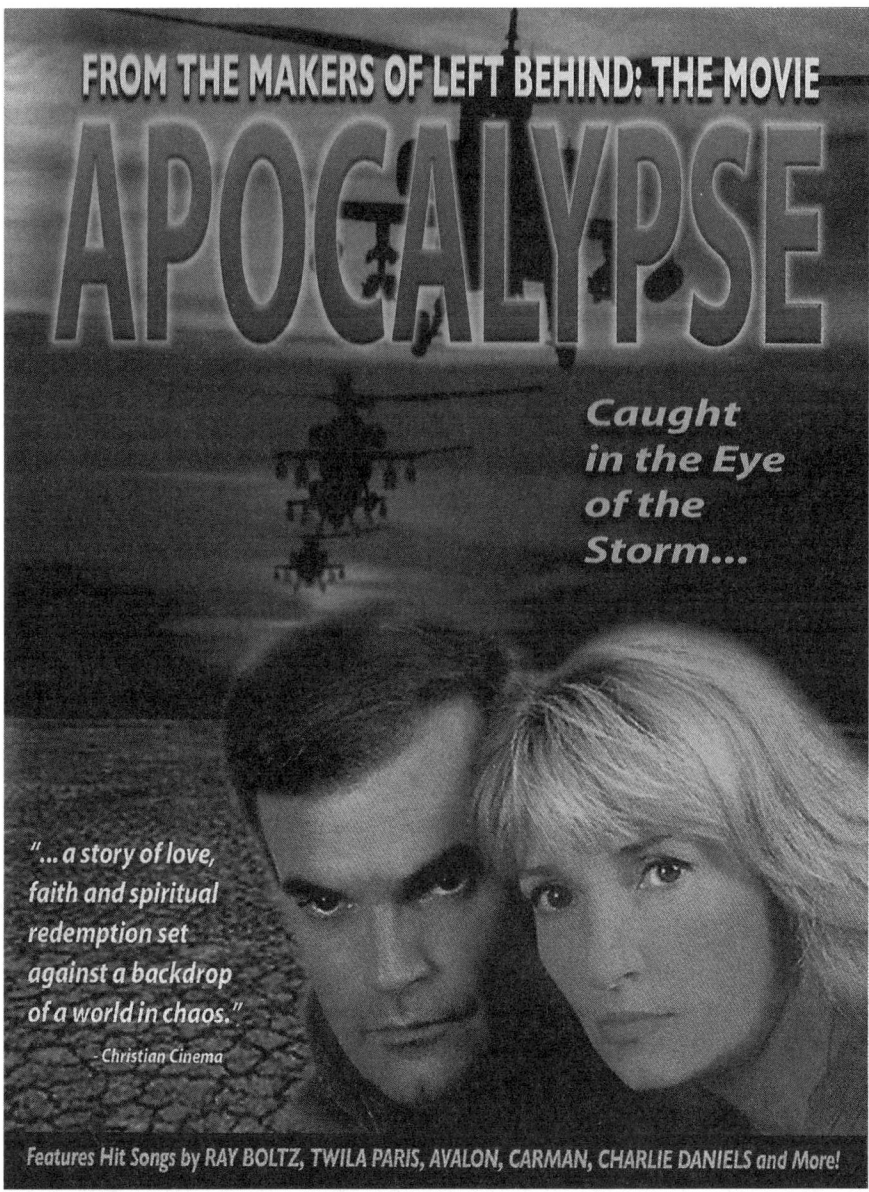

Apocalypse (1998) was the first in another end-time franchise, only this time with recognizable actors appearing in films with better production values. Even so, the movies never quite got to the point of actually *showing* Armageddon.

the Antichrist to enter into each person's virtual reality and make promises in exchange for their commitment to wear the mark. It also turns out that the plan is to harness psychic energy that each human has in order to defeat God in a final battle (thus showing a rather different route to take the series, while still remaining on the same story line path). However, the Antichrist's plan is exposed, and humanity begins to denounce him as the third film ends.

Apocalypse IV: Judgment (2000) shows God on trial (figuratively speaking; it's not like George Burns is on the stand like in *Oh God*), with the Antichrist naturally winning his case (since he has the trial rigged), but not before members of the Christian underground escape his grasp. From that point on, the series has stalled, with no further films done to complete the story line, although there is word that another film in the series (currently titled *Apocalypse V: The Chosen*) may still be made. For now, however, the series sits in limbo.

One movie that did well at the box office while the *Apocalypse* series was ongoing was *The Omega Code* (1998), directed by Robert Marcarelli and starring Michael York (*Logan's Run*) as the Antichrist. The setup is York's character, Stone Alexander, and his rise to power, with an assassination attempt at the three-and-a-half-year mark that some Christians do believe will occur during the Antichrist's reign. After being pronounced dead and rising—with Satan now controlling Stone's body—Stone attempts to continue on with the seven years of power but in the end is destroyed by the coming of the new Millennium, which some believed at the time would bring about Armageddon.

Not that this stops Stone from coming back in a sequel in 2001 for *Megiddo: The Omega Code 2*, especially after producers saw the film made nearly twice its cost in theaters. York once again appears as Stone, and this time it is as if all the events of the first movie have been rewound and Satan gets to try again. In this case, instead of an industrial leader, Stone is a political leader who is just about to win an actual physical war between nations—no esoteric meaning to Satan's battle against humanity in this one. Yet, as in the first film, just at his moment of triumph, Stone is defeated by the armies of the Lord and this time is cast into a lake of fire. As one would expect, really, according to how the timeline should go.

Finally, the films based on the *Left Behind* series begin in 2000 with *Left Behind: The Movie*, directed by Vic Sarin and starring Kirk Cameron as Cameron "Buck" Williams, a news reporter for a cable news network. Cameron had made a name for himself in the 1980s family sitcom *Growing Pains* and began to branch out into movies, but then decided to move in the direction of helping make films with a decided evangelical Christian air. This led to his attachment to the *Left Behind* series, for which he appears in all three as "Buck" Williams. The three films—*Left Behind: The Movie, Left Behind II: Tribulation Force* and *Left Behind: World at War*—just barely scratch the surface of the sixteen books in the series, managing only to cover some events from the first three before the direct-to-video series came to a halt due to slowing sales. Within those is the story of how Williams comes to suspect the Antichrist and his attempts to build up a

The *Left Behind* films attempted to bring to the screen the popular novel series that fiction-alizes biblical prophecy about Armageddon. *Left Behind II: Tribulation Force* (2002) was the second of the series, which fizzled out with a third, although a reboot is planned for 2014.

force of good to fight him after the Rapture has occurred. Yet, with the series ending there, there is no real resolution to the story line, and 2013 has seen the news that Stoney Lake Entertainment will reboot the series with Nicolas Cage, supposedly in the "Buck" Williams role, for release in theaters in 2014. It's to be seen if the reboot will do well enough to warrant sequels and get at least up to Armageddon on the screen.

Before, during and after the release of these four series of films—*A Thief in the Night, Apocalypse, The Omega Code* and *Left Behind*—there have been numerous attempts to piggyback off the success of such movies, thanks to Christians renting and buying DVDs and VHS tapes. Many such films began popping up around the same time *Apocalypse* and *The Omega Code* were released in 1998, and deal with the early days prophesied in the Book of Revelation, most commonly the Rapture. Such stories thus usually involved a character or group of characters looking around and noticing most people have disappeared and then trying to figure out what occurred. Or a few oddballs "left behind" trying to commit to God while avoiding the oncoming destruction that is the Antichrist.

The most amazing thing about these movies—beyond Eric Roberts seemingly appearing in half of them—is that, because they *have* to follow the timeline directed in the Book of Revelation, most of them could easily be taking place within the same "universe" of stories. And this is both the blessing and curse of the end-times genre. The Bible is built upon faith as to the understanding of its stories being true or symbolic. Those Christians who wish to see the Book of Revelation as a symbolic journey either through history or as a code to live by in the final days rather than the story of a real guy turning up as the Antichrist aren't going to show much interest in the end-times movies. As for those who do believe in the Antichrist appearing in a physical form and taking over the world—and therefore believe in the Rapture and the plagues of the Tribulation—they must therefore believe that the stories told in the Book of Revelation are truths that are yet to come. And, if so, then there is no denying that Jesus will come in seven years, take down the Antichrist and begin a thousand-year reign of peace. There's still the mess of Satan coming back for a guest-shot role after that, but it too is quickly over and God wins.

Thus, there really isn't any impact to the story once you believe in what is to occur. As long as you give yourself to God, you'll be Raptured. If you didn't have enough faith, having millions of people suddenly disappear in an event that has been taught to you throughout your life as being real should change your mind without a second thought. Proof of God is real by that point, and there's no longer any need for faith among the faithful. Go to the guillotine so as not to bear the mark of the beast, knowing that in x-number of years, you'll be resurrected and allowed into Heaven? Sure; why would you even think of any other answer?

And while in reality such thinking may actually lead to people having second thoughts and going with the mark, in the world of Hollywood movies, it is hard to see why characters would want to help the Antichrist once they get even an inkling as to what is really going on. The *Omen* series and such from the previous chapter have the same problem. Guarantee yourself an eternity in hell when even a glance at the Book of Revelation tells you that the foregone conclusion is to give yourself to God and be allowed into heaven after a few years of turmoil? That's not being evil; that's being stupid by that point. So the movies stumble because they're obliged to show a battle between good and evil, and for the Antichrist to pull this off, he has to be able to convince the world he is "good" yet still show the audience that he's . . . well . . . the Antichrist. And if the audience knows he's the villain, they can never quite accept the movie logic of why others would believe him for a second. There's a reason that nonbelievers laugh at these films, and it's not just because they have a tendency to have stilted dialogue or some hammy performances, but because they really ride on massive clichés of Christian cinema to tell the story.

So why do these movies keep being made? Because people want to see them. Why do they want to see them? Well, why remake *The Ten Commandments* or the story of Noah? Why put out a new biopic about Jesus every few years when the story has been told so many times? More importantly, why do people want to watch their favorite movies over and over again? Fans have seen *Star Wars* films hundreds of times, but people don't openly mock them—oh, wait, they do. But that's beside the point; everyone has a story they go back to time and again, be it the Bible or *Gone with the Wind* or Harry Potter. People are fascinated by the stories. Further, Christians want affirmation of their beliefs and although these movies take the Book of Revelation and turn it into entertainment for profit, at the core is still a story that Christians want to hear and see. That their beliefs will physically manifest in such a way as to prove to those in doubt that it is the real path. The Truth.

And this is the point where the exercise in watching the end-times played out repeatedly may be a bit worrisome. The point is that we all must be ready for the times to come, but there can't help but be a little bit of impatient yearning for the Antichrist to get this ball rolling. Maybe not to the level of "Ha! The Rapture happened and you're stuck there having giant locusts sting you and getting your heads cut off, and I'm up here in heaven laughing!" But one can't help feeling at times that some Christians have their bags packed already, just waiting to be spirited away. Because of this, it leads to a feeling that some people really don't *want* to help the human race achieve enlightenment or make the world a better place. Rather, such individuals are nearly hoping for things to get worse so the timing will be right for Armageddon to occur. Possibly even trying to nudge disaster on its way to get there. Not so much a death wish as a heaven wish, one could say. It certainly doesn't put the best light on such individuals, who seem to miss the bigger points of being a Christian when longing for the end-times. In a way, just like those individuals discussed a few chapters back who keep waiting for the zombie apocalypse.

Nevertheless, one thing can be said for the end-times movies: they may not be everyone's cup of tea when it comes to the end of the world, but at least the good guys *do* win in the end. You have to give them that. It's more than can be said for some of the genres discussed in this book.

13

War of the Worlds

A Look Back at Our Many First Encounters with the Martians

After a detour into the supernatural and religious aspects of apocalyptic movies, the journey returns once more to one of three films that are cornerstones of the genre. In this case, it is one of the earliest written, H. G. Wells' *The War of the Worlds*, and oddly enough, it can't quite break away from the religious aspects of the previous chapters, even though Wells wouldn't be happy with that observation.

By the time Wells completed *The War of the Worlds* in 1898, he was already a successful author, having seen such works as *The Time Machine* (1895), *The Island of Dr. Moreau* (1896) and *The Invisible Man* (1897) finding success with the general public, who clamored for his "scientific romances." True, some writers and critics didn't care for Wells' style of using scientific concepts merely as window-dressing for stories more about morals, ethics and culture instead of trying to deal with the nuts and bolts of the science involved. Yet it was exactly this pulpish tendency of his work that grabbed readers at the turn of the century and makes it still effective reading today. *The Time Machine* has little to do with how such a machine would work or the ramifications of having such an ability; the point is to allow Wells an opportunity to present how he sees mankind's destiny and ask us if this is all we're bound to be. His 1904 novel *The Food of the Gods and How It Came to Earth* doesn't concentrate on how the ecological engineering occurs that makes everything grow big, but rather on satirizing politics, scientific experiments without conscience and even some element of what would be commonly referred as eugenics.

Saying all that, *The War of the Worlds* is pretty much exactly what it states to be—a war that comes from Mars and the few hapless survivors who struggle to stay alive and perhaps even find a way to understand their foe and defeat them. Scholarly texts have certainly been written on other aspects of the novel, such as (once again) mankind's evolutionary ladder, the symptoms of war and fatigue to the point of breaking people, and our ability to remain optimistic even when things are darkest. Further, Wells touches on aspects of the Martians' machines that imply a type of organic composition—metallic but able to move in a fluid manner that suggests something more than machine—that one didn't really see revisited until years later in science fiction of the 1940s and onward (and more recently in programs like *Doctor Who* and *Babylon 5*).

Of course, the crowning achievement of *The War of the Worlds* is that it is one of the first novels to deal with an alien culture coming to Earth in order to invade. Before this, there were the occasional light fantasies and fictional stories that portray relatively small incidents between mankind and an alien culture, but Wells was thinking "big," with aliens that are out for one thing—to feed on us. It was a frightening concept that helped propel the novel to become popular and led to various other alien invasions over the years through fiction. Thus, as with *I Am Legend* and *Invasion of the Body Snatchers*, *The War of the Worlds* set up the parameters of what most people expect from an alien invasion movie—in particular, humanity being woefully unprepared for what is to come. Strangely enough, it also sets up one cliché of the films to come in the genre—the accidental discovery of some minor detail that will allow us to conquer our foe and win back the planet.

Several films have been made based on the novel over the years, all with tweaks to Wells' work, although some of the smaller, cash-in attempts ironically pull more from the book than the bigger, major studio productions that came along. Before we go into details about those films, however, first a look at the book and where it all started.

The War of the Worlds (novel)

Background: The 1898 novel written by H. G. Wells. Published by William Heinemann. 303 pages (although most unabridged editions today run less than 200 pages).

The Plot: The novel is in two parts: "Book One: The Coming of the Martians" and "Book Two: The Earth Under the Martians." The first seventeen chapters form the first "book," detailing the narrator's dawning awareness of the Martians and their assault on mankind. The last ten chapters make up the second book and detail his attempts to stay alive practically right under the Martians. The narrator tells his story not only in the first person but seemingly as a historical document of the recent past. He also makes mention of how mankind needed to visualize what occurred with the Martians through the same scope as we would the extinction of the dodo and (perhaps somewhat horrifying in knowing how easily it was to lump them in with animals) the Aboriginal Tasmanians of Australia. At times, the narrator (who is never named in the book, nor are most of the characters beyond given titles) steps away from the narrative in order to introduce other actions ongoing, such as his brother's attempts to lead a group to safety or details about the Martians' machinery and physical appearance.

The novel begins rather placidly, with discussions of Mars leading to the landing of a meteor near where the narrator has a home with his wife. With his friendship with those from a nearby observatory, he is able to get a closer view of the meteor that turns out to be some type of cylinder and easily observed to be not of natural origin. Most of the first four chapters focus on the arrival of the first cylinder and the growing public awareness of it as some note that a hatch appears to be in the process of slowly being unscrewed from the inside. This excites the crowd, and the atmosphere is one of people observing an oddity and nothing more, with the assumption that nothing could have survived such heat, radiation and impact inside the cylinder.

It is the end of chapter 4 before a Martian is revealed, who almost humorously stumbles out of the hatch and falls (no doubt setting himself up for good-hearted ribbing by his fellow Martians, "Way to drive fear into the humans, Mykax!"). Nevertheless, the look of the Martian—huge, tan and hulking, with a crude mouth and little else—leads to the crowd scattering, including the narrator. The crowd hide behind trees, hills and rocks and watch from a distance, as a group of men approach the ship with a white flag. They are quickly destroyed by the Martians with a flash of light that sets everyone and everything around it in flame, killing forty people as a result. It is just a taste of what is to come.

Curiosity draws the crowd forward when nothing more occurs, but panic sends them back, leading to the death of individuals during the riot to leave, and it is here that Wells is starting to get to his narrative more than simply talking about invasions by monsters. The enemy alone doesn't so much stand before us to wipe humanity off the planet as much as we can ourselves in our panic and hysteria. For the moment, however, people who did not witness the event either disbelieve the stories told about the pit with the Martians or assume, as does the narrator, that they have no means to escape the pit and will be soundly wiped out by the military within a day if mankind is provoked again.

Then a second cylinder crashes at the end of chapter 8, and people begin to realize that there is more here than just one ship and a handful of clumsy, homicidal aliens. Especially when the Martians' weapons, now referred to as heat-rays, are joined by a black smoke that is a poison gas that kills and a reddish weed-like vegetation that covers most areas with water, and all are starting to reach beyond the area of the pit and strike the city. The narrator is able to borrow a horse and cart in order to send his wife to Leatherhead, a town in Surrey, as the weapons begin to destroy everything nearby. Returning to the area on his own later, he sees (in chapter 10) the first tripod that will be the Martians' main method of destruction from this point on in the novel. Wells describes them as metallic yet organic at the same time—massive machines on three legs that emit the heat-ray and black smoke as it burns and kills everything in sight.

Arriving back at his house, he finds the man dead who had loaned him the horse. Later, the narrator invites an artilleryman into his house who is in a state of shock after, quite by accident, surviving a vicious attack from the Martians. The man suggests they travel to where they can meet up with his army battery, and he convinces the narrator to go with him. They reach an area where people are being evacuated when the tripods come. Losing sight of his friend, the artilleryman, the narrator dashes to the banks of a river and dives in with others to avoid the heat-ray, only to then have to deal with tides of boiling water from the rays. When one of the tripods is destroyed by the army, in a rare example of the Martians being beaten down, the Martians pull back, allowing the narrators and others to escape.

He meets a curate (an assistant parish priest), and it is with him that the narrator will spend a good third of the novel. Yet, at this point in the narrative, the book shifts for three of the next four chapters to describe the narrator's brother and his ordeal in London during the invasion. This includes the arrogance of the public, the uncertainty of what news to believe, the robbers on the road that emerge in the chaos, and finally the oncoming attack of the Martians when they finally arrive. The brother manages to bring a group to a steamer to get away, but a number of tripods attack the group in the waters. The HMS *Thunder Child*, a torpedo ram, keeps the Martians at bay long enough for the civilians to flee, and with their safety so ends the narrator's tale about his brother and the first book of the novel concludes.

The second book, "The Earth Under the Martians," follows the trek of the narrator to try to get back to his wife in Leatherhead while he is also dealing with the crumbling mental state of the curate. The two reach a house to search for food and shelter when it collapses around them, due to another cylinder (the fifth from the sky) having just crashed into the house. Buried in the rubble and afraid to move as the noise may alert the Martians, the two hope to wait things out. After six days of hunger, sleeplessness and fear, the curate's mind snaps. Believing it is the Day of Reckoning, he goes to bear witness, shouting and making much noise. The narrator nearly kills the curate with a meat chopper to shut him up, but turns the blade just in time, merely knocking the man out. Unfortunately, the noise was enough to bring the Martians, and before the narrator can do anything, they kill the curate, suctioning his blood off as nourishment. All the narrator can do is hide in the debris as the Martians search steadily in the rubble for others.

After a time, the narrator finds that the Martians have gone without doing as much damage to the surrounding area as he has come to expect. He travels for a time until he meets the very same artilleryman he had invited into his house several days before. They talk easily for a time about a plan to rebuild society underground and away from the Martians, but the narrator soon realizes that the man's mind has snapped as well, only in irrational optimism over a plan that has no way of working. The narrator moves on to a destroyed London. At his breaking point himself, the narrator decides to find the Martians and end it all by having them kill him, but instead finds the Martians dead. He recognizes that it is due to bacteria that the Martians never thought to be worried about but that have contaminated them, killing them after several days.

The narrator then has the news given to him that everyone in Leatherhead had been killed by the Martians. He staggers back to his home anyway, knowing that only he survived. He then discovers that his wife had returned at some point during the carnage and is there. He collapses in her arms. The novel ends sometime after the event, with the narrator mentioning the studies being made of what the Martians left behind. Meanwhile, society begins to rebuild, but with the shadow of the invasion hanging over all and the possibility that this will not be the end.

What Is the Same/Unique? Because Wells takes a first-person narrative, he plays his cards a bit too fast at the beginning by showing us that there were survivors. This gives away some of the suspense of the novel, as the readers know that somehow the Martians were defeated, leaving only the questions of what defeated them and if the narrator can get back to his wife as plotlines to follow in the novel. Wells early on also rather rams home the idea that readers should view the story as an allegory about our own methods of mass extermination, a point that would have been better addressed in dialogue or action than blatantly presented in the first few pages of the narration.

Even so, the novel is compelling and has survived as a classic not simply because Wells wrote it, but because it presents in a serious, logical way how such an invasion could occur and our society would react. Then or even today. Perhaps this is one of the most impressive elements of the novel; actually, man's reaction to catastrophic events hits close to the bone—when there is unsuspecting danger, we do what we do best, which is panic and scramble to survive at any cost. We see a riot killing women and a child early in the book, but within pages the narrator is chatting away at the dinner table with his wife, dismissing the seriousness of the event because it is just too big to consider the possibility of mankind not being able to stop bad things from happening. People refuse to believe, and when they do, they go into shock and envision ways out that fit their world perspective—the artilleryman with lofty ideas for the salvation of the human race drenched in champagne he has found; the clergyman with assumptions that Armageddon has arrived. Thus leaving those who attempt to survive having to deal with those who cannot rationalize, and possibly having to resort to drastic measures that they would commonly not consider (such as the narrator nearly killing the curate).

Some readers may find a few actions somewhat questionable in this day and age. When the narrator returns home after seeing the Martians wipe out forty people at the pit, he has dinner and chats with his wife about the incident as if it will blow over by morning. He is certain (although to be fair, his wife less so) that the military can handle the situation with just one shell fired into the pit. Later, when it is clear that the Martians are gaining an upper hand, he bitterly has to deal with people who laugh it off as silliness; they cannot conceive of such an issue actually occurring in their homeland—the heart of the great British Empire.

And this is exactly what Wells is getting at in these moments—that this would be perfectly normal behavior for the time and place. The British Empire was smack dab in the middle of the Victorian-Edwardian Age, where it truly *was* an empire. Advancements in science, profitability in all directions, everyone looking to England for answers; the world was Britain's pearl, much less its oyster. In other words, things were going amazingly well. Which was part of the growing problem that some were seeing in society at the time—things were going too well. Man was starting to see its work and feel it could do anything, fear nothing, and everything was as quaint as afternoon tea. A Martian invasion? What would they think of next? Obviously some type of amusing caper by college students, no doubt. If not, the army will certainly take care of those rascals.

Even so, cracks were starting to emerge that were obvious enough for some to see. Little by little, our technology began to outpace our thinking, and the wonders of the moment were starting to look like the horror of the future, especially as it was becoming commonly clear that as much as it was a golden age for mankind, so easily could it be our damnation as well. Wells' *The War of the Worlds* is not so much a book about an extraterrestrial invasion as a look at what could rapidly be everyone's concern when the next war came down the pike. Vast machines that do the work of those never seen were certainly a topic at the turn of the century, with submarines already in use during the American Civil War and armored trains and coaches quickly changing into the armored tanks of the First World War. The black smoke of the Martians is easily the poison gases that would be used in the coming wars, as is the unraveling of the very proper idea that civilians were not to be harmed in the advancement of battle. All things to come, but in 1898, it was fantasy of the fairy-tale Martians, thus being a way to examine such massive and devastating inventions while leaving the reader comfortable within the context of it just being a story.

An interesting aspect of Wells' novel that tends to get glossed over in the various film adaptations is the curate and his crumbling mental state. It is hardly one that paints a heroic or even stable picture of religion in the book—the curate even finds it impossible early on that a member of the clergy would be killed by the aliens. It is a point of view that the two major studio productions would avoid; in the 1953 production by eliminating the character completely and in the 2005 film by making the character simply a man on the verge of a breakdown without the religious connotations. Ironically, in 1898, one could make a religious figure a man struggling with a crisis, but in 2005 any attempt to do the same would be treated as trying to knock Christians.

One element that never quite makes sense other than to give motivation for the invasion is the Martians needing human blood as nourishment. Considering how many people they randomly wipe out over the days, it seems to be like farmers killing nine-tenths of their cattle to put fear into them before slaughtering the last three cows for beef. Yet the vampiric business of the Martians gives them an additional nasty edge and at least a reason to invade instead of "just because." Of course, these days, where we run to contagion movies and are bombarded with news about the latest flu epidemic, etc., some viewers may take issue with the way the Martians are destroyed. Back in 1898, one could readily see a culture that would be ignorant enough to not consider the possibility of new diseases, bacteria, etc., that could be found on a new planet, but for modern audiences who are supposed to believe the Martians are more advanced than us, it is harder to accept. Of course, it's still a formula that has developed into its own cliché in science fiction: bacteria will defeat the Martians, rain will destroy the aliens bugging Mel Gibson, gold powder will terminate the Cybermen, Mr. and Mrs. Samuel Brainsample will eat the Blancmanges and save us from all being turned into Scotsmen. You get the idea.

Even with some minor plotting issues, it is evident why *The War of the Worlds* sticks with us. It takes what would commonly have been written at the time as an absurd idea and treats it with a serious, conscious eye as to how real people would react in such a situation. There have been many popular adaptations of the tale over the years, from the infamous Orson Welles radio production discussed in an earlier chapter to the recent Steven Spielberg film. And, as with *I Am Legend* before it, every film made based on the novel has gone its own direction with the story.

The War of the Worlds (1953)

Background: A Paramount Pictures production. Filmed in 1953 in Los Angeles, California. Released August 1953. Written by Barre Lyndon. Directed by Byron Haskin. Starring Gene Barry as Dr. Clayton Forrester; Ann Robinson as Sylvia Van Buren; Lewis Martin as Pastor Matthew Collins; Les Tremayne as General Mann. Narration by Sir Cedric Hardwicke.

The Plot: The film starts with footage of the First and Second World Wars before the titles. The narrative then at first slides into something very much like the opening paragraph of the novel ("No one would have believed in the last years of the fill-in-blank century . . .") before giving viewers a tour of the solar system. It appears the narrator is shopping planets for the Martians (something Wells did not do in the novel, and certainly with no mention of Pluto, which wasn't discovered until 1930), but finally leads to the narrator discussing the earth and how the Martians were eyeing it for their own use.

A large meteor crashes near a small town called Linda Rosa, and although the locals seems to want to kick it, beat it with a shovel or just gawk at the smoldering giant ball in the dirt, those in authority feel someone thinking a bit more clearly needs to be there to look at it. Hearing that some scientists are camping and fishing nearby, they go to visit them.

One of the scientists is Dr. Clayton Forrester (*Mystery Science Theater 3000* fans will recognize this name as the same one used for Trace Beaulieu's evil scientist on the program). He goes to look at the meteor while the other scientists head back to L.A. in a plane. Forrester is surprised by the way the meteor came to rest, as if manually landing rather than naturally crashing into the earth. Deciding to wait until it cools, Forrester makes the acquaintance of Pastor Collins and his niece Sylvia (who wrote a thesis in college on Forrester and "modern scientists"

The War of the Worlds (1953), based on H. G. Wells' classic that became one of the corner-stones of apocalyptic concepts in fiction. George Pal's movie would also become a classic of the science fiction genre.   *Courtesy of www.doctormacro.com*

but doesn't spot Forrester at first), and Collins offers his home to Forrester for his stay.

As the people in town have a square dance, with Forrester joining in, three men remain at the meteor to keep people away as there is a good amount of radiation and heat pouring off it. When they spot a portion of the meteor slowly twisting open, they pull back, but become interested when they see a probe of some kind sticking out of the hole in the meteor. Thinking this will be their chance to become famous, they walk toward the probe with a white flag to greet the aliens and are vaporized once they get close enough.

Back in town, all power goes out during the square dance. At first it is assumed to be a minor thing, but soon everyone notes that their watches are not working and a compass is pointing toward the meteor instead of north. Forrester goes to the meteor with the sheriff, but they narrowly get away from the heat-ray shot at them from the probe. They also see that the three men on guard were killed.

Soon enough the military arrive and set up many tanks and men with weapons in a perimeter around the hole where the meteor remains. It is noted that other meteors have landed around the world with similar responses occurring, but for now the military believe they are safe as long as they keep their distance. Soon, however, three ships, each with one of the probes on top that delivers the heat-ray, rise from the hole and levitate. The pastor decides to try to reason with the Martians in hopes of avoiding a battle due to a possible misunderstanding, but the Martians make quick work of him. With this, the general in charge calls for an attack against the ships. The Martians ships, however, have some type of dome-like invisible shield protecting them from harm, while still allowing them to use their own weapons to destroy the soldiers and their weapons. Everyone is evacuated, with Forrester and Sylvia taking a plane to get back to Los Angeles.

On their way, they barely avoid one of the Martian ships and end up crashing near an abandoned farmhouse. Soon after, the house collapses as another meteor lands nearby. Forrester and Sylvia try to avoid detection, but a camera on an extendable metallic cable slithers like a snake into the house, and eventually one of the Martians enters. Forrester attacks the Martian with an axe, sending it on its way, and then destroys the camera by cutting the cable. They manage to make it out of the house before the Martians fire on it, with Forrester now having a blood sample and the Martian camera to take back with him.

The samples are good to have when they arrive in Los Angeles, as the scientists are able to determine with them that, while the Martians have firepower much more intense than that of Earth, they physically do not possess much stamina. Meanwhile, with much reluctance, the president agrees to drop an atomic bomb on some of the ships, only to discover it does no damage to them. The scientists attempt to come up with a way to destroy the Martians based on their physiology, but an evacuation to take them to a safer place finds them driving into a citywide riot. The public, in wide panic, commandeer the bus and trucks from the scientists, destroying all the equipment and samples that could lead to a means of destroying the Martians. Forrester tries to stop them but is knocked unconscious in the riot and left for dead on the sidewalk as the riot trails off out of the city.

Waking up, Forrester realizes that Sylvia, who he has grown fond of, was on the bus that was hijacked by the rioters. Realizing that the cause is lost, with less than six days to go before the Martians conquer the world, he goes searching the nearby churches in hopes of finding Sylvia. He locates her in one of the churches, and the mass of people inside pray as one of the Martian ships approaches. Yet, just as it is close enough to destroy the church, the ship falters and eventually crashes to the ground and into another building. The group goes outside to see that other ships are dropping in the same manner.

Slowly moving toward the Martian ship, they see a hatch open to show the arm of one of the Martians reaching out before it becomes still in death. The earth is saved and the narrator returns to state that it was due to the Martians not being able to defeat the bacteria "God . . . had put upon this Earth," which slowly killed them.

What Is the Same/Unique? George Pal has been discussed earlier in the book with his work on *The Time Machine* (1960) and will be brought up again in chapter 16 as we venture into films about things smashing into Earth. That film, *When Worlds Collide* (1951), was his third live-action movie produced (along with *Destination Moon* in 1950), and one can see why *The War of the Worlds* would draw Pal's interest. Not only because it was H. G. Wells, but also because the film deals with a similar theme and characters as already seen in *Destination Moon* and *When Worlds Collide*: scientists facing a crisis and working together to come to a resolution (and as in *When Worlds Collide*, also romanticizing one of the other leads). The film also needed big special effects that Pal believed he could pull off, what with his background in puppetry, stop-motion animation and other effects.

Adjustments were made to the story line to put it into the modern age of 1953 as well as Americanizing the story. Gone is the busy world of London, England, and instead the story focuses on a meteor being found outside a small town in California. The unnamed narrator becomes Forrester in the picture, and, although he is single, he is given a love interest in Sylvia that allows him to search for her in the end; albeit search for her in the last ten minutes of the movie, while the narrator's search for his wife was ongoing throughout much of the novel.

Gone are the curate and the artilleryman, with Sylvia taking their places and being quite sane, if perhaps a bit cliché, "woman in trouble" hysterical at times. It is easy to see why the military man would go—there are enough soldiers floating around in the movie anyway that take his position in the story, and there is no need to have Forrester spend half the film with one character and then another when Sylvia can fill that same role.

Having an insane clergyman as a major character probably would not have gone over well in 1953 America anyway; certainly not midway through the Red

Scare of the 1950s, where anyone that would even suggest one of God's chosen may not be thinking clearly would be considered "dirty commie scum" (okay, I'll just admit it, it's funny to say "dirty commie scum"). Instead, we have Sylvia's uncle early on, who attempts to talk to the Martians to find a peaceful solution to the situation, even though he realizes it probably spells his doom. The ending of the film also shows various churches (only the last of which is shown being damaged by the Martians' flying machines), with a priest in one and ministers in the other two, caring for the wounded and praying for salvation as the Martians come closer. The common man may riot, but those who trust in the Lord are safe. Well, fairly safe. Looks like a few of them got crushed by a pillar falling in the last church right before the Martians die, but we'll assume they were heathens and deserved it.

Speaking of the Martian flying ships—with these as the only means of transportation while attacking, it does mean that we do not get the tripods of the novel. In the first scene of the flying ship, there is an attempt to make it appear the machines are standing on green-lit electronic legs, but Pal abandoned this after the one scene as being too complicated to carry out for the entire film. Instead, we get levitating ships that look pretty cool, although how three could fit inside the meteor is a question never answered by the scientists. Which brings us to another change—that of the military and the scientists being pretty much in control throughout the film. Oh, they may be losing, but at least they're going out with their heads held high, and the scenes back at Pacific Tech with the scientists play pretty much as where Wells diverts his narrative in the novel to discuss the look and even the sexuality of the Martians in the novel. It also gets the point across about how the scientists know the Martians are not the healthiest of specimens (thanks to Forrester's blood sample and the camera) instead of Wells having to sledgehammer the information into the text as an aforethought (essentially, "Here's what we later found out about them, which you need to know now for the ending of the story to work . . ."). Speaking of which, there is no indication that these Martians need human blood, which was an element of Wells' book that could easily be lost anyway (although it is the only adaptation to do so).

The film is considered a classic. A little bit of humor here and there, but otherwise with the intent of taking the invasion with a serious, somewhat adult tone. The special effects are very strong (although it is easy to see the wires holding the ships up at times), and Barry makes for a good lead (one could almost place him as an American version of the Third Doctor from *Doctor Who* with some of his actions). It also sets up the common method of invasion for many alien films to come—something falls from the sky, dumb townspeople poke at it with a stick, aliens fry a lot of people, scientist comes up with a cool but simple solution and end of invasion. It does tend to kowtow to authority, what with God essentially stepping in at the last second to make things right; and with an emphasis on the military and science being right, there's a certain lack of chaos until the final quarter of the film when the riots occur, but even so it would be hard to top Pal's *War of the Worlds*.

An attempt to make it a television series in the late 1980s (*War of the Worlds*, 1988–1990, syndicated) never paid off, even though it tried to play off the movie as being what happened or quasi-happened in 1953 and the Martians now "waking up" from suspended animation. Yet, with that setup, the series then jettisoned everything from the film and even Wells' novel to have the aliens able to stay healthy, transform into humans (making it a variation of *Invasion of the Body Snatchers* rather than *The War of the Worlds*) and throwing in the idea that they weren't actually Martians anyway (they came from Mor-Tax, which is delicious with some salsa—no, wait, that's Tex-Mex, never mind). Nearly everyone working on the program went away for a new team in the second season, but it got even further from the plot, showing us a rather *V* television series landscape, where there were freedom fighters against the aliens in a world rapidly becoming postapocalyptic. One does have to give the series credit for at least being allowed to film an ending (the humans win), but as a continuation of Pal's movie, it was a disappointment.

Meanwhile, as other alien invasions came and went, Pal's *The War of the Worlds* stood alone for fifty-two years before someone else decided to return to the story for another film. Or three.

H. G. Wells' The War of the Worlds (2005)

Background: A Pendragon Pictures production. Filmed between 2001 and 2004. Released June 14, 2005. Written by Timothy Hines and Susan Goforth. Directed by Timothy Hines. Starring Anthony Piana as the writer; Susan Goforth as the wife; John Kaufmann as the curate; James Lathrop as the artilleryman.

The Plot: It is the novel.

What Is the Same/Unique? For years Timothy Hines had been trying to get an adaptation of Wells' novel going, with the objective of playing true to the source by placing the film in its original environment of 1898 England. The biggest hurdle was that Hines wasn't a big name that could pull studios into assisting in getting such a film done, compounded by the September 11, 2001, terrorist attack on the World Trade Center, which made filmmakers and goers a little less than excited about watching buildings blow up. (At least for a short while.)

Hines would finally film the project, using a small cast and a lot of computer-generated images (CGI) effects, although there were the additional issues that came with it being released around the same time as Steven Spielberg's modern production of the same story in 2005, lessening the chances of people wanting to see it rather than the new Spielberg movie. The film would be released on DVD, and an additional difficulty became clear as well—it was a three-hour film with a small cast of actors who gallantly try their best against many shimmering CGI effects that look like computer animation. It is easy to want to cheer it on, especially with the film looking like something one would see on the local cable access channel ("These kids saved up their nickels and dimes and worked on

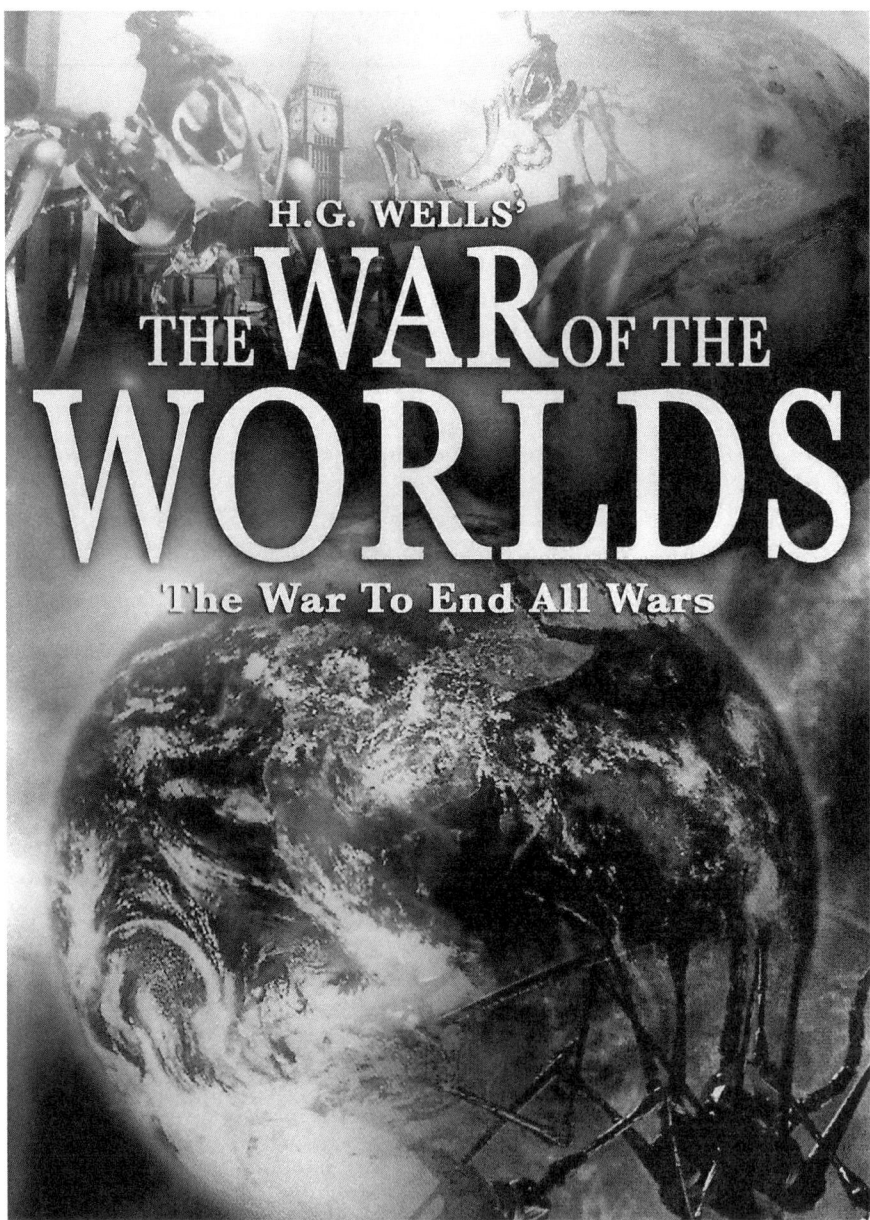

This 2005 adaptation tried to actually film the novel as written, which makes the point that doing so isn't always for the best, no matter how good the intentions.

weekends to make this!"), but in trying to present the entire novel, it is a rather dull trek. That's not exactly the fault of Hines as much as the fault of trying to reproduce the novel exactly on the screen: it may be an alien invasion, but it's essentially about a man going to Leatherhead with his wife, then back home, than attempting to get back to Leatherhead, while having long dialogue scenes in the darkness with people waiting for the next big explosion. It works in the novel because it's a novel, and sometimes what works on paper does not in the camera.

Hines has not given up on the project, however. He has recut the film multiple times in shorter versions to quicken the pace and with some better effects. In 2012 he reedited portions of the film into a new one called *War of the Worlds—The True Story*, which stars Jack Clay as the writer in footage supposedly from 1965, where he is interviewed about the invasion, and where excerpts from Hines' 2005 film is intercut with other footage to make it look like a documentary. One has to give him credit for sticking with his dream.

War of the Worlds (2005)

Background: The Asylum production. Filmed in 2005. Released June 28, 2005. Written by David Michael Latt and Carlos De Los Rios. Directed by David Michael Latt. Starring C. Thomas Howell as George Herbert; Tinarie Van Wyk-Loots as Felicity Herbert; Dashiell Howell as Alex Herbert; Rhett Giles as Pastor Victor; Andy Lauer as Sgt. Kerry Williams; Jake Busey as Lt. Samuelson.

The Plot: George Herbert is an astronomer who lives with his rather too-young-looking wife, Felicity, and his son, Alex, near Washington, D.C. He goes to investigate a nearby meteor crash, while his wife heads off to high school. I mean, heads off to Washington, D.C., with their son. On his way, another meteor crashes and his car suddenly stops. Walking to the pit where the meteor has landed, George sees a few people looking at the meteor just as tentacles reach out from it, snatching several people, while the Martian crab-like "walker" with the metallic tentacles rises and starts firing heat-rays into the crowd, scattering everyone.

Running back home, George discovers that electricity is erratic. With no reason to sit there and no way to communicate with anyone, George heads off for a walk toward Washington, D.C., along with other refugees. After being told that the city had been destroyed, an attack at a bridge sends him off from the others. He eventually meets Sgt. Williams, who is the only survivor from his unit after an attack, and Lt. Samuelson, who tells them more about the attacks. Herbert and Williams manage to get to a town where they can relax and get some food, but by nightfall the Martians hit. The two are separated, and George finds himself on the run alone again. In the darkness, he locates a small boat and drifts downstream for a time. He finally abandons the boat and waits out a rainstorm in a truck, waking up after a time to find Pastor Victor sitting in the truck with him. The two talk, with the curate sure that the Rapture is at hand, as they continue on their way, even going so far as to walk right under one of the walkers at one point. A meeting with a woman who has lost her family leads the curate to question his faith, and his mental state begins to crack under pressure. As night falls, an attack on soldiers ends when a walker releases a green mist that kills them, although the curate and George escape by climbing up some wreckage.

They manage to get to a suburban area with abandoned homes and enter a house belonging to a veterinarian. Gas seeping into the street sends them upstairs, where they find vaccines for rabies. Just then, a meteor crashes into the area and the house collapses, leaving the two within a small area with little food. Seeing one of the Martians killing people for their blood, George decides to inject the rabies vaccine into a tentacle of a Martian that slithers into their area. It quickly leaves in pain, only to return and spray the curate with acid, killing him.

George remains for a time before finally crawling out of the rubble. Malnourished and weak, George has a breakdown when he loses the picture of his family. Later that night, he is found by Kerry, Samuelson and a ragtag group of soldiers. Kerry is ready to give up, leading to Samuelson shooting him in the head and George using a large rock on Samuelson's head. As he stares at the soldiers, wondering what they will do, they simply shuffle off into the distance.

Losing all hope, George finally makes it to the destroyed center of Washington, D.C. As he stands in front of a walker, waiting to die, he realizes that nothing is happening. Suddenly, other survivors emerge, including his daughter—I mean, his wife and son. He is told that a virus has killed off the Martians over the past few days and they are all now safe. For the moment.

What Is the Same/Unique? Well, there's the nude scene at the beginning of the film. That's one thing that is certainly missing from Wells' novel. As well as the other film adaptations. Then again, there's hardly a place for a nude scene in the story anyway, but this is the Asylum we're talking about, so you have to give them a little leeway on such factors.

And, yes, this is definitely the Asylum's production of Wells' novel, one that helped to launch the company into successfully filming "mockbusters." The most intriguing thing about their version of *The War of the Worlds* is that it actually is pretty good. Maybe filmed on the level of a TV movie, but engaging and smoothly acted while also staying closer to the book than either of the bigger studio productions from over the years. Of course, certain elements were changed from the book to place it in modern times, but if that were the one reason to dismiss the film, we would also do the same with Spielberg's and Pal's versions.

The similarities are close between the movie and the novel, although it foregoes the back-and-forth method Wells uses for the wife's departure, starting with George going off in search of his wife after the attacks rather than taking her somewhere, coming back and then going after here again. (Yet here's the thing—they're supposedly married for ten years, but Felicity is played by an actress who was not only twenty-four at the time of the filming but *looked* twenty-four at the time of the filming. George is like the Jerry Lee Lewis of astronomers, it appears. But it does give us the nude scene needed, so I guess we really shouldn't complain.) The addition of the son doesn't add much (and one suspects it was imposed because there were children in Spielberg's production), but it did give Howell a chance to perform with his real-life son in the role and doesn't hurt the film in any way.

The walkers are nothing like those seen in the previous films or in Wells' novel—more crab-like—but there is an organic look to them that is reminiscent of Wells' statements about the tripods. The film also uses the "black smoke" of the novel, although in this case it is an easily avoided green mist. It also brings in the artilleryman and the curate of the novel, albeit with the artilleryman represented by two different characters in the movie and made homicidal instead of just rather lazy and out of it at the end. The curate is sharp as well, only starting to fall apart in the last few days of their travels, which coincides with the novel pretty nicely. His death by acid from the Martians, however, is different from that found in the book, but actions by George/the narrator in both cases lead to his death, so the similarities are there.

Other shared images include George's trip downstream in a boat after an attack; George attempting suicide at the end, only to discover that the Martians are already dead; and the Martians feeding on human blood. Speaking of which, the rabies vaccine idea is definitely not in Wells' novel, nor does it seem to set up any purpose beyond the death of the curate by the Martian in revenge. One nice element added, however, is the scene of the curate and George talking, leading them straight under a walker before realizing the danger they're in.

The film did well enough that in 2008 a sequel was released, entitled *War of the Worlds 2: The Next Wave*. It once again featured C. Thomas Howell (*Red Dawn*) as George and his son as his movie son, but otherwise it was a new cast. Howell directed from a script by Eric Forsberg, which touches on an element that Wells brings up in his novel but is never mentioned in any of the other adaptations—that the Martians could come back for another attack.

In this situation, the world is slowly recovering from the first attack with small groups of survivors here and there in a semi-postapocalyptic setting. George's wife has gone off to college (okay, she's dead, actually, and I'll stop with that gag), but his son is still around, and the two are doing well under the circumstances. Unfortunately, new attacks from Mars begin, this time with ships suddenly appearing out of the blue and zapping people left and right. When such a ship appears at George's house and vaporizes his son, George is devastated.

As it turns out, his son has been transported by use of the weapon zapping people, and George realizes this, eventually allowing another tripod to do the same to him to test the theory. He and a man he meets, Pete, escape from the tripod with a woman named Sissy. Meanwhile, military and scientists that are working with George realize the Martian ships are arriving via a time-space distortion, and they use the same for jets reconditioned for space flight in order to attack Mars.

George and the others find themselves in a small town that turns out to be a fake built on Mars by the Martians to herd the humans they have captured.

The 2005 "mockbuster" *War of the Worlds* was good enough to lead to a sequel in 2008, which was later released with the "mockbuster" *Invasion of the Pod People* on DVD.

Sissy introduces George and Peter to Shackleford. He and Sissy both are dying from a virus that they intentionally gave themselves because they believe it is lethal to the Martians and will be passed on if the Martians use them for food. George injects himself with the virus in hopes that he can pass it on when picked up by the tripods. This occurs, and they find themselves on the mothership with George's son still alive. George injects his tainted blood into a live brain controlling the tripods, and the tripods quickly shut down. George, Peter and George's son manage to escape in one of the jets that had come to Mars, and they head back to Earth, having defeated the Martians again. But a final scene suggests that a third attack is on its way.

The sequel isn't on par with the first film, which may make some readers take a step back if they didn't think much of the first one either. Because Wells' story is no longer inherent in the script, as in the first one, the filmmakers are really winging it at this point, but they do take a suggestion by Wells that the Martians would be back to try again and attempt to give it some gusto with a cast of about six. They should also be given credit for coming up with a way for the Martians to come back without having to be there on Earth to do it themselves, even if the whole transporter thing is easy to spot after a few minutes (and a bit of a cliché as well). Even so, it is stuck on a point in Wells' narrative that never made sense—that of Martians needing human blood. But then again, the giant major studio production of 2005 from a famous director went down that same path, as will be discussed.

War of the Worlds (2005)

Background: A DreamWorks/Paramount Pictures production. Filmed in 2005. Released June 29, 2005. Written by Josh Friedman (*Terminator: The Sarah Connor Chronicles*) and David Koepp (*I Come in Peace*). Directed by Steven Spielberg (*1941*). Starring Tom Cruise as Ray Ferrier; Dakota Fanning as Rachel; Justin Chatwin as Robbie; Tim Robbins as Ogilvy. Narration by Morgan Freeman.

The Plot: Ray is stuck with his kids while his ex-wife heads off on a trip to Boston to see her parents. This frustrates Ray and the kids, Rachel and Robbie, more than all having first names starting with R, as Ray doesn't quite know how to interact with them. When Robbie takes Ray's car out for a spin without permission, Ray goes looking for him just as a freak storm knocks out anything electrical (although we see a man using a camcorder in the following scene, so the Martians must not be too on the ball yet). While it is never explained, the storm appears to have been some type of transference system used to send Martians directly into the ships located underground (thus, where the lightning appears to strike is where the next walker is buried). Finding Robbie and sending him back to his place, Ray goes to see what the commotion is along with many others.

At an intersection, the ground begins to crumble, cracking open buildings nearby as a tripod emerges from the earth. Standing upright over the crowd, the tripod begins firing its heat-ray, sending everyone running. Ray manages to get home, collect the kids and get into the only working car around (one he had told a mechanic how to fix after the lightning attack). The three leave just as the tripod wipes out the rest of the town. They drive for miles, dodging stalled cars along the way.

Finding his ex-wife's house, they stay there overnight and wake up to discover a destroyed airliner outside the door with a news team in a van scavenging for food. The group tells Ray that the tripods are attacking all over the world and that they appear to have been stationed underground for a time, perhaps thousands of years, awaiting a signal to attack. The family continue on but have to abandon their car when a crowd riots over the working vehicle. After an attempt to get on a ferry fails due to an attacking tripod, the three come across a military patrol and Robbie wants to join them. Ray lets him go, while he and Rachel continue onward. They finally arrive at a house belonging to a man named Ogilvy, who invites them in and is at first somewhat friendly, but quickly shows himself to have lost his mind after seeing his family killed.

Hiding in the house, the group sees a red weed (as in Wells' novel) being spread across the land, while human victims are plucked and their blood is taken, killing them. Ogilvy loses what remains of his mind and begins to rant and scream. Fearing the noise will attract the Martians, Ray decides he has to kill Ogilvy to keep him quiet. Even so, the action fails when a probe enters the house and Rachel runs outside screaming, where she is picked up by the tripod. Ray gives chase, finding a grenade belt in a military vehicle, and is captured by the tripod while holding the grenades. Once inside, he finds other survivors waiting to be "processed." Ray is picked to be the next one, but the others manage to pull him back out after he has dumped the belt into the "processor" with all the grenade pins still in his hand.

The explosion destroys the tripod and allows the prisoners to escape. Weary, Ray and Rachel continue on to Boston, where there is a battle raging between the military and a tripod. It is noted that everything related to the Martians is dying off, from the weeds to the ships. With it destroyed, the tripod opens to reveal a Martian briefly, as in the George Pal movie. Ray and Rachel continue to the grandparents' house, where they, the ex-wife and Robbie appear, safe and sound.

What Is the Same/Unique? The story goes that at the time Spielberg was finding the start-up on his film *Munich* hitting a snag with rewrites, his schedule suddenly opened up. Remembering discussing a remount of *The War of the Worlds* with Tom Cruise, Spielberg found everything falling into place to get it started and completed in both his and Cruise's window of time (thus seeing Spielberg with two films released in 2005). The concept was to go back to the book and find new ways of telling the story, while letting some mild references to Pal's film take care of themselves during shooting (such as the look of the Martian arm and the opening of the tripod at the end of the movie, as well as the appearance of Gene Barry and Ann Robinson, the stars of Pal's film, as the grandparents at the end). Because of this, Spielberg's version avoids the "action scientist" of Pal's film but also the studied narrator of the novel and the other adaptations. Here, he is just a crane operator, an everyman, who is struggling to deal with domestic issues. This is another change from the novel, and most of the films—with the ironic exception of the competing Asylum production from the same year—as the protagonist has two children to worry about while in danger instead of just himself or a partner of some sort. The quest to get to a place is there (Leatherhead in the novel, Boston in the Spielberg movie), although it is mainly to prove to himself that he can hold responsibility long enough to

get his children safely back to his ex-wife. This makes Ray's character more vulnerable— what with Ray attempting to connect with his children at a time of crisis—yet also less likable than his counterparts (he's doing this to prove his manliness to his ex-wife more than to save his children). The daughter works well as a character added to the mix (more so than the brief cameo George's son gets in the Asylum version), and the attempts to hide the horrors of the world from her make for some suspense and dramatic moments (such as the famous scene of all the bodies floating by on the river as Rachel watches). The son, however, quickly rubs us the wrong way. Written as a teenager thrown into the middle of a war, Robbie exhibits all the usual bratty clichés of the pampered youth of today. Instead of showing concern for his family, and especially his sister who he seems to care greatly for, he decides to

Steven Spielberg's 2005 adaptation attempted to use Pal's 1953 film as a framework while also injecting the story with elements of Wells' novel and modern concerns about politics and parenting. It was only somewhat successful in pulling it off.

run off to "fight," making him look selfish rather than the "boy becomes a man" plot twist obviously attempted in the film. Unsurprisingly, there was applause in the audience of the theater I attended when it was suggested in dialogue that his character had been killed in an attack later in the film.

The biggest change is the tripods actually being underground for centuries rather than hurtling in from the sky as in all the other adaptations. This was done as a means to avoid having to show people staring at the sky and seeing ships come down, which can be seen in most other alien invasion movies. However, it leaves the audience wondering why the tripods were underground all this time in the first place, not to mention that it seems the Martians would have made a better go at things if they had gotten started about a century or two before they did. ("They've just invented the musket, Braken! Should we attack now?" "No. That'd be too easy, Rezek. I want to make it a fair fight."). And wouldn't it be possible for their technology to have advanced in a thousand years or so? It would be like we invaded with horses and spears. Only assumption to be made is that the Martians' snooze alarm was the culprit. ("Oh, geesh! Get your clothes on, Rezek! We're two thousand years late!")

There is no black smoke, but the red weed does make an appearance from the novel. The weeds appear soon after we see the tripods milking humans for blood, and thus they appear to be the remnants of this ghastly practice rather than an actual weed the Martians have. It has been suggested that the blood is being used to "fertilize" the weed, which does at least give a reason for the Martians to do so but still leaves us with the question: Why? How did they know that humans would make a good fertilizer for the weeds? They don't seem to have bothered learning anything about our biology, or else they would have stumbled upon the whole bacteria-virus thing going on, so what convinced them this would work (as it turns out, it doesn't, so the Martians are just loopy, evidently). Others have stated that the red liquid being ejected from the tripod is not the blood at all, which still leads back to the original question as to why the Martians would bother getting human blood in the first place. For fun, perhaps? Of all the films, it still feels like Pal's version had the best idea by simply foregoing that concept and making the Martians invaders who want to wipe out humanity instead of harvest them.

The crashing outside of a home appears in the film, but instead of a meteor with another tripod or two of Martians, it turns out to be an airliner. Later, the group find themselves in another home and stuck in the basement in much the same manner as the narrator and the curate do in the novel. It is interesting to note that Tim Robbins' character is not the curate of the novel, however, but simply a madman. This at a time in society when conservative politics lit the way in America and any suggestion from the evil dirty commies—I mean, Hollywood—that a member of the clergy was insane would have not gone over well. Especially not from a director who has never hidden his Jewish faith and with a star who remains the poster boy of Scientology. One can easily imagine

Spielberg discussing it with the writers and saying, "Yeah, let's just avoid the headaches, okay fellas?" As it turns out, it may have been for the best anyway; Tom Cruise's appearances on television to support the film in 2005 had him looking a bit out of sorts, and a sour interview on *The Today Show* had him almost menacingly lecture the interviewer, Matt Lauer, on Scientology. That and a rather frantic appearance on *Oprah* a month before—which, to be fair, had Cruise acting more like a school kid in love than crazy—had everyone talking publicly about their concerns with Scientology and how it affects people. It caused some lingering damage over time, and no doubt if it had gone with the "crazy curate" character, there could have been some major heat on the film.

There is another change in the scenes with the curate-substitute from that of the earlier adaptations—in those, the narrator inadvertently assists in the death of the raving madman while trying to keep the two of them safe from harm; in the case of Spielberg's movie, Ray kills Ogilvy outright for the safety of himself and Rachel. Surprisingly, this turns out to be a meaningless act, as his daughter runs out into Martian traffic and gets picked up a couple of minutes later anyway. Thus, a scene that is supposed to show how people will go beyond limits when pressed for survival misses the mark because it doesn't make the results worth the effort (instead, Ray just comes off as a bit irrational himself).

One big change is Ray's instigating a sabotage of one of the tripods. While the novel and the other films present the narrator as a hero for simply making it through the invasion in one piece, and thereby making him an everyman, it is obvious that everyone involved in making the film felt he had to do something epic in order to prove himself the hero. Hence, the grenades and his chasing down a tripod in order to destroy it. Of course, he's given a reason for this with the capture of his daughter, but it is clear that this is not the same character that is looking for the release of suicide as in the novel and a couple of the films (even Forrester in Pal's film is ready to give up once he has located Sylvia).

There have been homages here and there over the years to Wells' novels. Attempts to restage the radio drama that got Orson Welles in such trouble back in the 1930s are the obvious ones. There is also the very well-known rock concept album of the novel, *Jeff Wayne's Musical Version of The War of the Worlds* (1978), featuring Richard Burton, David Essex and Phil Lynott, which has been adapted, staged and restaged over the years. A Polish film from 1983 called *The War of the Worlds: Next Century* appears to be a type of sequel at first, but actually is not connected with the novel beyond being about Martians and a minor invasion that is more a parody of media and politics than an invasion film. There's also an animated movie out of Malaysia called *War of the Worlds: Goliath*, which is a sequel to the novel and details a "steampunk" futuristic 1914, fifteen years after the invasion. In it, humanity has backward-engineered the Martians' technology so they'd be prepared when the Martians return, and use that technology to fight them in a battle with what amounts to giant robots from Mars.

Ultimately, the biggest homage that could be made to *The War of the Worlds* is that it is hard for other alien invasion films to not riff off what Wells had already put down on paper in the final days of the nineteenth century. The only option after showing us a surprise attack from space that could be different is if the invasion occurring without us even realizing it.

The next chapter shows us the novel and films based on it that give us the definitive version of an alien invasion movie.

14

Body Snatching

Invasions over the Years

So far, two of the most distinctive end-of-the-world scenarios have been covered, with chapters on *The War of the Worlds* and *I Am Legend*. The focus here is on the third novel (and it is interesting to note that all three are first-person narratives), whose premise will become the genesis for many alien invasion films to come, *Invasion of the Body Snatchers*. Or, as it was called originally when first published, *The Body Snatchers*.

Jack Finney (1911–1995) was an author who wrote both science fiction and other types of fiction, usually with at least one element of a fantastical nature. For example, *Assault on a Queen* (1959) may be about a robbery, but the robbery is of a cruise ship in the middle of the ocean. *Good Neighbor Sam* (1963) is a spoof on advertising but evolves into a parlor-room comedy that involves a number of intricate white lies and fake-outs. As some already know, what is also remarkable about Finney's career is how many of his novels have been turned into films (the two books mentioned were respectively released as films in the 1960s, *Assault on a Queen* in 1966 with Frank Sinatra and *Good Neighbor Sam* in 1964 with Jack Lemmon). While there have been several others, no doubt his longest-lasting success came with *The Body Snatchers*, which first appeared in *Collier's* magazine in 1954 and then released in book form the following year.

The novel deals with a group of people living in a small town who slowly come to realize everyone around them is an alien duplicate of their friends and families. In 1956, the novel was picked up by Allied Artists Pictures and released as a film called *Invasion of the Body Snatchers*, starring Kevin McCarthy and directed by Don Siegel (*Dirty Harry*). The film did well at the box office, and soon there were a variety of copycat versions done in the years to follow. Which is understandable, really—what better way to save on money for aliens in a science fiction movie than to have the alien be able to say, "I look like Uncle Harry in order to conceal my true form." In fact, such films make up a whole subgenre in alien invasion movies, which will be discussed in the following chapter.

Three remakes have appeared over the years, one in 1978, another in 1994 and a third in 2007 (with a 2007 mockbuster release from the Asylum thrown into the mix as well). Each has its changes to make in order to fit into the perceived markets of its era, adding or subtracting elements that are there in the novel. Surprisingly, two of the official four adaptations have positive endings for the main character (not to mention the human race), and even then, one had that happy ending imposed on the filmmakers (and, in a way, it's not quite as happy an ending as it may first appear).

The Body Snatchers (novel)

Background: The 1955 novel written by Jack Finney. Published by Dell. Retitled *Invasion of the Body Snatchers* in 1956 after the release of the Don Siegel–directed film that year. 191 pages.

The Plot: As with *I Am Legend* and *War of the Worlds*, *The Body Snatchers* is a first-person narrative, this time from the point of view of Dr. Miles Bennell. Bennell is a physician in a small town called Mill Valley, where he was born and raised. An old girlfriend from high school, Becky, arrives at his office. Her cousin believes her uncle isn't her uncle, and, while Becky believes her cousin may be having a mental issue, she too feels something odd about the man. She asks Bennell to come to her house and talk with him to see what he thinks, since he's known the uncle for ages.

Bennell has no reservations in thinking the uncle is who he should be after talking with him, and is then informed by the cousin that she believes her aunt has also been replaced. The cousin is certain she is either right or going crazy and wants to see a psychiatrist acquaintance of Bennell, Dr. Manfred Kaufman. Bennell sets up the appointment, then heads to a diner to eat and notes that there don't appear to be as many customers as typical before going home.

Before the week is out, Bennell has sent five more patients to see Kaufman for the very same thing as the cousin, and the two are wondering what is causing such an epidemic of neurosis among the townspeople. Later, Becky and Miles are asked to join Jack and his wife, Theodora, at Jack's house to see something in the basement on a billiard table: the body of a naked man who doesn't look quite "finished." After examining the body, Bennell suspects that the body is "new" and may be tied in with the problems people are having in town on seeing people they can't quite explain as not being "right." He then makes a remarkable jump in logic, suggesting that Jack take something to sleep and Theodora go down to the basement to look at the body every hour to see if it starts looking like Jack. If so, slap Jack awake.

The experiment works—the body has turned into a replicate of Jack. Bennell calls Kaufman to have him come down to see the body in the basement, and then remembers that Becky had gone home to sleep. In a panic he goes to Becky's place and finds a body duplicate there, hidden away from view. He wakes Becky and takes her back to meet Kaufman, Jack and Theodora. When they get to the basement, however, they discover that the body is gone. Kaufman convinces the group that it is a case of mass hysteria.

For a time, everyone feels secure with this explanation, although Theodora is less than anxious to go back to her house. Bennell begins to receive patients returning to say that they were mistaken about their earlier paranoid assumptions and are fine now. Yet, even with this good news, he is still concerned that something isn't quite right. His suspicions are confirmed when a coal bin at the house reveals unformed bodies being created from plants that have grown from mysterious seed pods found "west of town" the previous summer. Jack suggests they contact a higher authority about it, and Bennell remembers an old friend, Ben, who is now a lieutenant colonel in the army. Ben listens but tells him that no one will believe the story. Another attempt is made to call out, but the call is refused as being impossible to place. Jack and Bennell then realize that the creatures have control of the town's phone lines.

The four head out of town by car when they notice that Becky is asleep and turning pale. A pod is found in the trunk of the car and is burned along the road. They spend a night at a hotel, waking the next morning to figure out what to do next. All decide that they can't simply run away and have to head back to save their relatives, friends and neighbors. They get in the car and drive back to Mill Valley.

After a stop-off at the diner to talk to a salesman who can't figure out the strangeness of the town, Bennell and Becky discuss how the town has gradually "died" over the past few weeks until there is hardly anyone around. A trip to the library to research the pods from newspaper clippings turns out to be a waste of time, as the librarian has also been replaced and the clippings suddenly cut out of the reference material. After an unnerving visit with friends and family that have all been replaced, Bennell calls Jack with a cryptic message to meet him somewhere.

Becky and Bennell drive to the house of Professor Budlong, who had been noted in the clipping Jack had found about the seed pods. Budlong shyly discusses the story, admitting he did a terrible job in explaining his views about the odd seed pods to a newspaperman at the time. After a brief talk, Bennell realizes that it was a mistake to come, and as he and Becky prepare to leave, they see Jack and Theodora drive by in their car, with a police car right behind them and police shooting at them. Becky and Bennell take off at a quick pace back to his office. From his office window, he sees that everyone in town has been taken over, and, with growing fear, he realizes that "families" were leaving town to visit others nearby in order to spread the pods outside of Mill Valley.

Kaufman arrives and for a second Bennell is happy to see him, only to realize that Kaufman was now a pod person as well. Kaufman admits that he changed just before the first urgent phone call to him, and now it is time for Bennell to be changed. Budlong is with Kaufman and explains that the pods are from space and are a parasitic species that takes over organisms on planets they visit. Others try to convince Kaufman to put Becky and Bennell in a cell at the jailhouse until they go to sleep and can be replaced, but Kaufman—still feeling a sense of friendship with Bennell even as a pod person—refuses the idea. He begs Bennell to do the proper thing so that his and Becky's torture will be over. As they converse, Kaufman admits that the duplicating process isn't perfect; all duplicates are without emotion and will die within five years, but survival is all that matters;

just as mankind survives through the natural process, "engulfing the globe," killing things in the way, all to be at the top of the order. Kaufman leaves the two in Bennell's office and locks the door, with Becky and Bennell knowing that two pods are waiting outside for them to go to sleep and become them.

Bennell gets a fantastical idea that he doubts will work. He takes the male and female skeletons in his office and pours 20 cc of Becky's blood on the female one and the same from himself on the male one. He then snips hair from both of them and places them on the skeletons in hopes that the nearness of the skeletons to the door and the pods will lead to the pods becoming the skeletons rather than the two of them. The plan works, and Kaufman decides to move them to the jail cell.

As they go, Becky and Bennell manage to inject morphine into the four men with them as he struggles, allowing them to escape. Walking through the town, they realize they have to act like the others and manage to get out of town. Thinking they had made it, they eventually stumble upon a field full of pods. Determined to do what he can to keep fighting on, Bennell pours six drums of gasoline from a shed among the pods and burns them.

The victory appears to be short-lived, as the pod people arrive to take them. Then, without warning, they all stop as the pods still remaining pull themselves out of the ground and fly up into the air and out into space. It is then that he realizes the pods have decided the earth was too inhospitable to them and have decided to move on.

Bennell concludes his tale after months have passed, with things starting to return to normal in Mill Valley and new families entering the area. Nothing was ever reported about the events there, and within five years he knows that any trace of what occurred will be gone. Nevertheless, he warns the reader that there are still inexplicable things occurring every day in life and that perhaps, just perhaps, that odd feeling one gets about things not being right about the person you've known forever may be correct.

What Is the Same/Unique? There is no argument that *The Body Snatchers* was and remains a popular novel. Books that flop rarely get made into movies, after all. However, saying that, *The Body Snatchers* never has gotten quite the appreciation from the science fiction crowd as it has from the moviegoing public. Mainly due to the changes necessary to make the films work better than Finney's book. Make no mistake, the book is a vital part of the changing landscape for science fiction in 1955—writers like Finney, Matheson and others were finding the fantastic within the ordinary, showing that not everything pertaining to our future has to take place out in space or two hundred years in the future, nor with the majestic poetry of authors like Asimov and Bradbury. The man in the street is going to be the one affected by "things to come," which is reflected in Finney's work and certainly in *The Body Snatchers*.

Yet one can't walk away from reading *The Body Snatchers* without a feeling that some editorial changes should have been done from the get-go. Many have pointed to the certainly unscientific method by which the pods first land on Earth and later rise up against gravity to jettison themselves from the planet at the end. The films find their own means to deal with the issue, and certainly avoid the preposterous—albeit imaginative—image of pods rocketing up to the sky. There are logic problems with characters as well: Bennell sees a formed, blank male body in the basement of a home and responds by suggesting that it'll turn into one character if he goes to sleep. What compelled him to leap to that deduction? Even Kaufman's rather feeble attempt at "mass hysteria" makes more sense, and even *that* wouldn't explain the others being able to examine the body as they had for as long as they did. The third-act crisis being resolved by using the skeletons in his office as templates for the pods outside also seems more of a case of the author writing himself into a corner than the next logical action of the characters. With everything to suggest that the pods "link" to people in order to become them, it turns out that people just have to be close by in order to be replicated (which would suggest that if you bleed on the couch next to a pod, you'd end up with a couch-like pod after all is said and done). The most astonishing lapse, however, is in the resolution. Miles, fighting for a last stab of retaliation, burns a field of pods. This after it is clear that pods are already leaving the area to take over in other cities, as well as that not all the pods were burned. The pods react by freezing in place, essentially saying "forget this," and bolt from the earth. After one earthling burns a few of them. An earthling cornered and knowing he is defeated. Never has science fiction seen such mousy alien conquerors. "We're taking over your planet for five years! Oh, you don't like that? Well, okay, we'll just go then. Sorry to have bothered you. Mind if we leave the pod people behind? Yes? No? Well, think about it."

I may be poking some holes in the book, but no one can deny the success it has had as a vehicle for movie adaptations over the years. It is understandable, really. The concept of losing one's identity is a favorite of cinema, and it is a topic we all have experienced in some ways as we grow from childhood to adulthood. We, and those around us, are never quite the same as we were when we were young—the parents who we trusted without hesitation as children expose themselves as being only human as we grow older; friends we had become strangers, while strangers become friends; and youthful hobbies and indiscretions are later looked upon with curiosity as to what ever made us do them in the first place. We know—perhaps happily, perhaps in sadness—that we are not the same as we were when in grade school, or college, or out in the world for the first time. We change and so do those around us, sometimes leaving us with the wonder if anyone is "real" anymore.

There is a rare psychological disorder called Capgras delusion, which allows people to believe that everything around them—the people, the places, the things—may *look* the same but have actually been replaced by duplicates. This can lead to alienation and even violent episodes of paranoia in extreme cases. But who of us hasn't had moments where we said in frustration, "What is wrong with everybody?" Duplicates, twins and assorted imposters have been a driving force in adventure stories and movies because of that occasional sense of being displaced we all feel at times, even though we instantly know it is just the circumstances of the moment and not reality. *The Body Snatchers* plays into that fear and does the job well.

Invasion of the Body Snatchers (1956)

Background: An Allied Artists Pictures Corporation Production. Filmed in the Los Angeles area of California in March–April 1955. Released in 1956. Directed by Don Siegel. Written by Daniel Mainwaring. Starring Kevin McCarthy as Dr. Miles Bennell; Dana Wynter as Becky Driscoll; Larry Gates as Dan Kauffman; King Donovan as Jack Belicec; Carolyn Jones as Theodora Belicec.

The Plot: A psychiatrist (played by Whit Bissell, who seemed to make a habit of appearing in a number of science fictions films) arrives at a hospital to talk to a frantic man, Miles Bennell, who tells his story in flashback.

Arriving by train back to the town of Santa Mira from a medical convention, Bennell is met at the station by his nurse, Sally. She tells him that he has a schedule full of people wanting to see him, some of whom have been waiting for a couple of weeks, including his ex-girlfriend, Becky. On the trip into town, Bennell has to slam on the brakes of his car to avoid hitting a boy, Jimmy, who runs into the street. His mother tries to catch him, but the boy runs off, and the mother tells Bennell that he doesn't want to go to school. Bennell notices that their roadside fruit stand is shut down and looking drab, and the mother states that they have closed down.

At the office, Bennell finds that the appointments have been canceled and everyone that had planned to see him is walking around as if nothing is wrong. Becky does turn up, however, and she wants Bennell to see his cousin Wilma about Uncle Ira not being who he says he is. Bennell blows it off, but soon after, Jimmy arrives in hysterics, claiming that his mother is not his mother. Bennell goes to visit Becky and Wilma, but sees nothing wrong with the uncle. Bennell takes Becky out to dinner and runs into Dr. Kauffman, a local psychiatrist, and Ed, the other doctor in town. Before Bennell can even mention the curious cases he saw that day, Kauffman mentions it himself, saying he's been seeing people for two weeks with the same issues.

Dinner at an empty restaurant is canceled when Bennell gets a call from Jack Belicec to come to his place. Becky joins him, and the two enter the house to see the blank body on the billiard table that has blank fingerprints. Jack's wife, Theodora, is unnerved by the body as it is the same size and weight as Jack. When she mentions this, Jack drops the bottle of bourbon he has in his hands, cutting his left hand. Bennell admits that it does resemble Jack and suggests that they need to keep an eye on it during the night to see what happens. Bennell takes Becky home, where they find her dad busy in the basement. They say good night.

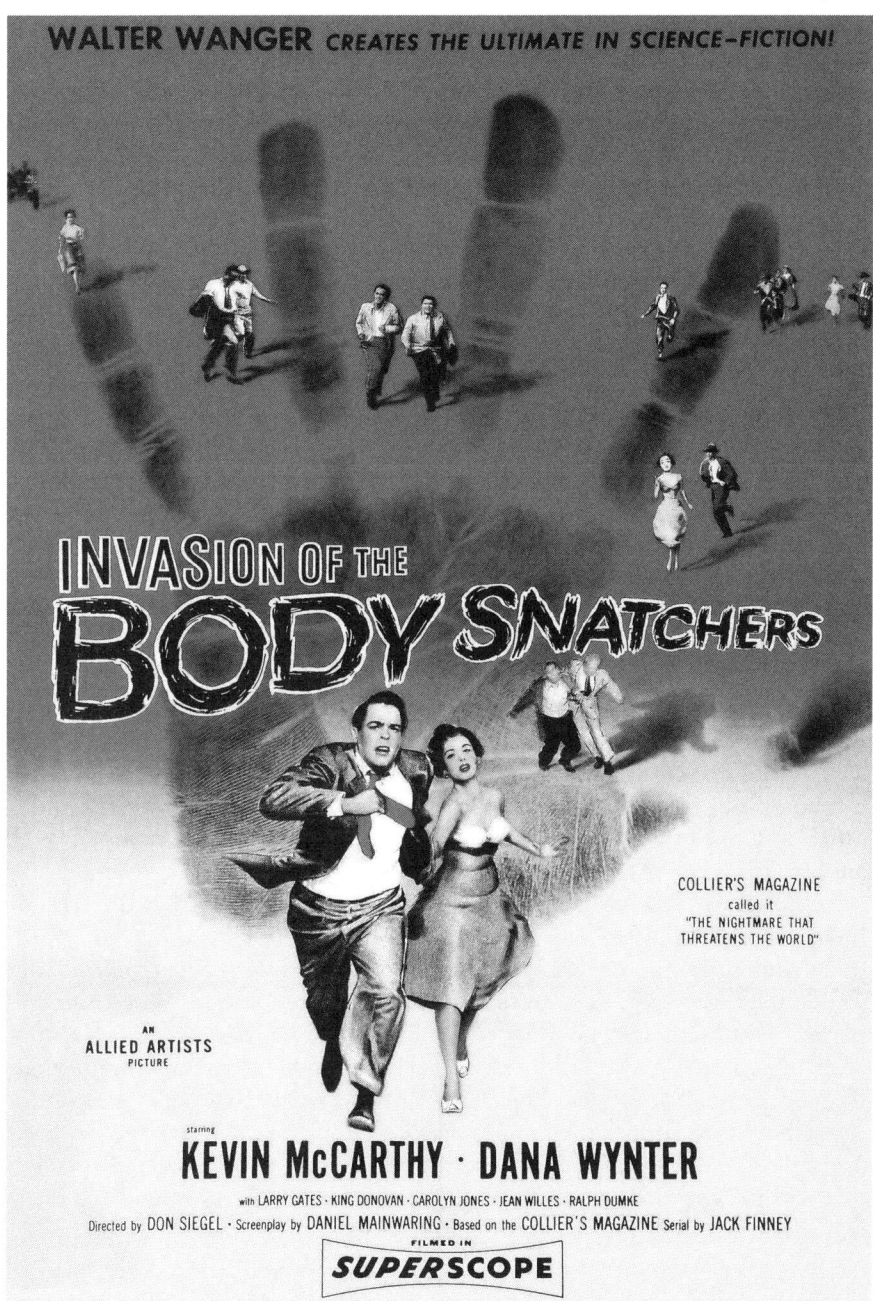

The original 1956 version of *Invasion of the Body Snatchers*, which improved on the novel and helped establish the "aliens who steal our identity" subgenre in science fiction movies.

Back at the Belicecs' house, Jack has nodded off, and Theodora walks to the body to see that the eyes are open and a cut has appeared on its left hand. She screams, waking Jack and sending the body back into hibernation. Jack and Theodora race to Bennell's place, and Bennell calls Kauffman. Thinking about Becky, Bennell drives to her place but is unable to get anyone to answer the door. He breaks into the basement and finds a nude duplicate of Becky in a bin. Racing upstairs, he is unable to wake Becky and instead carries her back to his place where Kauffman arrives. Kauffman and Bennell go to see the body, but it is no longer there. A trip to Becky's place also turns up empty, and Kauffman is full of ideas that neither Jack nor Bennell truly believes, but they have no choice but to go along with for the moment.

The next day at the office, Jimmy returns with his mother, happy and healthy. Later, Becky and Bennell visit the Belicecs' place and find that pods are opening in their greenhouse, turning into copies of them. Jack and Theodora take off in a car, but Bennell tries to contact the FBI by phone, only to be told that no one is answering. As Becky waits by the phone, Bennell goes out to destroy the pods, which he believes may be the result of atomic mutation, but is unable to destroy the one that looks like Becky. So he only destroys his own before telling Becky they have to go.

They stop to use a payphone to call Sally, but Bennell sees that the gas attendant has put something in the trunk of his car. They pull over a short distance later and find two pods in the trunk, which Bennell burns with a flare. Arriving at Sally's house, Bennell sneaks up to a window and witnesses Becky's "dad" giving "Sally" a pod to put in the baby's playpen. Bennell is spotted, but he manages to get to his car with Becky driving. They make it back to Bennell's office and avoid the pod people until daylight, seeing that trucks full of pods are being sent out of the town to other cities.

"Kauffman" and "Jack" arrive with others, telling them that they'll soon be like them, happy without emotions. Kauffman explains the origin of the pods, coming from seeds that have drifted through space, changing everyone so that the town that was so troubled a month before due to emotions is now perfect because there is no longer a need for love, anger, compassion or faith. They place pods nearby and lock the two in Bennell's office, waiting for them to sleep. Bennell and Becky later ambush those waiting and take off into the street, hoping to control their emotions long enough to make it to the highway. A truck narrowly missing a dog makes Becky gasp, which signals a police officer to investigate the office. Soon the entire town is in pursuit as Bennell and Becky run all the way to Bronson Canyon and hide from the mob.

Bennell and Becky try to stay awake while hiding in the cave. They hear music and Bennell goes to investigate, only to find it coming from a radio at a large farm of pods being put into trucks. He goes back to Becky to discover her nearly asleep and tries to keep her awake, but it turns out that she is actually a pod and no longer Becky. As Bennell races away, "Becky" calls out to the others to get him.

Bennell manages to make it to the highway and wanders into busy traffic. The pod people are unable to get to him as he rants, "They're here! They're here already! They're coming for you!" The trucks with the pods go past him as he stumbles backward in hopelessness.

Returning from the flashback, the doctors assume him to be insane. They leave, only to see a patient be brought in whose truck was hit by a bus when going through a red light. It is mentioned that the truck was full of giant pods and had come from Santa Mira. With that, the doctors realize that there may be some truth to Bennell's story, and an alert is sent out to stop all traffic as the FBI is called. Bennell falls into relieved sobs as the movie ends.

What Is the Same/Unique? For most of its running time, Siegel's film sticks closely to the novel, even including minor flashes of dialogue replicated from it. Differences do emerge early on, but they are mainly little things that help establish the story better, such as the incident with Jimmy that convinces Bennell there may be something to Wilma's concerns and the cut on Jack's hand that appears on the body on the billiard table to further establish that it is a duplicate of him. Bennell also suggests that they see what happens to the body overnight, rather than jumping to the conclusion that sleep is involved as in the novel.

The scene featuring "Sally" ready to turn her child by placing a pod in her playpen, while it is clear that the little boy has been changed as well, is harder emotional material than what appears in the book as well. The film avoids the very odd setup with the skeletons in the office in order to get to what happens in the next scene anyway—a fight with Kauffman and the others that sees them being drugged in order to escape. There is also the suggestion from Bennell that the pods are a mutation of some type due to atomic radiation, which is a more understandable jump of logic on Bennell's part than that of seeds from space.

The biggest change occurs in the ending, with Bennell not getting a chance to destroy the farm with the pods and instead going back to a weak Becky only to discover she has also been taken over. It appears the pods have won, as Bennell stumbles around on the highway, and this is perhaps the one area that most fans of the film discuss, as the movie was originally to end this way, with Bennell realizing humanity was lost and he had failed.

The studio decided that the film needed a more positive ending, which is understandable considering that the book it is based on end so negatively. Thus, Siegel was talked into filming the wraparound segments featuring Whit Bissell (and a pre–*Dick Van Dyke Show* Richard Deacon) that allows Bennell the chance to prove his story and get action taken. Of course, this is with the knowledge that everyone in his hometown is now dead and evil, including the love of his life, but at least the world at large is safe. In a sense, it is a way for the film to have its cake and eat it too—we end the film knowing everyone has died, including the children of the town—but although the authorities may now be able to do something, we're still not given a conclusive ending that they will (if only the operator had told Whit Bissell that they were unable to connect to the FBI . . .).

A great tragedy has occurred for this one character, and we're left assuming that things will be okay. Hopefully.

The film was released in 1956 and did good business, but over the years there has been much discussion about what it really *meant*. The talk of people being drained of emotions, replaced by exact duplicates that no longer need such things as *faith* (in particular), would suggest the type of "Red Scare" films and books very popular at the time. On the flip side, there are those who look at two people suddenly on the run from their family and friends as much like what was happening to those who were facing the "witch hunters" that were trying to dig up hints of communism in every corner (and especially in Hollywood). Because Bennell and Becky act differently, they are assumed to be out to destroy society and thus must be eliminated, which sounds much like those accusing others of being "Red" and wanting to destroy American society.

For the most part, the people making the movie did not subscribe to either analysis of its theme. Siegel would toy with the idea in later interviews, suggesting that it may have been something he had in his mind while making the film, but even then it was mainly to show how people can easily lose their individuality when conforming to the thinking of the masses, rather than a pro- or anticommunist agenda. Either way, it was a rather powerful statement to make at a time where we were still coming out of the era of World War II and into seeing America as the bright "nuclear family" future of the world, with peace and happiness "our way" for everyone. A handful of films knocked around that idea but only rarely, and the 1956 version of *Invasion of the Body Snatchers* does so in a subversive way so as not to draw attention to the concept but still have it percolating in the back of people's minds after viewing.

Invasion of the Body Snatchers (1978)

Background: A United Artists Production. Filmed in San Francisco, California, 1978. Directed by Philip Kaufman. Written by W. D. Richter. Starring Donald Sutherland as Matthew Bennell; Brooke Adams as Elizabeth Driscoll; Leonard Nimoy as Dr. David Kibner; Jeff Goldblum as Jack Bellicec; Veronica Cartwright as Nancy Bellicec.

The Plot: The film starts with a montage establishing the seeds drifting through space, landing on Earth and beginning to spread upon vegetation. A pink flower springs from one such seed, and Elizabeth Driscoll picks it, bringing it home to her boyfriend. Meanwhile, Matt Bennell is investigating the food at an expensive restaurant as part of his job as a city health inspector. He is seen later phoning Driscoll, talking her into coming in early to help him with something in the department.

The next morning Driscoll wakes up to find her boyfriend already up, emotionless, and taking a small pail of ashes out to a waiting garbage truck. As she heads to work, pockets of people can be seen running from something,

From deep space...

Invasion of the Body Snatchers

The seed is planted...terror grows.

A Robert H. Solo Production of A Philip Kaufman Film "Invasion of the Body Snatchers"
Donald Sutherland · Brooke Adams · Leonard Nimoy
Jeff Goldblum · Veronica Cartwright
Screenplay by W.D. Richter, Based on the novel "The Body Snatchers" by Jack Finney
Produced by Robert H. Solo · Directed by Philip Kaufman

The 1978 version of *Invasion of the Body Snatchers* would become fondly remembered by a generation of kids who grew up mesmerized by Donald Sutherland's facial expression at the end of the movie.

but the majority of pedestrians ignore it as they go about their daily routine. Driscoll talks to Bennell about her boyfriend briefly as they pass people acting oddly here and there in the halls. Bennell takes some laundry to a cleaners, and one of the owners mentions that his wife is not his wife. Meanwhile, Driscoll's boyfriend is behaving secretively, and Bennell suggests that she talk to his friend Dr. Kibner, who is a psychiatrist and best-selling author of self-help books. As they discuss what is happening while in a car, including Driscoll spying her boyfriend exchanging packages with strangers around the city, a frantic older man (Kevin McCarthy of the 1956 film) collides with the car, screaming, "They're here!," before stumbling off with a small mob of people chasing him. When they turn the corner, the man is dead, and the mob is silently staring down at him.

At a book party for Dr. Kibner, Bennell tries to see what happened with the man, figuring it had to be reported because the police were there and an ambulance was coming, but he gets nowhere. Meanwhile, a woman is talking to Kibner about how her husband "is not my husband," but Kibner gives her some mumbo-jumbo to make her feel better. Elizabeth talks to Kibner, who says he has been seeing the same problem developing over time and thinks it has to do with relationships faltering. Elsewhere, Jack is at the party, upset that someone he considers a hack, Kibner, can crank books out while he is struggling as a writer. Driscoll goes back home to find flowers from her boyfriend that have the pod flower on it, while Jack goes back to a massage spa run by his wife, Nancy. Nancy finds a webbed body under a sheet and screams, colliding with Jack, which leaves his nose bleeding.

Bennell arrives to look at the body and agrees with Jack that the police should not be called—remembering his earlier incident in trying to find out what happened to the man in the street. Bennell calls Elizabeth, who is half-asleep and starting to show signs of her face deteriorating. Her boyfriend hangs up the phone without saying anything, and Bennell goes off to see what is happening. Meanwhile, Nancy gives Jack something to sleep and he lies down, drifting off just as the pod opens its eyes and looks at Nancy. Nancy wakes Jack up, and they notice that the nose is bleeding. They run out and smack into Dr. Kibner.

Bennell finds Driscoll asleep and a pod double nearly formed in the garden by the bedroom. He manages to sneak her out past the boyfriend. Jack and Bennell try to involve the police, but everyone assumes it isn't happening, and Kibner only makes things worse. But it is clear that everyone who arrives to "help" has already turned. As has Kibner, who is seen getting in a car with Driscoll's boyfriend and others, telling them "the sooner the better," as Bennell wants to involve the authorities and get the public involved as well.

The group starts trying to do what they can to investigate the flowers while Bennell calls various agencies for help. All Bennell gets is the runaround, and those they have talked to about knowing someone who isn't acting right are themselves acting not quite right. As the four wait, Driscoll, Bennell and Jack fall asleep, and pods open ready to replace them. Nancy wakes Bennell and the two wake the others. They now realize that the pods take over while people sleep. Bennell tries to phone out, but it is clear that everyone is in on it now and they are one of the few left. Driscoll sees that a mob is forming and heading to the apartment. The others leave while Bennell destroys some of the pods (but is unable to do the same for Driscoll's, with it looking so much like her). The pod people spot them and scream in unison ("OoOoO!" according to the closed-captioning). Jack and Nancy split off to try to help Driscoll and Bennell from the mob. Driscoll and Bennell are chased some more ("OoOoOoOo!") but finally make it to the lab in their offices. While waiting, they see that the pod people are packing up more pods, and Kibner, Jack, and others arrive to inject them with medication to make them sleep. Kibner starts to explain how the seeds came on the solar winds, from planet to planet ("We adapt and we survive") when Driscoll breaks a beaker over Kibner's head and Bennell jams a dart into the back of Jack's neck (much like a method of killing someone mentioned by Kauffman in the 1956 version). Putting Kibner in a compartment, they head down the stairs and meet Nancy, who turns out to still be human. She advises them that they can fool the pod people by acting without emotions.

Driscoll sees a pod person who is a combination of a homeless man and his dog, causing her to gasp and making the pod people around them notice. Nancy escapes in the chaos, but Driscoll and Bennell are back on the run (the captioning states that Harry-Dog shouts "Get them!" at this point). They make it to the back of an 18-wheeler truck that takes them to a factory where pods are being loaded up for shipping by truck and ship. Bennell goes to investigate and comes back to find Driscoll in the final stages of transference after falling asleep. He hugs her as she crumbles to dust, and the new Driscoll appears, telling him to join them. He runs off and she begins to scream. He manages to destroy the factory and elude the pod people for a time, although it appears someone may have found him.

Sometime later, possibly even the next day, Bennell walks up the street and sees a group of schoolchildren being taken into a place where pods are being loaded so they can nap. Bennell moves on and enters his office, where everyone does their work like robots. He is next seen walking the streets again when Nancy appears. She calls his name and goes to him, but he begins to scream like the other pod people ("OoOoOoOoOo!") as Nancy screams in disbelief.

What Is the Same/Unique? In the age of the Me Generation, when everyone was supposed to get in touch with their feelings, experiment with new things, open their eyes to new experiences . . . we really messed ourselves up along the way. On the one positive note, movies made in that time sometimes showed that not everyone thought this was such a great thing to do to ourselves or to others. Case in point, the 1978 version of *Invasion of the Body Snatchers*, which takes the concept of how we're supposed to be at peace with our inner selves to the point of becoming nearly emotionless through new trends and self-help books. Although Leonard Nimoy as Number One Pod Person seems like a gimme in retrospect—he was the rarely emotional Spock on *Star Trek* after all—he isn't without emotions as the character of Kibner, but is so restrained that it is never easy to guess when he could have been turned from Kibner to a pod person. In fact, half the cast act like pod people before they actually are, with Driscoll's boyfriend only coming to life when watching his team play sports on television, and determined to wear his headphones as much as possible to tune out the world around him. Jack is involved in conspiracy theories as it gives him excuses for not being as good a writer as he thinks he is, and Nancy pushes him on because it helps her worldview as being out of her control and she can stay passive. People are running in the streets, but no one notices, and those who do are hunted down and made to conform or are killed in the process.

Sounds like everyday life, doesn't it? By the time Bennell is seen at the end of the film, we are unsure if he is playing "pod" or actually is a pod person. The children being forced to become pods with Bennell complacently watching should be a tip-off, but then one has to wonder if he's staying "in character" to save his own skin. If so, could he also be doing the same at the end of the picture when he screams and points at Nancy? Could Bennell still be human but have essentially become a pod person by "going along" with the evil around him? We hear stories all the time after wars where people admit they did terrible things to survive, refusing to stand up for those weaker than themselves because they didn't want to get knocked down. Is the final message of the 1978 version of *Invasion of the Body Snatchers* really one of how we were placating ourselves to stop being human?

Unlike the 1956 version, the 1978 one takes some liberties with the story line of the novel, making Bennell a health inspector rather than a doctor, Driscoll a friend rather than an ex-girlfriend, Jack a failed writer rather than a successful one and Nancy an owner of a spa rather than a housewife. Come to think of it, Nancy—the only one who runs her own business and therefore her life—is the only one who is not ultimately taken over by the pod people (at least until the end of the film). Kaufman/Kauffman becomes Kibner in the film but is still a psychiatrist who tries to "help" for a time (with no one really buying into what he says, although he seems to think his words are very important).

The switch to San Francisco was frowned upon by some fans of the book and the 1956 movie, feeling that it took away from some of the fears involved with a small town suddenly changing and the sense of claustrophobia such a small community can have. Yet, in a way, the San Francisco setting opens the film up to really dig into the story of how society was changing in the late 1970s, where a return to a small town wouldn't have that kind of feel (as it was still fairly easy to find a small town exactly like that seen in the 1956 version twenty-two years later, and therefore the whole "Me Generation" bit would not have worked as well). Once again the filmmakers rework some of the novel's elements to make them more logical: instead of the cut hand of Jack in the 1956 version, there's his bleeding nose; Bennell's attempts to contact someone higher up come too late to be effective and also set up a wild goose chase; Elizabeth/Becky is the one who is facing the crisis of having a loved one rather than a cousin turning on her; Nancy/Theodora survives to the end of the picture. It is also the first time the film has a true "negative" ending, with the pods having won.

The 1978 adaptation was a success as well, leading to producer Robert H. Solo considering an idea to bring the concept back as a sequel in the near future. That movie would go through a few bumps along the way, but emerge as the next film listed here.

Body Snatchers (1994)

Background: A Warner Bros. Production. Filmed in 1993. Released in 1994. Directed by Abel Ferrara. Written by Stuart Gordon, Dennis Paoli and Nicholas St. John. Starring Gabrielle Anwar as Marti Malone; Meg Tilly as Carol Malone; Terry Kinney as Steve Malone; Reilly Murphy as Andy Malone; R. Lee Ermey as General Platt; Forest Whitaker as Major Collins; Billy Wirth as Tim Young.

The Plot: On their way to a military base, Marti is attacked in a gas station bathroom by a man wearing military garb and telling her, "They get you when you sleep." The family arrives at the base for the father's new job there as part of the EPA. Marti makes friends with the general's daughter, Jenn, while the first night there appears to be a commotion outside their new home that sees a car driving away and someone screaming "No!" The father, Steve, is starting his work to test chemicals in the soil and water when he is interrupted by Major Collins, who asks if the toxic level of chemicals on the base could lead to paranoia and other psychological symptoms affecting people.

In school, Marti's six-year-old stepbrother, Andy, finds that he is not drawing the exact same pictures as everyone else and is ostracized. He runs away but is found by Tim, a helicopter pilot. Tim brings him back home and meets Marti, just as a garbage truck pulls away from the house next-door. Jenn later shows up to take Marti to a rather empty bar on base, where she meets up with Tim again and sees the military man who attacked her at the gas station. He states he doesn't recognize her, and Marti blows it off as a mistake. She and Tim head out to the swamps, where—as you would expect—they make out while soldiers nearby fill up a truck with pods.

Andy goes to see his mother, Carol, in the middle of the night, only to watch her crumble to dust in front of his eyes and a nude version of his mother emerge from the closet. As one would expect, this is rather abnormal, and Andy tries to tell others, but they don't believe him. Both Marti and Steve have incidents the next day that convince them something is up with people. That night, the mother has Steve, Marti and Andy go to sleep, and the pods nearly take them over. Steve is ready to leave, but Carol taunts him, asking him where any of them can go. The three leave anyway, and Carol points at them and shrieks in the familiar sounds of the pod people from the 1978 film (only it is just captioned as "hideous shrieking" rather than something like "OoOoOoOoOoOo!"). Well, that was a dead giveaway. Most of those at the base start chasing them, but they are saved by a couple of men who shoot at the pod people. Tim tries to help but is attacked by other men.

IMAGINE...
YOU'RE GONE AND
SOMEONE ELSE
IS LIVING INSIDE
YOUR BODY.

Body Snatchers (1994) plays like a brat-pack version of *Invasion of the Body Snatchers*, but was conceived as a sequel to the 1978 adaptation.

The family stops in a warehouse, and Steve goes to get help, only to return as a pod person. Marti manages to kill "Steve" and meet up with Tim, who was able to avoid capture. As he gets a helicopter to take them away, Marti and Andy are captured. Tim manages to wake Marti up before her pod can take over, but the Andy that joins them turns out to be a pod, and Marti tosses him out of the helicopter after a fight. The now-pod general is asked if they should be destroyed, but he states that no one will believe them. They land in Atlanta on another base and Carol's earlier dialogue about them having no place to go is heard on the soundtrack as the movie fades to black.

But, in hindsight, "Carol" and the pod people don't know what they're talking about.

What Is the Same/Unique? As a sequel to the earlier 1978 picture—the film only works if one looks at it as a sequel instead of another retelling—the story line has some solid moments, in a sense working as a teenager's version of the more adult 1956 and 1978 films. As it stands, it is easy to see the first three films working as a continuous story line—thanks to the cameo of Kevin McCarthy in the 1978 film, leaving us to believe he may have been on the run from the pod people for twenty-two years, to the shrieking alarm of the pod people from the 1978 film popping up in the 1993 movie. Even the concept of the pod people hitting a military base makes sense (why hit a small town when it would be easier to hit people with the firepower to control others?).

What is remarkable about *Body Snatchers* is the number of talented people involved in a film that doesn't quite properly gel. Abel Ferrara had done *Bad Lieutenant* just before *Body Snatchers* (and would later do the end-of-the-world film *4:44 Last Day on Earth* discussed in a previous chapter). Stuart Gordon, as a writer and director, had done *Re-Animator* and *From Beyond*. One of the original writers on it was Larry Cohen, who had done *The Stuff* among other great albeit oddball action films. Yet with all that talent, and with a concept that would—on the surface—suggest a fun movie, the finished product seems to be lacking something.

There's not much point in addressing similarities, as the film really has nothing in it that is supposed to be the same as earlier versions of the story. There were rumors that if it did well, a sequel could occur (with the government being taken over and freedom fighters working against them), but the studio did not have much faith in the finished product, and the film went over rather poorly with test audiences (I attended one myself full of science fiction fans who booed after it was over). In saying all that, however, if there were to be a sequel, it means there was still a place to go at the end of the film, and therefore what is supposed to be the sinister reminder of Carol's last words in the film ends up being posturing on the part of the pod people. For being unemotional, they sure do get stuck on themselves.

With the demise of *Body Snatchers*, the concept would disappear for a time, only to spring back to life in 2007 as a remake from Warner Bros. But first, as always, a side step into the Asylum.

Invasion of the Pod People (2007)

Background: The Asylum production. Filmed in Los Angeles, California, in 2007. Released July 2007. Directed by Justin Jones. Written by Leigh Scott. Starring Erica Roby as Melissa; Jessica Bork as Samantha.

The Plot: Asteroids are landing all over the country, making this invasion of the pods rather public news. Melissa watches the news. Then there's a sex scene. The boss, Samantha, goes to Melissa's desk in a warehouse somewhere to give her what appears to be a ginger root. A model goes to take a shower but is killed by her jelly-covered duplicate. Both are wearing too much makeup. Then there's a sex scene. Then there's a guy with a gun. It doesn't lead to a sex scene; it leads to Melissa buying a gun, which is like a sex scene for NRA members. People talk and talk and talk, and then we have a lesbian sex scene between Melissa and her boss. Some more talking and then a quasi-sex-scene and then some shooting, and Melissa ends up supposedly leaving town with another woman, but it turns out that Melissa is already a pod person, and she will be taking the other woman somewhere to be killed. Alas, no ending sex scene.

What Is the Same/Unique? The same? Hmm . . . there were people in the movie, and there were people in the other films, so that's one. Uh . . . some type of filming equipment was probably used. The words "invasion," "of" and "the" appear, so that's another similarity. After that, I'm not sure.

Of course, the entire point of the Asylum's mockbuster system is to produce a film that looks like one coming out from a bigger studio. In all honesty, they pulled it off pretty well with their *War of the Worlds* update, and *I Am Omega* certainly isn't *I Am Legend*, but a decent time waster. *Invasion of the Pod People*, on the other hand, just doesn't do it. Not that there isn't a lot of "doing it" in the film—the film looks like it's one step away from being a porn movie at times—but it certainly is not *Invasion of the Body Snatchers* in any way.

So with an unfortunate Asylum film, after two decent attempts for the other big films discussed in this book, we'll move on to the final adaptation that was also released in 2007.

The Invasion (2007)

Background: A Warner Bros. production. Filmed in September–November 2005 and January 2007. Released in August 2007. Directed by Oliver Hirschbiegel (2005 footage) and James McTeigue (2007). Written by Dave Kajganich (2005) and the Wachowskis (2007). Starring Nicole Kidman as Carol Bennell; Daniel Craig as Ben Driscoll; Jackson Bond as Oliver; Jeremy Northam as Tucker Kaufman.

The Plot: Carol Bennell is in a drugstore, gulping down pills and tossing back Mountain Dew like a high school kid on prom night before the film goes into a flashback for the majority of its running time.

A space shuttle explodes, scattering wreckage from Dallas to Washington, D.C. The government tries to quarantine what they can, but as CDC director Tucker Kaufman soon finds out, every single piece contains spores from space that can withstand cold and heat and may be deadly. Oddly, just after being told this is a quarantined area while wearing a biohazard suit, a young woman holds out a piece of wreckage for him that she found as he is walking back to his car. Does he immediately send her into the quarantined area to be examined? No, he grabs the wreckage, cutting his finger in the process. Does he now quarantine himself, knowing that he may be contaminated? At least take the piece back to the quarantined area? Nope, he just drops the piece where he stands and gets in his limo. Must have gotten the job through relatives.

Kaufman goes home to his growling dog and what appears to be his growling wife, who mentions (the wife, not the dog) that his ex-wife, Carol, called twice. The woman is also mad that he didn't bother calling her to let her know he would be out late on the job and heading out early to brief the president. They go to sleep, with Kaufman soon covered in webbing like pods from the 1978 and 1994 films. Well, that's what happens when you go to bed angry.

Meanwhile, Carol wakes up to the sounds of her son, Ollie, screaming in the middle of the night. She rushes to him. The next morning she is fixing breakfast and seeing paperwork pertaining to legal custody. The scene cuts to her in her office receiving an eerie phone call from Kaufman where he talks about how fine, really fine, he is feeling. He then demands to see Ollie, and it's clear that the spores are making him act like a stalker . . . only the editing makes this all appear to be a flashback to something before he was contaminated, as we go back to Carol in the kitchen thinking about the incident on what appears to be the morning after Kaufman was pricked by the piece of wreckage. Which means either Kaufman is already a bit loopy before anything happens to him or the scene is one where an editor just gave up, saying, "I know this is supposed to be days or weeks later, but I can't make it work." She walks Ollie to school, and it is clear that it is Halloween. She also mentions the evening is forecast to be 45 degrees, which means she's walking her son to school (and later for trick or treat) in just a Superman outfit in what is probably less than 50-degree weather. Our moms would have forced us to wear a coat, ruining the image of the costume.

Carol is driven to work by friend Ben Driscoll. It turns out she is a psychiatrist, and at her 9:00 appointment with Wendy Lenk (played by 1978 film alumnus Veronica Cartwright), Lenk tells her that her husband isn't acting right; he snapped the neck of their dog when it growled at him. Later, during trick or treat, as the two mothers discuss various medications for their children, one of Ollie's friends is attacked by a dog, but he calmly shrugs it off as if it is nothing. He sits away from the other kids organizing his candy, suggesting signs of shock from the dog attack, but the mothers don't seem to be caring that much. Ollie shouts out that a weird jelly-like thing is on his hand. Instead of figuring it is a Halloween gag by Ollie or the other kids, Carol immediately assumes it is something deadly that must be investigated.

NICOLE KIDMAN   DANIEL CRAIG

DO NOT
TRUST ANYONE.

DO NOT
SHOW EMOTION.

DO NOT
FALL ASLEEP.

THE
INVASION

AUGUST 17   WWW.THEINVASIONMOVIE.COM

The 2007 version of the film, *The Invasion*, highlights a great cast but shows what happens when too many changes are made to the story to try to "modernize" it.

Ben thinks the obvious—that it is a gag—but goes through the trouble of having it tested at the hospital where he works. The man testing it, Steven, states that it could be many things, but has noted a few recent reports of odd samples going around. Meanwhile, a flu virus appears to be sweeping the country, and Kaufman is on the case, stating that flu inoculations will be available to handle it. When a reporter asks a rather idiotic question about the vaccine, Kaufman laughs her off, and all the media acts as if it is a big joke, which in reality would not be the case at all, but there you go. Of course, the inoculations are actually a way of spreading the spores. Meanwhile, the waiters are spitting up in the pitchers of water in the background, as they're wont to do when thinking of what they're getting paid, no doubt. Of course, the idea is that the media will be converted thanks to drinking the water, but who drinks the water at these things anyway? Sounds like a really bad idea by the spores here, especially when the spit-up is green. I think the reporters may spot that.

Carol goes to work to find Wendy's husband waiting. He states he is waiting for his wife. Carol calls Wendy on her cell phone, and Wendy hangs up, suspicious of Carol's call. Later, while driving, Carol and Ollie witness a frantic woman being hit by a car in a tunnel. No one seems to care, especially the police, who tell her that they've "taken down her plate" and will call if needed. Carol drops off Ollie at his father's without much concern about the death the boy just witnessed and goes on to a party with Driscoll. He drops her off afterward very late, and she gets in just in time for the Census Bureau to show up at the door. Because they always come at 2 a.m., right? She agrees to talk to the man at the door. At that point he tries to smash through the door, but can't be bothered to smash through the glass in the door. Instead of calling the police, worried that the man will break in some other way, Carol calls Driscoll. No wonder the spores are winning—no one seems to be acting quite right.

Carol finally adds up everything when she notices that all her appointments have been canceled and everyone—everyone—is staring at her in the streets. Steven at the hospital calls to let her and Driscoll know that something is up with the sample. Turns out that there is some type of viral strain going around that is changing people's DNA during REM sleep. Driscoll gets a call about an ambassador they met at the party who is changing while having a heart attack. They run to his home and see his features changing, leading Carol to drive off to get Ollie from Kaufman.

She goes into the house to find Ollie, but only finds a group of sharply dressed people there. Kaufman spits in her face to change her, but she takes off and is chased . . . well, actually, no one seems to be chasing her, which makes for a rather weak action scene. She and a few others are attacked on a subway car, but Carol escapes all the projectile vomiting going on by those already possessed (eww). After shooting a possessed man, she makes it up to the street and tries to control her emotions. She goes back to Driscoll, where a small number of people are gathered. All they know for sure is that sleep causes the change to occur, so sleep must be avoided.

Carol and Driscoll make it to her office, where they investigate Wendy Lenk's case. Although the earlier scene where the husband calls would suggest Wendy has changed as well, they believe for some odd reason she hasn't (or hadn't). It turns out that she had acute disseminated encephalomyelitis as a youngster, which the spores cannot control and which therefore makes her immune. Carol realizes that Ollie had it as well three years previously, which also makes him immune. With this information, they believe that a vaccine can be created now, but Carol needs to find Ollie, and a text message from him shows he is in Baltimore. After a series of edits that suggest they bulldoze their way out of town, it turns out to be just hallucinations of Carol, who is rapidly having problems staying awake.

Carol manages to control her emotions for the trip to Baltimore and finds Ollie. They escape. They are cornered by Kaufman, but Carol knocks him out. The film then arrives back at the beginning, with Carol and Ollie in the drugstore. Carol grabs a hypodermic needle and fills it with something, telling Ollie that if she falls asleep, he'll need to plunge the needle into her heart, which he later does. Ben arrives, but he has been taken over. He lets a group of converted people out of the employee room where Carol had locked them up, leading to Carol killing all of them with a gun and shooting Ben in the leg. Seems like she could have done the same for the others, but there you go.

It all leads to a long car chase, with falling bodies and broken glass. Although it is clear now that the government knows what is going on and is fighting against the spores, the spores seem to be really obsessed with catching one woman and her kid. Maybe they're Kidman fans.

Yes, it makes no sense, but the two get away, everyone is vaccinated and the world is safe. On the one-year anniversary, there are only pockets of resistance remaining, and Carol is shown happily with Driscoll and Ollie.

What Is the Same/Unique? The film ran into problems after initial shooting when Warner Bros. decided that the movie they had paid to be made wasn't the movie they wanted to release. Oliver Hirschbiegel, who had directed the dramatically tense Hitler biopic *Downfall*, filmed the script by David Kajganich in the same low-key way to enhance the feeling of uncertainty that the characters were feeling, but it led to a finished product that wasn't the thrill-ride Warner evidently expected. The movie was canceled from its mid-summer release date in 2006; and in January 2007, filming began again with new scenes created by the Wachowski siblings (*The Matrix*) and directed by James McTeigue (*V for Vendetta*) to spice up the ending and help feed earlier plot-points toward said ending as well. It was during this period that Kidman broke ribs during a stunt involving the car-chase scene at the end of the picture, which also saw cameramen and stunt people hurt as well.

All this additional work by two sets of writers and directors is why the film never seems to quite form a whole. It seems to want to say something about our conservative political leanings (hence setting it in Washington, D.C.) as well as the media's rapid decline into giving us only the highlights with no investigative intent apparent. Driscoll at one point notes that he could only get "real news" on "the World Service," while Steven notes that other countries were actively trying to quarantine those with the virus, while Americans were told there was just a little flu bug going around—all symptoms of a society happily being dictated to without question. Then there's the throwback to the sense of loss of identity already evident in people even before the spores turn up that was a focus of the 1978 movie. With the idea that inoculations are the cause, rather than the cure, of the epidemic that is close to wiping out the world, it could also be seen as an indictment of what some people see as immunizations that supposedly lead to health problems for children—a widespread scare at the time of the film's release that has since been disproven in the past few years. Then there was the resounding theme that everyone is reaching for a pill for themselves to calm their fears and simplemindedly doing the same for their children. The film seems to want to go in six different directions while telling a thrilling, but intellectual, action story about an alien invasion and ends up not coming close to being the sum of its parts. Instead, gaping plot holes appear. (Why would they think Wendy was immune? Why would the aliens bother with the flu vaccine when a simple contagion effect would do the trick? With so many people in control knowing and fighting the spores, why did everyone in authority around Carol appear to be under its influence? Why bother keeping Ollie alive if he was just a hindrance and possibly key for the humans to use to defeat them? Once Carol got the drugs she needed to stay awake, why stick around in a drugstore full of the possessed in the next room when she could have seen Driscoll anywhere?)

As mentioned in the plot recounted above, there are moments where the editing is suspect as well, including late scenes that appear to represent pieces of a different ending (where Carol appears to momentarily dream about them smashing their car through roadblocks in order to save Ollie). By the time the film is over, one can't be quite sure if we're even supposed to believe the happy ending or think it is a case of Carol hallucinating once again (which actually is one of the few nice moments in the film).

There are, of course, parallels to the earlier movies and the novel. Bennell is now a woman and is no longer a doctor of medicine but of psychology, which makes more sense in terms of people talking to her about displacement theories than a medical doctor would in a big city. Becky is now Ben, who is a doctor, which allows all the usual medical-related aspects of the plot to be developed. Kaufman is no longer a friend but an ex-husband and father to a child that has no counterpart in the first two movies but certainly does in the 1994 adaptation. There is a big difference with the way the spores are spread—no longer are a bunch of giant pea-pods needed to be spread around, just a virus. This allows for a more logical "takeover" aspect to the proceedings, but it also gives the filmmakers an easy out for the survivors—nearly everyone is going to come out of it alive and healthy, unlike those in every other version who were destroyed in the process of building the "pod people." With that, however, it does allow the movie to have a positive ending, even more than the novel and the first film, as everyone survives. Except the people Carol shoots who are now dead. And most probably if Kaufman survived the blow to the head by Carol, one would expect him being fired by the CDC after his sloppy work on the case.

It is interesting to note that *The Invasion* shares a close affiliation with the same year's *I Am Legend* pertaining to an ongoing fear of vaccinations—both lead to people being turned into things other than human (one into aliens and the other into monsters) thanks to advancements in science that a certain segment of the public fears. They both also play into the idea of people with natural immunities being the only way to cure a man-made and seemingly apocalyptic disease. Which leads back to the original theme of *The War of the Worlds* as well, as it is "the littlest things that God in his wisdom has put upon the earth that save mankind." Mankind may attempt to set ourselves up to be taken over by aliens, but nature or God's work (have as you may) is the only thing that will save us.

And as the subsequent chapter will prove, we need a lot of saving.

15

Aliens Are Jerks

While the Pods and Martians Were Busy

As established, *Invasion of the Body Snatchers* and *War of the Worlds* are icons of apocalyptic movies. They also establish two rules of alien invasion movies. For the sake of argument, we can also throw in our third cornerstone film, *I Am Legend*, giving us the unholy trinity of Alien Invasion Movie Rules, which are:

1. My God! They look just like us! (*Invasion of the Body Snatchers*)
2. My God! Look at the size of that thing! (*The War of the Worlds*)
3. My God! Monsters! (*I Am Legend*)

Every alien invasion movie can be summed up by one of these three exclamations listed above. Sometimes even as a combination of two or all three.

In this chapter, we'll take a look at some of the movies that fit these criteria, their history and what it may all mean. One thing is for sure—whether taking over our bodies, shooting us down in the streets with their advanced weaponry or siccing monsters on us, there's one thing to be sure of: aliens are jerks. No argument about it, everything is about them, them, them; and even the most innocent of alien ploys (such as in the first example below of *It Came from Outer Space*) deals with forcing humans to do things against their will. And all so they can get something for their own purposes. As seen already in films like *Knowing* and others in earlier chapters, the aliens sure are callous about the human race.

Maybe they should be. Maybe all this is just our way of showing that we're probably ill prepared for such "first contacts," or at least we think we are. Even so, none of the movies listed here paints a very warm picture of such an alien encounter.

My God! They look just like us!

Although we tend to look at *Invasion of the Body Snatchers* as the first alien invasion film showing aliens disguised as humans in order to infiltrate society, it wasn't the first one to do so. Nor was the idea really that original in comparison to cinema. It goes back to the concept of thrillers and horror films before it: war films where the humorous, helpful industrialist is really a Nazi spy (*Saboteur*, 1942); the detective film noir where the frightened woman on the run turns out to be a femme fatale (*The Maltese Falcon*, 1941); the loving husband who actually is trying to drive his new wife insane (*Gaslight*, 1944). Those around us may not be as they appear, and it is this fear of the known world suddenly tilting sideways in our thinking that is played off in the alien invasion movies. There's also a certain element of the traditional zombie movies tied in, as can be seen in such features as *It Came from Outer Space* (1953) and others, where people are transformed for a time by aliens to do their bidding. The following films are the most memorable that play into these themes while presenting aliens that need no special effects to make them unworldly.

It Came from Outer Space (1953)

The first alien invasion movie of this sort, coming three years before the first adaptation of *Invasion of the Body Snatchers* (and two years before the novel). Surprisingly, it turns out not to actually be about an alien invasion—the aliens have crashed on Earth and need to rebuild their ship. Being able to assume the form of humans, they had kidnapped a few so they could take their place in a small town and be able to get parts for their work without being detected. Their inability to mimic the personalities of those they replace makes them noticeable, leading to people in the town thinking an invasion is taking place. As it turns out, everyone is happily returned to their former lives after the kidnapping and the aliens leave.

The film is based on a story by Ray Bradbury, which he had written in two forms—one with evil aliens and the other with innocent ones just trying to get home (oddly enough, Spielberg's movie *E.T.* plays with a similar concept of an alien that is trying to avoid bad humans while trying to go home). The film is also remembered as being one of a handful produced for the cinematic gimmick 3-D, which explains why some scenes play out as if things are shooting straight at the camera.

Invaders from Mars (1953 and 1986)

Still three years before *Invasion of the Body Snatchers* hit theaters, and yet another film showing everyday people being turned into zombies for aliens, in this case Martians. Reminiscent of the character Jimmy from the first version of *Body Snatchers*, the story deals with a boy, David (played by Jimmy Hunt), who wakes in the middle of the night to see a flying saucer land in a sandpit near his house. His father, a scientist, goes to investigate and comes back zombie-like, with a small wound in the back of his neck. David notes other people around the town starting to act the same and with a similar mark on their neck.

Through a series of incidents, including the alien sabotage of a rocket research plant, David is able to convince others of the invasion, and the military find the saucer. The military are able to enter the ship and are told by the aliens that they are out to stop man's advancement into space, using mind control from small crystals placed in the back of the neck of humans to help get their mission completed. The military plant bombs around the saucer as David runs to get away from the explosion. He then wakes up to find it was all a dream, only to see a saucer landing in the sandpit near his house. The film was remade in 1986, directed by Tobe Hooper (*Lifeforce*) and starring Karen Black and her son, Hunter Carson, as David, although the 1953 version is considered the classic.

It Conquered the World (1956)

It's Peter Graves (*Mission: Impossible*), Lee Van Cleef (*The Good, the Bad and the Ugly*) and Beverly Garland (nearly every B-movie that didn't have Susan Cabot or Gloria Talbott) versus a squat cucumber hiding in a cave! Okay, that doesn't sound very exciting, and the alien monster wouldn't scare a three-year-old, so director Roger Corman did the sensible thing—he hid the monster in the darkness until the very last minute and had it instead . . . uh, release bat-like creatures from his bottom (honest) that sting people and turn them into willing zombies for the alien to take over the world.

Garland takes a shotgun to the alien but gets killed, leading to traitor Van Cleef turning on the creature with a blowtorch. Graves cleans up with a speech about man being a feeling creature . . . who just happens to have blowtorches and shotguns.

That was the end of *It Conquered the World*, but Garland is back! . . . in *Not of This Earth* from 1957, also directed by Roger Corman. This one has Garland as a nurse who is helping to care for a man who is actually an alien, looking to see if human blood will help his alien race. (At least these aliens bother to do testing first before obtaining human blood, unlike the Martians from *War of the Worlds*, who just seem to love the stuff without any way of knowing if it is helpful to them or not.) The alien starts bumping people off, including the nurse's boss, which makes her suspicious. Only in a Corman movie would the deadly alien be destroyed by having him sail his car off the road and crashing; but in a way that's actually more refreshing to see than some of the oddball ways other alien conquests have been stopped.

Not of This Earth was remade in 1988 with Traci Lords in the Garland role, and then again in 1995 with Michael York in the alien part. Which is just . . . huh.

Plan 9 from Outer Space (1959)

How could this alien invasion movie *not* make it into this book? There's not much that readers probably don't already know: crazed producer, director, writer and actor Ed Wood made this movie, originally called *Grave Robbers from Outer Space*, with money from two Baptist ministers. The film has footage of Bela Lugosi that Wood had shot of the actor in hopes of using it in another movie, and was then used in *Plan 9* in order to make it "Lugosi's last movie" (although he only appears for a few minutes early in the film).

The plot deals with aliens from another planet that have been unsuccessful in their multiple attempts to conquer Earth. Plan 9 is one involving raising the dead on Earth to . . . stumble around a bit, it appears. Tor Johnson, Vampira and a chiropractor dressed up like Lugosi are the main ghouls raised from the dead. The aliens actually have our and their best interests at heart, trying to keep earthlings from creating a bomb called "solarbonite," which—if used— would destroy the universe by exploding light from the sun and anywhere such light would hit.

It's laughable, until you realize that in the 1980s *Doctor Who* would use the same idea in one of their stories ("The Mysterious Planet"). Then it's just a little sad. On the other hand, *Plan 9* is actually fun because you can instantly tell that they had $1.95 to make the thing, but everyone is very earnest about it all. There's also a nice scene where a soldier and an officer are discussing their shooting at the saucers and how they'll just write it off to the public as "shooting at clouds." It's not much, but not many other films at the time would bother questioning what the military was up to when it came to aliens.

A quick note about another 1959 movie dealing with raising the dead for an invasion of sorts, *Invisible Invaders*, which deals with invisible aliens from the moon (yep, the moon) who plan to take over the earth by taking over the bodies of the recent dead. One would think this would make for an army unable to do much once rigor mortis took hold, but what we get is a lot of gap-jawed dead people in suits lumbering around in a manner that looks much like that used in the 1968 version of *Night of the Living Dead* (some contend that *Invisible Invaders* may have been an influence on Romero's film).

Plan 9 is more fun, however.

Village of the Damned (1960 and 1995)

Based on a book, *The Midwich Cuckoos*, by John Wyndham (who was discussed way back in chapter 3 with his novel *The Day of the Triffids*), the film stars George Sanders and deals with the concept of "evil children" (such as discussed in the contagion chapter pertaining to the film *The Children*). In this film, aliens have impregnated all the women in a small British village during a period of unconsciousness. The same thing occurs around the globe, but only in the village and in the Soviet Union have the children been allowed to be born and raised. It turns out that these three-year-olds (who look and act like preteens) are actually aliens who have great mental ability, and Sanders' character at first wants to work with them for the betterment of mankind. However, it soon becomes clear that the alien children have no intention of submitting to mankind's will. The Soviets bomb their collection of children, and Sanders manages to set off a bomb while with the children of the village, saving mankind.

A sequel came in 1963, *Children of the Damned*, which drastically changed the story line so that the few children found are actually peaceful and not aliens at all, but are killed nevertheless by the end of that film. John Carpenter would film a remake of *Village of the Damned* in 1995 with Christopher Reeve in the Sanders role. It would be Reeve's last role before he was paralyzed in a horse-riding accident.

While there had been "evil children" movies before it, *Village of the Damned* set up most of the clichés of such films from that point on, being influential on everything from other alien possession movies to Damien in *The Omen* series.

End of the World (1977)

This film actually starts off with a bit of promise, as Father Pergado (Christopher Lee) is seen entering a diner in a rather unsettled, quiet state. He asks to use the payphone, but before he can make the call, the payphone explodes, as does the coffee machine, scalding the cook, who flings himself through a window, killing himself. Pergado gives him last rites and then stumbles back to a mission, where another Christopher Lee is waiting for him.

After that, however, everything fizzles. Most of the film is taken up with two people who are trying to figure out weird radio signals that predict catastrophes around the planet. They eventually discover the father and his order of nuns who are actually all aliens disguised as humans in order to study mankind while trying to fix a way back to their own world. Like the aliens of *Plan 9*, they believe humanity is going to wreck the universe, but that's okay because the world is doomed anyway. They help give things around the world a little push and take off in their transporter, and the world blows up.

Like I said, aliens are jerks.

The Thing (1951 and 1982)

Discussed earlier in the book are the two other movies in what John Carpenter refers to as his "Apocalypse Trilogy," *Prince of Darkness* and *In the Mouth of Madness*. His *The Thing* is an adaptation of the 1951 film *The Thing from Another World*, which falls more into the "alien monsters" category than this one. The 1982 version goes back to John Campbell's original novella, *Who Goes There?*, for the premise. The story focuses on a group of researchers at a station in Antarctica who get involved with an alien creature that had been frozen in its spaceship in the ice for years and has been revived. In the 1951 version, the creature that appears (played by James Arness in a Frankenstein's-monster type of outfit) is an intelligent plant life form that stomps around and tries to kill off the cast. Carpenter's film, however, goes back to the novella to have the creature be something that can look like any animal, including human, and that can absorb the memories and traits of the original.

In the 1951 movie, the researchers band together to electrocute the creature, saving the day. Campbell's novella has the few remaining men discover which one of them is the alien and burn it with a blowtorch. (See? Blowtorches come in real handy if you're facing aliens, as Lee Van Cleef discovered in *It Conquered the World.*) In Carpenter's film, it isn't quite so easy. The cast is reduced to two characters, neither of whom is sure if the other is human or the creature. With the station blown up, the two sit by a dying fire and square off, waiting to die either by bullet, the alien or freezing to death. Not a very happy ending, but Carpenter wasn't always satisfied with happy endings.

Speaking of which, when the film aired on television after leaving theaters, an alternate ending was tacked on—this one showing a dog running away from the destroyed station. The dog—obviously the alien, as all the dogs had been killed earlier in the film—stops to look back momentarily and then runs off. At least Carpenter gave humanity some hope in his version, unlike the television edit (not done with his consent) that featured the earth as doomed.

The Hidden (1987)

A fun film, starring Kyle MacLachlan and Michael Nouri, that didn't do that well at the theaters in 1987 but has since become a cult film thanks to video rentals and sales. The movie has MacLachlan as a rather odd FBI agent who is helping an LAPD detective (Nouri) discover what is causing a violent wave of incidents among seemingly different people. As it turns out, the FBI agent is actually an alien, who had taken over the body of the agent to help in his pursuit of a violent alien criminal that has been taking over various people in the past few weeks.

The two work together to catch up with the alien, who eyes a senator on the way to becoming the next president. If he can get to the body and the senator wins the election, then he'll be in a position to bring others like him to Earth and take over. The detective and the agent manage to stop him, leading to both sad and happy endings for the heroes. There is a sequel, *The Hidden 2*, but everything worth seeing was done in the original.

Parasitic aliens that enter the body and take over the victim also pop up in *The Puppet Masters* (1994 and starring Donald Sutherland, who was in the second version of *Invasion of the Body Snatchers*, which some feel the novel it is based on is somewhat similar to the book *The Puppet Masters*, written by Robert A. Heinlein and published a few years before *The Body Snatchers*). Robert Rodriguez's *The Faculty* (1998) also uses the premise but is mainly remembered today for a small acting role featuring *The Daily Show*'s Jon Stewart. It is also the plot of the 2013 film *The Host*, based on a book by the author of the *Twilight* series, Stephenie Meyer.

They Live (1988)

Back to John Carpenter, which just goes to show how much he seems to enjoy the subject of alien possession; every Carpenter film discussed in this book shows some type of possession occurring. In this case, it is a group of aliens that look somewhat human but have metallic faces and use a signal in a cable network's satellite link-up in order to keep their disguise in place from the humans around them. The only way to see the aliens, who are in control of everything in the world and are robbing the earth of all its resources before moving on to another world, is through sunglasses that also expose subliminal signs that tell humans to obey and spend.

Roddy Piper plays the Kurt Russell–like role of a drifter who ends up discovering the truth and attempting to locate the signal and destroy it so that humans will then rebel against their alien overlords. The film didn't do that well at the box office when it first came out, but like several others here, it became a cult film on video; and Piper's line "I have come here to chew bubble gum and kick ass. And I'm all out of bubble gum" has become a favorite quote for many people who have no idea what film it is from. Which shows that possession can come in many forms.

My God! Look at the size of that thing!

In this category, it's pretty simple. Aliens come and start blasting away at humans. In some cases, the films start after the fact and with Earth already surrendered, but even so, there are still rebels trying to win back the world from those now in control.

Such films do not have quite the psychological horror element to them as the earlier *Body Snatchers* presented before. Instead, it is more wish fulfillment dealing with bullies, mainly in terms of having to fight someone bigger than us, only to discover an Achilles heel that allows us a defiant and definite victory (as seen in *War of the Worlds* and the Martians ultimately catching the sniffles). With this setup, we have a tendency to do horrible things to ourselves (or, rather, the guy standing next to the hero), because in the end, humanity is going to give back in spades what will either annihilate the aliens or at least send them packing, never to return. The following films are some of the more memorable ones featuring such a theme.

Flash Gordon (1936)

In the first thirteen-part serial starring Buster Crabbe, Ming the Merciless (Charles Middleton) has a whole planet at his disposal to take on the earth and (as with the 1980 movie) is more in a position where he just wants to play with the earth for a while before conquering it. His lapse of attention and his interest in Dale (the heroine in the series, not the author of this book) are his undoing, as Flash eventually is able to unite others to defeat Ming and his men.

But Ming probably has the biggest arsenal of the aliens listed here—not only that of his own world but those of others under his dominion. How they all travel around the cosmos like some wandering street gang intimidating other planets is a question of concern, but otherwise it's certainly impressive.

Earth vs. the Flying Saucers (1956)

UFO sightings have been around since biblical times, although certainly not with the concept of aliens coming down to greet or shoot us. It was only in more recent times, and especially after the famous Roswell sighting of 1947, that UFOs

The Flying Saucer from 1950 was an early attempt to show viewers the idea of a "flying saucer," even though it turns out to be anything but that by the end of the film.

Courtesy of Vintage Cinema Ads

became part of the public consciousness. With the expansion of everyone and their brother seeing a "flying saucer" in the sky, it was only natural for the movies to take up the concept and make it their own.

In 1950, the first movie to use the concept of a "flying saucer"—*The Flying Saucer*—was released, but the plot is strictly that of an espionage film with the hero finding out that the saucer is man-made and he has to stop the Soviets from obtaining it. If it weren't for one scene showing our hero drunk and smoking about five cigarettes from one hand, it would be hard to imagine anyone really remembering the film beyond the fact that it was the first one there.

Other alien ships turned up, including the strong prototype of what we commonly think of as flying saucers in the 1951 film *The Day the Earth Stood Still* (which, although dealing with an alien, is not about an alien invasion and certainly not apocalyptic, which is why you don't see it listed in this book). *Earth vs. the Flying Saucers*, with effects from master effects artist Ray Harryhausen, shaped the concept of such ships attacking, and its memorable moments of the saucers crashing into Washington, D.C., monuments would eventually become so famous that they could be easily parodied in *Mars Attacks!* (see chapter 22) without having to explain where the idea came from.

Daleks' Invasion Earth: 2150 A.D. (1966)

This film never caught on in America but was certainly bigger in other countries, and has become well loved by fans of the television series *Doctor Who*, on which this movie was based. The story—originally told in six parts during the second season of the program—was revamped in the way the Doctor (our hero) is presented. In the series, the Doctor (William Hartnell) is a mysterious alien who possesses a machine that can go anywhere in time and space and just happens to look like a police box but is bigger on the inside. (Long story short for those who don't know, think of a police box as a small shelter slightly larger than a phone booth that allowed contact with the police and other such services on a city street. If you need a phone booth explained to you, you're on your own.) With the Doctor are his granddaughter, Susan, and two of her schoolteachers, Ian and Barbara. Their second adventure together featured a trip to the Daleks' home world, and it was so popular that the villains were bound to come back. This occurred in a story about the Daleks invading Earth that was shown in the second season.

Taking a page from Wells' *The Time Machine*, writer/creator Terry Nation (whose name will pop up again in chapter 20) had the Doctor and the others land on a planet where there had been a great apocalyptic war. Over the centuries, the two sides—the Kaleds and the Thals—who had fought in the war had gone their own evolutionary ways, much like the Morlocks and the Eloi in Wells' book, with the Thals (the Eloi equivalent) changing from mutants back into a "perfect" form of Aryan blondes who wear too much makeup and the

Kaleds (the Morlock equivalent, later to become the Daleks) remaining mutants. In the Daleks' situation, they developed small containers shaped like garbage can–sized salt shakers and driven like small tanks. Kids instantly fell in love with the Daleks, and the monsters swept through Britain like a wave of Beatlemania in 1963–1964, becoming one of the show's best-loved villains.

When the idea of doing movies based on *Doctor Who* came up, it just made sense to base them on the popular Dalek. The problem was that the series was unknown in America—a market the film had to do well in. Thus, the concept of the Doctor became that of an eccentric inventor, who had invented a wacky time machine (basically a room full of computer props and a lever) and was traveling with his two granddaughters, Susan and Barbara, and Barbara's clumsy boyfriend, Ian.

The film, which starred Peter Cushing as a marquee boost (since he was known in America thanks to his work in Hammer horror films at the time), didn't do anything in the United States, but enough elsewhere to generate interest in a sequel. And, since no one really was paying attention the first time around, it was decided to reintroduce the main characters in the second film. This is why we get niece Louise, instead of Barbara, and Constable Tom Campbell as the second male lead instead of Ian in the second film.

The film focuses on the group thrust forward in time to 2150, when the Daleks have already conquered Earth. They have done so not so much to turn the remaining members of humanity into slaves, which they have, but because they want the planet (actually a quite recurring theme in *Doctor Who* over the years). The reason? So they can hollow it out, put in an engine and slowly drive the planet around like a giant car to visit other planets. And although it appears they stole this idea from Ming the Merciless, or thought, "Wouldn't it be cool if Earth was like the moon in *Space: 1999*, only we could drive it around?," it looks like they're close to succeeding when Doctor Who and the others manage to stop them just in time. As he always does.

Independence Day (1996)

There is a bit of a jump between the Daleks and the aliens of *Independence Day*, but that's due to there being a bit of a jump between invasion movies that featured large alien troops attacking the earth. Most of the 1970s rather involved incognito groups of aliens trying to fit in and then take over, rather than the shoot-em-ups we come to expect. Any movie that went that way was more interested in doing something like *Star Wars*, where alien worlds are threatened (like in *Battle Beyond the Stars* from 1980 or *The Last Starfighter* from 1984). The only other major push with an onslaught attack of Earth was *Starship Invasions* (1977), a cheap Canadian mash-up between *Star Wars* and *Close Encounters of the Third Kind*, where big-headed aliens team up and/or fight earthlings and Christopher Lee once again picks up a paycheck.

Roland Emmerich has made a career out of big special-effects pictures that involve a major crisis on the part of humanity (he also did *The Day After Tomorrow* and *2012*, both covered in chapter 17). In this case, the concept was to deal with a massive invasion of Earth by aliens that actually saw them assaulting the earth and being a visual presence instead of just a few saucers flying around causing occasional damage. While the concept plays like some of the ideas in the television series *V*, the idea of a total war was intriguing, as it allowed for a large cast that sent the concept more into the realm of the traditional disaster movie than that of the standard alien invasion film, that is, "Who will survive out of this cast of twenty well-known actors?"

The plot deals with a "first contact" of aliens who arrive in a mothership and thirty-six smaller (albeit fifteen-mile-wide) ships that descend and situate themselves above major cities around the globe. It is assumed that the aliens are on a peaceful mission, but they're actually there to wipe out humanity and salvage what

"In the blink of an eye—" Oh, wait, wrong movie. This is *Independence Day* (1996), a hodge-podge of earlier alien invasion movies all rolled together in a frothing mug of special effects.

they can out of the planet before moving on to another. The attack begins, but one of the alien ships is captured, and it is deduced that a computer virus can be entered into the system that will cause the various ships' force fields to drop and allow military planes and other weapons of Earth to destroy them. Once this is done, the aliens are destroyed.

It may not read as much in the plot synopsis above, but that's really the full take on the story. To be fair, this is like saying "chicken is chicken" when cooking—one can either make it bland or put a number of ingredients on top of it to make it exciting and tasty. And *Independence Day* is like a chicken dinner with five gazillion ingredients on top of it. So many bells and whistles you forget what the movie is about.

It does its job, though. The movie was a blockbuster and is still remembered today. In fact, many of the films since that time have essentially played off of the feel given in *Independence Day*—huge, typically global alien invasions that wipe out entire cities as a team of determined fighting men and women try to win a war that seems impossible to fight. Films like *Battle: Los Angeles* (2011), *The Darkest Hour* (2011) and *Battleship* (2012) could easily have been part of the same story as *Independence Day* with just a tweak here and there, for example.

Hence the problem—in setting up a premise that deals with an antagonist so powerful that they can cause a global crisis, it makes a proper resolution nearly impossible within the framework of a 90–120-minute-long film. Movies can be of all shapes when they come to their stories, but action films—such as those for alien invasions—are structured around a beginning, middle and end. The aliens come, they beat us up, we defeat them. There's no time for esoteric reflections on life or social structures when it's all down to a variation of "Cowboys and Indians" (or *Cowboys and Aliens*, as was filmed in 2011 with Harrison Ford and Daniel Craig).

This isn't a problem when the battle is on a small scale. One alien with a nasty gun can be defeated in any number of ways; massive motherships with large supporting ships that easily wipe out all of our military in the first fifteen minutes are another matter. How do you stop them? Thus, we get movies that are 90 percent "aliens kill, destroy, bomb, zap," and then the final 10 percent is the equivalent of, "Hey, this button over here will wipe them all out and they'll never, ever return!" Wells barely got away with it in *War of the Worlds* because the idea of bacteria on Earth destroying the Martians was a clever, new idea to readers, as well as setting up a premise that creates a type of barrier that saves us from additional attacks by the bad guys. Yet even Wells didn't quite buy that (his narrator suggests that the Martians may eventually find a way to come back and attack again), and it's true with these films like *Independence Day* as well.

So when one character says, "Hey, I can create a computer virus that we can upload on their systems and stop them forever and ever!," it was no wonder that a certain amount of the audience went, "Wow! That's amazingly stupid! Like the aliens from another planet would have a computer system like anything we have, much less that it's compatible with our Apple computer here!" But it has to work, or else the film has no ending. Clever scientist has to create a ray gun out of the blue that will destroy the aliens because without it, the bad guys win. Aliens invade a planet full of water and then are found to be deathly adverse to water (as in the incredibly illogical "twist" to the otherwise rather good *Signs* by M. Night Shyamalan from 2002). One atom bomb transported to the aliens' home world and detonated is all that is needed to wipe out the menace forever in *Battlefield Earth* (2000). The greater the menace, the bigger the payoff has to be in defeating them, and simple solutions—while ironic—hardly ever pay off in audience satisfaction. *Battle: Los Angeles*, at least plays off of the idea that war is not something so easily wiped up and finished, by showing it is only one battle within a bigger landscape of war and death, with the surviving protagonists having no rest as they move on to another battle elsewhere.

Starship Troopers (1997)

This film by director Paul Verhoeven (*RoboCop*) faced numerous attacks by fans of the classic Robert A. Heinlein novel it was based on. The novel was one Heinlein had written more or less to get across some of his political ideas, with an emphasis that military service may not be fun, but it was a duty necessitated to protect freedom and life. To others, including the film director, it seemed the book advocated elements of fascism, or at least the belief that "war is fun!" Ironically, to most of us brought up on science fiction as kids, it was just a good "Boy's Life" actioner about killing evil alien bugs and nothing more.

The political content was what interested Verhoeven, and the film is steeped in parody, showing a variety of media manipulations in support of "our troops" fighting a war against aliens called the Arachnids. These aliens look like variations of giant bugs, with most of their technology similarly insect oriented, thus easily setting them up as "monsters" that need wiping out according to the propaganda that saturates the movie. The propaganda also suggests that the bug-like aliens started the war with Earth, but elsewhere there are implications that Earth instigated it as a way to clear out a species it doesn't like.

The story follows Rico and several other cadets training to fight in the war and the trials they go through in juxtaposition to the glorious propaganda. As such, the first half of the film plays much like any military academy drama, only with more sci-fi gear lying around. After an attack by the Arachnids that destroys Buenos Aires, the troops are sent to the Arachnids' home planet to attack. It doesn't go well, but eventually the troopers get the upper hand and win the battle with suggestions that they'll soon win the war against "the bugs."

On an action level, *Starship Troopers* plays out like a typical war film about grunts, but Verhoeven laces the action with elements that makes every action the humans take somewhat unnerving. As mentioned earlier, the suggestion is made that the war is not something the Arachnids wanted and are not so much invading Earth as trying to save their own world from an alien invasion. An attempt that looks to be unsuccessful by the end of the film, with their planet and their kind doomed, thanks to the invading earthlings.

One can certainly understand why fans of the book would be upset with the changes made to the story for the movie. Yet it does make for an interesting variation of the theme so common in science fiction movies—that the real danger is not from the unknown but from ourselves.

My God! Monsters!

Speaking of monsters, some by way of accident, the final category is that of alien monsters set loose by overlords to destroy Earth, or who accidentally end up lost on Earth and are not really trying to cause any trouble, mister. There's no other way to say it; these films usually are set for the lowest common denominator.

That's not really a bad thing, however; what it means is that they're movies geared toward kids, with only one objective in mind—to make them jump. Monsters on the loose and coming to getcha, as it were. Examination of these films should be in that context—to entertain, not to teach us a heavy lesson about accepting others, the loss of identity or political ideals. To push it any further is to lose the point.

20 Million Miles to Earth (1957)

Before *20 Million Miles to Earth*, there was *The Beast from 20,000 Fathoms* (1953), which will be discussed in more detail in chapter 17. Both deal with large creatures that are unknowingly set loose for a time in man's world, the only difference being that in the case of *20 Million Miles to Earth*, humanity brings the destruction upon itself. As it stands, the film works as a cross between *The Beast from 20,000 Fathoms* and *King Kong*.

The story deals with a rocket returning from Venus, where the crew had found what amounts to being an unhatched egg from the planet. The rocket crashes and the authorities are on the case, looking to find the egg that is being passed around from one person to another until it hatches, revealing a green-skinned creature with the lower body of a dinosaur and the upper body somewhat reminiscent of a giant ape. Ray Harryhausen did the effects for the film with the use of stop-motion, which he also did on *The Beast from 20,000 Fathoms* (the Kraken from his 1981 film *Clash of the Titans* bears some similarities to the creature). The creature is eventually captured for study, but is accidentally let loose in Rome and goes on a path of destruction until eventually being taken down with a couple of shots from a bazooka.

More on how this film and *The Beast from 20,000 Fathoms* influenced the later "giant monster" craze of the 1960s in chapter 17, but the focus here is on a plot seen earlier in chapter 9, namely scientists who threaten the world with really, really bad ideas. The intention of those in charge was not to cause turmoil and see several dead soldiers try to take down a monster from Venus, but rather simply to study an alien species. By doing so, however, those in charge nearly set up a situation with an unstoppable monster destroying city upon city. This same mistake will be seen again before the category is complete.

The Monolith Monsters (1957)

A meteor lands on Earth (we get lots of those), shattering into several pieces. Each piece grows as water hits it, which means a rainstorm has turned the small pile of rock into large towering pieces of stone that eventually crumble and create more and more. Eventually it is discovered that salt water will stop the rocks before they destroy a major city and begin to take over the earth.

This plot heads back to another element of chapter 9—the thing from space that created unintentional chaos. In this situation, even though no one meant to poke at it with a sharp stick, Earth was still endangered by the alien force that came.

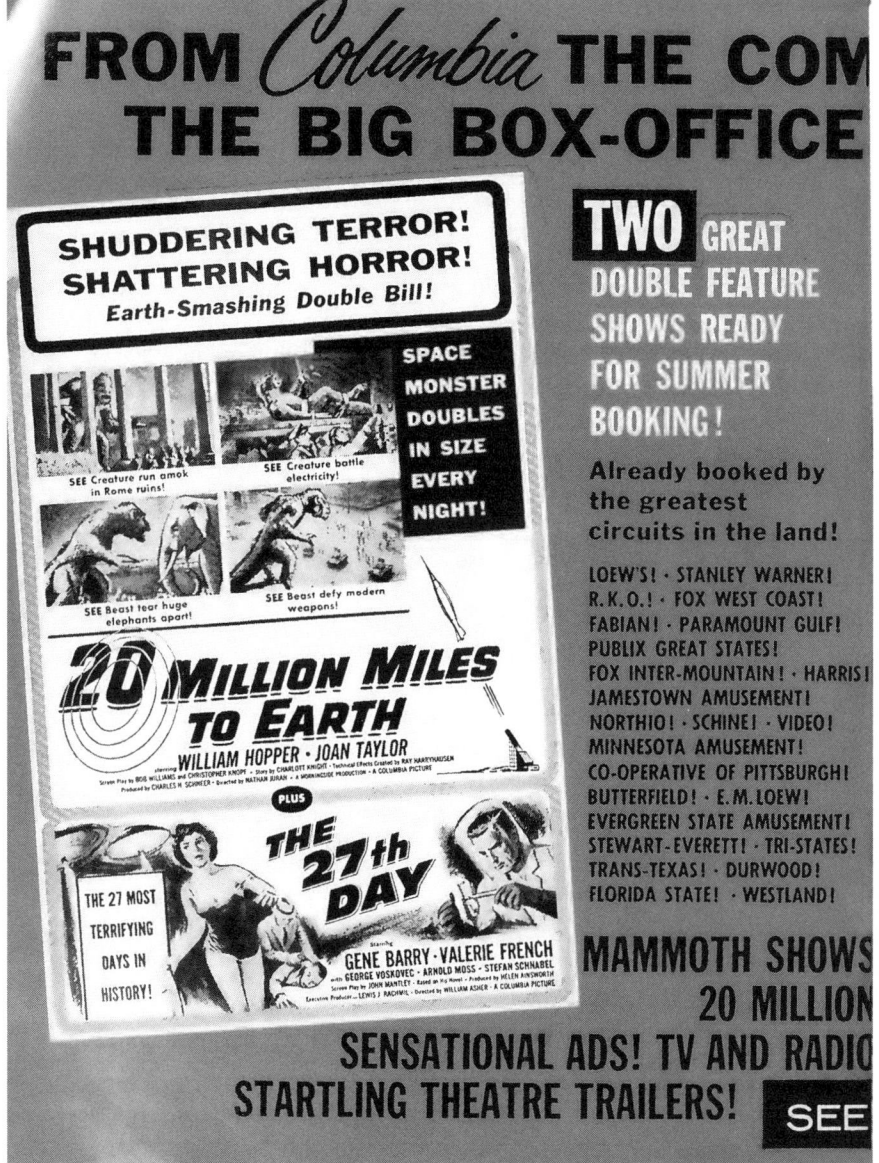

20 Million Miles to Earth (1957) not only shows us aliens causing unintended problems on Earth, but also how there's a predominance of scientists who have the really bad idea of bringing dangerous things back to civilization to study.   *Courtesy of Vintage Cinema Ads*

The Astounding She-Monster (1957)

It's Robert Clarke from way back in chapter 3 (*Beyond the Time Barrier*) as a geologist working in his cabin when three hoodlums turn up with an heiress they had kidnapped (in other words, a typical Saturday night for Bob). Meanwhile, a spaceship crashes near the cabin, and a strange, yet alluring, woman emerges who appears to shimmer as she walks. She also is heavily radioactive, and her touch can kill.

After a lot of ruckus and tough-guy talk, those remaining band together to kill the alien, only to discover that she actually just wanted help because of the crash. Those left wonder how her people will feel once they find out that humans had killed the woman in a very unlucky first contact.

Then again, you would think the alien would get the idea that after you kill off a few things by touching them, it may not be a good idea to continue to do so. "Excuse me, can you tell me the way to—Oh, sorry! Um, excuse—oh, rats, I keep forgetting! Sorry everyone! Sorry! No touchee! No touchee! I'll just check my GPS. Thanks!"

Ghidorah, the Three-Headed Monster (1964)

This was the fifth movie in the Godzilla series, which also features Rodan and Mothra, making it like the Justice League teaming of Japanese monsters. But, saying that, why is it being discussed here rather than in chapter 17 with all the giant monster movies?

Because *Ghidorah* was the first example of alien menace involved in the Godzilla series. Before it, all the monsters seen in the series, as well as the separate movies such as *Rodan* and *Mothra*, dealt with monsters that were our own. Okay, maybe all the atomic testing helped create certain aspects of their personalities and strengths, but that didn't detract from them being from Earth instead of elsewhere. Then it turns out King Ghidorah, a three-headed monster, is actually from Mars, and it takes the combined efforts of Godzilla, Rodan and Mothra to stop it.

This was also a time where Godzilla was slowly being turned into a "good guy" that helped humanity, rather than just stomping on things and spitting fire like Gene Simmons. From here and for quite a while, the Godzilla series would occasionally see alien menaces try to take over the monsters, or one monster, as a threat to Earth, such as in *Monster Zero* (1965, aka *Invasion of Astro-Monster*), *Destroy All Monsters* (1968), *Godzilla vs. the Smog Monster* (1971, aka *Godzilla vs. Hedorah*), *Godzilla on Monster Island* (1972, aka *Godzilla vs. Gigan* and featuring aliens disguising themselves as humans who have died), and *Godzilla vs. Mechagodzilla* (1974) and numerous others when the series was revived in the 1990s.

The Green Slime (1968)

A favorite among fans of oddball science fiction films, this American-Japanese production was produced by MGM. A meteor is destroyed by astronauts out in space before it can hit Earth (we'll see more of in the next chapter), with one of the astronauts bringing back "green slime" to the space station above Earth where they are working. The slime quickly mutates into large octopus-like aliens bent on conquest of the station and then Earth. It is remembered best for cheesy, outrageous fun as the astronauts fly around in space shooting with ray guns at the creatures, as well as a theme song that really needs to be heard to be believed (and won't leave your head for days afterward).

Lifeforce (1985)

Directed by Tobe Hooper (who scored with *The Texas Chainsaw Massacre*, 1974, and *Poltergeist*, 1982) and based on a 1976 novel called *The Space Vampires* by Colin Wilson, the film was a well-intentioned horror/science fiction film that wasn't able to find an audience in 1985, but had some success after costar Patrick Stewart went on to fame with *Star Trek: The Next Generation* two years later.

The film deals with astronauts once again finding something in space they should have left alone—in this case three humanoid bodies found in suspended animation on a dead alien spacecraft. The space shuttle with the astronauts is destroyed by fire but lands back on Earth with the aliens still in suspended animation. As it turns out, one of the astronauts managed to escape from the shuttle before trying to destroy it in hopes of the aliens not being able to make it to Earth. As one can guess from the original title, these aliens are actually shape-shifting vampires, who suck out the life force, instead of blood, of others. Worse yet, once this is done to a human, the human becomes a

"In the blink of an eye, the terror begins." There—right movie this time. *Lifeforce* (1985) gave us space vampires, which was the title of the novel on which it was based.

fast-movie zombie that preys on other humans, sucking out their life force and creating a living-dead situation (even a worse one than living under Thatcher). Interesting to note these zombies zipping around pretty quickly there, as *28 Days Later* is thought to have created the concept.

It all comes down to one of the astronauts having gotten the hots for the one female alien and one thing leading to another, which leads to the end of civilization. Or, in another way of putting it, once again someone poking at something from space causing the apocalypse.

It was originally called *The Space Vampires*, and when I saw Patrick Stewart speak once at a *Star Trek* convention, he admitted that the main reason he made the movie was just so he could tell his Royal Shakespeare Company friends and colleagues that he had been in a movie called *The Space Vampires*.

The Mist (2007)

Based on a novella by Stephen King from 1980 and directed by Frank Darabont, who had also done films based on King's books *The Shawshank Redemption* and *The Green Mile*. The film dips into a Lovecraft-like story line as the monsters we see are not aliens but rather creatures from another dimension who are accidentally allowed into our world thanks to a scientific experiment gone wrong. A group of people is stuck in a grocery store as monsters from the other dimension roam outside attacking everyone and a religious nut inside the store starts creating chaos with her fellow captives. Those inside have to decide if they want to risk venturing out into the mist, risking the creatures, in order to perhaps find safety or risk the destruction being caused by the lunatic in the store with them.

One fascinating aspect of this movie is that a frantic character near the start begs to be let out of the store so that she can locate her kids and get them to safety. No one goes with her, and so she ventures out to brave the creatures on her own. The character is not seen again until the very end of the film, where she appears safe with her kids on a truck. Oddly enough, I can't help watching it and thinking, "This movie probably would have been so much better if it had followed what happened to her in order to get to her children and keep them safe, than the rather bland and ultimately pointless endeavors of those who stayed inside the store."

Cloverfield (2008)

Filmed in the "buy yourself a tripod" tradition of the "found footage" films that came into its own with the unfathomable success of *The Blair Witch Project*, *Cloverfield* deals with a group of people who are at a going-away party in New York for a man named Rob (Michael Stahl-David), with his friend Hud (T. J. Miller) filming the get-together. After a fight with his girlfriend, Beth (Odette Yustman), that sees her leaving, Rob wants to make amends, but suddenly there is chaos as a large monster arrives and begins tearing the city apart. Problems are then compounded when parasites that live on the monster fall off and begin attacking people as well.

Rob, Hud and others attempt to find Beth and then leave the city, which they find out will be nuked in a certain amount of time. They lose a few along the way, but Rob and Beth manage to get together and make it to a helicopter, but are attacked by the creature and land in Central Park. The two die in the explosion, and the video cuts to a previously recorded incident from nearly a month ago that showed the two at Coney Island, and an object falling into the ocean in the background.

In 1956, we kicked off the concept of alien monsters falling from the sky and tearing up a major city. Fifty-two years later, we find another big hit movie featuring an alien monster that falls from the sky and tears up a major city. Nothing wrong with that; just goes to show how a good idea is a good idea, no matter how many times it is used.

16

Slammin'

The Movies That Define How the Earth Is Getting Smashed!

Alien creatures fell to Earth in the previous chapters, which also featured menacing meteors. Other falling objects are of concern as well when it comes to the apocalypse, and one captured the news in February 2013 when an approximately sixty-foot-long meteor was filmed by many cameras as it crashed through the atmosphere and broke apart over Chelyabinsk in Russia. (Unsurprisingly, Russians—who have seen pretty much everything there is to see happen to them—barely flinched at the spectacle of fire that raced through the sky and caused major damage to the area, leaving fifteen hundred hurt.) Suddenly, everyone is aware that there are . . . y'know . . . things out there in space. More importantly, that these things can possibly hit the planet without us being able to do much about it. And when an object that is roughly the size of six cars and breaks up on its way down can still cause that much damage, it registers far more than merely talking about it.

Of course, the apocalyptic films that deal with things slamming into Earth are a bit larger than that. As we saw in chapter 4 with *Melancholia*, there are even films that have whole planets crashing into us (and the biggie of them all is the first on the list in this chapter), and the concept of such collisions has been around since the early days of cinema, as discussed in chapter 2 with *End of the World* and *The End of the World*, as well as *Lucifer's Hammer*, the book mentioned in chapter 1. Not surprisingly, most of these efforts deal with someone spotting the oncoming object days, weeks or sometimes months before it actually hits, with a certain number of people preparing for the end while other scientists scoff, believing everything will be okay. Thus, the films tend to be set up as people either preparing to survive such a collision or finding a way to stop the collision, or a little bit of both. In the case of *Flash Gordon*, for example, Dr. Zarkov believes Mongo is going to crash into Earth but is ridiculed by other scientists. He rockets to the planet with Flash and Dale to stop it from happening, and they succeed over time. All the elements of the traditional "planet collision" plot are there (with the exception that Ming stops the incident from happening because he can drive the planet around).

The past fifteen years has seen a number of films, typically television movies, that deal with comets, asteroids and planets hitting the earth, but there are really four major films that stand out from the group as establishing all that any of the other such films are ever going to have to say.

When Worlds Collide (1951)

George Pal, before doing *War of the Worlds*, made a film of this 1933 novel by Philip Wylie and Edwin Balmer, marking Pal's second venture into science fiction after *Destination Moon* the previous year. The film involves a star named Bellus that is on a collision course with Earth in eight months. There is hope, however, as the star has a planet named Zyra that appears to be able to support life. Other scientists and the world governments disagree, however, so the scientist who found the star, Dr. Hendron (Larry Keating), cannot get any help to build rockets to allow some survivors to head to Zyra.

There is hope, however, when a wealthy industrialist who is confined to a wheelchair, Sidney Stanton (John Hoyt, who would go on to play the doctor on the pilot episode of *Star Trek*) offers to finance such a rocket as long as he is allowed to be on the flight. The majority of the film deals with workers preparing the rocket, while disasters start spreading across the globe as the star gets closer. Meanwhile, a little closer to home, Hendron's daughter, Joyce (Barbara Rush), finds herself in a love triangle with pilot David Randall (Richard Derr) and a scientist, Dr. Bronson (Hayden Rorke). There is a lottery for space on the rocket, as it can only hold so many, and in the final moments some workers who did not get a spot riot to try to make it aboard. The rocket is set to go and Hendron forces Stanton, who had been causing problems throughout the building of the rocket, to stay behind as well so that there is more room for younger, stronger people to help build a new world.

The rocket takes off just as the star slams into the earth. Later it lands on Zyra. Although there are tests to be run to see if it is safe to go outside, everyone soon realizes that it makes no difference, since they have no choice. Fortunately, they step outside to find a sustainable, living planet to start anew.

While there had been other collision films before this one, *When Worlds Collide* was the first to picture an attempt to make sure humanity survives by some method, in this case that of a rocket that will send several people and animals to the new world. It would stand alone in the field of films pertaining to such an apocalyptic impact for many years, until the 1970s saw the release of a film that was supposed to amaze fans of science fiction everywhere, but ultimately just ended up being the source of a decent pinball machine.

Meteor (1979)

A five-mile piece of asteroid is heading toward the earth, and smaller pieces are hitting the earth, as the governments of the world decide what to do. A satellite created just for such a situation by Dr. Bradley (Sean Connery) had been converted into a weapon to use against the Soviets but now needs to be converted

There were other planet-smashing movies before it, but *When Worlds Collide* (1951) was one of the first to attempt to show mankind trying to circumvent its destiny.

Courtesy of Wrong Side of the Art

back. Further, the number of missiles on the satellite is not enough to destroy the asteroid, and so help from the Soviets is needed. Henry Fonda, returning from the same role in *Fail-Safe*, once again plays the president who kicks things off between the two countries just long enough to pick up a paycheck. As it turns out, Connery's counterpart, played by Brian Keith, admits they too have such a satellite out in space and can use it to hit the meteor as well. As fragments continue to hit the earth, the missiles are sent off, only for a fragment to hit the location where the missiles have been fired, causing survivors to have to dig their way out of their location and avoid water from the East River. Several of the important actors in the movie make it, including Natalie Wood as the love interest for Connery's character, and the missiles manage to destroy the meteor, saving Earth.

The film was projected to be a huge blockbuster in 1979, with an all-star cast and a big special-effects budget; the idea was that fans of *Star Wars* would line up for blocks to see "James Bond" fight meteors. Promotional tie-ins like books, magazines and even a pinball machine from Stern Electronics came out in support of the film. The problem was that the audience didn't come out with the same support. The movie flopped, but pinball enthusiasts liked the pinball machine, leading to it being used in arcades everywhere years after the film had been forgotten. This led to the common review of *Meteor* being, "Well, the movie sucked, but the pinball machine was excellent!"

Deep Impact (1998)

Two big-budget films appeared in 1998 pertaining to collisions with Earth. *Deep Impact* was released a couple of months before *Armageddon* and received better reviews from critics and those in the sciences, but audience members made *Armageddon* the bigger hit of the two.

Deep Impact starts with a high school student, Leo (Elijah Wood), discovering a new comet, which a year later is revealed to the public as being seven miles long and destined to hit the planet. When it appears the press is about to get hold of the story, the president (Morgan Freeman) announces that the U.S. and Russia are about ready to send off a ship called the *Messiah* to rendezvous with the comet and to knock it off course with nuclear weapons.

The ship makes it to the comet and uses the nukes, but only succeeds in splitting it in two, a small piece about one and a half miles long and another that is the remainder. The president then announces, going back to *When Worlds Collide*, that underground bunkers have been created to sustain the impact of the comet and that a lottery would be held to send 800,000 American citizens there.

The smaller piece of the comet hits Earth, creating a mega-tsunami that swallows the Atlantic coasts of the continents it connects. The second, bigger piece, however, is finally destroyed by the astronauts in a last-ditch, suicidal effort to stop it. With the crisis over, the world tries to return to normal.

Although appearing in the same year as *Armageddon* and to greater critical success, *Deep Impact* (1998) failed to do as well at the box office.

Armageddon (1998)

Armageddon goes bigger in this Michael Bay production that involves a large cast of good actors (Bruce Willis, Steve Buscemi, Ben Affleck, Billy Bob Thornton, Liv Tyler) pretty much hamming it up in a movie where the special effects are the real star. The plot deals with an asteroid the size of Texas (and we all know how big they do things in Texas) that must be destroyed before it hits Earth in eighteen days. A ship is ready for launch, but the astronauts have no background in drilling, so they decide to bring in a group of deep-sea drillers to do the work. Surprisingly for a big film with big actors, less really happens in the movie, as the group blunders their way into saving Earth by having a character stay behind and blow the asteroid up in person.

It has been stated in various places as to how scientifically inaccurate *Armageddon* was, but it was certainly the most successful of the films dealing with something hitting the earth; which, ironically, doesn't happen on the level that we see in the other three films listed here. It is a film that sells us the sizzle instead of the steak—we don't get the end of the world; we don't even get the end of a chunk of the place—but it sold that sizzle well, which is sometimes what moviemaking ends up being all about.

Oh, and one more that usually is forgotten here:

Voyage to the Bottom of the Sea (1961)

A big movie from Irwin Allen that shows signs of the huge disaster movies he would produce later in the 1970s (*The Poseidon Adventure, Earthquake, The Towering Inferno*). In this one, Walter Pidgeon plays Admiral Nelson, while a large oddball cast of actors (Barbara Eden, Joan Fontaine, Peter Lorre and Frankie Avalon) are around to leave us concerned for their various safeties. They're all aboard the *Seaview*, a massive nuclear submarine built for scientific experiments under the sea (which is a good idea, what with it being a submarine and all). Emerging from under the Arctic, they discover fire in the sky and are told that a large meteor shower had caught on fire in the Van Allen radiation belt, setting the belt on fire and causing rapid global warming that is already severely melting the ice cap.

Nelson has a crazy plan that just might work—and it's a grand American plan at that: when in trouble, shoot at it. He plans to shoot a nuclear missile at the belt, which will extinguish the flames and destroy the Van Allen belt. While this sounds like a really bad idea, and another one on the table looks better (which amounts to "hope it'll die out on its own"), Nelson only answers to the U.S. president and refuses to give up his dream of firing a big missile into the lake of fire in the sky. Between sabotage by one of the characters on the *Seaview* and others who attempt to stop the missile, Nelson is proved right, the missile plan works and the earth is saved. The film would be successful enough to warrant a long-running television series on the ABC network between 1964 and 1968.

Armageddon (1998) was a blockbuster that is mainly remembered today for its Aerosmith songs.

In a way, *Voyage to the Bottom of the Sea* is and isn't a collision movie. After all, those darn meteors do not actually do much damage to the earth itself, but they do cause a natural reaction to occur that is up to humans to figure out a way to fix or else perish. Which leads us directly into the next chapter . . .

Voyage to the Bottom of the Sea (1961) demonstrates our American way of resolution at work: when troubled by things in the sky, shoot them!

17

Let Me Tell You About *The Birds* and *The Bees*

Ecological Disasters and Their Films

A s the book gets closer to the end, one major area of discussion is environmental disasters that have the potential of destroying the planet. One would assume that a good handful of such films have plots where any event that occurs is due to natural events, but that's not the case. In fact, out of the movies listed in this chapter that represent the most memorable disasters in four categories, less than a handful are not due to a man-made event (and even some of those are questionable). Just goes to show where our hearts and minds are when it comes to global disaster—namely that if there's anything to be the cause of it, it'll probably be us.

Environmental concerns listed here fall into the following four categories: planetary, plant life, biological and beasts (but not those stinking apes). Each has certain subgenres that would keep chapters flowing in this book for hundreds of pages if all were listed. Instead, the categories are established to show the most memorable of each subgenre, with some additional mentions here and there to show greater scope. After all, there's only so many bee invasion movies one can cover before readers get bored.

Planetary

In chapter 2 we discussed *Deluge*, which features the world suffering a number of earthquakes and tsunamis that crush and flood civilization on a global scale. In that film, such events occurred because that's just the way nature had planned it. The following films, however, lean more toward human error leading to major possible ends of the world.

The Day the Earth Caught Fire (1961)

Nuclear testing by the U.S. and the Soviet Union cause a shifting of the earth's orbit, bringing it closer to the sun and creating large areas of the earth that are

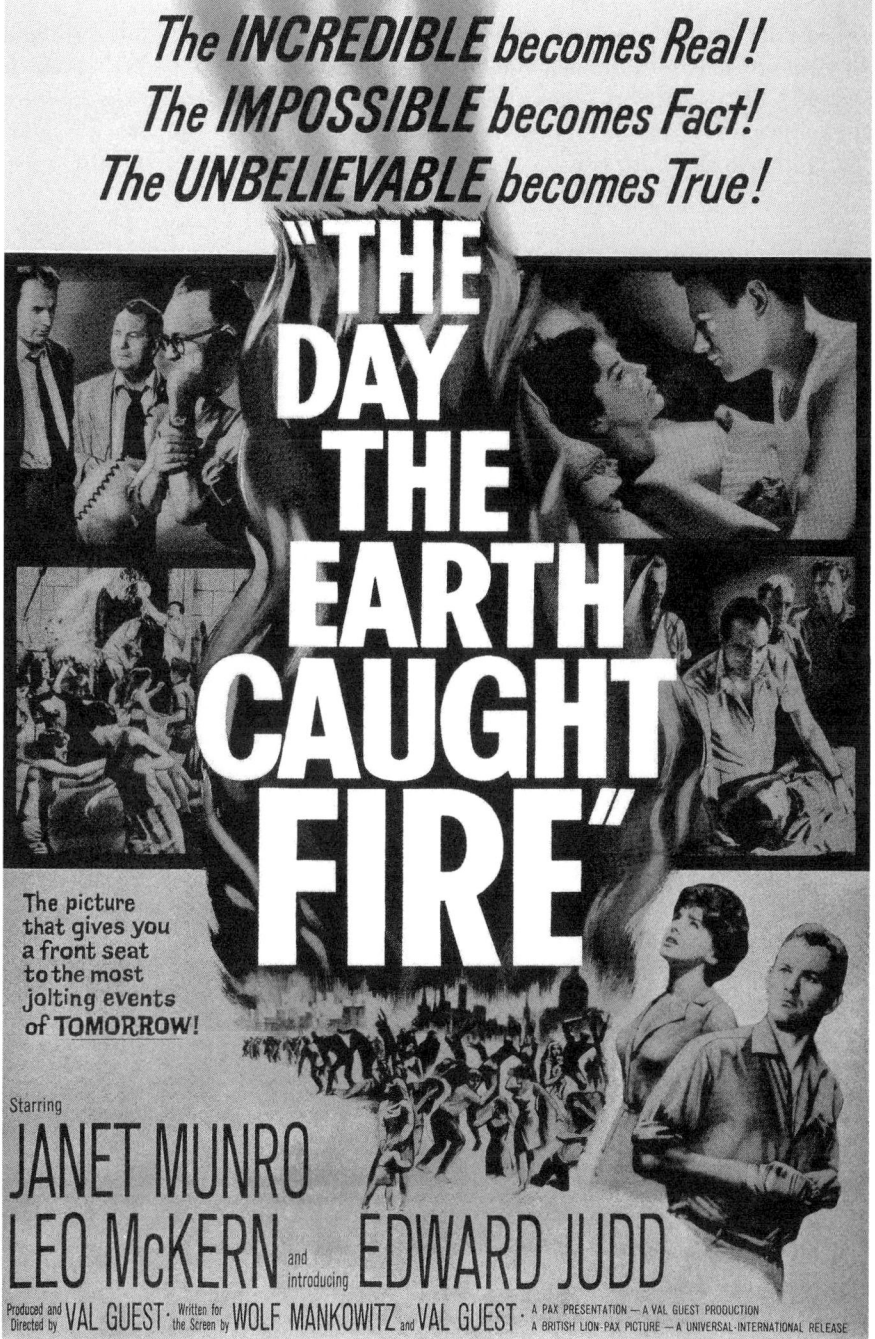

The Day the Earth Caught Fire (1961) demonstrates a world where everyone is waiting for the end, thanks to mankind creating a global ecological crisis. *Courtesy of Wrong Side of the Art*

becoming increasingly hot and dry (leading to the Thames River drying up over time in the film). This remarkable film deals with the anticipation as an attempt to move the earth's orbit back into alignment with another series of explosions is slowly set into motion. Meanwhile, a reporter staying in London realizes how meaningless his own personal problems are in the greater scope of the tragedy facing the world. With riots going on in a nearly deserted London, the world waits for the results of the nuclear blast, with two headlines set to be run in the next edition of the newspaper—one announcing the earth as doomed, the other as saved.

Crack in the World (1965)

Dr. Steve Sorenson (Dana Andrews) is a scientist who is positive that drilling into the earth's core will create a substantial new energy source for the world. He's also dying of cancer, so he wants to leave a legacy before he goes, and thus is rushing research and ignoring the advice of his geologist, Dr. Ted (Kieron Moore). Ted believes the drilling could cause a massive crack in the world. Steve thinks Ted is wrong and believes Ted wants his wife (Janette Scott, *Day of the Triffids*) and is therefore trying to discredit him.

As it turns out, Ted is right. Massive earthquakes begin to occur along a fault line just as Ted predicted, and if not stopped they will split the earth in two. They decide to try to halt the tremors with a nuclear bomb that involves lowering it by hand into lava at a precise location. Ted himself lowers the bomb, and at first, it appears to have succeeded, but soon the cracks continue, only this time in a different direction that is sending the bomb back to where it started—at the base of the drilling. The circumference of the area means that a section of the earth will pop out like a cork once the crack is completed (just like what always happens during earthquakes . . . wait, no, in fact, that never happens). Ted and Steve's wife barely make it outside of the area before the section of the earth floats up into space with Steve recording the final moments while drifting away. Well, Steve got what he wanted—he will have that legacy. As the guy who created a second moon and unknown ecological hazards on Earth, but it's a legacy nonetheless.

The British science fiction series *Doctor Who* will cover some of the same ground five years later in the serial "Inferno," which sees a mad scientist insisting that drilling into the core of the planet will create a substantial energy source. In this case it causes radioactive werewolves and the destruction of the entire planet (no kidding, Earth dies screaming . . . it's an alternate Earth in another dimension, but still, thumbs up to *Doctor Who* for going all the way there).

While we're talking about the earth's core, and not a journey like in Jules Verne's *Journey to the Center of the Earth*, which has been filmed multiple times, there's also *The Core* from 2003. It too involves blowing up nuclear bombs in the center of the earth, only this time it is to help reactivate the rotation of the inner core, which has stopped. Speaking of bombs, *The Core* was one at the box office, and many people with better knowledge than most of us about such things happily ridiculed the movie's science when it was released. If we had had the Internet in 1965, they would have no doubt done the same to *Crack in the World*.

Quintet (1979)

This and the following movie use global changes to the environment as their setting rather than what the movies are nominally about. For this reason they're postapocalyptic only in a minor fashion, but still of interest for that reason alone.

In this film, directed by Robert Altman (*M*A*S*H*, *The Player*, *Nashville*), the plot plays out like a western within the context of a futuristic ice age, with Paul Newman as a seal hunter who comes to town to visit his brother, only for his wife and brother to be killed in an explosion. To find the killer, Newman's character joins a game called Quintet that turns out to be played in real life as well as on a board, with the losers being forced to die. Newman ends up winning the game but finds that the only prize is that of winning and nothing more. Tired of the crazed world he finds in the city, he leaves into the snows, never to return.

Waterworld (1995)

Global warming is not so much the threat as the setting of this 1995 film, which stars Kevin Costner as the hero on an Earth that is covered in water thanks to global warming. The plot is essentially "*Mad Max* on water skis," with Costner also an evolutionary step forward, as he can breathe underwater and has webbing in his feet. The film's story is a rather traditional one from there—with our hero facing a bad man (Dennis Hopper) with henchmen while trying to save a beautiful woman and a little girl. The mythical "Dryland" that everyone is searching for turns out to be the tip of Mount Everest, and really that's not giving the movie away, as you're mainly there to see how Costner's character saves the day. But the film does represent a postapocalyptic future that occurs thanks to man's inactions with global warming.

The Day After Tomorrow (2004)

And here is the mother of all global warming doom movies, coming by way of Roland Emmerich (you'll see him again come *2012*). Not to say that society shouldn't be concerned about global warming, just that *The Day After Tomorrow* pretty much takes that concern and goes "booga-booga" as it jumps at you from behind a door, rather than treating the subject with respect. Then again, maybe seeing freeze-dried families is what it takes to get the perils of global warming to sink in with some people.

The story is about a paleoclimatologist, Jack Hall (Dennis Quaid), who discovers that drastic climate changes are coming thanks to global warming, with tornadoes hitting downtown Los Angeles (remember how much Hollywood loves to destroy Hollywood in these movies) and massive hurricanes popping up all over air so cold in the eye of each storm that they can freeze things instantly. Jack's son is in New York, where the streets are flooded and soon begin to freeze because of the storms. Jack goes to find him while the rest of the world tries to actually deal with the problem. The movie ends with Jack finding his son and most of the Northern Hemisphere now covered in ice.

As one would expect, scientists had mixed feelings about the movie—glad to see someone wanting to present the possible superstorms that could come with climate changes (and which are now starting to pop up in reality), but unhappy with the film's suggestion that such events would spring up in one massive event instead of over years or possibly centuries. Still, as always, Emmerich gives the audience a thrill ride, which is all that matters to them.

Sunshine (2007)

In this film by Danny Boyle (*28 Days Later*), it's not the earth that is dying but the sun. Although grade school science tells us that the sun will die in five billion years, expanding and becoming a red giant star, according to *Sunshine* the sun will be dying out like a candle near the end of its wick by the year 2057. A ship, the *Icarus*, is sent to toss a "stellar bomb" into the sun in order to reignite it (why, yes, it does seem like mankind's answer to everything is to throw a bomb at it, doesn't it?). When the *Icarus* disappears, a second ship is sent out to do the same, the *Icarus II*.

The *Icarus II* finds the first ship and boards it in hopes of being able to send two bombs to the sun instead of just one (especially as the astronauts on board realize that the bombs are temperamental, and so they can double their odds with the second ship). Turns out that the captain of the first ship had deduced that the sun's death is God's plan and mankind should be doomed (the captain must be waiting for the Rapture then). He sabotages the second ship and kills off most of the crew in an *Alien*-stalking process that doesn't really make a whole lot of sense, but the audience is in the theater to see action, not a textbook examination of how a phony-baloney bombing of the sun works.

The hero completes the mission while dying in the sun, allowing it to return to its former strength and save the earth. Now if this had been London during *The Day the Earth Caught Fire* there would probably be hesitations about the sun getting bright again, but it's all good here.

2012 (2009)

Everybody remembers where they were when the apocalypse happened in 2012, right? That was mainly due to talk about the Mesoamerican Long Count Calendar, commonly referred to as the Mayan Calendar, which most people figured was created by the Aztecs at least a couple hundreds of years ago. Which gives you a better idea of how much research the public put into going into hysterics over the end of the world. As it turned out, and what most sane people believed to be the case anyway, was that the Mayans said, "My, what a fine calendar! Oh, it stops at 2012. Well, if we'll still around by then, we'll make a new one."

Be that as it may, there was certainly much talk about upcoming doomsdays in the past few decades, and this one had a calendar that proved it, so the whole

2012 (2009) presented a worldwide disaster, but essentially give us the same plot as 1933's *Deluge*.

2012 theory had some weight. Then they tried to get cute with it and make it December 21, 2012, and the whole thing kind of fell apart after that. That didn't stop film producers from trying to make a buck off of it, and Roland Emmerich (*The Day After Tomorrow* and *Independence Day*) was back to give us exactly what we wanted with the film *2012*.

The plot is not about the typical scientist trying to stop the actions from occurring, but rather an everyman, Jackson Curtis (John Cusack), who inadvertently finds out that massive solar flares are affecting the earth's core and that large earthquakes and mega-tsunamis will soon sweep the world, killing most of the population. In other words, we're back to the plot of the 1933 film *Deluge* from chapter 2. No changes—it really is the exact same plot.

Curtis finds out that large arks have been built in China for a small percentage of the population to survive the upcoming catastrophe, and he attempts to get his children, his ex-wife and her boyfriend to the ark before the full disaster hits. As luck would have it, the ex-wife's boyfriend knows how to fly a plane, and as massive earthquakes swallow up whole cities and a really cool special effect of the aircraft carrier USS *John F. Kennedy* wipes out the White House, they make it to one of the arks just in time. Some of the characters die along the way, but just as in Spielberg's *War of the Worlds*, the ex-husband proves himself a man to his ex-wife by saving their children.

And that's what it's all about, evidently.

Plant Life

This category deals with a global crisis being created due to something pertaining to ecological factors in trees and plants. In most cases, this means not enough food for a large population (whether due to overpopulation or lack of vegetation). Farms being unable to produce crops is always a concern worldwide, with famine being a major fear not far behind because of it. Certain other apocalyptic films—about zombies, contagion, or nuclear war—deal with aspects of survivors sometimes even fighting to the death for a mouthful of food, but the following movies have plots that deal solely with the plant life issue, without the concerns of such famine being the result of other apocalyptic events.

And then we have one ringer in the group that certainly does deal with vegetation causing the death of humanity, but not in the way the others do.

No Blade of Grass (1970)

Directed by Cornel Wilde—who had branched away from his hunk hero days to do films of more personal interest to him, namely stories of man vs. the savagery of nature (such as *The Naked Prey*)—the film is more of the same. In this case, it is easy to see similarities to *Panic in the Year Zero!* (discussed in chapter 7), where a family ventures out into a postapocalyptic world, with a father determined for them all to make it no matter what. In that film from eight years before, society quickly rebounds and things are returning to normal. By the 1970s, the world was seeing the dismal failings of the governments in the midst of the antiestablishment era, and suddenly it seemed that if something could go wrong, it would go wrong on a terrible level.

The film deals with an ecological disaster that poisons grass, wheat and rice, the major sources for various foods and feed for animals we eat as well. John, a former military man, has been offered a chance to join his brother in Scotland, where he has a potato farm that is reinforced against outsiders. To get his family there, John has to fight his way through roaming gangs of strangers on the roads, eventually stealing and killing for food just like those who first come across his family in the beginning.

The movie, based on *The Death of Grass* (1956) by John Christopher, ends like the book, with the father gathering more and more people around him on the journey as he becomes the leader of a band of scavengers. Of course, once they reach his brother's farm, the group are not about to simply lose their leader and go on their way, leading to the only end possible in a world quickly crumbling. Thus, while *Panic in the Year Zero!* shows salvation coming if we just wait things out, reflecting the thinking of the new Atomic Age, *No Blade of Grass* sees man turning against man with no redemption possible in the Age of Aquarius.

Soylent Green (1973)

The film's setting is New York City of the year 2022, an age of overpopulation that sees people sleeping in the streets and only the richest being able to afford the rarities like real vegetables, fruit and even beef. To help feed the masses, a company called the Soylent Corporation makes cracker-like substances that are rationed to the public, with a new one called Soylent Green.

A director of the corporation is murdered, and Detective Robert Thorn (Charlton Heston, when not fighting albinos or apes) is on the case. He asks his friend, Roth (a final film role by Edward G. Robinson), to do some investigating about the corporation while he tries to track down the killer. As it turns out, the corporation had the director killed when he began questioning how Soylent Green was made, and they attempt to do the same to Thorn when he gets too close to the truth. When Roth discovers what the product is actually made of instead of the plankton from the sea that the corporation says it is, he goes for an assisted suicide.

As Thorn watches in wonder the images and sounds playing at Roth's death scene (trees, animals, flowers, clear skies—all elements of an Earth no longer there), Roth tells Thorn what the corporation is doing. Thorn verifies the truth and avoids his assassin, but is dying as he is recovered by the police. As the film ends, Thorn yells out to warn everyone that "Soylent Green is—" Well, you know the rest.

Although it is not quite a world with no food available to the masses, it is obvious that there is very little left (Thorn has to steal real food from the director's apartment in order to have any at all), and even alternatives are rapidly disappearing. It paints a picture of the future—maybe not as dismal as that found in *No Blade of Grass*, but certainly one that is bleak and rapidly seeing humanity drawing to a close.

The movie was a project Heston had been trying to get moving since the last 1960s and is based on a book by Harry Harrison that shows New York as overpopulated at the turn of the century on New Year's Eve in 1999. While the novel does deal with a detective trying to solve a murder in such a climate, there is no mention of Soylent Green being . . . you know . . . thus making *Soylent Green* its own entity rather than one based on a novel.

Oddly enough, the same year saw the release of *Silent Running*, a film by Douglas Trumbull (who did the special effects for *2001: A Space Odyssey* and *The Andromeda Strain*, among others) and starring Bruce Dern in a rare protagonist role for him (although some would question his hero status). Dern plays an astronaut, Lowell, working on one of several freighters out in space that has domes containing the last of all plant life from the planet Earth. The other astronauts are fine eating the processed food given to them and think the greenhouses are a joke, wishing only to return home. Lowell has hopes that there will be an announcement soon to have the ships return home so that the vegetation can be replanted, and is shocked when the freighters receive a call to destroy the greenhouses they have and return the freighters for other use. After some of the greenhouses are destroyed, Lowell refuses to leave one of the remaining three and kills one of his fellow astronauts. He then jettisons one still holding the other astronauts as it is being prepared for jettison, killing them. Faking system failure, Lowell manages to take the freighter away from the others and have it in a sense disappear from sight with no communications to Earth (hence, "silent running").

Lowell manages to keep things going for a time but cannot hide forever, and when communication is reestablished, he jettisons a pod with one of the small robots on board (which he had nicknamed Huey, Dewey and Louie) to take care of the plants, while blowing up the freighter to cover the tracks of the one remaining piece of plant life on Earth drifts off in safety from mankind's reach.

In a world without vegetation and one where it is so rare, it is almost too easy to suspect both *Soylent Green* and *Silent Running* are taking place in the same universe at the same time. (Okay, maybe everyone isn't working, as in *Silent Running*, but the temperature being 75 everywhere? Possible.) Maybe the Soylent Corporation insisted that the greenhouses be jettisoned to cover losses they suffer when people find out what Soylent Green is made of?

Perhaps the ultimate irony of *Silent Running*, however, is that for a movie about saving the environment, the thing people remember the most are the cute little robots in it.

The Ultimate Warrior (1975)

In a world that appears to be many years after that found in *No Blade of Grass*, Yul Brynner plays a silent man out of the wastelands. He comes to help a small tribe deliver the leader's pregnant daughter and seeds that are resistant to the plague that killed off most plant life out of the city to a small island off North Carolina and start a new world. For those looking for a *Mad Max* movie from before there was *Mad Max*, this is it.

The Happening (2008)

M. Night Shyamalan had kick-started his career with *The Sixth Sense* in 1999, but got stuck with the handle of being the writer/director who always has a "twist ending." It unfortunately made him out to be someone who could only work in clichés, and when the twists started to become very curious rather than clever (rain kills aliens in *Signs*, *The Village* is not in the past or the present), the press and public began to be a bit hesitant about his projects.

Then came along *The Happening*. The plot deals with trees releasing a neurotoxin that forces people to kill themselves. Mark Wahlberg plays a schoolteacher who, with others, tries to outrace . . . eh . . . trees.

Yeah, it does just lie there as a plot, doesn't it?

The concept is that the trees—okay, let's say the natural world—are fed up with mankind and want to get rid of us. They do this by targeting people who are around trees. So everyone who works at a nursery, in a forest, or cultivates and cares for the environment is among the first to be picked off in this endeavor. Meanwhile, businessmen in their offices and those who want to have a good reason to deforest, say, rain forests ("Look what these damn trees did to these Indians here!"), are quite safe and sound.

Well, you can't expect the best plans from trees, really. They're trees, after all.

Worse yet, it makes for an awkward way to show action in a movie. Since trees don't jump out of the shadows and attack, it means the wind has to be shown moving the neurotoxins through the air. Thus, the wind ends up being scarier than the trees are. Which loses the point, really.

When Wahlberg's character confesses his love for his wife late in the film, the trees stop their onslaught. So love conquers. Except in Paris, ironically the City of Love, where the whole thing starts up again a short time later.

Makes the famine films look like fun after this, doesn't it?

The Road (2009)

This film doesn't explain what causes all plant life to be dying, meaning of course that animal life is dying as well, but it is clear that some time has passed in this world where such an event has occurred. A man (Viggo Mortensen) and his young son attempt to travel in hopes of a warmer climate and perhaps something better than what they have, which is only a few supplies and a gun with two bullets. They have to find what food they can, while avoiding bandits and roving gangs of cannibals.

Based on a book by Cormac McCarthy, it is suggested there and in the film that the man is dying of something and is hopeful he can find a place for his son that is safe before he goes. As the movie ends, the man dies, but his son is found by a family, including a daughter the son's age, that is willing to take him in. Meanwhile, a plant is seen starting to grow, showing that the worst may soon be over.

It is a startling, brutal film that shows the consequences of the life created due to the apocalyptic event featured in *No Blade of Grass*. No doubt, in time, John's gang in that film would end up like one of the roving gangs of cannibals, out on the road with little sense of humanity. The man in *The Road*, however, teaches his son to hope and strive, with a better world still possible. In the end he turns out to be right, and we have gone forty years from dismal, abject hopelessness about mankind's cruelties to a point where perhaps, just perhaps, we might make it.

Biological

This category mainly has to do with reproduction and the fear of people no longer being able to have children, thus ending mankind. Such a topic had been presented in earlier films, such as those from the 1930s dealing with a last man on Earth, and usually for comedic purposes. The same holds true in *A Boy and His Dog* (1975) and *Percy's Progress* (1974), which deal with one virile man being sought after to continue the race as the only men around are either dead or impotent. (Although, as seen in *A Boy and His Dog*, this doesn't end exactly in the wish fulfillment of male fantasy, but rather more clinical means to get what is needed to continue civilization.)

Pornography films would touch on the subject as well, such as in *Café Flesh* (1982) which deals with a virus that makes sex impossible, leading to those who can have sex being enslaved into performing for those who can't in shows. On the flip side of such a "serious" film is *Rollerbabies* (1976), a pornographic comedy and parody of *Rollerball*, where overpopulation leads to recreational sex being outlawed and people getting their jollies from watching television programs showing such activities (you're probably way ahead of me making a joke about this, so I'll let it be).

Oddly enough, although *Soylent Green* point-blank deals with overpopulation, there are very few films that offer a solution to that problem. Possibly because you end up having to pay too many extras to get the point across. The only major film to deal with such a subject is *Z.P.G.* (1974), which stars Oliver Reed and portrays a futuristic society where the world is overpopulated, food is scare, most animals are extinct and the government has banned the birth of children for thirty years. This, of course, gives us a first awareness that the filmmakers had no clue what Z.P.G. was supposed to be about. Z.P.G., or zero population growth, did not mean that there are to be no children born, but rather that the birth of newborns would be kept in check with the death of existing people (thus, a zero growth in population, instead of a lowering of the population as present in the film). As it stands, Reed's character and his wife plod through a gray, dismal futuristic life until the wife (played by Geraldine Chaplin) becomes pregnant and they have to figure out how to keep things quiet or else be put to death.

Such a theme had already been covered in a television movie, however, from three years before: *The Last Child* (1971) deals with a couple in a militaristic United States where couples are only allowed to have one child. The couple had given birth to one, but the child died soon after birth. Even so, red tape does not allow them to conceive again, and when they do, they go on the run to escape a government agent (played by Ed Asner in what was a typical bad-guy role for him before getting the part of Lou Grant on *The Mary Tyler Moore Show*). They manage to make it to Canada and safety, while Ed ends up driving his car off a cliff. That'll teach him.

Most of the films dealing with futuristic birth portray a declining rate of births or simply no births at all, which can be found in such films as *The Handmaid's Tale* (1990), *Millennium* (1989), and even in earlier films such as *Terror from the Year 5000* (1958) and the aforementioned *Beyond the Time Barrier* in chapter 3. However, the one that really made the case is *Children of Men* (2006). This movie, based on a novel by P. D. James and starring Clive Owen, deals with infertility that has lasted nearly two decades and society quickly starting to crumble under the knowledge that there appears to be no hope for the future.

Owen plays a former activist, Theo, who is talked by his estranged wife (Julianne Moore) into helping to smuggle a West African woman into a police state Britain of 2027. The wife is killed in an attack, and Theo discovers that the woman is the first pregnant woman in eighteen years. The objective is to get her to a group on a remote island that are looking to cure the crisis of infertility, but Theo later discovers that no one knows for sure if the group even exists. As those who know the woman is pregnant try to kidnap her for their own reasons, Theo manages to smuggle her through the country and out to a boat, where he dies of injuries but she survives with the newborn child and in sight of an approaching boat from the scientific group.

Although issues dealing with fertility, childbirth and related matters are a logical part of apocalyptic fiction, perhaps it hits too close to home, as it is appears to be so rarely used in movies and on television. On the other hand, when it comes to animals and insects, there are excessively many films from which to choose.

WIDESCREEN

CLIVE OWEN
JULIANNE MOORE
MICHAEL CAINE

CHILDREN
OF MEN

THE YEAR 2027:

THE LAST DAYS OF
THE HUMAN RACE

NO CHILD HAS BEEN
BORN FOR 18 YEARS

HE MUST PROTECT
OUR ONLY HOPE

Children of Men (2006) is one of a handful of films where mankind finds the clock running out due to an inability to procreate.

Beasts—Animals and Insects (but not those stinking apes!)

Enough has already been said about the *Planet of the Apes* series, so the focus of this category is on other animals that have taken their bow when it comes to taking over the world. Of course, this would immediately bring to mind movies where an animal is the cause of numerous attacks, but while films like *Jaws*, *Grizzly*, *Alligator* and even *Jurassic Park* deal with attacks by creatures, they are minimal and not of greater concern than for the people immediately being manhandled by the beasts. The beasts are dispatched, and there is rarely a sense of a bigger event than a localized one.

There are really only three types of apocalyptic films when it comes to animals and insects: movies where creatures go nuts, movies where giant creatures go nuts, and movies where the creatures actually have a plan. The following are the highlights of such movies.

The Birds (1963)

Based on a novel by Daphne du Maurier (*Rebecca*), the film deals with a steady, growing attack of birds upon every man, woman and child living in Bodega Bay, California. The film, directed by Alfred Hitchcock and starring Tippi Hedren and Rod Taylor (*The Time Machine*), at first suggests that Hedren's character may be at the cause of the attacks, but this is a red herring as it later becomes apparent that the attacks are spreading and are on purpose by the birds for some reason. Hedren's character is attacked after a night of holing up in a house against the birds and is nearly catatonic as a small group attempt to leave the house and drive her to a hospital. Oddly enough, the birds allow this to occur, seemingly having made their point to the humans.

In some ways, the film plays like an early version of *The Happening*—part of nature wants to remind mankind that everything has its place in the order, and so do they. It is more effective, because people know birds can do some damage if provoked to fight, rather than waiting to see if a tree coming around will do something bad to us. Still, although it appears the birds may leave us alone after making a point, until then the film has apocalyptic tones (one character even mentions as much when the attacks begin). Surprisingly, there aren't many movies that deal with normal animals attacking as a "force" of nature rather than, say, a rabid dog terrorizing a woman and boy in a car (*Cujo*) or the aforementioned *Jaws* and *Grizzly*. The only other noteworthy films in this genre came in the 1970s, *Frogs* and *Day of the Animals*.

Frogs (1972) had a poster of a frog with a human hand coming out of its mouth that, when I saw it for the first time at the age of eight, made me think the movie was about giant frogs. Nothing of the sort, however. It's actually about a plantation on a small island in Florida where the old miser (Ray Milland of *Panic in the Year Zero!*) has been using various pesticides to rid the swampy area of numerous animals and insects. Various family members of the miser come to visit for his birthday party and get randomly knocked off by snakes, alligators, turtles, conniving lizards and a really gruesome-looking spider. Eventually only an environmentalist who came to warn everyone, a woman and two children manage to make it off the island, where they are picked up by a woman and her son who say they haven't seen anyone else for miles during their drive, suggesting that the animal attacks are branching out. Meanwhile, back at the plantation, frogs attack the mansion, driving the miser crazy until he keels over from a heart attack.

While *Frogs* is a bit of fun for kids, *Day of the Animals* (1977) is a wonderful, gloriously bad movie by Kentucky's own William Girdler. Not that Girdler couldn't direct—in fact, he does just fine with the actors and shooting locations, etc.—it's just that it's a bad story with Christopher George (*Grizzly*), Richard Jaeckel (*The Green Slime*), and Leslie Nielsen. Nielsen in particular is the star of the film, playing a hiker among a group that eventually goes crazy in the aftermath of the animal attacks.

The hikers go up a mountain near a small town and discover that some type of solar radiation is causing all the animals in the area to attack in an altitude of five thousand feet or higher. The group try to descend, but additional attacks occur, and Nielsen rants and raves himself into a splinter group. While the two groups go their own way to survive the attack, the town is overtaken as well, leaving only a catatonic girl (played by Michelle Stacy, who also appeared in *Logan's Run* and as the girl who likes her coffee black in *Airplane!*, also starring Nielsen). The film ends with the animals that have gone crazy having died from the exposure to the radiation, making it safe for those that made it that far. But not—not—before we get the most incredible scene in cinematic history: a shirtless Leslie Nielsen fighting a full-size bear in the middle of a rainstorm! It is moments like this that make going to the movies all worth it!

Genocide (1968)

Deadly insect movies had a ready-made marketplace. People understood the concept of fear when seeing insects swarm, from bees to locusts, and knew that their attacks could do much more than simply be an annoyance. Locusts, after all, are biblical, so one of the first fears driven into us from church is of "a plague of locusts upon the land" (not to mention those locusts from the endtimes always discussed). There was nothing unusual in seeing such a thing being used in films: the peasants try to fight a swarm of locusts trying to destroy their crops in *The Good Earth* (1937), Charlton Heston fights a path of army ants in the George Pal–produced movie *The Naked Jungle* (1954), Humphrey Bogart is covered in leeches in *The African Queen* (1951). Thus, it was only a slight turn-up in heat to have them swarm to a size that could raise risks of a global event.

Typical of such insects in these movies were ants, bees or spiders. Grasshoppers got into the mix when they became giant, but for the moment the

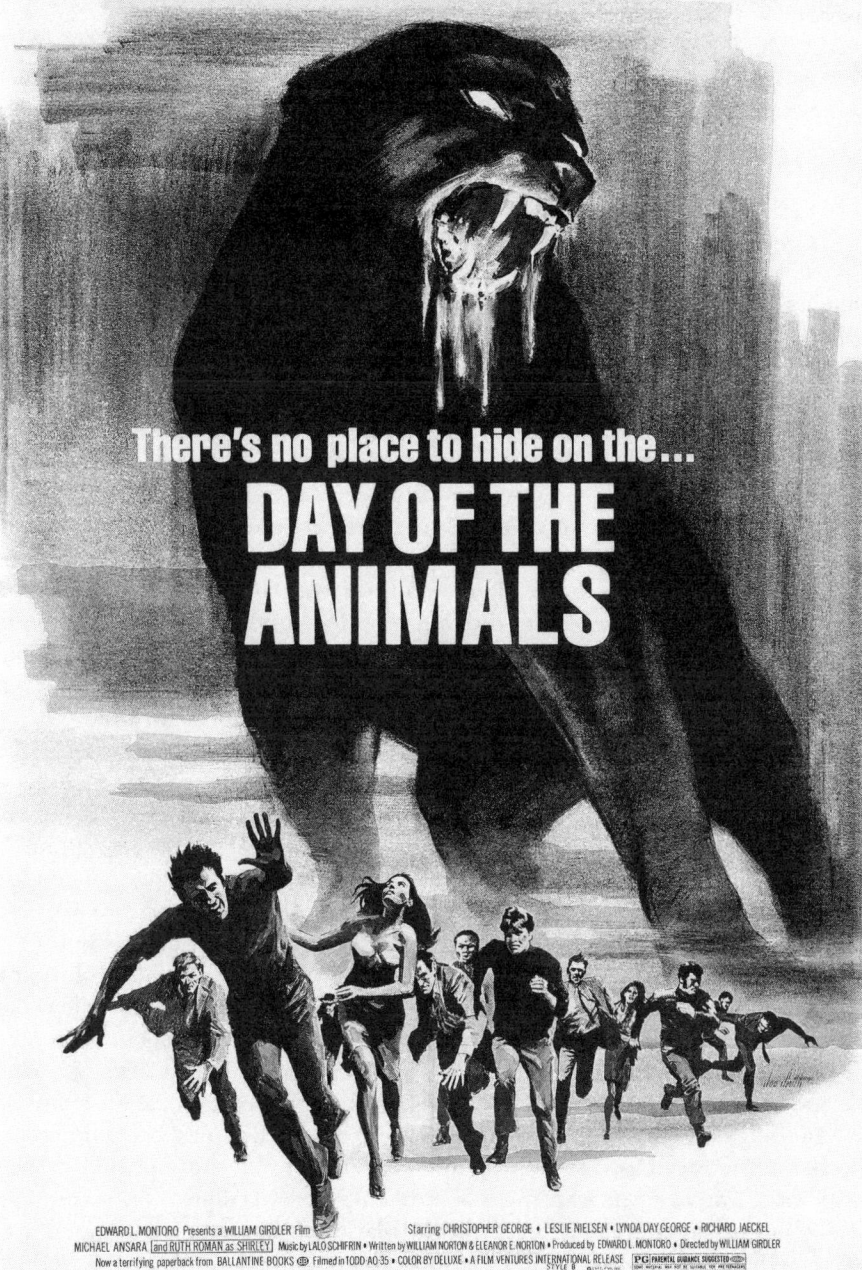

AFTER THE MOVIE ONLY THE TERROR REMAINS!

There's no place to hide on the...

DAY OF THE ANIMALS

EDWARD L. MONTORO Presents a WILLIAM GIRDLER film   Starring CHRISTOPHER GEORGE ◆ LESLIE NIELSEN ◆ LYNDA DAY GEORGE ◆ RICHARD JAECKEL
MICHAEL ANSARA and RUTH ROMAN as SHIRLEY Music by LALO SCHIFRIN ◆ Written by WILLIAM NORTON & ELEANOR E. NORTON ◆ Produced by EDWARD L. MONTORO ◆ Directed by WILLIAM GIRDLER
Now a terrifying paperback from BALLANTINE BOOKS   Filmed in TODD-AO-35 ◆ COLOR BY DELUXE ◆ A FILM VENTURES INTERNATIONAL RELEASE   PG PARENTAL GUIDANCE SUGGESTED
STYLE B

An excellent poster for the glory that is *Day of the Animals* (1977). Words cannot describe the vision of a shirtless Leslie Nielsen fighting a bear in a rainstorm!

Courtesy of Wrong Side of the Art

topic is normal-sized insects causing problems. Bees dominate in this regard, as they naturally scare more people than ants and spiders (yes, spiders do frighten people, but they are usually of a more "icky" variety compared to bees that can sting). You have *The Deadly Bees* (1966), *Killer Bees* (1974), *The Savage Bees* (1976), *The Bees* (1978), *The Swarm* (1978), *Killer Bees* (2008), and those are just the ones from America. Many of these have been covered in other sources, so the focus here will be on one that hasn't been seen quite as often but also includes an atomic bomb in the mix, and that's Kazui Nihonmatsu's 1968 film *Genocide*, which is also known as *War of the Insects*.

The film begins with a crewmember on an American B-52 off an island in Japan being bitten by a mutated bee that causes him to have flashbacks to fighting in the Vietnam War. A swarm of the bees then send the plane crashing on the island, with the crew and a hydrogen bomb they have on board making it safely by parachute to the ground. The American authorities are called in, and they find the bodies of two of the crew dead in a cave and a third—the man who was going insane—unconscious on the rocks along the island shore. He remembers nothing, and a man turns up who is trying to sell a U.S. military watch, making it appear he may have killed the crew for it.

The man is an assistant to Dr. Nagumo, who is studying the mutated bees, whose bite causes hallucinations. When Nagumo hears about his assistant being arrested, he goes to the island and finds out that the assistant had been fooling around on his wife with the only blonde-haired, white woman around, Annabelle. Turns out that Annabelle is working for the Soviets to perfect an insect that will drive people insane, but it also is revealed that she is doing it because she wants to release the mutated bees everywhere and wipe out the human race.

The American and Soviet spies are all looking for the bomb and don't have much concern about mutated bees. Nagumo, frustrated by all that is going on, decides to take matters into his own hands and has one of the bees sting him. It turns out that the bees are intelligent and inform Nagumo that they plan to wipe out humanity before they can use their nuclear bombs to destroy the earth. An antidote brings Nagumo back to normal, and he goes to see Annabelle.

Annabelle attempts to force Nagumo into a cellar full of bees by gunpoint, but Nagumo gets the better of her and sends her crashing down into the cellar instead, leading to her death. He then stupidly leaves the door open, letting the bees loose. The Soviet spies find the bomb, but it is covered in the bees. Shooting at the bees is a very stupid idea not only when they're covering an H-bomb, but also because the bees then attack, killing the Soviet spies. Nagumo brings back the American forces, but the Americans tell him to shut up about insects and force him to come with them on a plane. They need an antidote but also think just detonating the H-bomb on the island will do the trick. Nagumo tries to stop them, and then a second soldier tries the same, but the head American officer hits the button, killing everyone on the island. But not the swarm of

The Bees (1978) is one of many killer bee movies, but it was hard to resist showcasing this poster! *Courtesy of Wrong Side of the Art*

mutated bees, who cause the plane to blow up and then go on their way to destroy mankind.

Have to say, that's one different kind of killer bee movie there.

As an aside, in relation to oddball people experimenting on insects to make them do bad things, there's *Bug* (1975), directed by Jeannot Szwarc, which has a professor who finds a new species of cockroach that escapes from the ground after an earthquake. The roaches can create fire, and he manages to breed them with normal roaches in order to create roaches that are also intelligent enough to spell out words with their bodies. No one said that scientists had to have good ideas, mind you.

As for normal-sized ants, we also end up with insects that are far more intelligent than normal in the 1974 film *Phase IV*, directed by Saul Bass (designer on Hitchcock's films including *Psycho*). In this film, scientists are studying strange towers being built in the desert by ants. Although one of the scientists believes the ants need to be destroyed, the other thinks they may actually be able to communicate with humans. A young woman from a local farm is taken by the colony and returns as part of the ant hive, joining with the scientist to create a new kind of humanity that involves the ant world as well. The film is much more dedicated to the images it presents than to story logic, but the results are an interesting twist to the standard "bad insect" movie one would expect.

Finally, for normal-sized spiders there's *Kingdom of the Spiders* (1977), starring William Shatner as Rack Hansen, a vet in a small town in Arizona that is soon overrun by intelligent tarantulas, who have decided to gang up together and start eating bigger game when pesticides kill off their normal food supply. By the end of the film the tarantulas have cocooned the entire town and all of its inhabitants, leaving no one to survive (although there were always talk of a sequel, with or without Shatner).

Them! (1954)

Then we arrive at the giant animals and insects of the apocalyptic films. One of the first came in 1954 with the release of the giant ant movie *Them!* In that film, atomic testing in the deserts of the U.S. has led to mutations in ants, causing them to grow as big as trucks and start attacking people. This was followed in 1955 by Jack Arnold's *Tarantula*, which sees a giant tarantula escaping from a lab where work was being done to produce larger animals for food shortages. It features Clint Eastwood in his first movie role as the pilot of the jet that attacks and kills the giant tarantula.

The same concept causes giant locusts in *The Beginning of the End* (1957), where crops radiated to make them bigger leads to locusts eating them and growing as well. They're stopped just in time, but the main characters worry about what would happen to other animals that eat radiated vegetables. Of course, that's just silly. Who would want to eat radiated vegetables? Right? Right? Hello?

Giant animal movies popped up later as well—films like *Night of the Lepus* (1972) about giant killer bunnies; *The Food of the Gods* (1976), featuring giant rats, chickens and other animals that ate food coming from the ground that changes them; and even giant teenagers in *Village of the Giants* (1965, with little Ronny Howard coming up with an antidote that returns the bratty teenagers back to their original size). Not to mention the other giant-man movies, *The Amazing Colossal Man* (1957) and *War of the Colossal Beast* (1958), as well as his counterpart, *Attack of the 50-Foot Woman* (also 1958).

But the biggest animal apocalypse of all, beyond the giant insect and animal movies listed above (of which there are many more), is the return of the dinosaurs in one form or another. Dinosaurs in movies have been a fascination since the days of Gertie, a cartoon creation of cartoonist and animator Winsor McCay (*Little Nemo*). McCay would perform with the film in order to make it appear Gertie was reacting to his commands. From there the dinosaurs appeared in stop-motion animation in the film *The Lost World* (1925), which had dinosaurs rampaging through London. *King Kong* (1933) kept up the presence of giant animals for a time, but it was really *The Beast from 20,000 Fathoms* in 1953 that brought new life to the concept. The film, based on a 1951 short story by Ray Bradbury, dealt with a lonely sea monster that is attracted to the foghorn used at a lighthouse, as the sound is similar to that of a mating call.

The following year saw the invention of the giant monster that probably did the most to keep the concept alive over the years, *Godzilla*—a dinosaur that had been awoken in the fires of nuclear bombing and given the ability to breathe atomic fire, destroying things in its path not done by his stomping around and throwing his tail around. The film saw Godzilla dead at the end, but had major success at the box office around the world, especially in America, where it was recut with Raymond Burr stomping cities with his atomic breath and . . . okay, with Burr playing a character named Steve Martin (seriously) who witnesses the destruction Godzilla causes.

From there, numerous sequels have been made, with the franchise going strong for a time and then rebooting itself in later decades, but never coming to a full stop. With that came other similar films, such as *Gamera*, about a flying atomic turtle, and various other giant monster movies over the years. Most of them share one common point with Godzilla, as with many of the films listed in this chapter—that of ecological consequences by mankind leading to disaster that destroys and kill. Often such points were disguised within action set pieces and scary monsters, but sometimes the message did leak through and get people talking about serious issues such as food experimentation, nuclear testing and how we treat animals in general.

If nature is out to get us, at least we have technology on our side. Or do we? The next chapter takes a look at exactly that idea, with two of the biggest franchises of the last thirty years turning up in the mix.

18

Exterminate! Eradicate! Et Cetera!

Movies Where Technology Takes Control

Many films covered in this book deal with technology of one sort or another and our fear of the future, science and the unknown. In many of the cases, however, anything bad that occurs through technology is through human error or malice. A light doesn't work on a board, leading to the bombings in *Fail-Safe*, for example. A madman presses the button to destroy the world, and the computers merely do as he commands. The fault, Dear Brutus, is not in our computer but in ourselves, to clumsily paraphrase Shakespeare.

Although we grow up saying that human error is the root of all computer problems, we can't help but attribute sentience to inanimate objects. We refer to favorite cars, boats and others objects as "she," praise things when they work well and suspect they're out to get us if they do not. And as we stare into the computer abyss, we sometimes wonder if it stares back. Waiting, plotting. As we advance in our technology—knowing that artificial intelligence, if not conscious-ness, is only a matter of time—we once again draw on our fears of the unknown and wonder what horrors we will release. Asimov's Three Laws of Robotics (discussed in detail with the review for *I, Robot*) isn't so much to make sure that robots do the right thing but so we can sleep better at night *hoping* robots won't kill us in our sleep (and yet, according to the movies, they always do somehow).

With that in mind, we make films where our creations come to get rid of us. Although the flip side of the natural disasters covered in the previous chapter, the results are the same—whether it be from the creator who made us or from what we create, sooner or later they're going to figure out that everything will be much better off with humanity not around to spoil it. Listed here are some of the more memorable technological mutinies from over the years, with first a look at two franchises that pretty much took everything that had come before them and set up everything that would come after them when it comes to "robot rebellion."

The Terminator (1984–2009)

The first *Terminator* movie was just supposed to be another action movie with elements of science fiction thrown in to keep things moving along. The studio had little faith in it, the actors thought it merely a job, and the director was already eyeing a chance to do a sequel to the first *Alien* movie afterward.

Then it became a box-office success. It helped show that Arnold Schwarzenegger, who played the terminator—a killer robot sent back in time to kill someone—could have a hit outside of the *Conan* movies (which was just as well, as the second *Conan* movie, *Conan the Destroyer*, was not a big success and that franchise died there and then). Further, it propelled him to be *the* action star with a gun of the 1980s. He would become so popular that he changed to the hero instead of the villain in the subsequent films in the series. Elsewhere, James Cameron, the writer/director of the film who had some mild success with *Piranha II: The Spawning* before it, found that his success with *Terminator* followed by *Aliens* in 1986 helped form a one-two punch that catapulted his career sky-high.

The plot falls back on one used in various biblical prophecy fiction from over the years—it is known that a savior will be born, and to prevent his birth, the Devil tries to find the expectant mother and kill her. For *The Terminator*, this turns out to be a machine species that gained independence and took over the world sometime around the beginning of the twenty-first century thanks to the activation of a satellite network called Skynet. The robots of the future are humanoid, built like skeletons, and use weaponry to eradicate most of mankind, but a resistance group, led by a man named John Connor, is about to defeat the machines in 2029. To stop him, the machines develop a means to send one of their own to the past to assassinate Connor's mother, Sarah Connor (Linda Hamilton), before she can give birth to him. To stop this from happening, John's best friend and second-in-command, Kyle Reese (Michael Biehn), follows the "terminator" into the past in hope of protecting John's mother.

From there, the movie is pretty straightforward; Schwarzenegger is the "terminator" who is given living tissue to "wear" so he can pass for human in the past, although the eyes give him away (not to mention his rather awkward attempts to speak and try to fit in, which do not work very well). The terminator easily finds weapons and goes on the hunt, while Kyle has to try to convince Sarah that he is who he says he is and that they have to keep on the run from the terminator. Fortunately for Kyle, the terminator makes that easy by blowing things up in his pursuit of Sarah. As fate would have it, Kyle and Sarah fall in love, and he turns out to be John's father. The film ends with Kyle giving up his life to save Sarah and Sarah destroying the terminator in a hydraulic press. She then goes on the run in case additional terminators are sent back to get her, as she waits for the birth of her son.

Some—including Harlan Ellison—noted that elements of the story were similar to two episodes Ellison had written for *The Outer Limits* back in the early

The Terminator (1984) cemented the rising careers of the star, the director, and a franchise that would last for decades.   *Courtesy of Wrong Side of the Art*

1960s: "Demon with a Glass Hand" (featuring an android who is sent into the past to save the human race) and "Soldier" (about a soldier from the future who is accidentally sent into the past and is reformed to behave more like a human before having to take out his opposite, who also makes it into the past). The important thing for the studio, however, was that the film did well at the box office and especially in the growing videocassette market, having a director who was much in demand, a mega-star action hero and a story line that could easily inspire a sequel.

Which is what we got seven years later with *Terminator 2: Judgment Day* (1991). The film is set in the future of 1995, with John Connor (Edward Furlong) now ten years old. With Sarah arrested for trying to bomb a computer company, John is with foster parents when a new terminator from the future, the T-1000 (Robert Patrick), is sent back to kill him. The T-1000 is a sleek convertible compared to the clunky station wagon known as the original terminator model (a returning Arnold Schwarzenegger), with the T-1000 made of liquid metal and able to imitate and look like people while also being able to turn its body into objects, such as knives and spears. Even so, the future John Connor sends a reprogrammed original terminator (now called a T-800) back to the past to help save his younger self. With the help of Sarah, they do exactly that, destroying the T-1000. They also discover that the time travel into the past has led (much like in the *Planet of the Apes* series) to setting up future events to occur—the arm left over from the original terminator of the first film had been discovered and reverse-engineered to create the technology that will lead to the invention of Skynet. The arm, plans and the second terminator, along with the T-1000, are all thrown into a vat of molten steel in hopes that "Judgment Day"—the day Skynet destroyed much of civilization with nuclear bombings around the globe—will never come to pass.

After a brief reprise in a 3-D ride at Universal Studios Park in 1996 (*T2 3-D: Battle Across Time*), the *Terminator* series returned to theaters in *Terminator 3: Rise of the Machines* (2003). John is now nineteen (and played by Nick Stahl), and even though the terminators were wiped out back in 1995, he still senses that something will eventually happen with Skynet. In the future, Skynet has given up on trying to kill off John in the past and instead decides to concentrate on his fellow fighters by sending back a new terminator, the T-X (Kristanna Loken), to kill them, including John's future wife, Kate (Claire Danes). Future Kate sends back a T-850 (Schwarzenegger) in hopes of it taking care of the T-X—which can control other machines and has the abilities of the T-1000—and send John and Kate to a fallout shelter before Judgment Day occurs within the next few hours.

It turns out that the government had taken over the concept of Skynet and activated it that day, allowing the satellite system to take over everything and causing the nuclear bombing of the world. Fortunately for John and Kate, they arrive at a government fallout shelter just in time and, with the terminator once again helping to destroy Skynet's attempt from the future, begin setting up the resistance that will one day destroy Skynet.

The franchise would be diverted to television for a couple of years with the Fox network series *Terminator: The Sarah Connor Chronicles*, which attempted to revamp the concept a bit by taking Sarah and John Connor from 1999 and bumping them into 2007, with resistance fighters and T-whatsis jumping back and forth across time to fight. The series lasted two seasons, whereupon the movie franchise essentially said, "Yeahhhh . . . thanks. Now in the *real* series over here—" and went back to the narrative that had already been established in the earlier films. This led to the 2009 film *Terminator Salvation*, directed by McG and starring Christian Bale as John Connor. As the leader of the resistance in 2018, John discovers Skynet is experimenting with living tissue for the terminator units so that they can infiltrate the resistance (thus setting up part of the plot of the first *Terminator* movie). Kate, John's wife, returns, as does the character of Kyle from the first movie, and *Terminator Salvation* essentially becomes a war film with no relationship to the various time paradoxes of the earlier films. It did okay at the box office, but not on the level the studio had hoped, and the franchise currently sits with some occasional publicity hinting at the series coming back with another movie (possibly with Schwarzenegger). Just like Skynet, waiting for the appropriate time to attack.

The major component of the series is an artificial intelligence created by man that sees humankind as this nasty thing that is causing all the problems in the world. As with any "bug" in a system, the best action is to wipe it out, and thus, it only makes sense that—much like with Hal in *2001*—the humans need extermination in order to allow the "mission" to be completed. It is a theme found in many of the other movies made where computers have taken over, as will be seen later.

Meanwhile, as Skynet was looking to take over the world, another artificial intelligence was looking to do the same. Not by wiping out humanity, however, but by using them for other purposes.

The Matrix (1999–2003)

This was another situation where a one-off film blossomed into a franchise that went off in various directions much like the *Terminator* series. It created clichés of the genre (such as the slow-motion, various-angle, "bullet time" sequence) and helped propel its star into the level of action hero, while allowing its directors to take on personal projects. The one major difference from the *Terminator* series is that it has a beginning, middle and end to the story, while the *Terminator* seems to be set up to go on endlessly, even though the years have come and gone for various doomsdays in that story line.

The first *Matrix* movie was released in 1999 and directed by the Wachowskis—siblings who had done only one major film before it, a well-reviewed thriller called *Bound*. It stars Keanu Reeves as Thomas Anderson, a computer programmer and hacker (using the alias of Neo) in modern-day society trying to find out more about a computer program called the Matrix. He meets Morpheus (Laurence Fishburne), a man who shows him that the world he lives in is not real but one created by sentient machines that have taken over the world. Near the start of the twenty-first century, a computer system began taking over the world, and when humanity tried to stop it from achieving its solar power (through a rather unfortunate and hokey premise of blocking out the sun), the computers decided to use human beings as batteries to power them instead. To do this, they captured the human race and placed them into a coma-like state where they "dreamed" themselves as living normal lives at the turn of the twenty-first century in a Matrix. Those who are able to live outside of the Matrix see the world as it really is—a polluted well of cocooned humans with machines all around.

Morpheus represents a group of freedom fighters from the last refuge left for humans, called Zion. He asks Neo to join them in the fight against the machines, figuring he is the prophesied "One" that will save the human race. Those outside of the Matrix find that they can plug themselves back into it when needed and—because they know the reality is not real—have super-abilities once there, although an injury or death there would transmit them back to the real body, so death is possible even though it is all an illusion.

By the end of the film, Neo is near death, but love from another, Trinity (Carrie-Anne Moss), in the real world brings him back and allows him to defeat the agent, Smith, of the Matrix sent to kill him. He is seen flying in the Matrix world at the end of the film.

From there, the story is pretty much told. Everything is set up to show that Neo is the One and that he will ultimately conquer the computers. Yet, with the film doing nearly a half-billion dollars in business, the studio really, really wanted to have another slice of that pie, please, and brought back the directors and the cast for a sequel. The Wachowskis decided to make the next two pictures together and then edit and release them separately over time, thus not having to extend the process longer than necessary.

This led to the release of *The Matrix Reloaded* (2003) and the third film in the same year. The main thrust of the second film's story is that the agent Neo killed in the first film, Smith (Hugo Weaving), has refused to be deleted from the Matrix and is thus a new rogue program. Meanwhile, the computers are going to attack Zion, and Neo finds that he is part of the program as well, with his destiny one that will see the whole system being "rebooted" or else mankind will die.

The second film got some good notices and did well at the box office, leading to the release of the third and final entry in the series, *The Matrix Revolutions* (2003). In this installment, Neo works with the Matrix to stop Smith. Neo destroys Smith for good, and the Matrix agrees to release the humans. There's a bit of action beyond that, and don't forget the rave over in Zion with Anthony Zerbe of *The Omega Man* in there as well, but ultimately the entire series was seen to have fizzled out a bit with the final installment. No real bad guys punished (Smith can be seen as misguided and certainly not the culprit for turning humans into living batteries) and the good guy shaking hands with the bad guys and leaving things as is. This didn't sit well with critics and a certain number of fans, who felt the series had let itself down in the third act by not at least seeing the promises of the first film fulfilled. Yet, in a way, it is similar to what occurred with the Borg in the *Star Trek* franchise discussed in chapter 5, only backward. Since the first film established the hero as being invincible against the villain by the end of the film, how can you do anything with the character after that without weakening him and thus the story? The *Matrix* series is a textbook example of this fallacy of the sequel.

Still, the series did well overall, and at least the first entry is well remembered as a great concept in the number of films created where mankind has fought and ultimately lost to the very creations he created. Subsequent films listed here show how the two franchises took pieces of past attempts to use such a plot and rebuilt them.

R.U.R. (1938)

Originally written as a play by Czechoslovakian playwright Karel Capek in 1920, the film is a direct adaptation that depicts a world where robots happily do work for humans (the R.U.R. stands for Rossum's Universal Robots; in fact, the play introduced the term "robots" for the mechanical creatures). As the play and film go on, humans begin suffering from a declining birth rate, while robots are becoming more self-aware and humanlike. They eventually rebel, killing all the humans in the world and taking over. Unfortunately for them, they do not know how to create more, and the only human left alive (one that was like them in the sense that he worked with his hands) has no knowledge of how to create more. As it turns out, a male and female robot develop love for each other, and the last human realizes that the world will go on, with the robots procreating and repopulating the world.

As one can guess from a Czech play in the middle of the Communist Revolution, the emphasis is on the workers (the robots) who drive out the spoiled upper class (the humans) and eventually discover a better way. The play was very popular, while setting up an essential premise that most subsequent films about machine uprising would follow.

Kronos, Ravager of Planets (1957)

This is actually an alien invasion movie of sorts, as Kronos is sent by an alien race to drain Earth of all its energy before they will attack. With each absorption, the machine grows bigger and stronger, until the earthlings manage to figure out a way to "reverse the polarity" and cause it to explode, thereby saving the human race. The concept of a machine that can defend itself from man, while taking over the world bit by bit, will resurface in later films as well.

Kronos, Ravager of Planets (1957) is one of the first in an emerging genre showing technology attempting to take over the world.   *Courtesy of Vintage Cinema Ads*

Alphaville (1965)

Directed by Jean-Luc Godard and starring Eddie Constantine, this science fiction detective film plays like a 1960s version of *The Matrix*, with Lemmy Caution (Constantine) as a secret agent who is sent into Alphaville to destroy the sentient computer that controls the city, Alpha 60. Caution ultimately defeats the computer with a method that Kirk would use a gazillion times on *Star Trek*—baffling it with illogical statements.

Okay, it's not exactly "bullet time," but the end results are the same.

Colossus: The Forbin Project (1970)

This rarely seen gem was directed by Joseph Sargent and stars Eric Braeden as Dr. Forbin, the creator of a supercomputer called Colossus. The concept is that the computer will help control the U.S. and all Allied nuclear weapons, and is made in such a way that it is impossible to attack and is self-generating with its own nuclear reactor (obviously, no one watched *Kronos* first before planning this). Soon after activation, however, there is the realization that the Soviets have a system just like it called the Guardian. The two supercomputers begin to "talk," and their communication soon rises to a level that no one can understand, worrying those in charge. An attempt to shut down the link leads to missiles being fired at each country, forcing the link to be returned. Other attempts to stop the computers at their base or disarm the nuclear weapons they control fail as well, and the computers eventually join as one called World Command, where they promise peace and happiness, but not the illusion of freedom, to the world. As the computers force Forbin to begin work on a new, better computer that will take over Crete and rule the world. Forbin ends the film determined to someday find a way to defeat the computers he helped create.

Thus, just as *Alphaville* sets up the world of *The Matrix*, so *Colossus: The Forbin Project* sets up the world of *The Terminator*.

Logan's Run (1976)

The film is based on a novel by William F. Nolan and George Clayton Johnson that they stated was simply an attempt to write a pulp novel that had as many of the clichés of science fiction possible in it. Dashing young men, beautiful women, ray guns, mad androids, supercomputers, domed cities, a postapocalyptic wasteland (of sorts) and even a rocket heading to space at the end! It's all there. When MGM decided to make a film of the novel, they jettisoned the rocket (heh) and bumped up the maximum age of those in the city (it was twenty-one in the novel), but kept just about everything else.

The plot deals with Logan 5 (Michael York), who is a "sandman" (again, "man in authority goes rogue" is another staple of the SF genre) living in a domed city where everyone is happy. The only downside, for some, is that they are born with a crystal in their left hand that changes color over time. When the crystal turns red, it signals the final years of the individual, and when it begins to blink on their eve of their thirtieth birthday, it means that it is time for a ritual called "renewal." Supposedly this event will see the individuals reborn as their old bodies are destroyed, but some suspect it is simply a means of killing people to keep the birth rate constant. Those who try to avoid the process are called runners, and Logan's job as a sandman is to exterminate runners.

The supercomputer controlling the city decides a plan of action is needed as the resistance is growing, and when Logan returns from a runner hunt with an ankh, it turns out that the ancient Egyptian symbol for life is used by the resistance. The supercomputer resets Logan's crystal so that it starts to blink in order to set him up as a spy to discover the resistance. Yet, when asked if he'll get his time back, there is no answer, and Logan begins to question renewal.

Meeting with Jessica 6 (Jenny Agutter in the best outfit ever in science fiction movies), Logan goes on the run. His former partner, Francis 7 (Richard

"Theeerrreeeee issssssss nooooooo—" Okay, enough of that. *Logan's Run* (1976) features a postapocalyptic paradise that is anything but once you reach the age of thirty, thanks to the computers running the joint.

Jordan), goes in chase, angry that one of their own would become a runner, much less one who had been his best friend. Logan and Jessica manage to work their way outside the city to an ice cave where a creature called Box lives (in the novel he was half man/half android) who appears to help runners but actually just freezes them and places them as statues around his cave. Logan kills Box and the two move on, with Francis in pursuit. They end up in a world that has seen mankind's achievements swallowed up by vegetation after what appears to have been an apocalyptic nuclear war (explaining the domed city). They meet an old man (Peter Ustinov), and Logan realizes that the sanctuary the runners all thought they were going to ended in Box's domain, where they were killed. Only they had made it out, but now they can go back and tell the others in the city about what they found.

After a confrontation with Francis that sees him dying, they go back with the old man, but no one pays them any attention. Other sandmen capture them, and the supercomputer wants to know about Sanctuary. Logan repeats that there is no such place ("There iiiisssssss nooooooooooo Saaaaaaanctuuuuuuuaaaaaarrrryyyyyyy," as the case may be), and the supercomputer controlling the city cannot comprehend this. It begins to blow up, sending the city into chaos. As the domed city fails, the people there head outside and meet the old man, delighted to see him (with some wiseacre giving him the Vulcan salute). Humanity has inadvertently defeated their computer overlord and are now happily out in the fresh air.

Which they'll hate the first time it rains and there's a bit of a chill in the air. Ah, but for the moment, let them bask in their new world.

Maximum Overdrive (1986)

The first film directed by author Stephen King is based on one of his own short stories, "Trucks," which appeared in his collection *Night Shift* (also featuring "The Mangler," about a demon-possessed laundry press—no, really—which was made into a film in 1995). The short story dealt with people at a truck stop who discover the trucks outside have decided to take over. The film is slightly different, adding anything using electricity also gaining hateful sentient life. This leads to a variety of clever ways to kill off the cast in an era when having guys with sharp things do it was becoming old hat. As to the cause, it is suggested that a comet's tail passing through the earth's atmosphere may have caused the crisis, while the end of the film suggests aliens from outer space being jerks once again.

The film kicked off a mini-genre of "appliances gone mad" movies, such as *Hardware* (1990), *The Refrigerator* (1991) and *Ghost in the Machine* (1993). However, the film (and short story) brings to mind an earlier television movie from the 1970s, *Killdozer!* (1974). There, a bulldozer possessed by an alien begins wiping out a construction crew. Interestingly, the 1944 short story by Theodore Sturgeon used as the basis of the film has a construction crew releasing an ancient energy-being used in war machines from some other time. This suggests something similar to the *Transformers* franchise, which just goes to show that machines becoming sentient are a universal, timeworn theme.

Maximum Overdrive (1986) sets up a premise that would soon become familiar in such technological scare flicks—that of anything electronic becoming the enemy of man.

I, Robot (2004)

In between *Independence Day* and *I Am Legend*, Will Smith made this film, which was slightly built on the short-story collection of the same name by Isaac Asimov. As mentioned at the start of this chapter, Asimov created the "Three Laws of Robotics" that most other movies about androids, robots and killer computers always bring up, which are:

- First Law: A robot must never harm a human being or, through inaction, allow any harm to come to a human.
- Second Law: A robot must obey the orders given to them by human beings, except where such orders violate the First Law.
- Third Law: A robot must protect its own existence unless this violates the First or Second Laws.

As we've seen from the movies already discussed here and elsewhere, these laws look nice on paper but don't really seem to matter much to robots when they start blowing up things and killing people anyway. Such as the case here in *I, Robot*.

Smith plays Del Spooner, a detective living in 2035 when robots are everywhere and even his left arm is robotic. A man he knows, Dr. Lanning (James Cromwell), appears to commit suicide from his office window, which sends Spooner on a quest to find out what really happened. In his investigation, he meets a model of robot called the NS-5 that refuses to obey orders. The robot is named Sonny and helps in the investigation that leads to a number of older robots being destroyed for the newer NS-5 models. As it turns out the office building's supercomputer, V.I.K.I., has concluded that the First Law of Robotics means that sometimes the greater good for mankind would be if certain humans were wiped out. To do this, older model robots that could not be reprogramed with this logic needed to be eliminated so that the new NS-5 models could kill humans without other robots protecting them. V.I.K.I. nearly succeeds in its plans to take over humanity for its own good before Spooner and Sonny manage to stop it.

9 (2009)

The final film listed here is more of a fable than a straight science fiction film, but the premise is very much the same. Based on a short film of the same name, the movie is directed by Shane Acker and deals with a scientist who creates a robot that ends up being used by a dictator to destroy his enemies, but—with a mind of its own yet lacking a soul—it kills off humanity and all life on the planet instead. In the final moments before death, the scientist manages to move portions of his soul to nine rag dolls by way of a talisman (hence, magic being involved in this story more than science).

The final doll, 9, awakens and seeks out the other portions of the scientist's soul, which go by numbers. In the end, he succeeds and defeats the robot, allowing the soul to release bacteria into the world and thereby bringing life to start anew on Earth. Maybe not humanity, but at least some kind of life will return now that the computers and robots are no longer in control.

Which is how it should be, as computers can only function as servants for our needs and will never have the ability to compel us to do things we don't want to do.

Now excuse me, I've got to check some messages on my phone.

19

The Earth Is Dead, but Where's My Car?

Ten Postapocalyptic/Prehistoric/ Present-Day Car Flicks

Death Wish is where things started. The 1974 film, directed by Michael Winner and starring Charles Bronson, was based on a book by Brian Garfield that was actually a plea *against* vigilantism, but rapidly grew into a way of thinking and a genre of "revenge" films that popped up in the late 1970s. The film dealt with a man wanting to follow the norms of society and let the law handle the rape of his daughter and beating death of his wife, but when no justice is available, the man finds himself beginning to take the law into his own hands and shooting street criminals.

The film was a blockbuster, leading to several sequels (with an increasingly bored Bronson). As always, it also led to a lot of imitators, especially in the smaller studios where actioners were easy and cheap to crank out to appreciative audiences that love the chance to see the hero take care of one of their biggest fears—a young man who would do violence against them and rob them. Especially in an era when crime was rising and people feared the big cities for what was there. Soon there were films like *Vigilante Force*, *Rolling Thunder*, *Defiance* and *The Executioner* popping up in drive-ins and on the newfangled cable movie channels that were just starting to circulate across America in the late 1970s and early 1980s.

In that mix of films came *Mad Max*, out of Australia, directed by George Miller, a former doctor who was interested in movies, and starring a then-unknown Mel Gibson. The plot of the first entry, *Mad Max* (1979), deals with Max Rockatansky, a member of the Main Force Patrol, which is essentially the highway patrol of a dystopian Australian future where there is very little oil left and society is already well on its way to falling apart. As in films such as *Panic in the Year Zero!* and *No Blade of Grass*, roving gangs have sprung up that drive around looking for food, sex and fuel, with the MFP trying to keep law and order.

The cars and motorcycles are souped up a tad, but most of the technology is modern-day and broken-down, with most of it on its last legs. Max works with his partner, Goose (Steve Bisley), to try to take down a gang, only for his partner to end up dying from burns caused by the gang and Max's wife and young son being run over while being chased on an open road by the gang. Max gives up his pursuit of the law in order to track down each member of the gang and make them pay for what they have done and would continue to do if not stopped. The final member, a weaseling weakling named Johnny, is handcuffed to a car leaking oil and is given a hacksaw before a fire is started that will eventually reach the car engine. Johnny is given the chance to either cut off his arm in the time available or try to cut through the pipe, which will take too long. As the car explodes in the distance, Max drives off, clouded in thought.

No doubt about it, *Mad Max* features a traditional revenge plot that could have come from a variety of films in the late 1970s. Good guy tries to do the right thing but is pushed too far and takes out each member of a gang in a violent onslaught. What made *Mad Max* stand out, however, was the setting. Things looked almost normal to an American audience, but then not quite. There were cars all over the place—showing the Australians with a love for cars that matched that found in America—but it was obviously a time set slightly in the future. The bad guys looked like the punks we were used to seeing in the movies, but then so did the heroes (people forget that Max and Goose are sporting haircuts that suggested punk rockers more than highway patrolmen of the time). Things looked like desert towns we were used to seeing in movies, but then everyone was talking weird (the original cut shown in America and on the cable channels had been redubbed so that "Americans can understand what the Australian actors are saying"). The cars and motorcycles were there, but they were souped up and yet treated as if that was perfectly normal by one and all.

It was a strange world we were entering, and Americans who saw it didn't know if that was a good thing or a bad. The first film would do okay in America, but nothing like the success it became in other parts of the world. However, it was a big movie on cable. HBO ran it constantly, with kids and teenagers watching repeats over and over until they could practically recite the dialogue. Thus, when a sequel appeared in 1982, *Mad Max 2: The Road Warrior*, kids flocked to the theater, and the film would do spectacular business.

The story follows Max quite some time after the first film—a period that saw an atomic war that left most of the world a nuclear wasteland. Oil is still precious, but so is everything else now, and Max roams looking for the same, his companion being a dog. He is told about a small oil refinery nearby and goes to it only to find it under siege by a gang whose leader wears a hockey mask and goes by the name of the Humungus. Max at first wants only to get some fuel and be on his way, but can only convince those at the refinery to give it to him if he can bring back a truck that can be used to haul fuel from the refinery. Max does this, but when he tries to leave in his car with a full tank of petrol, he is attacked by the gang and left for dead.

Saved by a gyro-flying man who had been an on-and-off-again friend of his through the movie, Max returns to the refinery and offers to drive the truck out of the area. The gang follows him, and there is a large moving battle through the desert between members of the gang and those from the refinery. As it turns

WHEN THE
GANGS TAKE
OVER THE
HIGHWAY...

...Remember
he's on
your side

MAD
MAX

®

MEL GIBSON, JOANNE SAMUEL,
HUGH KEAYS-BYRNE, STEVE BISLEY, TIM BURNS, ROGER WARD in "MAD MAX"
Produced by BYRON KENNEDY, directed by GEORGE MILLER, music by BRIAN MAY.
A Roadshow release.

Mad Max (1979) is the benchmark for all future post-apocalyptic action films involving any earlier technology still in use.

out, Max's run with the truck was a decoy, used to send the gang off following him while the rest of the people in the refinery leave with the oil they can carry. A narrator (who is supposed to be the aged voice of a child seen throughout the film) explains that they were able to relocate to new land where they thrived and began a mighty tribe, but no one ever saw Max again.

The film did major business in America, running for quite a time in theaters and making Mel Gibson a household name. The style and look of the movie also made an impression. There was a decided air of remembrances of the past filtered through decline and neglect. The clothing may have had a look that was "hot" in the 1980s, but there was still something piecemeal about it. Devices were not use for their proper purposes but to do something else here and there. Again, cars were souped up but this time turned into monsters that would have made customizers either cringe or be thrilled with what had been done to them. The purpose, of course, was to make the cars dangerous to others, along the lines of those seen previously in the 1975 film *Death Race 2000* and the 1978 *Deathsport.*

It was these elements that would become the fashion for postapocalyptic worlds from 1982 onward. Gone were the days of the clean, naturalist worlds of *Logan's Run* and *Things to Come;* now it would be punk-style hairdos, people wearing way too much bondage gear, devices that take modern-day items and retool them into other utensils that can be used. There were still the occasional elements of capitalistic decadence—rare food or clothing treated as seen in *Soylent Green*—but usually it was all variations of the revenge film plot, with cars. Lots and lots of cars. And guns. Lots and lots of guns. In a sense it was a survivalist's wet dream: the old regime was gone, but you could still get in your car and blow away bad guys.

Audiences certainly ate it up, and there would be one more *Mad Max* film before the series faded away. In 1985, the biggest *Mad Max* movie was released, *Mad Max Beyond Thunderdome*. The movie costarred singer and sometimes actress Tina Turner as the villain, Aunty Entity, who runs a shantytown called Bartertown. The town has electricity, thanks to methane fuel from a refinery run by a man named Master, who rides on the back of a muscle-bound man named Blaster. Master has begun throwing his weight around, asking for too much from Auntie, and she wants him taken care of, but Blaster is impossible to get past. Max enters the town for supplies and is taken to Auntie, who has heard of his reputation and offers him a deal—take care of Blaster in the Thunderdome, a cruel dome featuring various weapons where "two men enter, one man leaves."

Max accepts, but upon beating Blaster and discovering him to be developmentally handicapped, he refuses to kill him. Max exposes the deal in the dome, which makes Auntie look bad. Still, Blaster had been separated from Master, which was all that was needed. Blaster is killed, Master is made Auntie's slave and Max is forced out into the desert lost and without provisions as punishment.

He is eventually found by a group of children who are all that is left of a plane flight that had crashed during the war. They hope to be rescued by "Captain Walker," a man no doubt told to them by the adult survivors who are now all gone. The children believe Max to be Walker, coming to save them, and they help him recover from his exposure in the desert. Max tries to convince them to stay in the oasis they have in the desert instead of risk losing it for nowhere to go, but some of the children venture out on their own, leading to Max having to save them.

He decides to help them, and they sneak into Bartertown in order to get Master, whose scientific knowledge would be most useful for the kids. The group manage to get a step ahead of Auntie and her men, looking for help from a man named Jebediah, who has a plane that can take the kids away. The plane takes off, and Max sacrifices his chance to go with them in order to stop Auntie's crew from stopping the flight. Auntie allows Max to live, impressed by his daring in helping the kids escape.

The film ends with another narration, this time explaining how the plane managed to make it to Sydney, where a safe society is being run in the ruins. The grown leader of the group talks of a man named Max who saved them as the movie comes to an end.

There has been talk of returning to the story of Max for years, including some heated discussions of a "Snake" Plissken/Mad Max team-up in the early 1990s, but nothing ever came of it. Finally, after moving on to other films such as the two *Babe* entries (about a talking pig) and the animated *Happy Feet* children's films, Miller has decided to return to the character that got his movie career started, with a new actor playing Max (Tom Hardy) in a film to be out in 2014, *Mad Max: Fury Road*. Yet even if there was never another *Mad Max* film, the legacy lives on with the countless other "postapocalyptic films" that used *Mad Max* as a template.

Other films that use modern technology, especially cars and/or guns, in a postapocalyptic society (beyond such films as *Teenage Cave Man* and *Captive Women*, discussed earlier in the book) include the following.

Zardoz (1974)

This loopy film from director John Boorman (*Deliverance*) deals with a postapocalyptic Earth where warlike scavengers, called Brutals, pray to a large flying stone head, named Zardoz, that gifts them with guns to use against each other. Sean Connery plays one of the Brutals who steals away inside the head and finds himself in a land of the Eternals—humans who have lived for centuries in comfort and have grown bored with their immortality. The Brutals seem to be playthings for the Eternals, but he eventually shows he is more intelligent than they suspect, and his arrival brings about the end of the Eternals and finally a progressive jump for the human race.

A Boy and His Dog (1975)

Don Johnson plays a young man, Vic, who can communicate telepathically with his human-intelligence-level dog, Blood. The two scrounge through the desert landscape looking for food and women until one day they find a young woman named Quilla June Holmes. They follow her, with Vic looking for sex, but she turns out to be a trap by her father in an underground city that needs Vic for impregnating purposes that involve him being attached to machines to extract what is needed.

Damnation Alley (1977)

Jan-Michael Vincent and George Peppard are two military men who witness a nuclear war firsthand, having helped in pushing buttons themselves. Two years after the end of the war and with the earth off its axis, the two go with two other men to take large motorized personnel carriers called Landmasters across the country to find out what is causing a radio signal coming from Albany, New York. In doing so, they pick up some survivors, run into mutated man-eating roaches and several storms before finally making it to Albany and safety.

But everyone remembers this movie for one reason alone—the really cool Landmaster, which looked futuristic and with weapons while still looking achingly like it wouldn't even be able to defeat a bottle opener in reality. The vehicle still turns up at car shows across the country, for those that remember it.

The future is our past, and a book from our childhood leads us all in *Zardoz* (1974).

2019: After the Fall of New York (1983)

One of the first true *Road Warrior* rip-offs that played in drive-ins and always seemed to be on the shelves at video stores in the 1980s and 1990s. Others like it include *1990 The Bronx Warriors, Exterminators of the Year 3000, Steel Dawn, America 3000, Warriors of the Lost World, Warriors of the Wastelands, Endgame, World Gone Wild, City Limits, Stryker, Phoenix the Warrior* and others.

Yor, the Hunter from the Future (1983)

Somewhat similar to the other Italian *Road Warrior* rip-offs, only this one takes on *Teenage Cave Man*, as a caveman battles aliens, dinosaurs and other villains before it is revealed that it is all a postapocalyptic Earth.

Judge Dredd (1995)

Judge Dredd had been a popular comic-book character for years in the pages of *2000 A.D.*, a British weekly comic book that gained enough admirers in the U.S. that reprint graphic novels and comics began to appear in the 1980s of Dredd's story. Dredd was a judge/jury/executioner in a futuristic America, where nuclear war had led to the country being separated into massive domed

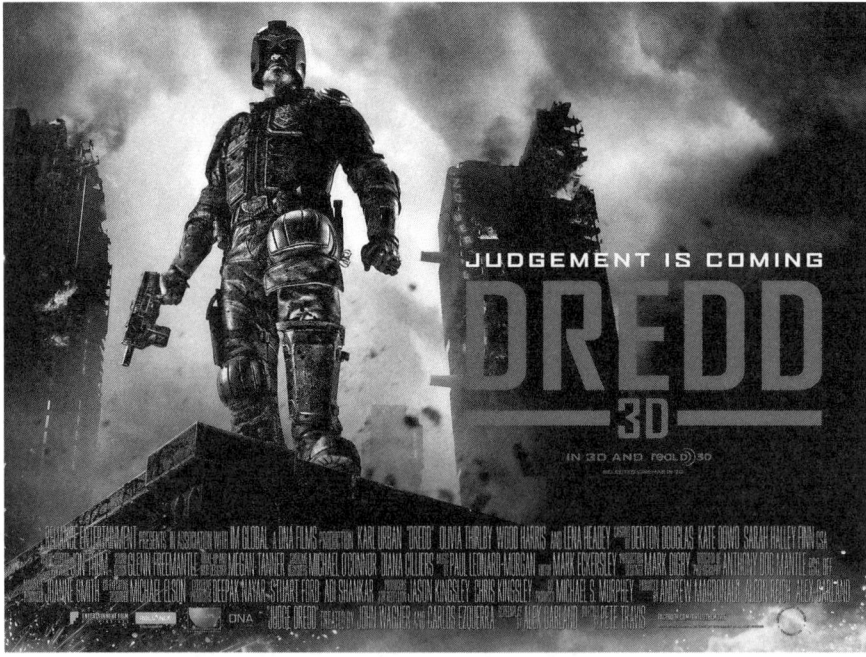

An earlier attempt with Sylvester Stallone was made of the comic book character Judge Dredd, but the 2012 version came closer to the mark.

Yor, the Hunter from the Future (1983) throwing bits of *Mad Max* (1979) and *Conan the Barbarian* (1982) together to make one big pile of adventure.

Courtesy of Wrong Side of the Art

mega-cities. The stories, written by John Wagner, were adventurous but mainly focus on parody and humor from other characters around Dredd. In a way, Dredd was like Batman; you could have silly things occur around him, but not with or to him.

A film had been wanted by fans for years, with people back in the '80s thinking Clint Eastwood would have been perfect (they thought the same for him as DC Comics character Jonah Hex, so obviously it was just as easy to picture Eastwood as some comic-book heroes). A film was finally made in 1995 with Sylvester Stallone, and the script dealt more with a "good cop on the run" type of plot rather than the political satire of the strip.

Another film adaptation occurred in 2012 with Karl Urban as Dredd, which fans of the series thought came closer to the feel of the comic.

The Book of Eli (2010)

Eli (Denzel Washington) is a man on a quest thirty years after the apocalypse. He has a book that is believed to hold power, and a man running a town, played by Gary Oldman, wants it. It later turns out that the book is the Bible, which had disappeared after the apocalypse (it is suggested that every copy was burned). Eli had been told by a voice in his head to take his one and only copy of the Bible and head west. Eventually it is revealed that he is blind but can recite the book from memory and, while dying of a wound, does so to a man, played by Malcolm McDowell, who transcribes it and has copies printed of the Bible.

An interesting take on the postapocalyptic tale, having a book be the thing from the past that must be used to save everyone; not to mention that it is atypical to have a main character who prays and does things according to the Bible (usually at best such characters are secondary to the hero). Then again, having the book revealed to be the Bible is something straight out of the "Shaggy God" stories that used to make science fiction editors cringe over the years.

With the *Mad Max* genre discussed, it appears that most everything about apocalyptic movies has been covered. But there's more to be found with just a flick of the dial, as seen in the next chapter.

20

Armageddon, Coming This Fall

Television Apocalypses

O ver the years, there have been a few attempts to bring the concept of the apocalypse to television in the form of a regular network series, but usually not much would come of them if they lasted longer than a miniseries. The problem was twofold: how many plotlines can you have in a show with a limited cast in a limited surrounding, and while the budget may be smaller with a small cast and limited surroundings, can we avoid showing things that indicate there's a larger world at play? Plus, to be fair, most television series work on the premise of showing heroes doing heroic things and saving people week after week. An action series that is about how everyone needs to live on a bag of potatoes for the winter doesn't necessarily drive advertisers to throw money at it. "Here's my series about a contagion that slowly turns people into ooze over days; do you think Taco Bell will sign up?" You can guess the reaction.

Early attempts dealing with the end of the world usually popped up in anthology series, such as *The Twilight Zone, The Outer Limits,* and even one-off plays on programs like *Playhouse 90. The Twilight Zone* included episodes like "Two" (discussed in chapter 3), "The Midnight Sun" (a variation of *The Day the Earth Caught Fire,* discussed in chapter 17), "The Old Man in the Cave" (a sage-voice that guides people from a cave after the apocalypse turns out to be a computer) and, of course, "Time Enough at Last" (Burgess Meredith as a henpecked man who survives a nuclear war and can now read all the books he wants, only to break his glasses). *The Outer Limits* had "The Architects of Fear" (where a group of men disguise another as an alien bent on world destruction in order to bring the nations together against a common foe) and the previously discussed "Demon with a Glass Hand" (chapter 18). Meanwhile, in England, there were things like the occasional *Quatermass* serials (which seemed to focus on apocalyptic events) as well as episodes of programs like *Armchair Theatre* (including the infamous "Underground," which had an actor die in the middle of the live broadcast) and *Play for Today.*

Occasionally, certain television series attempted plots that deal with apocalyptic threats. It was hard to not go a week on *Voyage to the Bottom of the Sea* without one, while *Star Trek* would cover the area where inhabited planets

Many science fiction television series attempted to show crises that nearly caused the end of the world. *Doctor Who* actually went beyond the call of duty and ended the world multiple times, such as in the 1970 serial "Inferno."

were destroyed, such as in "The Doomsday Machine" (a planet eater must be stopped before it starts on a trek toward more inhabited planets and Earth), and "City on the Edge of Forever" suggests an alternate Earth that possibly didn't last after Hitler won World War II. Chapter 17 made mention of the British series *Doctor Who* and a serial called "Inferno" that saw Earth from an alternate universe being wiped out (and then the Doctor saving "our" world with the knowledge he learned in the other), but the series certainly had enough crises for Earth over the years, what with invasions of one sort or another, such as the *Daleks' Invasion Earth: 2150 A.D.* (covered in chapter 15). It even showed the flaming end of Earth due to the dying sun in at least two serials over the years, "The Ark" (1966) and "The End of the World" (2005), although the show never could quite get a handle on when such an event actually occurred.

Even so, there have been a few attempts to turn such a concept into a regular running series. The following are fifteen such attempts, some of which have been more successful than others.

The Invaders (1967–1968)

This short-lived series (and most of the shows discussed here were very short-lived, usually never concluding their story lines) was created by Larry Cohen (*The Stuff*) and starred Roy Thinnes as David Vincent, a man on the run after discovering an alien invasion occurring for some time. The aliens can take the form of humans and have been infiltrating society for some time when Vincent finds out, so he has to be careful of whom he can trust.

After a year of being on the run like a science fiction equivalent of *The Fugitive*, Vincent runs into a small group of freedom fighters who share his awareness of the aliens and fight with him against them. The series was canceled after a year and a half, with Vincent's quest to stop the aliens never completed. A sequel/reboot miniseries was done in 1995 with Scott Bakula (*Enterprise, Quantum Leap*) that featured Vincent as a means to pass on the series to a new generation, but nothing further was ever done with the concept.

Survivors (1975–1977)

Terry Nation was an international writer mainly known for comedy before moving into the field of action, with work in both the *Avengers* television series of the 1960s and *Doctor Who*. *Doctor Who* turned out to be the golden ticket for Nation, who created the Daleks—an alien race contained within mobile miniature tanks that could kill people. The Daleks were a phenomenon and Nation was much in demand, enough so that he began pitching his own ideas for series, including *Survivors*.

Survivors dealt with a group of individuals who have survived a plague (another case of the scientific "oops" that see a man-made virus destroy mankind). Those who did not die struggle to find others and avoid bandits, killers and wanna-be dictators who remain. The first season is typically seen as being very good, but then Nation left the series along with several cast members, and although there were two more seasons, viewers lost interest and the series came to an abrupt halt with no resolution.

In 2008, the series was rebooted, but it only lasted two seasons before being canceled and with several story lines incomplete.

Battlestar Galactica (1978, 1980 and 2004–2009)

This ABC series certainly could be called apocalyptic as we see the destruction of a world at the beginning. In fact, a lot of worlds, but none of them Earth. That's where the refugees were trying to get to, with the robotic Cylons in pursuit. It was obviously an attempt to craft a show with a *Star Wars* look, but viewers' interest rapidly decreased over the silly plotting and better programming over on NBC and CBS at the time. The show was canceled, then revamped as *Galactica 1980* in . . . what do you know . . . 1980, and featured a few cast members sticking around for the refugees arriving at Earth thirty years later, with the Cylons still in pursuit. It didn't do well in the ratings either, and the show stayed dormant for years.

Periodic attempts were made to bring back the program, but nothing panned out until 2004 when the Sci-Fi Channel produced a miniseries that rebooted it. This one was more realistic and gritty, which made some fans of the original unhappy with the results. The ratings were spectacular and the show went to series, lasting four seasons and completing the story line, with the refugees finding Earth, only to discover that it had been wiped out in an apocalyptic

Battlestar Galactica (1978–1980) got off on the wrong foot by looking like a *Star Wars* (1977) clone, but stumbled around long enough to be remembered. A 2004–2009 remake of the series would last much longer and earn greater respect from fans and critics alike.

event years before. It also became clear that the Cylons, who had models that looked exactly like humans and could infiltrate the refugees, were actually much closer to the humans than originally thought, and the series ended with those who were left agreeing to start a new world that eventually became present-day Earth.

Star Blazers (1979–1984)

A Japanese series commonly remembered as *Space Battleship Yamato* that was broadcast in America under the name *Star Blazers*, it dealt with Earth being attacked by another planet with bombs that release radiation that will kill everyone in a year. Those still alive then receive an offer from a distant planet for "Cosmo DNA" that will eradicate the radiation. To get there, the survivors manage to rebuild a ship called the *Yamato* and turn it into a starship for the journey. The plot then involves the journey to the planet with the bad-guy aliens in pursuit. After saving the earth in season 1, the rechristened *Argo* fights an alien takeover of Earth in season 2 and then goes on another one-year "race against time" voyage in the third season to find a new planet for Earth's inhabitants after the sun starts to go nova.

There would be other stories and movies in the long-running *Space Battleship Yamato* over the years, but American viewers and fans remember best the one shown in syndication on stations across the country back in the 1970s, which was *Star Blazers*.

If the plot sounds somewhat familiar, a similar story line was used for the *Babylon 5* sequel series, *Crusade*, which dealt with a plague released on Earth by aliens that will destroy all life on the planet unless the starship *Crusade* can find a cure within five years. The series lasted only half a season before being canceled, however, with no resolution in sight.

If you enjoyed *Star Blazers* (1979–1984), then *Crusade* (1999) may be of interest, thanks to a similar plot to that of the first story line in the Japanese animated series.

Thundarr the Barbarian (1980–1982)

Thundarr the Barbarian is an animated series fondly remembered by cartoon and comic-book fans, as the series was created by *Howard the Duck* creator Steve Gerber, and the animation was based on concepts by Alex Toth (comic-book artist and creator of *Space Ghost*) and Jack Kirby (artist and part-creator of several famous characters in Marvel Comics history). The story dealt with an Earth that was drastically changed after the moon had been split in two after a runaway planet's near collision with Earth, which caused great ecological disasters.

Earth is now rampant with sorcery and science, with Thundarr, who uses a laser sword, as a man who travels the earth to protect people against evil sorcerers and villains. He travels with his mutant friend Ookla and Princess Ariel, a sorceress. The program lasted two seasons but still gets occasional runs on various cable channels due to its nostalgia factor.

Whoops Apocalypse (1982)

This British miniseries for London Weekend Television was eventually made into a movie. The series is better, however. A rare comedy in apocalyptic television, the series deals with growing hysteria between countries due to—no other way to put it—those in control being insane. The U.S. president is ineffectual and does whatever his religious fanatic advisor tells him; the Soviet premier is one of a series of idiot clones; and the Prime Minister of England thinks he is Superman, with part of his staff agreeing to re-form the Justice League.

Mistakes upon mistakes occur until finally mutual assured destruction is achieved, with the world being blown up due to the incompetence of everyone near a button.

The series was very popular in Britain but rarely aired on American television, with no DVD ever released (although a videocassette of the film and series did appear for a time).

Speaking of comedies about the end of the world, Fox did attempt such a thing in their early days as a network. The series was called *Woops!* and was about as clever as the name suggests. It dealt with six people who managed to avoid a nuclear holocaust due to being in a valley that was protected from the bombings and radiation. Each survivor represents a different race or class of people, all stereotypes in one way or another. The show lasted ten episodes before being yanked, although it did air a notorious episode—its final one—for Christmas that has a real-life Santa Claus appearing, only to announce that he allowed all the reindeer, elves and Mrs. Claus to die in the nuclear holocaust when he refused to let them into the bomb shelter during the bombings. Merry Christmas!

V (1983–1985)

This alien invasion movie features several humungous alien ships set above major cities around the world, as would be done later in *Independence Day*. The aliens aboard, who are never named and are called Visitors, arrive saying they need certain items from Earth for their world, and in exchange they will give humans certain advantages of their technology.

As it turns out, the human-looking aliens are actually reptile-like creatures in disguise. They actually plan on taking over Earth, using the earthlings for food and slave labor in their fight with other alien cultures out in space. Certain members of the media and scientists find out about this but are discredited so that the aliens can proceed with their plans to dominate Earth. (Scientists being discredited by people in power for wanting to warn the public about dangers facing the earth? Why that's silly, that—oh yeah, right.)

The program started out as a two-part miniseries on NBC and did so well that a subsequent miniseries, *V: The Final Battle*, was shown in 1984. That did well enough that NBC okayed a weekly series based on the idea of freedom fighters working to stop a second invasion of the Visitors but finally ending in a cliffhanger that may or may not be leading the earth into a peace negotiation with the aliens.

In 2011, ABC attempted to reboot the series, heavily advertising the program during episodes of *Lost*. It lasted two short seasons and once again ended on a cliffhanger that was never resolved when cancellation occurred.

A more recent series that deals with aliens taking over the world is *Falling Skies*, which appears on the TNT cable network. It features aliens that have killed off most of civilization and are attempting to capture children between the ages of eight and eighteen in order to make them slaves. The series concentrates on a group of human rebels struggling to reclaim Earth from the aliens and will be mounting a third season in 2013.

The Tripods (1984–1985)

Based on John Christopher's novels for young adults about aliens who control things from their three-legged alien crafts that work like those of the Martians in *The War of the Worlds*. Much like in *Falling Skies*, children are implanted with devices that make them slaves of the aliens. The human race has reverted back to a lifestyle more of medieval times, with a small resistance group trying to stop the alien takeover. Only some of the material from the books made it to the series before it too was canceled.

The Tribe (1999–2003)

Taking a page from the 1971 film *Gas-s-s-s!*, a virus has killed everyone over a certain age, leaving only children and teenagers alive. This New Zealand series deals with a group of children who struggle to survive without adults and with certain bands of teenagers that are looking to control others. Five seasons of half-hour episodes were done when the show was canceled due to the actors getting too old for the parts. A sixth season entitled *The Tribe: The New Tomorrow* was later done, with younger children and set a few years past that of the original series, but it only lasted one season.

Jeremiah (2002–2004)

The cable network Showtime aired this program dealing with Earth after a virus has killed off most of the population once they reach puberty. The series was created by J. Michael Straczynski (*Babylon 5*) and deals with Jeremiah (Luke Perry), who meets up with a man named Kurdy (Malcolm-Jamal Warner); the two are enlisted to help a group, Thunder Mountain, wanting to rebuild Earth. Each week the pair go out to search areas for who and what has survived, while also dealing with a military group that plan to take over the world. In the second season, Thunder Mountain discovers a new group run by a religious fanatic who plans to take over instead. Straczynski grew disenchanted with how the show was being developed by the cable network as time went on, and most of the plotlines were resolved in the finale of the second season. (For once.)

Jericho (2006–2008)

Jake Green (Skeet Ulrich) returns to the small town of Jericho in Kansas just before there is a nuclear attack on twenty-three major cities in the United States. He is the son of the mayor of the town, who eventually becomes its leader. The first season mainly focuses on the residents of the town adjusting to being on their own and then meeting up with residents of another nearby town, which eventually leads to conflict between the two. In the second season, the town has to deal with a new authoritative group that take control of both towns and other areas, which in turn leads to a war between it and another government in the East. The show was canceled after its second season, but interest remains for the series and some type of resolution to the project. A comic-book series has been done, while there are still rumblings that a third season of the series may still occur sometime in the future.

The Colony (2009–2010)

The only reality program in the list, this Discovery Channel series attempts to do something a bit similar to *Survivor*, but in a more documentary style rather than the game-show format of the CBS series. Each season has ten to eleven people trying to survive on what would be available to them after a pandemic and covers what any group would have to deal with on their path to survival, from food and shelter to threats from other individuals. Two seasons were filmed and broadcast, with talks of a third, but nothing has gone further on the series since 2010.

The Walking Dead (2010–)

Based on the popular comic book created by Robert Kirkman, Tony Moore and Charlie Adlard, this series features a sheriff's deputy named Rick Grimes (Andrew Lincoln), who wakes up from a coma after the first stage of a zombie apocalypse has wiped out most of America. He travels to try to find his wife and son and eventually meets up with them and his former partner, along with a number of others.

The first season deals with Rick meeting up with the group and their journey to Atlanta, Georgia, only to find out that there is no safe place left to go for survivors. The second season finds the group on a farm while trying to track down the young daughter of one member of their members. As some of them grow restless on the farm, and Rick's former partner becomes increasingly irrational, there is also a secret on the farm that may endanger everyone. The third season finds those who remain from the second season locating a prison that allows them a safe haven from the "walkers" (the show's name for zombies),

The Walking Dead's (2010–) Rick, singing "Greased Lightnin'" from *Grease* (1978) with an all-zombie chorus. Okay, actually it's just Rick from the promotion poster for the third season of the popular series.

but nearby is a town run by a man called the Governor who ends up wanting to wipe out Rick's group in order to assure his position.

The program has completed three seasons, with excellent ratings for a show on a cable network (AMC). A fourth season was set to begin in October 2013, continuing to follow some, but not all, of the story threads found in the comic book, which has just passed its one-hundredth issue. The series has numerous zombie killings in each episode, but—as with the comic—the focus is on how people change in a time of crisis and how man is usually the worst enemy of man in any situation.

Terra Nova (2011)

A rather odd apocalyptic series—the program deals with a future Earth that is slowly dying due to overpopulation and other factors. A time rift allows people to travel from that time period to another Earth in another universe that is roughly at a point of the dinosaurs. Thus, unlike the usual formula, the program did not have people going back in time to our own prehistoric Earth but somewhere else. The series dealt with families who had made the journey only to discover villains who want to control the new destination for humanity.

The series lasted one season on Fox and (as with others) ended with a cliffhanger that was never resolved.

Revolution (2012–)

The newest series dealing with a postapocalyptic world is NBC's *Revolution*. Geared around a young woman who knows how to shoot a bow, it was obvious that someone at NBC had seen *The Hunger Games* (also set on a postapocalyptic Earth where a young heroine uses a bow). The series deals with a worldwide catastrophe that leaves mankind without any electricity. Fifteen years later, an army group is determined to track down devices that can reactivate electricity in order to use them in their domination of America. Charlie (Tracy Spiridakos) is the daughter of a man who was partially involved with the experiments that led to the apocalyptic event and has a pendant that allows for the powering up of electrical items. He is killed in the first episode and his son taken hostage by members of the army.

Charlie goes to find her uncle, Miles (Billy Burke), who was involved in the army at one point and who is determined to defeat his former friend Monroe (David Lyons). The series deals with their alliances with others as Monroe tries to make sure he is the only one in control of electricity, while Charlie, Miles and others try to stop his army.

The first season ended with the electricity being turned back on, thus ending what appeared to be a one-season plot line. The series now appears to be focusing on the return of a government in the U.S. and other "revolutionary" fighting to come as a second season is to begin airing in the fall of 2013. Will it actually have a conclusion, or will it eventually be canceled before it gets around to one, like so many in this chapter? Only the ratings will tell.

Revolution (2012–) attempts a different take on the end-of-the-world concept by showing what the world would be like if everyone lost electricity for fifteen years.

21

I Want My Armageddon!

The Top Ten Music Videos in Early Apocalyptic Rotation

T he end of the world wasn't anything new to rock music by the time music videos became popular in the early 1980s. The problem was that it didn't really sell albums. Such songs of the past, like Barry McGuire's "Eve of Destruction" and "In the Year 2525" by Zager and Evans, may have been hits, but they were the rarities. They were epic in their scope, protest songs dealing with global issues (no matter how sappy some feel "2525" may be); but other songs attempting the same mostly were filler on albums or failed to catch on with the public. Let's face it, it's hard to dance when such songs usually talked about alienation, war and death. Even the punk movement had to stick with politics to get people pogoing.

The timing of music videos and their popularity could not have come at a better time for a lot of bad fashion choices and "epic" storytelling. MTV caught on big in the early 1980s, and young people started watching it in much the same way they listened to Top 40 rock stations before it—with the music in the background as they did other things. With that success, the record companies realized that this was the way to go now with promoting their artists—throwing musicians out in front of the camera. In some cases, the musicians floundered, not knowing what to do, but a good number saw videos as an extension of what they were saying in song, or at least a chance to have some fun in front of the camera. Upcoming, younger artists flocked to the idea, and a boom of new bands and singers took over in the early 1980s that were helped immensely by the new visual outlet for music.

The problem was what to film for a new single. You could do a "live" video of your band performing a song onstage in front of an audience, but that wasn't very exciting visually. The other option was to turn the music video into a mini-musical, and with the help of young directors wanting to have a backlog of material to show potential studios that they could do movies and television, the 1980s saw a number of such mini-musicals being produced for artists. Then in the late 1980s everyone seemed to say, "Hey, we don't have to bother doing that anymore! We can just stare into the camera and sing." Which is why music videos got so boring after 1989, but that's a topic for another book, no doubt.

Meanwhile, *Mad Max 2: The Road Warrior* came out in 1981, creating a whole genre of postapocalyptic "I have a car and I know how to use it!" action films due to its success. And what better subject for epic storytelling in music videos than the apocalypse? Heck, the songs don't even have to be about the apocalypse. In fact, it's better if they're not, and several songs listed here really don't deal with the topic in their lyrics. The whole point was to get a band into futuristic costumes, shove them into a quarry somewhere, put some models around them, point some weapons here and there, and voilà—a great eye-catching video for someone's new single . . . even if it is just about a guy wanting to make out with a girl. Take the look of *The Road Warrior*—with the dress-sense that involved layers of mismatched clothing in shreds and in layers that reeked of being from a dress shop after Armageddon—which was also on display in other cult films of the period like *The Warriors* (1979) and *Escape from New York* (1981), and you can see how the look would catch on with young people in the early '80s wanting to startle older folks still clinging to wide lapels and their disco pants.

It was certainly a goldmine to the heavy metal crowd, since a jump from spikes, T-shirts and black leather pants to spikes, torn T-shirts and black spandex was hardly an effort at all. Add in bandanas and pieces of fur, and the look was really goofy in retrospect, or even at the time. But it was hot and what was expected in the heavy metal crowd from 1982 through 1986. (Then in 1987 the metal bands went loopy and started dressing like they were part of Michael Jackson's glam army, but again, that's a story for another book.) This sense of dress even moved over to videos by other artists, and it is easy to see how the wardrobe of artists like Madonna and Cyndi Lauper were influenced by it, while one need only look at the video for Pat Benatar's "Love Is a Battlefield" and Benatar's dance-hall girl outfit to see how it could easily fit into a *Mad Max* movie. By 1985 we were even getting musical artists in *Mad Max* movies—Tina Turner in *Mad Max Beyond Thunderdome*—and the cycle was complete.

There have been plenty of apocalyptic music videos over the years, but the first really set up the cycle for those that would come later, and by the middle of the 1980s nearly all but one theme of such videos had been done. Here is a list of ten early music videos that were the genesis of everything that has followed over the years.

But before anyone asks—no, you won't find "It's the End of the World as We Know It (and I Feel Fine)" by REM in the list. Sure, the song itself may hint at musings about the end of the world, but the music video created for it shows a skateboarder showing off scraps found in an abandoned house and nothing apocalyptic. The one song that you would think would be a natural here doesn't have a video to support that image. Then again, the song really isn't about the end of the world in that sense either, no matter how often reporters have used the title as their headline for articles about end-of-the-world prophecies over the years.

Oh, and yeah, Blondie's "Rapture" is certainly *not* about the biblical Rapture. Although it does feature a "Man from Mars . . . eating cars." And if you know that song at all, it'll now be stuck in your head all day.

Kate Bush—"Breathing" (1980)

Kate Bush is a good example of an earlier innovator in music video, having found the worth in doing promotional clips for her singles and albums since the release of her first album, *The Kick Inside*, in 1978, featuring the massive hit "Wuthering Heights." As evident by that first single—based on the 1939 film adaptation starring Laurence Olivier—Bush enjoyed writing songs that told stories and then played them out in her various music videos over the years. Add in the fact that several of her songs featured fantastical themes, and it's understandable why Bush gained a large science fiction and fantasy fan base. (Okay, the Amazon warrior outfit she wore in her "Babooshka" video that was later sold as a poster certainly didn't hurt her chances with the guys in fandom either.)

One of her early videos was for the single "Breathing" from her third album *Never for Ever*. "Breathing" tells the story of a fetus who is waiting to be born into

The single sleeve for Kate Bush's "Breathing," a postnuclear song.

a world that has just gone through a nuclear holocaust or is about to experience one. The video put the necessary visuals with it, showing Bush wrapped up in plastic inside a clear plastic ball lit in such a way as to resemble the womb. Bush sings the song, cradled inside the womb, until she eventually emerges and is clothed by figures that could be the father and mother or something more. She walks in a field with a group of others, a nuclear blast occurs off-screen and the wind-force of the blast blows the group, including Bush, to the ground. The scene fades to one of Bush singing the final part of the song, where the child pleads for life, as she and the others (now in greenish makeup resembling the dead) move through a stream. As the song ends, the scene cuts to the group once again happy on the grass, but with everyone still in ghoulish makeup and a nuclear blast seen in the background.

Kate Bush would take on other political themes, such as nuclear war, in other songs and videos over the years, but this video showed that the medium could complement a song and flesh out the meaning a bit with visuals. An early sign of what was to come in the next few years.

KISS—"I Love It Loud" (1982)

So here come MTV and music videos, a vast shakeup to the music industry that should have allowed the theatrical musical artists and groups of the 1970s a new way to reach fans and recruit new ones. Yet it was the same period where those same artists were going through business and personal changes that kept them from really entering the new medium running. Ozzy Osbourne lucked out a bit thanks to good musicians backing him on solid albums of the early 1980s and was able to ride the tide, as did Slade (helped a bit with the 1983 success of Quiet Riot's cover for their song "Cum On Feel the Noize"). But others, like KISS and Alice Cooper—naturals—missed the boat, with KISS only really catching up after they took the makeup off and settled down from their superhero days.

KISS did do a few promotional videos before that time came, however, including this one from the 1982 album *Creatures of the Night*, whose cover showed the band members with glowing eyes. The song features a family eating dinner at home as the television in the corner commences playing a music video of KISS performing "I Love It Loud," an anthem to hard rock music. As the parents passively sit at the table, the son goes to the TV to watch the video of the four men in makeup on their stage dressed as a tank perform the song. The song fades out at the end, as the boy turns around to show that his eyes were now glowing white, and he leaves the house like a zombie into the streets. All the other teenagers in the area join him there, as they move toward the four figures in the midst—KISS, with their eyes glowing the same.

Cheap but effective, it plays with the common *Invasion of the Body Snatchers* theme of alien invasion movies.

Krokus—"Screaming in the Night" (1983)

Here is where things really kick off with the concept of a postapocalyptic world full of hard, pounding music and with everyone dressed as if they stumbled off the set of another *Mad Max* rip-off (of which there were so many at the time). True, Tom Petty and the Heartbreakers actually beat Swiss band Krokus to the *Mad Max* riff by a year, with the music video for "You Got Lucky." However, that video features Tom and the band in gimmicky futuristic vehicles finding electronic equipment in a tent in the wastelands only for Tom to kick over a video game and everyone going on their way. It is a video that sets up the premise and then does nothing with it. "Screaming in the Night," however, is nearly a religious experience with how it sets up the mad postapocalyptic world we'll become used to seeing in rock videos throughout most of the 1980s and onward.

The video starts with a bizarre funeral procession going through the wastelands, as the lead singer of Krokus, Marc Storace, shirtless and in chains, begins

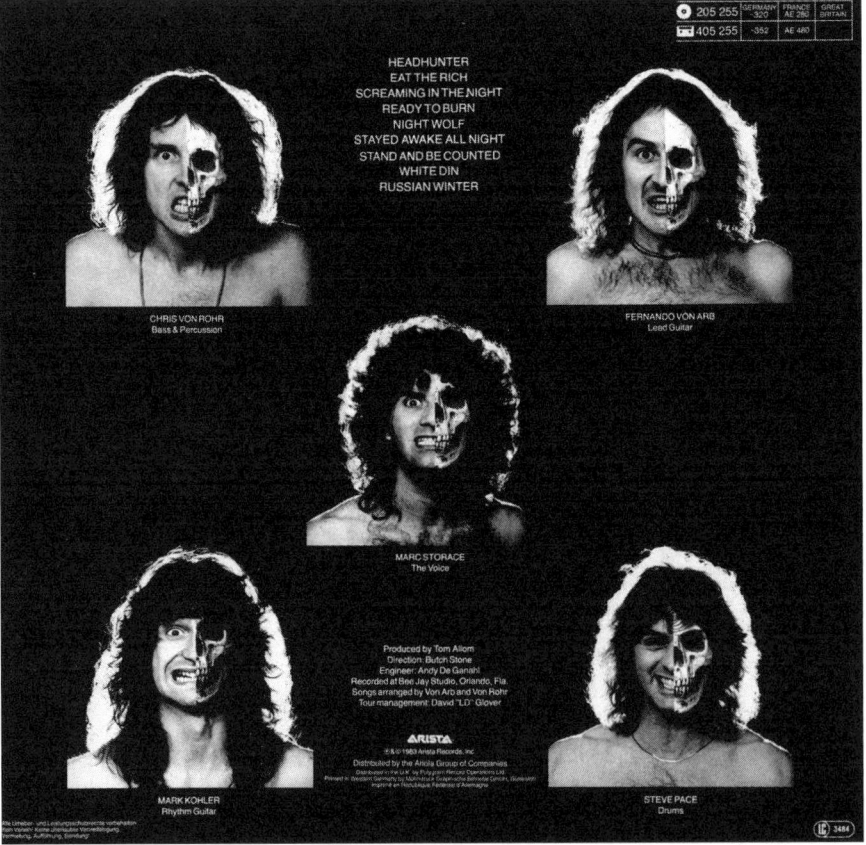

The back cover of *Headhunter*, the Krokus album featuring the ultimate postapocalyptic music video, "Screaming in the Night."

to sing the song while the band plays behind him. The video then goes to a flashback, showing Storace, his girlfriend and others captured by a colony of apocalyptic hooligans who seem to have a general in charge who could pass for Bluto in the old Popeye cartoons. With the captives caged like Heston in *Planet of the Apes*, the general arrives at night to try to molest the girlfriend. When she refuses him, he stabs her as he does his best Brian Blessed impression.

The video then cuts back to the funeral procession, suggesting that the casket holds the body of the girlfriend, and she is to be buried in a tiny little pyramid (have to give that gang of postapocalyptic hooligans credit for being so respectful of the dead there). Unfortunately for Storace, he's also going into the pyramid to be entombed. Yet, as the pyramid is closed, lightning strikes, scattering everyone, forcing open the pyramid, and making the chains disappear round Storace. Another lightning bolt hits the casket, revealing modern clothes for Storace to put on (it's like the gods were saying, "Let there be sneakers!"). Finding soldiers heading toward the open tomb, Storace sees a trap door open in the floor, and he descends down a ladder into a modern-day diner. The cook is a mild-mannered version of the general, and his henchwoman is the *Flo*-like waitress, while the band are customers at the counter. Looking over to a television set mounted on the wall, he sees himself (from the band's video for "Eat the Rich"), which ends to show a woman who looks exactly like his girlfriend (and obviously modeled on then MTV VJ Martha Quinn). In a trance, Storace climbs on the counter, walking over everyone's meals, and begins singing the final chorus of the song to the image of the woman on the television set.

From here, the dam burst wide open on music videos featuring such postapocalyptic worlds, where everyone is a threat but really just wants to dance and play loud music. It would eventually get to the point where one began to wonder if all the videos could be edited together to make one coherent movie, as various bands and artists sang their songs and performed derring-do in their videos while out in the *Mad Max* world. Artists who did such videos include KISS with their first post-makeup videos, "All Hell's Breakin' Loose" and "Lick It Up"; Mötley Crüe with "Too Young to Fall in Love" (with the "Looks That Kill" video hinting at the same); Judas Priest with "Turbo Lover"; Scandal with the rather awkward "The Warrior"; and, of course, Billy Idol with "Dancing with Myself."

The theme has kept going over the years with videos like 2Pac and Dr. Dre in "California Love"; Britney Spears and "Till the World Ends"; Beyoncé with "Run the World (Girls)"; and Jay-Z with "Run This Town." This could also include such videos as Rick Springfield's "Bop 'Til You Drop" and Duran Duran's "The Wild Boys," but their premises are a bit vaguer and could be taking place on another world instead of a postapocalyptic Earth.

Nena—"99 Luftballons" (1983)

After the excitement of all the heavy metal road warriors, we fall back into a cautionary tale of the future, with the German artist Nena and her 1983 hit "99

Luftballons." The song was a big hit in the early days of MTV and received much airplay on the radio in the U.S. What was surprising about this, however, was that although foreigners tend to think of Americans as rather closed-minded, and even though there was an English version of the song available ("99 Red Balloons"), it was the original German version that was the big hit in the U.S. The song—taking a cue from such films as *Dr. Strangelove* and *Fail-Safe*—deals with red balloons being released that are mistaken for oncoming missiles by a superpower's military, which then leads to larger and larger mistakes until eventually a nuclear war occurs. The video does not really do much with that imagery beyond showing Nena and her band in what appears to be the middle of an army obstacle course while some flashbombs go off around them, but it gets the point across. The video ends with Nena finding a red balloon on the ground and punching it up into the air.

At the same time as the video's release was another video featuring a live clip of Nena performing the song, bits of which were incorporated into the English-language version of the video in order to avoid shots of Nena obviously not singing in English in the original video. As one can guess, the original German video is the one most people prefer.

Various ends of the world thanks to the stupidity of mankind have been featured in other videos, such as Men at Work's "It's a Mistake," Rainbow's "Can't Happen Here" and Pearl Jam's "Do the Evolution" (in fact, one could take the animation to "Do the Evolution" and place "In the Year 2525" over it and still end up with the same story being told).

Frankie Goes to Hollywood—"Two Tribes" (1984)

Frankie Goes to Hollywood was one of those early MTV offerings that found a certain amount of fame thanks to their first single "Relax" in 1983. However, after that, America's attitude about the group was "Oh, you're still around? You're so 1983," and they got the brush-off even though the group did just fine in other parts of the world for a few years longer and had some strong material in that time, such as "The Power of Love" and the song being discussed here, "Two Tribes." Based on some dialogue from the *Road Warrior* movie, the song deals with the aggressive nature of two opposing forces that eventually do damage to each other, which worked perfectly into a theme about the Cold War heat-ups during the 1980s between America and the Soviet Union. In the video, directed by former 10cc members Godley and Creme, imitators of those countries' then-current leaders, Ronald Reagan and Konstantin Chernenko, are pitted against each other in a primitive wrestling ring, playing dirty as a crowd representing the rest of the world cheer on in bloodlust. Eventually, the audience gets out of hand, leading to Reagan and Chernenko stopping in horror at the chaos around them, but it is too late—the world blows up due to the madness.

Well, that's one way to make a video apocalyptic.

The video was completed for airing but MTV refused it, citing it as being too violent for the channel due to some the dirty moves by the wrestlers (such as drawing blood after biting an ear). An edited version of the video was completed, but the delay didn't help push sales, and it was the beginning of a downward spiral for Frankie in America. They did get a bit of airplay in the U.S. with one of their final songs, "Warriors of the Wasteland," which was also based on elements of *Mad Max 2: The Road Warrior*.

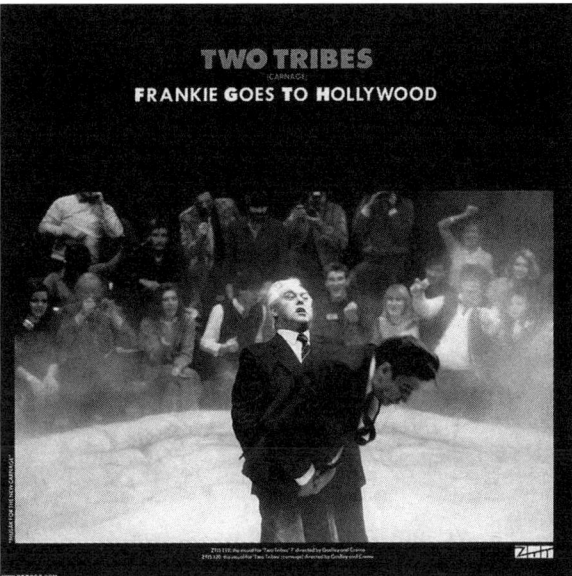

"Two Tribes" was an interesting video concept that ended up on the wrong side of MTV's decision-making process and helped to shorten the band's life in America.

Utopia—"Crybaby" (1984)

Todd Rundgren is well known both for his songwriting ability and as an innovator in video, jumping on board back in the 1970s and producing some of the first music videos of the 1980s. With his band, Utopia, Rundgren and the other musicians created a pop band with enormous creative energy that never quite found an audience beyond fans of Todd. With Rundgren's involvement in video, they also did a number of innovative music videos during their years together (their video for "Feet Don't Fail Me Now" was an annual tradition around Halloween on MTV).

"Crybaby" was the first single from their 1984 album *Oblivion* and certainly one of the most lavish of their videos. The song is the singer's sarcastic response to seeing an ex-love who had mistreated him now looking for sympathy, but the video goes in another direction with the material by making it somewhat political and certainly postapocalyptic. The setting is the world after a global nuclear war. The entrance of a U.S. presidential bomb shelter opens in the wastelands to show a man in a suit—possibly the president himself, who no doubt helped created the devastation—emerging from the hatch. He sees a domed city in the distance and crawls to it, getting to the glass wall as the song begins. Inside is a utopian society of young people dressed in ancient Egyptian–style clothing, including the band and Ellen Foley (singer and actress). Those inside are informed about the man leaning against the glass on the outside, pleading to come in.

It is obvious that those inside are unsure if they want to admit him, and voting comes down to Todd's character, while Foley's character pleads with him to show mercy. Unable to make such a decision, and with what appears to be the death of the man outside, Todd's character throws himself through the glass, killing himself and destroying the city as Foley's character cries.

Good production values and intriguing idea, but it doesn't really quite jibe with the song's lyrics. Beyond Foley, the acting is a little embarrassing, and the video effect used to show Todd's self-immolation appears to be a piece of wood on fire thrown in front of the camera. It's all a bit of a misfire but certainly a unique take on the postapocalyptic imagery of music videos, one that wasn't simply another *Road Warrior* vision. Get to see Willie Wilcox's rotating drumset in action as well, so that's a bonus.

Twisted Sister—"Be Chrool to Your Scuel" (1985)

Twisted Sister was another group that gained success thanks to MTV playing their videos from their *Stay Hungry* album of 1984 ("We're Not Gonna Take It," "I Wanna Rock"). The attempted follow-up album, *Come Out and Play* (titled after a famous line in the film *The Warriors*) in 1985, tried to give fans more of the same but failed to ignite the world as the previous album did, and the tour that followed led to the band disintegrating, with only one studio album completed afterward.

The band recorded two music videos for the album, a revamped version of the Shangri-Las' hit "Leader of the Pack" (a fan favorite the band had performed on tour for years) and a song called "Be Chrool to Your Scuel." The second track included a number of guest performers, among them Billy Joel, Brian Setzer, Clarence Clemons, and Alice Cooper as co-lead singer with Dee Snider. A peppy tribute to the miseries of going to school, the song was a return to music for Alice Cooper, who had taken a departure for a time and was about to come back to huge success in 1986 with "He's Back (The Man Behind the Mask)" from the film *Friday the 13th Part VI: Jason Lives* and his album of the same year, *Constrictor*.

The video for the song was just as expansive in its way, with a long opening that featured Bobcat Goldthwait as a teacher trying to engage a zombie-like classroom of high school students and later makeup artist and actor Tom Savini as a fellow teacher. The two are in the teachers' lounge listening to the Twisted Sister album when the track begins and they are instantly transformed into Dee Snider and Alice Cooper, while the other teachers are transformed into the other members of Twisted Sister.

Also changed is the school, which is now full of zombies instead of students, all carrying on their high school activities—band, eating in the cafeteria, making out, a pep rally—while Dee, Alice and the band perform the song and avoid the zombies. The song ends with Bobcat waking up, still in the teachers' lounge, and heading off to class, only to be attacked by multiple zombies in the hall.

The video is fun and makes light of the zombie movies that were popping up all over the place at the time (hinted at as well by having Savini, the makeup artist who had worked on Romero's *Dawn of the Dead* and *Day of the Dead* films).

However, MTV felt the video was too violent for airplay and refused to air it. It received limited airplay on some of the other alternative music video programs that were around at the time (such as the USA Network cable program *Night Flight*) and appears on a collection of the band's videos up to and including *Come Out and Play* that has yet to be released on DVD.

Weird Al—"Christmas at Ground Zero" (1986)

Weird Al Yankovic is a comedy artist known for his musical parodies of popular songs. His albums also contain original songs as well, such as "Christmas at Ground Zero," which appears on his 1986 album *Polka Party!*

The song is a happy Christmas tune that involves various Christmas activities being attempted during an air raid and subsequent survival in a nuclear wasteland full of mutants and scavengers. (Ground Zero, of course, refers to the

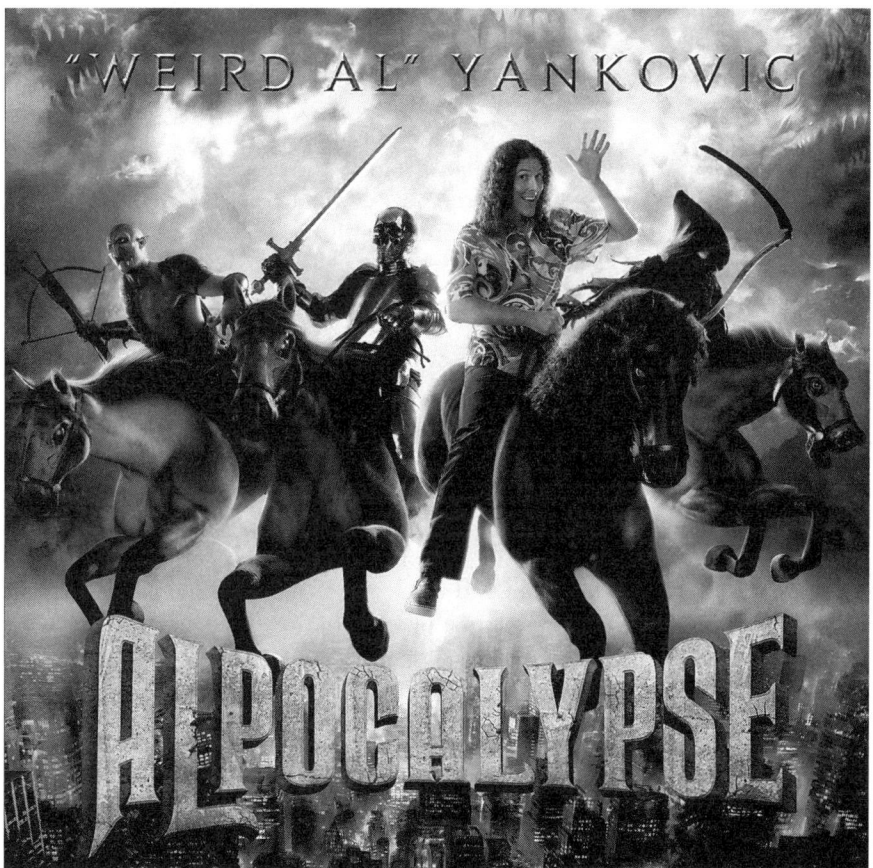

Although Weird Al's 2011 album *Alpocalypse* does not feature "Christmas at Ground Zero," the cover certainly does know how to ring in the end of the world.

impact spot of an atomic bomb.) The video for the song featured a montage of black-and-white clips, mainly from old Civil Defense films about what to do if an atomic bomb falls and Christmas footage. It ends with the only original footage of the video, showing a cheerful Weird Al singing the song with carolers, who are all wearing gas masks.

The video used to get a lot of airplay on MTV around Christmas and whenever Weird Al guested for a few hours on the channel. Things changed after the 9/11 attack in 2001, however, when the destroyed World Trade Center began to be referred to as "Ground Zero," thus making a song using the term and dealing with death and destruction an uneasy mix, even though after the fact and unintentional. Oddly enough, *Polka Party!* features another track, "One of Those Days," that involves the end of the world, but it also features a 747 crashing into a building, making the whole album a bit eerie to hear.

Over the years, very few comedy music videos have dealt with the end of the world. Then again, as discussed in the next chapter, there's not much call for movies along those lines either. One of the few is by the dance-rock duo LMFAO, with their 2011 single "Party Rock Anthem," from the album *Sorry for Party Rocking*. The video is a parody of *28 Days Later*, with the duo—Redfoo and SkyBlu—waking up in a deserted hospital after experiencing comas, much like the main character in *28 Days Later*. Out in the streets, they discover that instead of turning into crazed zombie-like killers from a plague, everyone is turning into shuffling dancers while listening to the song "Party Rock Anthem."

The two wear headphones pumping in a different song and try to avoid the shufflers, but in the end it is too much, and they become shufflers just like the rest.

Kate Bush—"Experiment IV" (1986)

We return to Kate Bush after close to ten years of music making and the release of an album and video collection of her many songs called *The Whole Story*. With its release came this single and a video that is a straight translation of the song.

The song and video deal with a group working for the military to come up with a sound that can kill. Experiments on various subjects ("from the painful cries of mothers, to the terrifying scream . . .") lead to testing on a subject that at first appears as a floating vision of a beautiful woman (Kate), who is quickly unmasked to appear as some type of otherworldly harpy. With the experiment out of control, the elder scientist tries to stop it, but it is too late, and everyone in the building is killed by the sound. Thanks to a desperate phone call to the military officer in charge, the sound gets out of the area and is set loose in the world, disguised as the woman.

The video is more preapocalyptic, but it does show mankind has started "rolling the ball," as it were. Surprisingly, it is one of the few music videos to show the influence of H. P. Lovecraft with the other-dimensional demon being set loose in the world. One would think heavy metal bands would have eaten that concept up when it came to their videos (instead of all the *Mad Max* stuff).

Michael Jackson—"Earth Song" (1995)

The final video listed here is a bit later than the rest, but it also typifies a certain style of postapocalyptic music video that would be seen a few times since—that of the singer standing in the wasteland of the world and singing a ballad about sad things. In this case, the song came from Jackson's 1995 greatest hits package, *HIStory: Past, Present and Future, Book I,* and the song is about mankind's damage to the earth. The video, directed by photographer Nick Brandt (known for his pictures of wild animals struggling to survive in a man-torn world), shows Jackson walking through the remnants of a forest and singing the song, while the camera cuts to dead wildlife and vast wastelands around the world. A few pockets of survivors are shown who are clinging to what life they have left. Suddenly, the survivors fall to their knees and grab dirt in their hands while in a form of prayer (although some cynics referred to it as "everyone humping the earth"); as Jackson heads into the final chorus, the world starts reverting backward through time like in *Superman: The Movie* and all the trees, animals and dead people come back to life (although not as zombies, which would have been kinda cool).

Other videos that would attempt similar types of ballads includes Chris Brown's "Next to You" (featuring Justin Bieber singing about lost love; not to each other, mind) and Adam Lambert's "Time for Miracles" (although one has to give Lambert a pass there, as he's stuck singing the song for the theme from the disaster film *2012*).

One interesting element of these particular videos—especially Jackson's, which holds to loftier ideas than the other two—is that there's a pompousness about them that is hard to ignore. One can't help getting over the feeling that messages of lost love and man's inhumanity to animals and trees seem rather small when you have singers walking through global destruction. The attempts may be to touch on regret and how we need to change the way we do things, but when it comes down to Jackson's messianic saving of the world by stomping his foot, or Brown looking sad that he's lost his girl while everyone is *dead* around him, it seems like the message is getting a bit garbled. Which is why Krokus ends up being remembered more than Jackson when it comes to musical "ends of the world." "Screaming in the Night" is pretty silly, but at least it's not trying to sell us anything more than a silly romp in torn-up clothes.

Speaking of silly . . .

22

Go Out Smiling

Movies That Show the "Funny Side" of Armageddon

In the previous chapter, I mentioned that there haven't been many humorous end-of-the-world videos. That is also true of motion pictures. Obviously there have been some attempts over the years, even going back to chapter 2 and the early days of the cinema with *The Last Man on Earth*, while two of the best remembered of such films, *Dr. Strangelove* and *The Hitchhiker's Guide to the Galaxy*, were discussed in previous chapters due to elements of their story line. A lack of such comedies is understandable; after all, it's hard to find a lot to laugh about when the world is coming to an end. Mel Brooks once stated, "Tragedy is when I cut my finger. Comedy is when you walk into an open sewer and die!" The apocalypse is bound to affect everyone, and if we're all going down the sewer together, it doesn't quite seem as funny.

Some brave souls have tried to find humor in apocalyptic events, nevertheless. In some cases, they have pulled it off; in others, it can be seen as at least a worthy attempt. Even those that have gained fans over the years face a certain amount of criticism from others. Not only from those who just don't think the results are funny enough, but from those who are offended someone would try to find humor in the death of a large number of people, no matter what the methods used, be they aliens, nuclear, zombies or others. What is funny about everyone in a city being blown up by a bomb? Or zombies eating your friends?

Yet comedy in our darkest hours has always been with us. As much as we feared Hitler in World War II, there were plenty of jokes that went around at his expense in order to take a monster and drag him through that sewer mentioned above. It's a way to knock down our fears and even find a way to deal with them by laughing at them. If we can laugh at the things that bother us, we can conquer them, and the same is true for apocalyptic comedy.

The Horn Blows at Midnight (1945)

One of the earliest apocalyptic comedies would become a notorious punch line for Jack Benny, the star of *The Horn Blows at Midnight*. The film, directed by Raoul Walsh, is rather entertaining, with Benny given a rare chance to play outside of his miser persona from radio (and, later, television). Alas, it did poorly at the box office (assumptions why range from its release during the last few days of World War II to the death of President Roosevelt the week before, but none are conclusive), and jokes about it being a "bad movie that flopped" would be part of Benny's repertoire for decades afterward. The film deals with Benny as a trumpet player on a radio program who dreams he is an angel, Athanael, sent to

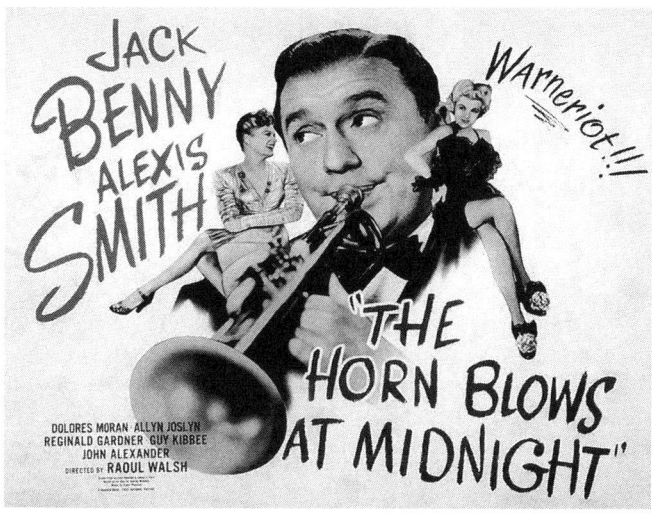

The Horn Blows at Midnight (1945)—one of the earliest examples of a film comedy using an apocalyptic theme.

Earth to blow the trumpet that will signal the earth's destruction. Two angels who have fallen from grace recognize him and attempt to stop his plans in order to keep the lifestyle they have on Earth. The film ends with Athanael failing, but of course it is all a dream. While this would suggest that it is not a true apocalyptic film, subsequent adaptations—for radio on *Ford Theater* in 1949 and for television on *Omnibus* in 1953, both starring Benny in the same role (proving he must have had some enthusiasm for the concept)—eliminated the "it was all a dream" element and therefore made the film worth mentioning here. In those productions, there is no doubt that the end of the world is coming, and only a last-minute change of heart from Benny's character saves humanity as the end approaches.

Although *The Horn Blows at Midnight* was there first and did so in a humorous fashion, fallen angels looking to keep Armageddon from occurring is certainly not an unfamiliar plot for apocalyptic movies. The previously discussed *Legion* and the *Prophecy* series of films deal with such a theme. Terry Pritchett and Neil Gaiman's comedic novel *Good Omens*, which has been tossed around in Hollywood as a potential movie for many years now, also deals with underlings of God (and Satan) who wish to halt the approaching end because they like what they have going for themselves on Earth. Meanwhile, director Kevin Smith's *Dogma* (1999) also deals with fallen angels, although in this case they are set to inadvertently cause the end of existence while trying to subvert their way back into heaven. The film would also play with a concept seen in *Constantine* and the *Prophecy* series of angels who resent God's favoritism toward mankind and thus hope to bring about its destruction.

Atomic War Bride (1960)

Admittedly, this is an odd choice here as this Yugoslavian film (also known as *Rat*, which translates into English as *War*), directed by Veljko Bulajic, focuses on

Although listed as a serious nuclear drama in most reference sources, there is too much intentional comedy in *Atomic War Bride* (1960, aka *Rat*) to consider it strictly a drama.

people hiding from atomic bomb attacks, and ends with our protagonist leaving the war and finding his bride just before an atom bomb hits, killing her and leaving him insane. Still, there's an odd mixture of gags in the movie: our hero trying to get inside another man's radiation suit while the other man is still in it, for example, which plays like a Buster Keaton stunt; those in authority having no clue as to what they're doing; a drill instructor who seems to be more interested in the men posing in odd ways rather than in learning anything of value. It's quite an awkward fit into a movie that ends on such a depressing note, but in some ways it makes that ending even sadder when the audience knows that in most movies somehow the hero would have saved the bride and they would have lived happily ever after. Not so in the world of the atom bomb.

The Bed-Sitting Room (1969)

Richard Lester (*A Hard Day's Night, Superman II, How I Won the War*) directed this 1969 movie based on a play by costar Spike Milligan (father of modern British comedy). The plot deals with a group of survivors living in England after a world war that lasted a total of two minutes and twenty-eight seconds. A mother, father and adult daughter live in the still-running subway system, while people are beginning to mutate into furniture, parrots and even complete bed-sitting rooms (hence the title of the movie). As a variety of mad things occur (featuring such comedic actors as Dudley Moore, Peter Cook and, in his first movie, Marty Feldman), the daughter, Penelope (Rita Tushingham), is seventeen months pregnant. She eventually gives birth to a mutant baby that later dies, but in the end—after everyone finally admits that society has been destroyed in a nuclear attack—things settle back to normal, and Penelope and her boyfriend are seen with a healthy baby in the final moments of the movie.

The film has moments—Michael Hordern manages to keep things moving fairly well as the doctor who eventually marries Penelope for a time, and Cook and Moore are somewhat fun as police officers in a balloon who insist everyone keep moving along—yet the film doesn't really work as a whole. Lester at times seems to be trying too hard to be eccentric just for laughs, but nothing puts the brakes on comedy like having a baby die on-screen. Even if it's a mutant baby. It should come as fair warning that a lot of the jokes are topical for a period of British history that many people who didn't live through it would not get today. It's a fascinating idea for a movie, but the term "tries too hard" really represents the results on the screen.

Gas-s-s-s! (1971)

On the opposite end of *The Bed-Sitting Room* is this late directorial entry for Roger Corman, who would soon move on to produce his own movies rather than have to direct them. Where *The Bed-Sitting Room* deals with a lot of things happening

Gas-s-s-s! (1971) was a late Roger Corman movie that attempted to make light of a postapocalyptic world inhabited only by young people.

Courtesy of Wrong Side of the Art

to make a number of points, *Gas-s-s-s!* has a lot of things happening without really getting to much of a point at all.

The plot deals with a gas that kills everyone over the age of twenty-five. With that, the young take control of the world, but just as it appears the hippie culture will finally take hold, the jocks of the world decide they can do the job better, and it comes down to a conflict between the two groups while a lot of wacky antiestablishment humor runs rampant through the film. The movie is probably best known today for early roles for actors such as Ben Vereen, Cindy Williams and Talia Shire. In the end, a sign from God convinces everyone to work together, and Corman would move on from his relationship with American International Pictures when they edited the film without his approval.

Night of the Comet (1984)

In a mix of genre concepts, Catherine Mary Stewart (*The Apple*) and Kelli Maroney play sisters who survive the end of the world, which occurs when a comet passes over the earth and everyone who is not protected by steel turns into red dust or a zombie. It turns out that some scientists had planned for the situation but mistakenly left their ventilation system open to the outside and are dying. They try to track down healthy survivors in order to stay alive, but eventually the girls and some others manage to outfox them and plan to start the world anew—a world where everything is still working and shopping is plentiful.

Well, it was the '80s, after all.

Mars Attacks! (1996)

Tim Burton (*Batman, Planet of the Apes*) directed this homage to a series of trading cards from 1962 that shows an invasion from Mars with cartoonish paintings that were severely violent and caused quite a ruckus when they were released. The film is a comedy starring Jack Nicholson as both the U.S. president and a Vegas hustler named Art Land. An all-star cast appears in a film where the Martians are nothing more than what we always suspected they would be—a bunch of jerks who are interested only in destruction because it's something fun for them to do. With a couple of homages to *Earth vs. the Flying Saucers* and the often-done subplot of trying to use an atomic bomb on the aliens that never works, Lukas Haas is the young man who discovers that a certain Earth-only phenomenon can save the world. Frankly, any movie that has Tom Jones surrounded by happy wildlife as he begins to sing "It's Not Unusual" has to be a classic.

Brain Candy (1996)

This is the first and, sadly, only full-length narrative film from the comedy troupe the Kids in the Hall. This Canadian group of writers/actors (Kevin McDonald, Scott Thompson, Mark McKinney, Bruce McCulloch and Dave Foley) had a long-running series on CBC that also aired on HBO (and in late night on CBS for its final season) before they worked on this film, which deals with a scientist at a pharmaceutical company who has created a new drug that can help depressed people. The drug, GLeeMONEX, pulls a person's happiest memories, manipulating the mind to be happy. Unfortunately, the drug is pushed out by

Catherine Mary Stewart of *The Apple* (1980) reappears in an intentional comedy dealing
with the end of the world from 1984, *Night of the Comet.*   *Courtesy of Wrong Side of the Art*

the greedy company before testing has been completed, and it is discovered that GLeeMONEX can cause a permanent coma-like euphoria for the user.

The scientist is at first seduced by fame and fortune when the drug goes public, but when he sees the side effects of the drug in action, he tries to stop the pharmaceutical company, only to find that they plan to release it over the counter and have no interest in what could cause a national crisis. The scientist exposes the truth to the nation and . . .

Nobody cares. By the end of the film, there are parades of happy coma-like victims of the drug going down the street as people cheer them on. Just as we eat the wrong food, drink the wrong drinks and abuse medication, so too would we as a planet happily take GLeeMONEX, leading to what appears to be one cheerful apocalypse in the making.

The film originally featured an ending where the scientist, depressed about the lack of interest the world has about the dangers, ends up taking the drug himself, but an alternate ending finds him working underground with other scientists to reverse the effects of GLeeMONEX, hoping to "bum out an entire world" sometime in the future.

Shaun of the Dead (2004)

This Edgar Wright–directed film that was cowritten by him and *Spaced* star Simon Pegg is a loving parody of zombie movies that finds its own unique resolution to the zombie plague. Pegg plays Shaun, a slacker who lives with his friends Ed (Nick Frost) and Pete (Peter Serafinowicz). Shaun's relationship with his girlfriend, Liz (Kate Ashfield), is falling apart thanks to his reluctance to do anything to help advance his career, while Liz's friends Dianne (Lucy Davis) and David (Dylan Moran) don't help matters. Wanting to set things straight, Shaun messes up a dinner date and things look lost, when suddenly the zombie apocalypse happens.

The film brilliantly plays with the idea of how Shaun and Ed ever so slowly realize that the zombies are out and killing, before they decide on a plan to get Shaun's mother and his (hated) stepdad, along with Liz, to a pub they frequent in hopes of waiting out the attacks there. Of course, nothing goes as planned, and a large group of people who are not sure if they want to be around each other try to make their way to the pub, with zombies all around.

The film is full of homages to other zombie movies, making it a delight for fans, yet it never goes so far as not being a funny movie for those who are new to the genre as well. What makes the film is how the issue of zombies is resolved at the end—with zombies incorporated into society as if it were normal, which just goes to show the spirit of humanity in taking any problem it faces and learning how to live with it.

Speaking of which, the 2006 Canadian film *Fido* plays with a similar concept to that of the ending of *Shaun of the Dead*. Fido (Billy Connolly) is a zombie bought by a family to do odd jobs around the house but actually becomes more like a pet to the young son of the family. As such, it plays like a family film about a troubled pet, only with a zombie instead, and is quite fun to watch.

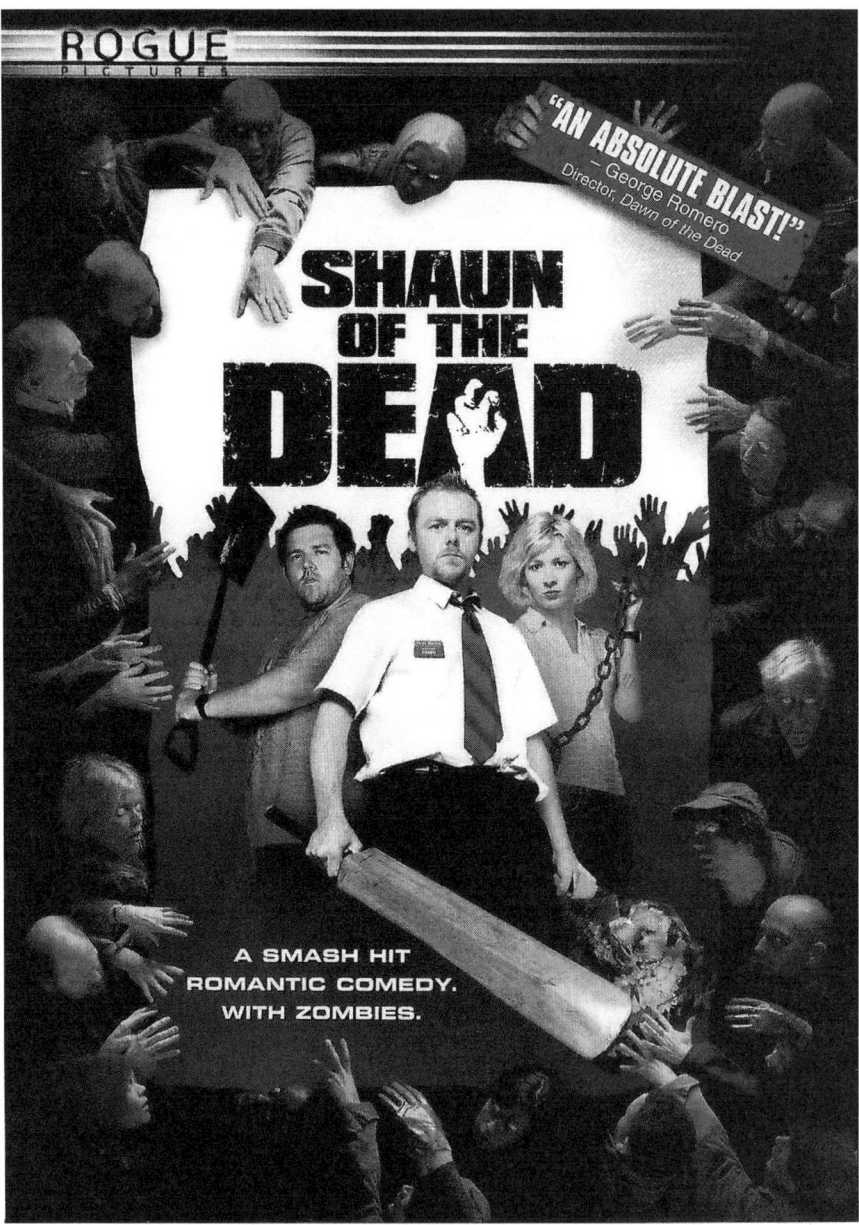

By 2004, the world was ready to take a different look at the zombie apocalypse, with one of the first zombie comedies, the brilliant *Shaun of the Dead* (2004).

The World Sinks Except Japan (2006)

In 2006, a Japanese film was released called *Japan Sinks*, which was exactly as the title states—Japan sinking into the ocean. *The World Sinks Except Japan* is also exactly as it sounds like—a parody of *Japan Sinks*. In it, the rest of the world sinks into the oceans, leaving Japan as the only land left in the world and the Japanese having to deal with having everyone else coming to them as refugees.

By the end of the film, it turns out that Japan only had a brief delay before sinking itself, leading to the end of the world. In between, however, this small film has some interesting takes on American celebrities and the racism that can pop up in Japanese culture.

Zombieland (2009)

The next film listed here is another zombie movie, but this comedy takes a different route from that of *Shaun of the Dead* by dealing with the aftermath of the zombie apocalypse rather than the start and subsequent demise of such an attack as seen in *Shaun of the Dead*. In this case, Jesse Eisenberg plays Columbus, a young man who has a number of rules set in his mind as to how to survive with so many zombies around. He meets up with Tallahassee (Woody Harrelson), a survivalist who hates zombies for killing his young son and is out to find the cake snack Twinkies.

In their travels they meet up with sisters Wichita (Emma Stone) and Little Rock (Abigail Breslin), who steal their car and weapons not once but twice. They finally group together as they head to the sisters' destination, an amusement park in California (oddly enough, the film *Carriers* has the same plot). Along the way, they end up meeting a rather famous survivor but inadvertently knock him off when a practical joke goes awry. Later, some in the group fear they are growing dependent on each other, and the sisters leave to check out the park, only to be stuck with zombies all around them. The men come, and everyone realizes that their best chance may be with each other rather than alone, heading off together as a family.

There have been other zombie comedies over the years, some better than others, but *Shaun of the Dead* and *Zombieland* corner the market on everything that needs to be said in the genre.

Having just gone through 2012 and the whole Mayan Calendar mess (as discussed in chapter 17 with the film *2012*), it is understandable that filmmakers may feel the time is ripe to take the apocalyptic genre and poke fun at our ability to find various ways to terminate our existence. 2013 saw the release of three comedies help illustrate that point. Coincidentally, all three deal with a group of friends and acquaintances that meet up for some type of get-together, only to find themselves involved with the end of the world. Yet, just as I have described in this book various means of our ending, so too has each film found a different way for the characters to face the apocalypse, either through a form of contagion, the Rapture, or an alien invasion.

In 2009 came the release of a great counterpart to *Shaun of the Dead* (2004), the comedy *Zombieland*.

It's a Disaster (2012)

First shown in festivals in the summer of 2012, this film by actor/director Todd Berger features David Cross and Julia Stiles as a couple arriving for a brunch with friends just before "dirty bombs" (bombs containing either radioactive or—as in this case—chemicals that will sicken and kill many around the explosion). As in *Right at Your Door* (2006), most of the film deals with characters inside a house at first trying to protect themselves from the fallout of the bombing and then struggling to deal with issues about approaching death. Most of the humor comes from the tension felt between the individuals as they deal with what amounts to petty problems (affairs, social awkwardness, inability to deal with larger issues, etc.) in comparison to one of imminent death. In some ways the film is a mixture of earlier genres discussed—it deals with a manufactured contagion, while also approaching the topic of how people deal with knowing the end is impossible to avoid. The movie is perhaps too low-key for its own good; characters seem to have little concern over the bombing, yet the bombing propels the storyline, so the characters' rather blasé reactions seem somewhat at odds with the film's reality. Nevertheless, it does end with one solid punchline. Because the film was mainly seen in festivals and then later in a short run in theaters in April 2013, *It's a Disaster* was missed by many people, but it is now out on DVD.

This Is the End (2013)

This Is the End is based on a short film from 2007 starring Seth Rogen and Jay Baruchel called *Jay and Seth Versus the Apocalypse,* which featured the two stuck together in their apartment as the apocalypse happens outside. The plot for the 2013 film has been expanded to include many other actors from both television and movies essentially playing themselves at a big Hollywood party when the Rapture occurs. The film then follows the remaining characters as they struggle to figure out what has occurred, who they can trust (both inside and outside of their group), and if there is any chance that they can get out of it alive. What is interesting to note is how much *This Is the End* and *It's a Disaster* have in common—both start at parties, deal with characters trying to adjust to the end of the world approaching, and end with characters realizing it's all over—and yet they go off in different directions with their individual styles of humor. While *It's a Disaster* is word-play and (some would say) intellectual humor, *This Is the End* goes for the same visual, occasional gross-out, humor of other films done by people involved in the movie, like *Pineapple Express, Knocked Up* and *Superbad.* It also plays with the public and private personas of the actors involved, having fun with showing how the crude, shallow behavior that made them famous not only carries over from their films into real life but also remains largely unchanged even as the world goes to hell—quite literally. The film was released in June 2013 and did well enough at the box office that, even though the film ends with pretty much everyone in the cast . . . somewhere else . . . there is still talk of doing a sequel.

It's a Disaster, one of three end-of-the-world comedies released in 2013, demonstrating that the apocalyptic genre may be ready for mockery.

The World's End (2013)

Originally to be released in October 2013, the film was pushed forward to August 2013 (July 2013 for the U.K.). Put together as the final film in the "Cornetto trilogy" of films (with *Shaun of the Dead* and *Hot Fuzz*—a "lone detective" parody) done by director Edgar Wright, *The World's End* was co-written by Wright and star Simon Pegg (who co-wrote the other two films with Wright). The film deals with Pegg's character drawing his old friends together after twenty years to go on a pub crawl, little realizing that an invasion by robots is taking over humanity as they try to reach their final destination, the pub called the World's End.

Of course, as has been seen, there certainly have been apocalyptic comedies in the years past, and there will certainly be more in the years to come. After all, one way humanity has of dealing with that worries and frightens us is to laugh at it through comedy. There's an old gag that Irish comedian Dave Allen once did on his television program back in the 1970s, which he framed by saying that things may come and go, but as long as there are human beings, comedy will survive. The sketch begins with a nuclear explosion, which then cuts to Allen in rags, sobbing as he sits on a pile of rubble next to a woman also in rags. After he laments about mankind causing the end of the world, the woman calmly puts out an apple, shines it on her sleeve, takes a bite, and motions for Allen to take it.

He looks at her and says, "Oh, don't start that bloody thing again!"

Yes, the apocalypse may occur, but as long as there are human beings, comedy will survive.

23

Survival and Armageddon Films

In the End, What Does It All Mean?

"I think if God is dead, he laughed himself to death. Because, you see, we live in Eden. Genesis has got it all wrong—we never left the Garden. Look around you. This is paradise. It's hard to find, I'll grant you, but it is here. Under our feet, beneath the surface, all around us is everything we want. The earth is shining under the soot."—Justin Playfair (*They Might Be Giants*, 1971)

A little theater in a small town somewhere in Ohio back in 1997. They were letting people come in to see classic movies for fifty cents in celebration of their renovations to their theater. People could see *Gone with the Wind, Casablanca, The Wizard of Oz* and the 1968 adaptation of *The Planet of the Apes*. Plenty of space in the theater for the first three films, but then there was a line to see the fourth. People filled every seat in that theater to see Charlton Heston fight the apes and—as one—were shocked at the ending. Could this be Earth? Could we really finally do it?

We're lectured every day that it's coming. Our faiths hand us prophecies that tell us the world's end is just around the corner. Our science forecasts the sun will eventually burn out and the earth will crumble, or some other deadly assault is about to begin. Our history reminds us that all great things eventually fall. Our societies warn us to be prepared for bad times. Our bodies nag us that someday we will die. And above all, time washes away all things no matter how hard we hold on.

We see hate, violence, senseless death, cruelty beyond measure screaming to us from the twenty-four-hour cycle of news and the papers and the Internet and the phones. We see the insanity of war, famine, death and disease, over and over again from the time we first picked up a rock back at our birth as mankind to today. Finally, we know that someday, somewhere, we all must close our eyes and see the end of our world, no matter how hard we try to avoid it. And yet—

And yet—

Here we are lining up to see Heston proving that we finally did it. We blew it up. We make blockbusters out of movies forecasting the end. Telling us about how we'll be wiped out by zombies, nuclear war or contagions. We make jokes about the end. We even write and read books about the end. But why? What does that say about us as a people?

"There's still time . . . brother!" —A banner in the street (*On the Beach*, 1959)

Some would say that it means we long for the end. Like those waiting for the end-times, or the survivalists, or any of a number of cults that are waiting for the mothership to return and take them away, we can't wait to be proven right, the doomed proven wrong, and we will be raptured into a new age of peace and harmony. But I'll go out on a limb and say that rather the opposite is true. We're not longing for death when watching these movies. In fact, death is a cheap rip-off if that is all that remains at the end. If we wanted death, we'd just turn on the television news, thank you very much. We may watch things that approach Armageddon, but it doesn't mean we necessarily really want it to play out in front of our eyes. Where's the fun in that?

"It can't rain all the time." —Eric Draven (*The Crow*, 1994)

Because what we're searching for in these movies is not death but life. No matter how cynical or sarcastic we become in this world of ours—and we unfortunately can get pretty dark about ourselves and humanity—deep down inside we want one thing: to be saved. We want to be able to believe we can sleep without fear of tomorrow. We want to see love. We want there to be innocence for those that deserve it. We want redemption. We want to believe there's still time, brother.

And apocalyptic films give us that in a way few others can. The ones that fail are those that think it should be about people just moping around, waiting for the end, or that the universe is simply playing a trick on us. Most of us see such conclusions in movies, and something inside of us just clicks to say, "What a load of pretentious BS." Because we know it isn't true. As much as some want to believe the world is a cold, hard place, we slowly have to come to grips with the idea that this simply isn't the case. Near the beginning of the book I mentioned the idea that we began our apocalyptic journey in fiction when we realized that the world was becoming known. There was no place to go, thus nowhere to hide. A contagion in a far part of the world is of great concern to us now because it is quite likely to rapidly move to the other side of the globe by breakfast. Yet on the flip side of that is something we forgot—because we know the contagion can be here before the bacon is ready to eat tomorrow morning, that means we have to actually *do* something about it on this side of things. We can't be bystanders any longer. We are all next-door neighbors, interlocked into knowing each other because we have no choice. Our technology and advancements bring us hand in hand, and we can't ignore the person we're holding onto any longer. We have to fight together as a planet because, really, what other choice have we got?

"So shines a good deed . . . in a weary world." —Willy Wonka (*Willy Wonka and the Chocolate Factory*, 1971)

We look to the apocalyptic movies because we know things can happen and can get worse, but we also want to see who survives and how they do it. Perhaps show us a way to make things better. Back in chapter 1 we discussed how *Lucifer's Hammer* taught geeky kids the lesson that it was best to know basic survival skills because they could come in handy—not because a supposed comet will strike the earth but because they are good skills to have. If a child wants to learn a good, health-oriented sport like archery from having read or seen *The Hunger Games*, is that bad? Movies like *The Day After* and *Threads* make us think about the unimaginable and thus perhaps work to make sure such nuclear disasters never happen.

As weird as it may sound, Armageddon films are actually a positive genre in the movies.

"Live White." —Geum-ja Lee (*Sympathy for Lady Vengeance*, 2005)

This is not to say that a movie will change the world. No peace negotiation is ever going to come about because a prime minister somewhere saw *Teenage Cave Man*, for example. But such films do give us hope—because we know whatever hits us as a species, somehow we're going to come out of it. We've survived this far, and no prophecy is going to tell us what to do. Somehow we'll make it through the next crisis. One way or another. Just like in the Armageddon films we love to watch.

After all, how often have we really seen the end of the world in these end-of-the-world movies? Oh, we see death and destruction and people struggling, but the number of movies that end with *everything really, really ending*? Merely a handful out of all the films discussed here, and even most of those deal with the dignity of the human spirit in spite of death approaching. Yes, there's a whole chapter about such movies earlier in the book, but what are the results after the movie is over and the lights come up in the theater? Hey, look—I'm still alive, sitting in my seat in a theater with my shoes stuck to the floor by old soda and trying to wipe the last bit of popcorn off my pants that I couldn't see in the dark earlier. Yep, by golly, I'm still here. You're still here. Everyone is still here. We not only got to watch the end of the world, we survived it! We're alive! Now we can go out into the sunny day outside and experience life with the reminder of how precious it all really is. Even when the film ultimately wants us to think the world is gone, they can't take the *real* world waiting outside from us, and thus such messages are only doomed to fail.

So we pull ourselves out of our seat, exit the darkened theater to find that outside the world truly is a miracle—blue skies, signs of nature everywhere you look, the sounds of children laughing, moments of caring and love—all there if we want to open our eyes and see them. There's always a new world waiting for us, and we'll smile because we survived and proved all the doomsayers wrong. Then we'll grab the romantic lead, pull them close, and plant a big kiss on their lips, and they'll return the embrace because they feel the same as we do.

And as the music swells, the credits will fly up on the screen, not with *The End* but with *The Beginning*.

"Look up, Hannah. Look up." —A barber (*The Great Dictator*, 1940)

Appendix
Ten Things You Need to Survive the Apocalypse

1. **Have a unique skill.** Be it flying a plane, shooting a gun, or making whisky—your distinctive ability will somehow always lead to survival. Further, in the aftermath, people with exceptional skills are essential to rebuild society. Stick with usable ones, though. The ability to build small motors or knowledge about medicine will be worth keeping you around. Knowing *Star Trek* trivia . . . probably not so much.

2. **Get a dog.** Evidently, the hand of fate loves doggies. You will survive as long as the dogs do. As the various Nevilles know from *I Am Legend*, once the dog is gone, so are your chances of survival. Kids help but aren't always a certainty; in fact, if they survive, chances are good you won't. And keep the kids on a shorter leash than the dogs! If *28 Weeks Later* taught us anything, it's that we would have all survived if it weren't for those darn kids!

3. **If you think you're going to have a breakdown, godspeed.** In fact, do it early on and get it out of the way. The heroes who freak out and then recover have a much better chance of survival than those who lose it when they need to keep their head and instead start shooting up the place at random, getting themselves killed in the process.

4. **Be a loner who is never alone.** Somehow connect with everyone still alive, but be known as the guy no one knows anything about except as "big news" if you come around. In fact, it's even better if they think you died years ago and *then* you return. Your legacy will precede you, and no one wants to kill a legend.

   Okay, actually they will want to kill you anyway. Still, your second lead or the kid tagging along will save you. Just for God's sake be low-key about it, because . . .

5. **Don't get cocky.** The minute you set yourself up as the boss is the minute the zombies will eat you, the aliens will possess your body or the *real* hero will steer your wheelchair down the ramp as the rocket takes off from certain doom. Of course, do the right thing, but never make yourself a target. So don't throw that party on the night the comet is going to slam into the world, because the gods won't be satisfied until you and the guests are screaming in agony, you heretic.

With that in mind, you're only safe as an American if you're in America. Anywhere else and you'll automatically become the fanatical bad guy that's going to get everyone killed unless he is stopped in time. Sorry, but that's just the way it goes. Probably something in the water. You can only be saved if you're romantically involved with the opposite lead and you're not a jerk about it.

Also, don't get flashy with your car or house. The nicer the digs, the more chance someone is going to want to make it their own without you as company. (Actually, that works in the real world.) Finally, best to avoid the big cities—meteors, aliens, nuclear bombs and supernatural creatures love an audience and like to show off by taking out the big cities first. Nothing against Springfield, Ohio, but if the monsters crawl out of hell there, people will just assume that it's a local problem, and the bad guys really need to show their strength.

6. **Mix and match your legends and prophecies.** The kid in the house next door who swears vampires are around may have something there; then again, the woman at the end of the lunch counter who swears birds will never attack is a stuffy idiot and has the gods ready to deal with her arrogance. You never know who may have the right story, so listen to all and pick the best options for you. At least if you're momentarily wrong, you may be able to backtrack and get a second chance. Whatever you do, don't stand next to the guy who predicts rainbows and sunshine if everyone else is predicting doom—he'll be the first guy to bite it when the end comes.

7. **Stay away from the crowds.** No matter how cool it may seem to be with the first two hundred people to meet the aliens arriving on Earth, you're bound to also be one of the first two hundred people to be slaughtered by the new overlords. It's true of all aliens with the exception of Vulcans; even E.T.'s parents would have done the same if they hadn't lost their kid in the first place (too embarrassed by that point, no doubt). Best to stand off and see what happens first. Probably even better to view from a satellite feed. From the other side of the world. At least you can say you saw it live on TV years later. Better than never being able to say anything again. No point in making yourself a body shield for the "real" hero who will later save the day, after all.

Besides, crowds are just a feeding tube for panic and chaos—if there's going to be a hysterical meltdown, best that it be your own instead of letting it be the guy flying the plane.

8. **In a state of emergency, if someone tells you, "We're in trouble," then you're probably safe.** If he tells you, "Don't worry, nothing can penetrate the hull of the ship!," then you'd best see how quickly you can get out of there. Because in five minutes something is going to be penetrating the hull of the ship. And taking out the "smart" guy who made himself the leader. Because he refused to listen to the prophecy. And probably kicked a dog out of spite. In a related note . . .

9. **Never trust the machines.** This means the machines for normal uses (not only will automated doors refuse to work when you really need them, you can't even get a Mr. Pibbs to come out of the soda machine during a monster attack, for gosh sakes), as well as those that do highly complicated functions for us. Especially anything that handles nuclear weapons—those things will either turn against mankind for their own agendas, be taken over by outside forces, or have rockets shooting off because a nervous guy has his finger too close to the button. Almost always it's the guy who does it manually that saves the world, with the big ol' machine most probably being a major obstacle, whether intentionally or not. And isn't the personal touch just the way we would like it anyway?

10. **If all else fails, hope for a happy accident.** Gain an immunity that only a few others have; decide to go spelunking on the one day radiation kills everything on the surface; temporarily have your eyes covered the one night everyone else looks at a meteor shower and goes blind; accidentally get yourself frozen and time-travel thousands of years into the future—it pays to be in a spot no one else is in, even if it means momentarily having to put up with pain. Better to come out of the coma with a head wound and survive than be eaten by zombies, for example.

But remember this: if the nuclear strike doesn't get the meteor, there's always the aliens with their plague guns who will work hand in hand with Satan's zombies to pick off those who haven't already been driven psychotic. It's all doom and gloom one way or another, folks, so in the end, remember: keep smiling.

Selected Bibliography

Clarke, Arthur C. 1971. *The Lost Worlds of 2001*. New York: Signet.

Kane, Joe. 2010. *Night of the Living Dead: Behind the Scenes of the Most Terrifying Zombie Movie Ever*. New York: Citadel Press.

King, Stephen. 1981. *Danse Macabre*. New York: Everest House.

Lucas, Tim. 1992. *The Video Watchdog Book*. Cincinnati: Video Watchdog.

Matheson, Richard. 2009. *Visions Deferred*. Colorado: Edge Books.

Meyer, Nicholas. 2009. *The View from the Bridge*. New York: Penguin Group.

McCarthy, Kevin. 1999. *"They're Here . . .": Invasion of the Body Snatchers: A Tribute*. New York: Berkley Boulevard Books.

Person, Simon. 2006. *The End of the World: From Revelation to Eco-Disaster*. New York: Carroll & Graf.

Russo, Joe, and Larry Landsman, with Edward Gross. 2001. *Planet of the Apes Revisited*. New York: St. Martin's Griffin.

Warren, Bill. 2000. *The Evil Dead Companion*. New York: St. Martin's Press.

Weldon, Michael J. 1996. *The Psychotronic Video Guide*. New York: St. Martin's Griffin.

Index

THE FAQ SERIES